D1106458

AMERICAN PANORAMA

AMERICAN PANORAMA

A Revised Edition of
Fads, Follies
and
Delusions of the American People
Including
New Diets, Quick Cures,
Campus Bloodshed, the
Cults, Jogging,
Skyjacking, Millionaire Athletes,
and Much More

By Paul Sann

CROWN PUBLISHERS, INC./NEW YORK

OTHER BOOKS BY PAUL SANN

Americana
PICTORIAL HISTORY OF THE WILD WEST
  (with James D. Horan)
THE LAWLESS DECADE
FADS, FOLLIES AND DELUSIONS OF THE AMERICAN PEOPLE
THE ANGRY DECADE: THE SIXTIES

Crime
KILL THE DUTCHMAN! THE STORY OF DUTCH SCHULTZ

Novel
DEAD HEAT: LOVE AND MONEY

Sports
RED AUERBACH: WINNING THE HARD WAY
  (with Arnold Red Auerbach)

Revised edition of *Fads, Follies and Delusions of the American People*

© 1980 by Paul Sann

Inquiries should be addressed to Crown Publishers, Inc., One Park Avenue, New York, N.Y. 10016
Printed in the United States of America
Published simultaneously in Canada by General Publishing Company Limited

Library of Congress Cataloging in Publication Data

Sann, Paul.
  American panorama.

  Edition of 1967 published under title: Fads, follies and delusions of the American people.
  Includes index.
  1. United States—Popular culture. 2. United States—Civilization—20th century. 3. National characteristics, American. I. Title.
E169.12.S237 1979   973.9   79-15791
ISBN 0-517-53773-7

*This book
is for my daughter
Eleanor
and the
woman I love,
her daughter
called Brandie*

ACKNOWLEDGMENTS

THIS IS THE EASY PART. I want to say thanks here to the people who helped. First, to my son Howard, a toiler on the Philadelphia *Evening Bulletin* when it all began. He did a healthy share of the legwork and the library research for this book. Second, to my nephew Arthur Berman of the Los Angeles *Times*. He did the Berkeley Revolt in the chapter on the campus, and he did it well. Beyond this pair of mercenaries, I owe a debt to a tireless volunteer named Jackie Spitzler and to the many colleagues who dug into their memories in the hope, however remote, that not too many things would be left out of this rambling history. Put cousin Ruth Preston, the fashion watchdog, down here too. And while I am loath to say anything nice about a book publisher, I must note that the idea for this bruising journey on the American merry-go-round came from Nat Wartels of Crown, and Nick Lyons of his staff had all the better ideas when it came to the organization of the original material. So much for the text. On the picture side, I am indebted, notably, to Dorothy Schiff, then publisher of the New York *Post*, for the liberal use of the files reposing in that journalistic vineyard. For this revised edition Myron Rushetzky and David Hubler performed valorous labors, and such newspaper types as Alan Whitney (just an editor) and sportswriters Maury Allen and Hugh Delano also lent needed hands. Finally, throw in Ms. Ellen Datlow, who, along with some splendid ideas, had the unspeakable nerve to edit my new words.

PAUL SANN

CONTENTS

WHAT IT'S ALL ABOUT

In its original concept in mid-1960, the stress here was on the more engaging fads, follies, and delusions which had occupied this land of the free for over a half-century or so. The test was not duration but interest. How many of us, in the tens of thousands or in the millions, suddenly started doing the same things, turning on to the same things, buying the same things, shouting ourselves hoarse over the same things, *believing* in the same things? What accounted for it? Thus, to cite one example, I dealt at length with that once-commonplace extracurricular campus phenomenon: the panty raid, taking notice along the way of its transition to the other kind of raid—not on the co-ed dorms but on the commonly accepted, more sacred precincts of our educational foundries. I dealt with the 1964 uprising at the University of California at Berkeley, where the prize was not milady's undergarments but, of all things, *free speech.*

Then, spurred first by racial unrest but eventually torn almost completely asunder by that "dirty little war" in Vietnam, the American campus came under another, infinitely more explosive siege. National Guardsmen, GIs, tear gas, bloodshed and the ultimate infamy: the senseless 1970 slaughter by the Guard at Ohio's Kent State that grew out of a mass student protest over Mr. Nixon's "secret war" in Cambodia, quickly followed by a trigger-happy police bloodletting at all-black Jackson State College in Mississippi to put down a minor brick-and-bottle-throwing demonstration that had less to do with our young dying on far-off battlefields than an understandable discontent with the place where they were at that moment in history.

Now, well beyond a perfunctory updating, I have expanded this chronicle into a six-decade history on a scale broad enough to take it well beyond its original title. I have turned what I hope is an adequately surgical probe upon such more recent phenomena as the born-again boom (throw in Watergate's Charles Colson, pornographer Larry Flynt, Black Panther Eldridge Cleaver and a couple of members of the Charles Manson murder family) and the evangelicals who have followed Billy Graham into the American living room via the little screen—and the Moonies, and the mad messiah called the Reverend Jim Jones, who took more than 900 of his disciples to death with

him in the Guyana jungle in 1979. I have examined the new sex therapy pioneered by Masters and Johnson and that other therapy—in the gutters, the pornography scene. The sports front—what turned the sweat-stained baseball players into union men with so many millionaires in their ranks and brought the lawyers, agents and accountants into the other professional games—is here now. So is the new "in" drug, cocaine, and the dreaded Angel Dust. And the communes that flowed from the time of the Hippies and the Flower Children. And the fly now, pay later skyjackers. And the health food explosion—along with the fresh arrivals on the quack diet front, another one of our growth industries. The Patty Hearst story is in these pages too, because that saga wasn't a simple kidnapping but a horrifying innovation in social protest that seemed worthy of examination. On another level, I have included the runners, both the legions of joggers and the streakers who flashed briefly across the horizon a few years back in their birthday suits. And the new army on roller skates.

We're up to date, then, so let's go back and start with some definitions, disposing of the follies first. All of us know what folly is. It is what you or I *think* it is, because folly is perforce in the eye of the beholder; it may be an act of consummate wisdom and brilliance to the person involved in it. Whatever it is, the record will show that it is never in the private domain of any particular segment of the populace. Emerson said that "Each age has its own follies, as its majority is made up of foolish young people," but folly by its very nature cannot repose exclusively in the young. Folly is for people of all ages.

Now the fad is something else. For the most extensive survey ever made in this field, one has to go to Dr. Emory S. Bogardus, founder of the University of Southern California journal, *Sociology and Social Research.* He started his study in 1914 and was still at it when he stepped down as Dean of USC's Graduate School nearly half a century later. Twice a year over that period Dr. Bogardus had his students collect information on whatever nonsense happened to be current in the land. Some 3,000 fads came under scrutiny in that process, and the professor found that most of them had a tendency to disappear within six months to a year, although he made allowances for the ones that somehow come and go and come back again, such as the Yo-Yo or the raccoon coat or the Ouija board.

"As soon as most fads are widely adopted, they no longer attract attention and they are dropped," Dr. Bogardus tells us. "Another factor helps to explain fads as a current phenomenon. They flourish only in social environments in which people are looking forward and seeking progress by trying out new things and ideas. In countries tied down by customs, rituals and the like, fads have no standing. In countries whose eyes are forward looking, fads are adopted by the many, and even at the hands of their devotees they are quickly discarded for a newer, and, if possible, more glamorous object."

The psychiatrists, of course, go a little deeper. "Most fads meet a kind of neurotic need," says Dr. Gerald T. Miles, of New York's Karen Horney Clinic. "When the need is either met, or it is discovered that the particular fad doesn't meet the need, the fad is over." Webster's New International, predating the vogue of the head doctors, describes the fad as "a custom, amusement, *or the like*, followed for a time with exaggerated zeal...." Note the italics, because the license in these pages derives from those three words. This history has to do with the American crowd, young and old, and an assortment of the items which have managed to seize its attention, however briefly, from time to time. *Or the like* covers an immense ground, because there simply is no way to account for the crowd and its tastes.

On one level, the children find themselves irresistibly drawn to Batman and the adults want to know what kind of foolishness is this and then wind up rooted in front of the television screen themselves and suddenly fighting their way into the movie houses to see the revived Superman. The children discover the Hula Hoop and the Frisbee and have to do battle to get them away from the grown-ups. The children all set up a clamor for the Davy Crockett coonskin cap and make a fad out of bubble gum, and the adults, for quite another reason (*even your best friend won't tell you,* the ads used to say), turn to chlorophyll. Thus one turn-on or another crosses the lines, with variations, between the generations.

On another level, the children go for the high-speed, ground-based adventure of the skateboard, and the adults go for the stationary, way-out-there spooks of the Ouija board. The children, sure bait for the Good-over-Evil hucksters, go for Zorro in the nickelodeons and the adults, in the tabernacle, for a Billy Sunday riding circuit against the devil. Similarly, the children go for Hopalong Cassidy and the adults for the Reverend Dr. Graham. Now these must seem to be irreverent comparisons, undoubtedly invidious to some, but there they are: The same hunger for the Good continues to manifest itself on the divergent plateaus of age, intelligence and even faith. Our heroes play different roles on different stages. Billy Sunday, uniquely, made it on two distinctly separate levels; he was the fastest man in baseball before he became the homerun hitter of the hell-robbers. Billy Graham had the looks, wit, grace and natural talents to make it on any performing level he might have chosen, except that his abiding beliefs took him down a road paved both with redemption and gold.

Beyond all this, strange happenings in the American social arena often derive from the bewildering variety of promises unfailingly held out to the panting masses. Oh, those promises—something for nothing, easy money, mental contentment, just plain physical health, boundless vigor in the boudoir, and on and on and on. Thus the young have gorged themselves on Wheaties just to collect the box tops and mail them in for almost anything, anything at all, and the senior citizens in their time mailed *ten cents* a month (it added up to millions) to a doctor named Townsend because he was going to lay *$200* a month on them, *every* month, unto infinity. Another army paid their dues, a good deal heftier, to a Howard Scott, whose banners heralded a nice $20,000 a year for all the happy workers under the splendid mirage of a thing called Technocracy. Once the blacks, in the thousands, faithfully followed a Father Divine into a sin-free Valhalla-on-earth, plunking down every last penny of their poor wages for the privilege; later, in the multitudes, they fell into step beyond a minister named King, who gave up his very life in another kind of commitment. Not just a bland, or perhaps even blind, contentment, but *equal rights.* Once the well-heeled lavished dollar bills on a Frank Buchman to carry the torch for some vague moral reawakening that is still somewhere out there beyond our grasp. Once, deep in the heart of Dixie, a supersalesman named LeBlanc coined a fortune peddling a whisky-spiked thing called Hadacol to fix up our insides, while in the supposedly more sophisticated regions Dr. Wilhelm Reich struck it rich peddling the manifold wonders of his Orgone Box for the sexually ailing. Nationwide, because the gambling fever is always upon us in this get-rich-quick society, the TV hucksters hooked the gullible on the cliff-hanging drama of a Van Doren literary scion's adventures in high finance, quiz-show style, and sold tons of cosmetics and tired-blood remedies in the process until the law stepped in because that one was just another crooked wheel. Obviously, there was more wisdom than pun in Barnum's "Every *crowd* has a silver lining." It turned out to be true whether the crowd was sitting at home before the little screen or standing on line to buy tickets for a freak show.

The crowd alone is the key because when you talk about fads, follies or delusions (any attempt to define the latter term seems unnecessary here), you are in areas of momentary madness, of moral epidemics, of emotional contagion and of collective behavior that have been a source of wonder down through the ages. "Anyone taken as an individual," the poet Schiller wrote, "is tolerably sensible and reasonable—as a member of a crowd, he at once becomes a blockhead." Much later, in 1852, Britain's Charles Mackay said it in another way in the preface to his classic work, *Extraordinary Popular Delusions and the Madness of Crowds*: "Men ... think in herds, while they recover their senses slowly, and one by one." Mackay had a strong basis for that conclusion, having made an exhaustive study of the human merry-go-round up to that point in history. He took for his text such swindles as the South Sea Bubble, the ephemeral stock deal which left the British masses all but bankrupt early in the Eighteenth Century, and the infamous Mississippi Scheme through which John Law, holding out the promise of overnight fortunes to be wrung from the precious metals supposed to abound along the great river's banks, emptied the purses of the French. Mackay also examined such phenomena as the Crusades, the witch mania of the Thirteenth to the Fifteenth Centuries, and the mumbo-jumbo of the fortune-tellers, astrologers and cure-all fakers of early Europe. France's Gustave Le Bon addressed himself to the problem of the crowd fifty years after Mackay, and Dr. Freud also brooded over it. In our time, Elias Canetti, the Bulgarian sociologist, pondered the same problem in *Crowds and Power*.

Why does the crowd behave the way it does? Why do millions of people, all at once, fix their eyes and their hearts upon a given thing and follow it blindly down an unchartered road? Why does a rage to gamble seize the crowd? The early British and French experiences had their counterparts here in the Florida land boom of the Twenties and the stock market fever that exploded into 1929's Black Tuesday and the Great Depression. The get-rich-quick syndrome reappears, with tragic effects, in all the ages of man, right into the here and now, vicariously or otherwise. Without it, we couldn't have been lassoed into the phony game called the Quiz Show; we would not have believed it in the first place. Why is the crowd seized by a rage to believe? A rage to love? A rage to hate? Why does the crowd seek out witches and infidels at one stage in history and heroes in another? Why does the crowd suddenly and inexplicably fall into an orgy of public weeping and hysteria over the remains of a Rudolph Valentino? Hopefully, you will find some clues in this examination of the curious things which have transpired in recent decades on the rich acres which the wheeler-dealers of another day, with another set of promises, heisted away from the Indians.

There are some passing phenomena omitted for cause in this study. I left out dating by computer, which *Mademoiselle* magazine once described as "the biggest American fad since the Hula Hoop," because I knew that no tin can could banish the trial-and-error methods of our own springtimes. I skipped the beanie out of sheer despair; who could begin to fathom why 30,000,000 little caps topped with spinning propellers and flying saucers turned up on the heads of the nation's small fry in 1952? I passed on the *Executive Coloring Book*, and all the others, because that flash fire hardly lasted long enough for the flash. I shunned the recurring fast-gun craze because we all know the male animal won't ever stop firing slugs into his own limbs in the process of emulating the overblown quick-draw artists of the Wild Frontier. I left out the T-shirts emblazoned with the likenesses of such as Brahms, Beethoven and Bach because I knew the music wore better (but you will find Patty Hearst here in her PARDON ME T-shirt). I left out the "talking plant" foolishness of 1974 because no cluster of green ever talked to me no matter how tenderly I cared for it. I have included all the soothsayers from the Omnipotent Oom to Timothy Leary and the LSD Express because my own observations of that kind of history show a repetitive pattern worthy of comment. I made the full circle from the Rudy Vallee rage to Bing Crosby and Mr. Sinatra and the ill-fated Elvis Presley on to the Beatles and the Rolling Stones and the emergence of the Bob Dylan-Joan Baez folk-singers with their stirring, vibrant musical poems of a land without war and social injustice, because there is a pattern there too, from one generation to another. I threw out Punk Rock because that's all it is. And, finally, I have included a great many items which in my mind bear in one way or another on our peculiar and special capacity to go on shopping so assiduously in the marketplace of ideas, entertainment, quick cures, quick-cash (the new Chain of Gold letter) fun and games, instant salvation or what have you. This is an astonishingly interesting place—no, not to visit but to live, because there aren't many dull moments. That's what this book is about, now covering a good deal more ground than it did at its inception.

PAUL SANN

Part I

SOME TINSEL HEROES

Bob Kane, creator of *Batman*, waited twenty-five years for the payoff. *Paul Sann*

BATMAN:

Galahad in a Cape

BATMAN: My own parents were murdered
by dastardly criminals.
ROBIN THE BOY WONDER: Holy barracuda,
you mean . . .

ON MARCH 16, 1966, the United States' race-into-space against the Russians suffered its first real brush with human disaster. Seven hours into the mission and 180 miles up, over Red China, a short circuit in the tail of Gemini 8 touched off a rocket booster and the craft, linked by then to its Agena target rocket, started to tumble so violently that astronauts Neil A. Armstrong and Major David R. Scott could not steady it on its course. "It's rolling and we can't turn anything off," Armstrong told Gemini Control, and after thirty minutes, fearing that the fuel tanks might burst and incinerate the space twins in a giant fireball, Gemini Control ordered an immediate splashdown. Even then, there was danger: The men had used part of their reentry fuel in the vain effort to stop the wild tumbling. The drama began to unfold at 7:22 P.M. with the disclosure of the trouble and the order to Armstrong and Scott to ditch the mission and head for their unscheduled descent into the Western Pacific.

The next big bulletin after that came at 7:44 P.M.: SPACE TWINS DOWN.

This is where 1966's Superhero, Batman, comes into the picture. CBS Television had stayed with the space story all the way and was on the air with it when that bulletin hit but NBC and ABC had to break into prime-time programs to flash the welcome news. ABC, then enjoying the largest audience of all because it was showing the new Batman serial, preempted a total of ten minutes as successive bulletins came from Gemini Control. In those ten minutes, with the nation presumably on the raw edge waiting to hear whether the astronauts were safe and well, the switchboards on the networks' affiliate stations lit up like Christmas trees as Batman's fans set up a roar of protest. In New York, the emergency operators pressed into service by ABC couldn't handle more than 300 angry calls in that time; they took another 700 or so after Batman and Robin, having triumphed over the seductive Catwoman of that night's episode, played by the amply endowed Julie Newmar, had withdrawn to their Batcave. NBC was swamped too, because the real-life saga in the Pacific first intruded on its piece of Western make-believe, *The Virginian,* and then knocked the Bob Hope Show off the air altogether. CBS registered about 500 complaining calls just for having elected at the very outset to cover the big story even though it meant bumping such scheduled Wednesday night fare as *The Beverly Hillbillies* and the Danny Kaye and Dick Van Dyke shows, not to mention an item ironically titled *Lost in Space.*

1

ABC, of course, figured to be the prime target of the disaffected masses because that network, shored up with the newfound services of the wealthy playboy who deserted the fleshpots to enlist in the war on evil, was in the process of chalking up a whopping 31-point rating on the New York Arbitron against a combined 11.4 for the two bigger outlets.

Now we don't need to know much about those two astronauts who inconvenienced so many of us when they put their lives on the line. Dave Scott went onward and upward, doing his bit in the race for the moon, and all Neil Armstrong did was to go up there with USAF Colonel Edwin E. (Buzz) Aldrin, Jr., in 1969 and become the first man to walk on it. But what about the Batman story?

To go to its actual inception, it began thirty-two years before Gemini 8 when a ten-year-old Bronx boy named Robert Kane, son of an insurance broker, began making copies of his own favorite comic strip characters, Mutt and Jeff, Popeye and Flash Gordon. When he was fourteen, the boy came upon Leonardo da Vinci's sketches of his "ornithopter," a batlike flying machine with flapping wings propelled by human muscles, and tried drawing his own version of that contraption. Then, while he was a student at DeWitt Clinton High School, Kane found himself entranced by some related items: a movie called *The Bat,* adapted from a Mary Roberts Rinehart story and starring Chester Morris as the Good Guy (the Bat was the Bad Guy in those days), Douglas Fairbanks Sr. performing his incredible gymnastics in the dual role of Don Diego Vega and Zorro in *The Mark of Zorro;* The Green Hornet, the mysterious Shadow of the airwaves, flitting across rooftops in his long black coat and, finally, the newly arrived Superman, the one in the skintight long johns.

From high school, Kane attended Cooper Union briefly on an art scholarship and then took a fast course in anatomy in a commercial class, all the while putting in long hours at his drawing board sketching a character he called "Birdman." By the time Kane was nineteen, in 1939, Birdman had become Batman, making his bow, quietly, among the assorted offerings in the pulp *Detective Comics.* Within a year, Batman had become sufficiently imposing to emerge in a comic book of his own. He was unconquerable from the start. He never really needed the Boy Wonder, but Kane threw in the sidekick in the second year to broaden the muscular hero's appeal to the younger set. In 1943, Batman and Robin were launched as a daily strip but couldn't go against Superman, and by 1946 they were out of the newspapers and back between cardboard covers, earning just

enough to enable their lanky creator to keep eating, get married and raise a daughter.

But Batman—"just an average millionaire out there fighting master criminals," in Kane's own put-down— was not doomed to fight the good fight forever in relative oblivion. Virtue's reward came in 1965 as an offshoot of the increasingly spreading twin viruses of Pop Art and Camp. Blown up to poster size, Kane's meal ticket suddenly appeared in the novelty shops along with Superman, Flash Gordon and the other comic heroes. Susan Sontag, the Supreme Court of Camp on the strength of her *Partisan Review* essay on the subject, issued a verdict of Low Camp on Batman in the *New York Times Magazine* early in 1965 and, lo, somebody at ABC had a bright idea about Batman: buy the rights and let William Dozier's Greenway Productions play around with a pilot film on the Twentieth Century-Fox lot.

Come winter, the Batman boom enjoyed another shot in the arm thanks to Hugh Hefner, the *Playboy* magnate, and a little serial Columbia Pictures made out of the comic book in 1943. Hefner, or some other bright soul in that empire built on triple-decker photos of the girls who take their bras in the larger sizes (but hardly ever wear them), dug out long-forgotten clips and ran a couple of segments in the theatre under his Chicago Playboy Club on a rainy Saturday afternoon. The cliff-hanger, starring Lewis Wilson and Douglas Croft as the Caped Crusader and his helper, J. Carroll Naish as Dr. Daka, the Japanese agent, and Shirley Patterson as Batman's best girl, simply entranced the idle Bunnies and the other stray onlookers. Hefner followed that small triumph with *An Evening with Batman*, daring the customers to endure all fifteen chapters in one four-hour-and-seventeen-minute sitting. This time he filled all 634 seats in his Temple of Sex with his guests, alternately cursing that loathsome Dr. Daka or shouting words of encouragement to Batman.

In any case, Batman and his little helper hit the airwaves the following January 12 with a force that must have been borrowed from the Nuclear Power Atomic Pole that adorns their Batcave. The show's Trendex rating on its second night reached a splendid 58.8 (one home out of every three), the highest score since the Beatles had dropped in on Ed Sullivan four months earlier. By early February, on the strength of its first four episodes, it had nudged its way into television's coveted Top Ten, and it would keep its Number 1 or Number 2 rating in its own Wednesday and Thursday time slots right through the year even while eventually dropping down in the overall national listings. And it wasn't all kid stuff: The calls which came

J. Carroll Naish (right) played the villainous Dr. Daka in the old movie version. Shirley Patterson was Batman's girl and you know he got her back.

Burgess Meredith as The Penguin, another bad guy.

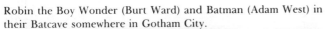

Julie Newmar was playing the Catwoman—and losing, of course—the night the drama in space intruded on Batman.

Robin the Boy Wonder (Burt Ward) and Batman (Adam West) in their Batcave somewhere in Gotham City.

in over the rude interruption caused by that poorly timed short circuit in space demonstrated this fact. The public was very much with Bruce Wayne (Adam West, ex-TV cowboy and bit player) and Dick Grayson (Burt Ward, age twenty, no previous record) in their relentless struggle against such supervillains as The Riddler (Frank Gorshin), The Joker (Cesar Romero), The Penguin (Burgess Meredith), Mr. Freeze (Otto Preminger), Evil Fingers (who but Liberace?) and such decorative female culprits as The Mob's Moll (Jill St. John) and that big cat Newmar.

What accounted for Batman's return from the grave? Dr. Charles Collins, psychotherapist, said he believed the underlying factors were "more pathological than nostalgic . . . people who have never felt a part of anything worthwhile cling to something familiar like the comic book heroes. It makes no demands on them and they can identify with it." Dr. Geoffrey Lindenauer echoed that view. "The whole thing is basically a question of identity," he said. "Modern man has so much free time that he is losing his sense of identity. He is existing in an emotional vacuum and he's looking for ways to fill it."

Child psychologist Eda Le Shan had a more serious concern. "To adults, the whole thing is a delicious joke; from the safety of their maturity, they look back with amusement on the hero of their youth. Children, on the other hand, particularly younger children, take the whole thing very seriously. For them the experience can be confusing." Dr. David Singer of Duke University's Psychology Department said that the grown-ups were tuning in to laugh at themselves because the Superhero they had turned to in the 1940's out of their own childhood insecurities had now become so ridiculous. Dr. Singer also offered a one-word analysis of the Caped Crusader's rampant new popularity: "Bat-taste." Maybe so, but a New York *Times* critic called it "the best therapy since Lawrence Welk's 'Champagne Music.'" The man couldn't have been far from wrong, for the Dynamic Duo never once ventured from Stately Wayne Manor in their atom-powered Batmobile without millions of their fellow Americans figuratively riding beside them—most of them no doubt chuckling but some perhaps taking it even more seriously than the very people who were behind the show.

William Dozier, whose previous credits included the much-honored Playhouse 90, conceded from the start that he was laying it on thick, Pop Art–style. He didn't want Batman in the bogus crime-doesn't-pay sweepstakes or in the by-then tempered race for ultimate violence on the home screen. Neither did the scriptwriter, Lorenzo Semple Jr. "There's none of the usual mindless violence," Semple said. "The show doesn't appeal to psychotics in any way. Of course, on a very sophisticated level, it's highly immoral, because crime seems to be fun." Indeed, they were simply following the path charted by Bob Kane. There never was any excessive bloodletting in Batman, just a succession of POWS! BAMS! KLUNKS! WHAPS! and KRAKS! to suggest that a spot of punishment was being meted out to the evildoer; nobody ever suffered the death penalty at the hands of that one-and-one-half-man law enforcement agency unwittingly sprung from the hand of Da Vinci four centuries earlier.

Our Russian cousins, of course, didn't see it quite that way. *Pravda*, dragging in the Vietnam war, assailed the Caped Crusader as a "representative of the broad mass of American billionaires who kills his enemies beautifully, effectively, and with taste, so that shoulder blades crack loudly and scalps break like cantaloupes." The Soviet newspaper found the sinister forces behind Batman "striving to brainwash the ordinary American, to get him used to the idea that murder is beautiful, that it is a worthy occupation for a real man, a superman."

Pravda overlooked the fact that Batman and Robin, far from administering homemade justice in the manner of the "lawmen" of the TV Westerns or, say, the shoot-now-talk-later method of Mickey Spillane's Mike Hammer, just tame the baddies of Gotham City and turn them over to Police Commissioner Gordon (Neil Hamilton) not only with an exemplary gentility but with a perhaps unwarranted compassion. Take the case of Mr. Freeze. This is a character who can survive only in subzero cold. He is determined to inflict his kind of chill on Gotham City, literally putting all the inhabitants on ice, which is no way to live at all. But when Batman rescues the shivering bathing beauty from the cake of ice (never mind how *she* got there) and puts the collar on Mr. Freeze, he insists that the Police Commissioner install him in a specially refrigerated cell so that he won't die. Why? "No man is all bad," says our hero. West, just a fair-sized six-feet-two and not the conventional ham-fisted TV muscleman, always played it straight. "If any actor plays it for laughs, he goes," Dozier said at the start. "He's got to act as if he's deciding whether to drop the bomb on Hanoi." Howie Horwitz, the producer, put it this way: "As soon as Adam West thinks he's funny, we're dead. It's Eagle Scout time all the way."

It was Camp time, too, of course, although Dozier couldn't stand the word. "It sounds so faggy," he said, doubtless bearing in mind the indictment drawn against Batman and his handsome ward back in 1954 in Dr. Fredric Wertham's withering study of the

Neither was movie director Otto Preminger, in the role of Professor Egghead, a/k/a Mr. Freeze, a match for the Caped Crusader.

Marsha, Queen of Diamonds (Carolyn Jones) used a magic love potion to lure our hero to the altar—but the wedding bells never sounded. Batman had too much to do to kill any time with the other sex.

comic books, *Seduction of the Innocent*. "Only someone ignorant of the fundamentals of psychiatry and of the psycho-pathology of sex can fail to realize a subtle atmosphere of homoerotism which pervades the adventures of the mature Batman and his young friend Robin," the psychiatrist had said. "It is like a wish dream of two homosexuals living together." Revived when the TV show was on its way to the home screens, the Wertham suggestion of twisted sex in good old Wayne Manor brought forth the most strenuous rebuttals.

"To me," Kane told the author, "Batman is the epitome of virility and manliness—just the opposite image of the fag. I'd like to be Batman. A lot of guys would like to be him. *You* would like to be him. Wertham read homosexuality into this thing because I portrayed a man and a boy living in a big house together—in the same bedroom—with just a butler and no female around. The doctor read the homosexuality into it, through *his* eyes, but for that matter he also put down the Wonder Woman comic as a Lesbian invention. Hell, beauty and evil and even homosexuality are often in the eyes of the beholder. It was all hogwash but I had to do something about it anyway.

So I changed their bedrooms and I added Aunt Harriet—sort of a mother to both of them. Even so, I suppose the homosexuals like the TV show because of those tight outfits Adam West and Burt Ward wear. I imagine they sit around watching them on the screen and slap each other on the knees with the sheer joy of it all, but what can you do about that? I can't change the characters because they weren't homos in the first place and because you have to be crazy to fight success."

Dozier also testified for the defense. "I never saw anything like that in the comic book," he said. "There's no doubt that Batman and Robin like girls, even though they may be too busy fighting crime to have much time for it." Burt Ward, in the young married set himself (twice, in fact), took up the echoing Wertham challenge with this: "If anything, Batman and Robin represent the wish dream to be good. I don't think it's wrong to go out and catch crooks." Not even Dr. Wertham could argue with that concept, but the other side eventually went to even greater lengths. In time, Batman lost his head altogether and let a woman in his life. The Queen of Diamonds (Carolyn Jones) fed the guy a magic love potion and he went all the way to the altar, on the air, before finding out that she was up to no good. The deceitful Queen had to go, of course, but the point was made: Kane's crimebuster had all the more desirable instincts. Lest anybody doubt it, a full-time Batgirl—Yvonne Craig—was written into the script for the fall 1967 season.

The esoteric quarrel over the sexuality of the new TV heroes evidently had little impact. When Batman and Robin went back into newspaper syndication they quickly picked up more than two hundred clients, in itself a sure testament to their masculinity; what editor on a red-blooded American daily would buy an adventure strip with a homosexual theme? For that matter, would Carroll College in Helena, Montana, put back its Evening Rosary for Batman if the guy wasn't all man? Would that Methodist Church in Bella Vista, California, switch the hours on choir practice to let the kids see a TV show with that kind of undercurrent? Perish the thought.

And how about the American breadwinner? It was quite plain that he bore no animus toward the Dynamic Duo. The Licensing Corporation of America, handling the inevitable merchandising boom as the fad caught on, had no less than a thousand Batman items on the way to market from a small army of manufacturers well before the spring of 1966. You could take your pick: Batmasks, Batcapes, Batguns, Batcars, Batbelts, Batplanes, Batmobiles (model size), Batjackets, Batman posters, Batman LP's, Batman guitars, Batpaper (for the kid's room), Batlamps, Batman rain capes, Batkites, Batpens . . . name it. Jay Emmett, LCA's president, talked about sales of 75 to 100 million dollars' worth of Batitems in the first year. While there was nothing on the list to compare with that very special product Clark Kent was responsible for,

Superman Enriched Bread, a rash of sideline gimmicks did turn up. Thus you could dance the Batusi with a girl who had just had her hair done in the new Batman cut, and in a San Francisco bistro you could be entertained by Batgirl (topless, of course) and The Batmen. Things like that.

And the craze, obviously, wouldn't be lost on the Pop Art set. Early Batman comic books soared in price so wildly that the first edition went to 100 dollars a copy. Bob Kane himself not only couldn't find one to buy but heard that the more affluent collectors on the West Coast were offering as much as 500 dollars per copy. Neither was he knocking the high price on his own creation. "Batman has a certain place in history," he said. "It's American culture. I feel it's High Camp—*High Class Camp*—but I was Camp twenty years ago. There's a Batman comic book in the 1939 World's Fair time capsule. I will admit that I didn't see too much in Pop Art at first. I couldn't see the point of enlarging Superman's head twenty-five times. Now I can. After all, Pop Art brought Batman back for me, and you know you don't analyze something like this, you accept it."

The people, young and old, traditionally on the side of the angels in the war between good and evil, accepted it. But, alas, nothing in our society is more fickle than the love of the television viewer for last year's heroes. The jury at ABC was out quite a while before the show was renewed for the fall 1967 season because the ratings were dipping. Batman needed his whole arsenal to combat such a formidable enemy, and before 1968 expired Mr. Freeze would win that battle. Bill Dozier never should have let the Caped Crusader put him in the icebox.

SUPERMAN:

Muscles to Burn

"Rarely have so many identified
themselves so profoundly with
anything so vague."
—HEINZ POLITZER, discussing
Superman in *Commentary* magazine

JUST FOR OPENERS, Hercules throttled the Nemean lion with his bare hands and dispatched the nine-headed Hydra and those man-eating Stymphalian birds without working up a sweat. Samson, tricked into losing his Beatle cut by that whore Delilah, tore down the temple of the Philistines. Closer to our time, but not one to shrug off by any means, Tarzan hurtled through the towering trees and handled the beasts of the jungle like so many lapdogs. And in the very moment in history under discussion here, Douglas Fairbanks Sr. made mincemeat of the human beast, in any shape or form.

To Jerry Siegel, a peace-loving teen-ager taking his lumps on the streets of Depression-torn Cleveland because the other kids were bigger and stronger, there was inspiration in that oddly assorted quartet assembled out of legend, the Bible, fiction and the silver screen. Nursing shiners in his own private world of fantasy, he dreamed of a muscleman who would make those guys look like pantywaists. He dreamed of six-footer Clark Kent, who wore glasses, like himself, and toiled as a meek and shy reporter on the *Daily Planet* until trouble loomed from some quarter, *any* quarter, whereupon he would slip swiftly into some secluded place like a telephone booth, strip down to his blue and red shorts, drape his beautiful frame in a form-

fitting jumper with what looked like an athletic supporter on the outside, and go "smack down the bullies of the world." He dreamed of Superman, known more modestly as the Man of Steel and even more modestly as the Man of Tomorrow. And the next step? Siegel, son of an immigrant clothier (Man of Cloth, you could say), got lucky. In Glenville High School there was another boy—smaller and even more fragile—who had a pen to match young Siegel's endlessly vivid imagination. Joe Shuster, born in Toronto and son of a tailor, put Superman on paper to the Siegel specifications, but it wasn't easy to get the new one-man police force (all right, throw in the FBI and Interpol) off the ground. The comics editors of the time, evidently much less daring than one would have expected in *their* fantasy world, had their doubts about that hooded, flying wonderworker. How do you like that? They had no trouble buying the exploits of the Shadow, the Green Hornet or the Lone Ranger, let alone such pre-Sputnik spaceship jockeys as Flash Gordon and Buck Rogers—but Superman? A character who could lift an ocean liner out of the drink with one hand, set the Empire State Building right when it started to topple, shake off Death Rays, push over mountains, outrun bullets, bounce cannonballs off his chest, crack safes with his fists and walk

Jerry Siegel (standing) concocted a character blessed, all at once, with "super-courage, super-goodness and super-justice"— Superman, who else? Joe Shuster happened to be on hand to do the drawing. Shown in 1941, the pair made the mistake of selling the rights to their Man of Steel before he took off, so they wound up broke. *WWP*

through steel doors like they were made out of Kleenex? Silly. The kids would never believe it. Thus Superman, who started out as just an average healthy boy from the planet Krypton (with self-propulsion, X-ray vision, skin you couldn't bruise or cut and rabbit ears tuned in on the whole world) before he took a paying job and acquired the dual role of Clark Kent, kept coming home to his pint-sized creators as fast as they sent him out for inspection. The McClure Syndicate itself turned the strip down six times in three years. And then the lightning—Superman could handle that too, by the way—struck. *Action Comics* needed a filler for its issue of June, 1938, and bought thirteen pages of Superman's adventures for a modest ten dollars a page. Iron Jaw did nothing less than double the magazine's sales. McClure saw the light and started selling the guy to the newspapers—like 300 of them, in time—six months later. A bimonthly *Superman* magazine ran up sales of 1,500,000 per issue and a *Superman Quarterly* hit the market. By 1940 Superman was a radio star, and the next year, under lease to Paramount Pictures, he emerged on the screen as

an animated cartoon, in time to turn live in the person of George Reeves and later, in 1966, to emerge on the Broadway stage as a musical comedy hero. Before the war, Superman comic books were being published in seventy-six countries in thirteen different languages. In this country, estimates of the fans drawn to the Siegel-Shuster creation in its numerous outlets ran as high as 35,000,000. In 1941, 200,000 children joined Supermen of America, pledging themselves to "aid the cause of JUSTICE" and, for a ten-cent fee, acquiring a fancy membership certificate, a Superman button and a secret Superman code. And the two guys who dreamed it all up? Siegel and Shuster sold the rights to their cartoon hero in 1948 and both wound up close to destitution while their Man of Steel got richer and richer. In 1975 Siegel was eking out a $7,000-a-year living as a mail clerk in Los Angeles with his ex-model wife, Joanne—the original inspiration for Lois Lane—and a daughter to support. Shuster, a bachelor and legally blind, was being supported by a younger brother in New York. The National Cartoonists Society stepped in at that point and wangled a deal from Warner Communications, present owner of the Superman empire, to pay each of the two sixty-one-year-old artists $20,000 annually for the rest of their lives.

How far did Superman's influence extend when he turned his attention from such bush leaguers as Superbum Luthor, nipped over to the war-torn Continent, smashed the West Wall with one of those ham fists of his, scooped A. Hitler out of Berchtesgaden and Stalin out of the Kremlin and hauled them before the suddenly come-to-life League of Nations to get peace restored? *Liberty* magazine had a journeyman reporter look into Clark Kent's other life, and the man wrote this in September, 1941:

Superman unquestionably has many millions of grown-ups as followers. Eighty-six percent of the parents into whose homes he enters Sundays read him as they do the Bible. Several hundred West Pointers, midshipmen, coastguardsmen and draftees have actually become Supermen of America and follow the secret code messages. Joe Louis reads him faithfully, and his devotees include a du Pont, a LaFollette, a Roosevelt and, since both LaGuardia kids are Supermen of America, it is to be expected that the Little Flower himself derives inspiration from the man he so obviously emulates!

Extravagant, but you had to believe that last part; those of us who knew Fiorello LaGuardia, the last real good Mayor of New York, had no trouble buying it. As far as any of the others went, there were no denials forthcoming from any du Ponts, LaFollettes or Roosevelts. Nor from the heavyweight champion, the one citizen in the lot who happened to be stronger than Superman at the time.

What made Superman fly so high, in any case?

In *The Comics*, published in 1947, cartoonist Coulton Waugh put it this way:

This has been a superage. We have had (ah, me!) super prosperity, super slumps, super salesmen, super cars, super peanut butter and super flypaper. Superman was an inevitable concept, the obvious top to the super trend. The simple and marvelously effective idea back of Superman was to take one of the interplanetary heroes, who, as we have seen, had added super-normal powers to their sex-bursting physique, and allow him to whip through the setting of our place and time. The world, life itself, has come to be fearfully difficult for millions of people. The body of the great public is highly disturbed; it would like to do something about it, but it doesn't know what to do. The individuals who make it up feel their own smallness, their soft brains and bellies—then along comes Superman.

Waugh saw Superman as a modern-day Paul Bunyan. To sociologist Heinz Politzer, in a 1949 *Commentary* article, he was a "Li'l Abner without Mammy Yokum and without popular background, a hillbilly without the fertile background of folklore or remnants of creed . . . he has merely put on his credo like his winged cloak." Politzer, indeed, was terribly worried about the guy.

Superman, in fact, is a figure of dual identity. . . . But the dual identity motif is the schema of Dr. Jekyll and Mr. Hyde—a pattern bordering on that of the pathological swindler and criminal. For a popular figure, it is not without its dangers. The double face and the split personality are symptoms of a disease that has attacked our civilization. And, more often than not, it is also an attribute of modern dictators, perhaps of the tyrants of all epochs. Superman has become anchored in those sections of the population that are most naive, most capable of enthusiasms, and most susceptible to revolutionary impulses . . . [and] has it in him to become a political figure. To play with him is to play with the dynamite of our times.

A long, long way, obviously, from Jerry Siegel's own simple concept: "We got the idea for Superman when we both decided that all comic strip heroes are sissies. We do not stress the intellectual side of Superman. People do not dream of being superintelligent. A boy dreams of being strong enough to whip the guy who took his girl . . . or something like that." Something, but no high politics.

Looking back from the vantage point of 1959, Stephen Becker, in *Comic Art in America*, weighed the scales between those who saw Superman as a force for good and those who saw him as a dangerous peddler of the concept of absolute power and came up with this judgment:

Superman may have been partly a wish fulfillment: hesitant to accept battle with the evil loose in the world, parents quietly approved the presence of this fictional strong man who would have been such a comfort had he existed. And then there were legitimate elements of suspense and melodrama. Superman's origins were mysterious and otherworldly. Set down on earth, he had become an American, which was properly patriotic. When war broke out, the country went through the necessary psychological preparations for battle, which included the process of persuading men that they were heroes. Irresponsible social philosophy or not, Superman was the sensation of the early forties (during which time many of the staid, conventional children's magazines were quietly laid to rest).

And to Jules Feiffer, in *The Great Comic Book Heroes* (1965):

The particular brilliance of Superman lay not only in the fact that he was the first of the superheroes, but in the concept of his alter ego. What made Superman different from the legion of imitators to follow was not that when he took off his clothes he could beat everybody up—they all did that. What made Superman extraordinary was his point of origin: Clark Kent.

In that connection, there is a noteworthy item which must have endeared the *Liberty* reporter's Bible-reading adults to Superman. We're coming to sex, but something less than Supersex, now. For the best part of three decades—decades that have seen so many of the moral codes swept into the discard—Clark Kent has lusted after sobsister Lois Lane with what must be described as Superdesire.

But he never made the pass, Mother, even though the babe made no secret of how much she hankered after him. He had more important things to do, and he never swerved from his duty. And so he did great honor to the Fourth Estate and, indeed, to flag and country and what's left of the tattered ideal of the American woman. He was never banned in Boston and never called any bad names by Dr. Wertham either. Put Superman down as the Mr. Clean of the fads. For the first forty-two years of his life in the comics you had to list Superman as the Mr. Clean of the cartoon heroes, because the guy never took his pants off except in the noblest of causes. But, then, how long can the male animal hold out? In a 1975 comic book, No. 297 in the series, Mr. Kent turned up in a candlelit session with Lois in his apartment, and darned if there wasn't all kinds of smooching and Miss Lane plaintively asking, "Clark, where have you been all my life?" Earlier, the Krypton-bred reporter is shown stowing his blue, red and yellow serious working gear in his secret closet and saying, "Something's got to give . . . and I've decided that 'something' is my life as Superman."

No way. By 1974 Superman was in the hands of the moviemakers again in what started out to be a little $8- or $9-million film, turned into *Superman* and *Superman II*, and passed the $35-million mark—a record—before it was ready for release more than four years later (But let's not brood over all that money. *Superman* grossed $32 million in its first three months and then soared past $100 million on its way to an all-time high.

The new Superman is six-foot-four Christopher Reeve, a twenty-six-year-old New York actor who had to spend six months in intensive body-building to fit the role. If you're wondering about that staggering production cost, well—there're all those sets, like the planet Krypton itself, location shooting in England, New Mexico, and New York, and a rather expensive cast surrounding Reeve, who collected a big $250,000 for two years of his sweat and came out of it a very bitter (super)man. Superman's father, Jor-el, happens to be Marlon Brando (only $3.7 million for twelve days' work, or $27,000 per hour) surrounded by such super- and near superstars as Gene Hackman, Valerie Perrine, Susannah York, Maria Schell, Glenn Ford and Trevor Howard. Mr. Kent's girl is Margot Kidder, and there's no dilly-dallying this time. "We make love right away," says the new Lois Lane, a slim brunette, "but it's tasteful."

Praise the Lord.

The new movie Superman, Christopher Reeve, dressed for the part . . .

. . . and in his other life as the newspaper reporter, photographed in the city room of the New York *Daily News*. Director Richard Donner is at right, and the new Lois Lane, Margot Kidder, is at the typewriter.

Who else could be the scientist Jor-El, Superman's father? That's Marlon Brando with the kid from the planet Krypton. Susannah York is the mother in the multimillion-dollar two-part movie. The baby is Lee Quigley.

ZORRO RIDES AGAIN
(and again)

"Bravery never goes out of fashion."
—THACKERAY

BEFORE SUPERMAN and before Batman, there was a Caped Crusader who did it all by himself. He didn't need X-ray vision or his own private Nuclear Power Atomic Pole. He didn't need an electromagnetic vest or a silly old Batmobile. All he needed was some cutlery, like a finely honed dueling sword ("a flame to right every wrong") and a horse. His name was Zorro. He was the one-man gang who kept things straight in California back in the 1820's when the Golden State was under the high heel of the Conquistadores, an even more terrifying breed than the American movie moguls who settled out there almost a century later.

Zorro came out of the pages of Johnston McCulley's novel, *The Mark of Zorro,* an item dashed off in six days. Like Batman, he had another identity. He was Don Diego Vega, the only son of the wealthiest hidalgo in California. In the daytime, he lolled around the hacienda having himself a high old time, as befit his station, but at night, watch out, baby. No evildoer was safe when Zorro put on his mask and cape, buckled on his sword and whistled for the raven-black Tornado (it came out Tornahdo when Zorro talked to the brave horse).

If there is such a thing as an imperishable commodity in Hollywood, it has to be Zorro. Douglas Fairbanks Sr., the All-American male, cut the mold in 1920, slicing the bad *hombres* down to size even when he had to vault over walls, swing from chandeliers or leap from balconies to get the job done. He didn't need any Boy Wonder to help him, or any Supergirl, for that matter. Two decades later, Twentieth Century-Fox brought back Zorro (well, Zorro *means* fox) in the person of Tyrone Power, for another generation to feast its eyes on, and Walt Disney rescued the caped swordsman from the celluloid vault again in 1958 to show him off on the *little* screen.

The television Zorro was Guy Williams, out of a bloodline which surely came closer to the role than that of his celebrated predecessors. Williams' square name was Armand Catalano and they said he was made to order for the role because he knew a thing or two about swords. The story was that his father, Attilio, had fought a duel of honor as a young man in Italy and taught Armand to fence when he was a boy. Mr. Disney, of course, didn't take any chances; lest the strapping Catalano-Williams cut himself while

11

dueling, he called in Fred Cavens, the durable Belgian fencing master who had coached both the earlier Zorros, to brush up his techniques. The new Zorro, a bit player and model who happened to be slightly broke when the McCulley hero enjoyed another resurrection on the Disney lot, was a huge success.

ABC-TV had the serial on 173 outlets across the American pampas, and the usual merchandising brains went to work on our pocketbooks for some 25 million dollars' worth in 1957 and 1958. While it lasted, there were Zorro capes, Zorro swords, Zorro T-shirts, Zorro gloves, Zorro rings, Zorro books, Zorro records and Zorro jigsaw puzzles, among other items. And in the plush Colony restaurant in New York, for those who had that much money left, there was Chicken à la Zorro.

Douglas Fairbanks, Sr., shields Marguerite De La Motte while preparing to cut down the cad Robert McKim in the original *Mark of Zorro*, filmed in 1920 by United Artists.

Linda Darnell and Tyrone Power in the 20th Century-Fox remake of *Zorro* in the Forties.

Boyd and his co-star, Topper. The actor died in 1972 at seventy-four.

GOLD IN THEM HILLS:

Hopalong Cassidy

"With fathers away from family life so much
in modern times, mothers are afraid
the boys will imitate them instead of their fathers
and turn into sissies; they encourage their little boys
to copy the current play ideal of masculinity."
—MARGARET MEAD, the anthropologist

THE THING ABOUT television's Hopalong Cassidy was that he would rather *not* fire a shot in anger. If sweet talkin' would do it, why go to the six-gun and shed another man's blood? Peace, brother, even on the lawless frontier, and darned if that soft-sell prescription—nonviolence in a violent time and place—wasn't worth a fortune. In the movies, with the conventional rough stuff, the old oatburner just turned a fair profit. Tidied up in 1949 for the little screen and all them willing captives at home, with the mayhem left on the cutting room floor, Hollywood's longest-running serial burdened the real-life Hoppy with the most awful tax problems. Even then the silver-haired Bill Boyd, who had the brains to see it all coming, didn't reach for his temper. He just wondered out loud what profiteth it a man to perform all those deeds of valor and decency and come out with such a strained purse when the revenooers got through with him.

How did it all begin?

When producer Harry Sherman bought the screen rights to six of Clarence E. Mulford's Bar-20 stories in 1934, he wanted Bill Boyd to play the dashing cowhand, Buck Peters, but the actor liked the role of Buck's sidekick better. That guy wouldn't shrink from the chase even after a rustler's bullet shattered his knee. "Oh, I can hop along with the rest of you," he told Buck, so they called him Hopalong. That's what caught Bill Boyd's eye. "Boy," he said. "Hopalong Cassidy! What a wonderful name for the kids."

It proved to be one of history's larger understatements.

In the next twelve years, Boyd made sixty-five of the small Western epics. The Illinois-born Mulford, who was toiling as a marriage license clerk in the wild environs of Brooklyn when he wrote his first Western and went on to turn out twenty-eight novels about the badlands before he ever set foot in the cow country, couldn't keep up with the whirring cameras. Sherman and Boyd had to call in spare writers after a while.

The last six Hoppy movies, slapped together on ninety-hour shooting schedules with penny-ante budgets, were made in 1947. The mine was all dried out by then but the real bonanza, courtesy of NBC-TV, lay ahead. The younger set embraced Mulford's Good Guy with so much fervor that the old film quickly ran out and Boyd had to saddle up the white horse Topper, a creaking sixteen years old by then, and go back before the cameras. In the custom-made version,

From an early oatburner: William Boyd has a friendly armlock on Gabby Hayes.

Author Clarence Mulford, creator of Hopalong Cassidy, was seventy-one when this photo was made in 1954. *WWP*

the kids never even saw an Indian bite the dust, but that had as much to do with plain economics as it did with Boyd's hearts-and-flowers formula. "The price of Indians is way up," he said in a doleful commentary on the America of the Fifties. "I used to get a whole tribe for practically nothing. Now they have a union." With or without the redman, without cussin' or bad words like "ain't" or such abuses of the English primer as "they went thataway," without anything stronger than "sarsparilly" to wet his lips, the strapping, silver-haired Boyd assumed towering proportions.

When the *Daily News* brought Boyd to New York in January, 1950, to promote the new comic strip fashioned after him, the line of small-fry admirers waiting to see their hero in the flesh stretched for blocks and blocks. The *News*, allowing for a smidgin of exaggeration, put the figure at 350,000. But you didn't have to blow up the numbers much; wherever he went, whole hordes turned out to hail the man in the white ten-gallon hat.

"Every kid needs a hero," said Cecil B. DeMille. "Hopalong Cassidy takes the place of Buffalo Bill, Babe Ruth, Lindbergh and all the rest."

The director spoke with understandable pride. Back in 1919 he spotted the young William Lawrence Boyd in an extra's role in a thing of his own called *Why Change Your Wife?* and got him signed to a five-year contract with the Famous Players-Lasky studio for a Model T-type thirty-dollar-a-week guarantee. Then he watched him pick up seasoning in some run-of-the-mill Westerns and gave him his big chance in 1926—the lead in *The Volga Boatmen,* followed by a fair part in *The King of Kings.* Boyd, an Ohioan who spent his youth in Oklahoma and worked as a tool dresser, surveyor, automobile salesman, lumber camp hand, orange packer and oil driller before heading for the movie mills, blossomed into star ranking on a $2,500-a-week contract with Pathé when the talkies arrived but his career was fading when the scripts wrung out of the Mulford novels fell into his lap. The

role of Hoppy didn't do much more than furnish him with $100,000 a year—enough to keep Boyd and his third wife, dancer Grace Bradley, in groceries and things—but television changed all that overnight.

Having had the foresight to buy the rights from Mulford in 1948, the actor cashed in beyond his wildest dreams. The TV royalties were secondary. In 1950, when he made his debut on radio and in a syndicated comic strip, Boyd drew 5 percent off the top on sales of millions of dollars' worth of Hopalong Cassidy items ranging from bicycles with built-in holsters to skates with spurs and jewel-studded straps, toy guns, snowsuits, cowboy outfits (all the way from $1.95 to $75), shirts, bathrobes, towels, raincoats, rugs, bed-spreads, candy bars, cookies, peanut butter, soaps, swimsuits, gum, tumblers, watches and wallpaper. Ninety manufacturers shared in that selling orgy.

In 1951, *Business Week* furnished this breakdown of Boyd's income: $600,000 from the commercial tie-ins, $350,000 from TV royalties (including pieces from England, France, Italy, Mexico and South America), $55,000 from Hoppy comic books (selling around 15,000,000 a year against total sales of 4,000,000 for all the Mulford novels), and $7,000 in record royalties. Personal appearances and other odds and ends boosted the take to $2,032,000 but the star's manager, Robert Stabler, produced figures showing that Boyd Enterprises couldn't possibly net more than $728,000 after taxes, shaking down to $140,000 when such items as payroll and expenses came out. Even that figure was impressive when you consider that Clarence Mulford picked up a neat ninety dollars when he sold the first adventure of his gimpy hero to *Outing* magazine back in 1907, but nobody was sing-ing hosannas. Boyd himself said he would sell off the whole shebang if any believer in Hopalong Cassidy's future came up with, oh, eight million dollars. He must have known that the kids were sure to get hooked on one new idol or another as time hopped along.

Like Davy Crockett . . .

The real Crockett.

THE KING OF NOTHING:

Davy Crockett

Born on a mountain top in Tennessee
Greenest state in the land of the free
Raised in the woods so he knew every tree
Killed him a b'ar when he was only three
—THE BALLAD OF DAVY CROCKETT*

WAS HE KING of the Wild Frontier or just another dissolute, blabbermouthed, rum-soaked bum? In 1955, you could have your pick. There were two Davy Crocketts—one celebrated on television by Walt Disney and so wildly embraced by the pre-teen set that all manner of products were being sold in his name, the other torn to shreds in the literary marketplace of the grown-ups who knew their history. Start with John Fisher, the erudite editor of *Harper's*. Appalled by the highly embossed Disneyland version of old Davy, Fisher coldly described the revived folk hero as a juvenile delinquent, a runaway, a wife-deserter, a shiftless tiller of the soil, a tin soldier who weaseled his way out of the Creek War by hiring a stand-in to finish his tour of duty, a justice of the peace singularly bereft of any acquaintance with the law of the land, a failure in politics, a hack writer (with a ghost, no less) and, perish the thought, a violin player. Fisher did give Davy Crockett credit for dying at the Alamo, although he saw more bungling and stupidity than heroism in that "blood-splashed ruin," but came finally to this harsh verdict:

He never was king of anything, except maybe

the Tennessee Tall Tales and Bourbon Samplers' Association. When he claimed that he had shot 105 bear (stet) in nine months, his fellow tipplers refused to believe a word of it, on the grounds that Davy couldn't count that high.

Fisher wasn't alone. In his syndicated column, Harry Golden conceded that Crockett was a frontiersman but observed that "he was out on the frontier only because it was an easier place to live than in a home with a growing brood. Davy had a flock of children and he left them and his wife and never bothered with any of them again. He set the cause of married life back about 200 years." Murray Kempton, in the New York *Post*, observed that "Davy grew up to be a very brave young man, who would bear any hardship to escape a routine day's work." More in humor than anger, Kempton made the point that the new TV hero put in two months with the Andrew Jackson forces in the Indian wars, never fired a shot at a redman in anger, and went home. "He was a tosspot and a brawler," the columnist said, adding that when Crockett saw his first bear he ran like a thief even though he was practically a grown-up eight-year-old. This was perhaps the cruelest cut of all, but there was more to come from other spoilsports. One quoted President Jackson's open denunciations of Crockett while Davy was enjoying a Congressional absentee record that wouldn't be paralleled until men like Harlem's Adam Clayton Powell came on the scene a hundred years later. Another recalled that a Missouri newspaper had charged Davy with such deplorable derelictions as drunkenness and adultery. Others coldly noted that the whole legend derived more from the potboiling Crockett autobiography and the fabricated Crockett *Almanacs* published between 1835 and 1856 than from anything that ever happened on the real frontier.

You couldn't tell that to the small fry, of course. The long-striding, straight-shooting Davy Crockett they saw on the home screen in those frilly buckskins fresh from the dry cleaner made Dan'l Boone and a whole array of earlier American giants look like five-and-dime-store models. *Their* Davy Crockett happened to be the impeccably upright Fess Parker (six-feet-five upright), who shaved every day, very likely bathed every day, killed off some of them bad Mexicans every day and never, never let either the Demon Rum or a bad word cross his lips. *Their* Davy Crockett *was* the King of the Wild Frontier—Walt Disney's frontier. When Disney had to let him perish at the Alamo (well, Davy was on hand when Santa Anna's cavalry swept down on the ill-fated garrison), the kids set up such a roar of protest that the man in the coonskin hat had to be brought back to life in a full-length movie, *Legends of Davy Crockett.*

The Crockett boom lasted seven months. In that time the "Ballad of Davy Crockett," theme song of the TV show, was recorded in sixteen different versions (including the "Davy Crockett Mambo") and 4,000,000 copies were sold. In book form, the newly revived legend sold 14,000,000 copies, and for a while there was nothing much harder to buy in this country than a raccoon tail, because coonskin caps were selling like popsicles. The price of raccoon tails, a long-slumbering item until Texas-born Fess Parker came out of a bit player's obscurity, went from twenty-five cents a pound to as much as six and eight dollars. In the name of the dauntless enemy of the Big Black B'ar, retailers pushed something like 100 million dollars' worth of merchandise across the counters in hundreds of items ranging from toy flintlocks to knives to bows and arrows to leggings to moccasins to wallets to plastic powder horns to jigsaw puzzles to playroom rugs to bedspreads to towels "the kids will beg to take a bath with" to guitars to school lunch boxes to bathing suits and baby shoes and every other conceivable item of wearing apparel. When coonskin ran short for the caps, the resourceful, prospering furriers switched to Australian rabbit, skunk and silver fox. And when the Borg-Warner Corporation decided to push its sales of Norge refrigerators and other appliances by giving away Davy Crockett pup tents with every purchase, the little old tentmaker couldn't make them fast enough; what parent could pass up that kind of giveaway and face his children in the morning?

Vincent H. Jefferds, merchandising manager for Disney in the United States (oh, yes, the fad had its overseas partisans too), watched the great buying wave pass the earlier booms in Mickey Mouse, Hopalong Cassidy and Daniel Boone items and described the thing as "absolute madness." So did the happy buyers for such retail outlets as Macy's and Gimbels as orders swamped their stores. Another buyer, badgered until his nerves were frayed, lost his cheer. "The next person who mentions Davy Crockett to me," he said, "gets a Davy Crockett flintlock over his head."

Sylvia Porter, the syndicated financial columnist, looked over the phenomenal singsong of the cash registers that spring and made this observation on the fabulous selling power of television: "The youngsters always have had a vital influence over the family's spending habits—but now even the pre-reading ones are developing definite buying habits. We're creating a nation of spenders from infancy." Miss Porter detected something else in the frenzied shopping spree.

"It tells as much about us in 1955 as the original tall tales about Davy Crockett told about America in 1835," she said.

But the boom had to end. Before the year was out, the small fry lost interest. The buying wave tapered off and then came to a dead stop and Davy Crockett was the *ex*-King of the Frontier, relegated to the faded folklore hero of his pre-TV days. What happened? "Manufacturers were shipping Davy Crockett items as fast as they could make them," said Jerome Fryer, president of the Toy Manufacturers of the U.S.A. "Then one Monday morning the phones stopped ringing and the orders stopped coming. Don't ask me why everyone picked that day. They just did." The National Retail Dry Goods Association, doubtless mindful of all the member outlets suddenly stuck with newly replenished stocks, observed in mournful tones that "kids are more fickle than women." Professor Paul F. Lazarsfeld, chairman of Columbia University's Department of Sociology, offered a more learned explanation:

A fad satisfies a need for status and common experience among kids. Parents welcome it, too—sometimes subconsciously. First, because it helps keep kids out of their hair. Second, because the hunger of children for new experience usually is far beyond the inventive capacity of even the most devoted parents. And a fad provides a clear-cut line of gratification: "If you're good, you'll get a Davy Crockett cap." But a fad disappears when its function has "functioned" long enough. Function is a term the sociologists invented to avoid saying "good" or "bad." The more pressure behind a fad, the more quickly it'll run out.

Variety put the matter in much more vivid terms. "Davy," said the show business weekly, "was the biggest thing since Marilyn Monroe and Liberace but he pancaked. He laid a bomb."

Of course. Davy Crockett was back where he started, the King of Nothing.

They let Parker die with glory at the Alamo but then, prompted by the outraged cries of his young fans, brought him back on the big screen in *Legends of Davy Crockett.* Here Walt Disney, who died in 1966, visits his star on the set. Parker enjoyed another rebirth in 1964 in the role of Daniel Boone, the authentic backwoods trailblazer whose explorations of the Indian-infested Kentucky frontier opened up major settlements in the 1870s. Dan'l, celebrated in Lord Byron's *Don Juan,* had to take a back seat in his own land until the Crockett boom ran its course. *All Fess Parker photos © Walt Disney Productions*

Fess Parker, the TV movie Crockett.

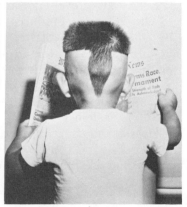

Three-year-old Robert Eugene Powell of Wichita Falls, Texas, didn't need a coonskin cap. His father simply cut his hair in the necessary style.

007:

Licensed to Kill (and sell)

"I have a rule of never looking back.
Otherwise I'd wonder, 'How could I write
such piffle?' "
—IAN FLEMING

Ursula Andress and Sean Connery with Ian Fleming on the set of
Dr. No in 1963. The author died at the height of 007's fame on
the screen.

THE THIN MAN cut the cane seat out of the armchair
with his clasp knife and made James Bond strip. Then
Le Chiffre came back, carrying a pot of coffee, a
three-foot carpet beater in twisted cane and a carving
knife. He settled down next to the armchair with the
cut-out bottom. Now go on with the story—

Bond stood stark naked in the middle of the
room, bruises showing livid on his white body, his
face a grey mask of exhaustion and knowledge of
what was to come.

"Sit down there." Le Chiffre nodded at the
chair in front of him.

Bond walked over and sat down.

The thin man produced some flex. With this
he bound Bond's wrists to the arms of the chair
and his ankles to the front legs. He passed a
double strand across his chest, under the armpits
and through the chair-back. He . . . left no play
in any of the bindings. All of them bit sharply
into Bond's flesh . . .

He was utterly a prisoner, naked and defence-
less.

His buttocks and the underpart of his body

protruded through the seat of the chair towards
the floor . . .

Le Chiffre lit a cigarette and swallowed a
mouthful of coffee. Then he picked up the cane
carpet-beater and, resting the handle comfortably
on his knee, allowed the flat trefoil base to lie on
the floor directly under Bond's chair.

He looked at Bond carefully, almost caressingly
in the eyes. Then his wrist sprang suddenly upwards on his knee.

The result was startling.*

Startling, indeed.

The little exercise in torture Le Chiffre had devised for 007, quite a guy with the girls, was almost
too ghastly, too hideous to contemplate. Except for
the merciful arrival of the hairy assassin dispatched
by SMERSH to kill the double-dealing Le Chiffre,
007 would have come out of that experience in *Casino Royale* talking in a high-pitched voice and looking the other way every time one of those gloriously
stacked Ian Fleming babes came into view. Try to

* From *Casino Royale*, by Ian Fleming, Macmillan, New York.
© 1953, Glidrose Productions, Ltd.

imagine that. Solitaire, Gala Brand, Tiffany Case, Tatiana Romanova, Honeychile Rider, the tireless Jill Masterson, Pussy Galore, Domino Vitali, Vivienne Michel, Tracy (the one the spy loved), Kissy Suzuki. All wasted, and what a waste.

But that's not the point of this bloody essay.

We have dealt in this section with the likes of Batman, Superman, Zorro, Hopalong Cassidy and Davy Crockett—just so many sissies alongside Mr. Fleming's boy. Batman uses all those gimmicks, Superman has fists of steel, Zorro's got a better blade than Wilkinson, Hoppy has a six-shooter he simply hates to use and Davy's toting a Winchester. It's all so elementary. James Bond—licensed to kill by his government—came equipped with all the latest refinements in mayhem. Novelist Kingsley Amis summed it up best in *The James Bond Dossier:*

> On my computation, he shoots, throttles, stabs, buries in guano, causes to be blown out of the broken window of a high-flying aircraft, or in some other way directly encompasses the deaths of thirty-eight-and-half bad men: he and a barracuda share responsibility for the death of a thirty-ninth. Spread over thirteen books, this is not a large figure, and Bond's range looks restricted when we notice the seventy or so other individuals who, without his intervention, are blown up, burned in wrecked cars, eaten by piranhas, cyanided, pushed down a bobsled run without a bobsled, buried in an avalanche, chopped up in the snow-fan of an Alpine locomotive, choked with a fish, hurled into a river by the dynamiting of a railway bridge, hit on the nape of the neck with the brim of a hurled steel hat, and so on.*

Mr. Amis counted another 500 dead, roughly, in the warfare touched off at Fort Knox when Mr. Bond thwarted Auric Goldfinger's efforts to dip into that perfectly marvelous cookie jar and in the soggy mess which must have ensued when Sir Hugo Drax's homemade A-bomb in *Moonraker* dropped into North Sea shipping lanes because the spoilsport Bond didn't want his beloved Britain blown apart.

We're talking, then, about violence—let alone sex, which is mostly a nonviolent thing—on a rather large scale. Your Mickey Spillane hero, who might casually put a .45 slug into a woman's midriff, pales by comparison. That's what made Ian Fleming such an in-

teresting man for our times, but he had an answer for those who would quibble over the bloodletting and rampant lovemaking which flowed from his pen. "We live in a violent era," he told Ken W. Purdy in one of his few interviews. "In our last war, 30 million people were killed. . . . As for sex, seduction has to a marked extent replaced courtship."

Put it down if you will. For Fleming, a product of Eton and Sandhurst who served in the British Naval Intelligence during the war and then had a successful low-pay career as a journalist before trying his hand, tentatively, as a London stockbroker, it meant the highroad. Before a bad heart killed him in 1964, the tall, lean Englishman with the bashed-in nose could himself afford all the lush ways of the supergambler, supergourmet and superlover who came into being in 1952 when he decided to write a book "as a counter-irritant or anti-body to my hysterical alarm at getting married at the age of forty-three." It is perhaps noteworthy that the woman in the case—Lady Anne Geraldine Charteris, pilfered away from a husband no less distinguished than Lord Rothermere, the newspaper giant over there—looked upon Fleming's booze-and-broads Pop hero with something less than open-eyed admiration. The lady wasn't alone.

When Bond came to life on the silver screen, played by the perfectly cast Sean Connery, who has described himself as a red-blooded Scotsman with Irish blood and an appropriate interest in the other gender, he fell into ultimate disfavor with the love-'em-to-death crowd on the Left.

In East Germany, the Communist youth paper *Junge Welt* asserted that "the business being done with James Bond is a business based on the cold war, business with the lowest instincts, a dirty business in favor of fascist brutality and ignorance." The paper charged that the West had created 007 to soften up the world for "the gas war in Vietnam, the murder of civil rights demonstrators in America and the blackmailing of young African nationalist states." Fleming himself was put down as "a hater of everything progressive, a man of sadistic fantasy," while the party newspaper *Neues Deutschland* complained that in the selection of his Bad Guys he was peddling "all the obvious and ridiculous rubbish of reactionary doctrine" and had made socialism "synonymous with crime." *Lumea*, the Romanian foreign affairs weekly, noted that "the handsome James Bond moves in a world peopled by splendid women and hideous, evil men and, mind you, these men are never English or American. They are, in particular, colored men." This was a slight overstatement, of course, since the Commander in his time had only two colored archvillains

---

* © 1965 by Kingsley Amis.

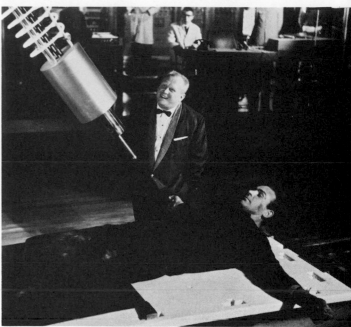

Pussy Galore (Honor Blackman) drops Bond with a judo toss in *Goldfinger* (left), a soft touch compared to the ordeal Auric Goldfinger (*Gert Frobe*) put him through with that laser beam (above).

to dispose of—Mr. Big, the massive black master criminal of *Live and Let Die*, and the mixed-up Chinese Dr. No.

Fleming had some trouble in Rome, too. *L'Osservatore Romano* deemed the elegant Briton guilty of stirring a dangerous mixture of "violence, vulgarity, sadism and sex." Conceding that its views might seem old-fashioned, the Vatican daily protested that "we find ourselves confronted with an authentic contraband of immorality. . . . Evil, presented in an alluring manner, has a most strong attraction on poor human nature weakened by original sin."

For the defense, John Kenneth Galbraith, the Harvard economist who served as President John F. Kennedy's Ambassador to India, had a more up-beat view. The sex-violence-sadism bit didn't bother the professor at all. He put 007's larger international aspects first. "In a world where the enemy is hardboiled, tough-minded and disillusioned," Galbraith told scholars assembled in 1967 at the University of London's Institute of American Studies, "we have been taught that we must be tough-minded, hardboiled and disillusioned, too. To succeed against the Communists, one had to be capable of behavior as repulsive as anything they manage. Our principal teacher, of course, was the late Ian Fleming." The liberal Galbraith evidently had no quarrel with the summary way in which James Bond disposed of all those unfriendly guys in the Soviet's SMERSH (*Smiert Spionam*—Death to Spies) and in SPECTRE (Fleming's long-winded Special Executive for Counterintelligence, Terrorism, Revenge and Extortion).

The public, in any case, couldn't get enough. Before he died, Fleming's books had chalked up a sale of 21,000,000 copies in the English language with *You Only Live Twice,* set for a record first printing of 2,700,007 in paperback, still to come. And the returns on the Bond movies won't be in for years to come. The first four—*Dr. No, From Russia with Love, Goldfinger* and *Thunderball*—speedily brought back $150 million on an investment of $12 million for producers Harry Saltzman and Albert R. (Cubby) Broccoli, with Connery often on the point of parting company with them because his slice seemed a trifle inadequate against those telephone numbers. That breach was healed in due course, so the star hung in for ten years, or until he had enough in the bank to go and do some more serious acting. For Special Agent 007 in *On Her Majesty's Secret Service*, George Lazenby was imported on the strength of his work in an English TV commercial, but that one bombed so badly that the new James Bond repaired to a monastery to meditate on his future as a thespian. Britain's elegantly handsome Roger Moore, so long invincible as "The Saint" in that long-running TV serial over there, is the new 007, staggering under a huge salary and a piece of the gross and still trying to figure out how the lightning struck as he neared the half-century mark. The Bond films' gross stood at a billion in 1978, and there were some whispers abroad that Sean Connery had at least one eye on another shot at the role. For those who may wonder what accounts for the Golconda wrought by Ian Fleming, it is well to bear in mind that the movie Bond makes the paperback Bond look like a panty-waist by comparison; the scripts generally called upon the muscular Connery to dispatch some twenty assorted cads between frolics with a mixed bag of at least four immensely seductive and most willing sirens. (This is a record, incidentally, which could not even be matched by Israel Bond, Hebrew Agent Oy-Oy 7 in *Loxfinger* and *Matzoh Ball*, from the typewriter of Ian Fleming's kosher rival, Sol Weinstein.)

Since this history touches on the orgies of retail merchandising which so often attend our heroes, real or imagined, a passing note on the store-counter Bond is in order here. What happened when Sean Connery compounded the fame of Secret Agent 007 with his incredible feats of courage (even in the boudoir) in the celluloid version of the Fleming thrillers? It figured, of course, that someone would come up with a doll that had simulated death-dealing spikes protruding from her shoes, just like that awful Rosa Klebb in *From Russia with Love*. It figured that the stores would bust out toy attaché cases with guns, decoding machines, exploding devices, booby-trapped code books, pistol-and-silencer sets and everything else out of 007's arsenal, not excluding quilts, pillowcases, bedsheets, pajamas for the small fry (in size 003½) and "gold" lingerie for the more daring girls. But the 007 retail orgy, a 100-million-dollar item in 1966, went even further—into the realm of the things the man-about-town, or even the boy-about-town, is told he needs in his medicine chest. The advertisements for

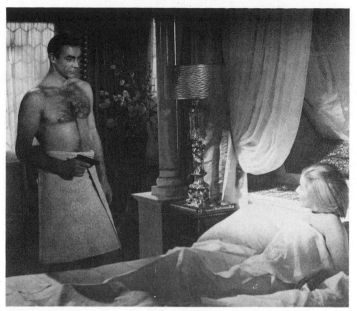

007 encounters the Soviet spy Tatiana Romanova (Daniela Bianchi) in his very own bed in *From Russia with Love*. She switched to his side in due course. Who wouldn't?

Mr. Bond's aftershave lotion bore a somewhat suggestive message: 007 GIVES ANY MAN THE LICENSE TO KILL . . . WOMEN, with the footnote you would expect to find under it, "Dangerous? Sure, but what a way to go." And this wasn't all. The 007 line, courtesy of Colgate-Palmolive, included the more intimate men's products, prompting *Life*'s Shana Alexander to observe that "the Bond image is now so potent that it even has the selling power to deodorize armpits."

All Ian Fleming wanted to do was to write a little action thriller to get his mind off the perils of the marital state. It's hard to say whether he would have shuddered or chuckled over that remark.

Part II

THE ENDURANCE FOLLIES

THE MAN ON THE FLAGPOLE

"Why should I worry? He knows what he is doing."
—Shipwreck Kelly's Wife

High above College Park, Maryland, in 1942, Shipwreck Kelly catches up with the news of the world downstairs. *WWP*

START WITH THE "pillar hermit," St. Simeon Stylites. A Syrian shepherd boy, he entered a monastery at the age of thirteen but his excessive austerities, such as week-long fasts, caused him to be expelled ten years later. He roamed the countryside for four years and then, in A.D. 427, put up a six-foot column of stone at Qalat-Serman in North Syria and ascended it as a forum for preaching to the heathens. Building slowly, St. Simeon eventually raised his lonely tower to a height of sixty feet, and there, in a railed-in enclosure, he passed thirty years in prayer and meditation as disciples bore aloft his simple needs. While a passage in Lucian tells of a Greek worshipper who ascended a pillar at Hierapolis twice a year to converse with the gods, there appears to be little question that St. Simeon, arriving on the scene later, set the endurance pace. In the years after his death in 459, tales of other pillar dwellers emerged both from Syria and Palestine, but none to compare with his story.

Now you skip some two thousand years, laying aside any religious motivation in the process, and you come to Alvin Shipwreck Kelly, the flagpole sitter who emerged on the American scene in 1924 or thereabouts and came to be likened to St. Simeon by some

of the less reverent but more learned reporters assigned to describe his feats of daring. Shipwreck Kelly did it for a living, nothing more. The best that can be said for him—or the worst, if you will—is that he started something in a decade that did not want for wacky stunts in the first place. He drew imitators by the score, even dipping into the ranks of the children. Right into the Thirties, there was barely a day when one hardy soul or another wasn't on some high perch striving to wean away a portion of Kelly's fame—and, of course, his paltry fortune. Even where it was just a teen-age stunt, there was generally a commercial interest helping the flagpole sitter to while away the tedious hours; like the television performers of a later day, they all tended to have sponsors who had something to sell.

It wasn't easy to tell how it all began, because Shipwreck Kelly seldom told the same story twice. Thus he said once that he got the idea in 1920 when he was down South to see a Jack Dempsey fight. "There was a bunch of foreigners there, foolin' around. They got playful and threw me out of a third-story window. I hit a flagpole and hung on. That got me started." Reminded that Dempsey didn't fight in the South in 1920, Shipwreck said the incident

Since thirteen was his favorite number, Kelly picked Friday, October 13, 1939, for this stunt atop one of Manhattan's early skyscrapers, the Chanin Building. Pushing doughnut sales, he downed thirteen sinkers in this position. *WWP*

really happened on the eve of the heavyweight champion's soft defense against France's Georges Carpentier on Boyle's Thirty Acres in New Jersey in 1921. He said he was thrown out of a hotel window there for defending Dempsey over some slurs but a flagpole broke his fall and *that* gave him his idea about flagpoles. Still another time, he said it all began when the champ chased him up a palmetto tree in Florida in 1922, and it occurred to him (Kelly, not Dempsey) that he had a talent for shinning up to high places and staying there without excessive discomfort. Mr. Dempsey, for his part, told the author that he may

have met Shipwreck somewhere along the line but positively never chased him up a tree.

There is a more plausible story about the origins of the strange Kelly career. In this one, datelined Hollywood, 1924, the little Irishman from New York's Hell's Kitchen, turning thirty-two, performed a risky feat as a steeplejack in a stunt role for a movie and somebody on the set asked him whether he thought he could do ten hours or so on a flagpole. The answer was yes, and pretty soon Shipwreck found himself on a mast outside a Los Angeles theatre as a shill for the epic then on display. He stayed up thirteen hours and thirteen minutes, pocketing a side bet with the theatre owner, and then slid down to the ringing cheers of a medium-sized multitude in the streets. Now he had a career. Before then, counting his labors as a movie double, Shipwreck listed a round total of thirteen "dangerous" occupations. The other twelve: merchant seaman during the war, rigger, structural iron worker, human fly, high diver, prizefighter, aerial athlete, licensed pilot, navigator, soldier of fortune, sign painter and window washer. Once he said he had been in thirty-two shipwrecks and once the figure came out sixty-two, but his nickname did not necessarily derive from any such harrowing experiences. The story was that when he boxed, calling himself Sailor Kelly, his five-foot-seven-inch frame was on the canvas so much of the time that the fans took to chanting, "The sailor's been shipwrecked again."

To go way back into Shipwreck's life, it needs to be noted that he was an orphan. Before he was born his father, a rigger, was killed in an accident caused by another worker's carelessness. Then his mother died in childbirth, and the man responsible for the elder Kelly's death adopted him. The boy ran off to sea when he was thirteen and put in the best part of the next sixteen years on the bounding main, interspersed with the landlocked occupations listed above. Parenthetically, Kelly liked to say that in addition to surviving all those disasters at sea he had managed to emerge unscathed from two airplane crack-ups, one railroad wreck and three auto accidents. With the eventual onset of his fame, he billed himself as "The Luckiest Fool Alive." It was no exaggeration, at that, because the career he ultimately settled on wasn't made for lesser men. Just for a quick sidelight: On October 13, 1939, when he was at least forty-seven years old, Kelly stood on his head on a plank jutting out from the roof of the fifty-six-story Chanin Building, then the tallest skyscraper in midtown New York, and ate thirteen hand-fed donuts to draw attention to National Doughnut Week. Reporters observed a twelve-inch brakedrum in the plank as a headrest and a leather thong securing the daredevil's left wrist to the board, so the papers made light of the stunt. But did it take courage to go out on that plank suspended over the Manhattan skyline (and eat all those doughnuts), even with the safety devices? One has to say that it did.

There were safeguards atop the flagpoles, too, for that matter. When Shipwreck stood on the six- to eight-inch disk that served as his platform, he had stirrups attached to the pole so that he wouldn't tumble to the ground if he fell asleep and lost his balance. Sitting, he used a cushioned eight-inch seat fashioned from a Ford brakedrum, either locking his thumbs into special holes or keeping his little fingers between his teeth so that he would instantly react if he dozed and started to waver. He said he trained himself to take five-minute catnaps on the hour to keep his strength. He took nourishment regularly, mostly liquids hoisted up to him on a rope. A fastidious sort, he always kept shaving equipment on hand, and when he found one so daring, a manicurist would be hoisted up to trim and polish his nails.

In 1927, Shipwreck did seven days, thirteen hours and thirteen minutes (you must have noticed that the man had a contempt for superstition) on a flagpole atop a thirteen-story building in St. Louis and then switched to the St. Francis Hotel in Newark to better his own record. He said he would stay up eight days, fasting on coffee to show that people didn't need to eat so much, but he stayed on that fifty-four-foot flagpole for thirteen days. There was money in the extra time, of course. Shipwreck not only was collecting handsomely from the hotel and cutting in on the receipts from the rooftop admission charge but had a coffee sponsor as well, while his manager, Emmett MacDonald, was peddling a pamphlet describing the earlier Kelly feats in rather flowery terms.

Shipwreck made $6,000 on that date in the murky Jersey sky but had to suffer a small domestic problem on the side. He had a brand new nineteen-year-old bride, the former Frances Vivian Steele, and she grew understandably impatient after a while, submitting that she was being cheated out of her honeymoon. The groom counseled patience, reminding the girl that their love had flowered on a flagpole in the first place. This was the story: Shipwreck was welcoming in the New Year atop a chilly pole over a Dallas hotel where the little redhead worked as an elevator operator. A scornful Texan stepped into her car and asked, "Is that damn fool still up there?" Miss Steele slapped the man's face, saying "He's not a fool." The hotel

manager threatened to strip the spirited elevator operator of her chevrons for that act of impertinence. Hearing the tale from rooftop sources, Shipwreck bid the girl to his side—with rope and tackle, of course—and rewarded her with a handshake which in turn led to the altar almost as fast as the daredevil could descend to level ground.

Alas, Miss Steele became distressed not only over the abbreviated honeymoon but found her soul mate's extended flagpole meditations constantly more trying as time went on. Shipwreck was exceptionally busy in the upper reaches in 1928, his spreading fame having boomed his fees to $100 a day, and he topped all his own records in the banner year of 1929 by putting in a total of 145 days on one precarious perch or another in the process of coining something like $29,000. The child bride, by then the mother of Alvin Jr., called Little Shipwreck, occasionally was hoisted topside for brief discussions of domestic matters and perhaps a peck on her trembling forehead, but it wasn't enough. Her disenchantment led her to the divorce courts the following year. "What's the use of having a husband unless he comes home nights?" she said in plaintive tones.

One of Shipwreck's more spectacular feats in that year—in December—kept him on a flagpole atop the Paramount Hotel in New York for thirteen days, thirteen hours and thirteen minutes. He took a dreadful beating from the weatherman—zero cold, snow, sleet and freezing rain along the way—and he was bitter when he came down. Only thirteen copies of his pamphlet had been sold in all that time. "Flagpole sitting ain't what it used to be," Shipwreck said, trying to rub the cold off his squashed-in nose. "I thought I had a Depression-proof business but I know better now. I could have stayed up there forever but I wasn't making any money."

By then the woods—or the flagpoles—were crawling with imitators. Doing a stint atop the Plaza Hotel in Long Branch, New Jersey, Shipwreck was horrified and embarrassed to find a minion of the law stationed below him waiting to serve the papers in a seventy-five-dollar nonpayment suit filed by some press agent. Descending, the belligerent Irishman discovered that the legal document really was intended for a flagpole sitter of decidedly lesser renown who also happened to be toiling under the name of Shipwreck Kelly. He found the imposter tucked between the sheets in the Plaza Hotel in that very town and swiftly exhibited a copyright filed in Washington giving him sole and exclusive right to the name in the United States, Argentina, Australia, Austria, Bolivia, Czechoslovakia, China, Canada, Great Britain and all the colonies (there was still some Empire left then), and a few other outposts.

"Looks like I made a little mistake," the bogus Kelly murmured.

"The trouble with you," said the real article, his 144-pound frame quivering with rage and his gray eyes flashing, "is that you haven't got any ethics. How do you think I felt when I read in the papers that a constable was waiting for Shipwreck Kelly to come down so that he could serve a seventy-five-dollar judgment? Me, who has never beaten a bill. You have hurt the profession."

"I'll tell you what," the Long Branch Kelly replied, "if you just let me sleep I won't use your name anymore."

His honor intact, Shipwreck departed, but there was no peace. He was standing off a small army of challengers now. A character named Hold 'em Joe Powers, who had put in sixteen days and three hours atop the flagpole of Chicago's Hotel Morrison back in 1927, dared Kelly to match a stunt of his 647 feet above street level in the Windy City. Shipwreck scoffed, observing that the perch supporting Hold 'em Joe had so many of the comforts of home that the man could stretch out and sleep like a baby on it. He may have had a point there, because a woman named Hattie Stenecko had offered to ascend that pole and pay the hotel its top room rates for each day she fell short of Hold 'em Joe's record. And Tim Belucos, a steeplejack, said he would be willing to take his best girl up on the pole and get married there, but the Morrison eventually decided that all it wanted on that overburdened mast was Old Glory, no more non-paying guests.

Hugo Bihler, claiming some kind of a fancy record on a pole in his native Germany, offered to bet Shipwreck $6,000 that he could outsit him anywhere—choose your flagpole, Herr Kelly—but the square-chinned champion shook that off, too. He had no patience for the other guys' claims, whatever the variations. If they were on the level he would pass them in due time. H. V. Crouch of New Bedford, Massachusetts, put in seventeen days and two hours on a rig over a dance marathon floor in 1927, and Robert Hall, billed as the Phantom of the Flagpole, immediately topped that performance with an eighteen-day stint. Shipwreck bided his time and signed on for Milton Crandall's dance marathon in New York's Madison Square Garden two years later and stayed on his perch—standing on an eight-inch disk for twenty-one hours a day—until the marathon closed down twenty-two nights later. In the summer of 1930, he put in forty-nine days and one hour atop Atlantic City's Steel Pier just after some pretender to the throne had set a forty-two day record in Baltimore. Shipwreck said he came down not out of any weariness but only because he was beginning to miss the little woman (that was the year the marriage came asunder).

Not long before that, another challenger's efforts came to a most embarrassing short stop in Chicago. Bennie Fox passed eighteen days on a rig atop the Masonic Temple, in excellent shape and headed for all kinds of glory, when wisdom dictated an unscheduled retirement. An army of creditors had set up a clamor over past debts, and Mr. Fox found it expedient to slide down the pole in the dead of night and make a getaway while sleep overtook the detective assigned to collar him. In Los Angeles, Bobby Mack, a twenty-one-year-old stunt aviatrix, did twenty-one days on a flagpole before the City Council passed an ordinance outlawing that kind of foolishness. In Boston, Frank S. Holl lasted just two days on a pole above Tremont Street when he was hauled down and fined twenty-five dollars for causing a public nuisance. In Denver, Leroy (Spider) Haines did 300 hours in the air and claimed a new record, but nobody paid any attention because he wasn't even in Shipwreck's class. Nobody could be, in truth, after that tour de force on the Steel Pier. That performance came to a total of 1,177 hours, 600 more than Shipwreck had ever bothered to do before, and there were 20,000 well-wishers on the boardwalk when the ocean-sprayed hero, who had weathered three thunderstorms and a hailstorm, made his slow and painful descent.

The bubble burst for Shipwreck Kelly after a while. The public evidently having had its fill, the big fees became elusive. In 1934, in need of something to revive the waning interest in his exploits, Shipwreck let it be known that he was prepared to plunge off the George Washington Bridge on a greased rope. The journalists and newsreel cameramen arrived in force —but so did the police. Kelly's rope happened to be fifty-two feet short of the 250 feet needed to deposit him in the Hudson River in one piece, so the law canceled that trip and now the hard times were really upon the orphan from Hell's Kitchen. In the shadow of his own birthplace, he found himself reduced to doing brief stints above a saloon to bring in the thirsty legions. By 1942, things were so bad that Shipwreck took on an assignment to paint the flagpole at Palisades Amusement Park in New Jersey; careless, he fell five feet one day and got hurt.

Cleveland baseball fan Charlie Lupica brought along all the necessities when he ascended this high perch in 1949 and vowed to stay there until the Indians knocked the Yanks out of first place. He stayed up for 117 days, but it didn't help. The New Yorkers were too tough then. *WWP*

Whipped by summer rains and fierce Atlantic winds, Shipwreck managed forty-nine days on Atlantic City's Steel Pier in 1930. *Hess Photography*

The end came on a chilly October day in 1952 when the police encountered a body between two parked cars on a street in Manhattan. The man was a heart case, and a pocket stuffed with yellowing newspaper clips identified him as Alvin Shipwreck Kelly, whose name had once graced the marquee of Madison Square Garden, just a block away. The police said Shipwreck was living on home relief in his old neighborhood. And they said his listed age—fifty-nine—wasn't true. They said he was really sixty-seven. You had to accept that as something of an epitaph,

because if they were right it meant that for a good many years Mr. Kelly had performed endurance stunts, way up there, that nobody his age had a right to gamble on.

In the time of Shipwreck Kelly, for some inexplicable reason, the city of Baltimore suffered the worst consequences of the flagpole sitting fad. Avon O. Foreman, a lass of fifteen, set the pace in 1929 when she mounted an old ironing board on a pole in her own backyard, repaired to that haven and settled upon it for ten days, ten hours, ten minutes and ten seconds, alternately sleeping on the board and waking to the plaudits of some 4,000 friends and neighbors. From that moment on, it seemed as if nearly everybody in Baltimore between the ages of eight and eighteen was heading for the nearest high place. There were so many children striving to cling to one perch or another, and suffering assorted broken bones and lesser ailments in the process, that the police had to set up a special detail to check all flagpoles and make certain that they were safe for human occupancy.

The liberal *New Republic* took note of the spreading "mania" with an article that struck out boldly at the town's elders. "The parents of most of these children," the magazine said, "exhibit a distinct pride in the performance, protected by ignorance and stupidity from appreciating the possible consequences, physical and otherwise, of these idiotic vigils ... moralists, in the larger sense, have an opportunity for prolonged and depressing speculation as to the essential significance of the Baltimore phenomenon. They can meditate on the dullness of lives which find relief in the spectacle of twenty children squatting on the top of improvised flagpoles throughout the city; on the low estimate a skillful politician with further ambitions must have made of his fellow citizens before he decided to take up these Stylites in a serious way; on the vacuity of adults who wear collars and own automobiles and permit their children to astound the neighbors in this fashion; on the strange evolution which makes an outbreak of this sort, to be expected in Los Angeles, possible in a conservative city like Baltimore. . . . A hell of a thing for the second port on the Atlantic seaboard!"

The Baltimore *Evening Sun,* by contrast, was far from disturbed. When Jimmy Jones and Willie Wentworth, both twelve, passed little Avon's records, the *Sun* spoke in glowing terms of the "crown of sitterdom, with its splendor, its claims and prerogatives, its titles, its dignity and glitter." It was evident that the city's staid old newspaper and its Mayor—William F. Broening—were on the same wavelength.

The kids, of course, got over it fast enough. The grown-ups, if you could call them that, carried on in the Kelly tradition, in dwindling numbers, as long as there was a dime left in it.

In the spring of 1949, on a bet made in his friendly neighborhood tavern, a baseball fan named Charlie Lupica deposited himself on a pole over a Cleveland delicatessen and vowed to stay there until his beloved Indians either made first place or tied the then-terrifying New York Yankees. Nothing could have been more futile or unrealistic, so Lupica came down

on the 117th day, September 25, with the Indians mired in fourth place. It wasn't a total loss, however. Escorted to the ball park, the man bathed in the cheers of 33,977 fans and went home with a Pontiac car, a tricycle for his son, a stroller for the baby and a four-poster bed, among other assorted gifts.

For $50 a day, John Lynch settled on a four-foot platform six stories above the Chicago streets in 1958 as a shill for a used car dealer. Lynch came down after fifty-two days. "I got sick and tired of looking at the same old neighborhood," he said.

In 1951, in a switch on the flagpole bit, Erma Leach of Eugene, Oregon, clad in a bathing suit, spent the best part of 152 days in a champagne bubble bath in San Francisco to push an automobile dealer's wares. Her rewards supposedly included a world title of some kind, $7,500 in cash, a Cadillac and a fur coat. In 1955, quite pregnant, Kathleen Donham did 169 days on a sixty-foot pole in Parkland, Washington, to push a commercial enterprise of some kind and help pay for baby. She had a radio, telephone and all the other comforts of home and survived the ordeal nicely. Four years later, in Indianapolis, Mauri Rose Kirby, a seventeen-year-old carhop, set up housekeeping atop a seventy-one-foot pole in a wall-to-wall rig similar to Miss Donham's and managed to stay there 211 days. "I've missed going places and doing things," she said when she came down, lugging her guitar. "I don't know why in the world I climbed up there." In any case, she wound up with the world's squatting record for females, whatever that may have been worth at the time. In 1961, Little John Gregory settled down in a tent above a shopping center in Rockford, Illinois, trying to beat a 211-day record he himself had set in Fort Smith, Arkansas, but he had to be hauled down by a small army on the eighty-fourth day because he had ballooned up from an otherwise crisp 419 pounds to an alarming 499. Little John's medical advisers back home in Wisconsin evidently didn't want him over that dangerous 500-pound mark.

Somewhere, of course, sex will rear its ugly head, and this is where this chapter has to end.

In a certain Texas city in 1958, a disc jockey repaired to an improvised tent home sixty-five feet above a used-car lot, saying that he was prepared to stay quite a long while and play records and that sort of thing. He stayed thirty-six days—and came down to face a charge of statutory rape. It seemed that a fifteen-year-old girl admirer, languishing at the base of the pole, had been invited up on three or four moonlit nights to share the lonely hours—and all those records—with the swinging character in the tent.

On doctor's orders, Little John Gregory, also shooting for seven months, had to come off an Indiana flagpole on the eighty-fourth day because he was putting on too much weight he didn't need. *WWP*

Mauri Rose Kirby is hauled down after nearly seven months on a flagpole in Indianapolis. *WWP*

The accused man beat the charge. It turned out that his playmate had a rather speckled background, for all her tender years, and her own testimony did not hurt the defense cause at all. "I knew what he had in mind when I climbed up there," she told the court.

You have to assume that Shipwreck Kelly turned over in his grave when those words were spoken. It demeaned everything he ever stood—or sat—for.

THE BUNION DERBY

Well fortified against the muddy turf, C. C. Pyle urges his runners on. *UPI*

The Marathon is a romantic revival of a fatal run made in 490 B.C. by a Greek soldier bearing the news of victory from the battlefield of Marathon to Athens. This gallant soldier ran the whole distance (twenty-six miles, 385 yards) at a terrific pace, arrived before the Acropolis in Athens, delivered his immortal message: "Rejoice! We conquer!" and then dropped dead.
—ROBERT L. RIPLEY, 1928

THIS, THEN, IS HOW marathon racing, first revived at the 1896 Olympic Games in Athens, really began. It is well to know this before delving into the saga of C. C. Pyle and his famous, or infamous, transcontinental Bunion Derby, but to do that you have to start with a certain football player.

When the fabulous Red Grange elected to become a college dropout in 1925 and go make some money, having labored free of charge for three arduous seasons in the backfield of Bob Zuppke's Illinois eleven, he was granted an audience by the somewhat taciturn President of the United States. This is the full text of that historic session:

CALVIN COOLIDGE: Howdy, where do you live?

HAROLD E. GRANGE: Wheaton, Illinois.

CALVIN COOLIDGE: Well, young man, I wish you luck.

The young man didn't need luck. He had made the acquaintance of C. C. Pyle before going through that White House swinging door. This man, briefly the impresario of a barnstorming semipro basketball team and a little theatrical company before acquiring movie houses in Kokomo, Indiana, and, happily, the campus town of Champaign, had observed No. 77's heroic deeds on the gridiron in considerable awe. He was there that crazy afternoon when the kid—in a single quarter—tore off four touchdowns against Michigan on runs of 95, 67, 56 and 45 yards. Damon Runyon saw Grange as "crashing sound . . . poetry . . . brute force." What the crafty Pyle saw was pure gold, and damned if the great open field runner wasn't a regular patron of his nickelodeon. Since the boy was so far from affluence that he had to carry ice in the summers to keep his pockets replenished, Pyle staked him to a pair of passes and then, in his senior year, stopped him in the lobby one night and spoke as follows: "Young man, how would you like to make a hundred thousand dollars or maybe even a million?" The young man was so impressed that he decided he didn't need to wait around for his sheepskin to make good in the world. And so "The Galloping Ghost" turned pro and in no time at

29

all put the sagging professional game—and C. C. Pyle—on a more solid footing.

The athlete himself, truly one of the towering figures of sports' Golden Age, did not suffer in the process, for no man ever drove a harder bargain than his dapper, fast-talking forty-four-year-old sponsor. Pyle got the Chicago Bears to pay Grange $12,000 to fill up their ball yard—an unprecedented sight—one Sunday afternoon and then signed him to the Papa Halas eleven for an eighteen-game tour calling for nothing less than a down-the-middle split of the receipts. ("We were also allowed to bear all the expenses," the wry Mr. Halas recalled this year in his autobiography, *That's How the Ball Bounces*). The halfback, son of a Wheaton sheriff's deputy, took down $125,000 for letting that five-foot-eleven-inch frame endure the abuse of the big bad pros—all on starvation wages—on that historic, SRO journey. Pyle, a stranger to football except for a little junior varsity experience before he departed Ohio Wesleyan University, pocketed almost as much on his deal with Grange (60 percent for the bruised and beaten ball carrier, 40 percent for the brain trust).

It was only the beginning, of course.

On the side, Pyle promoted endorsements and commercial tie ups with such zeal that you could buy, among other items, Red Grange helmets, Red Grange caps, Red Grange sweaters, Red Grange candy bars, Red Grange dolls, Red Grange shoes and, for the stronger stomachs, Red Grange sausage sandwiches. And you could see Red Grange on the silver screen, first in *One Minute to Play* (football, of course) and then in *Racing Romeo* (autos, for a switch). Grange's take in his first three semesters out of Illinois came to a cool million, the very number his sponsor had mentioned that fateful night in the nickelodeon.

In 1926, branching out to tennis, Pyle talked France's Suzanne Lenglen into abandoning her amateur standing to star for him in a cross-country professional tournament. He guaranteed Mlle. Lenglen $50,000 and made $100,000 on the tour himself. He also got Vincent Richards, Howard Kinsey and Mary Browne to turn pro but couldn't make a deal with Bill Tilden. The net game's giant wanted too much of the take. Pyle, son of a Methodist minister in Ohio and steeped in the virtues of frugality as a boy, did not care for the grasping sort.

In this period, the marathon had come into its own. All kinds—walking, running, dancing, talking, drinking, eating, even a kissing marathon now and then. The running variety seldom involved anything more strenuous than a couple of hundred miles or so but C. C. Pyle had a much larger idea—a foot race that would really cover some distance, like from Los Angeles to New York. The purse: $25,000 to the winner and $23,500 to be split among the next nine men strong enough to survive the rather taxing jaunt across the American countryside. And who would the lonely long-distance runners be? Pyle said he would dispatch agents across the seas to import all the world's best to supplement the native contestants. He said each runner would have to pay a twenty-five dollar fee for the privilege (relieving him of the necessity of digging into his own purse before the race began to produce its financial rewards) and he expected no less than one thousand entrants. And where would Pyle get the loot to feed and house that running army, raise the prize money and have a little something left over for his own simple necessities? He explained it this way to John Kieran for an article in *Life* magazine:

We'll run through thousands of towns, cities and villages. Spectators by the thousands will be attracted to those places to see the race pass through. That will mean money for the towns, especially where the race halts overnight. It will help the sale of everything from mousetraps to grand pianos. Each town will be assessed so much for the advertising, or we won't run through it. We'll run through a rival town. You know what that means. Local pride comes high. The smaller the town, the higher the pride and the higher the price. Then we'll sell a million programs, easy. You can't tell the runners without a program. I'll get $100,000 for the advertising in that. I'll have a traveling vaudeville show with the race. Admission will not be free. I'll make money on that, too. In fact, it's the easiest thing I've ever seen.

Splendid. Now how about those 1,000 runners? It turned out, perhaps happily, that there weren't that many crazy runners, or even walkers, on the face of the earth. The $48,500 Pyle spectacular, immediately christened the Bunion Derby by the more caustic sportswriters, did draw 275 hopefuls but only 199 were on hand when the three-week training grind ended and, on March 4, 1928, the man's most lucrative single promotion, Red Grange, gave the signal for the start from the mud-soaked turf of the Ascot Speedway in Los Angeles. It was a distinguished international field at that, boasting such large names as Herbert Hedemann of Austria; Willie Kolehmainen of New York; Jüri Lossmann of Estonia, second-place winner in the 1920 Olympic marathon; August Fager of Ohio, another Olympic runner; Arthur Newton, the 100-mile champion from Southern Rhodesia; and such celebrated heel-and-toe men as Italy's Paolo Brune and Guisto Umek and Canada's Philip Granville. The world titleholder in the walking department, Willie Reinbold of New York, who had once strolled Manhattan's 31.6 miles in a trifling five hours and fifty-nine minutes, couldn't start because a mad dog bit him during training.

The contestants, ranging in age from sixteen to sixty-three, began to show the strain in no time at all. Their tall and elegant sponsor, a resplendent dresser whose ensemble often included pearl-buttoned spats, derby and walking stick, not to mention a delicately trimmed Adolphe Menjou moustache, had no such problem. He traveled in the advance guard in a specially designed $25,000 "land yacht," *The America,* with two deluxe sleeping compartments, two baths and a kitchen. Wherever the mad hegira was headed, Pyle had to get there first to set up the sideshow tents where the local citizenry, hopefully, was expected to plunk down twenty-five cent pieces in large numbers to be entertained by something passing for hula girls, surrounded by assorted reptiles and beasts, a trained police dog named Kah-Ko, some tropical birds and an item reputed to be the mummified corpse of an Oklahoma outlaw, followed by Red Grange's introduction of the Bunion Derby braves. Pyle had quite a few other things going, or at least coming: $100,000, or maybe $60,000, from the U.S. No. 66 Highway Association for the privilege of running his race over that road and thus spreading the fame of the towns along the way, bonuses from manufacturers who had the contracts to supply the runners with shoes, foot powder, liniment, sunburn lotion and chewing gum, a cut on all roadside concession stands, and his program sales.

On the very first lap, a mere sixteen-mile jaunt to Puente, no less than seventy-six of the 199 starters fell victims of the harsh, hot pavements. Forty-year-old Willie Kolehmainen, a sinewy Finn, covered that lap in one hour and thirty-six minutes and led the field. Behind him, in order, were Gunnar Neilsen (not to be confused with the Great Dane of the same name who emerged in the mid-Fifties as one of the world's top runners), Saul Richman of New York, and Nicholas Quomawahu, a Hopi Indian from Arizona. On the third day, when the course reached California's towering Cajon Pass and dipped down

to the Mojave Desert, Kolehmainen suffered a muscle injury and Arthur Newton moved to the front as the boiling flatland began to take its toll. The runners now had to contend not only with the animal life of the desert but also with an occasional hit-run driver and, worse, with the larger problem of their care and feeding.

Somewhere in that week in the unfriendly Mojave the outfit engaged to feed the troupe at two dollars a head per day suddenly demanded three dollars on the grounds that the athletes' taxing endeavors were producing excessive appetites. Pyle thereupon canceled the contract and installed football player Ralph Scott as the entourage's chef. The runners welcomed this innovation but shortly began to complain that Scott was feeding them the same Mulligan stew day after day out of dishes that were never being washed. Pyle met that rebellion head-on too. He farmed out the feeding contract to the fly-and-mosquito-ridden beaneries along the way, allowing the panting contestants a grand total of two thirty-five-cent meals a day with a couple of extra sandwiches thrown in for good measure. In the land yacht, the cuisine was considerably better and the runners, increasingly disgruntled, knew it.

When the ever-dwindling sand-covered troupe reached that charming little sweatbox called Needles, whose only known virtue is that it can get you *out* of California and into Arizona, Pyle got a bad break. Newton, winner of nine of the first thirteen laps and holding a nine-hour lead on the field, twisted an ankle and had to quit, yielding the lead to Andrew Payne, a part-Cherokee farm boy from Claremore, Oklahoma, who in turn was passed by Arne Souminen, a Finn from Detroit, as the runners crossed the Continental Divide.

In Albuquerque, New Mexico, the Bunion Derby ran into the first of a series of troubles which would beset it more and more even as the runners still managed, one way or another, to stagger through their assigned forty miles a day. The Chamber of Commerce reneged on its promise to pay $5,000 for the privilege of having Pyle's charges grace the town with their presence, having decided it couldn't possibly be worth the price, so Pyle, giving nothing away, rerouted his leg-weary band into the desert outside of the town.

Across New Mexico and into the Texas Panhandle, where touches of rain, sleet, snow and hail washed the grime off their backs, the runners drew disappointing crowds. Then, fortunately, Souminen suffered a tendon injury and young Payne took the lead just as the Derby, suffering now from mounting fi-

The 1928 Bunion Derby kicks off from Ascot Speedway in Los Angeles with 199 hopefuls. The finish line: New York. *UPI*

nancial problems, reached his native state. Pyle lost his $5,000 guarantee from the Oklahoma City Chamber of Commerce when Ralph Scott, the unfrocked chef, sued to tie it up, alleging that the promoter owed him that much. For all his native cunning, Pyle outsmarted himself in that legal hassle. When he was slapped with the papers in the suit, he tore up his guaranty so that both he and the Chamber could swear in court that there was no $5,000 owed to him and therefore no such sum could be attached. John Kieran described the sad ending this way: "It turned out that it couldn't be collected either, for when Mr. Pyle asked for it in a friendly way, the Chamber of Commerce representative pointed out that it would be perjury for them to pay it. This announcement was greeted with laughter, in which Mr. Pyle, for some reason, failed to join."

It was only money, of course, and at that the Bunion Derby did enjoy a brief boon in the oil city. The town was so proud of Andy Payne, running his little legs off just to retire the mortgage on his old father's farm, that another one of its moderately well-known sons, Will Rogers, paid him homage, and hordes turned out for a peek at the marathon-to-end-all-marathons. Pyle knew how to deal with the free-loaders. He routed the race around to the State Fairgrounds, where the natives had to pay to see his charges do their stuff.

There was also a brief unpleasantness in Oklahoma. The runners threatened to strike unless the management began to produce some money for special prizes in the daily laps. Pyle simply stared them down, and the marathon headed through Kansas to Missouri and into his familiar Illinois, where a most disconcerting thing happened. With the crazy endurance contest past the halfway mark, completing its second month and able to boast that some seventy mortals were still slogging through the paces, a deputy sheriff slapped a writ of attachment on Pyle's floating overland mansion just because the gentleman celebrated by the nickname of "Cash and Carry" owed an item of $21,500 to the Illinois Trust and Savings Bank's branch in Champaign, his old stamping ground. Pyle happened to be a sure winner: The land yacht was a rented vehicle and didn't belong to him, so it couldn't be seized by any old bank.

But the worst was yet to come.

In Chicago, Pyle found that the U.S. No. 66 Highway Association had changed its mind about shelling out all the loot he had been promised, maintaining that the Bunion Derby had strayed from Route 66 too often to merit any bounty. Now, suddenly, there were estimates that Pyle was in the hole for something like $150,000 to $200,000 and might have to scuttle his caravan before it reached New York and its grand finale in Madison Square Garden, a scant

1,000 miles away. Here a Good Samaritan appeared in the person of Freeman F. Gunn, a wealthy Chicago sportsman who happened to have a twenty-two-year-old son in the marathon and a $75,000 side bet to go with him. Gunn had two buses and two trailers following the race all the way from Los Angeles to minister to the needs of his prodigy, Harry, while he roughed it in his own Pierce-Arrow roadster. He had bet on the family standard-bearer—a walker, not a runner—to finish the race, come hell, high water, bad feet or bad weather, so he elected to pay off Pyle's more pressing debts and foot the bills the rest of the way. Pyle, always good-natured in financial matters, graciously accepted and turned to some fresh problems. For one, Red Grange, who had taken a bath with Pyle earlier that year in an unfortunate venture into a rival operation to go against the National Football League, got off the merry-go-round in Chicago and that once-rich relationship ended. For another, the runners were unhappy again. They had the option of bedding down for free in Pyle's tents, on Pyle's bunks, under Pyle's blankets, or paying for their own lodgings in hotels along the way. Now they protested that the bunks had not been cleaned, nor the blankets laundered, since that cruel odyssey's first night, some 2,500 miles ago, on the outskirts of spotless Los Angeles. The ingrates contended that the blankets were itchy, to say the least, and said they wanted either some fast dry-cleaning or some hotel money from that point on. Pyle, now being described as "Corn and Callous" in the sports pages, managed to wriggle his way out of that one as the endurance contest wended its weary path through Ohio, Pennsylvania and New Jersey toward its ultimate destination. In Ohio the field shook down to fifty-five—with that remarkable Payne boy back in front after losing the lead briefly to a bearded entrant from England named Peter Gavuzzi. Payne, indeed, spread his lead to a very comfortable seventeen hours and twenty-eight minutes over his nearest competitor, John Salo, a sturdy thirty-five-year-old Finnish shipfitter from Passaic, New Jersey, perhaps proving that there was more to be said for a touch of Cherokee than 100 percent of any other known breed.

Salo helped in the stretch, because his adopted hearth, flag-bedecked and on a half holiday, turned out in a body at a moment when the derby was under mounting attack. The Newark *Evening News* viewed the runners as "emaciated, unshaven, unshorn scarecrows," and the New York *Evening Sun* termed the marathon "the flop of the century" and a "tinhorn side show," while the *Herald Tribune*'s W. O. Mc-

Geehan dismissed it as "The Aching Dog Caravan." To the proud town of Passaic, none of this made any difference. Thousands cheered as Salo was made a member of the police force in honor of his achievement, even though he was still fourteen hours behind that upstart from the Will Rogers country. Leaving Passaic, heartened by the acclaim for their colleague, the runners dashed onto the Weehawken ferry, sucking in the refreshing May breeze wafted up from the Hudson, and somehow managed to summon the strength to leap off on the Forty-Second Street side in Manhattan—to something less than wide public acclaim. There was hardly anybody there to greet the fifty-five runners, and a bare handful watched them make their way up Tenth Avenue and turn east for the Garden, where only 4,000 paid their way into the 18,000-seat arena. Pyle, undismayed, wanted his tattered troops, many of them taped and bandaged, to do a snappy twenty miles around the board track but had to settle for ten laps. With the newsreel cameras whirring, the survivors, all newly shaved and tidied up, just about made those ten laps as Pyle moved along the track screaming, "Come on, you fellows. Streak it, boys. Streak it. Show 'em what I've brought to New York. Show your mettle, boys." Instead, most of the runners limped to a halt to refresh themselves with sandwiches, bananas and pop sodas. On the sidelines, Morris Munitz, official shoe repairer for Pyle, let it be known that he would now do all his work without charge—for those who had no money, that is. Why any of the runners would want their shoes refurbished at that point—eighty-four days and 3,422 miles out of Los Angeles—was not at all clear. The finale was set for the following Friday in the Garden—June 1—and that gala night didn't draw more than 500 fans. Pyle said he had lost between $75,000 and $100,000 on his cross-country adventure but he paid off the winners.

Andrew Payne, still only nineteen years old, accepted the $25,000 first prize and then wandered into a concrete pillar and fell unconscious—almost but not quite paralleling the dramatic exit of that gallant Greek soldier at Athens centuries before him. His winning time for the whole wacky run: 573 hours, four minutes and thirty-four seconds. Salo, second by fifteen hours or so and the only one of the eleven Finns in the race to finish, got the $10,000 second prize. Philip Granville, forty hours behind the Oklahoma boy, took the $5,000 third prize back to Ontario. Mike Joyce, a bartender from Cleveland, picked up the $2,500 fourth prize, and $1,000 apiece went to Guisto Umek of Italy, William Kerr of Minneapolis, Louis Perrella of Albany, New York, Ed Gardner, a

1926: Pyle is flanked by two of his chattels, Red
Grange and Suzanne Lenglen, the French tennis
great. *WWP*

John Salo, the pride of Passaic,
New Jersey, doing an indoor lap
for local fans. *UPI*

Back in Oklahoma, Andy Payne, winner of the 1928 footrace, is
greeted by an uncle, William Burgess, while Payne Sr. stands by.

black from Seattle, Frank Von Flue, a Californian, and John Cronick of Saskatoon, Saskatchewan. Oh, yes, Harry Gunn was there too—out of the money but in excellent shape at home. He had saved his father's $75,000 bet.

Pyle, watching all that good money disappear into the hands of the winners, had this to say to the assembled journalists: "There has been a lot of talk about how much these boys suffered. There is not one of them who suffered more than I did. Their feet were sore sometimes, but my arms were sore all the time, from digging down in my pocket and shelling out cash."

Later, in better cheer and more like his debonair self, he amplified those remarks to set forth the larger lessons of the Bunion Derby. He said that the world had just witnessed not merely a sporting event but history's most notable experiment in chiropody. He said that, thanks to C. C. Pyle, the Golden Age of the Foot was at hand and, as if to prove it, he decided to push his bad luck into 1929, setting up a reverse marathon from New York to Los Angeles for a $60,000 purse. He found himself ninety-one starters, most of them veterans of the earlier extravaganza, and that seventy-eight-day jaunt, another fi-

nancial disaster, proved to be a two-man duel between John Salo and Peter Gavuzzi. The durable Passaic shipfitter won the $25,000 first prize that time but not long thereafter, policing a sandlot baseball game, he was killed when he was struck on the head by a foul ball.

Pyle, now doomed to spend years in a footrace with his creditors, went into radio on the West Coast, leasing transcribed programs, and put on the Ripley *Believe It or Not* exposition at the 1933 Century of Progress Exhibition in Chicago. In this period, his wife Euphemia divorced him, charging desertion, and he married Elvia Allman Tourtellotte, a thirty-two-year-old radio comedienne. He died of a heart attack in Los Angeles in 1939 at fifty-five. He had enjoyed eleven years of high life, rich and poor both, from the time he took Red Grange out of the amateurs. He could have sold ice to the Eskimos, or even Bermuda shorts, if he ever put his mind to it, but he had to find out the hard way that he could not mine gold out of the American hinterland just by having a band of men run, walk and stumble from one coast to the other in a grotesque charade. It was one of the few things you could not sell in that dizzy time.

Fresh and strong, the men of the 1929 derby leave the ferry from Manhattan on the Jersey side. Only 3,000 miles left to go. *UPI*

SHALL WE DANCE?

The Marathons

How often have I blessed the coming day,
When toil, remitting, lent its turn to play,
And all the village train, from labour free,
Led up their sports beneath the spreading tree!
. . . And still, as each repeated pleasure tired,
Succeeding sports the mirthful band inspired—
The dancing pair that simply sought renown,
By holding out to tire each other down. . . .
—OLIVER GOLDSMITH, *The Deserted Village*

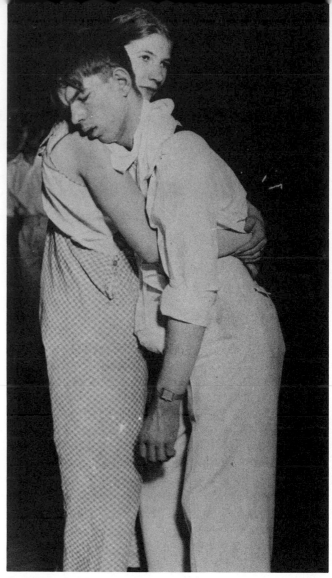

What it was like. Joe Rock is sound asleep on the shoulder of Margie Meadows in the 2,760th hour in Chicago's Merry Garden Dance Hall in 1930. *WWP*

IT MAY SEEM the long way around, but those lines from the Irish poet bring this narrative, almost two centuries later, to Milton Crandall, sometimes called Professor, sometimes called Doc, sometimes called other things. Under the inspiration of C. C. Pyle's Bunion Derby (see the connection?), Milton Crandall pushed the Dance Marathon to a brief but epic height. It wasn't a sport, of course, and it wasn't a case of the "dancing pair . . . holding out to tire each other down." The trick—for a little prize money and a touch of short-lived fame—was to hold each other up.

Crandall came to this dodge by a circuitous but somehow logical route. Briefly a newspaperman in his native Pittsburgh, he turned up in Hollywood as one of the more imaginative press agents. Thus reporters summoned into the presence of Theda Bara on some pretext of his found the dark and sultry temptress seated alongside a skeleton. Why the skeleton? It was Miss Bara's one true love (the name had to be kept secret to protect the innocent, presumably). "Not even the grave can separate them,"

Crandall explained to the bewildered but dubious journalists. It was this flair for zany promotions which the man brought to the Dance Marathon. Columnist Jimmy Cannon, an early observer, put the thing down as a "pageant of fatigue," but Cannon was kind. Richard Watts Jr., later to become drama critic for the New York *Post*, called the Professor's hustle "a macabre modern equivalent of a homicidal Roman gladiatorial spectacle."

Blinded in an accident as a boy of eight, Crandall did not regain his sight until he was sixteen, and thereafter had to use glasses with extremely heavy lenses. Pudgy and balding, he wore especially tailored low-cut vests to show off what passed for a diamond belt, and this gear, combined with the spectacles, endowed him with an appearance that hovered uncertainly between the very sinister and the very innocent when he burst upon the New York scene as the Lawless Decade was drawing to its bleak ending. His "Dance Derby of the Century," staged on a groaning board floor in Tex Rickard's Madison Square Garden, ran for 481 hours before the Board of Health moved in and stopped it. That 'round-the-clock affair opened on Sunday, June 10, 1928, with ninety-one couples shuffling along to the strains of such stirring melodies as "Let Me Call You Sweetheart" and "Sweet Sue, I Love You." The floor was a riot of color and what passed for fashion—short skirts and bobbed hair for most of the girls and lavender blazers, white flannels and silk shirts for the men, not to mention a tuxedo here and there. First Prize: $5,000.

The rules were simple: You danced an hour and took a fifteen-minute break on a canvas cot set up in a tent on the edge of the arena. There were trainers and Swedish masseurs on hand to tend to the weary, along with a variety of salesmen peddling remedies for bad feet as well as replacement shoes and hose. One couple lasted just two and a half hours before deciding that it couldn't possibly be worth it—not even with a $5,000 first prize dangling before the pair that went the distance. In the next five days or so, another sixty-two couples also retired from the field of combat—and there was no absence of combat, by the way. A survey taken in the Marathon's 131st hour purported to show that half of the twenty-eight remaining couples hated each other but the other half still had some love left in their overstrained hearts. That had to be a rigged figure, because tempers evidently were fraying all over the place. For your $2.20 ticket, you had a pretty good chance of seeing some rather unfriendly displays as the hours wore away. The Manhattan newspapers chronicled the developing warfare with something approaching the diligence applied to the gangland bloodletting of the period.

On the seventh day, Albert Kish, an import from Youngstown, Ohio, fell asleep on his feet and drew a hard kick in the shins from the pointed toe of his partner, Helen Augusta Clark. Thus awakened but by no means happy, Kish danced the girl around the floor with such renewed vigor that she had to be dragged off to her cot in a state of collapse; she never made it back. Around the same time, Phyliss Colbert developed a fierce dislike for her co-entrant, one Don Alfred Echeveirria of Spain, and began to flail away at him. It took four men to stop the assault and remove the weakened Spaniard to the tent serving as an emergency hospital. He recovered, but Miss Colbert's unsportsmanlike conduct caused the couple to be disqualified. Short of physical violence, Olive Goss had a similar problem. She couldn't stand the sight of Alois Bruhin after a while and kept turning his head away. When Bruhin resisted, Miss Goss began to scream uncontrollably every time his face came into full view; this drew her an eviction

notice after 206 hours. Fred Martino, in utter despair after begging Harriet Gluse to quite the arena because his feet hurt, lost his aplomb and punched the girl, so he had to go. Joseph Tartore gave Helen Schmidt permission to keep rapping him in the jaw when he began to doze. The sturdy Helen, fiancée as well as dancing partner, whaled away with rights and lefts under that license but Tartore sank to the floor on the ninth day anyway, all tuckered out. Charlotte Kush had a bad time when she began to slap Dominick Laperte and stomp on his toes because he was leaning on the bandstand and just pretending to dance. Laperte thereupon hauled off and hung a shiner on the girl's eye. "You're no gentleman," Miss Kush told her unchivalrous partner. "I suspected it before." Mortimer Jack, dancing with Billy Rogers, developed hallucinations in the 211th hour. Convinced that an army of the light-fingered was sweeping his flannels clean, Jack suddenly took off into Eighth Avenue in pursuit of one such imaginary pickpocket. When he came panting back into the Garden, he found that he had been ruled out for leaving the arena. Victor Tomie and Della Kenne, sagging badly in the second week, took to fanning each other with flowers retrieved from the littered boards, but these exertions took so much out of them that they had to withdraw from the sweat-stained competition.

As that week drew to a close and the Crandall charges began to topple the records of earlier marathons in such way stations as Pittsburgh, Chicago and New Kensington, Pennsylvania, the city's Department of Health sent in a small task force to look over the remaining thirteen couples and see whether anybody was in imminent danger. The medical men found the walking dead—well, you couldn't call it dancing anymore—in reasonably good condition, all things considered, although one of them had a small reservation. "They'll be all right," this doctor said, "if they escape insanity. This music may get them, but otherwise they should last." The man had a point there, since the Professor never dipped into his gate receipts to squander any large sums in that area. His musical ensemble consisted of one saxaphone, one banjo and one trombone, bolstered by a kazoo and alternating with a victrola playing the same dreary waltzes and fox trots over and over and over again.

The dancers did enjoy two brief respites, by way of a change of scenery, thanks to Tex Rickard's more serious commitments to the less savage art of boxing. A bout between welterweight Jimmy McLarnin and Phil McGraw, a Detroit florist on the side, moved the Marathon into the Garden basement.

Milton Crandall: His feet never got tired. *WWP*

For this woman, a brief trip to dreamland.

That one didn't help enough, as it happened, because the great McLarnin took out the other gladiator in one round and the ring was removed in jig time. The dancers also repaired to the basement the night light heavyweight champion Tommy Loughran entertained a visitor from Italy known as Armand Emanuel. The challenger managed to survive ten rounds but there was some grumbling in the dank regions below. The Brothers Ringling had stored some of *their* animals on the premises not long before, and the Crandall minions weren't too happy with the lingering circus odors.

On the seventeenth day, somewhere around the 420th hour, Texas Guinan, the town's most celebrated heroine of the Prohibition wars, marched into the arena and announced that she would give $1,000 apiece to any of the remaining couples who would quit the Marathon then and there. Miss Guinan felt that the Professor was not splitting enough of his profits with his footsore charges; hence the openhanded offer to dispense with some of her speakeasy earnings in behalf of the toiling masses. "Compared to Milton Crandall," said the flashy Tex, "Nero himself was a neophyte. He [Crandall, not Nero] came over to my club the other night and I told him I believed it was my duty to serve him ground glass. Such unpaid tortures as he instigated hurt my feelings." Nobody dared to question the qualitative difference between ground glass and Miss Guinan's brand of bootleg liquor, of course; the woman had an abundance

Texas Guinan, with lawyer Arthur Kaufman on one of her endless trips to court during the Prohibition wars, did not approve of those vulgar marathons. *New York Post*

of friends in all circles of New York life—high, low and journalistic. She was not the first to offer to rescue the dancers from their servitude, by the way. Earl Carroll, the Broadway producer, beat her to it. Famous both for his *Vanities* and the brief prison stretch Uncle Sam made him endure over the private on-stage party in which he featured a shapely seventeen-year-old damsel in a bath of excellent but illicit champagne, Carroll dropped by one morning and offered $100 apiece to any couple that would walk out. There were less than a dozen on the floor then and there were no takers—not with that $5,000 prize now seemingly within reach. Peggy Hopkins Joyce, even then a tested veteran of another kind of marathon, called matrimony for short, was herself a regular in attendance then but did not join in the Carroll-Guinan mercy drive. A four-time loser (or was it *winner?*) in the marital sweepstakes by then, Miss Joyce said that not a dime of her alimony was going on the line in that kind of cause; she was enjoying the thing too much. This was also true of the Countess Phyliss de Dauvis, proprietor of Manhattan's Mimic Club, who set some kind of record as an after-hours, night-long spectator in the Garden. What did she see in the Dance Derby of the Century? "Listen," the Countess said, "I am goofier than those kids."

Professor Crandall was getting a little goofy himself around that time because a touch of mutiny had rent the foul air. The rumblings began to be heard midway in the third week of the endurance test. Mary Promitis, a Pittsburgh entrant known as "Hercules Mary" to her many admirers in the stands, stamped herself an open leader of the rebellion with a fighting declaration.

"I'd like to take a shower and go to a real dance with lots of swell partners," said Mary, a waitress in her other life. "A lot of pineapples we are—dancing here and Crandall getting all the money. Next time we don't enter anything without a guarantee of so much a day."

Her partner, Bill Busch, a veteran of the Bunion Derby, nodded in drowsy assent. He could hardly challenge the diminutive Greek blonde in any case, because he had started to falter on the eleventh day only to find that he had a forbiddingly strong and determined female in his sagging arms. First Mary tickled him to keep him awake. When that lost its effectiveness, she held smelling salts under his nose, whereupon Busch took the bottle from her and hurled it across the floor. Later Mary pressed an ice pack against the back of his neck, causing Busch to lose his cool altogether and chase her around the arena in great anger. Even at that, the girl hung in and Busch

didn't dare to quit. He had a somewhat tattered reputation to maintain: Although disqualified from the Pyle derby after a mere 1,700 miles, he had claimed the world's record for a transcontinental run in 1927, parlayed with such items as a nonstop 188-mile jaunt from Boston to New York and a backward dash (now *there's* a record) along the Connecticut countryside from Bridgeport to Stamford. Still, he was going up against an unfair advantage. Beyond her sheer strength and will, as it turned out, "Hercules Mary" had something of an edge over Busch for all his prior accomplishments. Her trainer, Joey Reynolds, had soaked the girl's feet in vinegar and brine for three weeks before the Marathon. This time-tested device (the bare-knuckled fighters pickled their hands that way to toughen them) evidently had done wonders for Miss Promitis.

The "mutineers"—so labeled by the Professor—demanded a fee of $400 a day to keep shuffling their blistered feet into a fourth week. Crandall in turn announced that he would have nothing to do with any of those ingrates forever after. "What one of them could have made as much in three weeks?" the promoter asked, submitting that the remaining twelve couples already had earned lavish amounts of cash in the waltz sprints and other special events staged to keep the customers coming through the turnstiles and tossing coins to the contestants.

In any case, the mutiny shortly gave way to a larger problem in the person of Health Commissioner Louis I. Harris. Fairly early in the proceedings, the Commissioner had denounced the Marathon as "the sort of folly which the law has no power to control," lest it infringe on personal liberty. Now the guardian of the city's well-being found something to bolster a court move—the case of Frank M. Quinn, only twenty-one, suddenly on the critical list back home in Wilkes-Barre after giving way to the grueling Garden pace. Quinn had collapsed on a street corner there, vomiting blood, and Harris, citing the verdict of the Pennsylvania physicians in attendance, attributed his condition to a bleeding ulcer brought on by his exertions in the Marathon. Crandall entered a quick demurrer.

"Quinn left the dance in the 257th hour because he and his partner had been fighting," the Professor said. "He was well when he went out. In this land of the free and the home of the brave no one ever got stomach ulcers from dancing. He must have had it before he started, but to say that his dancing aggravated it isn't fair. He was a soda jerker and had been used to standing on his feet." Crandall got no help from Quinn's partner, Mary Goddess. A dance hall hostess, Miss Goddess scoffed at the talk of discord and said the youth had suffered prolonged dizzy spells while piloting her around the floor. Harris accordingly pressed his claim that the Marathon truly was menacing the life of its participants. "This is a disgusting spectacle, having neither artistic merit nor sporting interest," the Commissioner said, noting that he personally didn't have the stomach to go and witness the atrocity himself. "High-strung persons are apt to crack under the strain of such competition. You cannot tell whether they are going to suffer permanently." Going further, Harris observed rather acidly that Crandall had pocketed some $65,000 on other marathons before invading New York. The Professor did not deny that he was more interested in the currency of the land than its health or culture but did protest that his otherwise "refined" show had been ruined by the Manhattan tabloids, not to mention the dancers "who went union on me."

Harris won the argument, emerging from the courthouse with an order empowering him to shut down the endurance contest at midnight on July 1, in its 482nd hour. Crandall then said that he meant to call the thing off at 2:00 A.M. the following morning anyway. Indeed, there were dark hints to the effect that a dwindling gate had impelled the Professor to get a friendly newspaperman to go and steam up the Health Commissioner in the first place. While this may have been true, there were 7,000 customers in the joint when the end came, although all Crandall had left on the floor by then were nine couples—walking, limping, shuffling around in assorted states of exhaustion. There were a few bordering on the unconscious, too, but under the Marathon rules you didn't have to be conscious; you just had to keep moving, if not indeed simulating the dance. For that matter, only Joe Lopez, a transcontinental runner from Mexico, and his partner, a sturdy Pole named Airelar Ksohnin, appeared to be dancing. "We believe in obeying the rules," said Miss Ksohnin. "Mr. Crandall said this was a dance. We believe it is, even though some of the others don't. Maybe that's why we haven't had any trouble with our feet or muscles." The Professor's resident podiatrist did not share this diagnosis, for he detected a badly fallen arch on the Polish delegate and disqualified her just as the end neared. Miss Ksohnin was not pleased. "My arch," she said, "is no more fallen than Mr. Crandall's head. I intend to sue him."

For at least one other couple—Gunnar Neilsen, another Bunion Derby loser, and Hannah Karpman, a Brooklyn physical education teacher—the Marathon didn't end a moment too soon. Miss Karpman had a rather plaintive grievance. She submitted that Neilson had treated her with a towering indifference in the early stages of the contest only to turn overbearingly affectionate as the long days and nights dragged on. She said she would have withdrawn from the arena in defense of her honor except that (a) she had bet the runner $100 that he would quit before she did, and (b) she needed the prize money to get her nose bobbed so that she could retire from that musty school gym and try the stage. Unlike the Neilsen-Karpman duet, there were a few couples in at the finish prepared to demonstrate that a man and woman could waltz around together for the best part of twenty-one days and then, no kidding, go out dancing. Jimmy Scott and Olga Christiansen, for example, went right from the Garden on a round of the pleasure palaces—Texas Guinan's, the Silver Slipper, the Charm Club and wherever else there was music. Jimmy Priore, a furnace stoker in real life, took his partner, Florence Carlough, on a round of the cabarets even though there had been some concern over the strain imposed on her heart in the service of Milton Crandall; for a time, they had a nurse checking Miss Carlough's pulse on the half hour while the husky Priore cradled her head on his shoulder. Tommy Nolan and Anna King, both well known in the ballrooms for their mastery of the Charleston, also were back on the boards just as soon as the court order doused the Garden lights. Miss King, by the way, must have been a quite remarkable woman. While Red Cross functionaries in attendance estimated that the Crandall charges had lost a total of seventy-two and a half pounds over the grueling course (the Amateur Athletic Union estimated that the dancers were covering forty miles a day), Miss King proudly announced that she had managed to add a pound and a half to her sparse frame during the ordeal.

Now on the tawdry matter of the dollar again—
There were two sides to that story.
The Professor confessed to gross gate receipts of $121,000 but said he had netted only a skimpy $25,000 for himself after expenses. The conflict came in the distribution of the prize money. In one account, Pittsburgh's gift to America was credited with paying the last nine couples $995.56 apiece—a matter of $8,960.04, nearly double the $5,000 he had pledged to give away. In another, the windfall came out to $277 and change for each of the surviving eighteen, which is more like that original $5,000. For some reason, it was never quite clear which figure was cor-

The much-married Peggy Hopkins Joyce was one of the more devoted fans of the 1928 Garden marathon. Here she's dancing with the Met's Nino Martini in a nightclub. *WWP*

With the Garden whirl moving into its final stages, a nurse tends Anna King and Tommy Nolan. Note the bandages on Miss King's swollen feet. *UPI*

Broadway's Earl Carroll, who couldn't abide a long-stemmed beauty in disarray, also got some publicity mileage out of the Crandall spectacular. He beat Tex Guinan to the punch in offering dancers money to quit the contest.

rect. Either way, Crandall took a characteristic bow. "I'm a square shooter and no small-town piker," he told the press.

Commissioner Harris, for his part, wasn't content to rest on the laurels earned in his triumph over his stout little adversary from Pittsburgh. He went up to Harlem three days later, clutching another court order, and closed down an all-Negro marathon then in its sixteenth day. The Harlem grind, set up to compete with the lily-white Garden show, had started with twenty-four couples but was down to its last eight do-or-die dancers when the padlock went on. It wasn't a total loss, however. One couple in it had so much fun they took an hour off and got married midway through that marathon.

Milton Crandall, no quitter, retired from the scene only long enough to regroup his forces for a fresh raid on the Manhattan pocketbook. He brought in another dance the very next year, all dressed up with safeguards designed to keep the law off his neck. The new rules permitted contestants to take twenty-minute breaks after every two-hour stint, plus complete rest and refurbishing from 5:00 to 7:00 A.M. daily.

The 1929 extravaganza also boasted some new wrinkles for box office purposes: Shipwreck Kelly standing on a flagpole fifty feet above the floor with nothing more than a sleeping break downstairs from 5:00 to 8:00 A.M. daily; Dr. Alexander Meyer, billed as the "prewar rocking chair sensation of Russia," rocking back and forth on a straight-backed chair on a platform in the center of the arena, prepared to take on all comers, and Art Hoffman, a champion endurance driver, shackled to a steering wheel and pledged to stay awake as long as the last dancing couple kept going. Kelly celebrated what passed for his thirty-sixth birthday on his eight-inch disc amid the rafters, using the occasion to pour scorn on the couples whirling below him. "They are crazy," was the word Shipwreck sent down to the journalists. "They make me dizzy."

Doctor Meyer, actually a hospital orderly when he wasn't rocking, had no complaints to speak of, especially since his 213-pound bride often rocked beside him to keep him company and his one challenger, Doctor George Palmer, so called because he had once functioned as a rubber in the six-day bike races, quickly folded up. Hoffman, however, couldn't take it beyond the second day, even though he was a twice-decorated infantry veteran of the World War.

"I'm not afraid," he said. "I can stand drum fire and poison gas with the best of them but if I had to sit here for one more minute, watching those dancers,

Shipwreck Kelly and that guy Meyer, I would go crazy." So they took off the handcuffs and let him go.

Beyond the sideshow attractions, Crandall's twenty-eight starting entrants not only boasted such familiar names as Tommy Nolan and Anna King, Gunnar Neilsen (with blonde Ida Coleman in his burly Finnish arms in place of Hannah Karpman), and Jimmy Priore with a new partner, Jeanne L. King, but also introduced an all-girl team from Brooklyn, Irene Schroeder and Peggy Fitzwilson. Even so, Crandall ran into something even more formidable than Commissioner Harris: poor health at the box office. The natives just weren't ready for another Crandall spectacular. While the 1928 show had started off slowly, there was one twenty-four-hour stretch when some 18,000 fans bought their way in. The return engagement, by contrast, started off badly and stayed that way and Crandall shut it down on the twenty-second day, this time without any prompting from the authorities. Kelly, still on his perch although at one point he had thrown a scare into the house when he fell asleep on his feet and began to sway as he snored, accepted the closing announcement with a show of contempt. "Time to quit already?" he called down. Meyer, well beyond the sixty-six hour record he said he had set back in 1914 in Tomsk, Russia, was still rocking too, despite a last-minute dispute which arose over some attempt to cut him down to what he termed a "Soviet wage scale" because of the dwindling attendance. The six couples still shuffling around in the gray half-light of the Garden split the $2,500 first prize as Crandall withdrew from New York to seek greener dancing pastures elsewhere.

Other dance marathons were flourishing with one degree of success or another in all kinds of outposts at the time. In Wildwood, New Jersey, a bleeding-foot spectacular ran for eighty-one days. What made it truly newsworthy, however, was not its duration but the fact that a husband-and-wife team, Mr. and Mrs. Tom Day of St. Paul, Minnesota, won it. No more compatible married pair ever emerged on the American scene, before or since, unless you wanted to count the couple credited with winning a kissathon in Chicago in 1934 with a nonstop performance lasting six hours and thirty-seven minutes.

The Windy City, incidentally, put on a combined skating and dance endurance test which ended, suitably for that shoot-'em-up town, in a burst of gunfire. It happened on the thirty-second day when an armed "collection agent" on the premises, out on bail in some pistol play at the same affair several weeks

Some of the Crandall charges gather at the high-calorie chow line.

earlier, was cut down in a lethal hail of lead. The killer, discreetly identified as a business rival of the deceased, also wounded a policeman on his way out.

In an Atlantic City marathon, Frank Miller, a fifty-six-year-old grandfather, managed to stay in motion for the best part of 1,473 hours, hauling around a girl of twenty-two, because he needed the $1,000 first prize. In Wilmington, Delaware, there was a switch: Charles Curran went into a marathon to earn enough to pay off his back alimony and beat an arrest warrant, but he began to sag after 800 hours and decided he would rather languish in jail and save his feet.

In the same period, the nonstop dance—a cruel refinement of the marathon, if such a thing was possible—began to find some favor overseas, with endurance claims coming from places like Paris, Edinburgh, Marseilles and Sunderland, England. But those records—Paris led with a dance that lasted twenty-four hours and twenty minutes—quickly fell before the tireless Americans. Alma Cummings of New York, permitted to alternate partners, wore out six volunteers from the supposedly stronger sex in a twenty-seven-hour stint and followed it a week later with a fifty-hour performance. But within eleven days Helene Mayer, a Midwestern department store clerk, chalked up better than fifty-two hours, Magdalene Williams lasted just short of sixty-six hours in Houston and Vera Sheppard shuffled around nonstop for sixty-nine hours in East Port Chester, Connecticut, before she was carried off the floor, slightly unconscious. Then two Cleveland dancers topped her record, Magdalene Wolf with seventy-three hours and Arthur Klein with eighty-eight, only to lose the crown when another

durable Ohioan, June Curry, managed to keep going for ninety hours and ten minutes, dropping from a hefty 161 pounds to a hefty 149 in the process. The nineteen-year-old Miss Sheppard furnished as plausible an explanation as any when reporters asked how she had managed to stay on her feet that long. "I'm Irish," she said, "do you suppose I could have stuck it out otherwise?"

On the stage of the Bayonne Opera House in New Jersey, the fallen-arches craze had a tragic effect. Charles Gonder, twenty-six, of nearby Elizabeth, collapsed going into his forty-eighth day in a marathon and died a short time later, leaving a destitute wife and two children. In New York the following year, 1933, Governor Herbert H. Lehman signed a bill outlawing any dance which went beyond eight hours. For all of the massive social strides made in the Lehman administrations, you had to make room for that piece of legislation as one of his smaller monuments—one you couldn't ignore, in any case.

Charles Gonder was not the first fatality of the marathons, by the way. That woeful distinction went to Homer Morehouse, twenty-seven, of North Tonawanda, New York, and dated back to the earliest days of the dance lunacy, in 1923. To win a bet, Morehouse whirled around to the muffled strains of a country club band for eighty-seven hours. But then, leading his wornout partner off the floor, he fell into a heap and died.

New York, of course, wasn't alone in banning the round-the-calendar dances. Boston rendered the madness illegal five years before Milton Crandall and the other entrepreneurs found gold in them hills. On the

The lone dancer (background) in this 1933 marathon at Boston's Revere Beach was exercising an option some promoters permitted. With his partner out of it, he could solo for a specified time, hoping to acquire a new one if another male gave way to exhaustion.

The men's rest quarters in Boston. Number 6 is sleeping in an upright position, evidently afraid that he wouldn't be able to get up again if he stretched out during the brief break.

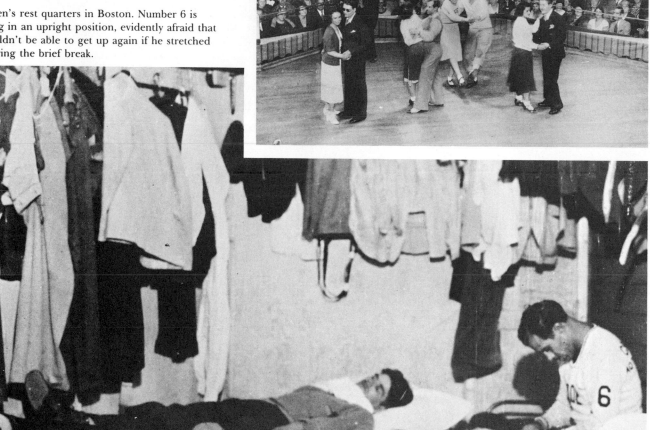

Pacific Coast, such cities as San Francisco, Los Angeles, Portland, Seattle and Tacoma followed suit. Back East, the law didn't step in until the competition for endurance records reached its peak in the early Thirties. In Pittsburgh, a dance marathon lasted 532 hours, with seven couples still on what was left of their feet, when the padlock went on. In Detroit, a marathon went into its 106th day before the police danced in and summarily ordered the five surviving couples to go home to their separate beds for no less than forty-eight hours. In Red Bank, New Jersey, the Society for the Prevention of Cruelty to Animals had a marathon promoter arrested, and the Justice of the Peace got a quick answer when he asked the ASPCA agent, Frank C. Moyan, why he had interceded. "We're interested in humans as well as animals," Moyan said.

Mayor J. Hampton Moore of Philadelphia issued a ban on all marathons in 1932, and the state itself followed suit in 1934.

The magazines and newspapers were rife with protest all along.

The New York *Evening World* put it this way: "Of all the crazy competitions ever invented, the dancing marathon wins by a considerable margin of lunacy. If the authorities are anxious to find legal grounds for stopping such exhibitions, the statutes in regard to the case of lunatics would seem obviously applicable." Hearst's New York *American* was even more exercised, observing that "No anthropoid ape could possibly have had descendants that could display such hopeless idiocy. If the Darwinists intend to maintain their theory they will have to call in the ape and substitute some other ancestor for mankind—the cootie, for instance." The Boston *Evening Transcript* hailed the local authorities for banning the marathons. "These contests are likely to cause overexertion on the part of many who are poorly equipped for trials of endurance," said the *Transcript*. "Long-distance dancing does not come within the scope of those tests of skill which serve a useful purpose." The *Literary Digest* also took a dim view of the whole business. "If such tests of stamina as the marathon dances ever were exacted as punishment they would be deemed cruel," the *Digest* said. "The treadmill was abandoned as too harsh, yet the prisoner was made to tread no more than six hours a day in fifteen-minute periods with intervals of rest. The dancers keep in motion for hours and hours at a stretch. They certainly earn their grotesque glory and the small purses that go with it, and fortunately there are enough hospitals and asylums in the country to take good care of them."

The *Digest* may have been echoing a point made as far back as 1923 by Surgeon General Hugh S. Cumming when he warned marathon contestants that their excesses could cause dilation of the heart and sudden death, or perhaps just cripple their hearts permanently or shatter their nervous systems and make them prey to all manner of afflictions. The Public Health Service chief traced the descent of the marathons to the Middle Ages, noting that in London,

five hundred years back, whole hordes of people would suddenly begin to dance feverishly in the streets for as much as five days at a time until they fell from exhaustion and many died. The doctor, of course, was referring to a dancing mania which evidently sprang from pathological sources.

The classic case occurred in Aachen, Germany, in 1374, when frenzied mass dancing in the streets left scores of persons in assorted states of injury and exhaustion. This outbreak followed the Feast of St. John the Baptist, which is always accompanied by public dancing but never before produced such senseless, uncontrolled fury. Set down in history as the Dancing Madness, it spread from Aachen to other Rhine Valley cities and then to Italy, where one theory traced the phenomenon to fear over the bite of the poisonous tarantula. The dancing fever was indeed described as "tarantism," but it appears that this label derived from the name of the town where the Italian outbreaks began—Taranto. Some historians traced the phenomenon to a mass anxiety neurosis, noting that in the latter half of the Fourteenth Century the Black Plague had virtually wiped out entire populations in parts of Italy, with casualties running as high as nine out of every ten persons in some of the stricken areas.

But, then, all this is far afield from Milton Crandall and the other marathon hustlers of his time. They were just trying to make a buck. Now, by way of a footnote, consider what happened four decades later, in 1965, when a New York discothèque called Our Place staged an endurance contest for the devotees of The Twist and all its wondrous variations, pelvic and otherwise. Nora Hayden, the owner, wisely elected to let the participating dancers pace themselves through their wild gyrations so that the marathon wouldn't end too soon. Fifty couples entered, competing for assorted gifts, and in the thirty-sixth hour Harvey Zaimoff, a Brooklyn clothing store salesman, and his eighteen-year-old partner, Evie Asnes, appeared to have the field all to themselves when little Evie was prompted to make this observation:

"Pretty stupid, isn't it?"

The competition ended shortly thereafter, the girl's remark having gone unchallenged.

JUNE HAVOC

Winner and Still Champion

"We lift up a solemn note of warning
and entreaty . . . . against dancing."
—THE DOCTRINES AND DISCIPLINE OF THE
METHODIST EPISCOPAL CHURCH, 1932

The girl is June Havoc—Jean Reed then—in a 1933 marathon.
She broke all the endurance records and had enough left to go
on to a stage career while her sister, Gypsy Rose Lee, made it as
a stripper.

TO STAY WITH the marathon craze for a moment, there was an actress on Broadway in 1966, appearing in a revival of the Kaufman-Ferber *Dinner at Eight*, who might be considered an authority on the subject. She holds the all-time record. She dances 3,600 hours, just about five months, in a marathon in West Palm Beach in 1934. She was seventeen years old when she went in and eighteen when she came out, clutching her winner's purse—a whopping forty dollars, which is what was left after the promoter dipped in for his deductions for such items as laundry, dry cleaning, shoe repairs and that sort of thing. She didn't go back; she had done her time. She went on from there into movies and the theatre. She didn't happen to be a stranger to show business. She and her sister danced in vaudeville long before they were ready for kindergarten. She was billed as Dainty Baby June, the Pocketsized Pavlova, but she became June Havoc (from Hovick) later on. Her big sister achieved fame as Gypsy Rose Lee, the stripper.

June Havoc turned up in her first marathon, in 1933, quite by accident. Slowly starving as a single in vaudeville, she went out one night to do a tap dancing bit as a fill-in during the rest period in a San Fran-

cisco marathon. It wasn't a very glamorous booking but she needed the five-dollar fee. She happened to look the way any marathon promoter wanted his contestants to look—"you know, anemic, like you're about to drop dead; it was good box office"—and so she was talked into putting her taps away and going after the big prize money that was supposed to be floating around in those days.

Dancing under the name of Jean Reed and making futile stabs at the Broadway chorus lines between marathons, she served a hard and bitter apprenticeship on the way to that big forty-dollar purse—sweetened with what little was left of the money tossed on the floor by the fans for the singing chores she did on the side. The six marathons which preceded that unconscionable Florida grind included a thirty-three-day stint in Somerset, Massachusetts, sixty-six days in Boston's Revere Beach and eighty-three days in Old Orchard Beach, Maine. Along the way the deceptively sturdy Miss Havoc encountered two other dancers destined to go on to larger things—Red Skelton, who did some clowning on the floor, and Frankie Laine, who sang for audience handouts in the entertainment periods. She also danced in the company of

46

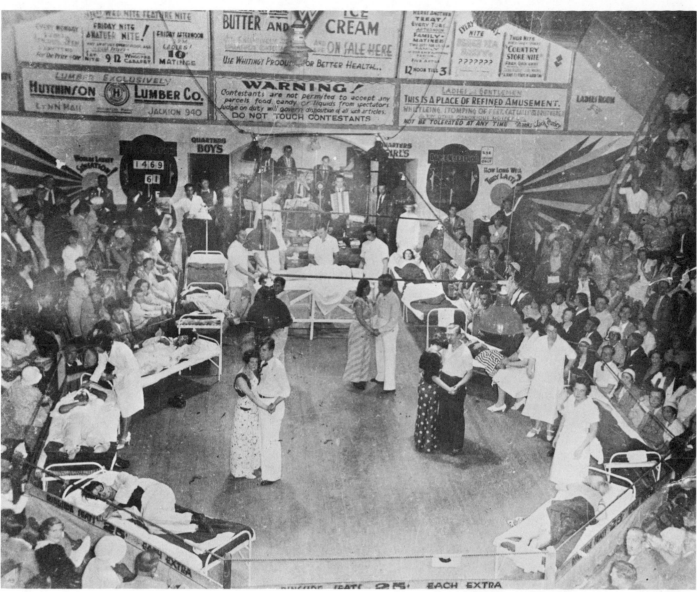

That's the teen-aged Havoc on the cot in the lower right-hand corner on a well-earned sleeping break. The photo is from her own collection.

1967: Starring on Broadway in a revival of *Dinner at Eight,* Miss Havoc looks over a clipping from her days in the marathon wars. *Paul Sann*

such widely known marathon figures as Boston's Joe Rock, who wore his wife down on the dance circuit and then drafted his daughter as a partner and was still hitting the boards when he was sixty-five, and Marvin (Hobo) Hobaugh and his wife Patsy, an Illinois couple. Miss Havoc herself was a star, as distinguished from the "horses" who just danced their feet off in one grind after another for the will-'o-the-wisp prize money, by the time she deposited her scant belongings in the crummy dressing room of the converted fight arena where that West Palm Beach endurance contest, sponsored by the American Legion, was to unfold on its incredible course.

Miss Havoc talks about that 3,600-hour record today as casually as the rest of us might talk about a long night on the town or a hard afternoon on the tennis courts. "Of course," she says, "you were always on the verge of falling down, the way you do when you're untrue to your system, but you kept going somehow. The sound of the band or the scratchy old phonograph records, amplified a hundred times in those tinderbox arenas and rollerdromes, helped to keep you going when you were dragging. The audience helped too; you kept going because they cheered for you." For a girl as fragile as she was in those days, actually, her feat was calculated to make the most rugged athletes green with envy. In that marathon, constantly chewing on such things as lettuce and celery strings to keep awake (gum was barred), the contestants had to keep going forty-five minutes on the hour around the clock, broken only by eleven-minute rest periods with two minutes to get to their sleeping cots and two minutes to get back to the floor. It sounds impossible, but the dancers beat it by sleeping on their feet a good deal of the time. In this process, called "lugging," the contestants stayed in motion with the help of their partners, striving not to get caught with their feet still for more than the three seconds which meant disqualification. Miss Havoc danced with Elmer (Sparkplug) Dupree of Minneapolis, only twenty-two but even by then a thoroughly tested—and thoroughly flatfooted—veteran of the marathon wars. He slept on his poor feet more than the rail-thin blonde, but there was a reason. "Sparkie needed the rest," she says, "because he was also one of the marathon's top clowns and had to do two shows a day, matinee and evening. He took an awful lot of falls in the process, while I just shuffled around the floor." So she had to carry him much of the time but she developed a simple trick, somewhat unappetizing, to keep him from collapsing. She kept a pinky in one of his nostrils.

Miss Havoc recalls that the eleven-minute breaks actually were surprisingly refreshing for most of the dancers because they had trained themselves—"it was a kind of self-hypnosis," she says—to fall asleep as fast as they hit the cot and then roll off it refreshed when the wake-up sirens went off. "I've always believed that you can train yourself to do anything," says the pretty stage star. "To stay alive in those marathons, you had to get the most out of those eleven minutes or run the risk of going 'squirrely'—out of your head, cuckoo—on the floor. That's a risk you couldn't afford to run because then you might fall for some dirty trick and find yourself out of the marathon, like another dancer waltzing up behind you and whispering some terrible thing—'your mother's dying, go home,' or something like that—and hoping you'd dance right out the door in your stupor." That last stunt, which had any number of variations, wasn't calculated to work very well once the Palm Beach grind passed its thousandth hour, because after that the dancers were chained to each other, with dog collars binding their wrists together so that even a sleeping partner might detect an unexpected move, like a sudden collapse, on the part of a teammate.

Miss Havoc pulled no punches when she told the story in her book, *Early Havoc* (1959), and later in *Marathon 33*, a play produced by the Actors Studio in the winter of 1963 with the brilliant Julie Harris in the starring role. In both works, the dirt and grime of the marathons, as well as the vicious infighting among the contestants, were vividly related. "I didn't exaggerate a bit," says the former Dainty Baby June. "I didn't have to." In 1969 that time of madness was brilliantly re-created on film in *They Shoot Horses, Don't They?* with Jane Fonda, Michael Sarrazin, Red Buttons, Bruce Dern and Gig Young, who won an Oscar for his portrayal of the oily promoter.

To close out this chapter, one conclusion is inescapable, and it has to do with the legend that often hung on the arena walls—THIS IS A PLACE OF REFINED AMUSEMENT.

There was nothing refined about the dance marathon, nothing at all.

THE CONTEST MADNESS

"Who leaves the game loses it."
—FRENCH PROVERB

IN 1929, before the bad news from Wall Street turned American minds to somewhat more pressing items, like where's that next meal coming from, the countryside was rather liberally sprinkled with men and women engaged in one form of endurance contest or another. The variety of these competitions, inspired by the headlined deeds of Shipwreck Kelly and the blistered and bleeding combatants of the Bunion Derbies and the marathon dances, appeared to be endless. How long could you rock in a straight-backed chair. Or talk nonstop (the women were big in that sport)? Or listen to the radio? Or eat? Or roller-skate? Or—imagine this—kiss?

Clara Wagner, poor hard-luck Clara Wagner, made news that year. She passed the best part of nineteen days (minus ten-minute breaks on the hour and two hours at dawn for napping) gently rocking back and forth in a Chicago contest and then, with fame and some small reward within her grasp, gave way to exhaustion. Removed to a hospital, where she was deemed to be in "dangerous" condition, the twenty-five-year-old sweetheart of the rocking chair set was the inadvertent cause of a sweeping piece of restrictive legislation in nearby East Chicago, Indiana. There, citing Miss Wagner's plight, Mayor Rollie

Hale summarily shut down a rocking-chair derby then in its forty-seventh hour with three men and a lone woman still left among fourteen starters. The city fathers also closed the little metropolis to flagpole sitting, gum-chewing contests, marathon dancing, roller derbies, or long-distance talking or hand-holding competitions, even in the cause of sweet charity.

"Something must be done to curb this menace that is sweeping the nation," said Mayor Hale. "East Chicago will lead the way."

The menace wasn't quite curbed, since the Corn Belt was rife with rocking-chair derbies at the time. In Champaign, Illinois, an outlander from Kansas City, J. Bruce Hanley, dared to take on the local champion, Mrs. H. B. Schmidt, and had to go home in disgrace. Hanley fell asleep after 280 hours and 30 minutes. Mrs. Schmidt kept rocking until she hit 400 hours. In that contest, unlike those being staged at the time by the old dance marathon maestro, Milton Crandall, real rockers were used instead of the straight-backed chair, which was less likely to usher a competitor off to dreamland in unduly quick time. Crandall, by the way, staged a talking marathon in Boston that year. He had thirty starters but the thing was a bust, ending after a mere ninety-seven hours

49

with Betty Wilson and Howard Williams in a dead heat and all talked out. The Massachusetts capital took no official stand on that piece of folly but did act with characteristic firmness after Joe Scully, eight, competing for a prize of a huckleberry pie, kept a rope swing in his own backyard going for eight hours and five minutes and touched off a rash of similar competitions in the town's playgrounds. Just like that, Boston banned that sort of contest as a menace to the people's health.

By contrast with what was happening in the so-called adult population, the kids made sense, actually.

Competing for a $200 prize offered by a department store in Louisville, Kentucky, Mrs. Mildred Daniel listened to a radio for 106 consecutive hours. Before she could go home to her two infant children, Mrs. Daniel had to spend two days in a hospital to shake the twin effects of exhaustion and delirium with which she emerged from the ordeal.

Farther west, even stranger things were happening. Bill Williams, of Hondo, Texas, spent thirty days pushing a peanut twenty-two miles up Pike's Peak with his nose to win a $500 bet. Thus inspired, two other Texans, C. G. Hart and L. R. Rose, decided to whack an assortment of croquet balls all the way from Galveston to New York. Before those Lone Star stalwarts were 100 miles out of Galveston, H. P. Williams of Texas City, presently dubbed "Hoopie" by the journalists, rolled out an iron hoop on the sweltering afternoon of July 31 and announced that he was going to push it over that same 2,300-mile course, propelling it with a bamboo stick in the fashion of the hoop rollers down through the years. History was never quite clear on what happened to the croquet-swatting team but Hoopie Williams, traveling by slow stages, made New York early in January. Five months to poke a little twelve-inch band of metal over such a trifling course? Well, Hoopie said he had taken a total of sixty days off between rolls to replenish his strength and tend to his worn-out shoes and that sort of thing. In blasé Manhattan, the arrival of the hardy twenty-five-year-old Texan barely caused a ripple.

In 1930, far from abating, the endurance contagion spread, with the most marked effect in the juvenile ranks. A United Press survey that summer started in this fashion:

The nation's youth has gone marathon crazy. Boys and girls today sat in trees, teetered-tottered toward doubtful fame, pedaled bicycles in seemingly endless circles, danced far past the exhaus-

tion point and, to cap the climax, planned an endurance water-wing contest.

The UP traced the new tree-sitting epidemic—remember, there was a flurry of it when Shipwreck Kelly was in the full flush of his dizzy career—to a youth named Jimmy Clemmons of Racine, Wisconsin. Jimmy had just put in thirty-six hours on a bough, prompting immediate challenges. In Camden, New Jersey, the police counted no less than sixty boys perched in trees at one time. Vincent Morrisey and Anthony Scott claimed the national championship after a 100-hour stint in Camden's Old Stockton Park but two Kansas City boys quickly put them to shame. Jack Richards chalked up a 156-hour record and then Bill Kearney, ten years old, wiped it out with a 165-hour sojourn in his favorite cottonwood tree.

As ever, there were frowns of disapproval. In Philadelphia, the police announced that no tree-sitting would be tolerated at all. In the state capital at Harrisburg, all the title contenders were ordered down when the Weather Bureau observed that a tree was a bad place to be in, or up, if lightning struck. In South Bend, Indiana, the Board of County Commissioners was called into session to do something about Jimmy Sugonitis, thirteen, who happened to be perched in a maple on the courthouse lawn with an awning over his head bearing a commercial message from a local merchant. The board voted to dislodge the boy forthwith.

On the ground, briefly, marathon bicycle riding came into vogue, bothering the authorities just as much as the nature lovers in the trees. Larry Cagnon stayed on his two-wheeler for fifteen hours in New Britain, Connecticut, only to lose the title to Henry Carlson, fourteen, who passed his record by fifty minutes even while dodging the police, suddenly unhappy because there were five other marathon riders in action at that moment. The whole New Britain adventure, even with the extra element of the chase to make it more interesting, proved to be an exercise in futility a few days later when James Tsiorbas demolished all the records with a twenty-four-hour-and-forty-eight-minute performance in Manchester, New Hampshire. Then New Jersey came up with a switch—the team marathon. A quartet of relay riders led by a boy named Jimmy Dooley kept a bike whirling around a school playground in Hackensack for thirteen days. A Newark team led by Donald Mohr, challenging that mark, kept going for a week before the police, worried about traffic hazards, made them stop. In Montclair, another quartet, in its 300th hour, was hailed into court on charges of juvenile delin-

In this 1957 endurance contest in Belfast, Maine, the trick was to see who could eat more chicken. P. J. (Tiny) Terrill of Fort Lauderdale, Florida, the 383-pound behemoth on the right, quit after putting away 24 pounds and 9 ounces. Representative Albert E. Cote of Lewiston, a svelte 353, kept right on going. Still hungry, you know? *WWP*

Without missing a note, Heinz Arntz enjoys dinner, served by his wife during a marathon piano-playing performance which began in Germany and ended at New York's Roosevelt Raceway.

quency, of all things. In Hillside, the law put the brakes on still another record-seeking team, then in its 580th hour.

The girls were not idle at the time. In Evanston, Illinois, Mildred Borrey, twelve, and Ruth Emerson, fourteen, managed to keep a seesaw going for eighteen hours. "We would have kept it up much longer," said Miss Emerson, ruefully, "if our parents hadn't missed us."

The water-wing contest mentioned by the UP did not come off, perhaps fortunately, but there were enough nutty things in progress to prompt Nunnally Johnson, writing in the *Saturday Evening Post,* to describe it as the "Golden Age for Filberts." Johnson found America in 1930 "First in war, first in peace, first in tree sitting, gum chewing, peanut pushing, and bobbing up and down in water" (a St. Paul man had bobbed up and down 1,843 times to claim the record in that department). A newspaperman himself before his writing talents took him to Hollywood, Johnson blamed the papers for the spread of the tree-sitting fad, drawing this reply from one editorial writer: "Printing pictures of tree sitters no more encouraged tree sitting than pictures of generals en-

couraged wars. They sit in trees [the children, not the generals] because they love to sit in trees."

The Johnson article also remarked, with considerable dismay, on another kind of contest then drawing some attention—marathon eating. The standouts in this unappetizing department included Robert G. Baskell, a husky truckman from Bridgeport, Connecticut, and Charles Drayo of Leroy, New York. Baskell dropped into a restaurant in nearby Milford and downed 124 littleneck clams in twenty minutes to top the existing record of seventy-three in half an hour. When he asked for more, the proprietor demurred for fear that he would have a corpse on his hands, so Baskell put away half a cold lobster and went home. Drayo, no less spectacular, ate forty raw eggs in five minutes to show his contempt for Emile

A. Gillette, a Kansan who had won a contest at Racine, Wisconsin, by swallowing thirty-six eggs in eight minutes. For historians specializing in this field, two other giants must be listed here—Tony Laurentis, a Philadelphia barber, and Cadarino Nazareno, an ice cream maker from Chicago. One day in 1935, Laurentis, just moderately hungry, presumably, dashed off a repast consisting of four pounds of spaghetti soaked in cheese and tomato sauce, twelve spring chickens, two sirloin steaks and a platter of meat roast. To wash all that down, he had a gallon of wine and a gallon of beer before he waddled away from the table. Nazareno earned a place in the same dubious hall of fame the following year when he put nine opponents to shame by eating 1,137 feet of spaghetti—seven feet per minute for 162 minutes. Nazareno left the restaurant on his own power but some of the trenchermen foolish enough to go against him wound up in hospitals.

On the more cultural endurance levels, one cannot ignore Heinz Arntz, the durable piano player. This man enjoys three lines in the *Guinness Book of World Records* on the strength of a long-playing concert in Berlin in which he tortured the keys without pause (except for refreshment intervals) for 423 hours, or 17 days and 15 hours back in 1935, but this hardly does justice to the pint-sized pianist. To begin with, Herr Arntz was still in the warm-up stages of his career then, having switched from conventional piano to the long-distance variety just six years before. Playing in a Düsseldorf orchestra and known as an utterly tireless performer, the German was persuaded to take on Jack van den Build, the American marathon piano-playing champion, who had come to Berlin to meet all challengers. The match, in the Pharussaele Cafe, turned out to be a no-contest affair.

Van den Build, all tuckered out, had to quit after 72 hours. Arntz, who hadn't even raised a sweat, played on for another three hours, just to stay in shape, before arising to take a bow as the new champion, have his forearms rubbed by two masseuses, and pick up the winner's purse of 2,000 marks (about $180 then). It was better than pounding out the light classics in the cafes, so Arntz stayed with the marathon bit. He had a high record of 108 hours before the Berlin stretch which is listed by Guinness, and he ran up a string of 620 hours in Paris in 1955. The last time anybody was silly enough to challenge him was in 1960, when he took on Roger Rogère at Roubaix, France. M. Rogère staggered from the keyboard after 240 hours. Arntz, paid by the clock, presumably, kept going for another 566 hours. In 1965, sixty-six years old but showing no signs of wear at all, he ran off a 1,001-hour performance on his native soil and then beat that record by torturing the keys for 1,003 hours—better than forty-one days—in Paris.

Herr Arntz's fame spread to the United States the following year through the courtesy of Joey Goldstein, the highly intentive press agent for Roosevelt Raceway in Westbury, Long Island. Goldstein, a man with something of a marathon mind when it comes to grabbing space in the newspapers, conceived the idea of a transatlantic tour de force which would culminate at the Long Island Fair, held on the trotting track's plush premises while the horses and wagons were being rested between meetings. Arntz, five feet four and a trim 130 pounds, started in his favorite Düsseldorf cafe, kept playing on the Autobahn on the truck bearing him to Bremerhaven to board the *United States,* stayed at the baby grand in the ship's lounge all the way across, switched to his traveling spinet while another truck hauled him out to Westbury, and then settled down quite contentedly at the Fair.

With his wife, Leisel, in constant attendance, Arntz enjoyed all the comforts of home, like Weiner schnitzel and chicken soup, handfed while he went on beating the poor piano. The ever-attentive Goldstein furnished a barber so that the tuxedo-clad champion could be shaved while working and never miss a note as he ran all the way over the classical course from Bach to Tchaikovsky and back. When Herr Arntz called it quits on October 1 with a rendition of his favorite march, *"Alte Kameraden,"* he had been going for 1,054 hours—just under forty-four days since he sat down to that defenseless piano at Düsseldorf. Take away two hours a day for rest and refurbishing and you still have a stretch of continuous culture such as no racetrack in the world has ever enjoyed before.

This story has been told at length here not out of any overbearing love for the statistical side of things, but because there is a moral in it. Heinz Arntz started playing the piano when he was six, and his mother never had to tell him to practice. He practiced. It sort of makes you sorry you didn't listen to your mother when you were a kid—or does it?

~~~~~~

CROWD CLASSIC

THE VALENTINO FUNERAL

"Here was one who was catnip to women."
—H. L. MENCKEN

In *The Four Horsemen of the Apocalypse*,
where it all began for the once-
penniless immigrant.

IT WAS AN explosion of adoration and mass hysteria reminiscent of the Middle Ages. The New York *Times* described it this way:

". . . The rioting was without precedent, both in the numbers concerned and in the behavior of the crowd, which, in large measure, consisted of women and girls. Many of these suffered discomfort and rough handling for hours for whatever satisfaction it gave them to be hustled by the dead screen star's coffin and to gaze for an instant on his drawn, white face."

The dead star was Rudolph Valentino.

The date was August 24, 1926, thereafter known as Mad Tuesday.

The crowd numbered 30,000 at its peak. It stretched up Broadway in the rain from Campbell's Funeral Church at 66th Street all the way to 72nd, surging against police lines, barely backing up before repeated charges by the mounted forces, withstanding the blows of nightsticks, finally crashing through one plate glass window at Campbell's and another one in an auto showroom. But even with some of their number carried off in ambulances and scores of other casualties treated on the spot, only a bare handful left the scene while there was still a chance, up to midnight, to get a last two-second glimpse of that

drawn white face in the coffin. One woman made the full circuit three times, fainting each time she reached the bier, before the police told her she had to go home and make room for someone else to fall down in.

Who was the man that inspired this wild outpouring of public grief? There was some conflict about his background, but it came out this way:

Rodolpho Alfonzo Raffaeli Pierre Filibert di Valentina d'Antonguolla, born under a star on May 6, 1895, was the major production of the love match of the slight Beatrice Barbin, daughter of a Paris surgeon, and Giovanni Guglielmi, a dashing cavalry captain who doffed his uniform to settle down as a farmer and veterinarian in the little village of Castellenta in Southern Italy. There was an older brother, Alberto, and a sister, Maria, and the burden of their upbringing fell on their mother when Guglielmi's heart failed in 1908. In time, Rodolpho was sent off to the Royal Academy of Agriculture in Genoa but the farmer's life was not for him and he prevailed on his mother to send him to Paris for further schooling, perhaps looking toward a naval career. Alas, when he wasn't fighting off the advances of the French girls drawn by that striking face he gambled away his allowance at Monte Carlo, so Mama Guglielmi decided that her

The vanguard of the massed thousands outside Campbell's. *WWP*

Jean Acker, his first wife (foreground, head bowed) leaves the Valentino bier with her mother, Mrs. Martha Acker and sister Edith (center) following. But the classic scene in the funeral parlor was reserved for another player in this drama—Pola Negri. *WWP*

wayward son should go to America and try to make something of himself. He came to New York in 1913, eighteen years old and on his own.

Rodolpho went to work as a gardener on the Long Island estate of Cornelius Bliss Jr., got fired for smashing up a motorcycle belonging to another workman there; found a job tending the lawns in Central Park but lost it because he wasn't a citizen and couldn't take the Civil Service test; swept stores and polished brass so that he could pay for a room on the Bowery instead of sleeping on benches in the park; worked as a busboy and waiter and started to learn the barber's trade—and then got his break. A friend from Italy steered him to Maxim's, where they were looking for young dancers to pilot lonely matrons around the floor. There, playing what was essentially a gigolo's role, the youth came to the notice of Bonnie Glass, Clifton Webb's dancing partner in vaudeville, and she hired him when her act with Webb broke up. Rodolpho—Rudolph Valentino by then—made a hit on the dance circuit, first with Miss Glass and then with Joan Sawyer, and went to Hollywood after a while to try the movies. He got his break when June Mathis, the scenario writer, saw him in a bit role in 1921 and picked him to play Julio in her adaptation of the Blasco-Ibáñez adventure, *The Four Horsemen of the Apocalypse.* The Latin collar ad with the classic features, a trim and athletic figure just under six feet tall, made it on his first real shot. Then he went into something called *Unchartered Seas,* and the great Nazimova, watching him on the set, decided that he was just the man to play Armand to her Camille. And then came such vehicles as *The Sheik* (with Agnes Ayres), *Blood and Sand* (with Gloria Swanson), Booth Tarkington's *Monsieur Beaucaire* and in time, of course, *The Son of the Sheik,* opposite Vilma Banky, conservatively described in the studio handouts as the Hot Paprika from Hungary.

In that meteoric five-year stretch, nothing could diminish the image of Valentino as the Great Lover. For the men of the time, it was Clara Bow (just plain sex), Pola Negri (exotic stuff), Theda Bara (the vamp), Mary Pickford (the girl next door) and an assortment of other impossible dreams. For the women, in their secret hearts, it was Valentino alone. It didn't matter when actress Jean Acker, suing for divorce before the ink was dry on the marriage pact, alleged that the screen idol had struck her during a domestic quarrel. It didn't matter when Valentino let himself sink helplessly into the frosty arms of Natacha Rambova for a second disastrous adventure in married love; nor that the striking brunette—dancer, art

director and stepdaughter of cosmetics millionaire Richard Hudnut—should emerge as the party calling all the shots in the virile hero's career as if he was just a puppet on a string. Thus when he died his farewell scenes, like his pictures, were all sellouts. Even in death, he was still the Great Lover.

There was a nagging question about that carnival in Manhattan, and it persists to this day: Was it staged? Did clever press-agentry bring out the mob, or was it spontaneous? Well, to begin with, there was no question about the nationwide concern over the dashing figure with the long sideburns when a twin operation for an inflamed appendix and a perforating gastric ulcer put him on the critical list with peritonitis. As a slow-building suspense thriller, Valentino's fight for life in New York's Polyclinic Hospital outdid all the scripts written for him in the movie mills. The first flash came out on Sunday night, August 15, and for the next eight days the public fed on a stream of medical bulletins alternating between hope and doom. Barely hanging on in the forty-eight hours after surgery, Valentino rallied on the third day, only to take a turn for the worse at week's end when pleurisy complicated his condition. On Monday, August 23, the *Daily News,* obviously carried away with the high drama, led off its morning cliffhanger this way:

"The Great Director today stood ready to call Rudolph Valentino off the screen of life."

And the Great Director did—at 12:10 that very afternoon.

Now, with sound effects furnished by the roaring presses, the orgy began.

The *Evening Graphic,* tinted a suitable green in contrast to the unfortunately gay pink of the *News,* hit the streets with a photo of the departed Sheik being welcomed into Heaven by a rather hefty angel even before the sponsors of the public obsequies were ready to surrender the beautiful body. Tricky, no? It was one of the *Graphic*'s more indigestible "composographs," and the high-flying managing editor, Emile Gauvreau, said it was good for 100,000 extra sales. This tabloid, itself, doomed to live a scant eight years compared to Valentino's thirty-one, later produced a paste-up job showing the Great Lover and his countryman, Enrico Caruso, in white shrouds, reunited in that serene, cost-free shelter called Heaven. That one may not have been as farfetched as it seemed, for in due course Natacha Rambova, solidly wired into the spirit world, was to reveal that her lost love had indeed renewed his friendship with the fabulous tenor.

But to stay on the ground for a moment—

Although the scheduled first viewing was set for four o'clock in the afternoon, the lines began to form at Campbell's even before dawn lifted the black veil from the towers of Manhattan. Thus it was quickly evident that a new kind of Broadway spectacular was in the making. There were so many calls for police reinforcements that the Commissioner himself, George V. McLaughlin, went to the scene to take charge. As the rioting took form, Campbell's threw open its doors at 2:00 P.M. to relieve the crush along Broadway. First, however, S. George Ullman, Valentino's manager, took a further precaution. Fearing that souvenir hunters might strip the corpse, attired in full evening gear, Ullman had the silvered bronze coffin sealed to show only that once perfectly chiseled face. Thus foiled, the mournful viewers went after the appurtenances of Mr. Campbell's Gold Room itself, prompting that somber but practical dignitary to have the body moved to a less resplendent haven on the premises.

The next day McLaughlin's troops, having counted more than a hundred casualties from the opening engagement, including a few from their own sorely-tested ranks, found a way to maintain better order by forcing the crowd to line up four abreast in the streets above the funeral home. It was raining again but another 50,000—again, mostly women—showed up. There was no lack of drum-beating, of course, to help bring out the throngs. For example, Harry Klemfuss, a crafty press agent on the payroll to spread the fame of Frank Campbell, stationed armed Black Shirts around the bier to guard the remains, supposedly on orders from Mussolini himself. There was also a wreath on the scented premises labeled "From Benito Mussolini" but the Sawdust Caesar denied that he had ordered either the Fascist muscle-men (quickly chased by the local *carabinieri,* by the way) or the floral tribute.

In any case, the seemingly endless display of grief soon proved too much even for the publicity-hungry George Ullman, for he suddenly changed his mind about letting the body stay on view all through the week. "Because of the general disorder and lack of respect," said the harried manager, "this thing will not go on. It is more than I can stand." So on the third day the body was removed to a more private room, pending Alberto Guglielmi's arrival from Italy to participate in the arrangements for his brother's funeral, and the ultimate SRO engagement of Rudolph Valentino's career came to an end, leaving New York's masses free to turn their attention to another crowd spectacle: Mayor James J. Walker's ticker tape parade from the Battery to City Hall for Gertrude Ederle, all dried out and home in triumph after swimming the English Channel.

But the man in the bronze casket, momentarily sealed off from the mournful legions, wasn't spared. The buildup for the last big scenes went on apace—some of it tinged with the odor of high-pressure public relations and some genuinely tragic.

Peggy Scott, a twenty-seven-year-old British actress, took a lethal dose of poison in London and left behind an assortment of letters proclaiming her love for Valentino. "With his death," said one of them, "my last bit of courage has flown. . . . In 1922 Rudolph helped me to carry on. He told me a lot of his own sufferings. I have had lots of wonderful moments. There's a lot I cannot tell you." Friends of Miss Scott said she had met Valentino at Biarritz and thereafter always carried a picture of him sewn inside her dresses. Ullman, ever protective, insisted that the star had never met the girl.

A New York housewife shot herself to death with a batch of Valentino photos clasped in her hand, while another woman botched a suicide attempt. From Japan there was a report of two lovelorn girls leaping into a volcano because they couldn't live without Valentino, and Rome dispatches said Il Duce himself had appealed to the women of Italy to contain their grief and not take that last, fatal step.

United Artists, with a box office stake in the newly released *Son of the Sheik,* decided to furnish the departed star with some suitable last words to keep the publicity mills grinding. It came out, "I want the sunlight to greet me. Don't pull down the shades," supposedly a free translation of something the expiring Adonis had uttered in Italian to a doctor who did not understand the language. Oscar Doob, the UA publicity chief, originally settled on some last words a good deal closer to the role of the Sheik—"Let the tent be struck!" This was hastily dropped when a lesser studio functionary observed that it was dangerously close to the last words of Robert E. Lee. ("Strike the tent . . . tell Hill that he must come up.") When Doob dreamed up the line about the sunlight, nobody remembered, unfortunately, that *that* was pretty close to Goethe's dying *"Mehr Licht."* The truth in any case, appeared to be that in the agony of dying Valentino had neglected to say anything either worthy of passing on to history or suitable for the posthumous promotion of his movies.

Jean Acker, in Manhattan rehearsing for a play, summoned the press to her apartment and there, propped up in a bed of sorrow, revealed that George Ullman had spirited her into the comatose Valen-

The star lies in state—before wiser heads decreed that the body had better be installed in a casket and shielded from the coming throng. Eva Miles, a fan, pays her last respects. *WWP*

In this *Evening Graphic* composite, more damned than praised in the profession, Enrico Caruso and Valentino look on benignly in heaven as a band of new arrivals crosses from the river Styx. In the background, the towers of Manhattan, presumably the vessel's point of departure. The photo sold an extra 100,000 copies for the short-lived Bernarr Macfadden tabloid as the hysteria reached its peak. The star's second wife, Natacha Rambova, later insisted that he had indeed been reunited with his tenor friend on that celestial stage upstairs.

A quieter moment at the Broadway chapel after police restored order. *WWP*

Rambova ran out on her marriage with Valentino but embraced him in death, shaking off other claimants to his heart. Sixty-six, she died in Pasadena in 1966.

Not one to be denied, Pola Negri held herself to be the star's one true love, even while suing his estate over a $15,000 loan. She said they were planning to be married when Valentino died. In her mid-seventies and long retired to San Antonio, Texas, where she prospered in real estate, she was asked about the movie scene in 1970 when her *Memoirs of a Star* was published. The answer: "I do not like the nudity, the obscenity. I do not go very much. I was the first to introduce sex to the screen, but it was sex in good taste."

The woman is Nazimova, in *Camille*.

On his trusted Arabian steed, Jadaan.

In *The Son of the Sheik* with Vilma Banky, Valentino doesn't seem to be flipping his burnoose in this still, but Banky wasn't billed as the Hot Paprika from Hungary for nothing.

tino's room in Polyclinic for a very private farewell minutes before the end. "The shock of seeing him lying there was terrible," said the pretty brunette. "All I remember is that white face on the bed and his labored breathing. I wanted to do something to help him but it was all so hopeless. I had never seen anyone dying before." Miss Acker said that she detected under the sleeve of her ex-husband's silk hospital pajamas the silver slave bracelet she had given him in the days before their romance evaporated into that hit-run marriage. That in itself constituted something of a news flash, because the story till then was that Valentino had never taken off the slave bracelet hung on him by Natacha Rambova in happier days. Ullman, always anxious to help the newspapers, added another morsel to Miss Acker's hospital room scene. "She looked at him a while," he said, "and then bent down and kissed him. He stirred a little." But even with that kind of pulsating bulletin, Wife Number 1 wasn't destined to hold center stage very long. There was a flashing temptress in the wings waiting to stake her claim as Valentino's one and only love. This was Pola Negri, and she would leave no stone unturned and no tear unshed.

Although she was the one chosen for the necessary repair work on his shattered heart when Natacha Rambova spurned his pleas and went off to Paris to divorce him the year before, the sultry Polish import had remained in Hollywood during Valentino's gallant battle for life. "I would like to hasten to his bedside," she was quoted, "but I am in the middle of a picture." But when the ultimate word came, Miss Negri fainted and then, revived, betook herself to Valentino's mountaintop hideaway above Beverly Hills, Falcon's Lair. Why? Louella Parsons, Mother Confessor to the movie colony in joy or in sorrow, in sickness or in health, reported that the love nest of the Sheik was "the one place that offered her a solitary grain of comfort in her bitter anguish" as she summoned up the strength to journey East for the funeral.

Traveling by private railroad car in the magnificent loneliness of the long-distance mourner, the black-haired beauty was reported in a state of collapse a good deal of the time but did grant reporters in Kansas City and Chicago interviews from behind the sealed door of her floating steel chariot. The essence of the resulting communiqués was that when the Grim Reaper struck, Miss Negri was poised to star in a movie with Valentino and then give herself to the dashing Italian in holy wedlock and bear him the bambinos he so desperately wanted. Remembering the lady's track record in the romance marts,

Talk about bedroom eyes. This is from *The Sheik*, and the girl on Dream Street is Agnes Ayres. This 1921 epic, marked by scenes of torrid promise rather than performance, a process reversed in the Sixties, earned a million dollars for Paramount in a time when that was regarded as money.

there were those who scoffed. Miss Negri previously had enjoyed worldwide press display with an engagement to Charlie Chaplin—"My Sharlie"—only to announce after a while that "there are one thousand reasons why I should not marry Mr. Chaplin." On the heels of that one, there were broad hints—put down as extremely unlikely in the better-informed circles—of an alliance between Miss Negri and Big Bill Tilden, the tennis star. Blushing as she evinced a quiet rapture, the actress would not deny the story. "I admire Mr. Tilden very much," she said. "You must not ask me more." The athlete, no ladies' man at all, was more forthright. "There is nothing to it," he said, conceding that Miss Negri was "very, very charming."

If the suddenly amplified Valentino idyll did indeed bear the taint of a public relations operation, then Miss Negri's open travail in New York either belied it or entitled her to a special Academy Award for the best off-screen supporting role of 1926. This is how the *Herald Tribune* described her reunion with Valentino in Campbell's:

The coffin was opened and for five minutes Miss Negri stood rigid before the body. She then faltered and had to be supported. She regained her composure in a minute and asked leave to pray. She knelt before the bier and for fifteen minutes said the slow moving Litany of the Dead. When the last words were being uttered she threw her arms up and collapsed, white and drawn, across the rug on which the bier stood. She was unconscious twenty minutes.

Then came the funeral, marked by more crowd scenes—but no disorder—as a great horde lined the one-mile route from the funeral home to St. Malachy's, "The Actors' Church." Here, just another name in a glittering Hollywood galaxy led by such as Douglas Fairbanks and Mary Pickford, Gloria Swanson, Marion Davies, William S. Hart, Madge Bellamy, Richard Dix, Ben Lyon and Bebe Daniels, Norman Kerry, Marilyn Miller and Dorothy Mackail, Miss Negri shed tears in torrents but managed to contain

Jadaan, brought out of retirement for this mission, placing a wreath on the memorial in 1934.

The veiled Lady in Black paying homage in Hollywood Cemetery on August 23, 1947, twenty-fifth anniversary of the Latin Lover's death. This Lady in Black—there have been more than one—said she was Rita Flame, president of the Hollywood Rudolph Valentino Memorial Guild. *WWP*

herself. Jean Acker needed aromatic spirits to get through the ordeal.

Later that day, Miss Negri summoned reporters to the Ambassador Hotel to announce that she had a letter from a Polyclinic doctor, relayed to her by way of Miss Pickford for some obscure reason, revealing that when Valentino became aware that the end was near he was heard to say, "Tell Pola I have been thinking of her." This was at variance with reports of other smuggled communiqués suggesting that the one the Great Lover called for on his deathbed, the one who stayed in Europe and never came to him, was Natacha Rambova.

Be that as it may, Miss Negri kept the spotlight all the way from New York to the interment in Hollywood's Memorial Park. Riding the funeral train on a procession which was marked by suggestions that Valentino was outdrawing the crowds another headliner (Mister Lincoln) once drew on his last journey, the now-composed Pola further unburdened her heart. This is what she told Patricia Dougherty of the Chicago *Herald and Examiner:*

I have had many love affairs in my life, but Rudolph Valentino was the great love—the one I had been waiting for. I am a woman of temperament. Without love, I am hungry and cold and lonely. Love is the flame that burns in my soul and makes me a great artist. There are people who think that because I have fallen in love many times I regard love lightly. They do not know it was only that I was seeking the highest, purest love. Every man I met I measured with my mind's eye, thinking, "Could this be he? If love is here, dare I let it go?" But when I met Rudolph I knew. And he understood. Of all the men who have loved me he alone never reproached me. He never spoke about my past. He knew that all I had suffered was preparation for him. He loved me.

So much for those purple notes from the woman who once described herself as a "connoisseur of men." The next turn had to go to Miss Rambova, and the lady in the turban, initiated into the occult a

61

few years back, happened to be loaded with scoops from the spirit world when she sailed into New York harbor (on a boat, that is) in November. George B. Wehner, described as a "transmedium," was with her, and it turned out that he had a line in to Maselope, an Egyptian spook dead three thousand years but still working at his trade. Miss Rambova said that contact with the beloved "Rudy" had been established with Maselope's help. She said the old guy, working through Wehner, had tipped her off to Valentino's demise three days before the end. So much for that. What was the word from upstairs?

Talking freely, even cheerfully, the former Winifred Shaunessy, converted to Rambova by her own pen, said that while her ex-husband appreciated the world's homage, "he was quite put out at the holiday spirit with which many viewed his remains." Beyond that, it was "difficult for Rudy to reconcile himself to his departure" in the first place. But then "the guides on the Astral plane took Rudy in hand" and he found that he wasn't in such a bad spot after all. Indeed, his most recent messages had brought the glad tidings that he was seeing a great deal of Caruso —remember that *Graphic* picture?—and also enjoying the companionship of the great Sarah Bernhardt as well as Hollywood's Wally Reid and Olive Thomas, the showgirl. (In a later interview with *Photoplay* magazine, Barbara LaMarr was added to the list of Valentino's astral playmates.) "He is really quite happy 'over there.' He spends his time listening to Caruso sing, and he is going to theatres and lectures, too." Would Rudy act again "over there"? Yes, but only on the stage. Miss Rambova noted, sadly, that there was no movie equipment on that other plane.

OK. Now for the big one, lady. Whom did Rudy love? "Rudy still loves me," said his newly returned mouthpiece. "His messages tell me so. You must know that only the affections that really counted, the loves that really were, exist beyond." Well, did he ever mention that Polish babe? "Not a word," said Miss Rambova, her dark eyes flashing.

There were some pretty quick retorts from the other girls.

Miss Negri assailed the Rambova space bulletins as "shocking, profane and commercial." To Jean Acker, the whole thing seemed like so much hokum. "Rudolph did not believe in spirit messages," said Wife Number 1. "Even if such messages were received, they should have been too sacred to broadcast."

There the thing rested, passing in time into the custody of the worldwide Valentino fan clubs which, with and without the help of the spirit world, would keep the name burning ever so brightly. What is left in this chronicle is the infinitely depressed footnote which came four years after the funeral.

Brought into court when Valentino's brother and sister challenged his accounting of the actor's funds, George Ullman testified that he had staged the New York carnival so that the star could go to the grave in a more solvent condition than his finances otherwise would allow. He said the improvident "Sheik" had a half million dollars in debts hanging over him when he expired but that the reissue of his films, spurred by the great display of mass hysteria and adoration at Mr. Campbell's showplace for the dead, paid all that off and left a $700,000 balance.

"Rudolph Valentino's funeral was worked up for advertising purposes to aid the estate," Ullman told the court. He said he started the crush on Broadway by paying twenty women to set up that early morning line. He said he hired forty press agents to stir that mixture of saccharine and sorrow.

Did it really take a band of stand-in mourners and a battery of drumbeaters to bring out the last throngs? You have to wonder. The actor himself may have furnished the answer. "Women," he said once, "do not become infatuated with Rudolph Valentino. They do not love him. They are infatuated with what he stands for. They love the man they imagine he represents. They are in love with love. . . ." Maybe he knew something.

~~~~~~

Part IV

MONEY FOR THE MILLIONS

TECHNOCRACY:

$20,000 per...

*"The Constitution and our concepts of
social order ought to be
wrapped in cellophane and
put in the Smithsonian Institution for
future generations to look at."*
—HOWARD SCOTT

A LITTLE stage setting is in order here.

Once there was a war to end all wars, and the conquering Americans came out of it into an era of boundless joy and prosperity—the free-and-easy Nineteen Twenties. F. Scott Fitzgerald, flying high, called it The Jazz Age. To Westbrook Pegler, it was The Era of Wonderful Nonsense. Frederick Lewis Allen, its ablest historian talked of the New Freedom. Charles Merz called it the Dry Decade in deference to Prohibition, although the streets were running with bootleg liquor. Your present author called it The Lawless Decade, because his postmortem on that long night out produced little evidence that anybody had paid the slightest attention to the codes, moral or otherwise, which had governed the people's conduct in the horse-and-buggy days before the World War. By any name, it was nothing less than a ten-year binge without parallel in our history.

The hangover was a calamitous thing.

It set in first on Wall Street, mecca of the new get-rich-quick legions, in early September, 1929, just after the market had cascaded to its all-time high. The house of paper profits started to come down—and almost without exception the people in the best

position to know, in the Street and in the government of Herbert Hoover, failed to heed the ominous rumblings. On October 23—Black Thursday—an avalanche of selling smashed values down by five billion dollars. "There has been a little distress selling," said Thomas W. Lamont Sr., a partner in J. P. Morgan & Company, but six days later the crash came. There were 16 million shares traded on the Exchange and 7 million on the Curb and 30 billion dollars in open market values washed down the drain.

That was Black Thursday, ushering in the Great Depression. All at once there were bank failures and bankruptcies, shuttered gates on factories and brand new mortgages on the farms. In the cities, there were breadlines and hordes of new faces in the Skid Row soup kitchens. There were men selling apples for a nickel on street corners. And there was something new: home relief on a massive scale. The mounting disaster saw 4,500,000 Americans out of work by 1931—and unemployment tripled in the following year. So the voters ousted Mr. Hoover and turned to Franklin Delano Roosevelt and the New Deal. The new President launched a total assault on the Depression, using all the weapons in the arsenal of the federal government and inventing new ones where none existed. He put the stricken nation on the road to recovery, but the end results had to come slowly.

It was a time, then, for quick cures. It was a time for the economic medicine man, the guy with the one-shot, overnight remedy.

It was a time for Howard Scott, tall and taciturn and vaguely mysterious and bearing the most wondrous tonic of all—$20,000 a year for every able-bodied citizen over twenty-five years of age willing to work a soft four hours a day for 165 days of the year until he's forty-five. And then? The most golden of all retirements: the money, like Old Man River, keeps rolling along.

The name of that game was Technocracy, and at those prices you had to be pretty dumb to wait around for the man in the White House to produce his miracles. Technocracy, in time to come dressed up in a severe gray uniform with its own Youth Brigade and all those trappings, was for right now, or as soon as Howard Scott's Technate State of North America could come into being and grease the wheels. How many Americans paid the six-dollar membership fee and enlisted in this crusade behind a man who had been quoted as saying that "democratic methods are obsolete"?

Scott, an engineer without a sheepskin, wouldn't say just how crowded his Utopian caravan kept getting, but in 1935 he made this statement: "If our numbers continue at the present rate of increase we shall not be a minority when we take over. It looks as if we shall have sufficient numbers by 1940 to carry out our plans, perhaps by popular mandate."

There was evidently no room in those "plans" for the piece of paper drawn up by the Founding Fathers at Philadelphia in 1787, nor for the American brand of freedom, justice and liberty ("empty baubles of the social epoch of yesterday"), nor for the Congress we knew ("We could take any home of defectives, pick their inmates' names from a hat and so select our House and Senate and they couldn't do worse than we're doing now"). Strong language, but Scott disdained any personal political ambition. He said he just wanted to get all the busted Americans their $20,000 per, and then—

"You will never catch me kissing a baby, milking a cow, or standing near the rear end of a horse, like Tom Dewey. The only job I want is custodian of bears in Yellowstone Park. The bears hibernate in winter and are tourist-fed the rest of the year."

Two items of probable confusion need clearing up here: (1) That statement was made early in 1940 after Thomas E. Dewey had made his disastrous run against Mr. Roosevelt. (2) The bears were not to be included in the $20,000-a-year group in the coming Technate.

Who was Howard Scott? He was born in Virginia. That was a hard fact; everything else was cloudy. Once he said he had attended European universities, graduated from a Berlin engineering college and then held executive posts in the field in Europe and Canada. Later, under oath, he admitted that he had no college degrees. In the mid-Twenties he was operating a little floor-wax plant in Pompton Lakes, New Jersey, and espousing far-out economic theories in the Greenwich Village watering places at night. He told some rather elaborate stories about flying for the British during the war and then serving as an engineer at Boulder Dam and Muscle Shoals, but only the last item stood up. He had indeed been at Muscle Shoals—in a clerical job.

In 1932, around forty and graying prematurely at the temples, he turned up at Columbia University in a group of 106 engineers and architects engaged in something called an Energy Study of North America. Langdon W. Post, who was briefly associated with Scott and went on to do the spadework for public housing as the first chairman of New York City's Municipal Housing Authority, remembers him as "an egotist who thought of himself as a kind of Messiah come to earth in the midst of a deep depression with orders to remodel a decadent and demoralized economic and political system." Post, now with the Office of Economic Opportunity in San Francisco, said Scott demonstrated a phenomenal memory and considerable wizardry in marshaling and dramatizing the most complex facts but alienated the people around him by his high-handed methods. "He was determined to run the whole show himself," Post said, "but he really had very little idea what the show should be."

You couldn't tell that, of course, when Scott emerged from that splendid academic showcase at Columbia and proceeded to offer the masses his dream of high-salaried salvation. When Technocracy began to pick up momentum early the next year, the university hastened to disavow Howard Scott and all his works. Dr. Nicholas Murray Butler, Columbia's president, said he had simply lent some unused space to the research project, sponsored by the Architect's Relief Committee, to help the unemployed.

Just what was Technocracy? The water gets muddy here. The movement's own high priest put it this way:

Scott in the hungry time.

The word "technocracy," as representative of a new body of thought, means governance by science—social control through the power of technique. . . . Technocracy is a new approach to social phenomena. As such, a governance by science is one which would proceed from a methodology of determination and which would operate under a balanced load control of all functional sequences.

For those who had trouble knitting that together (Scott didn't like to answer questions), Technocracy had something to do with the fact that our machinery of production was by then so imposing that men didn't have to work more than sixteen hours a week to keep it humming along and furnishing them with a standard of living ten times higher than 1929's—if, of course, the technologists ran things. There were vague touches of Veblen somewhere in Scott's exposition, however murky. There were some other touches, too. In the March, 1919, issue of the magazine *Industrial Management,* an engineer named William Henry Smyth had advanced the argument that the war had converted the United States from a democracy to "the perfect industrial state," which perforce had to throw off the management of politicians and let the technicians direct the people's destiny by scientific methods. The word Smyth used happened to be technocracy, with a small "t." Beyond this depressing disclosure, John Macrae, president of E. P. Dutton & Co., charged that Scott had borrowed

liberally from a little-known book called *Wealth, Virtual Wealth and Debt, the Solution of the Economic Paradox,* by Professor Frederick Soddy of Oxford. The Professor, winner of the Nobel Prize in chemistry in 1921, had expounded at some length on the measurement of wealth in terms of energy. Macrae asserted that an article by Scott in the current *Harper's* bore the most remarkable resemblances to that portion of the book, published in 1926. Scott's public relations man, Charles Bonner, said yes, his client did like the Professor's work and had recommended it to many of his friends but, perish the thought, never intended to lift anything from it.

Whatever the origins, there was no question about the parallels between Soddy's energy theories and Scott's (the big guy was always talking about ergs and joules) and no question about the similarity between Scott's Technocracy and the lower-case technocracy of William Henry Smyth. The herald of the New Prosperity always insisted that it could be fashioned only by a self-perpetuating elite of engineers and scientists. On that score, he said in January, 1933, that he expected to draw no less than 20 million adherents under his banners within the next eighteen

Howard Scott, flying high.

months—more than enough to sweep out Washington and let the technicians get going. He said that, straight-faced, to an audience of 400 bankers, industrialists, artists and economists gathered at New York's plush Hotel Pierre in his honor by the Society of Arts and Sciences. The nation heard it on network radio.

What about the people who shook off that kind of loose talk about government-by-engineer (Herbert Hoover *was* an engineer) and demanded to know precisely how that abundant new easy-livin' society was supposed to come into being and sustain itself? "We don't have to answer our critics," said the retired floor-wax entrepreneur. "Time will tell who is correct."

Time never did.

Instead, Scott came under a massive attack over his bewildering assortment of charts, theories and figures on energy consumption, on the damage wrought by the big bad machine, on the price structure and on the real causes of the Depression. Apart from all the assaults issuing from the halls of learning and from professional quarters, Scott earned himself this withering piece of attention from Walter Lippmann, even then a large voice on the sociopolitical scene:

> The prestige of science, the mystification of scientific jargon, the prediction of disaster, and the promise of salvation have proved to be an ideal combination to impress a people who are disillusioned, frightened, and eager for guidance. It is a heartless pretense. . . . It is a vast inflation and pyramiding of generalizations and theories on a small base of substantial truth. . . . The prophesies and promises . . . are scientific hocus pocus.
>
> The delusion of grandeur which causes him (Scott) to look upon himself as the innovator of a new era in human thought and to say that "all philosophic approaches to social phenomena, from Plato to—and including—Marx, must functionally be avoided as intellectual expressions of dementia praecox" should not impress anyone. That is nothing but the pretentious ignorance of a crank.

Worse, Dr. Aaron Director of the University of Chicago revealed that Technocracy's supersalesman had lent his research talents to the radical International Workers of the World back in 1920. William Z. Foster, ex-Wobbly and ex-Communist candidate for President of the United States, said yes, the man had headed an IWW bureau charged with teaching the workers how to run industry after taking it over. Scott denied that. "I was not a member of the IWW," he said, "nor did I conduct a survey for them. I merely sold them some information as a consulting engineer. I would have sold it to anyone."

It was around this time that the staid old Dr. Butler told the Number 1 technocrat never to darken the cloistered halls again, and another band of rebels, led by Professor Walter Rautenstrauch, head of Columbia's Department of Industrial Engineering, left the Scott camp.

Dismayed but defiant, Scott withdrew to his borrowed Manhattan apartment (he always said he served his cause gratis and had no money), where his wife, the former Eleanor Steele, reported that the excitement had made him ill. Later this statement was issued from him: "The idea is bigger than any individual. The work will go on." And it did indeed. Scott cited large membership gains from a barnstorming tour he made through the West in 1934.

By then his Youth Brigade had flowered, complete with a military salute, and some of the grown-ups were in uniform. The model technocrat wore a double-breasted gray suit, in gabardine serge, gray hat, gray shirt, gray socks, navy blue tie and matching handkerchief, and plain-toed cordovan shoes of reddish horsehide. (Underwear was optional.) The outfit cost twenty-five dollars and you had to get permission from your local board of governors to wear it. The rule was that once you draped yourself in that Howard Scott gray you had to stay in it. And if you happened to be overweight you had another kind of problem. Scott, always lean himself, kept you in civies because he felt that fat technocrats didn't look good in double-breasted suits. The women weren't neglected, by the way; for twenty-two dollars they could hide their charms in drab single-breasted gray suits with blouses of gray or blue.

Was there a military purpose in all this? Scott said no—"It is not a uniform for parading. It is a uniform for living and working." Curiously, however, the man evidently had no distaste for the uniformed legions of Benito Mussolini. Asked once whether he thought Il Duce was in essence setting up a kind of technocracy in Italy, he said this:

> Mussolini has demonstrated his capacity for initiative and leadership. His position in the vanguard of European social action places him as probably the only figure in the Western European political world who has both the vision and the dynamic will to initiate the first national

move away from the old traditional structures in the management of human affairs.

Did the slightly suggestive military turn in Technocracy, not to mention the small plug for Italy's man of the hour, fatten the ranks? In 1937, Scott airily announced that his membership had skyrocketed by 461 percent in the past year. The natural question was 461 percent of what? And the answer, as ever, was, "We have never told and we never will." But even with that gigantic increase in the flock—461 percent of *something*—Technocracy fell into a slump as the nation's economy continued to turn upward in the second Roosevelt Administration. Recovery was indeed at hand; there was no longer any reason for the mass of Americans to pursue any economic will-o'-the-wisps.

In 1942, however, Scott emerged in elaborate new trappings. Somewhat gaunt in the old days, befitting his private economic distress, he was now puffy and bearing the facial marks of his long struggle to deliver the toiling masses unto the technocratic Eden. But he was also eating better, evidently, and that wasn't the whole of it. Full-page ads blossomed in dailies across the nation that spring urging FDR to name Technocracy's prophet, originally an isolationist, his "Director General of Defense." Scott told a Cleveland *Press* reporter that the advertising campaign, which called for "total conscription" of men, machines, material and money for instant victory, cost more than $50,000. Other sources said the bill had to come closer to $100,000. Moreover, the new drive wasn't confined to newspapers by any means. Scott bought time on ninety-two radio stations, published six slick-paper magazines and assorted pamphlets, and set up "continental headquarters" in a Manhattan skyscraper. Among Technocracy's new accoutrements were a motorcycle corps, "disaster squads" and a fleet of gray sedans serving its branches in San Diego, Detroit, Seattle, San Francisco, Phoenix and elsewhere, and always on hand to pick up the top man when he stepped off an airplane on his tours of his far-flung outposts. The uniform seemed more in evidence, too. Scott himself, long gun-shy about newspaper photographs, posed in one, noting that the garment was made of "superior cloth." Now Scott was called "The Chief." When someone asked how he had achieved that designation, he simply said, "I got here first." With the most, evidently.

Why was Technocracy suddenly being enlisted on the side of the war effort? "Our opposition to the Nazis," Scott said, "is not merely on the basis of ideology, but because Germany is built largely on human toil and ours is a power and extraneous energy society." But there were no tears for the dead and dying on either side. "Technocrats," said The Chief, "are not filled with any love of humanity or influenced by any ethical idea, but are primarily concerned with function."

The goals were roughly the same as before: the profit motive outlawed, the price system abolished, the politicians shelved (except "for laying cornerstones and receiving distinguished guests"), the engineers in charge, the short work week and that nice Twenty Grand, the new social order, the Technate State of North America (merging North America, Central America, the West Indies, Bermuda and Hawaii with the good old U.S.A.) and a pox on all "alien cultural intrusions." It was the old mouthful, compounded.

There was no evidence that the people were about to kick down the doors to get in, and the revived movement played no part in the war effort, even though there was some spooky talk from Scott about a "specially designed plane" and "specially designed tank," both courtesy of Technocracy, which could rout the enemy in no time at all. The President did not call in The Chief to take over the defense establishment—he had a pretty fair Secretary of War in Henry L. Stimson, borrowed from the Republican Party—and did not accept any guidance from him on the kind of total conscription needed for the conquest, in order, of Mussolini, Adolf Hitler and the Japanese.

In 1948, coming to the end of the line, Scott suffered a small embarrassment. Albert W. Atwater, formerly an assistant director of Technocracy, Inc., brought suit in Manhattan Supreme Court accusing him of pocketing "excessive compensation in the form of an expense account without proper authorization." Atwater said the organization then had 8,900 dues-paying members but that Scott made no financial reports on its annual income. Those figures looked pretty pathetic at that. You had to wonder where all the big money came from for that big push in 1942, but that's a question no one ever answered. After a while, it didn't matter. Technocracy, perhaps the most ominous of all our fads, receded into history without a formal burial.

DR. TOWNSEND:

The Good Life

The sign, held by the man who
thought it all up, said it all. *WWP*

"You and I have the world by the tail
on a downward pull on this thing,
if we work it right."
—FRANCIS TOWNSEND,
to his right-hand man,
Robert Clements

FRANCIS EVERETT TOWNSEND was born in a two-room
log cabin in Fairbury, Illinois, on January 13, 1867,
one of seven children. Educated there, he moved on
to Kansas to try to wrest a living from the soil as a
homestead farmer, teaching school on the side, and
then rode a freight to Colorado Springs in search of
"a better chance for survival." But it was no better
there, and at twenty-six he decided to become a
doctor. He moved on to Omaha, working his way
through medical school by tending the library for
the dean, cutting lawns in the searing Nebraska heat,
stoking furnaces in winter and picking up a steady
$3.75 a week delivering the Omaha *World-Herald*
along a seven-mile route. Tall, gaunt and rail-thin,
he got his degree at thirty and set up practice in the
Bearlodge country of South Dakota's Black Hills.
There, ten years later, operating a small private hospital, he married his nurse, Minnie Bogue, a widow
with a seven-year-old daughter. The Townsends had
twins, who died, and then a son, Robert. In World
War I, the doctor served in the medical corps as a
First Lieutenant, handling recruits in South Dakota.
In 1920, wasted by a bout with peritonitis and told
that he didn't have more than a year to live, he

moved to California and confounded his own colleagues. Nine years later, when the Depression came,
he was on the staff of the Long Beach Health Department, ministering to the needy. He described
the experience as a nightmare.

I saw such distress, pain and horror. . . . I
saw children, the children of Americans, doomed
to be weak, physical runts because of malnu-
trition. I saw them sent to school without breakfast because their parents were too proud to beg.
I saw men and women of comparative affluence
reduced to penury, their lifetime savings wiped
out.

The doctor left his municipal post after two years
and went to work for a forty-year-old real estate
man, Robert Earl Clements. Then, one winter's
day in 1933, something of great moment happened
to him. Shaving in his bathroom, he looked out of
the window and saw three haggard old women ran-
sacking garbage cans in the alley. It made him so
violent that he started to swear.

"There's a job that must be done," he told his

wife when he regained his composure, "and I am going to do it."

That's how the Townsend Plan, a matter of fierce controversy in the years ahead, was born.

The doctor, by now a cadaverous sixty-seven, took to thinking about the Perfect State of Edward Bellamy's *Looking Backward,* where every man was always assured of a living income and retired before he was sixty. Then he went to Clements and worked out a vague scheme under which the government would award pensions of $200 a month to all Americans over sixty. He got another friend to lend him an office for a month, put up a sign that said OLD AGE REVOLVING PENSIONS HEADQUARTERS, and spent the best part of his last $500 to advertise for volunteers to obtain pledges of support for his plan. He got a printer to set up a booklet about it free of charge. The booklet had no want of takers, even though that $200 a month looked pale indeed alongside the $20,000 a year Howard Scott was then holding out to the masses. There was a difference in the appeal, of course. The doctor was addressing himself to the forlorn elderly, and Technocracy's high priest to the young and able. Even with the great disparity in the promised cash rewards, the doctor's plan quickly drew a fanatical legion of dues-paying followers whose ranks would exceed Scott's by the millions in no time at all.

The first door-to-door canvassing in Long Beach brought in 20,000 members, each paying twenty-five cents for the booklet and pledging to send in ten cents a month to help the cause. Like a fresh summer breeze, the movement rapidly fanned out to the Far West and then into the Southwest, picked up broad backing in Minnesota, Iowa, Michigan, Indiana and Ohio, swept down to Florida and then began to make heavy inroads on the Eastern seaboard. After a while, there were ten thousand Townsend clubs in forty-two states with an advertised total of 5,000,000 members and a new national base of operations in Cleveland—with Dr. Townsend's son Robert on hand as treasurer and overseer of that incoming torrent of ten-cent pieces.

Just four years after he and Robert Clements hung their hand-painted shingle on that borrowed storefront, the doctor claimed 20,000,000 followers and boasted that he could put his own man in the White House in Mr. Roosevelt's place if he so desired. Himself, for example? No. He said he was just an inspirational force—"you might call me the Hammer of Thor"—and did not aspire to office. Columnist Westbrook Pegler observed that the soft-spoken old man was "too gentle and sincere" for the political gutters. Still, no one could argue the depth and intensity of the silver-haired crusader's popular backing. The lantern-jawed son of the prairie, a dignified figure with a close-cropped mustache and horn-rimmed spectacles, had a Pied Piper's appeal when he talked about making old age "a delightful golden autumn instead of a bleak and fearful winter" and generously added that there was no reason why such towering financial giants as John D. Rockefeller Sr., J. P. Morgan, Henry Ford and all the Mellons and DuPonts shouldn't share in the pension bounty if they wanted to give up *their* labors.

What would the Townsend Plan cost? Oh, so many billions a year. Where would the money come from? New taxes, different kinds of new taxes. And what would it do besides cushioning those hard years after sixty? The doctor said it would keep the indigent off the relief rolls and out of the poorhouses, solve the unemployment problem by taking millions of men out of the tight job market, boom industry and halt stagnation on the farms by requiring the estimated 12,000,000 pensioners to spend their $200 a month as fast as it arrived from Washington and—not the least, presumably—remove the incentive for three-quarters of the nation's ever-increasing crime. The thing covered so much ground that the spreading Townsend tent soon enfolded volunteers from such politically and socially conflicting groups as Huey Long's Share-the-Wealth movement, the Reverend Charles E. Coughlin's National Union for Social Justice, Upton Sinclair's EPIC plan, and, of all things, the battered but unbowed Anti-Saloon League, possibly drawn to the pension apostle because he shunned the hard stuff even after Prohibition was repealed. The doctor didn't shake anybody off; there was room for all willing hands without regard to previous servitude or conviction.

But you couldn't do it with numbers alone.

The jammed bandwagon ran into formidable stumbling blocks not long after John Steven McGroarty, California's poet laureate and a Republican Townsend booster in Congress on the side, put a bill before the House to write the pension plan into law. To pay for it, the measure called in the main for an additional 2 percent tax on business transactions and an additional 2 percent on inheritance and gifts. It denied the $200-a-month windfall to all persons whose net income exceeded $2,400 a year (this knocked out the Rockefellers, Morgans, Fords, Mellons and DuPonts, although there was no outcry from those lofty echelons) and required that any income under $200 a month derived from anything other than personal services had to be deducted from the government checks.

Would it work? The most devastating analysis came from the eighteen-member economics faculty of the University of Chicago, under Dr. H. A. Millis. In a thirty-page report, the professors noted that the sweet-sounding pension scheme would cost the taxpayers 20 billion dollars a year—40 percent of the nation's 1934 national income—and bring about a disastrous inflation. The report tore down all the new taxes advanced by the plan's backers as totally unrealistic and wildly short of that 20-billion-dollar tab. At the same time, the Twentieth Century Fund estimated that the principal item in the financing plan, the extra business tax, would not yield much more than 4 billion dollars a year—a far cry from the 24 billion Townsend himself had always talked about. It was already clear by then that the other proposed taxes couldn't possibly raise anything more than some scattered millions.

But while neither the McGroarty bill nor any of its numerous successors ever had a chance in Congress, the Townsend legions continued to multiply, and soon there were the inevitable questions about all those dimes pouring into that bustling GHQ in Cleveland. Early in 1936, with only four dissenting votes, the House decided to find out just how much was being collected "from those old folks" and how it was being spent.

It did not prove to be an easy assignment.

Robert Clements, just then suddenly and mysteriously eased out of his juicy post as national secretary of Old Age Revolving Pensions, Ltd., the corporate name of the Townsend operation, told the investigating committee that receipts between January 1, 1934, and January 1, 1936, amounted to $771,964.09 and estimated that another $180,000 had come in during the first quarter of 1936. That added up to $951,964.09 but did not include income earned by such dividend-paying subsidiaries as the Townsend *National Weekly* and the Prosperity Publishing Company, whose principal owners happened to be Clements and Dr. Townsend. Clements said he was sorry, but he did not have those figures. He did concede, under sharp questioning by committee counsel James R. Sullivan, that his own total earnings from the multiple Townsend operations during 1935 added up to $12,585. That was at sharp variance, to say the least, with a report made to a Townsend club convention in Chicago the preceding October by Ray McAllister, the OARP auditor. On that occasion, McAllister proudly told the delegates that the salaries

of Dr. Townsend and Clements had averaged "about seventy-four dollars a week." Sullivan noted the wide disparity for the record, which could not be altogether clear in any case, since the earnings of both men from the lush subsidiary operations didn't happen to be available; indeed, a team of five accountants from Price, Waterhouse and Company had failed in a valiant effort to unravel the Townsend books for the committee.

Even more embarrassing, Sullivan brought out that OARP had paid the rent on a Washington apartment occupied by Clements and the doctor, along with all the grocery bills, the wages of the servants and such assorted incidentals as an item of $1,475 drawn by Mrs. Thelma Clements as secretary to her husband. That twenty-eight-year-old redhead, fifteen years Clements' junior, did have the qualifications, by the way. She happened to be a stenographer when Clements left his first wife for her. She also figured in the blossoming Townsend Plan scandal in her own way. There were stories that Clements had been forced to leave OARP because he and his bride had been plotting to get the old man out, but another story was that Clements had been bought out so that he could take all the heat in the House inquiry. There was no question that some animus between Townsend and the slight, wiry, blue-eyed Clements—credited by some with being the real inventor of the pension plan—existed by then. The ex-real estate man had no hesitancy in implying to the committee, at any rate, that the doctor and his brother Walter, a background figure in the movement, had held OARP very tightly as a closed corporation, always selecting all the directors themselves.

Clements' principal trouble on the stand came over his net income. What about the personal expenses he drew? Clements said he could not say what he collected for traveling and other out-of-pocket items. Was that all "velvet"? Clements said he did not deal in such vulgar terms. Finally, the committee, increasingly impatient, ordered the witness to go dig a little harder and come up with some hard answers. The following month, back in the hot seat, Clements had to admit that his total income from OARP and those dandy privately held subsidiaries had come to something like $77,780 in a matter of two years. And Townsend? The assumption was that he had fared at least as well, because Clements made it a point to say that the two of them always took down the same salaries and dividends. Was there any money unaccounted for? "I have collected $850,000," said Clements, speaking for himself, "and I have accounted for every postage stamp."

The high moment in the investigation—the appearance of Townsend himself—began to unfold, rather explosively, on May 19. Sullivan brought in the name of Pierce Tomlinson, another departed associate of the doctor's, and this colloquy ensued:

SULLIVAN: Your friend Tomlinson swears that you started the Townsend Plan as a racket. Is that true?

TOWNSEND: It is untrue.

SULLIVAN: When a five-dollar bill was received, did you say, "This old sister has done her part. Stay with the movement and you'll get a hatful of money." Is that true?

TOWNSEND: It is absolutely untrue.

Another question, as to whether the witness himself had termed the movement a "racket" on another occasion and had referred to his followers as "old fossils," was lost in the shuffle when Representative John H. Tolan, a California Democrat and a Townsendite, moved to stop that line of inquiry. Tolan made the point that a "caravan" of the doctor's supporters had come all the way from the West Coast, was in the room with petitions of faith signed by 10,000,000 persons, but his motion lost by a four to two vote anyway. Under Tolan's own friendly questioning later, the beleaguered witness was able to get into the record the assertion that when he had said such things as "there might be millions" in his movement he meant millions for the cause, not for himself.

When the committee made him confirm salary payments of $16,577 from OARP and $32,500 in dividends from the Townsend *Weekly,* an admittedly incomplete summary of his take, he insisted that he had put back into the organization every dime he ever took out. He said he didn't have more than $300 to $500 in cash to his name at that moment. He had to concede, however, that his weekly, with 250,000 subscribers and heavy advertising (the patent medicine people simply adored the Townsend audience), happened to be worth millions.

The next day, Townsend treated his Congressional inquisitors to a stinging attack on President Roosevelt, terming FDR the "hostile force" behind the investigation and vowing to form a third party to protect the interests of the aged. The third session was more subdued, but then the lid blew off. That night Townsend and the Rev. Gerald L. K. Smith, who had taken over Huey Long's Share-the-Wealth clubs when Louisiana's gift to the United States Senate was assassinated at Baton Rouge the year before, issued an inflammatory joint declaration which hinted at a coming mass demonstration against the committee by their combined forces, while Smith put out a statement of his own assailing "the Communist dictatorship in Washington" and saying that "the persecution of Dr. Townsend calls for action."

When the hearing resumed with questions relating

Flanked by his wife Thelma and S. J. Elgin, editor of the *Townsend Weekly,* Robert Earl Clements announces that the old-age pension forces will run a third-party candidate in 1936 unless Congress enacts the Townsend Plan bill. Later, eased out of his ground-floor spot in OARP, Clements underwent some rough moments when the House investigated the organization. *WWP*

to his allegedly illegal use of the mails in soliciting funds, the doctor tried to read another printed statement but was cut off. Returning for the afternoon session in the old House Office Building, he announced that "in view of the unfair and unfriendly attitude" of the committee he would "rot in jail" before giving any further testimony. With that, he bid the startled Congressmen "Goodbye" and walked out of the caucus room. The old fellow plainly wasn't happy about Washington at all. The only thing he liked about the city on the Potomac was the Lincoln Memorial. "Just think," he said, looking at the majestic marble figure of the other tall man from Illinois, "they built that for him when he freed four million slaves. I wonder what they will do for me after I have liberated all of mankind."

That would have to wait, of course, because the doctor soon found himself adjudged in contempt of the Congress and facing a thirty-day prison sentence and a $100 fine. He seemed unconcerned. "Try as they can to imprison me, they cannot imprison that idea," he said. "The tide is definitely turning, and my 'crackpot idea' is becoming the idea which will save America from economic serfdom and will bring happiness and prosperity to our people." For all the brave words, he fought the contempt citation for two years, all the way to the Supreme Court, before finally coming back to the capital to give himself up and serve his term in prison. He did not have to; President Roosevelt elected to pardon the seventy-one-year-old firebrand.

Townsend's 1936 convention in Cleveland did not produce the third party which he had talked about so glibly when Congress had him on the grill. It did produce some embarrassment. Norman Thomas, an invited speaker, bluntly told the 11,000 delegates that the pension scheme was a quack remedy that wouldn't work. The old folks booed so hard that the doctor himself had to appeal to them to remember that fair play was a cardinal principle of OARP and let the Socialist leader finish. There was a happier moment on the platform. That was when Townsend, Father Coughlin and Gerald L. K. Smith joined in a three-way handclasp to signify their solidarity in the struggle against the evil forces they believed to be abounding in high places. Earlier, in Philadelphia, Smith had explained how he had joined forces with the doctor in the first place. "Last night," he said, "Dr. Townsend and I stood under the historic arch in Valley Forge and vowed to take over the government."

For his part, Smith must have been suffering some magnificent delusions. If he had to call on his own mass support at that moment (or, for that matter, even later when he went into the business of anti-Semitism as a full-time career), he would have had trouble taking over the corner pool hall, no less moving in on the seat of federal power. After all, as a Huey Long lieutenant, he had come from a minor league. The Louisiana rabble-rouser's Share-the-Wealth movement ("Every Man a King") never was in a class with the Townsend Plan. Long had made the mistake of putting too much icing on his pie-in-the-sky. He couldn't get enough Americans to buy the primitive notion that if the government simply dipped into the pockets of the Rockefellers and the Morgans every family head would suddenly begin to enjoy a guaranteed income of $2,500 a year, live in a debt-free home (with a car and radio thrown in) and pick up an "adequate" pension at the end of the rainbow. The "adequate" pension itself was nothing more than a cynical play on words. Listen to the plain-talking Gerald Smith, quoted in Stan Opotowsky's book, *The Longs of Louisiana*: "We originally promised $30 a month but we discovered we were running afoul of the $40-a-month pension advocates and the Townsend $200 pension advocates, so we decided to use the word 'adequate' and let every man name his own figure."

Now here was Smith, evidently having joined Townsend because he didn't know any way to outbid him, talking about some kind of revolution-from-the-Right. He was premature, for it was evident in the 1936 convention that the doctor himself did not feel that the time was at hand. Indeed, his own Utopia-bound caravan had slowed down appreciably in the wake of the House committee's disclosures, coupled with the Congressional finding that the pension plan was nothing more than a scheme in which 10 percent of the people would live off the toil of the other 90 percent.

There were some passing efforts in the next two years to put some life into the waning movement, but the bloom was off that $200-a-month rose by then; with better times at hand, not enough people seemed to care anymore. In 1939, another effort to get a pension bill through the House was soundly voted down while a dejected Townsend sat in the gallery. Remnants of his clubs somehow managed to stay glued together for years thereafter, with the doctor himself, a widower by then, still making occasional tours when he was ninety. By that time, incidentally, he was enjoying a touch of Franklin Delano Roosevelt's Social Security program. When that legislation was enacted in 1935, Townsend denounced it as "unfair and inequitable" and said he would have

Dr. Townsend in 1936 with a new-found ally, Gerald L. K. Smith, an import from Huey Long's moribund Share-the-Wealth movement. The Reverend Smith entertained visions of the Townsendites taking over the government but shelved them to concentrate on his one true love—anti-Semitism. *WWP*

The doctor waves presidential pardon from FDR sparing him from thirty-day jail sentence for contempt of Congress. *WWP*

none of it. Fifteen years later, at eighty-three, he changed his mind and applied for what was, after all, a government pension, even if it wasn't quite as plush as the one he envisioned when he saw those three women digging in the garbage outside his window back in 1933. His Social Security check came to $98.50 a month, and he was still collecting it in 1960 when he died of pneumonia in Los Angeles at the age of ninety-three. He had lived a quarter of a century more than those South Dakota doctors had said he would, and he had not wasted much of that borrowed time. No sir, the old guy had quite a run on all those dimes. Indeed, you could say that the Townsend Plan worked. It worked for Dr. Townsend.

EPIC:

Upton Sinclair's New Deal

"Why should I congratulate the winner?
This isn't a game . . ."
—UPTON SINCLAIR, after losing his race
for Governor of California

Upton Sinclair: the old order had to go.

EPIC STOOD FOR End Poverty in California. It was the brainchild of author Upton Sinclair, and in 1934, in the alphabet soup of the language then current in the land, it was just as much of a household word as the New Deal's NRA (National Recovery Administration), WPA (Works Progress Administration), FERA (Federal Emergency Relief Administration), AAA (Agricultural Adjustment Administration), HOLG (Home Owners Loan Corporation), CCC (Civilian Conservation Corps), FPHA (Federal Public Housing Administration) and all the others.

Upton Sinclair, a lifetime Socialist newly come to the party of Thomas Jefferson, won the Democratic nomination for Governor of California in 1934 on the strength of EPIC. In the same year, bear in mind, Howard Scott and Dr. Francis Townsend also were enjoying much public favor—Scott because Technocracy was holding out a dandy $20,000 a year to everyone over twenty-five who would rather work sixteen hours a week (not every week, at that) and the Doctor because he had a way to get a snug little $200 a month for every American over sixty.

EPIC, however, could not be equated either with the wild dream of Howard Scott or the much more modest Townsend Plan. Far from it. Sinclair simply proposed that the state of California rent the idle land and idle factories out there and put the unemployed to work producing necessities for their own consumption, paying them in "service certificates" and "warehouse receipts" which could in turn be exchanged for farm products, thus helping both sides of the economy. In a word, the jobless would not be working for money as such but for scrip which would enable them to sustain themselves through the Depression without benefit of government handouts. There were 1,250,000 people out of work in California then—a fifth of the state's population—and to them EPIC had the sound of salvation. It had such a good sound that the upstart Sinclair was able to intrude himself in California's Democratic primary that year and overwhelm the three party regulars competing for the chance to run for governor against the Old Guard Republican incumbent, Frank C. Merriam. The white-haired Sinclair, then fifty-six, couldn't go the whole way and win the election in November, but that's beside the point; his primary victory said enough. Indeed, it said so much that President Roosevelt himself felt impelled to entertain the apostle of EPIC at Hyde Park in a two-hour session that fall. The two men, seemingly so far apart in every way, had at least one common ground: When Mr. Roosevelt was a boy his mother used to read to him, and one of the books she read aloud was *The Jungle,* Upton Sinclair's searing study of the Chicago stockyards.

What a strange confrontation that must have been —the aristocrat Roosevelt and the radical Sinclair, suddenly come together under the same party banner. In *The Jungle,* Sinclair left the meat-packing industry in shreds. In *Boston,* he ripped into America's upper social strata. In *Oil,* he lashed out at Big Money. In *The Brass Check,* he damned the "capitalist press." Over the years, he ran for office time and time again on the Socialist ticket. Campaigning for the Democratic nomination in California, he made it clear that one of his first official acts if elected would be to free Tom Mooney, a *cause célèbre* of the Left ever since his imprisonment in the bombing of San Francisco's Preparedness Day Parade in 1916. This was the man now huddling with the high-born President.

EPIC did it. EPIC did it with its natural appeal to the jobless masses, but was there anything inconsistent in Franklin Delano Roosevelt and Upton Sinclair sitting down together? Not really. There wasn't much of a gulf between EPIC and the FERA's plan for subsistence farms and cooperative production of necessities by the unemployed. The New Deal, when you come down to it, was rampant with the kind of socialism that Upton Sinclair had preached all his life and still clung to until the day he died in 1968. The author was ninety then and left behind ninety books bearing his name.

THE CHAIN LETTER CRAZE

Mob scene as the people snap up chain letters. *Denver Post*

"Gaming is a principle inherent in all human nature. It belongs to us all."

—EDMUND BURKE

"PROSPERITY CLUB—IN GOD WE TRUST."

In God, that is, and the man down the street—and, oh, just 15,624 others.

This was the essence of the chain letter craze which had a noisy birth in Denver in the spring of 1935 and, like a prairie fire, swept out of Colorado across the Depression-wasted land. How could it miss? You put five names on a piece of stationery and added yours to the bottom. Then you sent out five copies of the letter and asked each recipient to mail a dime to the name at the top, strike it from the list, put his own at the bottom below yours, and send out five more copies. In the simple mathematical progression that followed, if no one broke your chain, the friendly letter carrier in time brought 15,625 letters bearing dimes. Net profit, minus the five two-cent stamps you invested: $1,562.50. Any questions? The first five letters begat twenty-five more and that twenty-five begat 125, which multiplied to 625, which multiplied to 3,125 and, presto, grew to 15,625.

Denver's "Prosperity Club" was barely off the ground—and in the United States mails—when the most touching stories emerged: a poor seamstress picked up enough money for a sewing machine even though some stone-hearted lout broke the chain she

started; a penniless widow netted enough to bury the remains decently; a new mother collected enough dimes to pay for the baby's birth and buy a carriage to boot; a woman went to a retired butcher and paid him a $50.40 bill she had run up in his shop years before; some families went in and "resigned" from the relief rolls because the chain letters were bringing in more than enough for them to live on. On and on, sometimes in reverse gear: a restaurant man swamped with 2,300 chain letters took a paid ad to let his neighbors know he wasn't sending one thin dime to anybody. Postal workers in the town, toiling around the clock alongside a hundred emergency employees as the chain letters poured as much as 95,000 extra pieces of mail into the bins in a single day, earned $20,000 in overtime in three weeks. Balancing that expense with some to spare, receipts were up $50,000. Still, the government wanted no part of this get-rich-quick scheme. Postmaster General James A. Farley saw an analogy between chain letters and taking a drink during Prohibition—"illegal but stimulating"—and hurried into court to enjoin the promoters. This was a fire you couldn't put out with court orders, however; you couldn't put it out until the people themselves got burned.

The citizens of Denver, eventually buying the letters from hawkers in the streets, got on the ten-cent bandwagon in such numbers that local postal officials said the thing couldn't be stopped short of arresting most of the people in the town. But it began to run down by itself toward May as the dreams of sudden riches dissolved, and on August 15 the Denver *Post* carried this requiem for the scheme: "The mortal remains of the chain letter craze, which sprang to mammoth size overnight here last spring and died with equal suddenness, are entombed in the great concrete vaults of the Post Office." And Postmaster J. O. Stevic, sitting happily on a hoard of more than 100,000 dead letters containing dimes, was a happy man again. "At the height of this thing," he said, "people seemed to have their minds completely unhinged. They would stick a letter into a mailbox with money in it and address it to John Jones, with perhaps no street or city address and without a stamp." There was also an abundance of incoming mail from other states containing either nonexistent names or wrong addresses.

Within weeks after the wild tales of Denver's ten-cent gold rush hit the wires, three chain letter "factories" in Springfield, Missouri, shunning the little dime for dollar bills, saw $18,000 change hands within five hours in scenes approaching riot proportions. The Associated Press correspondent, terming the town a "money-mad maelstrom," described that morning in May in this manner: "Society women, waitresses, college students, taxi drivers and hundreds of others jammed downtown streets. Women shoved each other roughly in a bargain-counter rush on the chain headquarters."

The Springfield *Leader and Press* reported that normal business had come to a standstill. "Fruit stands, paint stores, electrical shops," the newspaper said, "were packed with stenographers rapping out chain letters. Three printing shops on the street turned out 40,000 forms." Those shops were operating from dawn to midnight, charging fifteen cents for each two copies the customer might want made.

The next day's story—SPRINGFIELD SPINS MADLY ON FINANCIAL WHIRLIGIG—deserves to be quoted at length because nothing quite like it happened anywhere else in that wild spring:

After a frenzied night of speculation Springfield was still riding the chain letter merry-go-round.

Business was forgotten in the mad dash to get in on a chain before it's too late.

Chain letter exchanges popped up like mushrooms all over the business district and soon filled with milling throngs eager to turn dollars into thousands.

Hundreds of men dropped their legitimate business to gamble in the new city-wide lottery. They stuck with their chains, followed every name, and saw to it that the letters were kept moving. Some have been up day and night for several days.

There was an air of excitement everywhere you moved in the business district. It was a crowd of plungers, of gamblers caught in the mad whirl of speculation that swept the city.

Hatless men hurried along the sidewalks waving chain letters. They stopped everyone they saw, desperate to dispose of their wares before the urge to buy should die down.

In the exchanges far into the night and today, scenes rivaled those on the floor of the New York Stock Exchange in the explosive days of 1929. Men and women were waving papers above their heads, asking, pleading, demanding takers. Money was changing hands so rapidly it was difficult to keep track of it.

The fast moving money and the wild tales of wealth acquired in a few hours was a shot in the arm to the crowd whenever it rested for a moment.

There was a lot of money in the pockets of the throng. No one seemed to know where it came from, but letters were snapped up without a great deal of salesmanship being necessary.

Springfield was a picture so often conjured up by opponents of inflation—a picture of an entire city suddenly gone crazy in an attempt to get rid of its cash. Except it was not commodities that were being bought, but chances on a fortune.

Fees had risen all over town today. Where yesterday it cost 15 cents to have two printed copies typed, today the demand had boosted the price to 25 cents.

The flying fingers of swarms of stenographers who had set portable machines on every available table and window ledges of the exchanges typed a steady stream of quarters into the money boxes.

The crowd presented a fair cross section of Springfield's population. Cab drivers, debutantes, elderly matrons, business men, clerks, students and soda jerks.

The Springfield promoters left nothing to chance. They drew up chain letters in two-, three-, and five-dollar denominations, complete with names, and peddled them to the gullible from storefronts. It was as simple as pie. You bought a letter and the salesman led you to a notary, who enclosed your two, three, or five dollars in an envelope and mailed it to the person at the top of the list. You kept a copy, scratched off the top name, added your own to the bottom and made two carbons to peddle and start another chain going on its way. If you couldn't find buyers, the obliging salesman took on that chore—for a 50 percent commission.

Ten chain letter "factories" sprang up overnight. A three-dollar chain called "The Cream of the Crop" and a five-dollar chain called "The Pot of Gold Club" shunned the slow and footsore postman—not to mention the risk of prosecution—in favor of hand-to-hand selling. The idea was to get your name on a list and sell it to another man who would in turn peddle it to two others—in person. The amounts supposedly waiting at the end of the rainbow made Denver's ten-cent chains look like coffee-and-cake money.

The *Leader and Press* carried some pretty sour quotes from Springfield's School Superintendent, a gentleman with the astonishingly apt name of H. P. Study, who said he regretted that the people seemed willing to "surrender their minds to the collective mind" but expressed confidence that the whole structure would collapse of its own weight in no time at all.

He was so right.

From the next day's paper:

The dross was crusting Springfield's "pots of gold" today.

Persons who had invested heavily in chain letters found the market glutted and were desperate to dispose of their letters merely to get their money back.

Tales of easy money and quickly-made fortunes continued to spread through the city, but to the thousands who came in late they were tales and nothing more.

To those who got in early on the chains and made their killing yesterday and the day before money still dribbled in but most reports of large sums acquired last night and today proved unfounded.

The AP story out of Springfield that day summed it all up in a single sentence: "Sad-faced men and women walked around in a daze tonight, seeking vainly for someone to buy their chain letters."

What had happened? The "pass-a-buck" device had a beautiful sheen on it when the "factories" opened for business on the first morning; it was a seller's market because thousands of people were clamoring to get in on the ground floor but before the second day was over so many people had letters to sell that there were no buyers and they were stuck for their original investment. Within another twenty-four hours, end of joke, but even with the Post Office reminding the masses that chain letters came under the lottery and mail fraud statutes, carrying fines up to $1,000 or jail terms up to two years, or both, the craze continued to flourish clear across the country.

And the people, bless 'em, weren't at all shy about the kind of names they selected for their lists. More than two hundred "Send-a-Dime" letters came to the White House for President Roosevelt—an item not calculated to improve the disposition of his much-troubled Postmaster General. In New York, former Governor Alfred E. Smith received no less than a thousand letters and somebody figured out that if he had taken the trouble to send out $100 in dimes and keep those chains going—*and, of course, if nobody had broken any of them*—he would have netted a round $1,562,000. Since he didn't need the money, Mr. Smith threw all the letters away.

The basic defect in the chains had to be apparent on the surface, but in that spring of 1935 it was questionable how many people took this elementary fact into account: For everybody who made a dime, somebody had to lose one; you could not have all winners in that game. Even so, there was no want of players and no way to legislate it out of existence effectively. When the government hauled in three of the Denver promoters, producing evidence that the trio had used their own names or those of relatives on the "Send-a-Buck" letters they were handling, the Grand Jury refused to indict. And this was at a moment when another "factory" in the shadow of Pike's Peak was doing such a land-office business that it had handled 10,000 letters in one two-day period, netting a fast $5,000 for itself on the fifty-cent service fee the customer had to pay in return for the "guaranteed" profit in that chain.

The gullible legions did catch on in time. By July, the Post Office was able to announce, with a sigh of relief, that it was all over and that there were two to three million chain letters lying dead in overstuffed bins around the nation. The people, however slowly, had finally heeded the abundant warnings about the actuarial defects of the scheme. Dr. C. R. Fountain of Peabody College in Nashville, for one, had made a rather vivid case. He observed that a single chain confined to his particular county in Tennessee would bring 15,000 dimes to each participant but that to keep going it would have to reach each person in the county 15,000 times. The educator submitted that if he sent a dime each time he received one of the letters he would wind up with a $300 deficit in postage and nothing to show for his loyalty to his fellow townsmen.

The chains had the inevitable variations, of course.

The Rev. W. H. Allison of the Argentine Baptist Church in Kansas City, Kansas, enlisted the device on the side of the Lord. "The Apostle Paul wrote the first chain letter," the pastor said. "Today, this and every other church in the Christian world has it and is still passing it on. It is called Epistle to the Galatians." It was perhaps the first time that anyone had drawn a parallel between the Epistles and the chains, but the Reverend said it produced a 75 percent increase in his flock—and he had company in no time at all. Other men of the cloth cited the Old Testament –II Chronicles, 21: 11–12–as the original source of the chains. You know, Jehoram rose up by night and smote the Edomites and then "caused the inhabitants of Jerusalem to commit fornication," whereupon "there came a writing to him from Elijah the Prophet, saying, Thus saith the Lord God of David thy father, Because thou hast not walked in the ways of Jehoshaphat thy father, nor in the ways of Asa King of Judah. . . ." Well, that increased the flock in some American hamlets, or so we were told.

The GOP found a use for the chains too, shoveling this document into the mails:

If you believe as the writer does; if you are tired of the NEW DEAL, if you want a square deal, and if you believe it is time to revert to orthodox principles to gain RECOVERY, send a copy of this letter to five or more of your friends and ten (10) cents to

GEORGE F. GRETZ
Treasurer,
National Republican Committee

How far off the ground that drive got was never made quite clear, but some of the lobbies got into the act too. In San Diego, the Fighting Bob Evans Post of the American Legion started a chain in an effort to get 500,000 letters sent to President Roosevelt in the predoomed drive to change his mind about vetoing the tired old Patman bonus bill. In Boston, the ladies of

the Grand Old Party started a postcard chain to swamp the White House with protests over taxes in particular and that whole darn New Deal in general, just for good measure. Somebody else started a chain intended to put the heat on Calvin Coolidge to come out of retirement and perhaps save the Republic by making another run for the White House; you had to put that down as the most futile of all the chain letters, on more than one count.

There were lighter moments too, fortunately.

Out West, where men were men, a "Send-a-Pint" letter made its appearance. Get it? If nobody broke the chain your cup would shortly be brimming over with 15,625 pints of good American drinking whiskey. Of course, there was no evidence that anybody ever dropped the first pint in a mailbox anywhere. In Birmingham, Alabama, somebody started a "kiss chain"—for the unmarried only—which in some inexplicable way was supposed to earn each participant no less than 15,000 kisses and, somewhere along the line, turn up the ideal soul mate for a more permanent arrangement. There was no evidence that this chain worked at all. In the same vein, a "Send-a-Dame" letter turned up on the University of California campus. Eldon Grimm, a commerce senior credited with that dandy idea, submitted that the 6,000 coeds on the campus each would be dated 26,000 times if the 10,000 boys in the school cooperated to keep the chain going. A pretty item from the Delta Delta Delta sorority, Mary Kirk, enjoyed the distinction of having her name at the top of the letter but she estimated, somewhat sadly, that it would take her no less than seventy years to keep 26,000 dates. And what about conflicting dates for the belabored coeds? Young Eldon Grimm could only counsel "faith, hope and, of course, charity."

Variations on the chain letters have continued down through the years. In 1943, somebody started one with defense savings stamps. You mailed a stamp to the top name on a list of ten and if the chain wasn't broken you wound up with $750 worth. That one didn't get off the ground. In 1950, backers of Senator Robert A. Taft started a one-dollar chain to raise money for the reelection of Ohio's "Mr. Republican." The letter, hailing Taft as a "symbol of courageous statesmanship . . . singled out for slaughter by the AFL, CIO, Railroad Brotherhoods and left-wingers," brought in a few thousand dollars even though the Senator himself shunned the drive. On the lighter side, a so-called "Pantie Club" in Dallas tried to start a chain in 1951 which was supposed to produce thirty pairs of undergarments for the girl next door if no-

Denver Postmaster J. O. Stevic looking pretty unhappy about all those dime-laden letters. *Denver Post*

A chain letter clearinghouse in action when the craze was at its peak.

body broke it. Texas postal authorities quickly banned that one. And you had to count the nasty Russians in somewhere along the line, of course. Thus David Lawrence revealed in his syndicated column in the spring of 1954 that the Communist Party of the U.S.A. had no less than 25,000 secret agents dredging names out of phone books to start a chain letter to bombard President Eisenhower with demands that he halt all further tests of the H-Bomb. The Kremlin's minions, for all their reputed numbers, must have failed the task badly, for there was no evidence that the White House mailbags were sagging under an avalanche of Stop-the-Bomb mail at that time.

In 1958, in a throwback to that old defense stamp scheme, a new letter guaranteed to produce no less than $38,400 in bonds (maturity value: $51,200) for any trusting souls who would join in a chain involving the sending of $18.75 bonds. The promoters made the point that in this chain you helped yourself and your government as well, but the Federal Reserve Bank failed to see it that way and warned all its member banks against selling bonds for such a purpose. The Better Business Bureau cast a cold eye on the whole thing too, noting that nobody was going to come out with any $38,400 bonanza unless 2,048 persons happened to be thoughtful enough to ship those

$18.75 certificates along. That was the end of that dream. An effort to revive it three years later failed when the Treasury Department and the Post Office both put their big feet down.

Not only here but in such places as Japan, England, Germany, China, Abyssinia and other foreign outposts where it has flourished and died from time to time, the chain letter generally ended with some dark warning of dire consequences—or maybe just a little bad luck—for the person who broke the link. In this connection, it is perhaps appropriate to cite one which came to the author's desk some years ago:

DEAR FRIEND:

As you know, chain letters have been barred by the Post Office Dept.

This chain letter, however, is not illegal because it does not involve money.

In this chain you send your wife, because the purpose of the chain is not wealth but happiness.

Here is how it works: Send your wife to the man at the head of the list printed below, along with the names of five other husbands willing to participate in the chain. The man you select in turn sends his wife to the top name on your list.

POSTAL FORCE LABORS LATE INTO NIGHT SORTING 165,000 DENVER CHAIN LETTERS

SO THE PEOPLE MAY KNOW

THE DENVER POST

HOME EDITION — DENVER, COLO., SUNDAY MORNING, APRIL 28, 1935 — 88 PAGES

STAMP SALES ADVANCE 50 PER CENT AS FAD MAKES FRESH GAINS

Staggering Burden of Mail Predicted for Monday Despite Adverse Ruling by Government—Must Stop, Stevic Repeats

---

If the chain is not broken, you will eventually receive 3,246 wives, which should be enough for a normal lifetime, especially if you don't go broke. DO NOT BREAK THE CHAIN.

The man who broke the first chain in this series GOT HIS OWN WIFE BACK.

There were many variations, of course, but this is not *that* kind of history.

Actually, no wives were mailed and, it follows, none returned. That was just for fun, and much of the foregoing was nickel-and-dime stuff. The real sting came in 1978, more than four decades after that fifty-cent bit. This was the "Circle of Gold" letter that started on the West Coast and came east like a small gale. In that one the bite was an even $100. For that piddling outlay, you bought yourself a letter containing twelve names. The first $50 went to the nice person who sold you the letter, because he or she was going to keep 'em moving. The second $50 went to the party who graced the top of your list, whereupon you crossed that name off and added yours to the bottom. If you had half a brain, of course, you dealt only with people you knew and were willing to take an oath that they would not only dig into their wallets and follow your lead but let you go and watch when they mailed out their $50 bills. The way the promoters had it worked out, always assuming no cad broke the chain, your name eventually would appear on the lists of 2,048 of your fellow high rollers and you would wind up with something in excess of $100,000 in walking-around money. And, presto, the word was around in no time about John Doe picking up $30,000 and Jane Doe picking up a comparable fortune and all kinds of other Does making a fast $1,000 or so and chirping like birds. The postal ferrets put it down as nothing more than "the old pyramid scheme" but couldn't find anybody to prosecute because the folks behind the charmed "Circle of Gold" carefully avoided the mails and dealt hand to hand. As for the pie-in-the-sky types who bought the idea and did use the mails, you couldn't arrest them just for being true believers. If that one's still around, and it goes without saying that there were more losers than winners while the game was hot, the circle can't be very wide. Indeed, it had to narrow considerably in mid-1979, when the New York State Attorney General went to the law books and said, Oh, yes, there was so a way to prosecute anyone peddling that pipe dream.

Part V

SOME MIND-AND-BODY FADS

EMILE COUÉ:

The Twelve-Word Rx

Emile Coué: Greetings to America and its lost souls. *WWP*

"I am not a miracle man. I do not heal people. I teach them to cure themselves."
—EMILE COUÉ

IN 1923, the twin blessings of health and happiness came to our shores from Nancy, France, neatly packaged in one simple sentence—*Day by day in every way I am getting better and better*. Emile Coué, a pharmacist turned healer, carried over this prescription after a road show test in the loftier London circles had brought forth endorsements from Earl Curzon and Lady Beatty, among others. M. Coué, one of the more accomplished supersalesmen of the time, achieved his renown by advancing the simple notion that the imagination was man's most dominating faculty, a sure winner in any contest with the will. He called his system "Self-Mastery by Auto-Suggestion" and offered himself as its outstanding practitioner, casually observing upon his arrival here that he had enjoyed a most pleasurable voyage across the Atlantic despite a succession of storms that had left most of his fellow passengers positively green with seasickness. You can imagine what the Manhattan ship news reporters did with that one.

With that kind of start, bolstered by his lavish advance notices, the Pied Piper of Contentment had to fight off the economy-sized legions flocking to his side. Even though the American Medical Association denounced him as "a purveyor of cloudy stuff" and said

his system of healing was calculated to bring "tears of laughter and pity" from *real* doctors, he enjoyed a triumphal cross-country lecture tour which called for an encore in 1924.

By then, the Coué forces were proclaiming that their twelve-word magic formula could not only cure your varicose veins, among other assorted ailments, but also grow hair on bald heads. That item probably was thrown in to bring more men under the tent, since Couéism appeared to be suffering from an overabundance of female patrons. M. Coué, needless to say, didn't grow hair on anybody. He did lay claim to some smaller achievements, however. Thus he announced that a man suffering from a seizure of yawning had been able to cut his yawns down from seven per minute to one every ninety minutes under his ministrations. And he did take in hand two boys afflicted with stuttering and demonstrate that he could get them to say "Good morning" and "I won't stutter anymore" without tripping anywhere along the line. In a performance in New York's Knickerbocker Theatre, murmuring *se passe, se passe, se passe* (it is going away), he got an eighty-year-old victim of a trolley accident to walk without a cane for the first time in two years; the patient's doctor poured cold water on this triumph by saying that there wasn't anything wrong with the man's legs in the first place.

Even so, M. Coué drew so much notice that more than 3,000 people trooped into his Manhattan Institute in its first nine months, among them the celebrated Shakespearean actor E. H. Sothern, any number of Social Register types and some assorted captains of industry. Indeed, the Daughters of the American Revolution, impressed, put aside their vaunted native caution and invited the white-haired Frenchman to journey to Washington to display his powers; no cures were reported in that session.

On the broader levels, M. Coué ran into formidable opposition when he announced that autosuggestion could not only dictate in advance the sex of the newborn but also predetermine their careers. "If a mother wants a boy baby, she must bend her will to that effect, repeating with absolute confidence thirty or forty times a day, 'My child will be a boy.' If she intends him to be a great painter, she will insist on this to herself. She will visit art galleries and surround herself with beauty, and above all she will think beautiful things." While a necessarily indeterminate number of pregnant women very likely took to doing those things, Dr. Charles Burr, a brain specialist on the University of Pennsylvania faculty, led the medical community's quick put-down. Dr. Burr submitted that M. Coué was "scientifically out of bounds," which was another way of saying that he didn't know what he was talking about. Other authorities issued the same rebuttal when the Frenchman announced that autosuggestion, digging the bad notions out of the subconscious, could do much to diminish crime and vice on these sinful shores.

This, of course, is not to suggest, or even to auto-suggest, that the visitor did not find support in some high places. Dr. Henry Fairfield Osborne, president of the Museum of Natural History, offered the opinion that "American high-speed life needs the calming effects of Couéism." Dr. George Draper of New York's Presbyterian Hospital, submitting that M. Coué had "stripped disease of its dignity" by getting people to believe in their own regenerative powers, said it was wrong to pour ridicule on anyone who could do that. Some churchmen also came forward to say that both science and religion might profit from a touch of Couéism.

Just the same, the imported cure-all wasn't calculated to hold any sizable following here, for no matter how many times a day its devotees repeated the assigned words to themselves, the plain fact was that hardly anybody got *better and better*. Quite the contrary, the doctors kept insisting that the genuinely sick people in the Coué fold were bound to get worse and worse unless they cut out that silly business and went back to the old-fashioned remedies. Thus in due course the newly sprung Coué Institutes began to suffer from a want of customers, and the pudgy little man with the cute gray-black Van Dyke, the piercing eyes and the modest soft sell had to pack up his do-it-yourself happiness kit and go back to the Continent. There, too, by then, his twelve-word Rx, which had drawn as many as 40,000 "patients" a year to Nancy in his heyday, was beginning to slip; it didn't matter, because M. Coué, sixty-nine, succumbed to heart failure in 1926. One of the obituary writers summed up the story of Couéism in fifteen words: "It was conquered less by the scientists than by the demand for a new fad."

WILHELM REICH
AND HIS MAGIC BOX

"Every physician, almost,
hath his favorite disease."
—HENRY FIELDING, *Tom Jones*

TWO DECADES after Coué, the nation was treated to something that was much more engaging and on the surface infinitely more potent—and that happened to be the word—in the person of Dr. Wilhelm Reich and his "orgone box." In this saga, you have to start with the background of the man himself. Wilhelm Reich possessed credentials much more imposing than those of the Frenchman who came out from behind an apothecary's counter and managed to peddle a vague brand of psychotherapy spotted with touches of hypnotism and that concise dose of mumbo jumbo.

In his twenties, back in Vienna, Dr. Reich was in the select group of psychoanalysts gathered under the wing of Sigmund Freud. For six years he was director of the Vienna Seminar for Psychoanalytic Therapy, where he received credit for notable advances in treatment techniques. Somewhere along the line, rather early, the young doctor grew impatient and departed the Freud circle. Convinced that the analysts of that school, for all their probing, weren't *doing* enough about the sex problems afflicting society, he joined the Socialist Party of Austria and organized "sex-political" units to disseminate a program of "sex-economics" based on his own theory of orgasm. In

sum, this theory held that the business of perpetuating the race was just an incidental dividend of orgasm, whereas its real function was to release the sexual tension which in his view accounted for the unspent emotional energy that led to neurotic behavior. Reich held that the mental afflictions of the world could never be cured until more of the people began to experience orgasm—he called it "orgastic potency"—equal to the stored-up tension within. He had no trouble finding widespread support among the rank-and-file Socialists; indeed, there was so much interest in his "sex-economics" that the Party began to fear that its larger aims were in imminent peril of being shunted aside while everybody brooded over the more tantalizing problem of orgasm. The doctor and his sex-political units accordingly were thrown out in 1930 and he took his crusade into the Communist Party of Berlin, only to get the boot there too. Reich said the German commissars expelled him on orders from Moscow after his "orgastic potency" had been denounced as just plain un-Marxist bunk.

In 1934, openly challenged by Freud himself, Reich was banished from the International Psychoanalytical Association. After that, he turned up first in Denmark

Dr. Wilhelm Reich: The road was stormy. *New York Post/Tony Calvacca*

The Orgone Box in its upright position. Either way, problem solved.

and then in Sweden, running into the same sex-political difficulty in both places and finally settling down in Oslo, where he launched a series of electrical experiments on the erogenous areas of the body under sexual stimulation. This, very likely, is where his many-splendored Orgone Box had its earliest, tentative origins.

This contraption—roughly the size of a telephone booth—was trotted out for the inspection of the troubled masses on this side of the water a few years after the embattled Reich came over in 1939 and managed to satisfy the Federal Bureau of Investigation that he was not a bomb-throwing radical but just a man with some novel theories about orgasm. You can say what you want about the inherent caution and conservatism of J. Edgar Hoover, but the lifetime director of

the FBI evidently had no fear of the possible impact of the Austrian's brand of "orgastic potency" on the citizenry. Of course, Reich hadn't told the G-Men about his Orgone Box, if indeed it was ready for unveiling when he was being put through interrogation at Ellis Island.

What was it? Orgone was the doctor's word for orgasm—and orgasm, to the doctor, was cosmic energy. The wooden box, lined with zinc, was said to contain some secret property which would soak up orgone from the air and contain it so that it could be absorbed into the body and, presto, work wonders for patients troubled either with inadequate orgasm or no orgasm at all. But Reich did not always rely on the magic box itself. Treating patients in his office in Forest Hills, New York, the chunky doctor also applied manual pressure to numerous parts of the anatomy to drive away tensions; these treatments, by Reich's own published accounts, sometimes accomplished even more gratifying results—the ultimate, let's say—for the more responsive patients of both sexes. For those who preferred to seek relief without the personal touch, orgone boxes, also described as orgone "accumulators," could be rented for use in the home.

The trouble—you knew there was going to be trouble—set in when Reich began to go way beyond the initially heralded virtues of his strange contraption. Mildred Edie Brady summed it up in the *New Republic* in May, 1947: "With the discovery of orgone, the orgasm theory became, for Reich and his followers, a demonstrable corroboration of the work of Freud. But now the Reichites go far beyond Freud and declare that orgastic impotence is the primary cause of cancer, all neuroses, all psychoses, impotence, frigidity, perversions, cardiovascular hypertension, hyperthyroidism, constipation, hemorrhoids, epilepsy, peptic ulcer, obesity, narcotic addiction, alcoholism and the common cold." This summation actually did not include all the items mentioned at one time or another by the Reich adherents. Anemia, rheumatism, arthritis and high blood pressure were also listed as afflictions which the all-conquering box—and that real good orgasm—would forever banish.

In due course, the government dealt itself in. The Food and Drug Administration ruled that the orgone accumulator was a useless contrivance foisted upon the public under false claims and obtained an injunction barring its shipment across state lines. The same ban applied to the traffic in Reich's subsidiary energy-dispensing devices—he had a special blanket for bed patients as well as a "funnel" for use on the head and a "shooter box" for localized application—and forbade the mailing of his published works on "orgonomy." The doctor, then operating his Wilhelm Reich Foundation out of Rangeley, Maine, defied the injunction to force a court test. That was a mistake. The trial, in Portland, heard a whole array of medical men rip into the notion that one could lie down in a wooden box and soak up cosmic energy, or "orgone energy," or what-have-you, and emerge cleansed and purified and simply bursting with new-found "orgastic potency."

Reich and an associate, Dr. Michael Silvert, were found guilty of contempt of court and violation of the Pure Food and Drug Act. Reich was sentenced to a two-year jail term and Sivert to a year and a day, but the man from Vienna, on the highroad in psychoanalysis when he was admitted into Sigmund Freud's inner circle as a mere youth just out of medical school, did not survive his time behind bars. They found him dead of a heart attack in his cell in the Federal Penitentiary at Lewisburg, Pennsylvania, one morning in November, 1957. The doctor was sixty when that mixed-up, eventful and eventually prosperous career came to such an ignominious end. He would be remembered more for that incredibly wacky Orgone Box than for anything he may have contributed to our knowledge of the sexual function in his early scientific probings into this complex area. What a pity.

DIANETICS:

Freud on the Double

"Take the humbug out of this world,
and you haven't much left to do business with."
—JOSH BILLINGS

FOR THE HEALTHY legion of skeptics who wouldn't buy—or let us say rent—the Orgone Box, something less spooky, and more enticing, came along in 1950. It was "Dianetics, the Modern Science of Mental Health," from the book of the same name by L. Ron Hubbard, explorer, movie maker, naval reserve officer and science fiction writer. The key word came from the Greek *dianoia,* meaning "thought," but you needed an introduction to some newfangled English words to try to figure out what Dianetics was all about. You needed, first of all, to know about engrams, described by Hubbard as the "single source of aberrations and somatic ills" and beyond doubt the invention of the devil himself. Engrams was the word Hubbard used to describe the impressions left on our minds in that dark and wondrous time in the womb, later in the miracle of birth itself, and still later, say, in moments when we might be under anesthesia, or perhaps hit on the head, or maybe just undergoing severe emotional distress. Hubbard said the mind consisted of two parts, one analytic and thus rational and capable of remembering things and coping with the assorted problems of life, the other reactive and doing nothing more than recording impressions exposed to it while the analytic half is not working, as in the

instances cited above or in other periods of what Hubbard, thrifty with words, described as the "uncon."

The engram, you have gathered, is the villain of this piece. Hubbard, who dashed off his book in three weeks and watched it become an overnight best seller without benefit of any high-powered promotion campaign, said the analytic mind could do no wrong except insofar as wrong data from the engram bank in the bad mind might be fed into it. Got it now? We're all basically good and pure, too good to sin, too healthy to be plagued by our growing array of psychosomatic ailments—except for those nasty engrams in our other head, put there not because of anything any of us did but because of something that was done to us. You could read all this astounding stuff in Hubbard's book for four dollars, unless you happened to have been lucky enough to encounter it earlier in an article the husky, red-haired Father of Dianetics had dashed off for a magazine called *Astounding Science Fiction.*

You could read about it but you couldn't do anything about it. That is, you couldn't shake off your engrams without the help of a twenty-five-dollar-an-hour "auditor," or Dianetic therapist. That, happily, was easier than rolling off any square psychoanalyst's couch. All you had to do was to lie down, relax, listen to the auditor's patter, drift off into a kind of hypnotic state and then, in your dianetic "reverie," journey along the "time track" of your reactive mind picking up those engrams as they are fed to you by a factor labeled the "file clerk," let them pass in review with prompting by the auditor until more and more of them come to the surface, and then talk them out or, if you prefer, act them out. And then, lo and behold, your good old analytic mind disposes of all that trash, starting with the very first engram, the daddy of them all because it dates back to the very moment when those thoughtless parents of yours conceived you. When you got that engram, or any other engram, on the time track you just "bled" it off, in the words of the Dianetics Foundation, "never to return."

The individual sessions required two hours under the Hubbard formula but the man said that if you stayed with it through enough of those fifty-dollar mental workouts you would come out like new. The word for that was "clear," and you got "clear," by the way, ten times faster than your friendly neighborhood psychoanalyst could do it. This is the way Hubbard described the process:

Dianetics deletes all the pain from a lifetime. When the pain is erased in the engram bank and refiled as memories and experience in the memory banks, all aberrations and psychosomatic illnesses vanish, the dynamics are entirely rehabilitated and the psychological and mental being regenerated.

After that, of course, you wouldn't jump to any irrational conclusions or manifest any subnormal psychological drives, you wouldn't do any destructive things, you would shake off your sexual perversions if *that's* the way you had been getting your kicks, you wouldn't go around slopping up whiskey, and you wouldn't even catch the common cold. That was just for starters, of course. In your Dianetic "reverie," as long as everything hummed along nicely on the time track, you would also shake off such everyday nuisances as arthritis, hay fever, nonpathological eye trouble, asthma, migraine, ulcers, allergies, bursitis, tendonitis and anything that might be bothering the old ticker. And you would emerge bursting with peace and contentment, freed from all "major anxieties and illnesses," into a world of bouncingly healthy Supermen.

And what would happen then? The thirty-nine-year-old Hubbard said his new "science of the mind,"

with its "invariable" cures, would empty all the nation's jails and mental institutions as well as two-thirds of its hospitals.

Lots of people bought it. The book came out in July, and in September the publisher, Hermitage House, said that 75,000 copies had been sold and that it was on the way to a million. It surely was on its way to something big, because in no time at all there were "time tracks" busily operating in Hubbard centers in Los Angeles (where, like so many bright new notions, Dianetics caught on first), New York, Chicago, Washington, D. C., and Elizabeth, New Jersey. Indeed, the engram was on the run not only from coast to coast but across the blue Pacific in Hawaii as Hubbard's battle on the "uncon" became the going rage.

As always, just when something real dandy turns up, there were those who came in waving questions. Dr. Erich Fromm, the analyst and author, on hand to defend the Freudian ramparts, sailed in with considerable gusto. To begin with, the modest Hubbard statement that "the creation of Dianetics is a milestone for Man comparable to his discovery of fire and superior to his invention of the wheel and the arch" left the doctor cold. In his view, Hubbard wasn't making any contribution to the science of Man at all but was simply reshuffling some of the earlier Freudian theories and substituting "an engineering job" for genuine therapy.

"Freud's aim was to help the patient to understand the complexity of his mind and (thus) free one's self from the bondage to irrational forces which cause unhappiness and mental illness," said Dr. Fromm in a review of the Hubbard book. "Dianetics has no respect for and no understanding of the complexities of personality." He said the thing reeked with "oversimplified truths, half truths and plain absurdities."

Dr. Rollo May, consulting psychologist, observed that "Dianetics consists of guiding the patient into a realm where he can exercise any fantasy which pops into his head, somewhat as a person projects his own problems into the Rorschach ink-blots." He said it was full of "glowing promises" and shortcuts and no better than all the faith cures that had come before it.

While Hubbard claimed to have 270 cases of authenticated "clears" in his files before launching the new "science," the American Psychological Association called on its 8,000 members to steer clear of Dianetics until the man's claims could be evaluated. "What we have here," said the APA's E. Lowell Kelly, "is a man who claims he has discovered an exact science of the mind and developed a technique in therapy which goes far beyond that known to psychology, psychiatry and psychoanalysis." Dr. Kelly termed the Hubbard book "a hodgepodge of accepted therapeutic techniques with new names."

On Hubbard's behalf, it was said that he himself would have preferred more testing before unveiling his discovery but couldn't wait because he feared that another war might gobble up the world before Dianetics had a chance to save it. Art Ceppos, president of Hermitage House and executive vice-president of the Dianetics Research Foundation, echoed this view in an interview. "We are not crackpots," he said. "My interest in this book is not because I expect to get rich out of it. Suppose I make $50,000. That's a good sum, of course, but it's secondary. What does count are the things Dianetics can do for the world." Ceppos went on to observe that Freud himself, not to mention Galileo centuries earlier, had to bear the barbs of the skeptical in the beginning.

But the publisher wasn't around to defend his favorite science fiction writer too long. In October, 1950, the Hubbard operation began to come apart at the seams with the sudden defection of Ceppos, Dr. J. A. Winter, who had written the introduction to the book, and Dr. Mary McKee Roodenburg, a lay analyst who had switched to Dianetics because she believed that it could produce better results. Winter, who had no background in the field of mental health, said he was leaving because he had never witnessed an actual "clear" and because he didn't like the way Hubbard was running the foundation. Dr. Roodenburg, head of the New York branch, charged that Hubbard had refused to document his cases with medical supporting evidence and appeared to be more interested in the commercial side of Dianetics than in genuine scientific inquiry. The lady went further and said that Hubbard wasn't in the "clear" himself. "He was on his way, but he stopped to help others." There were also some things said about the type of people Hubbard had been qualifying as auditors (that course cost a round $500) as more and more people came in to shake off their engrams. Dr. Roodenburg said too many of the auditors were "low-caliber" types.

And so that bubble burst. Before the year was out, Dianetics, suddenly as soiled in the public mind as M. Coué's long-forgotten hocus pocus and Wilhelm Reich's portable all-purpose box, found itself reduced to a parlor game. Instead of plunking down their money for a joyride on the Hubbard time track, people took it up as another way to kill an evening, like Charades or Monoply.

It must be assumed that not too many engrams got flushed out in that process, but we had not heard the

L. Ron Hubbard in the early days. Still to come: endless prosperity with his Church of Scientology, but some trouble too. *WWP*

last of Lafayette Ronald Hubbard—not by any means. Born to a Navy Commander out of strong Nebraska stock, he would go onward and upward with an even better idea than Dianetics. He formed his very own church—the Church of Scientology—and has been in the public prints, or in the law courts at times, ever since. You can argue whether or not the word *church* is a misnomer. It is not to be confused with any old house of worship. Scientology is what the ocean-hopping Hubbard operation is all about, and the old Dianetic bit, engrams and all, is at the heart of it.

You don't go into Scientology to make your peace with God so much as to it get in the "clear"—for a price that may run into the thousands if you stay with it long enough at thirty dollars per hourly session. In 1959, four years after Hubbard and his wife, Mary Sue, set up their operation, the government ruled that it wasn't a religious organization at all, but something else, and was not entitled to tax exemption (this has since been reversed in the case of some units of the church). By that time the founders had repaired to England to preside over the movement from stately Saint Hill Manor in East Grinstead with "auditors"—and here and there men of the cloth—scattered around to minister to the believers. Hubbard has said (and in 1977 one of his "Deputy Guardians" put the number of listeners at 5,437,000) that with Scientology "the blind again see, the lame walk, the ill recover, the insane become sane and the sane become saner." Some of the movement's more modest claims are that it will arrest aging, improve the eyesight, raise intelligence levels and even cure the common cold. This sort of thing, naturally, has stirred vigorous dissent from such medical authorities as Dr. William Menninger of Topeka's famed Menninger Clinic, who has held that Scientology "can potentially do a great deal of harm." Disturbed by the growing number of converts flocking into the Mother Country in 1968, Britain's Health Minister, Kenneth Robinson, went before the Commons itself to condemn the Dianetic cure-all as "socially harmful, a potential menace to the personality and a serious danger to health." He could not have meant the founder's own physical health, or that of his purse. Now sixty-seven and said to have retired from the church in 1966 after collecting $240,000 for the continued goodwill associated with his name, Hubbard maintains a number of homes abroad but spends much of his time on the blue Mediterranean aboard a converted English Channel steamer said to be serviced by some two hundred crewmen and students.

In 1963 the FDA picked up a hundred of the Scientologist's "E-Meters," mechanical devices used to monitor answers given by persons enlisted in the Hubbard treatment, but the organization spent eight years battling the seizure and got those precious pieces of equipment back despite the FDA's claim that bogus curative powers had been ascribed to them. Lengthy as it was, that suit had to take its place alongside a whole passel of others, for the Church of Scientology is possibly the most litigious in the world, suing at the drop of almost any critical word. As Hubbard himself said once, "If you are foolish enough to have an attorney who won't sue, immediately dismiss him and get an attorney who will sue." The church has been on the other end as well, of course. It has been hauled into court by countersuits and on at least one occasion by a disaffected follower who claimed that he had poured a sizable fortune into Scientology without ever coming out in the clear.

At this moment the legal waters lapping up against Ron Hubbard's immensely prosperous creation are extremely muddy. Eleven of its ranking officials, including the still-active Mary Sue Hubbard, were recently indicted in Washington on charges of conducting a wide-ranging conspiracy—sort of a "little Watergate"—to infiltrate, bug and burglarize the Justice Department, IRS and other federal agencies to see what tidbits about the Church of Scientology's operations may be reposing in the files. The church has not claimed "total innocence" in the case. Quite the contrary, even before the twenty-eight count true bill was handed down a spokesman said the defendants would contend that any poking around they may have done was "in defense against a bureaucracy which has consistently acted against the civil and human rights of the church and its members." Your grandchildren may be reading about this one before it winds its way through the judicial mill.

The church's marquee, by the way, has not been without its share of headline names. *People* listed six of them recently: John Travolta, the kid skyrocketed into the seven-figure bracket with his performance in the movie *Saturday Night Fever*, followed by *Grease*; actress Karen Black, a ten-year veteran of Scientology; John Brodie, the ex-San Francisco 49ers quarterback turned NBC sportscaster; jazz bassist Stanley Clarke, Judy Norton-Taylor of TV's "The Waltons," and Lou Rawls—with a demurrer submitted by his agent, who told the magazine that while the singer is still on the Scientology rolls, "he doesn't want to be associated with those people."

We've been through some pretty heavy going here. Let us go on to something lighter—if that's the word. Like another item of endless torment and concern—the American waistline.

THE DRINKER'S DAY

"Imprisoned in every fat man, a thin one
is wildly signaling to get out."
—CYRIL CONNOLLY, British literary critic

THE GOOD TIME was 1965. Remember, fellas? *The Drinking Man's Diet.* All the booze you wanted, and all the food you could eat, too, and you kept getting thinner. *Thinner,* not fatter. Oh, what a year! You threw away the calorie counter and had yourself a ball, pulling in your belt all the while. It came out of a one-dollar pocket-size pamphlet cooked up by a trio of high-living San Francisco executives, Carroll Lynch, Herbert Drake and Robert Cameron, with the help of writer Robert Wernick and a pair of nom-de-plumes drawn from their middle names, Gardner Jameson and Elliot Williams. The subtitle on the diet, an overnight best seller, was HOW TO LOSE WEIGHT WITH A MINIMUM OF WILL POWER, and the beautiful secret was in your carbohydrate intake. The diet depended mainly on low-carbohydrate, high-protein foods which are low in calories, such as steaks, chops, pork, roasts, frankfurters, fish and chicken and such dandy afterdinner treats as strawberries and peaches.

You could eat those goodies all day long, smothering everything in butter, mayonnaise and salad oil, so long as you kept your carbohydrate intake to sixty grams, and you could drink like a sailor on shore leave because liquor is low in carbohydrates. Columnist Earl Wilson tried the happy new regime briefly and immediately renamed it the "Bacon, Butter and Booze Diet." Is it any wonder that there were perhaps a million copies of the Drinking Man's Diet in print, passing from hand to hand in the Corpulent Society, before more sober opinion—that is, the doctors'—began to prevail?

Dr. Frederick J. Stare, head of the Department of Nutrition at Harvard's School of Public Health and a world-famous authority in the field, put the new diet down as just plain ridiculous. Dr. Jean Mayer, also of Harvard, said that for middle-aged Americans it was "in a sense, equivalent to mass murder." What he had in mind were the effects of any system of dieting that prescribed an unlimited alcohol intake without reference to any offsetting nutritional balance. He mentioned the liver, the kidneys and even the poor heart. What about the fact that the preface to the *Drinking Man's Diet* counseled everyone to consult a physician before going on it? "You know darn well they don't," said the plain-spoken Dr. Mayer. "They just kill themselves alone." Dr. Theodore B. Van Itallie, Director of Medicine at St. Luke's Hospital in New York, had an equally low opinion. "It's just a passing fad, like the Yo-Yo or the Hula Hoop," he said, "and just about as worth while." More seriously, Dr. Van Itallie warned that any increased fat consumption on a low carbohydrate diet might tend to raise the blood cholesterol level, which in turn could accelerate atherosclerosis and lead to heart attacks. Other authorities hastened to point out that the 135 calories in a dry Martini were quite the same as the 135 calories in a fair-sized plate of spaghetti and constituted the same weight factor, regardless of carbohydrate content. The pall cast on the nation's grogshops by this kind of observation could not be measured, but after a while the drink-all-you-want diet ceased to be the rage, even though there were some living, breathing witnesses to its effects among the more careful gram-watchers of the time.

The fact is that a high-fat, high-protein diet changes the water balance in the body, causing the tissues to lose water and thus cutting weight. Nutritionists concede this, but almost always with this two-fold reservation: Such diets won't keep your weight down unless you're counting the calories, as in any diet, and they tend to become unpalatable too fast to keep the heavyweight eaters happy enough to stay with it for any length of time.

Actually, there was nothing new about the Drinking Man's Diet except that marvelous, selling handle—and the booze, of course. The Air Force for years had used a low carbohydrate diet, and a modification of it, passed around in mimeographed form, was actually what got the San Francisco quartet started on it. Naturally, the Air Force immediately disavowed any connection, since its diet always has been used only under medical supervision. Beyond this, it was ap-

parent that the government did not care to have the idea broadcast that if you wanted your son to be skinny, happy and also drunk, the place to send him was to the Air Force Academy; nobody, in a word, embraced the idea of linking our flying arm's down-hold on weight to unlimited imbibing. Nor would the flying service hold still for any other commercial straphangers, so a quick howl went up when an outfit operating out of Hollywood and Toronto started peddling an "Air Force Diet"—guaranteed to take off ten to fifteen pounds in thirty days OR YOUR MONEY BACK—for two dollars a copy.

In the same period, since 1965 happened to be a vintage year for the waistline, something called the *Mayo Clinic Magic Menu*—quite a piece of news to the Brothers Mayo—turned up in offices and on college campuses from coast to coast. This item, in mimeograph form or Xerox copies, acquired a solid underground circulation in no time at all because, like the Drinking Man's Diet, there were simply no limits on how much you could eat—short of dessert and potatoes. High on fats because "fat doesn't form fat but helps to burn it up," the anonymous authors of the *Magic Menu* said you could stow away a breakfast of twelve eggs and twelve slices of bacon, if you were so disposed, drown everything in butter all day long, and still lose five pounds a week. This quick pound-shedding gimmick, happily, didn't build up too much of a following, presumably because the early subscribers found themselves letting out their trousers or skirts after a while as the calories began, inexorably, to add up to inches.

The **Drinking Man's Diet** $1.00

OR

HOW TO LOSE WEIGHT
WITH A MINIMUM OF
WILL POWER

(ALSO RECOMMENDED FOR
LADIES AND TEETOTALERS)

A revolutionary reducing plan based on the new biochemical discovery that

CALORIES DON'T COUNT

...ed to eat fat if you are to be ...tissue. Dr. Taller explains the principles behind this new understanding of the body's chemistry and tells in full detail:

*How to eat three full meals a day and lose weight in the **safest** way possible.

*Why you must never leave the table hungry if you want to be slim.

*How you can eat "almost everything" while you watch those extra inches disappear.

*A reducing plan that includes a wide range of fried foods.

*How this radical new way of losing weight is linked to a low cholesterol count, better skin condition and resistance to colds and sinus trouble.

By Herman Taller, M.D.

This book ran into massive problems after selling close to a million copies, but there were two million in print before the diet ran its course—and you can still buy it in paperback now.

THE EATER'S DAY

"Nobody loves a fat man."
ANON.

THERE ARE TIMES when you have to ask yourself whether there is anything in the world shorter than the memory of an American, especially an American with a weight problem. The low-carbohydrate diets won their legions of loyal adherents just four years after the front-paged uproar kicked off by *Calories Don't Count,* the book by Dr. Herman Taller. Remember the magic safflower oil capsule called *CDC* (calories don't count, like the man said)?

Dr. Taller's opus came out late in 1961 and rapidly soared to the No. 1 spot on the nonfiction best-seller charts even though there were serious—and immediate—questions as to whether it belonged on that list or the other one. After a while, of course, Taller and his *CDC* pusher, Cove Vitamin and Pharmaceuticals, Inc., and his publisher, Simon & Schuster, had nothing but money to burn on legal fees as the need arose for defending what they had wrought upon the masses. Cove and S & S, indeed, had so much to spare that they wound up suing each *other* while fighting off the endless onslaughts of the Food and Drug Administration.

The fellow who started it all was a reformed obstetrician and gynecologist who once was a fat man himself. Dr. Taller, born in Romania and educated in Italy, sliced something like seventy-five pounds off his 265-pound frame on a high fat diet and then decided to let the public in on his secret: Take two safflower oil capsules and eat all you want so long as 65 percent of it is fat, 30 percent protein and a skimpy 5 percent carbohydrates. Why the capsules (just $6.49 for a month's supply)? Safflower oil, pressed from the seed of an herblike plant, contained linoleic, an unsaturated fatty acid which was supposed to chase your excess fats into your metabolism so they could get burned off instead of making you fatter. At that moment, there were no less than 55,000,000 Americans carrying around more weight than they were supposed to, so it is hardly any wonder that Taller's book —and his *CDC* pill—had no trouble at all finding eager takers. The doctor's burgeoning weight-control practice in New York—forty dollars for the first visit and the lab work, ten dollars a visit after that—did not suffer, either; a horde of round clients squirmed its way into his office.

The spoilsports were right behind them.

Dr. Stare said it was so much trash. Dr. Mayer found just one item in the Taller formula he could endorse—the suggestion that all weight watchers walk at least an hour a day. "Otherwise," said Dr. Mayer, "it is all very bad." Dr. Philip L. White of the AMA's Council on Nutrition called the whole thing "a grave injustice to the intelligent public." Dr. Willard A. Krehl of Marquette University dismissed it as "nutritional nonsense." The Rockefeller Institute's Dr. Edward H. Ahrens Jr. said that no scientists in the field could possibly take the calories-don't-count notion seriously. "You might lose weight [on the Taller diet] because fat is satiating," Dr. Ahrens said, "but if you did, it would be because calories *do* count, not because they don't." Barbara Yuncker, science writer for the New York *Post*, did a tough, probing series on the subject which raised serious questions about the efficacy of the *CDC* capsules.

The FDA lost no time dipping its own oar into the troubled reducing waters. Taller's book wasn't three months old before government agents, just testing, seized 1,600 copies—along with 58,000 *CDC* capsules—on charges that the book made false claims and that the pills bore misleading labels. This may have come as a shock to the increasing numbers of people who were buying the notion that safflower oil would not only make fat disappear but also lower and control the cholesterol level in the blood, prevent heartburn, improve the complexion, ward off those nagging colds and, for those with a shortage in that critical department, maybe even do something about sexual desire, among other things.

Did it make any difference? While the government was making its moves, and while the best-qualified people in the field were speaking out in pained tones, the S & S presses were straining to keep up with the demand for the Taller book and Cove couldn't shovel the capsules into the drugstores fast enough. In June, there was a break on that front, however. Cove withdrew *CDC* from the market, dropping its fight against the seizure order obtained from the Federal courts by the FDA. Edward Bobley, president of the pharmaceutical house, attributed his decision to "the refusal of Simon & Schuster to come to the defense of its own book" after selling something like a million copies and heading toward a sure second million.

In July, a stinging indictment came from George P. Larrick, FDA Commissioner. Larrick charged that *Calories Don't Count* was written just to promote sales of the capsule and that Dr. Taller and two vice-presidents of S & S acquired financial interests in the Cove company before the book came out. Larrick termed the capsule "worthless" and noted that the amounts prescribed by Dr. Taller would furnish only 5.5 grams of safflower oil daily—"an amount insignificant for any purpose," a point, incidentally, also

Dr. Herman Taller in Federal Court in Brooklyn in 1967. Six years after *Calories Don't Count* chalked up its raging success, he had to go behind bars on multiple charges stemming from the way the best seller was used to peddle reducing capsules to the overweight legions.

made in Miss Yuncker's series. As for the book itself, supposedly grounded on "sound scientific observations," Larrick remarked caustically that it was really the work of a layman. This was a reference to Roger Kahn, the top-drawer free-lance writer who had been called in to put the cloudy Taller theories in language the overweight layman could digest. (Kahn made the point that the plugs for *CDC* were inserted *after* he had done his ghost-writing job.) Taller elected not to answer the Larrick charges. Cove said the Commissioner had "overstepped his bounds a bit and made some promiscuous statements." S & S insisted that there wasn't "a scintilla of justification" in what the man said and submitted that only one of its vice-presidents, not two, had bought into the Cove subsidiary selling the *CDC* capsules, and that dignitary, the publisher added, had nothing to do with the book. The pharmaceutical house, on its part, ultimately pleaded

Behind the headlines: Beth Ann Wiener and Charles Simon, both interested in painting, met in 1961 at Rutgers. She was a student at Douglass College for Women and he was just hanging around the New Jersey campus after dropping out. They fell in love, got married, moved to a cheap flat on the edge of Greenwich Village—and then hit the drug scene: grass to hashish to cocaine to heroin to the amphetamines to LSD. In 1965, all but wasted, all the dreams blown away, they turned to the macrobiotic diet of the self-styled philosopher-scientist Sakurazawa Nyoiti of Tokyo, known as George Ohsawa to his followers in the States. That regime shunned all meat and relied almost entirely on whole grains—rice, wheat, corn, barley, rye, millet. Ohsawa's book *Zen Macrobiotics* promised cures for just about everything from dandruff to leprosy, including migraine, one of Simon's afflictions. The couple kicked drugs on that road, but in the process Beth, a beautiful girl, literally starved to death in less than ten months. Normally 120 pounds, she was down to 50 when she died. Simon, down to 105 from 135, vowed to stay with the cult diet. In more recent years a growing number of authorities in the field have come around to the view that there's something to be said for the macrobiotic way—in the proper balance—because there's nothing in that vegetarian diet that's bad for the system.

guilty to an indictment charging fraud in the sale of the pills.

The legal waters were further muddied when Cove sued S & S for a neat 6½ million dollars, alleging that the Messrs. Simon and Schuster had failed to keep an agreement to peddle the *CDC* capsules with the book, whereupon S & S promptly cited infringement of copyright and unfair trade practices and countersued for 7½ million. In time, the two suits canceled each other out, of course. Taller, for his own part, stayed out of that legal briar patch. He had his own troubles in the form of a jumbo-sized forty-nine-count indictment stemming from his masterwork. That case didn't come to court until 1967. The doctor, found guilty on twelve counts of mail fraud, conspiracy and violation of the Federal Food, Drug and Cosmetic Act, got off with a skinny $7,000 fine and two years' probation.

In late 1972, eleven years after that stormy Taller debut, history repeated itself with *Dr. Atkins' Diet Revolution*, a $6.95 item that drew 750,000 fatties to the bookstores in its first five months. The subtitle— *The High Calorie Way to Stay Thin Forever*—told the story, and the author, Manhattan's Robert C. Atkins, seemed headed for an income bracket in the neighborhood of a Jackie Susann or a Harold Robbins. His Rx came without any capsule gimmick but had a familiar sound nonetheless: what puts it on, folks, is the body's failure to metabolize carbohydrates properly, thus producing too much insulin, lowering the blood sugar and making you so cranky you keep slopping down food. The way to beat it? Simple. For the first week, a high-protein, no-carbohydrate, high-fat diet to produce something called ketosis, which filters incompletely metabolized fats out of your system via ketone-laden urine and acetone-tinged breath. After that, back to the carbohydrates (but no more than 40 grams a day) and you're still in ketosis and shedding those extra pounds even on a 3,000-calorie-a-day regime.

Oh, yeah?

The counterrevolution was in full bloom before the March winds started to blow.

Dr. Philip White, secretary of the AMA's Council on Foods and Nutrition, submitted that no one could forecast the long-term effects of that ketosis bit and, more seriously, there was some question as to just how many calories were being flushed down the *pissoir* in the process. That was just for starters. The Council, joined by all kinds of authorities, warned the cardiologist's devoted legions that any diet built on an unlimited consumption of saturated fats and cholesterol-rich viands could increase the blood fats to a point where the thinned-down customer might be tempting circulatory ailments or heart attacks. The Medical Society of the County of New York followed that blast with a charge that the diet was equally risky for persons susceptible to kidney disease or gout and could produce weakness, apathy, dehydration, calcium deficiency, nausea, lack of stamina and fainting spells.

The forty-two-year-old Atkins stood fast, mounting the barricades from a plush twenty-three room office (first visit: $200) that by then had begun to look like Penn Station in the rush hour. "Grossly unbalanced?" "Potentially dangerous?" The doctor said he would like to see some documentation from the critics of his anything-goes (except starch and sugar, of course) diet. He was still saying it two years later: "Ten thousand patients followed it with good results. I wasn't encouraging people to eat fats at all. I said the diet should have 60 per cent protein and 40 per cent fat. My success created enemies."

Cash, too.

The Atkins book kept selling, went into paperback, and is still very much around. Forget about that Taller opus. This one made *Calories Don't Count* look like a little book of poems carried on some publisher's list just to give it some class.

PROMISES, PROMISES...

"In all times . . . witches and old women and
imposters have had a competition with physicians."
—Francis Bacon, *The Advancement of Learning*

THE FAST-BUCK GUYS pointed toward the nation's bulging middle actually account for just a modest share of the staggering sums weaned away from the populace year after year by the small army peddling food fads and quack health cures. The story of the food fads is pretty elementary: If it is at all edible you dress it with some fancy language, and lots of Americans will swallow it, maybe millions. The primary ingredient can be wheat germ or vegetable oil, seaweed or brown rice, onions or garlic. It really doesn't matter; what sells it is promises, lots of promises. The thing is *good* for you.

The quack goes one giant step further. He stays up late nights worrying about what ails you; he wants to separate you from your physical distress—and some of your money too. He also stays up late to keep one step ahead of the government, which can never move fast enough to nail him in time anyway. The watchdogs in Washington may spot a quack as fast as he comes out of the woodwork but the chances are that a pretty resourceful lawyer comes ready-wrapped with the man's health formula, and our legal processes happen to be made to order for the people operating outside the law in this area. But this isn't where the problem lies. More often than not, the quack isn't violating the law, just the customer's insides. He's simply playing on our built-in gullibility. He's another happy prospector panning gold in a stream that never runs dry. The government's own figures on the fortunes mined in the twin wonderlands of the food fad and the quack remedy have reached sky-high proportions in recent years, accompanied by widespread publicity, without any apparent effect on the public. Back in 1959, William F. Janssen, chief of the FDA's information branch, estimated that the constantly multiplying assortment of health fads was fleecing 10,000,000 Americans out of $500,000,000 a year.

"This racket," Janssen said, "is based on mistrust of the facts of the science of nutrition. More people seem to believe more bunk about food than any other single topic in the health field. It is this widespread dissemination, and the zealous faith of the believers in nutrition nonsense, that make it difficult to combat. Food faddism today has aspects of an organized movement that is self-supporting and actively seeking new converts. . . . The old-time patent medicine man is back but this time he is a 'nutrition educator' who rings your doorbell and tries to persuade you that a shotgun mixture of vitamins and minerals, plus some secret factor which nutrition experts have not yet

Gayelord Hauser, Garbo's diet guru, in 1947. His Rx: blackstrap molasses. He came under heavy assault from the doctors—but maybe he knew something at that. He's still around, past eighty, and it's not all molasses. He's big on the high-protein low-fat diet and a whole carload of vitamins. D for the pituitary and thyroid glands. B_{12} "for a natural lift" and B_6 come the dark because it helps him sleep. *WWP*

identified, is the answer to your health problems."

Janssen singled out the raging vitamin fad in particular.

"It is dangerous," he said, "for anyone to assume that such products can be relied on to treat unidentified ailments."

But millions of people did—and still do—make that assumption.

Remember when carrot juice was being pushed upon us as a "liquid gold" good for almost anything that hurt? When grape juice—the "grape cure"—was foisted on the victims of cancer? When yogurt (perfectly nourishing) was supposed to cure all kinds of ailments? When honey was the answer? When Tiger's Milk was the thing? Tiger's Milk—and later Instant Tiger's Milk—came spiked with brewer's yeast, soy flour, blackstrap, fruit juice, wheat germ and powdered bone, or any combination thereof, and there was no faster way to knock off a whole mess of wonder foods in one big gulp. Remember when the ads said I COULDN'T STOP TORTURING HIM and it turned out that the woman in the accompanying photo was on the

verge of total social and sexual disaster UNTIL HE MADE ME FEEL A BRIDE AGAIN, thanks to those dandy mail-order pills? When "Royal Jelly," the food of the queen bee, was going to restore flagging sexual vigor, improve the old brain and even arrest your bride's fading beauty? While that one was the rage, briefly, Dr. Stare conceded that it might well have contained excellent properties for the queen bees, who lived longer and had more fun than the poor working bees. "But," added Harvard's resident expert, "it is in no way of benefit to humans."

The AMA and the FDA, meeting jointly, put the combined annual take of the faddists and the quacks at a billion dollars a few years ago. In those sessions nothing was spared, from the never-ending array of "cures" foisted on the sick to the vitamin bit. The conferees begged the people to note that no vitamin in the world could serve as a substitute for a balanced diet, that oysters and olives had no effect whatever on a man's potency, that you couldn't purify the blood with large doses of onions and garlic, that you couldn't slim down on "de-starched" potato chips because there isn't any way to take the starch out of potatoes, that raw beef juice couldn't endow men with rare courage and more virility, and that there was no "brain food" that would help the human brain.

Did it make any difference? In 1965, a Senate frauds subcommittee armed with 1,128 pages of testimony on food fads and so-called health cures satisfied itself that the public was still being taken for a billion dollars a year. Later estimates put the figure at two billion dollars a year, but then in this area it has long been apparent that you could write your own figure. In 1967, the AMA estimated that the quacks were prospering to such a degree that they were coining 300 million dollars a year from arthritis sufferers alone. This crippling disease has been traced to the time of the dinosaurs; Hippocrates accounted for the first recorded description of it 400 years before Christ, using the Greek words "arthos" for joint and "itis" for inflammation. The medical profession has struggled with it down through ten centuries, and still arthritis victims shell out money for fake "cures" as fast as they are advertised.

Even more pitifully, the AMA in 1967 took note of the increasing "cures" being peddled for the mentally retarded, such as the so-called "U Series" of treatments, when no cure is known to science. On a lesser scale, the AMA called attention to the growing list of overnight "cures" for everything from alcoholism to acne to wrinkles. But there was still no evidence that the recurring warnings from qualified sources produced any truly salutary effect.

This has always been the case, unfortunately.

Go back to Gaylord Hauser and the most wonderful of all the "wonder foods"—blackstrap molasses—in the early Fifties. Hauser, widely advertised as a friend of the svelte and ever-youthful Greta Garbo, which he was indeed, heralded the virtues of the sticky substance in his best-selling book, *Look Younger, Live Longer*. He said it would add five "youthful years" to your life, and pretty soon we were being told that it would perform all sorts of extra little miracles in the process: banish nervousness, chase that tired feeling, solve all digestive problems, correct menopausal difficulties, turn gray hair back to its normal color and even *grow* hair on heads where it was in short supply, among other things. Whole hordes of Americans accordingly turned to blackstrap molasses, which happened to be a by-product of sugar refining, rich in iron and inositol, a B-complex vitamin and an excellent repast for livestock. It turned out, of course, to be just what its name implied—a lot of

molasses. And that's the story of our food fads, then and now.

It would be nice if we could just write all this off to the quick buck and let it go at that—except that now and then a body count is in order.

Consider the recently flourishing liquid protein diet—*no food at all*—made from the by-products of cattle-slaughtering and selling for as much as $15 a quart. This was the new magic pound-shedder dropped on the fatties from heaven itself in the form of book called *The Last Chance Diet* by a Pennsylvania osteopath, Dr. Robert Linn. That one came out in 1976 and sold 3,000,000 copies in about five minutes, which shouldn't have come as a surprise to anyone, inasmuch as there's no way in the world not to lose weight if you don't eat. This is no indictment of the doctor; he's just a guy who came up with a flaming hot Rx. But before another year fell off the calendar FDA sleuths were burning the midnight oil checking into the deaths of thirty-six heavyweights who had died after prolonged hard times on that fad diet. In November 1977 FDA Commissioner Donald Kennedy hit out at the thirty-five manufacturers of that liquid goo with a charge that it had either killed or contributed to the deaths of sixteen women over a period of a scant few months. The FDA chief said that in ten of those cases the women, whose ages ranged from twenty-five to forty-four, had lost an average of ninety pounds only to succumb to heart irregularities either while on the diet or shortly after going back to solid foods. The cause, in the FDA view: a depletion of potassium leading to the short-circuiting of normal electrical impulses to the heart. One would imagine that the wonder-working $15 bottle—two tablespoons four times a day and you're on the way to that 32-inch waist—vanished from the shelves five minutes after Dr. Kennedy's front-paged press conference. No. There are doctors who are still prescribing it for the gullible thousands, very likely (let's give them the best of it) with the almost-always vain injunction that once you go off that potion and back to the three-meal-a-day bit you're going to have to watch those calories.

Once again, who listens?

The current count on the number of Americans lugging around too many pounds is about 70,000,000, and there are times when it seems that there are about that many fad diets as well. The record, unhappily, shows that more than 90 percent of all the weight-shedders put it right on again once they stop whatever regime they have chosen—Weight Watchers, the ever-popular Stillman diet, the Mayo diet, the rice diet, the ice-cream-only diet, the grapefruit diet—name it. Nothing sells like a diet, not just for doctors but the media too, especially the slick magazines. From *Harper's Bazaar* in recent years: the Flab Away Diet, the 1400-Calorie Good Sex Diet, the After Divorce Diet, the Erotic Diet and that old standby, the New Nine-Day Wonder Diet. From *McCall's*: the No-Will Power Diet and the Beautiful Skin Diet, to cite just two without overlooking the one *Redbook* came up with a while back—the Do It Together Diet.

At this moment, of course, the big boom is in health foods, with restaurants and retail outlets proliferating in carload lots. That industry hit the 600-million-a-year level in 1974 before a slight leveling off, by no means permanent, set in. Unless you've been off on a trip to Mars, you know this bit: whole grains and breads, unrefined sugar and unbleached flour, herbal tea and honey, dried fruits and nuts, pure juices, fertile eggs, raw milk, yogurt, peas, peanut butter, and, perish the thought, no preservatives or additives, no bleaches or dyes, no sprays. If that's the answer, you have to ask yourself why you run into so many chubby types who are hung up on the health foods. Another question arises when you come to the ginseng craze, born in the Orient centuries ago. This miracle herb—converted to instant tea, ground into powders, dried into chunks, pressed into pills, soaked into your favorite brandy—has been heralded as a "supervitamin" that will keep an airline pilot awake on a nonstop round-the-world flight, enable a so-so athlete to become one of the new millionaires or set up a rock star to keep pounding it out until the paying multitude falls into a collective sleep, not to mention what we're told it will do for the flagging lover's sex life.

Maybe.

By the time this book comes off the presses there may very well be something even better on the market. Keep your wallet handy. On the weight bit, it might be advisable to keep something else handy. It came from Dr. Neil Solomon, Maryland's Secretary of Health, during a television debate with the prospering prophet of ketosis, Dr. Atkins:

"The crazier the diet, probably the more weight you'll lose, the more harm you'll end up doing to your body, and the faster it will come back when you're through."

That seemed to say it all in one low-calorie sentence, but a mail-order ad turned up in some of the more tawdry weeklies in 1978 that grabbed the eye with this chunk of headline type:

I LOST 61 LBS. OF EXCESS FAT . . .
BY JUST RELAXING IN MY BATHTUB . . .
AT HOME. . . I ONLY TOOK 5 BATHS . . .
EACH BATH LASTING ONLY 15 MINUTES!

Below it, silhouetted in black, appeared the anonymous woman who supposedly wrote that glowing testimonial. You know what she looked like: on the left, gross enough to throw terror into a wrestler like Gorgeous George, and on the right, presto, the curvaceous doll a man would leave his wife for in five minutes. Clean, too, what with those trips to the tub. And how was that transformation accomplished? Elementary, fatso. It was a "new European miracle liquid" called W-L-40—$11.98 for a single dose, $20 for a double order, $27 for a triplet and $35 for the family size. And that's all you bought. No pills. No capsules. And you threw away your calorie counter because you would never need it again as long as you had hot water and lots of the "pleasantly scented" W-L-40. You see, that potion, so the ad told us, made the fat nearest the skin's surface disappear and then attacked the deeper layers, expelling what's left of the enemy "through the skin's pores." Now there was a bet no one—woman, man or beast—could lose.

If that excess flesh didn't melt away on the first shot, you sent back what was left of your stash of W-L-40 and got a "FULL refund" from the Florida-based outfit that was and may still be peddling it. Very tempting. And by the way, fellas, W-L-40 is not just for the girls. Works on the beer-barrel male belly too. The ad said so.

So there you have our diet fads, then and now. Skimmed, to be sure, since there have been no less than 3,000 books on the subject. Just two items remain. The first is the success story of Richard Smith, a thirty-seven-year-old native of New York's high-calorie Catskill-Mountain area, who worked as a busboy as a kid in the Borscht Belt up that way. Smith went to college briefly and then labored at occupations ranging all the way from tractor driver to women's underwear buyer for Alexander's in Manhattan before going into public relations and lo, most likely at night, coming up with a truly inspired idea. It was just a fun poster labeled "The Sensuous Dieter's Guide to Weight Loss During Sex." This is not the place for the details on that item. The thing is, it sold in large chunks and led to a book—*The Dieter's Guide to Weight Loss During Sex*—that zoomed to the top of the trade paperback best-seller list in the winter of 1978 and stayed there well into 1979. Smith was only kidding, of course, but a guy can get rich that way. And so with his sex-and-weight spoof still selling as fast as his publisher, Workman, could grind it off the presses, he came up with the other side of the gold coin—*The Bronx Diet*. In that one, you can find out where to gorge yourself on the heaviest Italian dishes available in The Borough of Colleges. One assumes that the moral is eat now, have your sex later. Are you waiting to hear that Richard Smith is the happiest 300-pound author and makes Mario Puzo look like a skinny man? Wrong. Smith is six-foot-one and weighs a neat 200 pounds. His secret? He runs sixty miles a week. The rest of the time, when he's not at his typewriter, he walks to the bank a lot.

Finally, the no-kidding, no-running, no-nonsense slimmer-downer which at this writing is sweeping the country with nary a dissenting sound anywhere in the air is *The Complete Scarsdale Medical Diet*, created by Dr. Herman Tarnower and turned into an instant $7.95 best seller with the help of Samm Sinclair Baker. This diet, grounded less on how much you're eating than on the chemical reaction between the prescribed foods, is limited to fourteen day spans meant to shake off up to twenty pounds per go-round for the faithful legions. The doctor, an internist and cardiologist, created it for his own patients—*minus* the heart cases—in the chic community in New York's Westchester and had to be talked into putting it between covers for all the strangers out there in the hinterlands. One wonders why, because it took no time at all for that skinny little book to soar to the number one spot on the *New York Times* nonfiction list.

For those who may want to travel the Tarnower route, you start with a set of restrictions undoubtedly painful in one degree or another to most of those taking the plunge: no between-meal snacks except celery and raw carrots, no butter, oil or mayonnaise, no sugar in your tea or black coffee and no alcohol (not even a thimbleful). Actually, that's the least of it. If you're in the meat-and-potato set, the worst is yet to come, starting with a breakfast that's always limited to half a grapefruit, one slice of dry protein toast, coffee or tea with a sugar substitute if desired, and this kind of week:

MONDAY

Lunch: Cold cuts (lean), tomato slices, coffee or tea (with all your meals, by the way).

Dinner: Broiled fish, salad with all the vegetables you want, that protein toast (just one slice, remember), grapefruit.

TUESDAY

Lunch: All the fruit salad you can eat.

Dinner: Lots of steak (lean), tomatoes, lettuce, celery, olives, brussels sprouts or cucumbers.

WEDNESDAY

Lunch: Tuna fish or salmon salad with lemon and vinegar, grapefruit.

Dinner: Two lamb chops (lean, baby) celery, cucumbers, tomatoes.

THURSDAY

Lunch: Cold chicken, raw or cooked spinach.

Dinner: Two eggs, cottage cheese, cooked cabbage and that one slice of toast (look, it's *always* one).

FRIDAY

Lunch: Assorted cheese slices, raw or cooked spinach, toast.

Dinner: Broiled fish, that big vegetable salad, toast.

SATURDAY

Lunch: That big fruit salad again.

Dinner: Cold chicken, tomatoes, grapefruit.

SUNDAY

Lunch: Chicken (hot or cold), tomatoes, carrots, cooked cabbage or broccoli or cauliflower, grapefruit.

Dinner: It's steak night again, plus celery, cucumbers or brussels sprouts, tomatoes.

While the dinners are subject to no change, Dr. Tarnower does permit an out—is that the word here?—if his lunch regime leaves you cold it's okay to switch to a half cup of low-fat pot cheese plus one whole tablespoon of low-fat sour cream with sliced fruit and throw in six walnuts or pecans with a diet drink.

Now if you've done all that for two weeks, and the word-of-hungry-mouth testimonials from Scarsdale were themselves best sellers before that book hit the stalls, you can go off the diet for two or three weeks. Well, mostly off. No potatoes, no pasta, no sugar, no more than two slices of that dry toast per day, and a fat ounce and a half of drinking liquor if you're one of those people. And, oh yes, desserts: fruit, diet gelatine or sherbert. And then, if your dressmaker or tailor can handle the action, back to that Spartan fourteen-day regime. Any cheating and all bets are off or, at the least, you don't melt away anything like twenty pounds again.

HADACOL:

Cure with a Kick

Dudley J. LeBlanc: The mixture was worth a fortune.
WWP

Now ONE IS reminded (hic) of the beautiful binge
that went by the name of Hadacol back in 1950. In
that banner year, State Senator Dudley J. LeBlanc
of Louisiana, who invented the stuff, hauled in 24
million dollars, most of it from his own neighbors in
the Cajun country and its environs. The wonder is
that the portly little politician didn't do even better,
because Hadacol happened to be more like a cocktail
(make it two cocktails, and see what the boys in the
back room will have) than a patent medicine. What
the Senator stirred up in that barrel in his barn, using
a boat oar, was a very special blend of vitamins, minerals, honey and just plain ethyl alcohol—12 percent
alcohol, pal. Dudley LeBlanc was no piker when it
came to mixing. He wasn't exactly stupid, either.
With that high alcoholic content, he had himself a
remedy laced with a strong appeal for the Bible Belt,
where a man with a real thirst had no place to turn
but to the sometimes elusive moonshiner.

You see, you could get yourself a little edge with
Hadacol, or you could take it for what the testimonials
said: anemia, arthritis, asthma, diabetes, eczema, epilepsy, gallstones, hay fever, heart trouble, high blood
pressure (or low, for that matter), rheumatism,
cancer, paralytic strokes, pellagra, pneumonia, tuber-

culosis or them naggin' ulcers. If you took enough in
one sitting, nothing was going to hurt—at least not
for a while. And if you happened to be a perfect
specimen but simply weren't up to snuff, you could
swill down some Hadacol—if you believed the man
with the golden boat oar, that is—just to get some
color in your cheeks and restore that youthful feeling.
Maybe the murky brown potion tasted like bilge water and smelled worse, but the half-pint bottle cost
only $1.25, and for $3.50 you could get the twenty-
four-ounce family-size jug. Except for the Skid Row
winos, who could ask for more? Down in Dixie, it
sold like Manischewitz.

The Senator was something more than a medicine
man, of course. He was a supersalesman. Born in the
time of the Puritans, he would have peddled the first
firewater to the Indians. Plunked down on a farm in
French-speaking Vermillion Parish in southern Louisiana in 1894, son of the penny-poor village smithy
and barefoot till he was ready for primary school in
Erath, he pointed himself toward the world of commerce at an early age. He sold things people needed:
tobacco, patent medicines, burial insurance. He was
such a good tobacco salesman that he was able to put
four brothers through college, in his footsteps, on the

proceeds. After that, following a stint in the Army, he peddled patent medicines and then went into burial insurance (one dollar a month and we'll take care of the body). Operating his own company, he nailed down 200,000 subscribers so fast that he was able to sell out for a neat $320,000, only to lose the bundle in the mild stock market tumble of 1937.

An old hand in politics by then, alternately in the Huey Long camp and threatening to clamp the King-fish behind bars if the people would just make Senator Dudley LeBlanc, called Couzin Dud, their Governor, he turned his selling talents after a while to a product he whipped up called the Happy Day Headache Pow-der. That proved to be a headache for the owner himself because the FDA took the view that the label on the bottle promised more than any little old pow-der could possibly deliver to the suffering masses.

Couzin Dud didn't quit there. No, sir. The ills of his own flesh prompted him to stay in the therapeutic service of the people. Stricken with rheumatism, in 1943, he enjoyed some relief from a Vitamin B com-plex and proceeded to dig into the pharmaceutical manuals to find out what his doctor knew. Now the legends diverge when you come to the particular concoction which in short order would make Dudley LeBlanc both rich and famous as a healer of the afflicted. The first one, in the simple tradition of the American entrepreneur and thus rather pedestrian, is that Hadacol actually was developed by an outfit called Wonder Medicine, Inc., but didn't get on the high ground until the silver-tongued Senator took it over and applied the old pitchman's know-how. The other is the man's own story.

In that one, and you have to buy it, Couzin Dud's own tireless researches led him to the conclusion that our flagging systems were crying out not only for vita-mins but also for minerals, and so—

He goes into hock for $2,500 for the raw materials, rolls up his sleeves, disappears into his barn, flicks on the weak overhead lamp, finds an empty barrel that's reasonably antiseptic, and puts his fleshy shoulder to the aforementioned oar. Hour after endless hour, pouring sweat in the choking heat of the Louisiana night (where's that damn Gulf-borne breeze?), he toils to bring succor to his fellowman. A touch of thiamin hydrochloride (B1) and riboflavin (B2), a spot of niacin, a dash of pyridoxine (B6) and pan-tothenic acid. A spot of likker. A sprinkling of iron, manganese, calcium and phosphorous. A taste of honey. Another jigger of booze to loosen up the mix-ture. Hmnn. The old ethyl ain't Bourbon but it sure is more than a preservative. It goes down kinda nice.

And so the Senator comes out of the barn with Hadacol, high-octane Hadacol. Good for all your parts, it is perforce the ideal product for Dudley LeBlanc's Happy Day Company.

Happy days, indeed, were right around the corner.

From a trifling $75,000 start in 1947, Hadacol sales rose to a couple of million dollars in 1949 and then, with working capital in the till, the Cajun medicine man proceeded to give those slick advertising guys up North some lessons in selling. He put the show on the road, like the circus. Never mind the freaks and the animal acts. LeBlanc got himself some headline names and organized the Hadacol Good Will Caravan. Names? You might see Mickey Rooney ("Andy Hardy uses Hadacol"), Burns and Allen, Chico Marx, Connee Bos-well, Carmen Miranda, Jack Dempsey belting a stiff around in an exhibition, maybe Bob Hope or Jimmy Durante on a quick one-shot (if you'll pardon the ex-pression) for Dudley LeBlanc's cure-all. And music? Only Roy Acuff and his Smoky Mountain Boys or Sharkey's Dixieland Band. And girls? Just a modest chorus line of fourteen high-steppers "direct from the Chez Paree in Chicago."

Traveling in air-conditioned buses with a convoy of a hundred spanking white Hadacol trucks and thirty sedans and five airplanes overhead to trumpet the message of health and everlasting well-being from the skies, the Senator's caravan swept through eighteen Southern states putting on extravaganzas in ball parks and arenas that had never before housed anything bigger than a two-bit carnival. And the price of ad-mission? Just a Hadacol box top, and you could buy the box right off one of those trucks and swill that dandy syrup right on the spot if you got thirsty (well, the half-pint model had as much alcohol in it as a fairly dry Martini). Couzin Dud picked up all the other tabs and threw in Hadacol lipstick for the women, Hadacol caps and T-shirts and Hadacol cowboy hol-sters for the kids (the ads said the juice was good for them, too). On the side, torchlight parades, the sound of calliopes and a hillbilly band banging out the "Hadacol Boogie" ("Down in Louisiana in the bright sunshine/they do a little boogie-woogie all the time /they do the Hadacol Boogie")* or that other specially commissioned whooper-upper, "Everybody Loves That Hadacol."

All that, of course, was just a "live" adjunct to an advertising campaign of staggering proportions. The Senator didn't pass up any bets. He blanketed the daily and weekly press in thirty-one states with thou-

---

* Chicago Copyright 1949, Bill Nettles-Wing Music.

sands of testimonial ads, making Lydia Pinkham look like a piker. RELIEVE THE CAUSE OF YOUR AILMENTS, said the big type, and around the smiling photo of Hadacol's discoverer there might be pictures of a couple of dozen satisfied Hadacol users, all the way from the golden years down to the teens, who had indeed been relieved of every conceivable ailment (in the small type). Couzin Dud also used the magazines and a thousand billboards or so, not to mention the sides of all the available barns, while pouring a small fortune into spot commercials on as many as 819 radio stations and on any number of television outlets, moving all the way up to a $75,000 network special with Groucho Marx in Los Angeles in an abortive effort to float Hadacol out of the provinces and into the big time. On that show, Marx asked the Hadacol King, known more locally as the King of the Cajuns in his less affluent days, what his bottled elixir was good for. "It was good for five and a half million for me last year," the Senator said.

Well, maybe it wasn't Mint Julep, but it was harder to buy in 1950. In areas where the Senator couldn't fill his orders, Hadacol went to two dollars a bottle on the black market. What a year that must have been. Hadacol's 24 million dollars in sales flowed from a production cost of 7 million and oh, maybe a million a month in that high-powered promotion campaign and the usual odds and ends in administrative expenses.

The way things were going then, the ebullient owner and proprietor saw no reason why he shouldn't push 75 million dollars' worth of Hadacol on his distressed fellow citizens in 1951, but he neglected to take into account those snoops in Washington. The slow-but-sure Federal Trade Commission sampled the Bayou highball in due course and decided that while it undoubtedly was very good for the Senator's bank account, it couldn't cure a damn thing. In a word, the government's chemists found that the mixture had no therapeutic value for the endless variety of bodily ills it was supposed to wash away and at best could do no more than help replenish certain vitamin or mineral deficiencies in the legions hooked on it. Undaunted, LeBlanc gentled down his advertising to take out his larger miracles and push this somewhat more modest line: "Don't be satisfied with symptomatic relief. It's possible to relieve the cause of your ailment when lack of Vitamins B1, B2, iron and niacin cause stomach disturbances, gas, heartburn, indigestion, annoying aches and pains, and certain nervous disorders."

LeBlanc, then in a second futile effort to capture Louisiana's executive mansion, insisted that dark political motives lay at the root of his troubles with the FTC. "If I wasn't running for Governor this complaint never would have happened," he said. "I know there's going to be more harassment, trying to embarrass my candidacy. I wouldn't be surprised if I was investigated for income taxes." The sly old political medicine man must have known something, because after a while the government filed a $656,151 tax lien on the Hadacol operation on top of a New Orleans indictment which accused Couzin Dud of evading $58,000 in personal income taxes during 1950. The Senator beat those raps.

In 1951, in any case, the Hadacol caravan started to slow down to a crawl, mired in a series of intricate financial maneuverings and legal complications, and LeBlanc suddenly announced that with taxes eating up all his profits he had decided to sell his depleting gold mine to something called the Tobey Maltz Foundation of New York for $8,205,000, staying on the payroll as sales manager at a comfortable $100,000 a year for fifteen years. The Foundation said no, it hadn't bought the cure-all but had just been dealt in for a royalty cut for cancer research. Then it turned out that Hadacol really belonged to a Maryland corporation organized by a vague band of "Eastern investors," but in October the new owners filed in bankruptcy, listing liabilities of $4,200,000 against assets of $2,600,000. This, of course, produced raised eyebrows (one of the few things you couldn't take Hadacol for) in so many quarters that Couzin Dud, sitting comfortably on his capital gains profits after paying Uncle Sam a 25 percent tax on that 8-million-dollar bonanza, professed to be very deeply hurt. "I'm just a poor country boy who worked his way through school," he said. "I didn't want to sell my company." What's more, he said he would return the purchase money to those Eastern slickers if he could just get his property back—an academic gesture, however florid, now that the whole shebang was destined to be tied up in the courts for years in an agonizingly slow bankruptcy process while creditors' claims against the new corporation mounted to $3,000,000.

The bitter aftermath of the sale was perhaps doubly embarrassing because earlier in that very year novelist Stephen Longstreet, preparing to put the man's success story between covers, had hailed the Senator as embodying in that one ample frame the tradition of Huck Finn, Daniel Boone and, of all people, Jesse James. That unfortunately sweeping endorsement, by the way, came on the heels of a rather delicate en-

The Hadacol Caravan hustling goodwill and the sure cure on a stopover in Columbus. This is Carmen Miranda under the floodlights in the Ohio State Fairgrounds. Senator LeBlanc made a pitch for his "dietary supplement" between the acts. *WWP*

A Hollywood model helps Couzin Dud push his product during 1951 sales drive on the West Coast. *WWP*

counter between Couzin Dud and the AMA, touched off when doctors around the nation began to receive letters signed "Leslie A. Willey, M.D.," identified as Clinical Research Director for The LeBlanc Corporation, offering them samples of Hadacol to be used as an ethical preparation in their practices. The AMA hung out a very fast storm signal, noting that (a) Hadacol was just another "alcoholic elixir" and therefore anything but ethical and (b) Mister Willey was not a doctor at all but just a male nurse who once got arrested for "conducting some sort of emergency hospital" in Newport Beach, California. The reference to an "alcoholic elixir" found some support around that time when the Chicago suburb of Northbrook took steps to confine the sale of Hadacol to liquor stores—and tax it accordingly—on the grounds that too many high school students were getting stoned on it.

While Couzin Dud has been out of it lo, these many years, the last chapter in the giddy Hadacol epic is yet to be written. The thing keeps popping into the news. In 1960, it received some notice when the bankruptcy proceedings finally dragged to a close with $55,000 left in the rusty till—all of it owed to the army of lawyers in the case.

In 1962, a "New Super Hadacol" turned up on the market out of Chicago, guaranteed to be better than anything the doctor ordered for that "let-down, no-life feeling," sleeplessness, nervousness, anemia, exhaustion, iron deficiency, colds and aches and pains in general. In the crucial pep-and-vigor department, the ads suggested that Southerners needed the "blood tonic" more than us Yankees because of dietary deficiencies and climatic conditions, of all things, down there in the land of cotton. This time the government moved much faster than it did in the days when Dudley LeBlanc, who lived to a comfortable seventy-seven before a stroke felled him in 1971, was coining all that money. The FTC pounced on New Super Hadacol with a cease and desist order right off the bat.

THE TIME OF THE GREEN

"I have perfumed my bed with myrrh, aloes, and cinnamon. Come, let us take our fill of love until the morning."

—PROVERBS VII:17–18

Dr. Benjamin Gruskin, chlorophyll's pioneer, didn't live to see the revolution-in-green.

CHLOROPHYLL MAKES the plants grow. Chlorophyll traps the sunlight and transforms it into the chemical energy used, in turn, to manufacture sugars and starches from the carbon monoxide in the air and the water in the soil. Chlorophyll replenishes the atmosphere with the oxygen that sustains the animal and vegetable kingdoms. Chlorophyll is so wonderful that nature itself holds the patent. It is one of man's ever-lasting blessings.

And that's not the whole story. In 1952 chlorophyll was bigger than Scrabble and bigger than almost anything. In 1952, the green gold from the plant world, known to scientists for centuries but never fathomed, came over to our side on a mission fraught with good: It was going to make us all kissing sweet. Hell, it was going to make our 22,000,000 dogs kissing sweet, too. The United States wasn't going to be half safe; it was going to be the most fragrant nation on earth, free of body odor and free of bad breath, a paradise where a man could stuff himself with onions and garlic and inhale bad whiskey and foul tobaccos all day and then go smother some girl with soul kisses and watch her swoon in his arms. Oh, bring back 1952!

There was chlorophyll in eleven toothpastes and tooth powders, thirty-one lozenges and tablets sold as breath sweeteners, nine chewing gums, four mouthwashes, three stick deodorants, one cigarette and eight name-brand dog foods (for dogs who *cared*). There was chlorophyll in mothballs, candles, toilet tissues, soaps, lotions, skin ointments, shampoos, popcorn, mints, diapers, sheets, socks, cleansing cream, inner soles, mints, bed sheets, socks and bubble baths (Schiaparelli's Chloro-Cologne, with Schiaparelli's Shocking fragrance, five dollars for six-ounces).

In a word, we were literally bathing in chlorophyll.

And the end was by no means in sight.

Somebody was talking about introducing the green goddess of the plant world to men's shorts. Wally Frank, Ltd., was trying to find a way to slip chlorophyll into its smokes. Hebrew National went to work on a chlorophyll-treated salami (one cynical observer said the *wurst* was yet to come), and in the Mother Country chemists were toiling to produce a chlorophyll-tinted beer so that a bloke could have a few on the way home without the missus ever knowing it.

Now go back a step from that beautiful year, back to the unsung Finnish-born doctor who found a way to turn chlorophyll into a form soluble in water. Leaving aside the rampant commercial exploitation of his discovery, this man, Dr. Benjamin Gruskin, made a substantial contribution to medical science because chlorophyll, under the trade name of Chloresium, happens to possess true virtues. Lieutenant Colonel Warner F. Bowers of the Army Medical Corps tested it on 400 cases of ulcerated wounds and infections in the mid-Forties and reported that it not only speeded healing and served as an antiodor agent in those cases but halved the time needed for the healing of burns. Gruskin was on the medical faculty of Philadelphia's Temple University when his researches led him to believe that water-soluble chlorophyll, until then in use only as a "safe" coloring agent, could both fight bacteria and stimulate the growth of tissue. With the help of a grant from the Lakeland Foundation of Chicago, he left his teaching post to pursue his quest.

In 1938, the Foundation took out a patent on the discovery in Gruskin's name but the pharmaceutical houses spurned the projected new healer when it was offered to them, and Lakeland let the patent expire. Then, in 1941, an advertising man named O'Neill Ryan Jr., looking around for a small business to invest in, heard about Gruskin's work, talked to both the doctor and the Foundation's people about it, and took out a "use" patent to see what he could do with the chlorophyll formula. Along with Henry T. Stanton, like himself a vice-president in the J. Walter Thompson agency, Ryan organized the Rystan Company. Rystan marketed Chloresium ointment in 1945 but the AMA, viewing the evidence of its therapeutic powers as "insufficient," withheld its blessings for the product until December 9, 1950. Four days earlier, old, all but blind, and yet to realize any real material rewards from his long and lonely labors, Benjamin Gruskin had died in Chicago. Beset by failing health, the doctor had retired from the Rystan Company in 1946. By then, Ryan and Stanton had sunk $650,000 into Chloresium and were staying above water only with the help of Mrs. C. Haskell Bliss, the Dodge heiress, brought in for money transfusions.

Ryan dreamed up the idea of a chlorophyll toothpaste in 1945 but couldn't sell the two top dentifrice manufacturers on it. Later Rystan put out its own toothpaste as an ethical product, chalking up embarrassingly modest sales, and in 1950 the Pepsodent division of Lever Brothers elected to gamble on the idea. Chlorodent, Lever's green toothpaste, hit the market in the winter of 1951 like a fresh breath invented by Coco Chanel. The other big companies swiftly followed suit, and by June of the following year so many Americans were hung up on the green that chlorophyll toothpastes were accounting for 30 percent of the 135-million-dollar-a-year market. By August, the first chlorophyll-flavored dog food was in the stores—along with about a hundred chlorophyll-scented products for those of us outside the canine world.

And, as ever, the debate was on.

Did chlorophyll fight tooth decay as well as sweeten the breath?

The American Dental Association said it did not. Dr. Thomas J. Hill, professor of oral pathology at Western Reserve University and head of the ADA's Therapeutics Council, pointedly asked how long the public would "place its confidence in products whose effectiveness is not in keeping with the values suggested by cleverly prepared advertising copy."

The other chlorophyll products drew much the same verdicts.

The Food and Drug Administration said with a sour breath that there was "no conclusive evidence" that chlorophyll deodorized anything. Dr. Andrew A. Eggston, president-elect of the New York State Medical Society, observed that "chlorophyll has certainly claimed to have swept the nation clean, not only of odors, but by so doing of money as well, and the public is made the innocent dupe of pseudomedical claims besides suffering financial loss." The AMA *Journal* asked doctors to remember that goats somehow smelled pretty bad even though they fed on plant life loaded with nature's own chlorophyll as distinguished from the product the manufacturers were extracting from alfalfa meal for the commercial market. The *Wall Street Journal,* on the same theme, weighed in with this jingle:

> *Why reeks the goat*
> *on yonder hill*
> *Who seems to dote*
> *on chlorophyll?*

Ryan himself wasn't in ecstasy over the excessive exploitation of the Gruskin researches but he had an answer for that kind of barb. He said chlorophyll could be assimilated by the body only in water-soluble form and that a goat would have to eat five tons of grass a day to improve its smell; unfortunately, there were no goats at the time willing to risk their shapes on such a heavy diet.

Chlorophyll products sold at a multimillion-dollar clip all during 1952 even while a rising chorus of medical opinion was striving to drive home the double message that the green stuff couldn't combat body odors because it was not absorbed into the bloodstream and couldn't do anything about such sworn enemies of the breath as onions, garlic and alcohol because those fragrances had their true home in the lungs rather than the mouth. On top of that, a Glasgow University chemist pitted chlorophyll against the odors of foul gases, skunks, onions, garlic and perspiration, and in his report in the *British Medical Journal* put the new American fad down as a loser. That was early in 1953. By September, the price of alfalfa-derived chlorophyll had skidded from $110 a pound to $45 as the green tint began to disappear from the marketplace at a precipitate rate. Two years later, a New York *Times* survey rendered this gloomy verdict: "Chlorophyll is no longer green gold." The *Times* found chlorophyll products down to sales of a paltry 10 million dollars a year—mostly in toothpaste, chewing gum and dyes for soaps—against 120 million during the very green years of 1952 and 1953. Today you can still buy green toothpaste and chlorophyll gum, among other chlorophyll confections, and you can still buy chlorophyll-treated delicacies for your dog if you think it helps. But don't try to find it in men's shorts, kosher salami, beer or tobacco. The color-it-green fad didn't run rampant long enough for any of those items to reach the market.

Part VI

FUN, GAMES AND NONSENSE

THE WONDERFUL OUIJA BOARD

Julia Migenes story: playing one of Zero Mostel's daughters in *Fiddler on the Roof* in 1966, she asked her Ouija board, "What opera will I perform?" The board spelled out *A-N-I-N-A*. "The only Anina I knew was in some Mozart opera I didn't particularly care for, so I passed over that and I kept asking and finally the board spelled out *S-A-I-N-T*." That was in May. In September, Conductor Vincent LaSelva invited the little soprano to sing the lead—Anina— in a revival of Gian-Carlo Menotti's *The Saint of Bleecker Street*. The Mozart thing is something else. You can't blame Ouija for that. *Paul Sann*

"You scoundrel, you have wronged me," hissed the professor. "May you live forever!"

—AMBROSE BIERCE

THE BARON ERIKA KULE PALMSTEIRNA, Swedish minister to London, told this story back in the Thirties in a book called *Horizons of Immortality:*

Not long before his untimely passing in 1856, Robert Schumann entrusted a new concerto to Joseph Joachim, the Hungarian violin prodigy, and told him that he did not want it published for a hundred years. So the manuscript was turned over to the Prussian State Library in Berlin, sealed with the great German composer's injunction, and there it stayed for more than half a century—until Joachim himself died and ran into Schumann in the spirit world. Reunited, the two musicians talked about that concerto, the only one Schumann ever wrote for the violin, and decided there was no reason why it should be withheld from the other world any longer. Simple enough. How does one get that kind of message delivered with no Western Union boys around? Well, that proved to be a fairly elementary trick too. Joachim remembered the family's dependable old Ouija board and slipped the good news along to his grandniece, violinist Yelly d'Aranyi, who dashed right over to the library and fished out the fading score.

That's the way the Baron had it. Miss d'Aranyi said no, there was no such intermediary as Joachim. She said Schumann himself, in direct spirit messages, ordered the manuscript exhumed in March, 1933, while Joachim simply passed the word along that he was all for it. The ill-fated Schumann's own daughter, Eugenie, put down both the Ouija board bit and the other one with a secret she had kept since her childhood. She said the score in question was entrusted to Joachim after her mother, Clara Wieck Schumann, the pianist, fearing that it revealed traces of the deepening insanity evident before the composer's death, discussed it with the violinist and their mutual friend Brahms and decided that she did not want it ever published. To complete the record, the library acquired the Lost Concerto when Joachim died in 1907, a German publisher bought the rights from his heirs in 1933 (over Eugenie Schumann's objections), and Yehudi Menuhin introduced it over here later that year. It is the Concerto for Violin and Orchestra, in D minor, and, alas, it found little favor. Critic Olin Downes, while conceding that the composition had a wistful quality and moments of festive jubilation, strongly suggested that it should have stayed lost.

This brings us, the long way around, to the story of the Ouija board, since the Baron wanted all the credit for the unearthing of Schumann's last work to repose with that interesting little device.

Invented in the gaslit era, the Ouija (we'ja) board was a best seller in this country during World War I, when thousands turned to it in the belief that it could tell them whether loved ones in uniform had survived, and it had a pretty good run a quarter of a century later when another generation of young Americans set sail to fight and die on foreign battlegrounds.

For the Ouija board, we are indebted—if that's the word—to the Fuld brothers, William and Isaac, a pair of Baltimore toymakers who in their more serious moments evidently were paying some heed to the spirit world. William Fuld, in any case, must have had some experience with the table-tipping mumbo jumbo of the mediums of the time, for he was the one who got the bright idea that there ought to be a simple contraption of some kind which would serve the same purpose without the medium's gimmicks and, indeed, without the medium. With Isaac's help, he devised a lapboard the size of a breakfast tray, adorned it with the letters of the alphabet, the numerals from one to ten, and the words "yes" (oui is French for yes and ja is the German for it, hence ouija), "no," and "good-bye." With the board came a tiny three-legged table, called a planchette—the key to the whole thing. All you had to do was place your fingertips lightly against this planchette and it would commence to move across the board, stopping at certain letters—or numbers, if you needed numbers instead of words—until it spelled out the answers to your questions and delivered the message being conveyed to you from the spirit world.

What made the planchette perform such wonders?

The brothers, tight-lipped as well as modest, confined themselves to saying that the "involuntary muscular action" of the players, or "some other agency," did the trick. Other true believers in the spiritual said that thought transference accounted for the planchette's strange capacity for carrying messages from the dead to the living, forecasting things to come, directing necessary courses of action, or even on occasion delivering some rather forceful orders. In his posthumous autobiography, Gilbert K. Chesterton, the English essayist and novelist, termed the Ouija board an instrument of unnatural or supernatural mental activity, and he happened to be a student of spiritual and terrestrial activity himself. In any event, living

devotees of the board told not only of prophecies, learned summations of world events, songs and poetry emerging from the tireless planchette but also of being confronted with such blunt messages as, "What morons you are," "Why don't you use some sense?" or "Go to bed, I'm sick of this."

William Fuld patented his board in 1892, leaving brother Isaac's name off the papers and causing a rupture which was never fully healed, but it took the Great War to get the invention off the ground. This is understandable. Our experience tells us that the mystics, mediums, tea-leaf readers, fortune-tellers, the seance set and all other spooks tend to flourish during periods of crisis when widespread anxiety, distress and uncertainty afflict the masses. Thus when Woodrow Wilson's soldier boys went off to war the Baltimore factory couldn't turn out Ouija boards fast enough to meet the demand even though William Fuld, anticipating large things when his own favorite board told him to "prepare for big business," had enlarged the plant well before the rush set in. The fact is that so many people wanted to know when—or if—Johnny would come marching home again that the United States Senate decided that the Fulds' interesting little gimmick merited the 10 percent tax the Internal Revenue Service happened to be collecting on games at the time. The brothers resented this view so strenuously that they fought the levy all the way to the Supreme Court, only to find those hard-headed Nine Old Men standing four-square behind the government's jaundiced view of their multipurpose invention.

Game or no game, the Ouija board by this time had acquired an ally almost as helpful as the war itself in the person of Mrs. John Howard Curran, wife of a businessman in Mound City, Illinois. Mrs. Curran, who claimed no previous interest or acquaintance with the occult, was entertaining some friends over her board one night when the letters began to spell out Old English terms mixed with some fancy Elizabethan prose. It was several nights later, following successive sessions, before Mrs. Curran could string the board's difficult language into coherent messages—and then she revealed the secret. The words were coming from an uncommonly prolific writer named Patience Worth, who was born in 1625 in Dorsetshire, England, and migrated to New England, where she was done in by some Indian cad before she could take up her quill and commit her great abundance of words to paper. The murdered spinster did not identify herself to Mrs. Curran until she was satisfied that she had found herself an able ghost writer—to use the word the way it should be used, for a change. Once

Mrs. John Howard Curran, the earthly voice of Patience Worth—very dead but grinding out words in torrents via that board. *UPI*

Dorothea Turley, released from Arizona State Penitentiary pending a new trial in the "Ouija Board" death of her husband, conferring with her lawyer, Greg Garcia, in Phoenix in 1934. *UPI*

the introductions were over with, the prose began to flow in a torrent never equaled before or since, not even, say, by the living John O'Hara.

The housewife with the world's busiest Ouija board ultimately reported to the world that between 1913 and 1919 the pent-up Patience had transmitted to her no less than 1,500,000 pearls of wisdom heavy with moral and religious dissertations, garnished with 2,000 items of blank verse and oh, six novels. Mrs. Curran said that on one busy ten-day stretch alone her whirling planchette recorded 30,000 words. She said she could take 2,000 words an hour off the board when both she and the virginal Puritan were on the right wavelength.

In 1919, Dr. James H. Hyslop, secretary of the American Society for Psychical Research, invited Mrs. Curran to New York to perform her wonders in public. Rising to the challenge, the woman reeled off a varied assortment of her distant associates' effusions—Hindu Vedas, Upanishads, some passing observations about such diverse competing scribblers as Confucius and Walt Whitman, and a smattering of Elizabethan tavern tales—but encountered much skepticism in her audience. Dr. Hyslop, of course, happened to be hung up on his own dodge. He was

very large for trance mediums; indeed, he was the man responsible for the depressing revelation that there wasn't a drop of good drinking whiskey, or any drinking whiskey, for that matter, in all of the spirit world. But then the doctor was by no means alone in putting down Mrs. Curran. From many other sources, psychical and otherwise, there were wide suggestions abroad that the long-departed Patience Worth was but a figment of an excessively lively imagination and that Mrs. Curran was batting out all that lore and purple prose with no help at all from the Fuld brothers' contraption. Some psychologists, such as William James of Harvard, mentioned the "alternating personality" situation in which, say, a person sits down at the piano for the first time (while they all laugh) and proceeds to spin out a performance worthy of a virtuoso, or the one in which some other lucky soul, without benefit of Berlitz, suddenly begins to babble with ultimate fluency in a whole assortment of foreign tongues. As far as this sort of thing goes, it was a fact that nothing in the education or background of Mrs. Curran indicated any bent toward the writing trade. It is also noteworthy that Mrs. Curran's emergence coincided with the revival of spiritualism led by

For Mattie Turley, Ouija spelled
tragedy. The girl said the board
instructed her to kill her father
so that her mother could marry
a handsome cowboy.

search, on hand for the demonstration, confessed to
reporters that he found the short-order verse "worthy
of the greatest poets who ever lived." No comparable
endorsement came from the literary circles of the
time. And the first Patience Worth novel, *The Sorry
Tale,* also fell on deaf ears in that lofty community
although the manner of its reputed origins did stir
some interest in the bookstores. So much for Patience
and her tireless transmission belt. Mrs. Curran, who
moved on from Mound City to St. Louis to Fort
Worth and finally to Los Angeles as her fame spread
and her bounty increased, died in December, 1937, at
the age of forty-six. Miss Worth never called to the
bench for a pinch hitter, so the great Niagara of
words ended there.

The Ouija board enjoyed considerable notoriety,
in isolated situations, many years after its World
War I popularity and the boost it got from the Worth-
Curran team. The most celebrated case involved
a beauty contest winner named Dorothea Irene Turley, a New York girl who went into an ill-conceived
union with a sedate old retired naval officer, Ernest
J. Turley, bore him two children, Mattie and David,
and found herself plunked down on a ranch in Arizona, of all places.

On the lonely Southwest plain, so far from the
high life of her native habitat, Dorothea Turley
needed some diversion to help while away the slow
hours. She found two—a Ouija board and a strapping
cowboy. The two objects, animate and inanimate,
happened to go together like milk and honey, and
the board, in fact, had an answer for the fading,
troubled beauty's gnawing dilemma: kill. Kill Mister
Turley with a shotgun. Daughter Mattie, then fifteen,
described how it happened:

Mother asked the Ouija board to decide between father and her cowboy friend. As usual,
the board moved around at first without meaning
but suddenly it spelled out that I was to kill
father. It was terrible. I shook all over. Mother
asked the Ouija board if the shooting would be
successful and it said that it would. She asked if
he would die outright and it said no. We asked
what should be used in the shooting and it said
a shotgun. We asked if we would have the ranch
and it said yes. We asked about the law, and it
said not to fear the law, that everything would
turn out all right. We asked how much the insurance would be and it said five thousand dollars.
I tried to kill Father the next day but I couldn't.
I lost my nerve. A few days later, though, I

Sir Arthur Conan Doyle, Sherlock Holmes's man in
his other life, and Sir Oliver Lodge in the wake of
the war when so many people wanted to reach into
Flanders Field and the other burial grounds to communicate with their lost loved ones. Sir Arthur, by
the way, enjoyed the support of another writing man
on this side of the Atlantic—Basil King, an Episcopalian minister turned novelist. He submitted that a
"spirit personality" had guided his work for many
years but would not identify the man except to say
that he was "very famous."

As for Mrs. Curran, she enjoyed a more favorable
reception in New York in 1928. Bid to the fabled St.
Mark's in the Bouwerie to show off her wares, she
performed before a house packed with disciples, producing poems on split-second notice in response to
requests from the audience. You picked the subject:
Mrs. Curran tuned in Patience Worth and rattled
off something to fit it. Dr. Walter Franklin Pierce,
president of the Boston Society for Psychical Re-

followed him to the corral. I raised the gun and took careful aim between the shoulders but then I lost my nerve again. But I thought of dear mother and what all this would mean to her. I couldn't fail. My hand was trembling awfully but I raised the gun and fired.

Riddled with buckshot from the close-range burst, the hardy old officer summoned up just enough strength to say a thing or two about the deadly contraption wrought by those Baltimore toymakers. He breathed a curse on the Ouija board and said it was always making his wife and daughter do things against their wishes and at times had even compelled him to act against *his* own best judgments. Then he expired.

On the witness stand in the ensuing trial, the single-minded Mattie Turley could not be shaken loose from her story. Was the murder plotted without benefit of the Ouija board and that hell-bent planchette? Was the Other Man in on it? Didn't Mother simply hand her the blunderbuss and tell her to go do in the old guy? No, sir, it wasn't that way at all. "The Ouija board told me to do it so that Mama can be free to marry a handsome cowboy, that's all that happened." Didn't she know that the law dealt with people who killed other people, even when it was in the family? "Mother told me the Ouija board couldn't be denied and that I would not even be arrested for doing it."

While there had been some strange court rulings on the immunity of the magic board elsewhere, such as the Chicago decision which held that a woman could not be prosecuted for uttering a slander against a neighbor on good old Ouija's directions, the Arizona jury found mother and daughter guilty of murder. Mrs. Turley drew a ten- to twenty-five-year prison sentence but three years later, in 1934, the higher courts reversed it and turned her free. The hand that held the rifle was in reform school then, having been consigned to those unfriendly premises, so dreary in contrast to the pretty little Cross Bar Ranch out there under the sky, until she should attain the age of twenty-one.

In 1932, while those determined Turley women were safely locked away, an even more doleful story of the evil inherent in some Ouija boards (do you suppose the factory goofed now and then?) came out of Kansas City. Herbert Hurd, a seventy-seven-year-old railroad worker, did away with his wife Nellie because—

The spirits told her through her Ouija Board that I was too fond of another woman and had given her fifteen thousand dollars of a hidden fortune. The Ouija board lied. I never was friendly with another woman and I never had fifteen thousand dollars, but Nellie beat me and burned me and tortured me into confessing all those lies, so finally I had to kill her.

In a less gory and more patriotic context, the Ouija board came into the news briefly in 1941 when John Geotis, a filling station attendant from Madison, New Jersey, presented himself for enlistment in the armed services.

"I want to learn a trade," the youth said, "and my Ouija board told me the Army was the place to do it." What with war on the horizon, the recruiting sergeant eagerly accepted the proffered signature, but then a catch developed. Geotis said he really didn't mean to join up unless he could take his Ouija board with him. The sergeant called on higher authority but found there was nothing in the regulations to cover such a contingency, so a test of the board's efficacy was deemed to be in order. A nearby department store furnished one and the halfway recruit went to work on the planchette. Well, damned if the board didn't spell out a most welcome, double-barreled, backward-to-forward communiqué: The Nazis would lose the war, and those beleaguered but sturdy Greeks would hold out until the blue Mediterranean froze over, or something like that.

The Army thereupon decided to take John Geotis *and* his Ouija board.

On the home front, once the infamy of Pearl Harbor was upon us, the Fulds' long-playing lapboard, with the brothers expired and very likely not even talking to each other in the spirit world, enjoyed a healthy commercial resurgence. Turned out by a dozen companies or so, the board picked up sales so steadily that in one five-month stretch in 1944 Macy's alone pushed 22,000 across the counters in its games department, and that represented a very small proportion of the sales around the nation in that year. The thing sold well right into V-E Day and V-J Day and then went back into the racks. Again, years of nominal sales lay ahead, but the end was nowhere in sight. Parker Brothers, appropriately situated in Salem, Massachusetts, acquired the patents in 1966 and found the board moving nicely in the three- and four-dollar and deluxe seven-dollar models.

The projected 1967 sale—without heraldry of any kind—came to 2,000,000. How much did the constantly escalating Vietnam war have to do with it? Nobody could say with any authority.

The Ouija board did enjoy a brief but spectacular excursion into the news columns in 1956. The will of Helen Dow Peck of Bethel, Connecticut, disclosed that she had bequeathed the bulk of her earthly holdings, a respectable $178,000, to lucky John Gale Forbes, whose name had been spelled out for her by her trusty board way back in 1919. Well, there were two things wrong with the best-laid plans of this moderately well-heeled matron as she departed our vale of tears at the age of eighty-four. First, a court-ordered search failed to turn up any John Gale Forbes in the real world. Second, nine nieces and nephews of the deceased, banded together in the common cause, engaged counsel and argued with some passion that even if the outlander turned up among the living, the full proceeds of Mrs. Peck's estate properly belonged to the kinfolk. They won their case.

It was the most stunning reversal suffered by the Ouija board since Eugenie Schumann blew the whistle on that spooky Swedish Baron.

But there was more to come, like the case of Clara Hoover, seventy-one-year-old heiress to a tanning industry fortune, who liked to while away the hours around that Fuld plaything in New York. With her friend and masseuse, Mrs. Margaret Faulkner, doing the translating, the widow was directed to start shoveling some cash along to a gypsy named Yuma, go-between for an unidentified "good angel." When the tab reached $59,285 Miss Hoover's faith in the board began to wilt. The next stop was the State Supreme Court, where a jury drew a sour notice for using forty minutes before bringing in a 10–2 decision directing the "good angel"—Mrs. Faulkner—to give all that money back. Justice Jacob Markowitz said three minutes should have been sufficient for passing on a case so "palpable with fraud." The gypsy—a commission merchant, no doubt—wasn't named in the civil suit and got off scot-free.

THE YEAR OF THE HOOP

YOU SEE, the Australians had this three-foot bamboo ring they were using in gym classes, just to keep everybody limber, and in 1957 the thing started to sell in the stores and the tidings somehow seeped across the Pacific to California. Richard P. Knerr and Arthur K. (Spud) Melin heard about it, and they run an outfit called Wham-O in San Gabriel. Now a company with a name like that could only be making a breakfast cereal or toys, and Wham-O made toys. So Knerr and Melin had the shop slap together some Hula Hoops out of scrap wood.

"First we tried it on our own children," Knerr explained, "and then we took it into the neighborhood, the best testing laboratory there is for toys. Well, the kids just wouldn't put the hoop down. It had the longest 'play-value' we had ever seen on any toy we produced, so we put it out on a test basis."

And how about the grown-ups privileged to know the two thirty-three-year-old proprietors of the Wham-O Manufacturing Company?

"Well, we tried it out at cocktail parties," said Knerr, "and we found the folks had to have a couple of drinks in them to take a whack at it."

Martinis, one has to assume.

Anyway, Wham-O's new Hula Hoop for the masses, in brightly colored polyethelene plastic, selling for $1.98 and costing about 50 cents to produce, took off more like a rocket. Turning out 20,000 a day, Wham-O fell way behind on orders. Pretty soon there were about forty competitors in the field, among them Art Linkletter's Spin-a-Hoop, the Louis Marx company's Hoop Zing, and Brian Specialties' Hooper Dooper—and that wasn't enough to fill the demand when the craze reached its peak in the spring of 1958. It is conceivable, one may suppose, that our Cold War friends in the Kremlin viewed that fact as some kind of commentary on our vaunted production machinery, but there is a limit. The Toy News Bureau reported that 20,000,000 hoops—say 30 million dollars' worth—had been snapped up by September. Later figures put total 1958 sales at 45 million dollars, suggesting an almost total saturation among the 30,000,000 youngsters the manufacturers were aiming at in the five-to-fourteen-year-old market. It was the Year of the Hula Hoop, and why not? Along with its low price, the plastic ring wished on us by the Aussies had the great virtue of simplicity. "Hug the hoop to the backside. Push hard with the right

114

Actress Rita Gam and TV's Steve Allen made one hoop do at a party in Sardi's Manhattan restaurant in 1958. *New York Post*

Movie actress Jane Russell had no trouble with it.

Neither did Sister Mary Pius, cheered along by other Benedictine Sisters at the Christ King Convent in Oklahoma City. *WWP*

Starlet Roberta Shore put her English sheep dog through the paces as the fad swept the movie colony.

This is a playground scene in New York. It was duplicated all over the nation. *New York Post*

The monkey on the left couldn't quite handle the thing.

In spring training, the Los Angeles Dodgers' Steve Garvey loosens up with the hoop.

hand. Now rock. Don't twist. Just swing it." Nearly everybody got into the act. Hollywood's Jane Russell exhibited her considerable skill with the hoop for the still cameras; so did Debbie Reynolds. Red Skelton performed in one on TV, the medium most responsible for its wild sales. Françoise Sagan, then somewhere pretty close to the line between the kids and the grownups for all her literary fame, took to it in France. Max Schmeling, the aging ex-heavyweight champion, mastered it in Germany. In Japan, where it was fated to be barred from the streets as a dangerous instrument, a "hura hoopu" was presented to Prime Minister Kishi on his sixty-second birthday.

But the adults were just butting in, as usual. The kids ran off with all the prizes. In Boston, Bobby Travers, ten, ignoring the handicap of a broken arm, kept a hoop whirling for four hours (18,200 turns, somebody figured out) to beat a record set by little Suzy Gliddens down in Knoxville, Tennessee. Suzy had managed 13,000 turns before exhaustion set in during the third hour. In Jackson, Michigan, an eleven-year-old boy scoffed at those achievements because Bobby and Suzy were using a single hoop, whereas he could keep fourteen going at once without even raising a sweat. As usual, not everyone was amused. One school board in New Jersey barred the hoop on the grounds that the kids who were hooked on it came to class too wound up. In Akron, Ohio, there was dismal news on the adult front: A fifty-eight-year-old matron broke a hip working out with one of the plastic rings.

The cables at the time also were sizzling with assorted items of intelligence about the hoop.

The *British Medical Journal* reported an increasing incidence of neck pains and wrenched upper abdomens. The Indonesians, more concerned about morals than minor injuries, banned the hoop altogether, having found that the contortions of its devotees "might stimulate passion." In Taipei, Formosa, a hoop demonstration drew 7,000 persons to the local stadium and almost caused a riot. The Russians, in character, viewed the innocent toy as a further demonstration of "the emptiness of American culture" and termed it a capitalist-inspired fad aimed at degrading the masses. The Red Chinese News Agency (Moscow and Peiping were getting along better in those days) damned party newspapers which were "boosting the nauseating craze." Tito's Yugoslavia, maintaining its independence from the rest of the Communist world, let the hoop in. So did Poland and East Germany.

Over here, there was much probing into the meaning of the Hula Hoop explosion. Dr. Gerald T. Miles, head of the child guidance unit at the Karen Horney psychiatric clinic in New York, explained it this way: "When a child first begins to draw a human body, it starts with a circle. A favorite game—ring around the rosy—is played in a circle. The child feels secure in the family circle." Hence the affinity for the circular hoop, see? Other deep thinkers were rebelling against their parents for some vague reason. It was not clear, of course, what the adult Hula Hoopers were rebelling against.

For better or worse, we didn't have to find out.

The Hula Hoop, perhaps the greatest flash-selling item in all the history of toys, began to fade from the scene with a speed equaling its dizzy flight to popularity. A nationwide survey by the *Wall Street Journal* in November, 1958, produced a headline that said HOOPS HAVE HAD IT and that obit notice stood up—but only for nine years. The never-say-die Melin and Kneer resurrected the thing in 1967, and you know what happened. A new generation of little ones began whirling around. The Hoop is still with us today, albeit in more modest numbers.

THE WAY THE
BALL BOUNCES...
AND
THE FRISBEE FLIES

Super Ball isn't
really that dangerous.

STAY WITH Wham-O for another minute. You know that an outfit like that doesn't just lie down and die over a little reversal in its fortunes. An outfit like that knows that somewhere, in some top secret laboratory, some superbrain—tireless, totally dedicated, totally brilliant, totally and purposely obscure—is toiling into the dark hours to produce some little thing, *any* little thing, which will help his fellowman.

And it happened.

This time civilization's benefactor proved to be Norman Stingley, a research chemist for the Bettis Rubber Company in Whittier, California. Toying around with high resiliency synthetics in his spare time, Stingley fashioned a crude rubber ball, dropped it from shoulder level and observed happily that it would keep bouncing for a minute or so. You know that even a tennis ball won't stay in action for more than ten seconds unless you're flailing it with a racket, but there was something even more wonderful about Norman Stingley's creation: The ball took the craziest bounces. Stingley offered it to his employers but the word from on high was no, the thing keeps falling apart. So the man took his brainchild to

Wham-O and it went back to the drawing board. Another year of concentrated effort solved the problem of durability. Now Wham-O had a ball that would last approximately forever. What would you call a ball like that? Super Ball, of course, bouncing longer and higher—indeed, as high as three stories—and more unpredictably than anything ever known up to that time.

The rest is history, however fleeting. For the boy, or the man, who had everything, Super Ball (98 cents, counting Norman Stingley's one-cent royalty) was *the* thing to buy in 1965, and millions bought it. "There's no mystery to this fad," Richard Knerr said. "We just stimulated the people."

It was a pretty good piece of stimulation at that, reaching into the most exalted levels. The word was that no less a personage than McGeorge Bundy, then Special Assistant to President Lyndon B. Johnson for National Security Affairs, had developed the habit of repairing to the basement of his Washington home every night to shake off such cares of state as that "dirty little war" in Vietnam, getting bigger every day by then, with a Super Ball. This intelligence in itself was

118

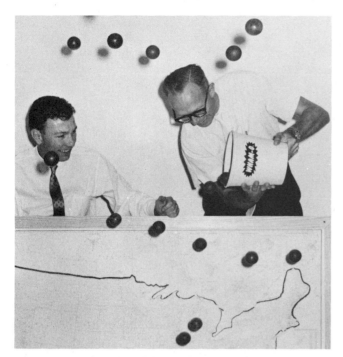

Wham-O's Spud Melin and his research-and-development director, Ed Headrick, test the Super Ball.

And who's this? Only Jimmy Carter. The President happened to wander out to the White House's South Lawn during a staff picnic in June 1978 and somebody threw him a Frisbee. No, he didn't catch it. *WWP*

The winners in the 1978 World Frisbee championship competition: Krae Van Sickle, seventeen, of New York (above), and Laura Engel, eighteen, of Venice, California (top).

enough to make Wham-O forget that damned Instant Fish Kit, even though that ball lost its bounce in the stores after a relatively short run and had to go back to the warehouse—mothballed, you might say—for a twelve-year rest. Brought back in 1977, it started to sell again in satisfactory if not sensational quantities. But, then, that's the way the ball bounces with our fads.

Wham-O, named for a long-forgotten slingshot which was the company's first product when it ventured into the fiercely competitive toy jungle in 1948, must also be blamed for the Frisbee. If you haven't been hit in the head by one of those playthings in the past decade, you've been indoors too much. This plastic flying saucer doesn't always take kindly to direction. Properly thrown to the party on the other end, however, it will go as far as 75 yards or so and come back to you unless some small boy runs off with it. The Frisbee Baking Company of Bridgeport, Connecticut, said the idea must have come from one of the hundreds of satisfied customers who long ago ceased to return its tin pie plates because they found it was more fun to play catch with them. Wham-O, for its part, disdains any link with anything as mundane as a pie plate, noting that the idea was brought in by Fred Morrison, a Los Angeles building inspector and former Air Force pilot who never in his life hooked anything from Frisbee & Co. The flying saucer, by the way, was a very hot item on such Ivy League campuses as Princeton when it came out, although the college set tired of it with more than its usual speed.

A small matter.

The Frisbee, a seventy-nine cent item at the outset and now $1.59 unless you want to splurge on the more professional intermediate disc that costs $3.99, was here to stay. Today it is Wham-O's top-selling product, with several million a year moving across the counters and total sales past the 100 million mark to build Wham-O's 1977 income for all of its products up to $20,776,000. The Fifth Annual World Frisbee Disc Championships, complete with a catch-and-fetch competition for dogs, was staged at the Rose Bowl in Pasadena in August 1978 with the world's top hundred performers on hand. Some of the events, beyond distance, accuracy and MTA (maximum time aloft): Disc Golf, with hazards and obstacles to skirt; Guts, a team game where the trick is to get your saucer up to 90 mph or so to deny the enemy a clean one-hand catch, and Ultimate, which is some kind of mixture of football, basketball and soccer.

Frisbee mania, needless to say, has not failed to produce at least one physical malady. This is the Frisbee finger, the middle one on your throwing hand—apt to blister, tear or turn embarrassingly callous because the disc develops rough edges bouncing along concrete surfaces. The better medical minds know of only one cure: complete abstinence until that finger is in one piece again. A tall order for the true Frisbee addict.

THE SKATEBOARD RAGE

Anyone for skateboarding? Here's Katharine Hepburn on an outing in Beverly Hills in the Sixties. Her sister's son, Jack Grant, got the athletic film star hooked on it. He made the picture.

Grab your board and go sidewalk surfin' with me,
Don't be afraid to try the newest sport around,
It's catchin' on in every city and town.
So get your girl and take her tandem down the street.
Don't you know you're an asphalt athlete?
—LIBERTY RECORDS
Sea of Tunes Publishing Co.

JAN AND DEAN recorded that one in 1965 and no less than 700,000 people bought it. How could it fail? The only item missing in the raging skateboard fad at that moment, since there was no shortage of plaster casts, splints and tapes in the hospitals, was its own theme song. In some cities around the nation, police were confiscating skateboards as a menace to life and limb, but the things were selling so fast that the trade publications listed the industry in the 100-million-dollar-a-year class. The Nash Manufacturing Company in Beverly Hills, running full blast six days a week, was shipping 100,000 a day that spring and, on the side, waging a successful battle to keep the Burbank City Council from passing an ordinance to outlaw the skateboard. A Philadelphia toy manufacturer, Leon Ponnock, president of the Metal Masters Company, confessed his own bewilderment over what was happening. "Somebody showed me a skateboard last year and I thought they were nutty," Ponnock said, "but they're selling like popsicles. The craze has shot up like a rocket from Cape Kennedy. Orders are coming in so fast we're unable to keep up with them."

Where did it all begin? On the West Coast, where else? Back in 1961, California's surfers bolted skate wheels to tapered slats of wood to keep in trim and sharpen their aquatic skills on land with a variation of the old soapbox scooter, which dated all the way back to the ball-bearing skate wheel's first appearance in 1880. The surfers, of course, disdained handles or the orange crate the kids always used to support themselves on the scooters; for their purpose they needed the no-hands action, since the essence of surfing is balance. The wave-riding set enjoyed a kind of monopoly on the skateboards until 1963 when the thing came on the market in models ranging from $1.79 to $14. Did $14 seem expensive for a piece of wood three feet long and eight inches wide with four roller skate wheels underneath it? Not in the plush economy of Mr. Johnson's blossoming Great Society. In no time at all, as the "asphalt athletes" emerged in full force, Macy's in New York showed off a thirty-inch "full precision board" with fiber-glass wheels and special bearings for a nice round $29.95. For the even more affluent, one company put out a motorized "Tiger Skate" priced at $49.94. In all, there were ninety-two manufacturers in the field by 1964—and that wasn't enough to keep up with the demand. It was as if someone finally had discovered the better mousetrap.

Fourteen-year-old Laurie Turner of Berkeley, California, won one of the scholarship prizes in the International Skateboard Championship at Anaheim in 1965. *WWP*

You had to watch yourself on the streets when the skateboard made its comeback in the mid-Seventies. This is a Los Angeles scene. *WWP*

This is the belly whopper, performed by Mark Strickland of St. Petersburg, Florida.

Nobody less than Hollywood's Katharine Hepburn, then in her fifty-sixth year, was photographed on a skateboard. Her sister's son, Jack Grant, introduced the actress to the sport while working on a book about it. The lithe Miss Hepburn, always in condition, quickly mastered the thing, but she had a question for her nephew: "Supposing I take a spill—and I am found there—what on earth would I say?" What, indeed? Perhaps fortunately, there weren't too many adults confronted with the problem.

The skateboard was strictly for the younger set— let's say from the cradle to the campus—as it fanned out across the nation and, incidentally, spread to Canada, Israel, Britain, Ireland and South America. The capital, of course, remained in sunny California. The First Annual Skateboard Championships, in May, 1965, drew 999 entrants and filled Anaheim's 10,000-seat La Palma Stadium for two days running. There every variety of skill went on display: the "coffin" (starting from a standing position but finally riding the board flat on your back with your arms crossed), hand and head stands, the kick turn (lifting the board's nose and piloting it left or right while pivoting on the back wheels), switching the position of the feet and, last but by no means the least risky, the little trick in which the highly skilled jumped over a four-foot "limbo bar" and came down, hopefully, on their boards instead of their backsides.

Inevitably, outside of the formal competitions, there was tragedy. The half dozen listed deaths included two five-year-olds—a girl who ran into a moving police prowl car while skateboarding near Manhattan's Central Park and a Philadelphia boy also hurtled into an auto's path. And everywhere broken bones were in evidence. In suburban New Rochelle, New York, doctors counted twenty-two fractures in as many days, while a single Los Angeles hospital reported an average of twenty-five cases a month. And so a howl went up. The California Medical Association put out a special bulletin called "Skateboards, a New Medical Menace." The AAA, backed by the more worried insurance companies, warned drivers against the new hazards confronting them. The National Safety Council joined in the outcry, observing that skateboarders were colliding at random with trees, autos, stone walls—and, of course, the innocent pedestrian.

And so the law went to work. In Bountiful, Utah, and Jacksonville, Florida, the police that spring began to confiscate all skateboards as a public nuisance. Niagara County in upstate New York barred them from the streets. New York City banned them from Central Park to safeguard the strolling masses. Fort Lauderdale, Florida, and Chattanooga, Tennessee, put sharp limits on the areas where the boards could be used. In Moorestown, New Jersey, they were barred from the shopping mall after two women customers were banged up in the parking lot. Cornell University ordered them off the campus, while the town itself, Ithaca, ruled them off the streets. In Hempstead, Long Island, the Superintendent of Schools made a public appeal to parents to take all skateboards away from their children. In Shrewsbury Borough on New Jersey's North Shore, the police impounded all the boards and then returned them with a warning that second offenders would get back only the wooden slat, not the skates.

There was no question, then, about the adult backlash, even as skateboard clubs were springing up everywhere and the *Quarterly Skateboarder,* the devotees' magazine, was confidently predicting a place in the next Olympic Games for the sport. That had a rather ambitious sound, especially since the fad began to erode in 1966. As with nearly all the other overnight sensations that spring up in our midst, we lost interest somewhere along the way. The hunk of wood with the wheels under it had seen its one and only 100-million-dollar year, but, alas, the story doesn't end there. Just six years later the skateboard turned up again—in its birthplace (where else?)—and kicked off another nationwide sweep, bigger than ever. So big, indeed, that in 1976 a World Professional Skateboarding Championship in the Long Beach Arena, backed by manufacturers of the device, drew contestants from all over the landscape and sent at least one youth home not only jubilant but $20,000 richer. He was Skitch Hitchcock, twenty-four, a native Californian from Laguna Miguel. But it was hard to tell how far ahead he stood. He said he had been riding those boards since he was in knee pants and used up as much as $10 a week just on new wheels.

So we're back where we started—in spades. With price tags now ranging all the way up to $125 for 60 mph fiberglass specials, the industry has sold as many as 15 million boards in a single year, which adds up to 300 million dollar's worth. What the medical profession has coined is something else. The skateboard made Number 7 on the list of our most hazardous products in 1977 (the bicycle holds the top spot). The National Injury Information Clearing House, polling data from hospital emergency wards, counted no fewer than 140,070 casualties for a single semester even with more and more of the addicts using safety equipment—crash helmets, wrist guards, kneepads—costing anywhere from $35 to $75. In 1978, citing at least twenty-five deaths and thousands of injuries, the consumer affairs division of the Americans for Democratic Action petitioned the Consumer Product Safety Commission either to ban the boards altogether or mount a campaign to get local laws passed restricting skateboarders to specially designated parks.

Dr. James Nicholas, director of the Institute of Sports Medicine and Athletic Trauma at New York's Lenox Hill Hospital but perhaps better known as Joe Namath's knee surgeon, virtually a full-time job when Broadway Joe was throwing the football for the Jets, put out a guarded word for the defense: "We think skateboards are good fun and develop agility and balance, but unless one is equipped with these there is a high risk of potential injury."

To put it mildly.

THE MAH-JONGG INVASION

You could go all the way with Mah-Jongg, like doing the whole Chinese bit. *UPI*

DID CONFUCIUS (551–479 B.C.) relax over a game of mah-jongg when his struggles against the tyranny of a corrupt feudal state wore him down? Or was the game unknown before the T'ang Dynasty (618–906)? Or was it evolved some five or six hundred years later by a Ming Dynasty general who needed something to divert his troops to keep them from killing each other when they had no wars to fight? Or was it the invention, long before all that, of a Ningpo fishing tycoon who wanted to take the minds of his hired help off the cruel sea?

Alas, Chinese history, heavy on culture, disdainful of such idle pursuits as gambling, furnishes no clues.

Mah-jongg came to America out of the blue in the early Twenties—an ideal import in the Lawless Decade because it was a splendid time killer which combined the strategy of poker with the luck of dice and the skill of bridge. Nobody asked how it

all began; the question was, where do we buy it? In 1922, Shanghai sent over 131,412 sets and didn't even come close to meeting the demand. The figure for 1923 was 1,505,080—in all shapes and sizes, including some with inlaid tiles selling for as much as $500. There were estimates that from 5 to 15 million people were hung up on the game, and there was talk of broken homes—or just broken noses—because mah-jongg is immensely confusing and thus subject to much argument. Regardless of the conflict, mah-jongg was suddenly *in*. The great mass of colored tiles, paying off on "honors," or points, had a particular fascination for the women. For a while, at least, the tired businessman didn't have to fret over his wife's whereabouts while he was at the office. She was hunched over a mah-jongg set with three of her neighbors, endlessly drawing tiles in the hunt for that elusive perfect fourteen-tile hand—four matched sets of threes and an extra pair. In China, men would gamble their last sampan in that quest, or even the clothes on their backs. There were stories out of the Orient about sums as high as $500,000 changing hands in a single night in the mah-jongg parlors. The National Christian Council of China urged United States churchmen to stand four-square against mah-jongg for this reason, but there were no dire consequences here. The game was too complex to Occidentals, apparently, for large-stake gambling. Its appeal on this side rested more on its exotic paraphernalia than any promise of sudden riches.

In the brief heyday of the game, mah-jongg was outselling radios, with the free-spending populace, fresh from a war and a brief depression, cheerfully paying the 10 percent tax the government imposed on all sets costing more than five dollars. Then, midway into 1924, the craze began to slide as fast as it had started. One of the prime importers found itself overextended and filed papers in bankruptcy, blaming another new fad—the crossword puzzle—for the overnight loss of interest in mah-jongg. By that time, the price of the $500 set had dropped to $100, and there weren't many takers.

But the game continues to have some devotees to this day. In 1941, the National Mah-Jongg League, organized by Mrs. Viola L. Cecil, put forth the view that our ever-mounting divorce rate could be cut down markedly if more couples played mah-jongg instead of bridge. The league said that pastime was generating husband-and-wife warfare on a scale virtually unknown among the wedded couples who were teaming up behind those little tiles. In 1949, the game won some notice in the public prints when the Chinese Reds outlawed it as a waste of time and, to make the point stick, picked up seventy underground mah-jongg players in Shanghai and condemned them to mop-and-broom duty in the public lavatories. No such dire measures would ever have to be invoked here, because mah-jongg never imperiled the republic in any way; it just kept millions of women out of the kitchen back in the Twenties, and it's keeping a few out of the kitchen even now. For some reason which eludes this author, mah-jongg always has had a strong appeal among women of the Jewish faith. Item: in the frigid winter of 1975 the first annual tournament of the American Mah-Jongg Players' Association was staged at the celebrated Grossinger Hotel in New York's Catskills and drew seventy women, some from as far away as Ohio. The crown went to Jane Snyder, a fifty-year-old housewife from Syracuse. But the lady paid a stiff price. She had ten pounds to lose when she got back home. All gained in three days—and all strictly kosher.

Peter Hodgson shows how his Silly Putty picks an impression off newsprint.

SILLY PUTTY?

PETER HODGSON—MARKET researcher, statistician in the Wendell Willkie campaign for the Presidency in 1940, copywriter—had the great good fortune one day in 1949 to drop into Ruth Fallgatter's toy shop in New Haven, Connecticut. The shop happened to be the last account of the expiring advertising agency where Hodgson was working at the time. The lady proprietor, on the lookout for adult toys, showed Hodgson a gumlike substance which a chemical engineer friend of hers, James Wright, had stumbled upon while working with silicon compounds in an effort to find a source of rubber for the General Electric Corporation. Hodgson didn't know what to make of the thing or what to call it, except a "gooey gupp," but he found it quite intriguing. It could be stretched into any shape, like clay, or molded together and bounced like a ball. It picked up the image of anything you pressed it against. What's more, you could make anything you wanted out of it, even a likeness of your mother-in-law if you had that kind of sculpting talent and craved a likeness of your mother-in-law in gooey gupp.

Well, General Electric wanted no part of it when Mr. Wright came up with the thing, and Ruth Fallgatter couldn't see fooling around with it. Hodgson could. He wrapped it in a plastic egg, called it Silly Putty and talked the Doubleday bookshops into displaying it. Did the adults buy it? "One manager," Hodgson recalls, "reported that it was the biggest thing in the shops since *Forever Amber* and *Peyton Place*." The kids took it away from the adults in due course, naturally, and after a while Silly Putty was drawing complaints about the thing sticking in hair curls and on dungarees, so Hodgson had the substance changed to prevent it from sticking or staining.

Fad? In this country, Europe, India and South Africa, 32,000,000 boxes of Silly Putty were sold in the first five years or so, and Hodgson had a 5 million-dollar-a-year business, since boosted to 7 million or so with separate manufacturing facilities in Frankfurt, Germany, to handle the overseas traffic. The Canadian-born Hodgson's home-base plant in North Branford, Connecticut, employed 125 people after a while, and until his death at sixty-four in 1976 he and his wife, Margaret, lived the good life on an eighty-eight-acre estate perched on a scenic hilltop in nearby Madison. In a word, there was nothing so silly about that putty.

ONLY
IN AMERICA:

The Pet Rock and Pop Rocks

Gary Dahl, filthy rich after his Pet Rock swept the country, enjoys a beer on the house in his own Carry Nation bar in California. *WWP*

SILLY PUTTY's one thing—even an art form, if you will—but how silly can you get?

Well, take the case of Gary Dahl, of Los Gatos, California. He was a free lance advertising man ("that's another word for being broke," in his own words) with lots of free time on his hands. He spent a fair amount of that time in bars, a natural habitat for him because his mother ran some watering holes in Seattle and Spokane, Washington, when he was growing up. A few years back, he was coming on forty and going nowhere when, over a drink, he had a good clean idea. Had to do with household pets. There's nothing wrong with cats and dogs, Dahl mused, but you've got to tidy up after your felines and take the hounds out in all kinds of weather, not to mention the incidental cash outlays. How about a pet that required no care and feeding, never had to be kept away from your more treasured furnishings, required no housebreaking, and made no demands of any kind on your love or your time?

Hell, any idiot could have thought of it, even without a blast or two to shake up his mental processes.

A rock.

Just a smooth little rock—say, the size of a hen's egg.

The Pet Rock.

Think about it, fellow workers.

You could carry it around, stroke it at will, teach it tricks—like, say, how to play dead or roll down a hill—or just keep it on the mantlepiece or your coffee table. Or anywhere, for that matter, even that empty pillow in your bed if you had a bed with an empty pillow. You would have to have rocks in your head not to dash out and buy yourself a companion like that for the lonely hours, no?

Yes.

Gary Dahl owns his own bar now and is doing his drinking at the wholesale price, because *the* hot Christmas item in the stores in 1975 was the Pet Rock, neatly packaged in a cardboard container and costing a piddling $3.89 even with a free manual thrown in on how to take care of it. At one department store in New York a dejected executive moaned to a reporter, "Oh, if we only had a thousand more . . ." This theme was echoed across the country and was still being heard here and there into the following year. Indeed, 1977 was upon us before the madness passed.

The former free-lance ad man had no complaints. He had made a couple of million dollars, even with the price on his brainchild dipping down to $2 before finally sinking to its proper level: no dollars.

In its heyday, the Pet Rock produced the inevitable spinoffs.

The Emerson Unitarian Church in California's San Fernando Valley set up $5 funerals for deceased—or let's say unwanted—rocks in a fund-raising drive. The services included the playing of the hymn "Rock of Ages" or, for the less bereaved, rock music. There is no evidence that any large influx of customers showed up for that drive.

In Detroit, Mrs. Jackie Hopper staked out some space in a parking lot and opened up a cemetery for used-up Pet Rocks with white concrete blocks to serve as headstones. She said the burial ground, free for all comers, drew twenty-three customers in no time at all, but you had to take that one with a grain of salt. The Hoppers owned a bar across the street from that lot. Dig? We bury your rock and you hold the wake at our bar.

Gary Dahl's brainchild, born in a bottle for all practical purposes, had come full circle.

The same could not be said for another "rock," not to fondle but to pop into your mouth, that actually dated way back but did not invade our homes on any awesome scale until the Pet Rock had started its downhill slide. This is the General Foods Corporation's Pop Rocks Crackling Candy, a source not just of some juicy income but some fairly heavy controversy as well. The credit for Pop Rocks—or the blame—goes to William A. Mitchell, a research scientist in food technology who wound up with no less than fifty patents in his name before withdrawing from the giant food cartel's laboratories in 1976 after thirty-five years of ceaseless toil spared from public view.

The wavy-haired, smiling Mitchell, now sixty-seven and still a consultant to GFC, stumbled upon his big, or little, brainchild twenty-three years ago, but the corporation waited two decades before test-marketing the product among school children in Canada and happily discovering that it was an item closer to gold bullion than candy. More than 500 million packets of the thing had been sold around the world before the calendar turned on 1978 even though the hard sell actually didn't even get under way until that December.

What is Pop Rocks? Are you ready for this?

That Mitchell creation isn't anything meant for the younger generation to eat. In fact, it can't be eaten, because all that crackling boxed candy does is pop and fizzle on the tongue and go away.

Like there is almost nothing to swallow. You might classify it with chewing gum, the only difference being that a stick of gum can satisfy its more ardent addicts for hours and hours whereas Pop Rocks disappears like a swig of soda pop. Not into the gullet, mind you, but into thin air.

Only a couple of months had passed, of course, before the inevitable rumors began to spread across the countryside.

Pop Rocks can cause cancer.

Pop Rocks can make your stomach explode.

Pop Rocks can blow you away.

The General Foods chiefs of staff assembled in their war room in White Plains, New York, didn't lose five minutes launching the counterattack, throwing the ever-cheerful and endlessly energetic inventor right into the battle line. The enemy was to be repulsed in a two-pronged assault.

General Mitchell himself, disguised in civvies, was dispatched on a speaking tour to assure the populace, old and young, that the secret ingredients in his baby all bore the stamp of approval of the best scientific minds in the FDA.

Simultaneously, a small fortune in fat display ads blossomed forth in forty-three newspapers, and not just in the hinterlands by any means. The heavy money went to such prestigious journals as the *New York Times* in the form of an open letter to parents, addressed "Dear Mom & Dad" and bearing Mitchell's personal imprimatur. A sampling from the crisply homespun big type should suffice here:

I have brought a lot of fun into the world with Pop Rocks, I guess, but I am writing this letter because I want to assure you that the product is a safe one. Safety is one of my real concerns. I have seven children of my own, and 14 grandchildren.

You have probably heard a lot of wild rumors about Pop Rocks. I can assure you that we have investigated, and there is nothing to worry about. It seems to be the nature of this "fun" product that it also attracts rumors. . . .

I think that is because it has the image of an exciting and mysterious product that causes funny little sensations when you put a tiny bit on your tongue. The expression on people's faces when they do this for the first time is fun to watch, as you know. . . .

Pop Rocks is a candy. . . . The carbonated fizz in

the candy, that causes the funny tingling, is equal to less than one-tenth the amount in a can of soda pop.

My seven kids grew up with Pop Rocks [Author's note: The text did not say how tall or how round the Mitchell offspring grew]. I invented it in 1956 and I would make a little bit of it every once in a while to have it around the house for birthday parties and other fun occasions. I became very popular in our neighborhood! . . .

You know, you hear a lot of people talk about how "serious" business is, that people who work for big corporations don't have very much "fun."

Well, "Pop Rocks" is a proof that this isn't so. This is . . . a safe and fun product.

That straight-from-the-heart summation for the defense closed with an invitation to one and all to write to the inventor-General himself at the General Foods GHQ if there were any questions left unanswered. The only thing missing was the ZIP code but, then, that may have just fizzled away because the copywriter had a mouthful of free Pop Rocks when he wrote it.

This segment ends abruptly.

Your correspondent is on the way to the nearest Mom-and-Pop store to lay in a stash of Pop Rocks and see if it will get some of the youngsters of his acquaintance off marijuana.

Singer Patti Page ponders move in a Scrabble game.

WAR OF WORDS:

Scrabble

Adz, or adze? zyme. la. girt. velum. zarf. yclad. yester. quid. quarto. kelp. huh. uppish. tzar. bike. avouch. xebec. nares. zax. undone.

What's archaic? What's a proper noun? What's foreign? What's contrived? What's an abbreviation? Wait a minute, wise guy, who's making the rules here? Who said you could use the Greek alphabet or the musical scale? Where's the *unabridged* dictionary?

For those who have had their share of quarrels over a Scrabble board, this is how it all began.

Alfred Mosher Butts, a New York architect, out of work, evicted from his apartment and holed up in a fifth floor walkup in Queens, set out to invent an adult game in 1933. What he had in mind was something in the neighborhood of anagrams but more challenging—"an alphabet game with a balance between all skill, like chess, and no skill, like dice." The bad times passed, and Butts went back to his profession but he kept right on working on that new game of his. In 1938, he had it: a board with 225 squares and 100 counters with the letters of the alphabet assigned point values according to the frequency of their occurrence in everyday words (one each for the vowels, three for *b* and *c*, four for *v, w* and *y*, eight for *j* and *x*, ten for *z* and *q*, etc.) and

squares designating double and triple scores. Butts cut the counters himself on an old jigsaw and made fifty sets for friends. Everybody he tried it on loved it but the game manufacturers all turned him away. So the thing remained something of a secret between the architect and Mrs. Butts and their own circle for nearly ten more years.

Then James Brunot, a social worker, came into the picture. Brunot, a friend of Butts and a long-time sparring mate in that new game nobody wanted, decided in 1947 that he was using up too many of the hours of his life commuting eighty miles a day from his home in Connecticut to his job in Manhattan. He wanted to stay in the country, so he talked Butts into letting him gamble on producing the maddening word puzzle for general sale. Then he named it Scrabble and went to work on it with his wife in the living room of his Newtown home. The Brunots managed to put 180 sets on the market during 1948, but there was nobody hammering on their door. Butts, collecting a royalty on each sale, sat back in his office at the architectural firm of Holden & McLaughlin in a mixture of wonder and disappointment—maybe the professional game people knew best, after all.

Brunot himself, by then operating out of a little

Connecticut plant with his books wearing a nice shade of R-E-D, was about to give up in 1952 when four years of word-of-mouth promotion by the devoted Scrabble underground suddenly and inexplicably began to pay off. Selling sixteen sets a day earlier in the year, Brunot found his orders running at a 411-a-day clip in the last quarter. And that was just the beginning: Sales in the first three months of 1953 reached 51,480 sets, nearly 2,000 more than the total for all of '52, and before the year was over there were a million sets—and a million arguments—in American living rooms. Scrabble became something of a status game as its fame spread. One observer made the point that the longhairs were playing it in three different languages at once, whereas in Hollywood some devotees were playing it with dirty words only.

In any case, Brunot couldn't handle the traffic after a while—"it was too big for us"—and so the rights were sold to Selchow & Righter, the New York games outfit which also had a little thing called Parcheesi, and now you could buy either the early three-dollar model with the wooden squares or the deluxe ten-dollar plastic job. Butts and Brunot contented themselves with a continuing piece of the action. While Butts always spoke lovingly of Scrabble as his nest egg, Brunot complained about the way the IRS eats into a man's sustenance.

"We didn't get rich," he said. "It's a living, but personal and corporation taxes murder you."

But he never had to go back to the eighty-mile commuting routine, and Helen Brunot took to raising Dorset sheep after a while, like a gentlewoman should. In a word, the Brunots—and Alfred Butts—didn't do badly at all. But, oh, the warfare in all those homes. Mah-jongg was never like that. Or Parcheesi. Or Monopoly. Or even bridge, for that matter.

Villain or hero? Alfred M. Butts started it all. *New York Post*

Hebrew scrabble. The late Gertrude Berg (left), then star of TV's *The Goldbergs*, in a match with two colleagues, Celia Adler and Joseph Buloff, in 1954.

THE SENSATION BALL!

THE LATEST PLEASANTRY IN THE PUBLIC STREETS.

THE TOY
FOR ALL THE AGES

From London's *Punch*, way way back, it is evident that boys were boys even in the old days. *From the New York Public Library Photo Room*

THERE'S NO USE trying to put down the Yo-Yo.

One of the more indestructible playthings, enjoying a long and honorable history, it is evident that it won't go away. In 1791 George IV, then the bad-boy Prince of Wales, was playing with his Yo-Yo when he should have been keeping an eye on the love of his life, Mrs. Fitzherbert. France's ill-fated Louis XVI has been portrayed with a Yo-Yo in his hand; the French called it *l'emigrette* and we're told that during the Revolution some of the less fortunate played with their *emigrettes* on the way to the guillotine—to reduce the understandable tension, no doubt. Another story is that Napoleon's frostbitten soldiers used to carry Yo-Yos to while away the hours during their wine breaks between battles, but long before that, in the Philippines, where it may have had its real origin, the Yo-Yo was more than a toy. It was a weapon. Made with flint rock and leather thongs, it served the hunter in pursuit of small game in the jungle—one whack on the head and the animal was ready for the frying pan. The Yo-Yo, called a disk then, also appears in the folklore of ancient Greece.

In the United States, the Yo-Yo—two round, flat-sided blocks of wood, plastic or metal connected by a dowel and run up and down on a string—is one of those rare fads which comes and goes but never dies. There was a run on Yo-Yos during the Twenties, a decade hardly short on diversions, and another flurry of interest in the mid-Forties. Fifteen years later, in 1961, there were times when you needed a connection to buy one even though the happy factory hands of Luck, Wisconsin, the Yo-Yo capital of the world, were toiling around the clock to produce them. What accounted for it? In early April, demonstrators shilling for the Yo-Yo industry made some television appearances, showing off such expert moves as the creeper, the spinner, the loop, the breakaway, the three-leaf clover, the bow bell, walking the dog (all right, you let the thing touch the ground softly and then bring it up, over and over again), tapping the drum and skinning the cat (oh, come, we don't know what that is). Within a month, the factories in Luck and elsewhere had more orders than they could fill. In June, sales in New York's metropolitan area for the previous eight weeks were put somewhere between 3½ to 5 million. Donald F. Duncan, the Midwestern manufacturer known as the Henry Ford of the Yo-Yo, put out a silver monogrammed executive model made of hand-rubbed walnut and selling for $7.50. For the executive who could do without the status symbol but had to have a Yo-Yo of some kind to help him work off his aggressions during the day, there was a plethora of plain maple models in the twenty-five-cent to one-dollar bracket. The company sold 15 million in a single year, but by 1968, with signs of rigor mortis setting in on that fad, Duncan elected to take a bundle of money from the Flambeau Plastics Corporation of Baraboo, Wisconsin, and get out. The new owners had to sweat for a few years, but they knew somthing: the Yo-Yo might go on holiday for a while but would never die. In 1972 Bruce Brenda, an eighteen-year-old freshman at West Virginia University, kept one going for eight hours and fifty minutes to break the eight-hours-and-thirty-two-minute record listed in the Guinness bible. The boy said he could have kept going indefinitely except that his string broke under the strain. The next year Tom Parks, a high school guidance counselor from New York, was billing himself as the World Yo-Yo Champion with a hundred variations—one- and two-hand—in his bag of tricks. And the Yo-Yo's still around, neon-lit and sold on street corners. Donald Duncan, who died in 1968, has to be whirling around in his grave. Like a Yo-Yo.

Shall we jump a couple of centuries now? This is Richard Nixon having trouble with a gift from singer Roy Acuff during a visit to the Grand Ole Opry in Nashville just three months before he stepped down as President in 1974. Watergate, you know. *WWP*

THE DOLL WITH STYLE

In 1967, keeping up with the times, Barbie emerged in a Twist 'n' Turn waist.

ELLIOT AND RUTH HANDLER had a daughter named Barbara—start with that—and they had a fair little toy business going for them in Los Angeles. Tinkering around with plastics in their own garage out there when he was a GI during the war and she was a stenographer for Paramount Pictures, they started with furniture for dolls, went on to toy ukeleles, took a bath with a strong-selling plastic piano when they underestimated their production costs, developed the first mass-produced music box for toys, and then went into a general line that included cap pistols, a replica of the Winchester rifle, toy rockets and that sort of thing. Then Mrs. Handler had a sudden inspiration in 1956 when she noticed that Barbara, called Barbie, liked to buy paper dolls and dress them with the cutout costumes in the package. The little blonde would also try to dress real dolls, but that was a difficult, frustrating chore. This gave her mother an idea— "Wouldn't it be nice if there was a three-dimensional doll which could be dressed in miniature fashions?"

It turned out to be very nice.

The Handlers went to work on a Barbie doll that would come with an assortment of costumes, say twenty-two or so to choose from, and launched it five years later. Barbie took a while getting started in the sales marts, but by 1965 the doll was a 97-million-dollar-a-year item for the Handlers' company, Mattel, Inc., with some fifty outfits ranging all the way from simple everyday wear—any old thing to throw on for a trip to the A & P, let's say—to the career girl's dress, evening gowns, sportswear, negligee, tailored pajamas and nurses' uniforms to mink jackets, the Mod-look miniskirt and all the other creations that lay ahead in the mad, mad world of fashion. In the beginning, of course, the inevitable question arose. Was Barbie just another fad or an American standby like the electric trains you once bought for your male offspring and then had so much fun with yourself? Well, it was pretty clear even then that Barbie, like her forebears who suddenly found their voices and started to say Mama in the Twenties, was going to be around as long as there were little girls. Of course, they said that when the Kewpie doll overran the Western world just before World War I, and they said it when the Shirley Temple doll was the rage in the Thirties until the child actress outgrew her own playthings. They even said it about the Shmoo when that roly-poly all-purpose blob emerged from Al Capp's "average Stone Age community," Dogpatch, in the late Forties. But, then, Barbie had an edge: She always dressed for *today*.

Maybe overdressed a bit, too. In 1976 Bill Barton,

And today she's got someone to hang around with—
Superstar Ken.

who claimed credit for designing the original model, complained that Barbie—seventeen then and soaring toward her 100 millionth sale—had been turned into a sex symbol complete with a bosom too big for her own girlish dimensions. "She has just gotten too sexy," said Barton, then running his own manufacturing business in Oakland, Oregon. "I really have some misgivings about what's happening today."

A few other things had also happened to Barbie by then, on Wall Street and in Washington. Early on, Mattel stood out on the Big Board as one of the more fabulous success stories in the money marts. The company reported pre-tax earnings of $34 million on sales of $272.4 million in 1971 with the Handlers' own piece valued at almost $300 million. But the following year it reported a loss of $29.9 million on the very same gross and in 1973 the red ink was

listed at $32.4 million. Two years later, under heavy scrutiny by the Securities and Exchange Commission, the Handlers resigned as the company's co-chairmen and somewhere along the line Mattel paid out $30 million to settle a flock of class-action suits brought by stockholders. Ruth Handler, three former officers and one current official were recently indicted on charges of engineering an elaborate scheme to falsify the Mattel books between 1969 and 1974. Elliot Handler was not named in the case.

But this is not a book about shenanigans in high finance. What you want to know is that the toy giant's new management listed net earnings of $30 million on $494 million in sales for fiscal 1979, and Barbie, who now has a brother named Ken, is doing just fine. The SEC left her out of the indictment too.

Still later, the doll went to some more expensive garb, like any growing girl.

Ruth Handler, who had the idea for Barbie, with her husband, Elliot. The doll pushed their little toy operation into a half-billion-dollar item with three plants in the United States and others in Hong Kong, Germany, Canada, Taiwan, England and Mexico. But then something went sour on the money end. Barbie's not their baby now.

Since this one's about dolls, this is your introduction to an eleventh-hour development in the field: Gay Bob, who not only came out of the closet in 1978 but brought it with him. Advertised as "the world's first gay doll for everyone," Gay Bob arrived on the scene with his best friend (no name, sorry) in time for the 1978 Christmas sales rush. He is the creation of a party named Harvey Rosenberg, who also has promised the gay lib set such other characters as Marty Macho, Executive Eddie, Straight Steve and Neurotic Ned, toting his own Valium. Not from Mattel's but from Gizmo Development Inc. of New York. And what you're looking at sells for a modest $18.

Part VII

~~~~~~

BETTER WORLD A-COMIN'

SUCCESS STORY:

The Omnipotent Oom

yoga [Sanskrit,-union], mystical system developed in
Hinduism, intended primarily to liberate the individual from the illusory world of sense perception. . . . The ultimate state sought is one of perfect
illumination. Yogis use physical disciplines to attain
it—purgation, cleanliness, concentration, exercises.
—THE COLUMBIA-VIKING DESK ENCYCLOPEDIA

"Doctor" Bernard instructing Lou
Nova in a yoga exercise to get him
ready for his heavyweight fight against
Max Baer. *International News Photo*

HE WAS A SLENDER, pasty-faced man with a high forehead, long nose and dimpled chin. He had a thin
upper lip and piercing blue eyes. He was known as
Pierre A. Bernard in Seattle and New York, where he
also called himself Homer Stansbury Leeds. In Chicago he was known as Peter Coon. But after a while
he was known, everywhere, as the "reincarnation of
the Supreme Being, Oom the Omnipotent," and it
made him rich and famous, because in that role he
had something that proved to be highly salable.

It began with yoga; where it ended was never entirely clear. This much was clear: Pierre Bernard was
the son of an Iowa barber, born around 1875. In his
earlier career, before the revelation seized him and he
became Oom the Omnipotent, he worked as a barber
around Chicago and California. In 1905, along with
one Winfield Nicholls, known to New York police
on the strength of a thirty-day conviction for cruelty
to animals, a discharge in an assault and robbery case
and a matter of indecent assault on a minor (fine,
three dollars), he turned up in Seattle as the head
man in something called the Tantrik Order of
America. There he also took himself a bride, Blanche
DeVries, a dancer.

The Far West, alas, must not have been too hospitable to the Tantrik Order, because by 1910 Oom
was exercising his mystic powers from an "institute"
on a drab street on New York's West Side. He had the
law to thank for his first real notoriety. Two teen-age
denizens of his spook parlor, Zella Hopp, a local item
on the premises with parental consent, and Gertrude
Leo, an import from Seattle, started the trouble.
Zella went to the police one day and said she had just
fled Oom, over his protests, and wanted (a) Gertrude's liberation and (b) the arrest of the master.
Furnished with the secret signal for admission, a complex series of taps on the bell, the men in blue broke
in. Downstairs, they found a bare room where Oom's
physical culture clients, paying a $100 bite, toiled
through exercises designed to produce the body beautiful. Upstairs, it got more interesting: There, on can-
vas-covered mattresses, Oom's inner-circle clients
participated in secret rites of some kind. The police
said the upstairs customers, following physical examinations, had to pay large sums and then sign their
names in blood before they could be initiated into the
cult.

The assorted charges against Bernard included kidnapping, Zella having alleged that Gertrude had been thwarted three times in her efforts to leave the institute. The Bronx girl's own grievances included an injured assertion that Bernard himself had conducted the preinduction physical on her person. She said the man took her into a private room, locked the door, dimmed the lights, lit a cigar, ordered her to strip—and then put his hand on her left breast to test her heart beat. Curtain. Now why did Zella, a tender nineteen, tarry after that incident?

"I cannot tell you how Bernard got his control over me or how he gets it over other people," she said. "He is the most wonderful man in the world. No women seem able to resist him."

There was a but—

"He had promised to marry me many times. But when he began the same thing with my little sister [Mary, age sixteen] I decided I would expose the whole matter. If it had only been myself I wouldn't have done it for the whole world."

Parenthetically, Zella noted with evident disapproval that Bernard sometimes staged open houses—he called them Bacchante evenings—where trusted outsiders would be invited in for eating and drinking, mostly the latter.

Both girls dropped the charges three months later. A married sister, Mrs. Jennie Miller, led Gertrude back to the more commonplace precincts of her native hearth, and Mrs. Hopp packed her daughter off to the Catskills for a rest cure. "Zella is too ill to prosecute the great Oom," the woman said.

Didn't Mrs. Hopp ever worry when Zella lingered in the institute for days at a time?

"No," she said, "because the man pretended to be of such high character and so absorbed in things of a higher nature. He came in our house and talked to us, and her father went down to his house to see. Everything appeared to be aboveboard. The treatments he gave her really benefited her health, and we were so grateful for that we were willing to believe it was really necessary for her to be away with him."

What the treatments were was never made entirely clear. Bernard said that his system, called Tantra, came from a Syrian named Hamati who had studied in India. He said he sat at the feet of Hamati for eleven years before branching out on his own some years before little Zella drew all that public notice to him. He described Tantra as a Sanskrit cult embracing magic and mysticism and derived from the dialogues between the Hindu god Siva and his wife, Parvutti. Reminded that those dialogues contained some rather salacious passages, Bernard affected a look of dismay.

"That's the trouble with people," he said. "They so readily misunderstand any true conception of the system."

And what was the system? These excerpts from the *International Journal of the Tantrik Order* furnish some clues to the hocus pocus which was to elevate Oom the Omnipotent to the highest high social and economic levels in due course:

Tantrik hypnotists recognize but three classifications of their art: fascination, drawing out love, and death.

When a Tantrik tries to invoke the Deity through the medium of the spirit of the dead, he sits over a fresh human corpse and keeps near him food and wine.

Tantriks worship the beautiful, the sublime, and sometimes select as an object of concentration a beautiful girl of about fifteen years, of fair hair and prepossessing appearance, in the best cloth and decked with the finest jewels.

Some Tantriks perform their daily service in their private chapels by placing before them an unclad woman.

The whole world is embodied in the woman.

Sex worship as a religion . . . constitutes the basis of all that is sacred, holy and beautiful.

Whoever has been initiated, no matter what may be the degree to which he may belong, and shall reveal the sacred formulae, shall be put to death.

There was no reason to believe, of course, that Bernard had ever had cause to go the whole way, as suggested in that last excerpt. He did attract some fresh notice from District Attorney Charles Whitman when he moved his operation into a residential area on upper Broadway. F. H. Gans, who occupied an apartment across the way, summed up the neighborhood grievances which had elicited Whitman's interest: "What my wife and I have seen through the windows of that place is scandalous. We saw men and women in various stages of deshabille. Women's screams mingled with wild Oriental music." Thomas Richardson, another tenant, said he hardly ever got to sleep before three or four o'clock in the morning because of Oom's revels, and the janitor submitted that taxis were pulling up at all hours to deposit fashionably dressed women on the cultist's doorstep.

Bernard's answer was crisp: "I am conducting a perfectly respectable Sanskrit school," he said, and the District Attorney went away. In time, Bernard did, too, emerging in 1919 as proprietor of something called the Braeburn Country Club in South Nyack on a site acquired as a gift from a former Episcopalian nun who was operating a girls' boarding school there until she became a disciple of Oom. Braeburn then had more than 100 members, who dressed alike in bloomers and sandals and could be seen from the roadside doing physical exercises. There was evidently lots of money behind those mild exertions, because in 1924 Bernard was able to produce $200,000 to buy the upper Nyack estate of the late Joseph Hilton. There, on a 265-acre spread, he set up the Clarkstown Country Club and settled down to stay. Over the years, Bernard, who had affected a turban and robe in his earlier days, became an affluent member of the riverfront set around Nyack and took to conservative English tweeds and a brier walking cane. By 1931, with 400 card-carrying followers—many of them in residence—and assorted well-heeled itinerants flocking to his sanctuary on the Hudson, he was at once president of the State Bank of Pearl River, treasurer of the Rockland County Chamber of Commerce, director of a trust company in Spring Valley and a junior partner in two manufacturing enterprises. The new Oom seemed to have shed the mystic overtones of the old. Joseph Mitchell, interviewing Bernard for the New York *World-Telegram,* produced these quotes:

> I'm a curious combination of the businessman and the religious scholar. I'm just a man of common sense in love with beauty and that sort of thing. There ain't no nudist cult here. No sir, nothing like that. Acrobatic exercises for men and women, lectures on art and philosophy, nice little things like that. We take sufferers from melancholia, old boys threatening to commit suicide, and build them up. Make new men out of 'em.

What about the club's membership roster?

"Just a lot of nice wealthy people interested in beauty and books."

Drawing on a fat cigar (Mitchell observed a brass cuspidor at the side of the desk), Bernard noted that his beauty-culture-and-spook resort had its own glass-encased swimming pool, its own dairy, its own theatre, a library of sacred Eastern books—and, oh, yes, a little seven-acre airport nearby for initiates being whisked to Clarkstown on his private plane. The place also had its own stable of elephants. The master of the retreat, then fifty-five, only recently had journeyed through the town of Nyack in a howdah

aboard *Mom,* queen of the small herd. This manner of transportation evidently befitted the potentate of Tantra, who by then boasted the ownership of 12 million dollars' worth of Rockland County real estate.

Later on in the Thirties Bernard indulged himself liberally as a gentleman sportsman. He built the Nyack Stadium and dressed up the opening ceremonies with Jack Sharkey, just relieved of the heavyweight boxing crown he had worn so briefly. For a wrestling show featuring Joe Savoldi and Ed Don George, the proprietor had Postmaster General Farley on hand as guest of honor. In 1939, the colorful Lou Nova, strong on yoga, trained on the congenial Clarkstown acres for his fight against Max Baer. Nova liked to talk about his deadly "cosmic punch," his revolutionary "bodily arc" and his perfect rhythmic stance. All so much mumbo jumbo, of course, but he did beat Baer. Yoga must have done something for Oom the Omnipotent, too. He lived to a ripe old eighty, dying in 1955. His wife Blanche, who had managed to avoid the public gaze down through the years, survived him.

And so did yoga—big. It's all over the place now without benefit of any such shenanigans as the Oom's. A 1976 Gallup poll listed 5 million Americans as adherents of the ancient Indian-based system of achieving self-mastery through both philosophical and physical exertions.

But yoga took only second place in that poll. Transcendental Meditation, hereinafter TM, introduced in this country in the late 1950s by the elderly, elfinlike Hindu monk Maharishi Mahesh Yogi, emerged with 6 million followers in Dr. Gallup's count. The Maharishi eventually had considerable help from the Beatles, you may recall. During the height of their fame the Liverpool quartet, heavily into Scotch-and-Coca-Cola and moving on from marijuana to some of the more exotic kicks, made a pilgrimage to his side in India to get their mopheads straightened out so they could fly right.

The TM set has since counted among its loyalists such diverse personalities as TV's Merv Griffin, brought into the fold by nobody else than Clint Eastwood (you didn't think Big Clint needed TM, did you?), Major General Franklin M. Davis, commandant of the U. S. Army's War College, William K. Coors, board chairman of that Colorado brewery, along with any number of Wall Street and business tycoons—even Joe Namath, who got into it in 1975 when that Golden Arm began to tarnish. "The thing I like about it," said Broadway Joe, "is the deep rest it gives you. I need it. I look forward to it." Namath had lots of company among athletes who didn't share his high-livin' booze-and-broads regime: golf's Gary Player, professional basketball's Big Bill Walton, Willie Stargell of the Pirates and the Mets' Jerry Grote, to name just a few. Paul Owens, the Philadelphia general manager, had about half of his sweat-and-money-stained slaves adhering to it for a while during the 1975 baseball season and damned if the team invariably referred to as the "lowly Phillies" didn't wind up that semester breathing down Pittsburgh's neck for first place in the National League East.

Unlike yoga, available to its devotees in all kinds of storefronts for a couple of dollars, the TM course has a $125 price tag. A rather stiff grunt, it would seem, just to learn how to sit down, close your eyes, relax your muscles, breathe through the nose and say "one" to chase away any distracting thoughts as you exhale. Two sessions a day, ten to twenty minutes apiece, and you've got the world on a string. The United Nations started regular TM sessions for interested delegates in 1976 under the ministratons of Sri Chinmoy, a forty-five-year-old Bengali who said he had come to these shores "in response to an inner command . . . to offer his inner wealth to aspiring seekers in the West." While the meditations may have helped some of the UN people, one must note that it hasn't done much for peace in the world. People keep on killing each other in one place or another.

THE MESSIAH WHO RESIGNED

Krishnamurti as he returned to India in 1927. "I have seen Buddha, I have communed with Buddha, I am Buddha," the Besant protégé said then.

"I could fake maybe, but this is no vaudeville act."
—Jiddu Krishnamurti

He arrived in New York on the liner *Majestic* on an otherwise ordinary day in August, 1926. He was just a slight wisp of a man, weighing only 100 pounds, and his thick black hair, parted down the middle, somehow heightened his frailty. He had a sensitive mouth and delicate chin, more like a girl's, and his dark eyes looked out of a narrow face that had an ascetic appearance perfectly suited to the rather unusual mission set for him when he was a mere stripling in India. Now he was thirty-one and he had the stand-in role in the Second Coming heralded for that December—on Christmas Day, if everything went according to the script. He spoke of himself as "the true successor to Jesus of Nazareth," without promising any miracles, and around the Waldorf, his abode in the Prohibition-time borough of Sodom and Gomorrah, the bellhops would come to refer to him as "that new Messiah fellow." It was easier than struggling over his square name—Jiddu Krishnamurti.

This particular Twentieth-Century Messiah, educated in the more fashionable British schools, accustomed to all the comforts, was anything but a tourist-class traveler. He didn't show up in a white robe and sandals, either. "Every Christ has worn modern clothes," he said in clipped Oxford tones, and he wore an impeccable gray suit tailored for him on Savile Row and touched off by expensive tan brogans. He made no apologies for his extravagant tastes; he had spoken critically of Gandhi for pushing the austerity bit. And while he was a vegetarian, a festive table had to be set for him, heavy on delicacies. He was strong on the body beautiful too: calisthenics every morning, tennis or golf as time permitted, no cigarettes, no booze, and no hell-raising. He said he had never heard of the Charleston before he came to this "jazz-mad" shore.

Jiddu Krishnamurti, one of the eight children of orthodox Brahmin-caste Hindus in Benares, India, could justly trace his considerable celebrity to his own hand. Hardly a slow starter, he dashed off a book when he was twelve. It was called *At The Feet of the Master,* and it contained all manner of wonderful revelations slipped to the youthful author in his dreams by a "world master" intent on bringing untold happiness and spiritual abundance to all. One story was that the boy got lucky when his spooky opus came to the attention of a spirited Englishwoman with a multicolored past and a rose-tinted present—Annie Wood Besant. The other was that this party came into his life *before* the book issued from his pen, so a word about her is in order here.

Annie Besant was the divorced wife of the Rev. Frank Besant, Bishop of Sibsey, Lincolnshire. A rebel in bobbed hair, she had been a member of the Fabian Society, an advocate of free thought and a battler for woman's suffrage. When she was thirty, in 1877, she risked trial on obscenity charges by publishing a forbidden pamphlet on birth control; she was acquitted. When she was divorced from the Bishop, the court took away her two children on the grounds that her open agnosticism made her an unfit mother. In time, she became a disciple of Helena Petrovna Blavatsky, the Russian occultist who had her own psychic hot line to the Mahatmas in India and enjoyed some renown as a co-founder of the worldwide Theosophical Society. Mme. Blavatsky's theosophy—from the root meaning of the two Greek words that form it, divinity and wisdom—spread the doctrine of the universal brotherhood of man, promoting comparative religion and philosophy and probing the mystic potencies of life through the occult. Under Annie Besant, who emerged as president of the new church's branches in India and America in 1907, the theosophists, 100,000 strong, began to talk about the Buddhist "Path" to Nirvana—the final goal of emancipation. Then Jiddu Krishnamurti's dream book came out, and the sect took another turn in the road. Mrs. Besant was operating out of the Society's headquarters in Madras then, and she was evidently very high on the "world master" bit, for it turned out that she had adopted the author, whose real name was Alcyone. His father, a magistrate's clerk, tried to regain custody later, submitting that Mrs. Besant "has been stating that the boy is going to be Lord Christ, with the result that he is deified and that a number of respectable persons prostrate before him and show other signs of worship," but he lost the case. Mrs. Besant took her ward to London for private tutoring and the following year, in Benares, set up the branch outlet which in essence was going to sponsor his life's mission—the Theosophical Society's Order of the Star of the East.

The timetable did not call for haste. Fifteen years passed before Mrs. Besant's prize possession was unveiled to the world. The setting was the Fiftieth Anniversary celebration of the theosophists at Madras, attended by 5,000 delegates from thirty-seven nations, and by a curious coincidence the man was then thirty years old, the same age Jesus attained before *he* began to spread the gospel. Annie Besant told the assemblage there was a new World Teacher on the way, embracing a new world religion, in the person of Jiddu Krishnamurti, and then he spoke. "I come for those who want sympathy, who want happiness, who are longing to be released, who are longing to find happiness in all things," he said. "I come to reform, not to tear down; not to destroy, but to build." If that last sentence had a familiar ring, blame it on Matthew's account of the Sermon on the Mount (5:17)—"Think not that I am come to destroy the law, or the prophets: I am come not to destroy, but to fulfil."

For that matter, there were some people on the premises that day, led by his sponsor, naturally, who professed to believe that the man from Benares was speaking in the very tones of the Saviour. "A voice of penetrating sweetness rang out through Krishnamurti's lips," Annie Besant said. Another witness said the crickets stopped chirping and all the other sounds of nature ceased as the words issued forth, while a hard-boiled British army officer insisted that he saw tongues of flame over the speaker's head.

The American unveiling came the following year, despite the efforts of dissident theosophists to have the new World Teacher barred on the grounds of moral turpitude, of all things. Mrs. Besant, a peppery seventy-eight, was at the side of her prodigy as he granted the ship news reporters an audience.

"I believe that I am to be the vehicle of the World Teacher," Krishnamurti said, "and that the Spirit has already made use of my body to carry to the world my message of happiness—a happiness that is found not in the material but in the spiritual plane." The timing of this proclamation was less than perfect, for a General Bible Conference was under way in New York then and the place was crawling with Doubting Thomases.

"I think this man has been hypnotized by Mrs. Besant," said the Rev. Dr. F. C. Meyer of London. "She is a woman of remarkably strong mind, and she has influenced him to an unbelievable degree."

"This 'Messiah' represents an old cult in which there is nothing new," said the Rev. Dr. David G. Wylie of New York. "His ideas are not modern, but are revamped from old Hindu doctrines and put in a modern form to attract the nonthinking. There is no place in America for such a cult. For this man to claim he is a Messiah is ridiculous and blasphemous. Possibly he may lead silly women and unthinking men into the wilderness of despair."

"America has always been the home of faddists," said the Rev. Dr. John F. Carson, pastor of the Central Presbyterian Church in Brooklyn. "This is merely one of the fads. I only wish Barnum were

Another view of the "Messiah" with the ever-present Annie Besant. On one occasion, in 1926, the tennis-playing Krishnamurti laughed when he was asked about the heavy burden of being called an incarnation of the Deity. "I should say it is rather a burden," he said, "but really I wish you would say it's all nonsense, that stuff about me saving the world and all that. I am just an ordinary fellow, and the thing I am most interested in just now is whether Suzanne Lenglen will be able to hold out against Helen Wills next year." (Miss Wills won at Wimbleton in 1927. The French star was eliminated in an earlier round.)

alive today to see this proof of his well-known statement."*

Krishnamurti came here to address the Theosophical Society's convention in Chicago but disdained it because he didn't like the setting.

"It is too noisy here," he said. "Why, the people even chew gum to be doing something. Could a Rembrandt set up his canvas on State Street and paint the rush hour? I think not. Could a poet produce sublime verse in a boiler factory? No. Is it something that can be turned on or off like an electric light? You think perhaps it is like inserting a new record in a phonograph—His Master's Voice? No, sir, only under favorable conditions can the inspiration, the divine afflatus, come. I could fake maybe, but this is no vaudeville act. I am no ventriloquist with a grotesque puppet. I should never feel right if I deceived my followers. There was not enough air in the convention hall and the people were restless, so 'The Voice' did not speak, that is all."

With that, he headed for California "to play tennis, to read philosophy and detective stories and the popular magazines, and to get out of this foolish confusion."

Like the Chicago address, the Second Coming didn't materialize either, and the following April, with a copy of Sinclair Lewis' Elmer Gantry tucked under his arm, Krishnamurti went back to Europe. There was no evidence that his sojourn here had boosted the Theosophical Society's membership to any appreciable degree, and three years later, in

---

* "There's a sucker born every minute."

convention at Ommen, Holland, the Order of the Star of the East suddenly and inexplicably went into the discard on the "Messiah's" own motion.

"It is useless to try to reestablish order and harmony while individuals in themselves are chaotic, unharmonious and disturbed," Krishnamurti said. "The transformation of the individual must come first. Man being entirely responsible to himself, creates by his own limitation barriers around him which cause sorrow and pain. In the removal of these self-imposed limitations lies glory and fulfillment of self."

Annie Besant bowed to the greater wisdom of her chattel. "Considering the special stress which has been laid by Krishnamurti on individual judgment and liberty, the dissolution of the order appears logical," she said. "My fundamental belief in Krishnamurti as the World Teacher makes me more inclined to observe and study than to pronounce an opinion on the method chosen by one whom I consider far my superior."

However cloudy the language, it appeared to the more realistic observers that Krishnamurti had in effect declined at long last the role for which Annie Besant had nurtured him since 1909. Indeed, he spelled it out himself in 1931 when, his black hair now streaked with a premature gray, he returned to the United States. Renouncing theosophy and the representations his sponsor had made for him, he said that while he once believed it was his vocation to be the "Voice of the Great Teacher" he saw his error when he matured.

"I learned that each of us must do his own think-ing," he said. "The Deity—the better life—lies within each and all of us. You cannot organize a system of truth; neither can you nor I set up a religious standard for another."

And the Order of the Star of the East?

"It was just another cult, another ballyhoo, like any other church," said the self-retired Messiah, noting that when he dissolved the Order he had returned all the money and property turned over to it by its disciples around the world. "I couldn't tell people to beware of their exploiters and then exploit them myself. They still ask me about truth, and God and immortality but I tell them they must learn for themselves. You can't point out paths to any of the real things in life, no matter how much you may want to. And besides, the only thing I really know even now is myself."

And Annie Besant? She died in India in 1933 and her body was cremated on a pyre of sandalwood. That's the way she wanted it.

Her spare, white-haired disciple is still carrying the message around the world, supported by nonprofit foundations in India, England, Latin America and the U. S. A. In 1974, then seventy-eight, he drew some healthy audiences to New York's Carnegie Hall for a series of four lectures. The message "Truth is a pathless land. You cannot approach it by any religion, any sect." The secret is "inward security." If you happen to be blessed with that "then outward security can be brought about for all of mankind." Now that would be nice, wouldn't it?

FATHER DIVINE:

God Comes to Harlem

Heaven and earth can fade away,
But Father Divine don't never fail.
—CHANT FROM THE KINGDOM OF PEACE

Wanted for questioning when one of his less peaceful helpmates took a knife to a process server, Father Divine fled to his branch heaven in Connecticut and had to be flushed out of a coal bin. Here he's in the Milford jail. *WWP*

BACK IN 1932 there was trouble in heaven, then temporarily situated in a rambling frame house in Sayville, Long Island, where Father Divine, the proprietor, provided for his small flock of "angels" or, as some said, vice versa. Arrested as a public nuisance on his white neighbors' complaints of late Sunday revels, the self-styled messiah ("If people believe I'm God, then I'm God to them") was hailed into the Mineola Supreme Court. In that earthly setting, standing before the bar as just plain George Baker, the defendant heard himself angrily denounced by Justice Lewis J. Smith as "a menace to society" and sentenced to a year's imprisonment and a fine of $500.

Four days later the judge, only fifty-five and in splendid health up to that moment, dropped dead of a heart attack.

In jail pending a successful appeal, the paunchy, five-foot prisoner sadly remarked to his keepers, "I hated to do it." And back in Sayville the angels sang, "Peace, brothers, peace! Our Lord has struck down the judge."

Father Divine, his fame multiplied in one mammoth stride, was on his way.

In years to come, as his flock grew and grew until no one heaven could contain it and a vast prosperity filled his days, this otherwise gentle little man would be credited (by his partisans, that is) with a whole assortment of wondrous and terrible acts of retribution. Thus, in 1935 alone: Will Rogers made a small joke about Father Divine on his radio show and then died with Wiley Post in that Alaska plane crash; Louisiana's Huey Long refused to see a delegation of angels and fell before an assassin's bullet; The New York *Times* ran a critical article about the new King of Glory and publisher Adolph Ochs passed away. And the next year England's George V ignored a cable Father Divine had dashed off to Buckingham Palace about one of his sidelines, the Righteous Government Movement, and pretty soon he was dead. *The Spoken Word,* published by the evangelist, linked George's failure to reply to that wire to his sudden departure for whatever heaven had been reserved for monarchs. Father Divine himself did not always lay open claim to such swift and irrevocable deeds as these. Generally, he limited himself to the fittingly modest statement that "the cosmic forces of nature work with me," or, more elaborately, "I don't have to say I'm God and I don't have to say I'm not God.

The Father's followers marching along Harlem's Lenox Avenue in 1938. *WWP*

I said there are thousands of people call me God. Millions of them. And there are millions of them call me the devil, and I don't say I am God, and I don't say I am the devil. But I produce God and shake the earth with it."

Who was this non-God God? His name was George Baker and there was some evidence that his parents were among the slaves owned by Benjamin and Samuel Baker of Savannah, Georgia. With an impish smile on his cherubic face and his doelike eyes twinkling, he liked to say that he was born in "the time of Abraham," but it had to be centuries later, like 1877 or so, for the Bakers settled their plantation around 1850. The boy did sixty days on a Georgia chain gang once but the offense, if there was one, was never known. Toward the turn of the century he turned up in East Baltimore, where he mowed lawns and clipped hedges for fifty cents a day and taught Sunday school in a Baptist church. It was there that he fell in with the man credited with pointing him toward his ultimate career—Samuel Morris, who by day drove a horse and buggy for a teamster and by night became Father Jehovia. As A. J. Liebling and St. Clair McKelway reconstructed that story in their 1936 profile of Father Divine in *The New Yorker,* the two men came together in a rather unusual way. Morris, occupying the pulpit as a guest

preacher in the church in which Baker had that class, was thrown out one night when, swept away by his own eloquence, he proclaimed himself "The Father Eternal." Baker helped him off the pavement and was invited to move into the boardinghouse Morris was living in, run by an evangelist named Anna Snowden.

Pretty soon both Morris and Baker were delivering the sermons in that establishment, and a party who called himself St. John Divine Bishop joined forces with them. That name is interesting because while Baker took to calling himself "The Messenger" (and he didn't mean Western Union) in Baltimore he had become, alternately, Major J. Devine and Rev. J. Devine when he turned up back in his native Georgia in 1914. There, on the streets of Valdosta, he began to identify himself as "The Almighty" and attracted a few followers before he was arrested on the complaint of two local black pastors and compelled to undergo a lunacy trial. Baker refused to give the police any name other than The Messenger, so they brought him in as "John Doe, alias God." In court, he was adjudged (hastily, it would seem) a person of unsound mind.

Ordered out of the state, he journeyed north to New York by slow degrees and there found St. John Divine Bishop, of all people, spreading the

Faithful Mary, having fled the cult, talks to a court officer during one of the many suits against Father Divine. *UPI*

What Purcell preached was nothing less than everlasting life: All the subscriber had to do was to shun sin, which, of course, included holding out money on "The King." Purcell enforced chastity, too, except that he permitted a special dispensation for the lawfully wedded and another dispensation, on the side, for the leader himself. Operating out of lavish headquarters in Benton, Michigan, he got jammed up in the Twenties when two girls in the House alleged that he had taken unfair advantage of their youthful charms. It turned out that "The King" had been sampling the more desirable flesh in his kingdom for years, occasionally sparing time for a wedding ceremony to avert the complications of illicit fatherhood, so he began to slip into the discard.

Another Divine forerunner was the Rev. Warren K. Robinson, a bearded six-foot-six preacher who had a string of heavens going in Long Island, Newark, Chicago and Indianapolis before he fell afoul of the Earth Man's law in Harlem in 1924 when an irate parent, citing the Mann Act, charged him with violating his teen-age daughter. It turned out that while *he* was freely denouncing the sins of the flesh, Elder Robinson's temple of worship was simply crawling with overactive females; indeed, twenty-three of them had been induced to produce issue for the busy giant. The government perforce felt it necessary to put the man in the Federal cooler at Atlanta for five years. A durable sort, the Elder came out in 1930, refreshed by his sojourn under Uncle Sam's watchful eye, and built his little empire into a 750,000-dollar-a-year operation. Then illness befell the great lover and his loyal assistants compounded it by refusing to let a square black doctor administer blood transfusions as the stricken leader lay on a silk-lined couch in his St. Nicholas Avenue throne room in Harlem. "This is God," the doctor was told. "No mere mortal's blood could be allowed to enter the veins of God." So that particular God was dead in the morning and in due course confined to an unmarked crypt in a Bronx cemetery.

Father Divine was the logical successor to Purcell and Robinson. Employing many of the same techniques, he made enough of a dent in Brooklyn to find the wherewithal to set up his Sayville operation in 1919. There he conducted what in substance was a free employment agency, sending his fifty or sixty resident angels into white homes as maids, cooks or gardeners. Among the happy, hard-working people, the word was "Father will provide," and he did indeed—with *their* money. Taught to shun not only all worldly possessions but even the more tantalizing

gospel in midtown Manhattan. Baker, still The Messenger, observed his old friend in action and set up his own shop in Brooklyn. Now it would be wrong to buy the elementary notion that George Baker's ultimate flowering in his chosen field derived alone from such minor-league associations as those he enjoyed with "The Father Eternal" and the excessively named St. John Divine Bishop. Somewhere along the way he must have read the larger lessons of the faith-peddling industry. He had to know, for example, about "King" Benjamin Purcell. Born in Kentucky during the Civil War, Purcell drifted to Chicago, and there, walking under the stars one night in 1880, it came to him that he was "The Seventh Messenger." Secure in this knowledge, he hastened to Detroit and enlisted in the cult of a character called "Prince" Michael K. Mills. The "Prince" ultimately found himself under fire over the handling of his sect's finances, whereupon Purcell moved into the seat of authority and set up the House of David, widely known in time for its bearded world-touring baseball team but actually something much more ambitious.

temptations of the flesh, the angels, resident or otherwise, brought all their earnings to "Father" and, in return, lived on a rather sumptuous level. That two-story "heaven" on the Sound boasted a magnificent table said to be styled after the early Christian love feasts and abounding in such rich viands as golden brown goose, baked suckling pig and roast duck, with all the trimmings. The meals were eaten in relays to maintain Father Divine's rigid separation of the women and the men, since he had freely denounced "sexual indulgence . . . lust and passion and all those detestable tendencies." Much stomping, ecstatic screaming and wild chanting ("Peace, it's wonderful! Ain't it wonderful! Thank you, Father") all but drowned out the steady singsong gospel from the man at the head of the table as the Gargantuan feasts proceeded.

By 1930, such great hordes were trooping out to Sayville from Harlem that the police could barely handle the Sunday traffic and Father Divine's neighbors, friendly for so many years, had trouble containing their dispositions. This is where the trouble began. The Suffolk County authorities planted two "converts" in the house to see just what accounted for all the joy within those thin walls but the girls weren't much help; after a while they decided to spurn the outside police state and stay in heaven. Before the revelation came to them, however, they may have furnished some of the information used in the court proceedings, such as the assertion that the man who always inveighed against the most "detestable" weakness of the flesh had someone passing for a wife on the premises while the real Mother Divine resided elsewhere. The Appellate Division, finding no basis in that sort of common dereliction for the severe penalty dealt out by the departed Judge Smith, turned Father Divine loose five weeks after the trial.

From that moment on, Sayville wasn't big enough for the man. He moved to a five-story heaven in East Harlem which proved to be a pilot plant for branches in Newark and Jersey City, Connecticut, Baltimore, Detroit, Philadelphia, Chicago, Los Angeles and other cities. There appeared to be no limit to the number of disciples, always including a handful of whites, willing to live under Father Divine's "International Modest Code": no smoking, no drinking, no obscenity, no vulgarity, no profanity, no gifts, no tips or bribes, no S-E-X and, indeed, no money. That last item tells you how you got to be an angel. You brought your pay to heaven. For the others, such as the jobless or the ones who lived and worked in the main heaven and its burgeoning

annexes, Father Divine had another classification—The Children. They kept their square names. The angels acquired new handles, such as Faithful Mary (more about her), Rebecca Grace (more about her, too), Angel Flash, Faithful Love, Peaceful Dove, Gladness Darling, Hozanna Love, Sister Glad Tidings, Satisfied Justice, Sincere Determination, Faithful Heart, Redeemed Love, Understanding Wisdom and Patience Simplicity. The men went by less flowery designations, such as Peaceful Samuel, Brother Simplicity and Onward Universe (he'll be back, too).

In Harlem in the very worst of the Depression, with perhaps a quarter of a million blacks bearing its worst stings and living in unbelievable squalor, Father Divine presented an incongruous figure. He wore expensive double-breasted suits with a gold button adorning one lapel and a pearl stickpin glittering from his silk ties. When he ventured onto the poor street from his fifty-room brownstone Peace Mission, people cried, "Father will provide"—and damned if the politicians hadn't come to believe it too. In the 1933 municipal election, both candidates for Mayor, the Tammany hack John P. O'Brien as well as the tough, independent Fiorello LaGuardia journeyed to the main heaven to pay Father Divine fulsome tribute and court the votes of his blindly loyal legions.

"John Doe, alias God," had come a long way indeed from the hostile streets of Valdosta. He not only had cut himself a healthy slice of the submerged black masses in Harlem; now he also meant something to the white establishment. Now, too, he had an income which could never be estimated because he kept nothing in his own name and never deigned to file tax returns like the mere mortals of the time. His army of angels brought in so much cold cash, supplemented by the rents from any number of Divine-owned tenements and the jingling cash registers of the many restaurants and stores operated on his behalf, that estimates of the weekly take ran as high as $10,000. Naturally, charges of profiteering and exploitation, and even some touches of hanky-panky, began to be heard in Harlem after a while. The dirty linen—the Divine empire included some dry-cleaning establishments, by the way—had to be hung out, and the aforementioned Faithful Mary, just plain Viola Wilson in her other life, tended to that.

A mountainous figure with a temper to match her heft, Faithful Mary operated Father Divine's Newark branch so efficiently that she had been imported to New York and placed in command of seven satellite heavens merged under one roof on West 123rd Street. This spirited woman, elevated to Angel Number 1

Heaven in Tarrytown, New York, in 1940.

and getting a little ambitious, had a falling out with the leader over some of the loose change in 1937 and left the fold in a huff. The burden of Faithful Mary's grievances, freely issued to the earth people from the newspapers, was that the piece of the Promised Land she was minding had to show net weekly earnings of no less than $500 to $700—or else. She submitted that Father Divine made the weekly collection in person and stashed the boodle away in his own living quarters on the premises. She said that if she was slow in making the delivery "Father Divine would roll his eyes until I gave it to him . . . and if it didn't come to at least five hundred every week turned over to him, he would ask how come." She also alleged that the "children" were ill paid for their endless toil in the heavens and that the angels were receiving the most paltry returns for the hard-won wages shoveled into the Divine kitty. And then the shocker came—

"Now the spirit tells me it is time to reveal that Father Divine had affairs with many of the good-looking women in the kingdom. . . . The women thought of them as blessings. They thought they had reached the highest peak of virtue when they submitted to Father Divine. He was the greatest living humbug on sex. He told all the women it was sinful to be with their husbands, but he told them also that they should come to him. This, he said, would be a blessing and not a sin. . . . He told it to me, but I would not submit to him. I felt it was wrong. But many of the women he sent to me—particularly the young and beautiful ones—actually boasted that they had been 'blessed' by an affair with 'God'—that is to say, with Father Divine."

All of this, naturally, led Faithful Mary to a much larger conclusion. She said she was now convinced that Father Divine wasn't God at all "but just a damned man."

For those who may remember what happened to Judge Smith for a lesser offense, the record will show that no final retribution was visited upon Faithful Mary when she let that blasphemy escape her lips. She did, however, suffer her share of bad times. Thus when she opened a rival heaven in an effort to bust Father Divine's monopoly on the available believers she speedily found herself bereft not only of the $25,000 she happened to have had on hand for the predoomed enterprise but also of the limousine and other appurtenances which had derived from her former high position in the Kingdom of Peace. The faithful, for one reason or another, stayed away from Faithful Mary in such numbers that the backslid Angel Number 1 had to withdraw to far-off California to nurse her wounds before eventually making a strange reappearance in the Divine fold seventeen months after she had aired the first hard suggestions that the lower-case almighty might have been prey to such mortal weaknesses as lust and greed.

The latter item brings us now to the story of Rebecca Grace (Verinda Brown) and Onward Universe (Thomas Brown). This notably thrifty and industrious butler-and-cook team entered the Sayville flock in the early days and in due course turned over to the celestial kingdom not only all of their earnings but also their material assets, including Mr. Brown's best tuxedo (he wouldn't need that garment anyway, because he wound up reduced to a furnace man in one of the Harlem heavens). It added up to a total of $5,660. Disenchanted after a while, the couple left heaven and managed to rally seventy-eight other ex-angels behind a Supreme Court suit to force the proprietor to render a financial accounting on the Heavenly Treasury even though he had steadfastly denied ever accepting any cash from his flock. The Browns testified that Father Divine sought to strip away their connubial bliss by announcing to them: "You are no more husband and wife because I never ordained that." Well, it was one thing for the resident angels in Sayville or in Harlem to live by that new precept, because they had to occupy separate boudoirs—that is, dormitories—but the Browns, employed by a Forest Hills family and sleeping in, had to battle temptation against the formidable odds of a double bed. There were nights, of course, when they lost the good fight—and didn't Father Divine know it the very next time they appeared in heaven? Mrs. Brown remembered what he used to say: "I see you have sinned. You cannot hide from God. I am everywhere. I see all. I know all."

On the more crass and mundane level of the American dollar, the Browns' case, tried in 1937, enjoyed authoritative corroboration. Faithful Mary, then newly split from Harlem's most affluent preacher, described at length the cash transactions in which she personally had been involved when she tended the extension heavens. Accordingly, Justice Benedict D. Dineen awarded the plaintiffs $5,949.57, even though the pint-sized messiah had said from the start that he would go to the electric chair before he paid those ingrates. In any case, a renewed effort to force the Divine operation into a receivership so that the State of New York could take a small peek behind the financial curtain floundered when the formerly bellicose Faithful Mary recanted her testimony. That fallen angel had been taken back into the flock by then in a Standing Room Only love feast in Heaven Number 1.

Faithful Mary's return to favor was hardly calculated to help the cause of the Browns or the other disaffected angels who wanted a chance to dip into the Heavenly Treasury they had helped to keep replenished in happier days. Indeed, nothing helped. Father Divine did turn up briefly behind bars, put there once for standing in contempt of the dog-eared court order to pay the Browns and once because an overzealous lieutenant stuck a knife into a process server who had dared to invade heaven, but his white attorneys never had any trouble getting him out. The evangelist was upset, understandably, by the law's recurring intrusions. Thus when another band of apostate angels entered its own vain suit for an accounting, one of the increasing legal assaults which forced the stubborn defender of the faith to quit Harlem altogether in 1942 and move his heaven to Philadelphia, an aide mournfully remarked, "Father Divine is so disgusted he has just about decided to evaporate for 1,900 years."

That did not happen. Quite the contrary, the Divine empire was much too far-flung by then for any absentee management. It was so far-flung, indeed, that it included its own Promised Land in a choice rustic setting just across the Hudson from President Roosevelt's Hyde Park estate. This expansion northward from the filthy streets and rotting tenements of the black ghetto began back in 1935 when Father Divine —or whatever disciples served as his stand-ins in Heaven's real estate branch—acquired a thirty-four-acre farm in Ulster County for $7,000. By 1939, so much of the adjoining property had been swept into the portfolio that the Promised Land represented an investment of $212,000—all paid in cash—and improvements running up to another $100,000. In 1940, Father Divine had picked up a feudal castle on a knoll 425 feet above the Hudson in Tarrytown, where the Duchess of Talleyrand and John D. Rockefeller Jr. also had little hideaways befitting *their* stations. The ivy-covered Tarrytown place served for a while as the evangelist's personal residence, but for the masses the centerpiece in his rustic compound, within hailing distance of baronial mansions bearing such blue-blooded names as Vanderbilt, Astor and Morgan, was a 550-acre site facing the Roosevelt place and graced with this sign:

KRUM ELBOW

PEACE TO THE WORLD AT LARGE

FATHER DIVINE

Excursion steamers puffed their way up the great river bearing the faithful in the good weather, often shepherded by the landed preacher himself and the towering Mother Divine. And while Mr. Roosevelt proved less than helpful when the Divine forces made an abortive effort to buy the estate of the late Fredrick William Vanderbilt, hard by his own retreat, the Messenger-turned-God showed no animus. Looking across the river from Krum Elbow to FDR's summer place, he would say, "I couldn't have a better neighbor, could I?" Come to think of it, who could? Mind you, that statement did not come from anybody out

The Father with the second, somewhat younger Mother Divine.
WWP

of the conventional mode in the American success story. It didn't come from a self-made tycoon of humble beginnings or from some shrewd and crafty manipulator who had found a way to beat the game they played in Wall Street. It came from a spellbinder whose triumphs seemed to come more from words (he coined more words than the generally acknowledged champion of the time, Walter Winchell) than deeds. It came from a man who could utter this sort of pseudoreligious mishmosh:

God is not only personified and materialized. He is repersonified and rematerialized. He materialized and he rematerializes. He rematerializes and he is rematerializable and he repersonifies.

Or this:

You are in a New World. Remember, we are not representing Heaven as a place geographically, but a state of consciousness, wherein all men can arise to, and recognize, God's Presence as Real, as Tangibleatable, and as practical as the principles of mathematics, it is indeed wonderful! Not only tangibleated but as tangibleatable; it can and will continue to materialize, and repersonify, rematerialize, and repersonify, for the great materializing process is going on!

So much for that. The end of this remarkable journey approaches.

Mother Divine, never in the newspapers much except for an occasional photo, was the first to go. This beefy, towering woman, whose name was Penninah, died of multiple ailments in 1937 or 1938 and was laid to rest without undue ceremony, lest the news of her demise raise needless questions about the widely heralded powers of her soul mate. Faithful Mary, outside the pale at the time, said that the leader slipped her a paltry $100 to get the deceased quietly buried. Years later, strangely, Father Divine revealed that before death overtook her Mother had bestowed her blessings on any future union in which he might choose to enter. This revelation came when the vest-pocket preacher and a twenty-one-year-old white girl, Edna Rose Ritchings, daughter of a florist from Vancouver, B.C., took the marriage vows in Washington in 1946. Miss Ritchings, a chesty blonde ex-stenographer, six inches taller than Father Divine, had come into the fold as a teen-ager. She was known as Sweet Angel, and the groom, probably pressing seventy then but a youthful forty-one on the license, hastened to assure his flock that the nuptials made them husband and wife in name only. "God is not married," he said, and for that matter the name on the papers handed to the Baptist minister who performed the ceremony in the capital was Major F. Divine, hopefully not to be confused with the Father Divine who on more than one occasion had denounced the wedded state as "legalized prostitution."

"There is no mortal marriage in the kingdom that I mean," Father Divine said, "United as one family and as one nation indivisible. I mean that this is not a matter of sample for everybody just because we have released just what our marriage is for. Of course, those that are living according to my teaching, they are redeemed from self-indulgence, human affection, lust and passion, and all those detestable tendencies."

Woodmont, the ultimate $250,000 GHQ of the cult.

As if to reinforce that old theme of his, he added that the new Mother Divine, bearing the transferred spirit of the old, would henceforth be known as "The Spotless Virgin Bride." Back in Harlem, the more fishy-eyed observers viewed that as a further device to forestall any mass defections from the movement or make recruiting harder, since the news of "God's" trip to the altar figured to do more harm than good.

Nineteen years later, when Father Divine fell victim to an assortment of mortal ailments and breathed his last at Woodmont, his seventy-three-acre country estate in Gladwyne on the Main Line in Pennsylvania's Lower Merion Township, Mother Divine emerged as the ruler *pro tem* of the Kingdom of Peace. Announcing the evangelist's passing on September 10, 1965, the cult's attorney, J. Austin Norris, said that Mother Divine would carry on but observed that "in this movement they don't believe that Father Divine's physical presence is necessary—his death is only the throwing off of the physical body, and he is still leader." The widow not only concurred but said her spouse wasn't even dead (the *New Day* wouldn't even spell out the bad word, reducing it to d-d because "God cannot die") and therefore she did not consider herself a widow. "Just like our marriage wasn't in the mortal caliber, Father Divine laying himself down cannot be classed in the mortal caliber. I'm still married to Father, as always—the same relationship." And, attentive as ever, she kept a glass of water on the man's desk at Woodmont because "there is no place that God is absent from." Mother Divine, by the way, said her momentarily departed spouse ("Jesus was resurrected after three days") married the first Mother Divine on June 6, 1882. This would have put him somewhere in his eighties when he married again and over the century mark when he d-d, whereas the record would indicate that he was closer to the proverbial fourscore and ten when such afflictions as diabetes and arteriosclerosis separated him from his earthly kingdom.

What was left? Father Divine once had talked of his sect's assorted holdings, mostly in real property, as a 20-million-dollar item. Norris put the figure at a more modest 10 million, but then it would appear that the movement had shrunk to some degree in the years after his legal difficulties had forced the lowercase messiah to move his GHQ to Philadelphia. God evidently became harder to sell toward the end. Either way, for Father Divine, Peace, it was indeed wonderful.

FRANK BUCHMAN:

The Higher Morality

There was a young man from Peoria
Whose sins they grew gorier and gorier.
By confession and prayer—
And *some* savoir-faire—
He now lives at the Waldorf-Astoria.
      —Limerick from the time of
        Dr. Frank N. D. Buchman

SOME PEOPLE put it down as an upset, but a spirit of religious revival began to stir such campuses as Princeton, Yale, Harvard, Williams, Smith, Vassar and Bryn Mawr early in the Twenties. There was a strange kind of "house party" going on, a party where undergraduates gathered not to carouse but to share their innermost secrets, lay bare the temptations assailing them and confess their sins. Their purpose was to achieve moral regeneration through "absolute honesty, absolute purity, absolute unselfishness and absolute love."

That ambitious prescription came from a struggling Lutheran minister who in time would go on to considerable renown with such things as the Oxford Group Movement and Moral Re-Armament (MRA). In those early days, he called himself a "soul surgeon" and stoutly shook off the cynical observers who tried to put down his spiritual operating room as just another religious fad.

"We are not a cult or a sect," said Dr. Frank N. D. Buchman, peering earnestly from behind gold-rimmed spectacles, "and we offer no newism."

Frank Nathan Daniel Buchman was born in 1878 in the Pennsylvania Dutch country. His father was a country butcher in Pennsburg then but later became an innkeeper and, without in any way diminishing his ardor for the Lutheran church, a dealer in wines and liquor in Allentown. His mother, Sarah Greenwald Buchman, a kindly, cultured woman, accounted for the deeper inspirational influences in his life.

The boy went from Muhlenberg College to the Mt. Airy Seminary, where he was ordained in 1902, and then took further studies at Westminister College and Cambridge University. Assigned a parish on the outskirts of Philadelphia, he established the first Lutheran Hospice in America before resigning in a dispute with his governing board. Then he traveled through Greece, Turkey, the Near East and Egypt and England, returned to serve as the secretary of the Young Men's Christian Association branch at Pennsylvania State College from 1906 to 1915, toured the Orient observing the work of the missionaries, and came home again to lecture on evangelism at Hartford Theological Seminary. His notions about a re-

154

Dr. Buchman addressing his first American Assembly in Stockbridge, Massachusetts, in 1936. *WWP*

1947: In New York with Admiral Richard E. Byrd, a supporter, and long-time associate Ray Foote Purdy for the premiere of *The Good Road*, a play dramatizing the virtues of Moral Re-Armament. *WWP*

ligious revival dated back to an experience in England on his grand sojourn abroad. In Keswick for a religious conference, he heard a woman preacher in a small chapel one night and came away with visions of a "changed life" deriving from a free confession of one's sins. This was the real origin of the house parties which would later stir so much attention on the campuses singled out for his attention as America settled into the postwar period.

"If you have a real love for men you should be willing to share your temptations with them," Dr. Buchman said. "You should be willing to confess your secret thoughts, to get alongside of their souls, to work with them to the end of redemption." And the man in charge? "When he is certain that the need for confession exists, the soul surgeon must be lovingly relentless in insisting that the confession be made." And at the end of the road? "The principles of the New Testament are practical as working forces for today. We believe in spiritual miracles in the form of life changes."

The minister's "spiritual miracles" did not sit well with the college powers once his strange house party confessionals began to lure more and more adherents. In 1924, Princeton's president, Dr. John Grier Hibben, told Dr. Buchman there was no room on that campus for his newfangled mixture of Christianity and mysticism. This dealt a blow to the revival, leaving the repairman of the soul with a bare handful of followers, but it did not deter him in the least. He moved his operations to England, built up a strong following at Oxford and Cambridge, and then mounted another invasion of the homeland.

Thus the movement came to life again at Princeton in 1926, and Dr. Hibben had to have the barricades mounted once more. This time he had some help from the student body itself. An open forum voted 253 to 85 to call for an investigation of the Philadelphian Society, the YMCA branch on the campus, for pushing "undesirable Buchmanism," which was described as "an approach to religion through an exaggerated emotional appeal with undue emphasis on sex." Dr. Buchman himself wasn't around when that storm broke. He was on something of a royal tour of Europe, spending weeks as the palace guest of Romania's Queen Marie in Bucharest when he wasn't staging his house party confessionals in England. For the trial *in absentia*, Dr. Hibben named a committee of three university trustees, three faculty members and three undergraduates.

The committee's assigned task was to investigate charges that under the aggressive brand of personal evangelism inspired by Dr. Buchman "the privacy of the individual has often been invaded, a confession of guilt with particularity has been set up as a condition of Christian life, various meetings have been held at which mutual confessions of intimate sins have been encouraged, and emphasis has been laid upon securing confessions of immorality." This indictment, springing basically from fears that the movement had inspired a morbid and hypersensitive interest in sex problems, did not stand up. The committee labored for several months and in January, 1927, produced a report clearing the Philadelphian Society of all those nefarious insinuations while at the same time slapping the wrist of its graduate secretary, Ray Foot Purdy, for having invited Dr. Buchman to the campus in the face of the long-standing Hibben ban.

It didn't matter to the founder by then, because his crusade, now the Oxford Group Movement, was flourishing in Great Britain, Canada and South Africa and attracting followers in all walks of life. Dr. Buchman in those days dwelt on three tenets of faith: "the need for unconditional surrender of the human will to the will of God made manifest in Jesus Christ as Lord and Saviour, the need for continuous contact with God through Bible prayer and listening for the voice of the Holy Spirit, and the need for every Christian to witness for Christ and to bring others to him."

For all the lush prosperity accruing from its well-heeled supporters over there, Buchmanism stirred wide debate. Oxford's undergraduate weekly, *The Isis*, saw nothing more than a "perverted religious mania" in the soul surgeon's sessions. "In an atmosphere hovering between giggles and fanaticism," said the campus paper, "restraint is flung aside, souls are laid bare by hysterical confession, and with a fervor which no longer pretends to be religious the tenets of the doctrine are discussed." On the other hand, *Truth*, the London weekly, cast aside the widespread suggestions that the minister was fostering nothing more than a surrender of the intellect to pious optimism. Perhaps sharing the view Dr. Buchman him-

self had once uttered in jest, "It's a hell of a life if you don't have the gospel of Jesus Christ," *Truth* insisted that the Movement was accomplishing much good.

On a personal level, there wasn't any question about all the good that was being accomplished. The once-humble YMCA secretary, who never married, traveled first class at all times, evidently the beneficiary of endless financial support and not only enjoying but insisting on all the comforts. "Good food and good Christianity go together," he said. Good living, too. In London, the minister dwelt in considerable splendor in a mansion in Berkeley Square, matched by elaborate diggings in Switzerland and a scattering of year-round rumpus rooms in such stateside way stations as Mackinac, Michigan, where MRA main-

Dr. Buchman finds a staunch supporter in the Hollywood movie mill. Yes, it's Mae West.

tained its North American training center; Tucson, Arizona; Los Angeles and the site of his young manhood, Allentown. An air of self-confidence accompanied his boundless well-being. Harold Begbie, the British author, described Dr. Buchman this way in the early Thirties:

> In appearance he is a young-looking man of middle life . . . upright, stoutish, clean-shaven, spectacled, with that mien of scrupulous, shampooed and almost medical cleanliness which is so characteristic of the hygienic American. His carriage and gestures are distinguished by an invariable alertness. He never droops, he never slouches. You find him in the small hours of the morning with the same quickness of eye and the same athletic erectness of body which seems to bring a breeze into the breakfast room.

In time, the Buchman brand of peace wafted in on that breeze, but a depressing footnote is in order first. It goes back to 1936 when the doctor, dropping in on his native country, made the mistake of saying that he "thanked heaven" for a man like Adolf Hitler. Oh, no, he did not go all the way. He said he was by no means sold on all of the guy's notions, but—

> Think what it would mean to the world if Hitler surrendered to the control of God. Or Mussolini. Or any dictator. Through such a man God could control a nation overnight and solve every last bewildering problem.

The minister evidently hadn't paid too much attention to his history courses. The New York *World-Telegram* reminded him that "Mohammed was a typical God-controlled Fascist dictator, and Torquemada worked from the same inspiration and along the same lines. They freely granted unbelievers the opportunity to embrace the true faith—or else the sword, the stake or the rack of torture."

In any case, it was Hitler's war that prompted Dr. Buchman's own peace offensive in 1947, launched in a "world assembly" at the plush Mountain House in Caux, Switzerland, MRA's GHQ. The delegates who flocked to the resort from thirty-five countries numbered among them members of the parliaments of Britain, France, Italy, Norway, Finland, Belgium and Holland as well as all kinds of influential private citizens. Dr. Buchman told them that a thousand years of peace could be achieved if every man would lay aside bitterness and greed and put his shoulder to the wheel in the interest of a better world and "try thinking and living as God wants."

It was the Moral Re-Armament way and it dated back well before World War II. Dr. Buchman's followers in high places included such dignitaries as India's Gandhi, King George of Greece, King Prajadhipok of Thailand, and even Mae West. Yes, Mae West. The chesty screen blonde, last best hope of America's middle-aged legions, bid Dr. Buchman to come up and see her in Los Angeles in the summer of 1939 and proceeded to give the Moral Re-Armament cause, launched on this side of the ocean the year before with a rally in Madison Square Garden, a substantial shove.

"It is a wonderful work," said Miss West, all but bursting through the confines of a sheer pink dressing gown. "I owe my success to the fact that I have been practicing this philosophy in recent years."

Plainly carried away by her zest for the movement, Miss West asked the minister whether he would take time to carry the prescription to W. C. Fields, with whom she was then making that minor classic, *My Little Chickadee.*

"This is just what Bill needs," she said. "By all means meet Bill and tell him all about moral rearmament."

"I'd love to," said Dr. Buchman, perhaps not aware that his newfound supporter was referring him to the one man in Hollywood least likely to come up out of his wine cellar for any kind of rearmament, moral or otherwise. The subject was dropped there, in any case, and Miss West went on with her tribute to MRA.

"Early in my career, before I discovered the importance of correct thinking and correct consideration for others," she said, "it was a hard and bitter struggle to get ahead."

Harder, perhaps, than Dr. Buchman's own struggle. He enjoyed nothing but the best and lived to the ripe old age of eighty-three before a heart attack felled him in Freudenstadt, Germany, in 1951. An MRA spokesman said these were his last words:

"The world shall be governed by God. Why not let God run the whole world?"

Why not, indeed?

BILLY SUNDAY:

The Devil Got Hell

"This man, Billy Sunday, for action, is
the Charlie Chaplin of the pulpit.
He is the Untired Business Man of theology.
He is the boundin', bloomin' Fuzzy Wuzzy
who'll break the Manhattan crust."
—IRVIN S. COBB, 1917

Billy Sunday: From the green playing fields to the
tabernacle. *WWP*

IT WAS A crucial game between Detroit and Chicago.
The Tigers, challenging for the pennant, were at bat
with the White Stockings clinging to a thin lead. Two
out. Two men on. Three and two on the enemy
catcher, Charley Bennett. Chicago's John G. Clarkson
wanted to blow a high curve in there but the pitch
came in low, just the way Bennett liked 'em. The
right fielder, Billy Sunday, only the fastest man in
both leagues, knew that ball was going a country mile
when it left the bat. He turned and started to run.
He hurdled a bench on the lip of the outfield and
kept running. Now he was backpedaling, looking for
the ball, and calling for help along the way: "Oh,
God, I'm playing on your team now. You know I am,
God. If you're going to help me, come on now." Then
Billy Sunday leaped into the air and threw up his
hand and came tumbling down on his back. The ball
was in his glove. Chicago won the game and went on
to nose out Detroit for the flag.

Billy Sunday liked to tell that story, and he liked to
tell how he got "on God's team" in the first place,
earlier in that 1886 season:

I walked down a street in Chicago with some
ballplayers, and we went into a saloon. It was
Sunday afternoon and we got tanked up and
then went and sat down on a curbing. Across the
street a company of men and women were playing on instruments—horns, flutes and slide trom-
bones—and the others were singing the gospel
hymns that I used to hear my mother sing back in
the log cabin in Iowa and back in the old church
where I used to go to Sunday school. I arose and
said to the boys, "I'm through. I am going to
Jesus Christ. We've come to the parting of the
ways." Some of them laughed and some of them
mocked me.

It didn't matter. The young outfielder followed the
Salvation Army singers into the Pacific Garden Rescue Mission on Van Buren Street and took that long
first step. It was to carry him to more renown—and
more rewards—than he ever could have known in
baseball or anything else. He was on his way to the
Sawdust Trail, where he would make his mark as the

Deeply religious herself, "Ma" Sunday was at the Reverend's side from the moment he took to the Sawdust Trail. *WWP*

In this kind of athletic stance, Billy Sunday generally was challenging the Devil to "come on up and fight it out if you dare." *WWP*

A little action for the flock. *WWP*

scrappiest, most flamboyant antagonist that "blazing-eyed, eleven-hoofed, forked-tail old Devil" ever had to go against. He made the pulpit rattle and shake with his one-man war on Hell's landlord. He had the guy overmatched. He boxed him and wrestled him and left him for dead, or practically dead.

Nobody ever batted in Billy Sunday's league before and nobody would for years—not until the call came to the more polished William Franklin Graham, also called Billy, to go forth from North Carolina and carry the word of Christ across the sinful land and to the heathens across the seas as well. Billy Graham drew more people, because he was plunked down here in the age of television and Instant Religion—*in the home,* if you were too far from the tent—but the Rev. Mr. Sunday set the pace if not the ultimate style. He carried the message to the pagan millions without mincing any words. "Come on, you miserable sinners," he would cry out, sweat pouring down his angular jaw, "get down on your knees. The Devil has two strikes on you already." He gave the drinkers hell, and the painted women, and the straying husbands, and the nonbelievers, one and all, and it worked for him. They said he brought whole legions of converts into the fold, all plucked from the yawning jaws of the abyss in the last half of the ninth. Hitting his high stride during World War I, with the Demon Rum in tow as another ready-made sparring partner alongside poor old Satan, the fire-eating evangelist listed city-by-city breakdowns on his conversions for those who would scoff—Boston, 63,716; Philadelphia, 41,724; Baltimore, 25,797; Syracuse, 21,115, etc., etc., etc. And that was in 1916, a year before the hoarse and rasping call to Christ would be sounded in Manhattan, U.S.A., the most fertile of all the proving grounds because it was so d - - - big it had to harbor more souls in need of redemption.

For that crusade, mounted from a specially built $65,000 tabernacle on upper Broadway, the showman-evangelist claimed 65,000 converts. When the Federal Council of Churches poured cold water on that statistic, insisting that not more than two hundred had stayed in the fold, Billy Sunday came back with a quietly scornful answer. "I never yet have been satisfied with the results of any campaign I have ever conducted," he said. "No business house does as much business as it would like to." It was an unfortunate equation, but then Billy Sunday was in business—the business of religion, and he didn't believe in the soft sell. "Get religion," he liked to say, "and get it hard." He always went for the spiritual jugular, swinging from the floor, and he brought his own vivid idiom into the battle. What was the story of David and Go-

liath? "David socked the giant in the coco, right between the lamps, and he went down for the count." The reformed base stealer wasn't one to offer apologies for the way he talked, either.

"I am a rube of the rubes," he said once, "I am a hayseed of the hayseeds. The malodors of the barnyard are on me yet, and it beats Pinaud and Colgate, too. I have greased my hair with goose grease and blacked my boots with stove blacking. I have wiped my old proboscis with a gunny-sack towel. I have drunk coffee out of my saucer and I have eaten with my knife. I have said 'done it' when I should have said 'did it,' and I 'have saw' when I should 'have seen,' and I expect to go to Heaven just the same. I have crept and crawled out from the university of hard knocks, and have taken the postgraduate courses."

It was an understatement, if anything.

William Ashley Sunday was born in Ames, Iowa, on November 19, 1863. His father, William Sunday, son of immigrant Methodists originally named Sonntag, was off with the Union Army then, destined to fall ill and die in camp without ever seeing his third son. Mrs. Sunday, the former Mary Jane Corey, was deserted by her next husband, and between the ages of twelve and fourteen Billy found himself alternately in the Soldiers' Orphan Home at Glenwood and the Davenport Orphanage. Then he was apprenticed to State Senator John Scott of Nevada, Iowa, serving as an odd-job man and stablehand in return for his board and a chance to go through high school. A trim five-foot-eight and a champion sprinter, he developed into quite a baseball player. Chicago's playing-manager, Cap Anson, one of the early greats, heard about the boy from a relative in 1882 and came to see him in a semipro game at Marshalltown. A quick look was enough: Billy could circle the bases in fourteen seconds and steal at will, and he was a pretty good outfielder to boot. Anson signed him for the White Stockings, then champions of the old National League. In the course of his five years there, before he was traded first to Pittsburgh and then to Philadelphia, Billy set a league record of ninety-five stolen bases in a season. He had one real good year at the plate, too, batting .359.

From the moment of his conversion, however, Billy's thoughts had turned from the playing field to the ministry. His marriage to the deeply religious Helen A. (Nell) Thompson in 1888 confirmed those feelings, and he started taking Bible courses at the Chicago Y.M.C.A. in the off-season. In 1891, a free agent, he turned down an offer of $500 a month from the Cincinnati team to take an $83.88-a-week job as the Y's assistant secretary. Later the Rev. Dr. J. Wilbur Chapman, a leader in the evangelical crusade then in progress in the Mississippi Valley, took him on as an advance agent and general helper, but Dr. Chapman accepted a pastorate in the Philadelphia Presbytery in 1895 and his protégé was cast adrift. The first of his four children had been born by then, and Sunday was in a precarious position. What did he do? "I laid it before the Lord," he said years later, "and in a short while there came a telegram from a little town in Garner, out in Iowa, asking me to come out and conduct some meetings. I didn't know anybody out there, and I don't know yet why they ever asked me to hold meetings, but I went."

That's how it all began.

Nurtured on the soft-sell preaching techniques of Dr. Chapman and the Rev. Dr. Dwight Lyman Moody, the Chicago-based Baptist evangelist who was the most towering figure in the field until his death in 1899, Sunday started in low key. Even so, he was an instant success in the country of the tall corn and soon had invitations from all over the Bible Belt. By the time he was ordained a Presbyterian minister in 1903, he had developed the style which would earn him his fame. Now his two-fisted reading of the Bible—the Scripture reduced to the language of the sandlot— came adorned with some acrobatics. Still at his playing weight, 145 pounds, the outfielder on "God's team" developed quite a fancy repertoire to go with his vivid tongue. He would strip off his jacket, tear open his stiff collar, stamp up and down on the tabernacle platforms, jump off chairs to furnish punctuation for his harangues, slap his hands together, shadowbox, throw one foot forward in the manner of a pitcher's windup as he hurled his challenge at the Devil ("he's on the job all the time"), fall to the boards with both arms outstretched to tag the bum out. In the athlete-come-to-Jesus, the Prince of Darkness had a terrible and relentless foe on his hands.

There was a notion abroad that the Reverend William A. Sunday's pyrotechnics wouldn't go over in the more sophisticated East, but you couldn't tell that to the man himself, nor to "Ma" Sunday, his business manager and Number 1 helper. With a large entourage headed by Ohio-born Homer Alvin (Rody) Rodeheaver, who could warm up an audience of Eskimos with his slide trombone, Sunday took the old-time religion into Philadelphia in 1915 and ran up quite a score. He preached two sermons a day for seventy-eight days, drawing upwards of 15,000 people every time, and came away with that claim of 41,724 converts. In Boston, the next winter, an even more frenzied revival produced a claim of 63,716 "trail-hitters" and at least one rather engaging sidelight for those times: Al Jolson, Cantor Yoelson's son, in town with the tryout run of *Robinson Crusoe, Jr.,* sent his chorus girls over to put the weight of their piping sopranos behind that hot Rodeheaver horn and the less flashy choristers in the Reverend's own touring company. The versatile Jolson girls had no trouble with the Sunday theme, "Brighten the Corner Where You Are"; they had the looks to go with it.

The tabernacle built for the shirt-sleeved Devil's adversary in New York the next spring had 20,000 seats, more than Madison Square Garden, but the man had no trouble filling them all. And his performances made the advance ballyhoo seem pale. The nonbelievers, cheerfully pouring cash contributions into the Sunday coffers for the privilege of witnessing the slaughter, not only saw Satan take one of the worst buffetings of his miserable life but also heard all the patented assaults on the "whiskey kings," the slackers, the German warlords and the suffragettes, along with some passing sideswipes at the local ministry ("warmed-over Christians"). The "whiskey kings," of course, were even then on their way to the perdition reserved for them, because Prohibition was just around the corner. Billy Sunday, a veritable pinup boy for the Anti-Saloon League, deserved as much credit as anyone for this idiotic detour on the American highway, but while it figured to deprive him of his Number 2 whipping boy he met that contingency nicely. He simply switched from his Demon Rum line ("The Brewer's Big Horses Can't Run Over Me," the song said) to a new stock sermon: "Crooks, Corkscrews, Bootleggers and Whiskey Politicians—They Shall Not Pass." They did pass, though, and in vast numbers.

In that period, the free-swinging revivalist's hold on the sinner loosened more or less in proportion to the way the Great Experiment itself was losing favor. While he did get some mileage later out of his one-man campaign against that whiskey-drinkin' Al Smith in the 1928 Presidential election, there was a noticeable shortage of souls available for saving via the hellfire-and-brimstone approach. The road ran downhill. but even at that nothing short of his own aging heart could stop the ballplayer-turned-God's-handyman. Billy Sunday was still on that Sawdust Trail when the end came in Chicago on November 7, 1935, just a week ahead of his seventy-second birthday. He had seven seasons in the big leagues and forty on the Glory Road, and he died in peace.

SISTER AIMEE:

Trouble in Eden

The long flowing silk gown
was a McPherson trademark.

ONCE AIMEE SEMPLE MCPHERSON doffed her flowing, ankle-length white satin gown and dressed herself as a traffic cop. Then she puttered down the aisle of her Angelus Temple on a shiny motorcycle, pulled up short of the stage, leaped off the bike and raised a gloved hand to her congregation. "Stop," the blonde evangelist shouted, "You're speeding to Hell!" Another time she came puffing onto the premises in football gear; she was carrying the ball over the goal line for her Foursquare Gospel. And another time, mindful of the high sports fever of the times, she had an illuminated scoreboard behind her on the lectern to chronicle God's triumph in the extra-inning game between Good and Evil.

Operating in the Twenties in the purple-green pastures of Los Angeles, suddenly host to great hordes newly wandered into a Godless territory, Sister Aimee saw her fortunes rise in the West as Billy Sunday's declined on the other side of the Mississippi. What made Southern California such an ideal prospecting ground for a roving grass widow preacher who had pulled into town in a broken-down jalopy with $100 to her name and a mother and two little children to feed? Perhaps H. L. Mencken understood it best:

The osteopaths, chiropractors and other such quacks had long marked and occupied it. It swarmed with swamis, spiritualists, Christian Scientists, crystal-grazers and the allied necromancers. It offered brilliant pickings for the real estate speculators, oil-stock brokers, wire tappers and so on. But the town pastors were not up to its opportunities. They ranged from melancholy High Church Episcopalians, laboriously trying to interest retired Iowa alfalfa kings in ritualism, down to struggling Methodists and Baptists, as earnestly seeking to inflame the wives of the same monarchs with the crimes of the Pope. All this was over the heads of the trade. The Iowans longed for something that they could get their teeth into. They wanted magic and noise. They wanted an excuse to whoop.

Sister Aimee had them whoopin' from the moment she began to scratch together the down payment on that garish $1,500,000 Temple of hers. No rickety old tabernacle for "The World's Most Pulchritudinous Evangelist." It had to be big enough to redeem 5,000 lost souls at a sitting. It had to have its own broad-

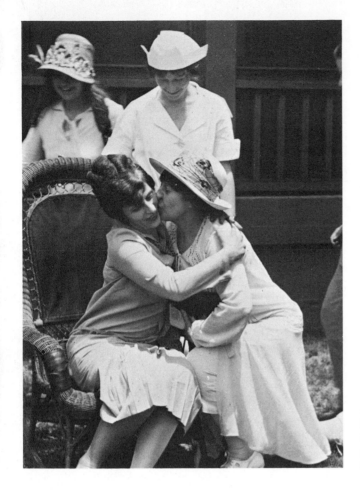

Kenneth G. Ormiston, the amorous radio operator of Angelus Temple, was in the thick of the scandal that followed Sister Aimee's "kidnapping" in 1926. *WWP*

On a hospital lawn in Arizona, Minnie Kennedy kisses her daughter while her children, Roberta Star and Rolf, await their turn. The reunion followed the soul-saver's mysterious emergence from the desert after her thirty-seven-day disappearance. *WWP*

casting studio and a marquee rivaling anything on the Sunset Strip. It had to have a Cradle Roll Chapel for the babies and a Miracle Room where the newly healed could cast away their crutches and braces. ("Jesus is the healer. I am only the little office girl who opens the door and says, 'Come in.' ") It had to have a bank of colored Kliegs like a movie set. ("Turn on the lights and clear the one-way street for Jesus!") It had to have a rotating, illuminated cross that could call in the troubled wayfarer for fifty miles around.

The strong-willed Minnie Kennedy, once a Salvation Army lass, brought Aimee into the world on a little farm outside of Ontario, Canada, on October 9, 1890, and dedicated her to the service of God right off the bat. At seventeen, Aimee lost her heart to Robert Semple, a strapping boilermaker who was a Pentecostal minister on the side. Semple, bent on missionary work, took his bride to the Orient, contracted malaria outside of Hong Kong and died just before their daughter, Roberta Star, was born. The young widow returned to the states, did some preaching around Chicago and then went East and lost her heart again, this time to a grocery clerk named Harold McPherson

from Providence, Rhode Island. That marriage lasted less than two years, producing a son named Rolf before McPherson departed, saying he couldn't cope with the hefty evangelist's "wildcat habits" in the home, whatever that meant.

Aimee hit the trail for good then, refining her Foursquare Gospel along the rustic byways and eking out a bare living from the sparse handouts of the faithful. She touched down in Los Angeles in 1918, went back and forth across the country, took the message across the Pacific to Australia and New Zealand, wowed 'em in San Diego and then went back to L.A. to build herself the monument called Angelus Temple, hard by Echo Park, in 1923. Between her Hollywood-style promotions and the lavish accounts of her vast healing powers, spread far and wide by her own radio broadcasts, she quickly moved into a position of preeminence as the Number 1 Hell-robber of the day.

It didn't last very long.

Sister Aimee, underneath the snow-white image much more the woman than "the little girl who opens the door," fell off the pedestal with a crash recorded on front pages all over the world.

The man in the case was Kenneth G. Ormiston. He

163

was the Temple's radio operator. His assorted impediments included a balding crown, a withered leg and a resident wife, but none of those items made enough difference to steer "The Beautiful Sister Aimee of the Silver Tongue" (her billing) away from a course fraught with peril.

The curtain raiser in this slow-building epic came on May 18, 1926, shortly after the evangelist drove off to the beach at nearby Venice for what was supposed to be a day of sun-splashed solitude and relaxation. She took her secretary, Emma Schaeffer, but sent her on an errand after donning a green bathing suit and settling down in a tent near the water. When Miss Schaeffer got back, her employer was nowhere to be found. This produced an immediate assumption that the evangelist had been claimed by that old devil sea. For her part, Ma Kennedy didn't even wait for the search parties to complete their labors. "We know she is with Jesus," proclaimed Ma, summoning the grieving legions. "Pray for her!" The faithful not only emptied their hearts but their pockets as well, since the Temple was not only offering a $25,000 reward for any information which would return Sister Aimee to dry temporal ground but also starting a fund to build her a modest $36,000 memorial (none of it ever returned, by the way).

What followed for the next month or so was an orgy of endless wailing in the Temple and scenes of sheer hysteria, lit up by bonfires and syncopated with such hymns as "Asleep in the Deep," along that lonely stretch of sand and surf in Venice. There was some needless tragedy, too. Long after the professional deep-sea divers abandoned their search of the ocean floor, the bereft were still hurling themselves into the blue Pacific in the vain hope of locating the remains. One youth drowned in this brave if futile endeavor and another died of exposure, while a girl in Sister's congregation reportedly killed herself out of grief. In due course, Ma Kennedy herself, underlining her acceptance of the inevitable, hired a small plane to scatter some lilies over the cruel waters.

For the more hardboiled observers, actually, an aroma of fish had settled over the Evangelist's disappearance just nine days after that shocking first bulletin from Emma Schaeffer. This is where the amorous radio operator, Mr. Ormiston, comes in, for it turned out on May 27 that he himself had been among the missing for assorted periods all the way back to the preceding January. What made that intelligence peculiarly noteworthy was that Sister Aimee herself had ventured forth on an extensive tour of Europe and the Holy Land earlier in the year and that Mrs. Ormiston, somewhere along the tangled line, had asked

the Sheriff's office to find her wandering soul mate. When this web of coincidence found its way into the papers, Ormiston showed up at the search headquarters on the beach. There he answered some perfunctory questions put to him by a detective, only to drop out of sight again as casually as he had reappeared.

Sister Aimee herself, somewhat bruised but reasonably buoyant, turned up on June 27—thirty-seven days after slipping away for that dip. First, toward 3:00 A.M., she aroused a slaughterhouse keeper outside of Agua Prieta, across the border from Douglas, Arizona. This man hastened to the door in his drawers and quickly withdrew to get his trousers, only to find his caller gone. Sister later rapped on the window of a cottage in the village itself and in due course a rickety taxi was summoned to deliver her to the Douglas police. The thriller which then unfolded proved to be a cliff-hanging saga of kidnapping and horror involving assorted players billed as Rosie, Steve and Jake, buttressed by an old Mexican (Felipe) in a bit role filled with interesting potential and a prop baby (no name). This is the way the bedraggled star of the drama described it:

Rosie slipped up to Sister Aimee's tent while Emma Schaeffer was off on that errand. Rosie said her baby (Rosie's baby, that is) was about to expire in a car just off the beach. Rosie said that Ma Kennedy had told her where to find Sister if she wanted a prayer said over the doomed infant. Would Sister do that? Sister would. Well, there was no baby in the car. Steve and Jake—just the driver and bereft of a speaking part—were in the car. Somebody pressed something against Sister Aimee's nose and she passed out. When she came to, she was in a shack somewhere in Mexico and that brute Steve was telling her that she happened to be the victim of a snatch but could buy her way back to her Temple, for, oh, a half million in cash (presumably in small, unmarked bills). And if she didn't care to come up with that king-sized ransom? Well, the trio, evidently short of walking-around money, would have to trade her off to the sinister Mexican (Felipe, like the playbill said) for whatever use he wished to make of her. Blackout. Thirty-six days later the kidnap band relaxes its vigil and their meal ticket slips away on a thirteen-hour march over the scorching desert to Agua Prieta.

Removed to the nearest hospital and furnished with a pink silk dressing gown in which to meet the assembled press, Sister Aimee exhibited burns on her fingers (somebody in the shack used a hot cigar to show that they weren't kidding around), bruises on her ankles (from the cord used to bind them) and

Joint defendants in the trial growing out of that kidnapping saga, Sister Aimee and her mother are shown in court. *WWP*

Months later, mother and daughter strike a pose that belies the fierce row separating them. "Affairs at the temple are the worst mess in history," Mrs. Kennedy had charged a short time earlier, capping a power struggle that went back years. She agreed to walk away from it all in 1927, but it took a battery of lawyers to work out the peace terms. *International News Photo*

blisters on her feet (from that long hike over the hot sands). Well, the reviews were simply dreadful, the critics noting:

• The damage to Sister's fingers and ankles hardly bore out her description of the indignities inflicted upon her.

• The blisters appeared much too mild for a thirteen-mile jaunt along the desert in ladies' pumps.

• The victim's dress, available for scrutiny, was strangely shy of the dirt or wear one would expect after all that time and travail.

Delivered back to her flock in a wicker chair due to her depleted condition, the evangelist was met at the railroad station by a throng of 30,000, surpassing the previous turnouts there for Woodrow Wilson, William Howard Taft and the King of Belgium. The motorcade to the Temple, led by the joyous Temple band, drew another 100,000 spectators.

But District Attorney Asa Keyes spoiled it all in very quick time. He said the still-missing Kenneth Ormiston and a buxom blonde who looked an awful lot like Aimee Semple McPherson had checked in and out of a whole flock of outlying beach hotels during late May and the first three weeks in June. This Odyssey, as Keyes told it, included a ten-day sojourn in a love nest in Carmel rented in the name of Kenneth Ormiston. While the woman used the name of McIntyre—Mrs. McIntyre, of course—her signature on the grocery bills was said to be very close to that of Sister Aimee.

"I am being crucified by the very bats of hell," the evangelist replied. "Any true man who knew the diabolical attempts to assassinate my name and great work by linking it with such a story would come out with a clear statement or communicate directly with our office."

Ormiston, a gentleman in the end, responded by mailing the District Attorney an affidavit which avowed that the shepherdess of Angelus Temple could not have been in Carmel with *him* because the babe on hand there happened to be a "Miss X." Keyes, a skeptical sort, filed a criminal complaint charging both Sister Aimee and her mother with obstructing justice in their appearances before his Grand Jury. This touched off months of furious recriminations, in and out of the courtroom. Sister Aimee alternately suggested that the "overlords of the underworld" had prompted the case against her and that dark forces in the Protestant and Catholic clergy were out to destroy her. She said the woman traveling with Kenneth Ormiston must have been made up to look like her. She said she couldn't possibly have run off with that man because her next husband had to be a preacher six feet tall or more who could play the trombone and sing and maintain "certain rigid standards" of personal conduct on top of all that.

The ensuing trial ("I am like a lamb led to slaughter," said Sister Aimee), ended on a note which, if possible, was even stranger than the events which brought it about. With what seemed to be an airtight case and with Ormiston flushed out in Pennsylvania and available for some sweating on the stand, Keyes suddenly moved for a directed verdict of acquittal. To this day, nobody has explained why, although a small clue emerged two years later when the prosecutor himself was slapped into San Quentin Prison for having taken a $100,000 bribe in a stock fraud case. This produced nasty suggestions that some stray cash may have been spread around in the McPherson case too.

Carey McWilliams, an on-the-scene observer, wrote the postscript to *L'Affaire Aimee* in *The Aspirin Age,* Isabel Leighton's book about the Twenties:

That Aimee's disappearance and return should have been one of the great news stories of the decade is not surprising. It contained all the right ingredients: sex, mystery, underworld characters, spooks, kidnapers, the ocean, hot desert sands, an escape, and a thrilling finale. It was a story made for the period, a period that invested the trivial with a special halo, that magnified the insipid, that pursued cheap sensationalism with avidity and passion. While admittedly quite a story, the kidnaping of Sister Aimee became invested with the proportions of a myth and the dimensions of a saga in the great vacuum of the age. It was a

kind of compendium of all the pervading nonsense, cynicism, credulity, speakeasy wit, passion for debunkery, sex-craziness, and music-hall pornography of the times.

There isn't much to the rest of the story. Sister Aimee's star dimmed rapidly. On succeeding tours along the Sawdust Trail, she had difficulty filling the tabernacle. She married again but her new beau ideal, Dave Hutton, could neither play the trombone nor meet the high moral standards Sister Aimee had set forth; he got his walking papers when another woman sued him for $200,000, alleging that he had been careless about some of the promises made under the stress of *their* romance.

Sister dropped out of the news after a while, and in September, 1944, she was found unconscious in a hotel room in Oakland under circumstances suggesting that she had been taking sleeping pills in excessive quantities. She died later in the day and in Angelus Temple the faithful serenaded her with the hymn called "In the Sweet Bye and Bye." For all the brave front in the good days, actually, Aimee Semple McPherson had more acquaintance with the bitter. Outside the Temple, she found love an elusive thing in the years when she needed it most.

The evangelist in New York in 1931 with her hefty new husband, Dave Hutton, her temple singer. The union quickly expired when an earlier romantic alliance of Hutton's suddenly surfaced and landed him in court. *New York Post*

Ma Kennedy had marital problems of her own. She tied the knot with the Reverend Guy Edward Hudson in 1931 and went on a $1,500-a-week vaudeville tour with him but then left him because he had "no taste for work" and, even worse, had another wife.*AP*

"I'm not an intellectual or a theologian. It's not me who draws the crowds. It's God." *WWP*

BILLY GRAHAM:

"Come quietly now..."

"I never thought simplicity
could cudgel us sinners so damned hard."
—CASSANDRA in the London *Daily Mirror*
after watching Dr. Billy Graham in action

BILLY FRANK GRAHAM Jr. didn't have to be dragged kicking and screaming to Christ, but he did put up an argument back there in North Carolina. He had to milk the cows before sunup and tend to all his other chores after school; he hardly ever had the time he wanted for basketball and baseball, or for showing the girls how fast the family sedan could roll along the open highway under the stars. So when Mordecai Ham brought his rip-roaring revival up from Kentucky into Charlotte, Billy Frank refused to tag along with his parents. Religion was a big bore to him but he was attending church and Sunday school. Wasn't that enough? The Grahams, Scotch-Irish Presbyterians, didn't press it but they did not fail to tell him about the colorful old evangelist when they came home, visibly moved. Finally, out of sheer curiosity, the boy went. He went every night for a month, and he couldn't sleep when he got home. The Rev. Mr. Ham was touching a nerve somewhere. "One night I went up and sat with the people who were saved," Billy Graham recalled years later, after his own fame was established as history's first globe-girdling evangelist. "I opened up my heart and knew for the first time the sweetness and joy of God, of truly being born again

. . . I belonged to Christ. The next morning when I went to school even the leaves and the trees looked different. It was a deep feeling."

That was in 1934, when the lanky farm boy was sixteen. While he wasn't sure about becoming a minister then, he enrolled in the Florida Bible Institute in Tampa after high school, and that's where it began to happen. Billy fell in love but he didn't seem serious enough about his studies and the girl spurned him in favor of a boy who was going on to Harvard Divinity School. Crushed, the rejected suitor took to prowling the school golf course late into the night—talking to the Maker. "God, reveal Your will to me," he would say. "Hear this prayer. What shall Your servant do?" Then, one night, "in the darkness, His answer came as clearly as a newspaper headline." Billy fell to his knees on the eighteenth hole, tears streaming down his face, and said, "All right, Lord, if You want me You can have me."

For Billy Graham, then, unlike Billy Sunday, it wasn't liquor and hell-raising; the torment of the heart and soul led him to the service of God. After that night on the golf course, he started to train himself to preach. He would steal off to a swamp on the edge of town or paddle up the Hillsboro River and find a secluded place and pretend he had a whole flock of sinners in front of him. "Standing on a tree stump," he recounted once, "I'd practice my sermon to the birds and the alligators. One day, I said, 'God, if You want me to preach, help me locate a pulpit.' Just then a fellow came up. He said he had heard me preach and they were having a gospel meeting down the road and the preacher hadn't shown up. He asked me if I would help him out. I looked up and knew that God had heard my prayer. I saved twelve souls that night."

That was the beginning.

To refine his techniques, Billy carried the gospel to the derelicts in the Tampa Rescue Mission on Saturday nights and spent his Sundays preaching in the trailer camps on the outskirts of town. Ordained in the Southern Baptist ministry in Tampa, he went on to Wheaton College outside of Chicago, and there he fell in love again. The girl, Ruth McCue Bell, China-born daughter of Dr. R. Nelson Bell, a Presbyterian medical missionary, had an abundance of good looks to go with her exotic background and bouncy personality. "Ruth was the campus belle," Graham has said. "She was a junior with suitors galore, and I was a freshman and a nobody. So I turned to God, asking Him to give her to me."

The wedding took place after Billy's graduation in 1943, and he accepted a forty-five-dollar-a-week pastorate in a tiny basement congregation in Western Springs, Illinois, but it wasn't what he wanted. He had his eye on the larger, more fertile audiences of the evangelist, and he got his break when a friend, Torrey Johnson, invited him into the newly founded Youth for Christ. Billy traveled widely for Johnson, bringing the gospel to bear in the war on juvenile delinquency, until he was offered the presidency of Northwestern Schools, a little Minneapolis college. Two years in the academic halls was all he could take, however, and in 1947 he turned evangelist again, assembling the nucleus of the team that would scale the heights with him: Grady and T. W. Wilson, schoolboy chums who had been converted with him in Mordecai Ham's tent; George Beverly Shea, the booming baritone gospel singer, and Cliff Barrows, his song leader. The Rev. Dr. Graham, blue-eyed, blond-haired and six feet two, made an imposing figure along the Sawdust Trail but there was nothing in those first couple of years to suggest that another Dwight Moody or Billy Sunday was upon us. Nothing, that is, until the Graham caravan dared to venture into Hollywood in the autumn of 1959. The waters, holy or otherwise,

get a little churlish here, casting methods being what they are out that way.

First, J. Arthur Vaus, wayward son of a minister, made his Decision for Christ under the driving force of the homespun gospel-according-to-Graham ("Some jealous guys were out to get Daniel, so they trained their spyglasses on him while he was praying with his Venetian blinds up"). J. Arthur, called Big Jim, made a most engaging convert because he came into the "Canvas Cathedral" staggering under a burden of sin that was inordinate even for the movie colony. An electronics expert of considerable talents, he put the special equipment in for his pal Mickey Cohen when all kinds of lowlifes were aiming cannons at Mickey's happy home. He installed the hidden listening devices when Brenda Allen, the red-haired queen of the call girls, felt the need of this modern appurtenance in her operation. And he tapped quite an assortment of telephones along the way. Anyway, the one-shot conversion instilled so much missionary zeal in Big Jim that he dragged Mickey Cohen along one night to hear Dr. Graham address a select gathering in the home of Jane Russell.

What came out of that session was a raft of headlines trumpeting the news that muscleman Cohen, of all the unlikely people, also had gone over to the side of the angels. "When I asked for people who wanted prayer to hold up their hands," Graham said later, "Mickey lifted his hand, and I am sincerely convinced that he wanted God." Another account from the scene was that Mickey was so moved that he began to moan, "Oh, pray for me, Oh, pray for me" even as the evangelist intoned his message of salvation. There were hints that Mickey might give testimony for Christ, as Big Jim had done, but the gangster didn't like that. "If I want religion," he said, "I'll go to a rabbi." There was also some talk of Cohen lecturing on juvenile crime under the Graham aegis but the aging delinquent had to forego that noble endeavor for fear that it would make him a sitting duck for all those unfriendly marksmen from the sun-drenched Hollywood underworld.

Even so, Cohen's near-break with the Devil received a display just short, say, of a declaration that the Gabor sisters, *en masse*, were chucking the high life to repair to a nunnery. The Hearst papers in particular, traditionally oriented toward the Golden Rule as a good clean circulation builder, simply went wild. And the Cohen saga, happily, was compounded by the redemption of the evil Vaus and the conversion of radio's Singing Cowboy, Stuart Hamblen, and Lou Zamperini, the ex-Olympic miler and World War II

too light and "needed a stake." Jones submitted that he wasn't excessively disturbed about the money. "My concern," he said, "is that Michael never really meant those things he said about accepting God. I feel sorry for him—terribly sorry."

Then Red Skelton, having dealt with little Michael when he was offered a chance to portray the real Mickey Cohen on celluloid ("I told him I couldn't see him as a tall redheaded fellow"), turned up with a fresh shocker. Called as a government witness in the Cohen tax-evasion inquiry, the comedian testified that the gangster once told him that the Graham organization had paid him $15,000 to sit in at one revival meeting and promised him $10,000 more if he would go all the way with his Decision for Christ. Cohen had indeed attended an open session, calling it a "wonderful experience" and proclaiming that "Billy has taught me to live correctly," but the Skelton story about the dollar bills drew a vigorous denial from Graham. Then in London, the evangelist said *he* had never paid or offered to pay any money to Cohen. He said it "would be blasphemy in the sight of God to offer one penny to anyone to attend a meeting or to make a profession of faith." He also said he was still praying "for the salvation of Mickey Cohen's soul," and there the matter rested. Little Michael, one way or another, was at least $5,000 ahead of the Crusade when the prison doors slammed shut on him once more. It was an isolated but nevertheless unseemly blotch on the Graham escutcheon, and it didn't end there.

The retired gangster dirtied the holy waters a little more in his autobiography, *Mickey Cohen: In My Own Words*, written with John Peer Nugent and published just a year before his death at sixty-two in 1976. Without touching on the coin of the realm, Cohen said Big Jim Vaus dropped in on him one night with Messrs. Hamblen and Zamperini and a fourth party—the Reverend Dr. Graham himself—"who just wanted to make my acquaintance, or maybe . . . he had it in his mind that he might convert me." That session, he said, was swiftly followed by a peremptory summons to the office of his long-time pal Jim Richardson, city editor of Hearst's Los Angeles *Examiner*, where

William Randolph Hearst got on the phone and told me in no uncertain terms, "Lookit, we're going to push Billy Graham, we're going to further Bill Graham's career, and we're going to use you, Mickey." He didn't ask *me* can we use you? He *told* me.

hero, who brought his bride into the fold with him. When the massive Hamblen saw the torch held aloft by Graham, he not only sold his racing stable but quit drinking and smoking and singing such naughty songs as "I Won't Go Huntin' with Yuh, Jake, but I'll Go Chasin' Women."

This rash of news quickly tripled the skimpy audiences of 3,000 originally drawn by the display ads heralding the arrival, with "glorious music" and a "dazzling array of gospel talent," of "America's sensational young evangelist." The handsome, personable toiler in God's vineyard was on his way, but there was an unpleasant postscript two years later. A Federal Grand Jury peeking into the Cohen exchequer heard testimony that members of the evangelist's organization had advanced $5,000 in loans to Mickey while they were talking to him about "accepting the Christian way of life." W. C. Jones, a Los Angeles member of the Graham board of directors, told the jury that the money—never repaid—was given to the hoodlum gambler in installments when he said he was traveling

Well, naturally, I'm not stupid. I knew they were going to use me with publicity, so I said, "Okay by me."

Cohen, whose labors for the evangelist included his appearance at a Madison Square Garden revival session to beef up the gate, said Graham paid a call on him in the L. A. county jail in 1951 when he was awaiting a hearing on his first income tax rap and personally tried to bring him into the fold, saying, "Mick, don't get hot about it, don't jump off the handle or anything like that, but you've tried everything else. Why don't you try Christianity?" This, as the book has it, was Cohen's answer:

"Listen, we've had an understanding that we're friends, but that it wouldn't get me into no religion bullshit or anything like that. Now I may not be considered by a lot of people as being a good Jew, but I was born a Jew. And that's it."

In any case, the Cohen saga had long since gone down as a sorry early chapter in the Graham success story.

The only other occasion for red faces had come in the highflying year following the Los Angeles revival. Drawing jam-packed throngs wherever he went, Graham ran into an embarrassment when the Atlanta *Constitution* juxtaposed two photos from his appearance there. One showed him in action, passionately calling the people to the Saviour. The other showed his chief usher laboring down the aisle toting a bag stuffed with $16,000 in "love offerings." It was the evangelist's introduction to the nagging question inevitably tossed at all the touring soul savers with the possible exception of Savonarola, who started it all back in Fifteenth-Century Italy—hey, what's happening to all the cash? To Graham, it was like a "kick in the stomach," so he besought guidance from the National Council of Churches and then decided to go on a straight salary—$15,000 a year, later upped to $19,500 and due to keep going up with the cost of living down here—with all "love offerings" clearly earmarked for the operation of the huge and ever more complex Billy Graham Evangelistic Association. "Money," the evangelist has said, "has no appeal to me. If I made religion commercial the Lord would take His hand off me." But this is not to deny that Graham ever underestimated the rich rewards of public relations.

No evangelist before Billy Graham ever boasted a pressure-cooker operation so finely attuned to Madison Avenue methods. He spent $225,000 on advertising and publicity in the six months before his New York "spiritual reawakening" pitched its tent in Madison

Betty Colleen Townsend, twenty-one then, walked away from a $1,000-a-week 20th Century-Fox contract in 1950 to turn evangelist. The Graham film organization then recruited her for its inspirational series. In *Mr. Texas*, billed as "the world's first Christian Western," she played the daughter of an oil tycoon who turned to religion after attending a Graham revival.

Square Garden in 1957 and another $400,000 for TV time in the six weeks afterward. "St. Paul didn't have television," Graham observed. "We can reach more people by television than the population of the world was then." He knew what he was talking about. His first live New York telecast outdrew the Jackie Gleason show and ran just two percentage points behind Perry Como. The returns on this mass exposure were very large indeed. Winding up a Yankee Stadium rally which attracted 100,000 persons, the only assemblage to top the crowd of 88,150 drawn to that temple of sweat in 1935 to witness Max Baer's futile effort to take the heavyweight title away from Joe Louis, Graham counted a total of 2,397,400 in his live audiences and listed 61,148 as converts prepared to abandon their pagan ways. In London, he drew 120,000 Britons into Wembley Stadium and even Cassandra, the sharp-tongued *Daily Mirror* columnist, had to concede that "this theatrical disci-

On the golf course with Richard Nixon, then the former Vice President. *WWP*

Houston, 1965: President Johnson and Lady Bird were on hand for the finale of a ten-day crusade there. *WWP*

ple, this Hollywood version of John the Baptist, has them rocking in the aisles."

How does a man of the cloth justify the frightfully expensive ballyhoo that has been used to help fill the world's largest stadia for Billy Graham? "We are selling the greatest product on earth. Why shouldn't we promote it as effectively as a bar of soap?" Why indeed? Money never was a problem, because there's just no ceiling on the amounts available to bring the Holy Spirit to the sin-ridden multitudes crying out for salvation.

For all the blockbusting promotion, of course, Graham won't go for the stunt. As a sin-splitter, he's a straight-from-the-shoulder preacher who never relied on the histrionics of a Billy Sunday or the burlesque antics of an Aimee Semple McPherson, but then neither is there any danger that he will ever be confused with Bishop Sheen. He'll warm up an audience with small jokes and say, "May God bless you real good," and he won't stand up there with his hands softly folded around the Word. He whacks his fists into his palms. He pounds the platform as his homespun gospel pours forth on the sinner in his magnetic, compelling tones. He summons up a potent anger as his deep-set eyes flash and he points an accusing finger and says, "Maybe nobody knows what you did in the parked car last night, but God knows." Or, "What about you? What does a man go to Hell for? Not for getting drunk, cursing, committing adultery, or lying.

Chatting with President Eisenhower after a guest sermon at Washington's National Presbyterian Church in 1955. *WWP*

The only thing that will send a man to Hell is rejecting Jesus Christ." Or, "I'll tell you you don't know what you're missing if you don't want God. He knows you. He wants you. He loves you. Will you do business with God tonight? This could be your last chance. This is God's night. This is harvest time." Or, in the voice of doom, "You can't come to Christ anytime you want to. You can only come when the spirit of God is drawing and wooing you. I beg of you to come now before it is too late. You know you need Christ in your life. Come quietly now and say, 'Billy, tonight I accept Christ.'"

How many have come forth (while the choir sang "Almost Persuaded")? It's all in telephone numbers now—like more than 50 million people have heard the evangelist's message in the flesh and more than 15 million of them—instant converts—came forward to dedicate the rest of their born, or born-again, lives to Christianity. How many emerged from the Inquiry Tent—Graham prefers "inquiry" to conversion—and then went into the church of their choice and stayed with it will never be known. The GHQ in Minneapolis keeps track of the reformed religious dropouts for just six months; after that, to borrow a phrase from Wolcott Gibbs, knows God. It is impossible to arrive at a figure in any case, because Graham's *Hour of Decision* has reached upwards of 15,000,000 television viewers in the United States and Canada on a single Sunday night and his tireless journeys across the seas even have penetrated behind the Iron Curtain. He broke that barrier in 1977 with five sparsely attended revival sessions in Hungary. How many, then, have come into the fold as permanent tenants? How many who hear the evangelist on his radio outlets around the globe? How many readers of his syndicated newspaper column? How many of the 3,500,000 $2-a-year subscribers to his monthly magazine, *Decision*? How many readers of his 1975 book, *Angels: God's Secret Agents*, which has sold 1.2 million copies at $4.95 for Doubleday and is now in its fifteenth printing with the Pocket Books paperback itself past the million mark? How many readers of the $6.95 *How to Be Born Again*, which hit the stalls in 1977 with a record first printing of 800,000 and drew a fast call for another 450,000 copies?

Graham himself once made an offhand estimate that 75 percent of those who see the flame wind up with what he likes to call "long-term contracts with God." He uses Billy Sunday's classic answer for those who say his doom-saying ministry produces no lasting effect on the penitent: "Neither does a bath, but it does you good to take one."

This kind of wit has been a Graham trademark since

he came out of the hinterlands to knock 'em dead—or is it knock 'em alive? Is he the Barrymore of the Bible or Gabriel in Gabardine? No, he is a simple servant of the Lord whose own prayers are uniformly answered except, he has said, when he's swinging a golf club. Is he God's Ball of Fire? No, he is God's Master of Ceremonies—"because I introduce people to the Lord." Why did God choose him? "I don't know. When I get to Heaven I'm going to ask Him."

Now touching sixty and the father of five, Billy Graham is a man clearly blessed with a charismatic quality. Perhaps Harold H. Martin said it best in his *Saturday Evening Post* article back in 1963: "He has become, around the world, a religious figure only slightly less well known than the Pope. In the United States he has become a symbol like the flag, a national institution like J. Edgar Hoover."

Yes indeed, but like the departed Hoover, almost equally sainted, this institution is by no means free of woes, large and small.

In 1974 Graham found himself tainted by the Watergate mess. A golfing buddy and live-in guru for Richard Nixon (with the Number One guest room, no less), he counseled the populace to keep the faith and stand behind the President as a good, wise and decent man. Oh, the red faces. Just thirteen days before he abdicated to beat an almost certain impeachment and close the book on the blackest chapter in American political history, Mr. Nixon had called the evangelist. "When I have a decision to make involving a moral issue, I counsel first with Billy Graham," said the Quaker nailed by his own tapes in the coverup flowing from his reelection campaign honchos' bungled 1972 postmidnight visit to the headquarters of Democratic National Chairman Lawrence F. O'Brien. "Maybe I was naive at that time," Graham said later. "Maybe I was used," adding that Nixon himself had not attempted to exploit their long relationship but "some of his staff may have tried to do so."

The evangelist was involved in another White House flap three years later when Rowland Evans and Robert Novak reported that Jimmy Carter had solicited his support when the media was pounding away at the tangled financial affairs of his soon-to-resign budget director, Bert Lance. Press Secretary Jody Powell, while admitting that the President had discussed the messy problems of his old pal Lance on the phone with Graham, heatedly denied the syndicated columnists' account of that pow-wow. Evans's answer: "We're not backing down from anything we wrote."

No matter how thick or thin the Graham–Carter relationship may be, it is quite obviously not shared by the entire Georgia clan. Son Jeff, then twenty-four, blasted the man during a campaign appearance for his father in Memphis just before that stunning Carter win over Gerald Ford. Asked for his view of a Graham statement warning voters against politicians who flaunt their religion before the electorate, Jeff said, "I think what people should watch out for is people like Billy Graham who go around telling people how to live their lives."

And that wasn't all.

The youth went on to knock the evangelist—remember there's one in the family, dad's sister Ruth Stapleton—as a man who had a "doctor of religion" degree anyone could get in the mail for, say, $2. A Graham spokesman quickly reminded the populace about that divinity degree from Baylor, not to mention a whole horde of honorary parchments picked up over the years.

Except for that Nixon stinger, of course, all of the above virtually fades into the trivia category against the affluent Bible thumper's more recent woes over the closely held financial affairs of his bustling organization. That headache surfaced in 1977 when North Carolina's Charlotte *Observer* laid bare the existence of a 23-million-dollar special fund unbeknownst to the minister's loyal and free-spending legions. Without laying on too much detail, the Reverend said that that bundle, called the World Evangelistic and Christian Education Fund and set up in 1970, had been regularly audited and its status reported annually to the IRS. He said its purpose was to "undergird evangelical ministries" and that it had been kept under wraps only to head off any deluge of requests for financial aid. He said that ever since 1950 his association had used sound business practices, even going so far as to put a ceiling on the salaries of the 425 toilers in the main tent to avoid an "Elmer Gantry image of financial irresponsibility and even dishonesty." He said "we are accountable to God" for every penny in individual contributions (an average of 2 million dollars per year) and that "extra precautions" had been taken "to be certain that everything is done with complete integrity so no dishonor might come to the name of Christ." The *Observer* reported that the special fund, with heavy investments in such blue-

chip stocks as Exxon, General Electric, IBM and AT&T, was underwriting just two major projects—a Billy Graham Center at Wheaton College in Illinois and a retreat center in North Carolina. While nobody has made any harsh noises about that great hoard, the Council of Better Business Bureaus in Washington has listed it among the forty-seven large religious groups which constantly have refused to pass along any hard information about its holdings.

It is to wonder.

In June 1978, George M. Wilson, the executive vice-president in residence in the main tent, reported that the Graham Association itself, along with five affiliates, had come out with $3.2 million in red ink during 1977 on combined incomes of $38.4 million against $41.6 million in expenditures. Wilson said the association was considering a chop in the number of radio stations carrying the head man's "Hour of Decision" and possibly cutting down his televised "crusade" specials. Wherever one turns in this success story, it would seem, that red ink specter rears its ugly wet head. Consider the situation of Word Books of Waco, Texas, the obscure religious house that publishes Dr. Graham's tomes. The American Broadcasting Company picked up Word in 1974 for 300,000 shares of ABC common stock, then listed at $23 per. But last year Word reportedly lost more than a million dollars while recording sales of $29 million. The ABC subsidiary, by the way, pays the evangelist $39,500 a year as a consultant, surpassing the level he reached some time ago in return for his evangelical labors. He waived that piece of change when he went on the Word payroll. But then, even with his large brood, he is hardly a candidate for food stamps. The 12½ percent royalty on his books—and there are two new ones on the way—has to make the Robbins, Wallaces, and Mailers look like authors working out of attics, and the Lord's messenger lives in a style befitting his station. His mountaintop estate in Minneapolis, guarded by a pack of killer German shepherds, has been valued at anywhere between $200,000 and $400,000.

On that note, our sermon proceeds to some of the hell-robbers who have blazed across the horizon in Billy Graham's wake.

BORN AGAIN:

The Number–One Growth Stock?

"The evangelicals have become the
most active and vital aspect of
American religion today."
    —WILLIAM MARTIN, Rice University
sociologist, in 1977.

THE ROSTER OF born-again Christians on these shores
has been put at 40 million and more—almost one out
of every five of us. Is this possible? Take away that
portion of the 48,000,000 Roman Catholics who
never strayed from the fold and have no need to
make a fresh decision for Christ. Take away that portion of the 22,500,000 blacks, mostly Baptist, who are
in the same position. Take away the 5,800,000 Jews
who don't need to be born again at all. And then
take away the millions who are either still in the cradle or not out of it long enough to have reached a
point where that walk down the aisle is either indicated or likely.

The conclusion is inescapable that the evangelicals
are counting some of the same people twice, which is
not to deny that the landscape is indeed dotted with
born-again Christians. The road to inner contentment
is patently too crowded to be put down as nothing more
than a numbers game. The old Bible-thumper's tent,
largely discarded for the all-encompassing airwaves, is
not only SRO but enjoying a boom underpinned with
some immensely diverse names. You start with the
White House itself and the nation's first born-again
President and go on to Charles Colson of Watergate
fame and the Black Panthers' Eldridge Cleaver and go

on to two members of the Charles Manson murder family and, of all people, smut king Larry Flynt, delivered
unto the Savior by Jimmy Carter's own sister. Now how
did that happen?

Ruth Carter Stapleton, who operates without a
church, without a microphone and without Madison
Avenue, came to her brand of "inner healing" full
time in the mid-Sixties on the brink of a marriage
that was collapsing after nineteen years and four children.

The self-made and remade Flynt came to his eminence by running a strip-joint newsletter into a multi-
million dollar pornography operation built around his
Hustler and *Chic* magazines, where it's all there, not just
in color photos and text but in sex paraphernalia for the
kinkier types peddled through the man's own Leasure
Times Products, Inc.

Enter now Joseph Wershba, a producer on the CBS
"60 Minutes" TV show who had done segments on
both those parties. Over lunch in September 1977, he
suggested to the evangelist that it might be useful for
her to have a talk with Larry Flynt. "Well, Joe," said Sister Ruth, "I've met all kinds of people. I guess I would
be pleased to meet that man." Her born-again husband,
Robert, a veterinarian, nodded in assent. Wershba

Sister Ruth addressing the International Order of Saint Luke, the Physician, at Little Rock, Arkansas. Her thing is love and "inner healing." *WWP*

Larry Flynt, pornographer, and Sister Ruth Carter Stapleton, evangelist. A most unlikely couple—but the *Hustler* publisher's conversion was for real, and the President's sister had a lot to do with it. *Charles Barksdale E/N*

passed that along to Flynt, who said, "Okay, I'll call that woman. Maybe we have something in common at that."

And darned if they didn't.

The October *Hustler* had an article linking child abuse to sexual repression. Sister Ruth found that theory "quite interesting" and invited the publisher to dinner at her home in Fayetteville because, as Flynt put it, "we're both interested in the business of influencing people." The then portly porn merchant, who seemed to Joe Wershba to be a deeply troubled man at that moment in a meteoric career that had made *Playboy* and *Penthouse* sit up and take notice, collected his wife and zipped down to North Carolina in his Israeli Jet Commander. The dinner went well and the Stapletons presently journeyed to the Flynts' palatial Ohio playpen in Bexley, outside of Columbus, seat of his empire. Come November, Flynt announced that he was turning to Christ and would tone down his skin magazines to promote a "healthy attitude toward sex rather than a perverted one." That flash, hardly calculated to help either the man's sales or advertising income, drew a rather sour notice from twenty-four-year-old Althea Leasure Flynt, a former go-go dancer who had gone to *Hustler* to grace its pages with her naked wares and stayed around to marry the head man and become associate publisher at a modest $500,000 a year. "When I told my wife that Christ had entered my life," Flynt told reporters, "she said 'twenty million is going to leave it.' "

There are separate versions, not all that disparate, of how that most unlikely supplicant, then (and still) appealing a seven- to twenty-five-year prison sentence on a Cincinnati conviction for pandering obscenity, joined the ranks of the born-again.

Sister Ruth's is that the two of them were in an airport cocktail lounge sipping soft drinks when she said, "Tell me what makes you, Larry Flynt, tick," and he started to describe his childhood down in the Kentucky Holy Roller country "and he began to cry and I began to cry—the faith healer and the pornographer, sitting in a bar, crying our eyes out. Through Christ's love, I could love a pornographer without really trying."

Flynt said it happened in his pink jet during a series of flights to California, the evangelist in the service of the Lord and he himself on some pedestrian flesh business. He said he spent five days confessing his sins, which means he must have had to talk pretty fast, and—

> I cannot describe it, except a serene feeling came over me. I felt like crying but I was very happy. I felt very much in tune with God, all filled with love, totally nonviolent, compassion for everyone. I begged forgiveness for hurting anyone, and I asked God to get into my life. Ruth didn't convert me—I just happened to be with her when it happened. Jesus stood right there in front of me. It happened and it changed my life.

The cynics said it was just a ploy to soften up the Ohio appeals bench or any blue-nosed jurors in Fulton County, Georgia, where Flynt had an even rougher case to face. This was patently ridiculous. Listen to the man: "Yes, I am a born-again Christian. But I am going to continue publishing pornography, and anybody who doesn't like it can go kiss a rope. I still believe in what we are doing. Women have got to lose their hangups about displaying their bodies." And *Hustler* (just $2.25 per copy) continued to hit the newsstands with the same oral sex, the same "love kits," vibrators, battery-operated dildoes for the lesbians, plastic penises in all sizes,

Flynt at his Columbus, Ohio, mansion with his wife, Althea, not long before the attempt on his life during his obscenity trial in Cincinnati in 1978. *WWP*

reviews of the new porn flicks by *Screw* magazine's Al Goldstein (don't wait for that character to be born again) and the exiled Soviet Nobelist Aleksandr Solzhenitsyn disgustingly portrayed as "Asshole of the Month" for saying some bad things about the U. S. A.

None of this, it turned out, was calculated to turn Sister Ruth away from her most celebrated (and unlikely) disciple.

When Flynt was paralyzed by a gun-wielding mystery assailant during his first no-win Georgia trial, the Stapletons flew to his side as he began the seemingly hopeless battle to walk again. Found guilty early this year, the publisher stood his First Amendment ground and refused to buy off a sentence of $27,500 in fines or eleven years in prison in exchange for an agreement never again to violate the Peach State's obscenity laws. Sister Ruth, nonetheless, continues to pray for him.

Such principles, alas, cannot be claimed for the evangelist's beer-soaked brother Billy, a born-again anti-Semite among his other character frailties. What the rotund family black sheep said after the murder attempt on Larry Flynt was, "If I had him shot from thirty feet with a rifle, he wouldn't be paralyzed," adding that if the man on the critical list was indeed a born-again Christian, "he's reborn a lot worse than he started out with." If there's a shortage of Christian charity anywhere in our First Family, it reposes in that man. One wonders whether he ever read Sister Ruth's best-selling

Brother Billy Carter, here guzzling his very own brand of beer, one of his flatter get-richer-quicker schemes, is something else. He was calling for Larry Flynt's scalp even after the Born-Again smut peddler came close to dying from an assassin's bullet. Later it turned out that the outspoken (and often obscene) Billy wasn't too wild about Jews, either. No, not in porn. Anyplace.

The Experience of Inner Healing, but this much is certain:

Jimmy Carter, beaten in his first race for governor of Georgia in 1966 and deeply depressed, went for a walk in the forest in Plains with his handsome blond sister, knelt at her side, prayed with her, and arose to go with God the rest of the way. It has since become clear that Sister Ruth took the wrong brother into the forest.

MR. COLSON SEES THE LIGHT

If this were a movie script or soap opera segment, it would open with a brilliant ray of sunshine poking through the bars in Charles W. Colson's prison barracks at the Maxwell Air Force base in Alabama. Sunshine and a vision of the Holy Spirit.

But that's not the way it happened for Richard Nixon's premier dirty trickster, low-blow artist, hatchet man and knife-in-the-back specialist. For Chuck Colson the vision came some two years before he was shipped down to Montgomery to do his plea-bargained penance for his role in the Watergate cover-up and for obstructing justice with his strenuous efforts to defame Daniel J. Ellsberg before the ex-Defense Department "whiz kid's" espionage trial for turning the Pentagon Papers over to the *New York Times* and a few other newspapers. It came in 1973 when Colson, facing exposure and in-

dictment, sat down with Tom Phillips, millionaire president of the Raytheon Company, and was persuaded that his salvation could come only from within. Before the 1972 campaign, with $60.2 million in the till, he had said that "I would walk over my grandmother if necessary to reelect Richard Nixon," who must have believed him, since Colson was the special hired hand put in charge of the White House's infamous Enemies List. Now, born again, he was trading in his mentor for the true God, not that he was going to do anything to hasten the impeachment or ultimate resignation of the man he had served since 1969 with such slavish dedication.

There were few believers when that word began to circulate around a capital inexorably being immersed in the nation's worst constitutional crisis. The common notion was that Chuck Colson, a six-figure Boston lawyer and anything but a birdbrain before he enlisted in the Nixon cause, was simply shifting to the side of Christ to soften the blow when the ax fell, dashing headlong for the prayer-breakfast circuit purely for the benefit of the sentencing judge in the hard-as-nails case against him. And why not? They were talking about the man who had helped out with the break-in into the office of Dan Ellsberg's West Coast psychiatrist, recruited the ex-CIA's E. Howard Hunt, Jr., for that amateur act in Larry O'Brien's office, suggested firebombing the Brookings Institution so the FBI could fish around in the files and casually carried out his share of the dirtier fund-raising and money-washing for the rotten business at hand. Hell, they were talking about the man Richard Nixon's own director of communications, Herbert G. Klein, once characterized as a "cobra."

But they were so wrong.

Chuck Colson was a born-again Christian when he pleaded guilty in the Ellsberg matter, drew his one-to-three-year sentence from U. S. District Court Judge Gerhard A. Gesell, and was shipped down to Alabama. He was a born-again Christian when he was paroled seven months later—just after the death of his father and a son's arrest on marijuana charges—and became one of the revival movement's more star-studded names. Gary Wills, the columnist and author, wrapped it up in one touchingly brilliant paragraph after spending much time with Colson and watching him in action as he strove to bring others into the fold:

If divine rescue is the central fact of the salvation drama, what better witness to this than the recently rescued, the shipwrecked man still dripping from his scrape with spiritual death. There-

Charles Colson preaching at the Sumter Correctional Institute in Bushnell, Florida. For this one, only 60 inmates out of 954 showed up, but the reborn Watergate-handyman's devotion to the prison circuit remains unshaken. *WWP*

fore, for millions of Americans, Watergate proves to have been the heaven-sent whale. Colson is Jonah, the man charioted toward life by that monstrous intrusion into the normal order of our politics. He is the crippled man who walks off the faith-healer's stage, holy and passing on holiness, touched by the Spirit, and touching others. He is the town drunk "witnessing" at the town revival. He is what it is all about.

He is indeed.

Colson's 1976 book, *Born Again*, both a confessional and the story of a moving pilgrimage, sold in the hundreds of thousands but couldn't put him anywhere near the gilt-edged neighborhood of all the other fallen Watergate figures who whipped out the tell-it-all books that fingered the other bad guys. There's no question that Charles Colson had an extreme distaste for men like John Mitchell and Bob

Haldeman but except for identifying Haldeman as the genius behind the White House taping system he let them all off the hook; the Devil led them astray. There's no question that he could have shredded the remnants of the Quaker Nixon's hopelessly tarnished history but he didn't; the Devil again. In the process, he passed up the real big bucks. Only forty-eight now, he is still spurning lucrative job offers to stay on the gospel trail. Beyond the prayer-breakfast service, he spends most of his time carrying the message to men doing time. Why?

"Alcohol is a prison, the country club is a prison, the executive suite is a prison, society is full of prisons," he has told the magazine *Christianity Today*. "I believe God put me in a prison without bars for a purpose and that is where I put my primary effort."

Charles Colson is paying a debt that seemed—and perhaps to many of us still seems—almost too heavy for one man to redeem. By contrast consider for a moment another recent born-again Christian of quite another stripe—Eldridge Cleaver, the veteran con (drugs and rape) who "fell in love" with the new trigger-happy Black Panther Party of Huey Newton and Bobby Seale on the West Coast in 1967. Cleaver never moved in circles quite as elevated as Chuck Colson's, needless to say. Off his earlier jail terms, he went to work with guns, not wit. He served eight years on an eighteen-year sentence in a 1958 case involving assault with intent to commit murder, turned to self-education in Folsom State Prison, eventually producing the moving *Soul on Ice*, but was ordered back into prison after a 1968 Oakland shootout in which a seventeen-year-old follower of his, Bobby Hutton, perished while Cleaver and two cops were wounded. Cleaver flew to the friendlier confines of Castro's Cuba rather than face that dismal prospect and later dwelt in some splendor in Europe and Africa before coming home in 1978 to throw himself upon the mercy of the courts. Awaiting trial and out on $10,000 bail, he turned up on the born-again circuit. His testimony is that after all those years in the grip of an all-consuming hate compounded by groundless revolutionary doctrines, he saw the face of the Savior in the full moon of Cannes one night during his long self-exile and was converted by a "God Squad" back behind bars before he was bonded. The obvious question, of course: Was Eldridge Cleaver another man in the toils embracing the faith to soften the rap? He would never answer that—except to note that he had no trouble understanding why some people wouldn't buy his conversion as the real thing. "They didn't believe in Jesus Christ either," he said.

Between Charles Colson and the reborn Black Panther Eldridge Cleaver, eighty-four-year-old Corrie ten Boom, a one-time Nazi concentration camp prisoner whose family saved many Jews, and Dr. Robert Schuller. The trio was invited to illustrate a Sunday morning sermon entitled "How to Climb Down a Mountain Without Falling." The enormously successful Dr. Schuller is one of the TV preachers who shuns the custom-made pinstripes for priestly garb. *Religious News Service*

John Travolta, one of the new millionaires after *Saturday Night Fever*, also was listed among the born-again recruits.

Susan Atkins and Tex Watson of the Charles Manson murder family both found God in prison. *WWP*

TRADE-OFF: FROM MURDER TO GOD

And now the pair who once embraced Charles Manson as their God and killed for him but have been born again in their separate prisons—Susan Denise Atkins and Charles D. (Tex) Watson. It was Susan, then nineteen and a reformed topless dancer, whose jailhouse babbling led to the apprehension of the band whose 1969 murder spree in Los Angeles took the lives of actress Sharon Tate, heiress Abigail Folger, hair stylist Jay Sebring, playboy Wojieiech Voytek Frykowski and a youth named Steve Parent, encountered in the driveway of the rented Tate mansion, followed by the similarly brutal knife-and-bludgeon slayings of wealthy supermarket owner Leno LaBianca and his wife, Rosemary. Held as a co-defendant in the earlier killing of musician Gary Hinman, Susan freely boasted about her role in the mutilation of the twenty-six-year-old actress—then about to bear a child by her husband, director Roman Polanski—and the others and was turned in by her confidantes, two hookers with friends on the police force. The bearded, pint-sized Lord High Executioner, Manson, was sentenced to the gas chamber along with Susan, Patricia Krenwinkel and Leslie Van Houten, but the four came out with life terms when the death sentence was ruled unconstitutional.

Susan, who waited until 1975 before her first expression of remorse, made her Decision for Christ in the Frontera Women's Prison and in 1977 Logos International, a Protestant evangelical publishing house, bought her memoirs, *Child of Satan* (another one of the cult's names for their thirty-five-year-old ex-con guru). Bantam Books reportedly paid $150,000 for the paperback rights, so the woman found the born-again path just as profitable for the purse as the soul. Eligible for parole by now, she may be expected to turn up on the faith-healing circuit one of these days. Tex Watson, twenty-four when he found his way to the deserted shack outside of Death Valley where Manson pronounced his random death verdicts, put his conversion between covers in a book called *Will You Die for Me?* He turned preacher in the California Men's Colony at San Luis Obispo and teaches a weekly class for fellow prisoners who have turned to Christ. Remember this: Tex Watson wasn't just some mindless mope in the Manson murder legion. He was the on-the-spot leader of the Tate–LaBianca missions, although he told a parole hearing last year that the leader himself had come along for the LaBianca slaughters. Born-again or not, Watson was denied his freedom as a man who "poses an unreasonable risk to society."

DIAL-A-CHURCH:

The Healer in the Living Room

"If there is no Hell, a good
many preachers are obtaining
money under false pretenses."—BILLY SUNDAY

BEYOND THE GRAHAMS and the other multinational hell-robbers, but by no means a candidate for food stamps, looms the cherubic figure of eighty-six-year-old Herbert W. Armstrong, founder of the Worldwide Church of God and a man who has the airwaves to thank for the bulk of the $85 million a year floating into his coffers. An ad salesman come on hard times after the 1929 stock market crash, Armstrong found something easier to sell than newspaper space—theology. His own, scooped up from a wide variety of the available sources. Some from Jehovah's Witnesses, some from the Seventh Day Adventists, some from the Mormons and a big chunk from the Jewish faith. In his church Christmas and Easter are pagan rites. His parishioners, indeed, are strictly kosher, observe Saturday as the Sabbath, celebrate their New Year on Rosh Hashanah and follow the Yom Kippur Day of Atonement ritual. Where they part with the Jews is on the matter of Christ's divinity and resurrection.

Starting as the Radio Church of God with some time bought on KORE in Eugene, Oregon, the Armstrong brand of evangelism, leaning in moderate but insistent tones on the end-of-the-world bit with the Four Horsemen of the Apocalypse right around the bend, bubbled forth on hundreds of radio and television stations with a special half-hour Sunday telecast beamed in translation all over the world. For its 70 million members, the message is rather expensive—a tithe of up to 30 percent of their incomes, which one may assume accounted for the heftiest portion of the estimated $75 million reportedly nestling in the Worldwide coffers in 1978. Bobby Fischer, long in the sect and far and away its most glittering name once he became World Chess Champion by dethroning the Soviet's Boris Spassky in their classic July-to-September match in Iceland in 1972, turned over 20 percent of his $250,000 purse to the church. In the years since, living in seclusion with Worldwide officials in their splendidly appointed $80 million, forty-acre spread in Pasadena, the contributions of the brooding, tousle-haired thirty-six-year-old ex-Brooklyn boy reportedly have added up to something more than $100,000 as his book royalties continue to pour in. It is solid chunks like that which account for the fact that the church-of-the-air's income is said to exceed the combined annual receipts of the Billy Graham and Oral Roberts organizations.

Much of the credit for that remarkable detail belongs to the founder's son Garner Ted, now nearing

181

fifty, even though he has been under relentless siege since 1972 when the stern old taskmaster "disfellowshipped" him on a rather serious charge in that Godly preserve—adultery, in abundance. "You have dishonored your human father and the Living Christ," came the pronouncement from the highest place, drawing this rather casual rejoinder from Worldwide's silver-haired and silver-tongued airwave voice: "If it will satisfy some people I'm willing to have a big billboard put up on the side of the road saying, 'Garner Ted Armstrong is a sinner.'" Before that schism in the family healed with reasonable speed only to come asunder again, Garner Ted's show "The World Tomorrow," beamed to 350 radio stations and 100 TV outlets, had claimed an audience of 30 million. And show was the perfect word, because that fashion plate never came on as a Bible-thumper pounding home the gospel of doom. His broadcasts, tilted sharply to the right, always dealt with the issues confronting our troubled planet, and you had to stay to the end to hear your personable host slip in a word or two about the Worldwide way home. If you didn't stay but switched to a Western or a rerun of Jackie Gleason's "Honeymooners" (still running), it was just another talk show, anything but a sermon or a fund-raiser and free of all churchly vestments. The supersalesman was excommunicated once and presumably forever in July 1978, this time not for the sins of the flesh but in internal warfare compounded by grave financial problems over the $20 million-a-year drain on the treasury accruing from the fallen heir's baby, Ambassador College in Pasadena, but by then he was comfortably ensconced with his wife and three children in his very own Church of God in Tyler, Texas.

Behind this depressing father-and-son scene, it turned out, lay an item more akin to an internecine power struggle in some multinational conglomerate. This was a battle for the succession between the straying son and the Jewish-born but converted Stanley R. Rader, a Beverly Hills lawyer whose reputed $175,000 a year plus expenses as Worldwide's general counsel wasn't all that embarrassing against the founder's $200,000-a-year draw. Dad moved the dapper, mustachioed counselor into his son's lavish office suite when the final break came and Garner Ted's bargain-counter $85,000-a-year paycheck presumably went into the discard. As for Bobby Fischer, once housed in some luxury in the Pasadena Taj Mahal but since removed—presumably by his own choice—to the basement apartment of one of the church's functionaries, he has had a few things to say about the high-living style of the Worldwide brass and the head

man's proselytizing methods, but they weren't meant for public airing.

Meanwhile, hardy old Herbert Armstrong—"retired" but very much in evidence, even to the extent of taking to the airwaves himself—has gone his own way in recent years, coursing the globe in leased jets and billing himself as "The Spiritual Kissinger" as he dropped in on prime ministers and heads of state in such distant outposts as Japan, Korea, South Africa, Belgium, India and the Philippines while Stanley Rader, most likely Worldwide's next rector general, minded the store at home. In his magazine, *The Plain Truth*, which boasts a paid circulation of 2.4 million, the founder has said that his purpose on those missions has not been to carry the message of Christ or convert the nonbelievers of international prominence but rather to "announce the news." Make room for more red faces. In 1972 the bulletin from the reformed ad salesman-turned-to-God was about the Four Horsemen around the bend—famine, disease, war and false religion. The latter, one had to assume, consisted of anything but the gospel of the Worldwide Church, and in any case that piece of "news" became rather moth-eaten as the years rolled by. Either that or the Four Horsemen took the wrong fork in the road somewhere along the line.

Come 1979 another band of horsemen, this time in three-piece double-knit suits bought on government salaries, rode into the picture. The California Attorney General's office, alleging that Armstrong and Rader has been liquidating church assets and diverting them to "their own use and benefit on a massive scale amounting to several million dollars a year," prevailed upon the courts to put Worldwide under a temporary receivership. Among other charges: the two men in the holy executive suite that very day were in the process of closing a $10 million deal for a former college campus of Worldwide's in Big Sandy, Texas, that had earlier enjoyed a book value of $30 million. The attorney general submitted that the church's honchos were in the process of "pilfering" its assets in a highly suspect manner, and threw in some fresh intelligence as well. He said Rader actually had a $200,000-a-year contract with seven-year renewable provisions guaranteeing him an even $100,000 per annum until the year 2003 if the world lasted that long. He also said the lawyer-turned-to-God's work had recently acquired a $225,000 home from the church and then resold it for $1.8 million, picking up a net profit of a million or so. The church fought back with its own array of lawyers, filing a $700 million damage suit against the Golden State on the side. Two months later a Los Angeles judge

Herbert W. Armstrong, founder of the Worldwide Church of God, outside his Ambassador College in Pasadena in 1978. Come 1979, Armstrong and his good right hand, attorney Stanley R. Rader, ran into trouble with the law over the way pieces of the $80-million theocratic empire were being sold off. *WWP*

agreed to lift the receivership if Worldwide could come up with a million-dollar bond pending a final determination.

Put Garner Ted down as a pretty lucky guy. He got the boot before the Worldwide turf turned so shaky.

CHRIST ON THE TALK-SHOW CIRCUIT

Leaving the Armstrongs to resolve their trouble in that rich broken family, what does it all add up to?

There are now more than 800 radio and TV programs nationwide devoted to Christian doctrines, the variety spanning such a vast range that not a single door to redemption has been left unopened. What will you have? Fire and brimstone? Pentecostal services? Instant cures for your physical ailments? It's all out there. The circuit rider of the old frontier has been replaced by the dial in the electronic era. What hath Guglielmo Marconi and Lee de Forest wrought? Perhaps the success story of North Carolina's Reverend James Bakker tells it best. He is the Johnny Carson, Mike Douglas and Merv Griffin of the faith-healing talk shows all rolled into one. His two-hour daily program from Charlotte is shown in taped excerpts to 20 million viewers on 190 television stations and 4,000 cable outlets. That sound like much? Well, when Telly Savalas as Kojak was burning up the airwaves a few years back one hundred seventy-eight stations bought that police show. Now there's one to ponder in a nation under never-ending indictment for its addiction to violence on the home screen.

The bouncy little Reverend Bakker, thirty-eight, son of a Michigan tool-and-die maker and a product of Minneapolis' North Central Bible College, needed just four years to pass the tough bald-headed TV cop in the numbers game. Savalas worked for an elaborate salary and all that juicy residual money out of the still-current reruns. Next to Bakker, pocket money. The Bakker show, spreading beyond these troubled acres into nineteen foreign countries, brought in close to $26 million in 1977. Not in pledges from the grateful throng out there, either born again or cured of one dread affliction or another. In the coin of the realm. The minister has a simple explanation for all this prosperity: he counts 30,000 souls saved during that boom year. And how many miraculous cures have emanated from this Lourdes operating out of a lavish broadcast studio? There can never be a count. The operators manning the sixty sky blue phones behind the master of those ceremonies will simply tell you from time to time about the cancer that went away or the growth that simply washed off a penitent's nose or the minds blurred by age or illness suddenly restored and just as sharp as ever. In his audience, men and women come to Christ often burst into tears of gratitude, and the man behind the Carson-type desk weeps joyously with them. And that is a desk, by the way, not unfamiliar to some guests of considerable note. Sister Ruth. Mahalia Jackson. Charles Colson and Dean Jones, nominated to portray him on the silver screen. Art Linkletter. Pat Boone. Dale Evans of the old horse operas. Senator Mark O. Hatfield, the Oregon Republican. Anita Bryant, the antihomosexual crusader. Lulu Roman of TV's "Hee Haw" and the fallen heavyweight champion George Foreman, to name just a few.

Once a disc jockey as well as host of a children's TV show with his diminutive wife, Tammy, who sometimes turns up on the screen to belt out a gospel, play the organ or do a puppet show, Bakker doesn't operate out of a church but rather something called The PTL Club. PTL originally stood for Praise the Lord, then People That Love, then People That Live, then People That Learn. But its lapel pins still say Praise The Lord. Some of the more caustic nonbelievers have translated those call letters of the Bakker PTL Television Network into something else—Pass The Loot. This is the price one pays for a score, religious or otherwise, that tends to become ostentatious after a while. The bushy black-haired

minister operates out of a $5 million, twenty-five acre estate modeled after Colonial Williamsburg and containing one building called Diamond House because it was built from gifts of jewelry. Back in 1976 the Charlotte *Observer* looked into the Bakker operation and headlined its front-page story this way:

THE HARVESTING OF SOULS. AND DOLLARS

The Reverend, carried on the PTL books with the mother of his young son and daughter for a combination salary of just $40,000 plus a car allowance, shrugs off that sort of cavil.

"You will find some pastors who disagree with this ministry," says the Pentecostal preacher-performer. "They relate anything on television to show business. I am sure the enemy of the gospel, Satan, would be delighted to keep us off television."

Jim Moss, Bakker's right-hand man, who formerly

Garner Ted Armstrong, the son and TV supersalesman who fell out of favor over his strong sexual appetites. *WWP*

Chess champion, Bobby Fischer, long devoted to the Armstrong church and a major contributor, has had a thing or two to say about the way it is run but didn't want it printed. *WWP*

operated a janitorial service in Charlotte, puts it another way:

"When I was cleaning commodes and making fifty thousand a year, I got criticism. Anytime you make money you get criticism."

Finally, a note on that telephone battery mentioned above. Those operators aren't just there to harken to the ills of your soul or physique. About two hundred times a year the PTL affiliates run fund-raising telethons. On those nights what's written down is your name, address and whatever you can spare to shoot along in the mail—10,000 pieces on the better days. The Bakker people say it costs a cool million a month to bring salvation to the troubled via the free air. All the circuit rider ever needed was a strong horse, a leathery backside and some oats.

FAITH AND THE MONEY MARTS

Before Jim Bakker, long before, there was the Reverend Rex Humbard and his Cathedral of Tomorrow. He still is around, too, although in that operation it is not all that easy to keep one's eye either on the tube or the message, because Humbard came on not just as an evangelist but a one-man wheeler-dealer business conglomerate as well. As often as not the public prints have been occupied more with tales of that man's own salvation—in the financial marts, that is—than in the surcease his weekly telecasts may have been delivering unto the masses out there. He has talked about the world's desperate need for an "old-fashioned, soul-savin', sin-killin' revival where the people get right with God," but his own problem for lo, these many years has been getting *himself* right with federal watchdog agencies like the IRS and the SEC, not to mention such privately funded nuisances as the Better Business Bureau.

Spawned by a wandering Bible Belt preacher from Arkansas but a holdout from Jesus until another faith healer converted him when he was thirteen, Rex Humbard blew into Akron, Ohio, in 1952 with $65 in his pocket and within six years had found the wherewithal—$3.5 million—to build a 5,000-seat cathedral-in-the-round that went on view in no time at all on some four hundred TV stations. Come 1965, however, the evangelist with a crew of hillbilly singers ran short of ready cash and found a most unlikely benefactor—the racket-ridden Central States Pension Fund of Jimmy Hoffa's International Brotherhood of Teamsters. Hmnn. The union doing business with the mob guys in Las Vegas and other sin dens now had a fundamentalist church on its IOU rolls, with the grunt eventually reaching a round $5.6 million. And what

was the Reverend doing with all that walking-around money? He was buying a girdle company in Brooklyn, two New Jersey plastics and electronics outfits, an advertising agency and typographical firm in Akron and finally, for $2 million and change, little Mackinac College on Mackinac Island in Lake Huron, Michigan, due to be converted into something of an educational resort with ski lifts, toboggan runs and that sort of thing. All this was just for openers. Finding willing bondholders among his followers, the evangelists came up with $10 million in 1971 to put up Akron's most elaborate building complex, the twenty-two-story Cascade Plaza. *Business Week* magazine, wading in Biblical waters not on its normal beat, took a hard look in 1973 and produced a rundown on a whole flock of cease-and-desist orders on file in Oregon, Wisconsin, Michigan, Indiana and Missouri against unlicensed brokers peddling unregistered securities both in the Cathedral of Tomorrow and Mackinac, the college of today.

The following year the cash started to flow the other way. Under a court order to repay $13 million to 4,000 divinely motivated investors who had been putting money into the Cathedral since 1959, Humbard managed to come up with $8 million (and still keep his family in proper style in a $250,000 Akron mansion) before the till was once again empty. One of the business trinkets the evangelist had to unload to work his way at least partially out of that financial jungle was his Realform Girdle Company. For his TV audience, he let it be known that he would henceforth devote all his time to the Lord's work rather than Mammon's. He said he had brought the good word to 646,000 souls in live appearances over the past four years and that 80,000 of them had made their decisions for Christ. Back on that crass financial side, Humbard later was able to go before his Akron congregation with a "Miracle Report" attesting that the church finally had paid off a whopping $12.5 million in unregistered bonds and notes and taken leave of the commercial marts altogether to concentrate on the larger problem at hand—hauling in the pagans. Everything went, even the college and the Reverend's two airplanes, and fifty overseas TV outlets were dropped from the colorcast to lop another million a year off the expense budget. This is not say that financial security was right around the corner. In 1976 the church still had $10 million in outstanding debts, including $5.5 million in mortgages held by the old Hoffa boys.

Come the next semester, the fifty-eight-year-old evangelist, celebrating his silver anniversary, had 543 stations on his TV network with an estimated audi-

The Reverend Jim Bakker does it all on the airwaves—and the money comes pouring in by the sack.

ence of 20,000,000, and he put it to them to send in $25 apiece—just one small dollar for each year of his labors in God's cause—to mark the occasion. What did the postman bring? The Better Business Bureau, which monitors that sort of tax-exempt operation, bid Humbard to join in a session in which such organizations as the Billy Graham Association, the Campus Crusade for Christ and the American Bible Society had agreed to discuss their finances.

The Reverend didn't show.

Nor did he send along any figures.

THE ORAL ROBERTS WAY

On quite another level, there's the saga, going back more than three decades, of Oral Roberts, an impressive six-footer who enjoys a hard-earned stature akin to Billy Graham's even without all that globe-girdling or his own key to the White House. You know there's more than one Oral Roberts. There's Oral Roberts the immensely successful Pentecostal preacher who in

1968 dared to risk some of his huge following by going back to the mother Methodist church of his birth, Oral Roberts the educator and number one cheerleader for the nationally ranked basketball team out of his own liberal arts college in Oklahoma, Oral Roberts of the National Bank of Tulsa's board of directors and—more familiarly—the prime-time television pitchman for the good Christian way.

Start at the beginning with a seventeen-year-old kid who stuttered, son of a Methodist preacher. Oral once ran away in rebellion against his deeply religious parents, and once dropped to the boards during a high school basketball game with his nose pouring blood. The diagnosis: TB, and this was in 1945, when the "white plague" was still claiming some victims. The boy hovered between life and death for six months. Then it happened. His sister drove him some distance to a tent evangelist, George Moncey, who laid his hands on him and "asked Jesus Christ to open my lungs," and—

"There was warmth at first, a warmth like warm water coming over me. It went into my lungs . . . but I took a deep breath . . . and I knew that a miracle was starting. And the man talked to me a moment, and he had me talk back, and I talked without stammering. . . . In a few moments' time I was standing straight and tall. . . . I was a healed man, and in my heart God's voice was ringing. "You are to take my healing power to your generation." Now, I didn't know how to do that. I've gone around this world; I've preached to crowds up to 100,000, and small crowds, middle-size crowds, on television and all over. And I've made many mistakes, and I've had lots of failures. But there are a lot of people today who know Christ, and who are healed, because God spoke to a boy, raised him up and put something in his soul.

Ordained in the Pentecostal Holiness Church, which shuns material possessions, Roberts was assigned to a pastorate in Enid in his native Oklahoma but left it after a while to hit the gospel trail as a faith healer. With the little tube about to invade the American living room, an excellent choice indeed. Skip a few years into another decade and the stocky evangelist is no longer perched on a wooden chair in a tent with his hands on the heads of the lame and the halt and calling upon God to make them whole again. No. Now he's wearing an impeccably tailored jacket and he's talking into the cameras. Talking to the millions. Offering gifts—plates decorated with

In his Cathedral of Tomorrow in Akron, the Reverend Rex Humbard calls his flock to his side in 1977, but his major efforts go into radio and television.

biblical quotations, replicas of Judean oil lamps. No charge, but if the spirit moves you send a contribution to further the good works of the Oral Roberts Evangelical Association. The spirit must have moved the hordes out there.

In 1963 Oral Roberts acquired five hundred acres of farmland on the southern edge of Tulsa and set about to build himself a university. What emerged two years later, dominated by a 200-foot blue and gold Prayer Tower that became the oil capital's premier tourist attraction, was a breathtakingly beautiful campus described by one wide-eyed observer as an "educational and spiritual Disneyland." Disneyland? Oral Roberts University, fully accredited, enormously respected, has a student body exceeding 3,500 today. And don't overlook its basketball team, always dominated by blacks although they represent only a small proportion of the student body. The Oral Roberts five has held its own in national tournaments, and don't think for a moment that the man who started it doesn't give the good Lord *his* share of the credit (of course, it also helps a bit if the kids in the short pants are tall and strong).

Roberts ceased his labors in that Prayer Tower—"the world's biggest revival tent"—in 1968 to concentrate his ministry on television. By that time he had a weekly half-hour program going to 275 stations in this country and Canada. Today his Sunday morning sermon is telecast nationally, but the big draw, four times a year on prime time that costs well over half a

million dollars a shot, is the evangelist's variety show. For the first half hour, entertained by such as Jerry Lewis, Pearl Bailey or the reborn Johnny Cash, you wouldn't know you had tuned in to a gospel show. That's the showman in Oral Roberts. He gets you settled down in the tent real nice before it's time for the message. Those specials have counted audiences as high as 60,000,000—among them evidently some pretty good spenders. The sixty-one-year-old Roberts is now building a $100 million, 777-bed hospital across the street from his university after beating off the local medical establishment in a protracted federal court battle.

Remember the flap when Jimmy Carter confessed in a 1976 *Playboy* interview that in his time he had lusted after women other than the good Rosalynn? Oral Roberts, married thirty-eight years then to an ex-school teacher who bore him two sons and two daughters, had a crisp answer for that: "The kind of life I lived before I found God and Evelyn, I don't like to recall. . . . My attitude [on that lust item] is that we can admire but not desire."

Roberts' youngest son, Richard, twenty-five, a regular on the broadcasts, is being groomed to step in when the evangelist calls it a day, perhaps to sit back and add some titles to his thirty odd books. After all, leaving out sex, scandal, the confessional, and the how-to market, hardly anything sells better than the Good Word. That's the one well that never runs dry. There are now some 5,000 evangelical bookstores doing a land office business. Throw in the reborn Christians' magazine subscriptions, T-shirts, religious records, and don't overlook the bumper stickers, and you have what the *Wall Street Journal* has described as a $2 billion-a-year industry.

It is an industry just as fiercely competitive as any other on the horizon. Thus the Grahams, the Robertses, the Armstrongs and the Bakkers just recently had to start looking over their shoulders at an upstart who arrived on their turf like a firestorm. This is forty-five-year-old Jerry Falwell, who once carried a football for the Baptist Bible College in Springfield, Missouri, and has shown the same bonecrushing power carrying the Message. Brother Jerry, whose grandfather was a bootlegger, started his ministry at twenty-two in a little ramshackle converted bottling factory in his home town of Lynchburg, Virginia, which he christened the Thomas Road Baptist Church ("Where the Old-Time Gospel is Still Preached"). Today there's room in that shrine for 3,500 communicants and it's the nation's second largest church in that denomination. But that's not where this success story lies. Once again, it's out there on the airwaves. This particular minister does not only

Evangelist Oral Roberts spread well beyond his faith-healing trail in recent years, principally into his own university in Tulsa.

In a 1976 Washington press conference, the Baptists' Jerry Falwell (standing) protested alleged attempts by the White House to pressure radio stations into censoring religious broadcasts commenting on the *Playboy* interview in which Jimmy Carter made those frank comments about the lust that had invaded his heart at times. Dr. Jack Hyler of Hammond, Indiana, is alongside him, and at right Dr. John R. Rice of Murfreesboro, Tennessee.

tell you that "you can stop the moral landslide if you invite the Lord Jesus into your hearts" but also brings back visions of the long-departed Senator Joe McCarthy of Wisconsin by vowing to get all them home-grown Communists shuttled off to the Soviet and to call forth large doses of hellfire and brimstone upon the homosexuals, smut peddlers and abortionists in our midst. He has 275 daily radio outlets and 310 TV stations airing his once-a-week "Old-Time Gospel Hour." He had a million dollars donated in 1971, watched it soar to $12 million in the next four years and hit a nice $32.5 million peak in 1978. Mary Murphy, one of *Esquire*'s roving editors, spent an afternoon in that boom year watching Brother Jerry's helpmates opening up the postman's goodies. Her report: "They pulled checks from mailbags in sums as large as $450 and as small as $14. The day's total was $339,000. The week's take was $1.2 million."

What does it all add up to?

Assorted evangelicals bought a half-million dollars worth of air time in 1977 (there were 1,200 radio stations and 25 TV outlets broadcasting *nothing* but the Message then) and claimed weekly audiences of 115,000,000 on the radio and 14,000,000 on the tube. If that half-million sounds like a lot of money, try to imagine how much income it generated. Your pocket calculator won't help because the numbers are too hard to come by, but there would not appear to be any losers toiling in the Lord's cause. Aimee Semple McPherson and Billy Sunday, predating the Big Sell with the microphone and the camera with the little red eye, were born in the wrong time.

Another phenomenon of the Seventies, with the jury still out has been the "Jesus Movement," so contagious that it has drawn hundreds of thousands of young people all over the nation. Wherever you are, you've encountered it on the sidewalks. In the top photo *(New York Post)*, a recent Jews for Jesus demonstration in Manhattan. Below *(WP)*, the legend on the girl's T-shirt in a 1971 "Festival of the Risen Sun" in Oklahoma City says it all. Much of the movement, generally lumped under the heading of "Jesus Freaks," has been traced to the remnants of the Hippie-Flower Children subculture of the Sixties, but churchmen studying it have found a much broader basis in those ranks without really nailing down what it means or where it's going.

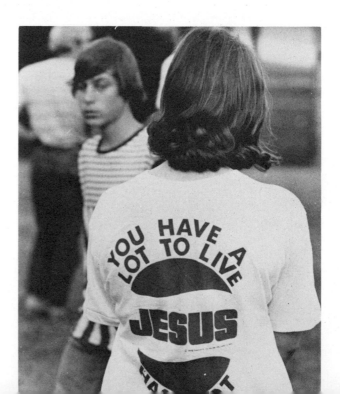

THE MOONIES:

Tomorrow the New World

"I am not saying, 'I am the
Messiah.' I am just fulfilling
God's instructions."
—The Reverend Sun Myung Moon

You see, the way it all happened was this: God installed Adam and Eve in the Garden of Eden to bring forth a perfect brood and establish the Kingdom of Heaven on Earth, but Satan, in snake's clothing, made it with the bride-to-be and that was the end of that. So God in his wisdom turned the big mission over to Jesus, but the Jews killed him before he could marry and get the job done. And then thousands of years passed before the heavenly father was able to find the man—boy then, actually—that he needed. He found him on Easter Sunday in 1936, praying on a mountainside in North Pyonyang Province, later North Korea. It was Sun Myung Moon, age sixteen, and what you have just read is not intended as a piece of sacrilege. This is the way Moon tells it, and while the head of the Unification Church never refers to himself as the New Messiah, neither does he ever fail to make it clear that he is indeed the designated hitter for Christ in the Second Coming. It's just a matter of time, and Moon, working steadily on his divine assignment since he ordained himself ten years after that session on the mountainside and became the Reverend Sun Myung Moon, is a man of infinite patience. Looking toward his sixtieth year come 1980,

he has yet to show the barest sign of wavering. Indeed, he can't. There are far too many devoted followers depending on him: a claimed two million led by 300,000 in his homeland, where he is not just God's messenger but also one of its wealthier businessmen, 210,000 in Japan and some 30,000 in his new stamping ground—where in 1973 he proclaimed that "The time of the second coming of Christ is near and America is the landing site!" When? The date Moon is using is 1981.

Who is this man who tells us that "I am the incarnation of Himself. The whole world is in my hand, and I will conquer and subjugate the world" but nonetheless finds it necessary to keep a battery of lawyers on hand to sue anybody who would gainsay him? The way some court dockets now look, it appears as if the first to be subjugated are the nonbelievers who commit to paper anything that falls short of glorifying the Unification Church and its founder. It is to wonder, since the count on those of us saved from hellfire and damnation via trials for alleged libels must be very scant at best.

In any case, from what the rather elusive record shows, it appears that Moon, a one-time harbor

With his wife, Hak-Ja-Han, alongside him, the Reverend Sun Myung Moon marches at the head of a graduating class of fifty-three at his Unification Theological Seminary at Tarrytown, New York, in 1977. *WWP*

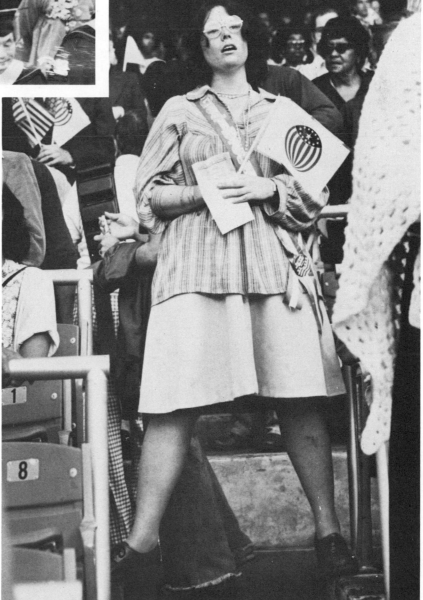

Any question about this girl's devotion? The scene is from the Moonies' "Bicentennial God Bless America" festival at Madison Square Garden in 1976. *UPI*

worker in Pusan, was jailed by the Korean Reds in 1948 on charges of draft dodging, promiscuity and adultery, which he has said actually were dreamed up because his anti-Communist activities were such that the regime then in power wanted him out of circulation. He served three years and founded his first church—the Holy Spirit Association for the Unification of World Christianity—in Seoul in 1954. On the side he must have possessed considerable acumen as a businessman, for today he is the chairman of no fewer than five Korean corporations engaged in such diverse pursuits as making rifles, machine parts, pharmaceutical products, paints, stone crafts and ginseng tea with an income variously estimated at anywhere from $15 to $30 million a year. He is also close to President Park Chung Hee, so he is quite apparently a good deal more than any old pulpit-thumping soul saver, although he much prefers to be called The Father than, say, an industrial tycoon. His assets in the United States have been put at well over $20 million, most of it in real estate in New York and California, and the tax snoops keep raising that nagging question as to whether the Unification Church is really entitled to its tax-exempt status.

So much for the crasser side of all this.

The sleek, round-faced prophet of the better tomorrow, who as of 1973 had fathered four sons and three daughters by the most durable of his wives, Hak-Ja Han, claims to have missionaries toiling in his behalf in no less than 123 nations. His heavily promoted public appearances in such arenas as Madison Square Garden and Carnegie Hall have not always drawn packed houses but his following here, however comparatively small in numbers, tends to be extremely devoted. The Moonies are the kids you see in the streets—often middle class with college backgrounds who seem to be direly in need of a good night's sleep—putting in long hours hawking such items as dried flowers, votive candles, peanuts and tea, and live a wholly austere existence. Smoking, drinking, drugs and premarital sex—"worse than murder" in the Moon doctrine—are of course forbidden. Postmarital sex, indeed, is deemed verboten for the first forty days, and you don't tie the knot in the first place in Moon-arranged marriages until you have confessed your sins to The Father.

The contrast in life-styles of The Father and his "children" is worth noting here. The Father, perhaps justly in view of his independent wealth, leads a lordly existence on an $850,000 estate in New York's bucolic Tarrytown ("God has been good to me," he says) when he is not on his fifty-foot yacht or delivering the message from one platform or another in his guttural Korean tones with his translator at his side. In Manhattan the Moonies now occupy the seedy New Yorker Hotel, which the Unification Church bought for about $5 million when it looked like a candidate for the demolition crews in 1976.

The Reverend Moon's more or less incessant troubles with parents seeking to reclaim their young have been heavily publicized. One of the targets of the Church's numerous lawsuits, just a $15 million item, is Ted Patrick, the forty-seven-year-old ex-middleweight boxer and ex-community relations aide to Ronald Reagan famed for his labors as a "deprogrammer," who is said to have collected fees as high as $1,800 for returning some inadequately brainwashed Moonies to their families. That particular suit names both Patrick and E. P. Dutton, publisher of a book of his aptly titled *Let Our Children Go*. The Moon litigation generally is built around a claim that the book defames the Church, thus depriving it of present and potential membership and slicing into outside contributions from true believers. One would think that publicizing such asserted defamations would be counterproductive, but the suits keep getting filed. The most recent target, in 1978, has been the *New York Times*, on the list for $45 million in compensatory and punitive damages over an article which the Moon barristers have claimed caused the Church the kind of irreparable "injury" cited above.

Speaking of the occasional hurts bound to befall a man of prominence (whether on the side of God or the Devil), the Reverend has also made the front pages in oblique ways emanating from the prolonged scandal involving bribes paid to various Congressmen by Tongsun Park, the Korean rice dealer. Late in 1978, as an outgrowth of it's three-year "Koreagate" inquiry, the House international relations subcommittee called for the setting up of a federal interagency task force to investigate the Moon organization for reputed violations of laws and regulations governing such matters as currency dealings, immigration, banking, export controls. That last item emerged as the most delicate because it involved a Moon enterprise called Tong II, a Korean government-designated defense contractor whose assembly lines turn out, among other weapons, the M-79 grenade launcher for the M-16 rifle, the South Korean Army's basic infantry weapon. While his own spokesman had denied that Tong II manufactured M-16s, the Washington ferrets learned that two top officials of the company—one of them the Reverend's second cousin, Moon Sung Kyun—had secretly met with officials of Colt Industries here in December 1977 to talk about shipping a supply of M-16s to these shores.

Somehow none of this squares with this statement uttered by the founder in 1976:

> Ladies and gentlemen, if there is illness in your home, do you need a doctor from outside? God has sent me to America in the role of a doctor, in the role of a fighter. For the last three years, with my entire heart and soul, I have been teaching American youth a new reverence for God.

The point here is that a doctor is one thing and a "fighter" is another and a wheeler-dealer in arms quite another.

Apart from the matter of the Second Coming, which should present no problem for any person of normal intelligence, it is not easy to pin down precisely what the Unification Church represents in religious terms. The best description may have come from Berkeley Rice, a senior editor of *Psychology Today* who has observed the Moon operation firsthand:

"While Church members accept Moon's theology as revealed truth, outsiders tend to find it a mind-boggling mixture of Pentecostal Christianity, Eastern mysticism, anticommunism, pop psychology and metaphysics."

There's a bit of broth. For some spice, you might throw in on the darker side of the moon a touch of the founder's patently clear anti-Semitism as expressed in his ever-peddled line about the Jews as Christ killers. It must be noted in this connection, however dolefully, that the Moonie net, spread with an $11 million operating budget against an annual income known only to God or his surrogate, has swept up a fair sprinkling of children from Jewish families and, for the dollar bill, even a Jewish lawyer of such note as New York's Roy Cohn.

And one small footnote: The Moon daily, *The News World*, treats its customers not just to the day's happenings and a spot of salesmanship now and then for the dictator Park back home, but also some action in the betting line, like the point spread in the professional games if you want to go against that perilous

Moonie Richard Schnorr struggles with police and private detectives in Greeley, Colorado, as he is led away for "deprogramming" on his parents' petition. *WWP*

wheel. And more. Not only the race results but its very own handicappers, often emblazoned in blue on its front page. And the paper has no compunctions about pocketing advertising dollars from the touts selling their services with betting systems guaranteed to retire you to a life something close to the Reverend Moon's. Well, there could be a solid historical background behind all this. The big brains in the Moonies may know that a lottery financed the Continental Army in the American Revolution, and that was a worthy cause indeed. Still, theres an inconsistency here. The notion that it is in no way sinful to go to the $2 window or call your friendly neighborhood bookmaker while you're waiting for the Second Coming is a bit hard to digest. Billy Graham wouldn't slip you a tip on a hot horse if you walked down the aisle twice a day.

The Reverend Jim Jones as NBC-TV's Bob Brown photographed him in Guyana not many hours before the Peoples Temple leader, pleading "die with dignity," led more than 900 of his followers into history's largest mass suicide-and-murder. Before then Brown himself was among those in Representative Leo Ryan's visiting party shot to death by the Mad Messiah's gunmen. *WWP*

JIM JONES:

The Cyanide Solution

TURNING FROM ALL of the aforementioned and by all means shunning even the remotest equation because none exists, this chapter on the better world waiting out there somewhere must close with the cult story that horrified the entire world on November 18, 1978.

Dateline: Jonestown, Guyana.

The event: The largest mass suicide and murder known to history, ordained by the Reverend Jim Jones of the California-based Peoples Temple.

The victims: More than 900 men, women and children—the vast majority of the adults utterly content to lay down their lives before the Mad Messiah put a pistol to his own head to lead them to the big sleep and everlasting peace.

Jim Jones was born during the Depression in Lynn, Indiana (population 900). That was Ku Klux Klan country then and his own father, a disabled veteran and part-time rail hand, wore the white hood himself, while his mother was a devout Methodist who didn't believe that salvation lay in lynching blacks. Lynette Jones, part Cherokee, worked in a factory to help put her only son through college—first Indiana University, where he dropped out, and later Butler State, where he earned a degree in education but then pointed himself toward the ranks of the Bible Belt preachers. Peddling such "miracles" as patently faked cancer cures, he launched his first Peoples Temple in Indianapolis in 1955. The temple was interracial and Jones's labors in the cause of desegregation earned him an appointment as head of the Indianapolis Human Rights Commission in 1961. He was ordained by the Disciples of Christ in that city in 1964, but three years later moved his small flock to Redwood Valley outside of Ukiah, 150 miles north of San Francisco.

That was the real beginning.

The Peoples Temple flourished to such a degree under its charismatic leader that the governor of the state himself, Edmund (Pat) Brown, felt it expedient to drop in on at least one occasion. While claiming no more than 5,000 disciples, Jones was able to help swing the 1975 mayoralty election to George Moscone, in turn winning an appointment to the San Francisco Housing Authority and swiftly becoming its chairman.

The move to the steaming bush in socialist Guyana came in late 1977 after *New West* magazine, followed by the San Francisco *Examiner*, laid bare the inside

Some of the dead in Jonestown, killed with a cyanide-laced potion which most of them willingly drank on their leader's orders. *WWP*

story of life in the iron-fisted Reverend's temple: savage beatings for minor infractions, suicide drills, heavy tithing and—something borrowed from the book of Father Divine more than four decades earlier—any number of situations in which the more dedicated turned all or most of their worldly belongings over to Father Jones. How much? The estimates on his Swiss bank accounts ran all the way from $7 million to $20 million. Now under assault in his own boudoir with both sexes while demanding abstinence of his flock, the married reverend dipped into his bankroll to spend a bit more liberally on legal help. His lawyers: the West Coast's Charles Garry, counsel for the Black Panthers and a darling of the left, and New York's Mark Lane, whose toil in the Jones cause—his idea of a true Socialist paradise—cost some time from his strenuous efforts to establish that an even more celebrated client by the name of James Earl Ray was not the assassin of Dr. Martin Luther King, Jr.

The indescribably gruesome end—with both Garry and Lane on hand but quick-witted enough to flee into the bush—came when Congressman Leo Ryan, along with several aides and a group of newsmen,

dared to journey to the jungle kingdom to see for himself the depths to which the Peoples Temple reportedly had descended. The courageous California Democrat saw—and when he left to return home on the night of November 17, taking sixteen defectors with him, he was cut down at the Guyana airport by gunmen from what had by then been turned more into an armed slave camp than the Nirvana of a man who called himself God. NBC News cameraman Robert Brown and Gregory Robinson, a photographer for the *Examiner*, perished with the fifty-four-year-old Congressman, father of five. So did defector Patricia Parks, forty-four. Ten others were riddled with bullets but survived.

Back at the temple after midnight, Jim Jones assembled his followers outside his own pavillion and, with the gentle strains of an organ serving as a backdrop to the taped proceedings, announced from his wicker-chair throne that he had ordered the airport ambush and the Guyanese army was on the way to wreak a frightful vengeance, and so—

"The time has come for us to meet in another place. To die in revolutionary suicide is to live forever."

195

The lethal potions had been prepared well in advance—fruit drinks laced with cyanide and stirred in a rusty tub cut down from an oil drum.

In the forty-three minutes that followed, the Pied Piper of salvation-through-death was only sporadically interrupted with pleas of mercy, wholly idle because the jungle haven had been ringed by guards prepared to use their automatic rifles before they took their last drink. Only a bare handful would slip away and survive.

Did the children have to die too? Yes, because if they didn't they would be slaughtered by forces "parachuting out of the air." The parents themselves had to administer the poison to the children who wouldn't take it; if they would not the ample medical suicide team on hand performed that chore. How many of the adults required the forced feeding, either out of paper cups or with needles, cannot ever be known. The tapes fed to NBC-TV and the *New York Times* by an enterpreneur about to peddle them on LPs and cassettes while both our government and the Guyana authorites in Georgetown were keeping the lid on them record the death throes of the cultists in the five minutes it took to depart the beautiful life held out for them by their hypnotic leader.

Who were the victims of the Klansman's son who built his early following by laboring with such dedication in the black cause?

Mostly black. But let it be said for Jim Jones that in his final high-pitched exhortation he did think to borrow the opening lines from the tombstone of Martin Luther King, Jr.: "Free at last."

~~~~~~

Part VIII

FOR $64,000...

Patty Duke, 12, who won $32,000 on the "$64,000 Challenge" last year, was given the questions and answers, her manager, John Ross, told the House TV probers. She is now starring in "The Miracle Worker" on Broadway. See Page 3.

THE CROOKED GAME

"A degree of deception is of considerable value in producing [quiz] shows."
—DAN ENRIGHT, producer, testifying before a House committee

WHAT YOU SEE here is the front page of the New York *Post* of November 4, 1959, and that jarringly poignant headline said an awful lot about the cynical men behind the Great Quiz Show Scandal. The nation knew the worst of this tawdry story before then—how Barry & Enright's *Twenty-One* had slipped a total of nearly half a million dollars to Charles Van Doren, Elfrida von Nardroff and Hank Bloomgarden under the guise of a contest of wits; how *The $64,000 Question* and its rich twin sister, *The $64,000 Challenge,* had nursed the impoverished Teddy Nadler to that crazy, all-time-record $252,000 pinnacle; how it was all part of the act when those freshly starched bank couriers showed up on camera with questions which supposedly had been residing in bank vaults until air time but actually had to be dog-eared from all that backstage handling; how *The Big Surprise* was less of a surprise to its contestants, prerehearsed, than it was to the viewer at home; how, perish the thought, one of Christ's own deputies on earth had been drawn into the bogus big money sweepstakes. The people knew that even such penny ante quiz shows as *Tic Tac Dough, Life Begins at Eighty, Dotto, Dough-Re-Me* and, yes, *Juvenile Jury* had

been rigged to keep the ratings up and do the best selling job for the sponsors' products.

Now, with the major revelations already on the record, little Patty Duke, by this time starring with Anne Bancroft in *The Miracle Worker* on Broadway, got caught in the TV net, too. It turned out that Patty had enjoyed the benefit of the most exacting rehearsal sessions in the process of taking down $32,000 as an "expert" on singing groups. The doleful tidings came out of the appearance of John Ross, the child's personal manager, before Congressman Oren Harris's Subcommittee on Legislative Oversight, which had jurisdiction over the operations of the none-too-vigilant Federal Communications Commission. Ross admitted that Patty had been recruited for her quiz show stint by Irving Harris, a friend of his, and then turned over to Shirley Bernstein, associate producer of *The $64,000 Challenge* and sister of Leonard Bernstein, for "coaching." Here are some excerpts from the questioning of the girl's manager by Representatives John B. Bennett (R-Michigan) and Steven B. Derounian (R-New York):

BENNETT: Did you tell her during these coach-

James Snodgrass (standing) and Hank Bloomgarden pore over reference works in bogus cram session for the *Twenty-One* giveaway game. The press didn't know then that the men had the answers before they looked in the books. Snodgrass turned in the show's producers after seeing $69,000 lopped off his $73,000 in winnings with a question he hadn't been handed in advance. NBC dropped that program after the *New York Post* published his confessional.

Herb Stempel, on the witness stand in Washington here, unloaded on *Twenty-One* because he was shoved aside for Charles Van Doren. Looking back in anger, Stempel accused the promoters of using the free air "deceitfully to exploit for private profit." His own take, before Van Doren arrived on the scene at the height of the quiz show craze, was $49,500. *New York Post*

ing sessions to take a pencil and paper and take notes on things that were asked her so she would not forget them?

Ross: Yes, sir.

BENNETT: Did you tell Patty that it was wrong for her to have gotten this answer [one of those that helped her win the $32,000] before the program?

Ross: No, sir.

DEROUNIAN: Do you think it is healthy for Mr. Harris to be parading around the city getting young children into situations like this where they are taught to cheat and lie for money?

Ross: No, sir.

DEROUNIAN: Would you have done this for your daughter if she had received the same opportunity?

Ross: It may not say much for me. I don't know, sir.

That answer could not have been more honest. It said something for the morality of our society, where cheating begins on the most affluent corporate and personal plateaus—the name of the game is How to Beat the Tax Man—and seeps down into every level of our lives. It said an awful lot. John Ross, drawing a 15 percent commission on pretty Patty Duke's earnings, whether out of honest toil or a rigged TV contest, had done only what nearly anybody else, with the possible exception of some Salvation Army recruits and card-carrying members of the DAR, would have done in the same deliciously tempting situation. It was such easy money. Could Patty Duke, sitting at the counsel table in a cute little jumper as her manager testified, have understood that? She was so young.

The quiz show was doubly reprehensible because it kept so many millions—as many as 36,000,000 in one sitting—transfixed before the magic tube, sharing vicariously in the cliff-hanging week-to-week ordeal of the performers as small fortunes changed hands in a crooked game. The man, woman or child in the isolation booth, fielding the questions upon which a whole lifetime might depend, never bit their lips or tugged at their forelocks alone; across the nation, the viewer suffered and died—or went into paroxyms of joy—with them. Patty Duke became America's sweetheart, the new Shirley Temple, when she was before the cameras supposedly summoning up all those answers from an eleven-year-old brain. Charles Van Doren in one brief stretch in 1956 and early 1957 had to have more fans than all the stars of stage and screen and television put together. Elfrida von Nar-

droff, hardly a sex symbol, was the envy of men and women alike while she was in there battling on that lofty intellectual level. Hank Bloomgarden, the serious, intense medical researcher who might well perform wonders for mankind with his cascading winings, had a nationwide cheering section. So did Herbert M. Stempel—until he was persuaded to settle for $49,500 and get the hell off the stage to let the more appealing Van Doren boy keep those ratings up. Stempel was cast as the poor struggling ex-GI and CCNY student who needed the money so badly.

How did this edifice built on paper money come crumbling down? Herb Stempel, pretty unhappy about that $49,500 kiss-off, told his story first to the New York Post and then to the New York Journal-American in the spring of 1957 but neither paper could nail down the corroborating evidence they needed to get his startling revelations past their libel lawyers. It took two lesser players in the TV drama to light the fire—more than a year later. First, Edward Hilgemeier Jr., an idle actor who was a standby contestant on Dotto, signed an affidavit for the Post swearing that a $4,000 winner on the show had been prefed her answers. How did young Hilgemeier know this? He found the woman's notebook on the studio floor one day—and it contained the very answers she happened to be rattling off on the air at that moment. The Post took Hilgemeier's affidavit to Federal Communications Commissioner John C. Doerfer on July 31, 1958. Eighteen days later the Columbia Broadcasting System quietly junked Dotto and the newspaper revealed the story behind it, prompting District Attorney Frank S. Hogan of Manhattan to start asking questions about the quiz shows. Stempel paid a visit to the Hogan truth factory ten days after that but the National Broadcasting Company kept Twenty-One on the air after Jack Barry, the Master of Ceremonies and co-producer of the show with Dan Enright, satisfied network officials that Stempel's soul-baring represented nothing more than the bleat of the sore loser. Enright, indeed, had a tape recording purporting to show that Stempel had tried to shake him down for $50,000 before blowing the whistle; he told the NBC brass the kid was just a nut.

But it didn't end there. An added starter turned up. James Snodgrass, an artist, emerged into the big money on Twenty-One in mid-1957 under the tender loving care of Albert Freedman, the Barry & Enright lieutenant on the premises, but balked when the time came for him to spill out a wrong answer and make room for another player. Well, there was a way to deal with that kind of maverick: You threw him a question from left field. So in one cold-deck session—

Eddie Hilgemeier, Jr., was the one who first pried open the door on the fixed shows. He's shown looking over checks he collected on *Dotto* before he discovered that a rival contestant was being prefed her answers. *New York Post*

his last, of course—the startled Snodgrass saw a nice $73,000 in paper winnings shrink to $4,000 in the coin of the realm. Now, a year later, the artist produced for the *Post* three registered letters which contained not only answers but stage directions for three of his supposedly extemporaneous appearances on the show—letters he had written and mailed to himself *before* going on camera on each of those occasions. NBC gave *Twenty-One* the hook three weeks after the *Post* published the Snodgrass confessional.

The Harris investigation didn't come until 1959— long after Frank Hogan's peek into the quiz shows had produced a massive file which must have set some kind of modern record for perjury. It was positively astounding how the contestants and the larger minds behind the TV Gold Rush, almost without exception, gave the wrong answers during the nine months when Mr. District Attorney was asking the questions. Their performance was surpassed only by the networks themselves and, more directly, by the sponsors of the big shows, one pushing a remedy for tired blood and the other selling beauty products, as they tried to wriggle off the line when it came time for all the soiled linen to be hung out on Capitol Hill.

Miss Von Nardroff, a thirty-five-year-old personnel consultant with on-the-air answers to burn, racked up the biggest single purse on *Twenty-One*—$220,500, a mere bagatelle, by the way, alongside the millions coming back as the viewers of that sham contest dragged themselves to the drugstores to get some Geritol for the aforementioned tired blood.

Charles Van Doren, lean and hungry at thirty-three as he struggled along on the meager salary of an assistant professor of English at Columbia University, settled for $129,000, but he was the big name. He came from one of the nation's most distinguished literary families—son of poet-critic Mark Van Doren and novelist Dorothy Van Doren and nephew of Carl Van Doren, biographer of Franklin. On top of that, he was by far the most engaging figure to turn up in the expanding quiz show cast since it burst upon the scene in 1955. He was the answer to a producer's dream and the darling of the ratings. So he drew the largest hosannas on the way to the television heights and the blackest headlines three years later—after the fall.

Van Doren did not help his own cause at all. He lied to Hogan's men. He lied to the newspapers. He held out on his lawyer. He lied to the NBC brass when the widespread whispers about hanky-panky finally penetrated the higher echelons in Radio City. The day after the Stempel revelations finally found their way into print, he lied on the Dave Garroway show where, thanks to his newfound fame, NBC was paying him $1,000 a week to dispense a fast five minutes of culture to the masses over the breakfast table; with a mixture of deep sincerity and deep hurt, he looked into the camera and said that he knew of "no improper activity" on *Twenty-One* and had never received any help with the answers. He lied to the Harris subcommittee, via Western Union, and then made the Congressional sleuths play catch with him before he came at long last to something his father had told him without even knowing the ugly story behind the family's sudden good fortune—"the truth is the only thing with which a man can live."

The truth which Charles Van Doren eventually unfolded on Capitol Hill was that his first appearance on *Twenty-One* was preceded by a very private powwow in the apartment of associate producer Albert Freedman, whom he had met before on a social level. Freedman said that Herb Stempel, the current champion, had to be deposed because he was becoming "unpopular." Freedman said Van Doren would have to accept a little behind-the-scenes tutoring to accomplish that necessary task because Stempel's

Charles Van Doren (left) and Herb Stempel playing their parts in the glass booth as they fielded pre-fed questions for the big money. *WWP*

great storehouse of knowledge made him practically unbeatable in any fair test. Van Doren said he would prefer to take the kid on cold but did not press it once Freedman explained to him that "the show was merely entertainment and that giving help to quiz contestants was a common practice and merely a part of show business."

When he bought that, the shy and scholarly scion of the Van Dorens was indeed in show business—up to his tousled hair. He may have been "sick at heart" and torn by an "intense moral struggle" but he was in show business the moment he took the first $1,000 for his debut on *Twenty-One*. In Albert Freedman, he had a drama coach as well as an endlessly generous benefactor. Freedman taught him how to hesitate over an answer, how to pass a question and come back to it to build up suspense, how to deliver his winning answers for maximum audience effect. Freedman was kind, too. In their closed-door briefings, he didn't always blurt out the answers to the harder questions. Sometimes he let his "human book of knowledge" go look them up because he knew the young college teacher enjoyed doing that. Freedman was even more thoughtful and considerate when his protégé, filled with fear and misgiving, begged leave to be freed from the increasingly oppressive confines of that air-conditioned isolation booth.

No longer able to console himself with the Freedman line that he was performing a service for the intellectual community by "increasing respect for the work of the mind," Van Doren asked out after "eight or ten" appearances, possibly even a little before that, but his friend kept him on the air until his

winnings had mounted to a new quiz show high of $143,000. Then, as the witness told it, Freedman fixed it for him to lose to Vivienne Nearing. The question he tripped over was a fairly simple one—who was the King of Belgium? Van Doren, who once said he could have answered 80 percent of the show's sticklers without benefit of those warm-ups, fluffed it honestly. He named Leopold instead of Baudouin and didn't have to wait for the rigged losing question that was coming later. Now, a few minutes ahead of schedule and $14,000 poorer, he could go home with his tainted $129,000—how much after taxes, $35,000?—and with the awful secret which would tear at his insides for the rest of his life.

The committee did not call Mrs. Nearing, an attractive thirty-year-old lawyer for Warner Brothers, especially imported for the prearranged dethroning of America's new TV idol. It did hear an intriguing piece of testimony on that score, however. Under questioning by committee counsel Robert W. Lishman, Edward Kletter, vice-president of Pharmaceuticals, Inc., sponsor of *Twenty-One*, said he was surprised at one point to discover that Mrs. Nearing had been paid an advance of $10,000 at a moment when her winnings on the show stood at only $5,500. This suggested a breakdown in the master plan somewhere along the line, for the blonde Portia wound up her stint on Channel 4 with that same $5,500 after reaching the $16,000 plateau and then losing when the string-pullers backstage sensed star quality in the glib, sure-tonged Hank Bloomgarden. The new Monday night whiz kid went all the way to $116,000 but settled for $98,500 on his fourteenth appearance when he named Primo Carnera instead of Max Schmeling as the man Jack Sharkey had beaten for the heavyweight title back in 1932. For Bloomgarden, it wasn't a total loss. All kinds of wonderful things besides money had happened during his brief sojourn in the limelight, like Marlene Dietrich, in person, stopping him on the street to wish him well in his stirring intellectual combat on the air.

Bloomgarden was spared an appearance before the Harris committee. So was Miss von Nardroff. So, too, was the biggest winner of them all—Teddy Nadler, the peppery little seventy-dollar-a-week Army depot clerk who never went past the eighth grade but collected $252,000 from the two modestly under-named "$64,000" charades and was still rattling off letter-perfect answers on widely assorted subjects when the headlines turned black and CBS, in cold blood, pulled the plug. Steve Carlin, Mert Koplin and Shirley Bernstein of Entertainment Productions, Inc., packager of the two shows, all confessed their fixing operations to the Congressional inquisitors. Koplin specifically described how Nadler had been spoon-fed in his remarkable ascent to the heights, but back home in St. Louis the dauntless "walking encyclopedia" scoffed at that kind of talk. "This whole scandal nonsense is like the witch scare in Salem, Massachusetts, in 1692 (he always gave places and dates). They'll have to drag me there to get me to testify."

Sitting comfortably if perhaps a bit uneasily atop what was left of his record haul after Uncle Sam chewed off the lion's share, the egotistic Nadler had professed contempt for the lesser brains responsible for the hard ones Sonny Fox, the Master of Ceremonies, used to toss at him. "The questions they asked me hardly scratched the surface of my knowledge," he said. "Sometimes this gift of mine is revolting." Revolting or not, the gift failed Nadler a year later. In what may have constituted the ultimate commentary on the three-year quiz show madness, he flunked a simple written examination for a $13-a-day census taker's job in St. Louis. Nadler was also responsible for the best joke to come out of that time, although you couldn't know it unless you happened to be on the inside. He offered to go head-to-head on the air against Charles Van Doren to settle once and for all the question of who knew the most. Who would have policed that contest—J. Edgar Hoover?

Teddy Nadler was not the only resident genius tarnished by the testimony of the high-salaried working stiffs whose double-dealing had helped to push Revlon cosmetics from a prequiz show level of $33,000,000-a-year to nearly triple that amount in 1958. The Harris committee also heard a few things about the care and feeding (answers, that is) of Billy Pearson, the jockey and art expert who won $174,000; Myrt Power, the little old baseball wizard from Georgia, winner of $48,000, and bandleader Xavier Cugat, who made $16,000 dispensing prestacked musical lore against the competition of singer Lillian Roth. There was even some mention of a couple of child spelling "champions" having been helped to some of the loot in the quiz show Klondike.

The hearings enjoyed a seriocomic respite when the Rev. Charles E. (Stoney) Jackson of the Church of Christ in Tullahoma, Tennessee, took the witness stand. The Reverend picked up a small bundle on the two $64,000 shows in the Great Love Story category after offering his services as an expert on football and the Good Book. Why did he stick around when he found that the programs weren't following the Biblical straight and narrow? He needed the money to repay a $25,000 debt incurred when he tried to set up a boys' home and make himself "the Protestant Father Flanagan." What about the ethics residing in a man of the cloth? "The fact that I was ordained a minister has not made me a saint yet." Why didn't he follow his best instincts when he was prompted to blurt out the truth on camera and expose the whole business? "I could not only see about six cases of apoplexy right there, but I could see my bullet-riddled body as I passed an alley someplace." (AUTHOR'S NOTE: There never was a shot fired in anger as the quiz show scandal unfolded.) How did he know when the money faucet was being turned off? "I suddenly couldn't get anyone to talk to me. I was perturbed. I asked myself, 'What's happened?' And then I realized, 'You've got the message. You're through.' And I was. They knew my weakness, and when they want you off the show they feed you questions that sixteen college professors couldn't answer. I finally realized I was not in a contest of intelligence at all, but a test of personality, of audience appeal. You would be kept so long as your appeal lasted, then dropped."

The Rev. Mr. Jackson's appeal lasted $16,000 worth on *The $64,000 Question* and $4,000 worth on *The $64,000 Challenge*. Tripped up in short order on the latter show, he got so angry over the whole business that he tried to return the $4,000, but there were no takers, so he was stuck with the whole dirty twenty grand.

The last chapter in the long-running, endlessly depressing quiz show follies was written in New York's Criminal Court on January 17, 1962. On that day, Charles Van Doren, Elfrida von Nardroff, Hank Bloomgarden and six bit players—including Dr. David

Jack Barry holds Elfrida von Nardroff's hand aloft in victory after she picked up $225,500, the record win on *Twenty-One*. At right is Barry's fellow producer, Dan Enright.

Psychologist Joyce Brothers, a boxing buff, made a fat $134,000 coming up with more correct answers than such fistfighters as Fat Tony Galento (left) and Tiger Jones. Dr. Brothers had the benefit of some special tutelage from the old master, Nat Fleischer, publisher of *Ring* magazine, but the House sleuths accepted her statement that it was all on the up and up. She emerged with a TV talk show of her own and a syndicated column on—no, not the fight game—the eternal problems swimming around in most of our heads.

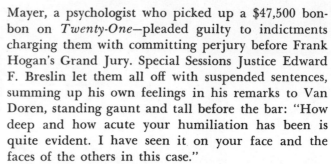

Mayer, a psychologist who picked up a $47,500 bon-bon on *Twenty-One*—pleaded guilty to indictments charging them with committing perjury before Frank Hogan's Grand Jury. Special Sessions Justice Edward F. Breslin let them all off with suspended sentences, summing up his own feelings in his remarks to Van Doren, standing gaunt and tall before the bar: "How deep and how acute your humiliation has been is quite evident. I have seen it on your face and the faces of the others in this case."

The judge knew that there was no punishment he could visit on those nine defendants, or on seven others caught up in the mess along the way, equal to anything they had already suffered. In the Great Quiz Show Scandal, the punishment fit the crime with no help from the bench.

Teddy Nadler, advertised as a memory whiz, made them all look like paupers with his score on the two big shows. The fix was in, of course.

The Reverend Charles E. (Stoney) Jackson manages a weak smile as he tells the committee he had a spot of help in winning $20,000 on the two $64,000 programs. *WWP*

Part IX

DREAMS FOR SALE

TIMOTHY LEARY:

A Religion Called LSD

1967 in San Francisco's Golden Gate Park, and the Leary theme: "Turn onto the scene, tune into what's happening, and drop out—of high school, grade school, junior executive, senior executive—and follow me, the hard way." Many did, and it was hard indeed. For some, that road led to madness—or the burial ground. *WWP*

"When I listen to Beethoven when I'm turned on, it makes me want to say, 'Oh, *come on,* Ludwig, get off it.'"
—DR. TIMOTHY LEARY

WHICH WAY TIMOTHY LEARY? He went from Lady Hemp to the LSD that comes from lysergic acid diethylamide to a new "religion" called LSD—his own League for Spiritual Discovery. His trip took him all the way from an argument over the forbidden weed to a psychedelic cult complete with yoga, the Hindu bit and vague references to Buddha and the Tibetan mystique. There was some mention of the Tantriks, too, so you had to ask yourself whether the early Oom, in the person of "Tim Leary, Guru," was playing a return engagement with a little extra lift from the highly questionable "mind-stretching drug the man from Harvard put on the front pages more than a decade after the Central Intelligence Agency, unbeknownst to the man in the street, had begun to use it in its quest for control of the human mind. Was LSD the new road to reincarnation?

While the League for Spiritual Discovery claimed a mere 411 card-carrying members when it sprang full-blown from the multiple-image Leary brain in the winter of 1966, the founder had no doubt that another million initiates would come in within a year, enjoying "trips" on that magic sugar cube only in seven-day

cycles but keeping their minds wide open in the interim with one-hour-a-day "meditation" sessions laced with marijuana. And the million happy people on Cloud Nine would represent nothing more than a bare start. "At the present rate of conversion," said the Guru, wildly extravagant with numbers, as time would tell, "more than thirty million Americans will have had a chemical religious experience by 1970. Our ultimate aim is to change the spiritual level of the United States and the world."

The agent of that "change," in the world of Timothy Leary, was to be LSD, of course. LSD, also known by such imposing names as The Chief, The Hawk and The Big D, would put our thirteen billion brain cells, a network now functioning well below capacity, into total operation for the first time. "The game is about to be changed," said the prophet of the new faith in something he wrote for the *Harvard Review* with Richard Alpert, one of his helpmates. "Man is about to make use of the fabulous electrical network he carries around in his skull."

Unfortunately, we couldn't all go on the big trip. The neurotics, for one, would have to stay the way

205

they were—unstretched. "I have taken LSD three hundred times," Leary said, "but I want to tell you that it is no business for neurotics to play around with. It is like a religious experience. It makes you see the most vicious things about yourself—that you're a liar, that most people are robots, that men are blind to the wisdom that is within their grasp. It's a ruthless microscopic view of how really ridiculous we perceive ourselves. LSD pulls the rug right out from under you. If you're not ready to look at the most unpleasant aspects of reality, stay away."

Leaving aside its perhaps demonstrable uses in medical science under stringent controls, was the wondrous newly publicized hallucinogenic agent just another fad? At least one authority, Dr. Sidney Cohen of UCLA, author of the LSD study called *The Beyond Within* and chief of psychosomatic medicine at the Veterans Administration Hospital in Los Angeles, didn't think so. "It is so seductive," said Dr. Cohen, "it is such a glorious, rapturous, blissful experience. A good trip is not going to go the way of goldfish eating." The doctor wasn't endorsing the Leary gospel, you understand, nor did he know that CIA operatives were laying the drug not only on some of our GIs and men in prisons but even slipping it to any number of poor souls into whose heads they were prowling around in the hope of ferreting out a useful secret here or there to ensure the republic's safety. "We are not in need of chemical Messiahs," he said. "We already have enough troubles."

The Leary view that the mind-blowing LSD was perfectly safe for the nonneurotics, whoever *they* were, drew wide assaults from the medical profession led, indeed, by Boston's Dr. Max Rinkel, the very man who introduced the powerful potion into this country for experimental purposes in 1949, eleven years after Dr. Albert Hofmann of the Swiss pharmaceutical firm, Sandoz Ltd., synthesized it from an ergot compound. Dr. Rinkel, a past president of the Society of Biological Psychiatry, warned that schizophrenia or suicide lay ahead for the campus thrill-seekers and the other high-flyers using LSD for kicks. "The truth is that we don't understand the chemical effect on the brain," he said. "Many people think they can find themselves through uncontrolled experiments. The fact is that nobody has found himself, and many have gotten lost."

To most observers, with a massive record building up in such urban centers as New York and Los Angeles, that was a mild way to put it. The little white powder put its share of victims in hospitals, including some in straitjackets, and a few in jails, too. New York experienced the most tragic case when a thirty-year-old medical school dropout turned on with LSD brutally murdered his mother-in-law. In Berkeley, California, a twenty-year-old youth on LSD walked out of a third-story window to his death. That boy may have been a suicide, but there were other reported cases of LSD users stepping out of windows because, under the drug's influence, they got the notion that they could walk on air; in Chapel Hill, North Carolina, a twenty-three-year-old youth with the magic sugar cube in him died of injuries sustained when he decided to "fly" over a post office roof from his second-story room. In Los Angeles a woman had her nineteen-year-old son committed to a state mental hospital after two suicide attempts traced to LSD. The Neuropsychopathic Institute at the Unversity of California started turning away hallucination cases late in 1966 because there just weren't enough beds to go around.

There, Dr. J. Thomas Ungerleider, a leading researcher, disputed the whole idea that LSD performs sheer wonders for the mind. "LSD has been called a consciousness-expanding drug," he said. "In fact it is quite the reverse. It decreases one's ability to select and pay attention. Therefore it decreases conscious functions. Sensations do become intensified. Perception, however, is not enhanced, and visual and auditory acuteness are not revolutionized but are distorted."

Long before that, in the early days of the LSD vogue, Dr. Roy R. Grinker Sr., chief editor of the authoritative *Archives of General Psychiatry*, warned that the drug's "deleterious effects are becoming more obvious. Latent psychotics are disintegrating under the influence of even single doses." The drug did find favor among some psychiatrists, because it lowered the barrier between the conscious and the subconscious and broke down the inhibitions of patients and there were a few doctors who found some virtue in it in the treatment of alcoholics or as the ultimate pain-killer for terminal cancer patients. But the hard question still was, and is to this day, Who do you use it on without turning his brain to mush?

Dr. Dana L. Farnsworth, director of student health services at Harvard, said in 1963 that there was no way of distinguishing between those who could safely take LSD and those who couldn't. This was after Leary, then a lecturer in clinical psychology at Harvard's Center for Research in Personality, and Dr. Alpert, an assistant professor of psychology, had been banished from the campus for using students as guinea pigs in experiments with hallucinatory drugs.

The religious bit came after that, although its origins went deeper. Leary, son of an army captain and raised as a Roman Catholic, started reading Eastern philosophy at West Point during a nine-month period when he was in Coventry, shunned by the Corps of Cadets over some infraction of the academy's code. He left the Point after two years, got his doctorate at Alabama University, served during the war as an army psychologist, and then traveled extensively. His introduction to mind drugs occurred in Mexico when he tasted some sacred mushrooms and found everything around him "infinitely greater, older, wiser and incredibly more beautiful." When he got to Harvard, Aldous Huxley, who popularized the hallucinatory mescaline in *The Doors of Perception* ("surer than churchgoing, safer than alcohol"), told him he could get the mushroom in its synthetic form, psilocybin. Leary used it in experiments on prisoners in Massachusetts, and then on the campus. LSD came later. When Harvard dropped him, Leary set up an LSD training center in Mexico, only to get thrown out. He had the same experience later in two British possessions, Antigua and Dominica. In 1965, crossing from Mexico into Laredo with his eighteen-year-old daughter Susan and what the trade calls a "dime bag" of marijuana (ten dollars' worth), the forty-five-year-old professor was arrested and slapped with an extraordinary sentence of five to thirty years and a $30,000 fine. The girl was ordered into a federal reformatory, but neither served any time. Out on bond pending appeal, Leary submitted that he was using the weed for religious purposes and the government was interfering with his Constitutional rights to practice his beliefs—Hindu then—with the help of those dandy cigarettes. He beat the case in the Supreme Court in 1969 but not on those grounds. The unanimous ruling held that his Fifth Amendment rights against self-incrimination had been violated and, more consequently, the two laws under which he had been convicted—importing grass without paying a $100-per-ounce transfer tax or without prior legal authority—were invalid. That decision embraced another hundred cases pending around the nation.

The law, of course, did not enjoy the same vision.

Within ten months after he beat the Texas case, denounced by California Superior Court Judge Byron K. McMillan as an "insidious menace" to society and a "pleasure-seeking, irresponsible Madison Avenue advocate of the free use of LSD," Leary drew one to ten years for possession of marijuana. His pretty new wife, Rosemary, twenty-four, was sentenced to six months plus five years probation on an LSD charge and his son John, twenty, was ordered into the Adult Authority in Chino for ninety days to have his head examined. The prophet himself didn't linger behind bars too long. Confined to the minimum-security California Men's Colony West in San Luis Obispo, the mahatma of the better world skipped the joint before the year was out, quite possibly with the help of the Weather Underground. With still another Texas case pending against him, Leary fled to Algeria into the arms of another fugitive, the even more-celebrated Eldridge Cleaver, but that union didn't take because Mr. Cleaver wasn't too high on the notion that our salvation lay in LSD. Leary then spent three years wandering through North Africa, Europe and Asia in search of asylum before one of our narcotics snoops caught up with him in Afghanistan after an interim arrest in Switzerland that didn't stick. With his Rosemary having dropped out somewhere along the way, he arrived back in the States with a new love, Joanna Harcourt-Smith, twenty-six, niece of the British publisher Simon Harcourt-Smith, who announced, "I know I am going to free him. Love is what it takes."

That woman evidently didn't know too much about the judicial system here in the Colonies.

The Guru, held in $5 million bond, collected another six months to five years for his escape and went back inside, eventually transferred to the maximum-security installation at Folsom State Prison near Sacramento. He was in the Federal Corrections Center in San Diego in April of 1976 when he won a parole, but that was proceeded by some embarrassment. Had the supersalesman of the turned-on generation been turned by the Feds? In a San Francisco press conference late in 1974, his own son John, Allen Ginsberg, Richard Alpert (a/k/a Baba Ram Dass by then) and Yippie leader Jerry Rubin all charged that Dr. Feelgood had been spilling his guts about the drug scene. Some of the milder references to the fifty-four-year-old fallen prophet: "cop informant," "liar," "paranoid schizophrenic." Young John was the roughest. "I would not be surprised if he testified about my sister or myself if he could. Timothy, by his deceit, is betraying the very meaning of trust." Rubin wasn't too generous either. "He has joined the forces that he opposed with his speeches about love and peace in the nineteen-sixties," said Rubin. "The specter of Tim is terrifying."

So much for Timothy Leary. He never did turn up on a witness stand to put anybody else behind bars and while LSD is still being peddled on a small scale, the drug had all but dropped out of the news until 1975, when the Center for National Security Studies, a private research organization, blew the CIA's closely-held secret with the help of fifty-nine documents obtained under the Freedom of Information Act. That scant bundle simply told us that the agency

Dr. Leary at his upstate New York sanctuary with his son John, seventeen then. Years later the boy would turn on him, charging that he was singing to the Feds to beat the multiple drug charges against him. *WWP*

Leary in Algeria with another wife, Rosemary, after his 1970 escape from San Luis Obispo prison in California in 1970 . . . *WWP*

. . . and in Los Angeles three years later following his capture in Afghanistan. *UPI*

The high priest of the LSD cult in San Diego with his wife, Joanna, when he got out on a $5,000 bond while serving a ten-year sentence for possession of marijuana. *UPI*

had been experimenting with LSD and other behavior-modification drugs all through the Fifties and Sixties. This was just the tip of the iceberg—sparked with at least one tragic morsel. That was the story of Frank R. Olson, an Army scientist who leaped ten stories to his death from a New York hotel window in 1953 after a dose of LSD was slipped into a glass of Cointreau he was drinking. The CIA paid the victim's family $1.25 million for that fatal test of the hallucinogen.

The full extent of the agency's mind-control labors began to emerge in 1977, when a team of *New York Times* reporters started sifting through 2,000 other documents and a Senate subcommittee headed by Ted Kennedy began asking some questions. The record sounded more like a B movie. The CIA maintained so-called "safehouses" in New York and San Francisco between 1953 and 1966, where unsuspecting subjects—sometimes lured to the testing ground by prostitutes—were treated to cocktails laced with LSD or other chemical agents while unseen operatives looked on, made films with hidden cameras and recorded their reactions. Why? The CIA believed the Russians, North Koreans and possibly other intelligence networks had used mind-altering drugs to pry secrets out of American agents in the Forties. And the CIA had company, like the Army FBI and the Federal Bureau of Narcotics. One rather embarrassing incident came to light through the testimony of David Rhodes, a former CIA man. He said he was sent to San Francisco with a colleague in 1959 to throw a large party and spray the air with liquid LSD-25 to see how that mixed with good drinking whisky. That one didn't come off because the particular "safehouse" chosen in suburban Mill Valley wasn't air conditioned and the weather was too hot to close the windows. As if that weren't bad enough, the aerosol

Frank R. Olson, the army scientist who plunged to his death from a New York hotel after the CIA quietly fed him some LSD in 1953 to see what the mind-bending drug could do for our intelligence apparatus. *WWP*

spray furnished to Rhodes and his helper wasn't working properly.

What it all added up to, with all the unsuspecting civilians, Army volunteers and nonvolunteers as well as convicts in various federal prisons, was a big zero. Neither LSD nor mescaline nor any of the other mind-expanders proved efficacious as agents of our security apparatus. All the tests stopped in 1967—and here we are twelve years later still safe in our own houses but without all those taxpayer-financed fun times.

THE NEW "IN" DRUG—COCAINE

... and Some Others

"Everything suggests that cocaine is becoming one of the routine luxuries provided by our consumer society."
— DR. LESTER GRINSPOON and JAMES B. BAKALAR in *Cocaine: A Drug and Its Social Evolution*

COCAINE'S THE THING NOW. From Hollywood to Broadway to San Francisco's Nob Hill to Nashville to Chicago's Gold Coast and, of all things, our Born-Again White House, with all the steps in between. At the more posh parties today, the perfect host may serve it up on a Tiffany silver spoon, but it does the same thing for you snorted off a plate through those wide straws dispensed with the soft drinks at McDonald's. The only problem here may be the cost—say, $20 or $30 for a twenty-minute high practically guaranteed to deliver you unto a euphoric dreamland, turn your brain into something that sees around all the corners, convert you into a super sexual athlete and work wonders for your creative powers. All without imprisoning you in the wicked addiction of the street people's heroin or burning out your brain like the amphetamines.

But there's something else about this champagne of illicit drugs. Dr. Robert L. DuPont, director of the National Institute on Drug Abuse, said in his $4-million, 223-page 1977 report on the magic coca leaf developed by the Inca Indians more than four centuries ago that cocaine stimulates the central nervous system, constricts the blood vessels, and acts as a topical anesthetic. Never mind what it does to the nose of the full-time snorter: plastic surgeons on both the coasts are now enjoying an SRO trade in the rebuilding of nostrils ulcerated because coke has eaten away the mucous membrane separating them. The doctor's larger point was that if you used enough of it often enough you were asking for depression, anxiety, sleeplessness, feelings of paranoia, hallucinations or possibly even a violence-inducing psychosis. And from Dr. Andrew Weill, a Harvard expert in ethnopharmacology: "Cocaine does not miraculously bestow energy on the body. It merely releases energy already stored chemically in certain parts of the nervous system."

How many users are there besides the star-studded names you read or hear about every other day? Dr. DuPont said 8 million Americans had sniffed coke at least once in the preceding five years, including 9.8 percent of the Class of '76 on the campus. His researches also counted one out of every five in the eighteen-to-twenty-five-year-old set as having sampled the drug in that same period—more than double the preceding five years. Put it down then as another one of the great growth stocks. And there's hardly any-

TV's Louise Lasser entering the municipal court in Beverly Hills in 1976 following her arrest for possession of cocaine. The sentence: six months in a drug diversion program. *WWP*

Linda Ronstadt, the dynamite singer, also made the list of the big names on cocaine. *WWP*

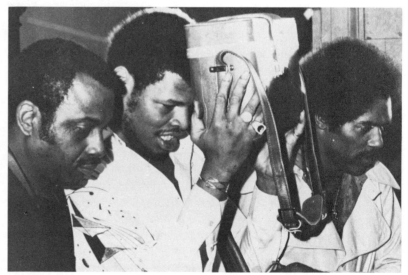

Leon Spinks, Olympic champion and briefly the heavyweight title holder before the tired and aging Muhammad Ali took back his title seven months later, leaves a St. Louis courtroom after being busted while still the champ in April 1978 when police said they found a "controlled substance"—coke—in his car. *WWP*

thing easier to get. Cocaine literally pours out of the Bahamas, where there are 700 islands and 2,000 cays and a grand total of four police patrol boats to cover a 750-mile area where the couriers of the happy dust and marijuana are busily plying their trade against a minimal risk. If you get caught the bail is $10,000 to $20,000 and you peel that off your roll and skip. Bolivia's an even happier hunting ground and accounts for the bulk of the U.S. supply. A $50,000 buy down there at $3,000 to $5,000 per kilo (2.2 pounds) is worth $300,000 by the time it gets to these shores, where it has a street value ranging from $1,500 to $2,000 an ounce. Stack that against what the hospitals and pharmacies pay for the legal product, often used in eye, nose and mouth surgery: $26 an ounce. Then throw in the fortunes the burgeoning "head" shops are coining along with the higher class purveyors peddling $150 spoons, fourteen-carat gold vials for as much as $350, or $90 razors to cut your cocaine lumps down into that dust.

All for the "in" set to whom that white powder has come to represent status, wealth and unbounded glamour. Not too many years ago you had to be some kind of drag to throw a party where your guests couldn't slip off into one of the bedrooms and enjoy a few tokes on a reefer. That's so pedestrian now. Today the evening's pièce de résistance is "tooting" coke and the DuPont findings have paled. A recent *Time* magazine survey put the current devotees at 2 million and the annual bill at $25 billion.

Until very recently the media's principal dosage for us peasants on the sidelines was studded with imposing names from show business, principally Hollywood and the Rock crowd: Louise Lasser of TV's "Mary Hartman, Mary Hartman." Singer Linda Ronstadt. Comedienne Judy Carne. Eighteen-year-old Linda Blair, star of *The Exorcist*, busted two years ago and not in the clear yet. Keith Richard, lead guitarist of the Rolling Stones. Anjelica Huston, John Huston's daughter and Jack Nicholson's girlfriend, who beat her own rap by testifying against Roman Polanski when the director was arrested on a sex charge brought by the parents of a thirteen-year-old girl. Nicholson himself, never in the toils but admittedly not unacquainted with the drug. Gregg Allman, Cher's second husband. Tommy Rettig, ex-star of the "Lassie" TV series, now thirty-seven. And some of the athletes as well: Leon Spinks, the babe-in-arms who took the heavyweight crown away from Muhammad Ali, was found with some coke in his car. Don Murdoch, the $2.5 million property of the World Hockey Association who became the New York Rangers' right wing and then was set down by the National

Hockey League for trying to bring some of the wonder flake in from Canada. Ernie Holmes, defensive lineman for the Pittsburgh Steelers—among many others from the sporting scene.

It may be said for our current crop of glittering snorters that, after all, they're simply following in the footsteps of such luminaries out of the past as Sigmund Freud (who used it an early age to combat depression and anxiety), Queen Victoria (who liked to slug down Mariani's Coca Wine, which was spiked with coke and contributed to the original formula for Coca-Cola), Pope Leo XIII (another fancier of that wine back in Victoria's nineteenth century), H. G. Wells, President McKinley, Emile Zola, Thomas Edison, Robert Louis Stevenson (just three days for the first draft of *Dr. Jekyll and Mr. Hyde* while under the influence) and such old-time stage greats as the "Divine Sarah" Bernhardt, Eleanora Duse and William Gillette.

But in the summer of 1978 the names on the celebrity register had to take a back seat. Dr. Peter Bourne, President Carter's $51,000-a-year chief advisor on mental health and narcotic policies, wrote a prescription for fifteen Quaalude tablets in the name of "Sarah Brown" (you remember the Salvation Army lass in *Guys and Dolls*, don't you?) that were really meant for Ellen Metsky, his twenty-five-year-old administrative assistant. Not very risky, except that a state pharmacy inspector happened to be in the suburban Virginia drugstore when a woman friend of Miss Metsky's came in with that Rx and he decided to check its origin. Bourne, a thirty-eight-year-old British-born psychiatrist who goes way back with Jimmy Carter, said he had chosen that device just to protect the identity of his assistant, who was suffering from insomnia and supposedly needed the drug. Well, it didn't seem all that awful, even though it bent a law or two. Bourne went on a paid leave of absence, and then the roof blew off. The doctor told James Wooten of the *New York Times* that marijuana—*and cocaine*—were not universally shunned by members of the White House staff. Then columnist Jack Anderson said Bourne himself had done a bit of snorting at a 1977 party staged by the National Organization for the Reform of Marijuana Laws. Bourne denied it. *Time* confirmed it—and then it turned out that the doctor had even turned on with a reporter or two from the Washington *Post* staff, whereupon the President's confidant resigned his key post. There's an embarrassment underlying all this. Just the year before, when the man from Georgia briefed the press on his Congressional bill to decriminalize grass in cases where possession of less than an ounce is in-

Carter Orders White House Staff To Follow Drug Laws or Resign

The New York Times/Teresa Zabala

Rosalynn Carter, at luncheon meeting, talked about problems faced by the President. Article, page A13.

INSIDE

Dollar Plunges Below 200 Yen

The exchange rate for the United States dollar plunged below 200 yen in Japan for the first time since World War II. Page D1.

By TERENCE SMITH
Special to The New York Times

WASHINGTON, July 24 — President Carter, responding to reports of drug use by White House employees, warned his staff today to obey the drug laws even if they disagreed with them or to "seek employment elsewhere."

"I expect every member of the White House staff to obey the law," the President wrote in a sharply worded memorandum distributed by the senior staff to the 351 White House staff members.

"Whether you agree with the law or whether or not others obey the law is totally irrelevant," the memorandum said. "You will obey it, or you will seek employment elsewhere."

'Deeply Concerned Over Reports'

The President said that he had been "deeply concerned over recent reports that some members of the White House staff are using illegal drugs." He added that he expected the senior staff to "convey my feelings directly and in no uncertain terms" to every member of the White House staff.

The President's admonishing memorandum, the first of its kind to the White House staff since he took office, came after a statement last week by his drug policy adviser, Dr. Peter G. Bourne, that there was a "high incidence" of marijuana use on the staff and "occasional" use of cocaine.

Dr. Bourne resigned last week after admitting that he had prescribed a powerful sedative for a member of the White House staff under a false name.

From the front page of the *New York Times* after Dr. Bourne told reporters there was a "high incidence" of marijuana use and some "occasional" flights on cocaine among members of the White House staff. Bourne said later that 8 million Americans had tried the white flake and 1.8 million were using it regularly.

volved, the man at his side was Dr. Peter Bourne. That Carter message, by the way, called in stringent terms for an end to all drug abuse.

In the case of cocaine, as with marijuana and the more dread heroin, there is no end in sight. You can't press a button on Capitol Hill or at 1600 Pennsylvania Avenue and make the drug culture—or counterculture—self-destruct. Not when our billion-dollar law enforcement apparatus is dogging the footsteps of the headline-name users or hauling in the minor pushers while the wide-open Mafia traffic in drugs is all but beyond the reach of the authorities. Apart from this woeful reality, where do you draw the line between the White House honcho, the party-throwing movie producer, the music tycoons slipping dope to the disc jockeys to get their records aired, the Jet Set types who simply adore the "society high" and can come up with junk just as readily as a new limo or the very sick guy in the tenement jamming a needle into his arm?

And now about those Quaalude tablets Dr. Bourne's aide had to have to go beddy-bye. That wonder pill—methaqualone or 2-methyl-3-tolyl4(3H)-quinazolinone in the long form—goes back to 1951 when it was snythesized for malaria cases. It became

Dr. Peter Bourne, the first man to tell Jimmy Carter he could make the White House and later his special assistant for mental health and the narcotics problem, briefs reporters on the President's drug abuse control message to Congress. It wasn't too long afterward that the doctor had to resign over some funny business with a Quaalude prescription he wrote for his administrative assistant. *WWP*

the dream sedative-hypnotic. Nonaddictive, too. In the late Sixties it was being fed to Ohio State football players to bring 'em down after that big Saturday afternoon. It didn't take too long for the nonathletes to get on that bandwagon, because "luding out," especially with a touch of the grape, quickly won substantial notoriety, like cocaine, as the ideal Rx for your problem with the other sex. It also killed some of its customers, unfortunately, and in 1974 the FDA put it on its list of "controlled" drugs. That cut the death toll down to sixty-one by 1977, but in the interim hospital emergency rooms counted some 5,500 Quaalude cases in a single year against 1,671 three years earlier. Freddie Prinze of TV's "Chico and the Man" downed five tablets the day he shot himself to death in 1977, and that boy out of New York's Puerto Rican slum hadn't passed up cocaine, either.

So there was nothing at all unique about what the pure-living Jimmy Carter's in-house drug-abuse aide had done. Doctors all over the horizon have been writing Quaalude prescriptions just as they have for all the other instant remedies for what-ails-you, and there's nothing easier to buy on the street if you've got anywhere from $3 to $5 in your jeans for the tablet good for the big sleep or the even better big bang under the covers—*if* you believe it.

What with its low death toll, one may classify Quaalude as about as innocent a drug as marijuana when you compare it with the revival now being enjoyed—if that's the word—in the high schools and colleges by the frightful PCP, or Angel Dust. This potion surfaced in the mid-Sixties in such resorts of the mind-benders as Haight–Ashbury but quickly went into the discard. The federal watchdogs list some 7 million users in the past couple of years and count at least 100 deaths and 4,000 emergency room cases. There is no precise record on the number of suicides or killings associated with this drug, even more unpredictable than LSD, but it has turned up as the basis for insanity pleas in a handful of murder trials.

PCP, the white middle class's equivalent of the black ghetto's heroin, stands for phencylidine, and was developed in the Fifties as a tranquilizer for animals. It was later distributed by Parke, Davis & Co. as a surgical anesthetic but withdrawn in 1965 because it produced such side effects as delirium and disorientation. It was called Sernyl then. Now, as Sernylan, a single laboratory is once more producing it for animals but there are very few vets who will use it because it's so potent it can knock out an elephant. The best thing about Angel Dust—also affectionately known by such names as hog, peace pills, rocket fuel, super weed, wobble weed, magic dust, flakes and goon killer—is its deliciously low price. You can buy a single dose of this white powder for $1 or a half-gram for $10 or $12, slop it down with mint leaves or parsley, take it in tablet form, snort it, lace your grass with it or use it with a needle if you think that's the faster buzz. The fact is, you don't need a spike with Angel Dust because your flight's leaving just as fast no matter how you take it. Destination? Heaven or hell itself, for PCP's effects range all the way from that beautiful euphoria to prolonged coma, violent rage, schizophrenic stupor, paralysis of the limbs, horror-stricken visions and now and then, in large enough doses, fatal convulsions. And there's nothing quick about that flight, as with LSD. PCP is so toxic that its effect can last for weeks, not infrequently with a touch of irreversible brain damage to prove it. Listen to Dr. DuPont: "The tragedy is that most people experience angel dust as some unusual form of marijuana and associate it with the benign patterns of marijuana, but it's anything but that. It's a real terror of a drug." Yes, that potion is another hallucinogen, but it's questionable whether many of its joy-riding clients know it until it's too late. The Drug Enforcement Administration's roster of the most dangerous narcotics now rates PCP right behind the much more expensive heroin. In truth, it has a right to the number one spot, because it doesn't have to be imported and never runs into one of those terrifying short-supply situations.

Angel Dust is whipped together in cellar, garage or storeroom "laboratories," known as "pig outfits," that blossom anew just as fast as the police or narcs shut them down. The West Coast, not surprisingly, is a major producer but the wobble weed's also coming out of such urban centers as New York, Detroit and even Washington, D. C., itself. And it's well worth the risk. The now defunct magazine *High Times*, an authority on our thriving narcotic underculture, put it this way last March in an article bearing the title "Angel Death:"

PCP has one of the highest profit margins of any drug. The basic chemicals needed for "cooking" a pound run to about $150; it then wholesales for about $16,000. A gram of pure PCP wholesales for about $130. Buffed, or cut, that one gram will yield $400 on the street; and with 28 grams in an ounce, and 16 ounces in a pound, a heavily cut pound of PCP now represents $58,000.

Quaalude, that delicious Q, didn't want for big-name customers either. Young Freddie Prinze, up from New York's Puerto Rican slum into the TV heights in the *Chico and the Man* series with Jack Albertson, swallowed a small handful of that drug before putting a bullet in his head in 1977. That's his wife, Katherine, estranged from him before his suicide. *WWP*

Steven Lerner, the San Francisco drug authority, says that a single gram contains enough Angel Dust to sprinkle on anywhere from ten to thirty marijuana cigarettes. On his figures, a $625 investment in PCP can earn as much as $225,000.

Pretty good money—and the busts are few and far between. The "pig outfit" is just about as hard to sniff out as the moonshiner in the hills or the bathtub gin purveyors who operated so freely—in their own homes, so many of them—during the Great Experiment known as Prohibition.

What a pity. In 1977 San Diego drug-abuse officials attributed nearly a third of that city's OD deaths to Angel Dust. And that's just one sampling. The PCP epidemic is moving faster than the people who keep the statistics can compile them. Indeed, it is only in the past year or so that the federal narcotics authorities started to make any noises about this revived scourge of our young. Who's minding the store? Who will save our children?

PART X

THE CHANGING SCENE

THE HIPPIES:

Nothing But Love

IN SAN FRANCISCO's Haight-Ashbury district in the mid-Sixties, row after row of once-proud Victorian dwellings housed a native slum population interspersed with a shifting band of boys and girls freshly resigned from our ever so complex society. Above the cracked stoop on one such building, a wayfarer observed this legend:

> DUE TO LACK OF INTEREST,
> TOMORROW HAS BEEN CANCELED

Haight-Ashbury, also called Hashbury and, more fittingly, Psychedelphia, was the western rampart of Hippies, but that sign did not tell the whole story of the dropped-out Flower Children.

Today had been canceled too, not just tomorrow.

To the Hippie, today was for the square on the nine to five grind (plus time and a half for overtime and maybe some pension money if he could make it to sixty-five). In plastic, prepackaged, deep-frozen, uptight America, today was for the working stiff scrambling to pay the mortgage on his split-level home—or meet the next installment on that super-hydromatic car with all those silly extras, or buy that twenty-four-inch color TV set, or dress his one and only wife in the best, or put the kids into that good private school. Or, poor bastard, to try to stay one step ahead of the tax man and still put a dollar away for that rainy day if he had a dollar left. Today was for the man scratching and clawing his way up the money ladder in the office or the factory or getting up with the dawn on the land. Today was for the drip-dry man-on-the-run who didn't know that the computer revolution was going to take it all away from him if the Bomb didn't do it first. It was for the pitifully *un*hip guy who didn't know that he could buy his way out of the whole rat race with a five-dollar trip to never-never land on a sugar cube dipped in LSD or, even simpler, just fly high and straight with a few pokes of marijuana or hashish.

The Hippies inherited the world from the Beat Generation, which didn't seem to want it either, but the new who-gives-a-damn school made the earlier one look industrious by comparison. The Beats, back in the Fifties, could at least point to the clattering glub-glub-glub typewriter of Jack Kerouac (*On the Road* was their bible) and the driving protest poems of Allen Ginsberg and Gregory Corso, among others, and claim a kinship of sorts with Mr. Hemingway's Lost Generation of the Twenties.

And the new breed? The Hippies couldn't point to

This sign in New York's Washington Square Park said KEEP OFF THE GRASS when it was put up, but the Greenwich Village Hippies altered the message. *Paul Sann*

couldn't end there. Where would you go from the love-in? What would you stand for? What would you want besides some inexpert advice on how to beat the draft or what to do if you freaked out on acid or came up with venereal disease or got busted? Nobody in his right senses could have bought the kill'em-all doctrine of an H. Rap Brown or a Stokely Carmichael, but the younger black flame thrower made an apt point about the Hippies and their cop-out in the summer of 1967. "Understand," said H. Rap Brown, "you have to fight back and you can't fight with flowers."

You didn't need guns or Molotov cocktails either, of course.

You did need something—even if your own private war skirted the explosive black–white issue and went beyond it into the more esoteric levels of our society. You needed something more than love, love, love. You couldn't love your way out of the collective madness of the nuclear age, out of collective suicide. You had to do something about it. You had to exert your will, your *collective* will, on the hell-bent nations. You weren't going to do anything abut the war without an end, far away in Vietnam, by sticking a button in your lapel that said LSD NOT LBJ. The Hippies did come to life, it must be noted, when they helped to swell the ranks of the battered and bloody legions who descended on the Democratic National Convention in Chicago in 1967 and turned the Windy City into a battleground against "Johnson's War." Even so, there was a classic misnomer in the label adopted by the Flower Children's drumbeaters—the Happening Generation. What was happening?

Was there a message for us squares in the vibrations which supposedly sustained the Hippie? Was some beautiful secret reposing in the inner universe of the Hippie? Was the blown mind going to lead us out of the twentieth-century wilderness? The Hippie, barefoot, broke, panhandling for food or pot or that sugar cube, told us that the American middle class was a corrosive, all-consuming monster and the way to banish it from the earth was to walk away from it: Turn on/tune in/drop out. Split, man. Find *your* bag. And the rewards? Timothy Leary told the kids that they would get to know God, really know God (on a first-name basis, one would hope). Timothy Leary conceded that there was a touch of Russian roulette in that spit-second LSD route to the side of the Maker but said, in essence, What the hell, "we're all gambling men." Allen Ginsberg, the oldest established Merchant of Pot, singing the virtues of acid as "the specific antibrainwash medicine," told us that the Hippies were breaking the shackles of the new

anything much. In on a pass, they were just sitting cross-legged on the grass (and smoking the other kind) and saying, in essence, "Oh, mother off, it's not worth bothering with." They were on the longest sit-down strike in our history. The Hippie, a long stride ahead of his Beat counterpart on Dream Street because with him marijuana was just a local stop on the LSD Express, was deep in meditation around the clock—around a clock, indeed, that had no hands.

The Hippie had flowers in his hair, beads around his neck and bells tinkling from his waist and just one word: *Love*. Love everybody. Splendid. Love is an item you can't ever come out against. Between the love-in of the Hippie and the hate-in, say, of the moral, racist dropout who got his kicks out of a thing like the departed George Lincoln Rockwell's American Nazi Party, the choice was crystal clear. But it

inferno into which our atomic toys and modern-day technology had plunged the world.

Well, we had heard some lofty things about the Beat Generation and its assault on the barricades, too, but for all the rampant nonsense, nothing stretched the unblown mind more than the notion that the Hippies, without so much as pausing to bathe away the dirt and grime of the battle, were leading a revolution of some kind. Thus Sidney M. Jourard of the Unversity of Florida told the antiestablishment American Association for Humanistic Psychology in 1966 that we were "in the middle of an unguided and uncoordinated revolution" whose aim was to end the rule of the "dirty old men between forty-five and sixty-five" who were pushing all the buttons. Jourard, a past president of the AAHP, said the Hippies, the college students, the girls and the blacks all felt "put down" by the "dirty old men." Some of us dirty old men were indeed willing to concede a smidgin of validity to that premise, but once we did that we had to go back to the concomitant question. What was the Hippie *doing* about it? On the New Left the alienated legions were locked in determined, resolute combat. They were against the war, against the Communists (too moribund), against the soft-line liberal, against the Johnson Democrat (especially that now-departed Hubert Humphrey), against the Goldwater, Reagan or Nixon Republican, against our giant educational foundries, against the die-hard lily white, against the CIA and, of course, against J. Edgar Hoover—and they were indeed on the barricades, full time. The Hippie was against everything except love and what was he doing?

In Haight-Ashbury, the Hippie was holed up in an incredibly filthy room in some kind of imagined tribal bliss, or padding along the mean streets with a song of joyous contentment hidden somewhere beneath his long locks, or spread out on the green acres of Golden Gate Park sucking in nature's vast free bounty while some of his more energetic helpmates were out hustling the store-keepers for the scrap meat and vegetables for the "Digger Stew" available out there on a handout basis once a day. In New York, in the East Village on the Lower East Side or in the comparatively richer precincts of Greenwich Village, in Tompkins Square Park or in Washington Square Park, the general scene was much the same, but let's not fret. The full-time Hippie population, not counting the school kids who beefed up the unwashed ranks in the summertime, was nowhere near as large as one might have inferred from its press notices. The San Francisco authorities insisted that there weren't more than 5,000 full-time Hippies out there, while in New York the figure—anybody's guess, actually—ran all the way from one thousand to six thousand. You couldn't put them all down as acidheads of course; a good many of them were getting all the kicks they needed out of the easy livin'—and the easy sex—of the Hippie cul-

The Haight-Ashbury street people felt like a parade that year, but the San Francisco gendarmes made a whole flock of arrests for unlawful assembly. *WWP*

This picture of Allen Ginsberg during a demonstration in the Sixties turned into a hot poster item in the stores. It was also prophetic. Today most law enforcement officials have taken up the slogan and agreed that pot should be decriminalized.

ture. They were doing their "thing," whatever that is, without getting zonked on drugs. Either way, it came down to love, flowers, Rock 'n' Roll or perhaps some Indian chants—and a button that said STAMP OUT REALITY. Now did somebody say something about revolution?

It was always abundantly apparent that our worst institutions had nothing to fear from the Hippies. Whatever *their* thing was it wasn't coming across at all. The full-time Hippie, so young and maybe not so hip after all, simply had moved into a new leisure class of his very own. He had retired without waiting to qualify for that little old Social Security check. In time, surely, he would have to emerge from that early retirement and get with today. Work on some creepy job. Pay the man—the landlord, the bank, the GM folks. Buy that color set. Love someone, just one someone and not the whole damn world—and dress her, too. Keep the kids out of those awful public schools. Put a buck away.

And it happened.

The Institute of Life Insurance polled 3,000 people between the ages of fourteen and twenty-five in seventy-two geographic areas in 1971 and found the vast majority dedicated to those boring old-fashioned virtues: the work ethic, bringing up baby, socking some cash away against that rainy day. And in 1976 Dan Rather dropped into Hashbury for a segment on the CBS "60 Minutes" show and found it more like a college town, with the barefoot street beggars and the other refugees from the American dream nowhere in evidence. Rather and his camera crew hunted down one reformed Hippie and asked what had happened. "It ended for me," the youth said, "the day I was walking down Haight Street and I saw a teenage girl eating a can of dog food in front of a psychedelic shop."

It must have ended that way for quite a few others.

THE BOYS:

How Could You Tell?

From the rear it looks like a couple of girls, but no . . . it's Kathy Tempel and Bill Craddock, classmates at San Jose State College in California. *WWP*

The School Board says he can't come to school no
  more
Unless he wears his hair like he wore it before
The PTA and all the mothers
Say he ought to look like the others
Home of the free, land of the brave
Why won't you let him be what he wants to be
    —HOME OF THE BRAVE. Words and music by
        Barry Mann and Cynthia Weil*

THERE WAS NO question where the guilt lay. The Beatles did it. The Beatles started the long-hair fad which took hold here in 1964 all the way from Greenwich Village to the remotest hamlets and then settled down for an extended run. In the beginning, the shoulder-length locks generally came accompanied by a guitar. Thus one of the first youths to find himself in conflict with the state over the length of his hair was George Leonard, who called himself Georgie Porgie when he was out there at night in front of his own six-man Rock 'n' Roll combo in Attleboro, Massachusetts. A high school senior, George was barred from class by a principal who didn't care for the Beatle cut. Since he would rather fight than switch back to short hair, George took his appeal all the way to the state's highest court. He lost.

There were losers everywhere, too numerous to mention, as the non-guitar-playing set began to join in the boycott of the barber. Except for such isolated instances as that of New York's progressive Walden School, which held that "the long hair rebellion is better than marijuana," our educational authorities veered heavily toward the old-fashioned locks. The American Civil Liberties Union, invariably on hand wherever the Constitution is in peril, contended that the penalties being visited upon the long-haired legions represented "an incursion upon student rights and the spirit of due process." The land of the free was fortunate at that; in Rio de Janeiro the police were picking up the mopheads in the streets and forcibly taking them in for haircuts, courtesy of the public treasury.

Arguing the cases of Kenneth Paul Ibsen of Marlborough High School near Newburgh, New York, and Glenn Arthur Wagner, a senior at Huntington High School on Long Island and a member of an R & R combination called the Cloud Walkers, the ACLU's Lola S. Lee cited an 1874 ruling once invoked by the state's own Commissioner of Education when he refused to let a principal bar a girl for coming to class in slacks. In the 1874 case, the State Superintendent of Public Instruction reversed a local school board

*© 1966, by Screen Gems-Columbia Music, Inc. Reprinted by permission. Reproduction prohibited.

which had expelled two students whose mothers refused to cut their hair. But in the 1965 cases Commissioner James E. Allen Jr. took the position that the local boards had the right to set their own standards of dress and conduct.

Confronted with a Nineteenth-Century ruling on hair which he himself had once leaned on, Dr. Allen might have dipped a little deeper into history. In the Harvard College Year Book of 1649, he would have found this stern admonition:

> Forasmuch as the wearing of long haire after the manner of Ruffians and barbarous Indians, hath begun to invade new England contrary to the rule of Gods word wch sayth it is a shame for a man to wear long haire, as also the Commendable Custome generally of all the Godly of our nation until within this few yeares Wee the magistrates who have subscribed this paper (for the clearing of our owne innoceny in this behalfe) doe declare & manifest our dislike & detestation against the wearing of such long haire, as against a thing uncivil and unmanly whereby men doe deforme themselves, and offend sober & modest men, & doe corrupt good manners.

Embattled on broad fronts as the long-hair craze continued unabated, the ACLU stepped in when the Richmond Professional Institute in Virginia barred three students who among them had beards, long hair, sideburns or a combination of all three. Two of the three buckled down to the school's will while the argument was in process but the third, Norman Thomas Marshall, said he would rather keep his beard and drop out of the Institute. Claiming an encroachment on academic freedom, the ACLU also plunged into the fray when two bushy-maned pupils in New York's Forest Hills were forced to sit in the principal's office instead of going to class. Superintendent of Schools Bernard Donovan reversed that ruling, whereupon the High School Principals Association accused him of encouraging anarchy among the young.

In suburban Detroit, there was more serious trouble. More than 150 students of Bloomfield Hills High School joined in a walkout to protest a crackdown on

Todd Nardin, Gary Fitzgerald and George Scott (left to right) were consigned to an unused study hall in New York's Oyster Bay High School on the grounds that their hairdos constituted a distraction in class. A trip to the barber settled that one. He fixed it so the boys' ears would show. *New York Post*

Barred from commencement exercises at Coral Gables High School in Florida over this coiffure, Gilbert Hall looks in a mirror to see what the fuss is about. Richard Hall saw nothing wrong with his son's mophead. *WWP*

Beatle hairdos and tight pants. School Superintendent Eugene Johnson, keeping his cool, wrote off that rebellion rather casually. "These kids are staging a mini-version of the social unrest they read about elsewhere," he said.

In Chicago, Dennis Conroy, a senior at the suburban Downers Grove Community High School and drummer in an R & R band, was ordered to cut away two and a half inches of his bangs or face suspension. He insisted that he needed the locks in his work. When the school suggested that he wear a wig on the bandstand, Conroy said that would be too expensive. Even with the ACLU advising him that he was wholly within his rights, the boy lost the argument. In Los Banos, California, the schools permitted no room for argument at all, posting a simple set of rules: For the boys, no bangs past the eyebrows, no hair below the shirt collar, no beards; for the girls, no skirts too short and no skirts too long. In Hartford, Connecticut, Edward T. Kores Jr. was not only ousted from school for wearing the Beatle cut but Dr. William J. Sanders, the state's Education Commissioner, urged the local board to take his parents into court. Kores Sr., a carpenter, was bewildered by the whole thing. "My son isn't even a Beatle fan," he said. "He just likes to wear his hair in bangs." In the Midwest, there was at least one parent who didn't have to be taken to court. Steven Gorz, a truck driver, asked Judge Fred W. Slater to order his son Richard, a premedical student at the University of Illinois and also a drummer in an R & R quartet, to get a haircut. The judge refused to tamper with the boy's constitutional rights to that degree. But in Kansas City, Federal Judge Richard W. Duncan held up dispensing justice to a sixteen-year-old offender with hair flopping over his eyes, ears and neck. "I refuse to sentence anyone I can't see," said the judge. "Take the boy out for a haircut."

Dr. Wladimir G. Eliasberg, German-born past president of the American Society of Psychoanalytic Physicians, had a thing or two to say on the mounting dispute over hair styles at that juncture:

"It's a passing fad—just a wave. I see no deep-rooted behavior disorders in the present tendency of girls to look like boys and boys to look like girls. It's not psychiatric. It's not neurotic. It is rebellion—rebellion of the youngsters against their parents and society. It is strictly a revolt against the world—starting with the parents first, then older people generally and finally the Secretary of Defense" (a reference to the draft-card burners).

The doctor, seventy-eight years old and therefore a witness to quite an assortment of passing hang-ups in his time, said that the girls "abhorred cave-man types and want boy companions who are subordinate to them in strength, who are sensitive and who talk a lot" and the boys, he went on, knew it. "This is their weapon against the popularity of the muscle-bound athletes. They let their hair grow, they adopt feminine attitudes—and the girls swoon." And at the end of this particular rainbow? Hope.

"The boy will let his hair grow and then cultivate a beard, which is very masculine," Dr. Eliasberg said. "The girls let their hair fall sexily over their shoulders—and then put on boys' pants. That proves there is nothing to worry about. Pretty soon the boys will start drifting toward the effeminate girls again and the girls will want their men to be strong again. Then we will sit back and wait for another wave." Marya Mannes, the social critic, also entered a brief for the defense. "Abundant hair, provided it is controlled at the nape and side," Miss Mannes said, "is a blessing to many boys who would otherwise look bleak and ordinary.... Let youth have its short span of freedom. If adults admired their long hair more, the young would probably cut it off themselves."

But the educators wouldn't yield. Carl W. Andrews Jr. of New York's Collegiate School, oldest secondary school in the nation, probably summed it up for that side as well as anyone else. "A sloppy head," Andrews said, "is indicative of a sloppy mind." In Hollywood, movie actress Martha Hyer dealt with another aspect of the problem. "It is getting so bad on the Sunset Strip that you can't tell which are the girls and which are the boys," said Miss Hyer. "It's not only confusing. It can be dangerous."

It was more confusing than dangerous, of course. A college principal in Peterborough, England, reprimanded a girl he caught emerging from the men's lavatory and then had to apologize because the "girl," full face, turned out to be a boy. Britain, where it started, had other troubles as well. A Southampton youth's $9.45 weekly dole was cut off on the grounds that only his long hair was keeping him unemployed, but the Ministry of Labor put the mophead back on the rolls. In a Durham factory, an engineering apprentice was fired when he refused either to wear a hairnet or have his locks cut, so thirty others went on strike, while the company pleaded that it had nothing against the Beatle hairdo but simply feared that somebody was going to get his head caught in a machine. Even Vidal Sassoon had a spot of difficulty over there. His posh lady clients began to suffer inconvenience because so many men—led by such long-hair types as the Duke of Bedford, Peter O'Toole and the Beatle's own manager, Brian Epstein—were dashing in to have their coiffures done. Sassoon met the issue head on, as it were. He asked the male contingent to confine their visits to the nighttime hours.

Confusing, yes, but the danger had yet to surface—just some more foolishness in all kinds of places, high and low.

1970: An Army unit expelled Eric Harris, a twenty-eight-year-old New York reservist with a law degree, for wearing long locks even though he tucked them under a cropped hair rug while on weekend duty. Facing eighteen months of active service unless he went to the barber, Harris headed for the federal courthouse instead, and there Judge Charles H. Tenney ruled that "plaintiff appears neat and soldierly in a shorthair wig." Also said a thing or two about his Constitutional rights.

1972: A restaurant owner in New York's upstate Tonawanda (named after a long-haired Indian tribe, by the way) refused to serve a man with shoulder-length hair and lost the case in court on the grounds of "discrimination based on sex."

1973: Roy Anthony Simpson, head football coach at the North Shore Junior High School in the Houston suburb of Galena Park, declaimed in an article for the monthly *Intellectual Digest* that long locks lead to "drug abuse, crime and sexual perversion." Cited all kinds of biblical authority, too, like how a proper interpretation of Revelation 1:14 would show that "the only visible person of the Trinity, Christ, had short hair." The Texas school was flooded with so many protests that the coach went elsewhere after a while.

1974: Lee A. Iacocca, president of the Ford Motor Company until his recent falling out with Henry Ford II, let his locks run long down the back but then decided that coiffure didn't fit his seven-figure position. Ditto the Minnesota Vikings quarterback Fran Tarkenton. Fire Commissioner John T. O'Hagan of New York banished both long hair and beards as dangerous for men toiling in burning buildings and a judge sustained that position. Over in Germany a GI named Louis M. Stokes was busted from Specialist 4 to private and then shipped to the stockade at Fort Riley, Kansas, for refusing to go along with the Army's tonsorial regulations. Stokes did two months before winning his freedom, but the verdict came on a technicality; the brass had tapped a telephone strategy powwow of his lawyer's.

1975: New York's Appellate Division overturned a Human Rights Appeal Board ruling which held that Page Airways of Albany had no right to ordain crew cuts for its male employees while their women colleagues wore *their* hair any way they wanted. "An employer has an important interest in the image which is projected through its employees and thus has a right to make reasonable rules and regulations," said the five-man panel.

1977: The Supreme Court—yes, the Supreme Court, 7–2—upheld the right of New Jersey's state police to stop long-haired drivers in the "hope of finding marijuana or other illicit drugs" in their cars or on their persons. Now there's a piece of information worth the price of this book. If you're thinking of taking your best girl, or even your wife, out for a spin and a few tokes in the Garden State, stop at the barber first.

THE GIRLS:

Where Will It End?

Jackie Kennedy went for the modified mini. Her sister, then the Princess Lee Radziwill, but Single-O now, is with her. *WWP*

IF MOHAMMED only knew.

Here we are in the time of the low neckline or no neckline, the no-bra bra, the low backline or no backline—or even frontline, for that matter—down just past the midriff, the peek-a-boo gown and the see-it-all gown, the woman wearing the pants (or just jeans and a T-shirt) and the more formal types in tuxedos. Now to find a point of reference in any discussion of what the girls are wearing or not wearing at this juncture in history you have to go back to World War I and the emancipation of what used to be called the weaker sex. Skirts suddenly went six inches above the ground in 1919 and *Vogue* observed that "not since the days of the Bourbons has the woman of fashion been visible so far above the ankle." The next year another three inches came off the hemline and the New York *Times* termed that "far beyond any modest limitation." But by 1927 the skirt had climbed all the way to the knee, and it wasn't going to start its downward flight again until everything else went down with the stock market prices to draw the curtain on the Lawless Decade and usher in the Depression-dampened, less adventurous Thirties.

In the next three decades, milady's skirt followed an up-and-down course from the ankle to the covered knee without occasioning any excessively stringent concern. You didn't need a scorecard to follow the plays: Suddenly there was closet room and you knew that your bride's most prized possessions were at the dressmaker's, going up again or down again in some mystique dictated by the Paris-based high priests of fashion.

Go back a step here, back to another war, for purposes of historical perspective. When this republic had to pitch in to stop A. Hitler, we needed all our fabric as well as our military hardware. The government decreed that skirts had to be restricted to two-inch hems, blouses couldn't have more than one patch-pocket, hoods and shawls were verboten, no skirt could extend more than seventy-two inches around, and cuffs on coats were a thing of the past. The fashion potentates responded with the convertible jacket, the soft blouse and skirt you could wear while tending your Victory Garden or convert to evening dress with a few touches. It was a time for Spartan wear marked by skimpy shirts and blouses without ruffles. Once Mr. Hitler took the easy way out in his bunker underneath Berlin and Paris was restored to its prewar proprietors, the middle-aged Christian Dior came rushing back in with his New Look—the long skirt. There were some howls of protest, of course. Mrs. Anna Rosenberg, a large name in public relations and labor affairs and an FDR confidante and appointee on the side, protested that the Dior skirt "shows everything you want to hide and hides everything you want to show." Mr. Dior, in return, writhed in agony. "My God, what have I done?" he asked. What he had done, of course, was to get rich again with a price tag running up to $450 on his long skirts before the better brains in New York's Garment Center switched from his silk creations to rayon and the smarter shoppers could look like Dior women for as little as $20.

Come the Fifties, the tube-length hooded dress appeared on the scene in hip-clinging knit with the skirts a good deal shorter but by no means in the peek-a-boo category, and then in the mid-Sixties the flapper came all the way back, and the knee, sometimes worthy of a satisfying glance and sometimes in the proverbial housemaid's category, came back into view. The upward flight, slow and tentative, started in a couple of British and French fashion temples while such a formidable American stalwart as Pauline Trigere was stoutly refusing to snip any more off the hemlines of her models. But then the pace-setting Courrèges in Paris decided that there wasn't any reason why the girls shouldn't go all the way and let the knee show, eliciting from famed anthropologist Margaret Mead a sour comment to the effect that "we are going through a period of extreme exhibitionism." That distinguished observer had a point at that.

The miniskirt was upon us.

Is it all the fault of Courrèges?

The author put the question to Ruth Preston, fashion writer for the New York *Post,* and drew a pitying look, like he didn't know anything. "Courrèges, of course," Miss Preston said, but then she herself was assailed by doubts and it turned out that you could still get an argument over whether the French designer got there first—first with the *least,* that is—or whether it was all started by little Mary Quant in her Mod-Mod boutique, the Bazaar, in London's Chelsea District. One school insists that the youthful Miss Quant was snipping things off skirts way back in ancient times, like 1955, and Courrèges didn't do it until 1964. The other says no, no, Courrèges started hacking things off his own Balenciaga line until there was daylight on the knee, and then the British designer went all the way, higher and higher. Betsy Talbot Blackwell of *Mademoiselle* reminded Miss Preston that the Quant stylings shown in the magazine's October, 1964, issue on ready-to-wear were not miniskirts at all, and that *Vogue* in March of that year had credited Courrèges with the new fashion.

Mary Quant, backed by all that's left of the British Empire, couldn't buy that but couldn't get violent about it, either, because she had a healthy respect for André Courrèges.

"Fashion since the last war has been logical, inevitable and universal," she told Miss Preston. "Tuned-in designers around the world have the same ideas at the same time. When we first started shortening skirts twelve years ago, we didn't go fast enough for the Chelsea girls who kept turning them up shorter and shorter." And Courrèges? "He's a genius. The look he started was purely original but the French girls were too conservative."

In any case, 1964 was indeed the year that the miniskirt got off the ground, so to speak, around the world. Perhaps logically, it came not too far behind the somewhat controversial topless bathing suit of Rudi Gernreich—oh, what a howl was raised over the tentlike one-piece bathing suit of the Twenties, something like a horse blanket next to the Gernreich creation—and it separated the just-plain females from our Go-Go girls, the French Yé-Yé girls and the English Mods. The chopped-off skirt, more like a bib worn below the waist, had its main appeal among the younger swingers, although an alert photographer from *Women's Wear Daily* caught nobody less than Jacqueline Kennedy emerging from a posh Manhattan restaurant in one of the new models on a crisp December day. Elizabeth Taylor also squeezed into the nonskirt, presumably with the full benediction of

France's André Courrèges. Did he raise milady's skirt or did England's mini-sized Mary Quant do it? The debate raged on in fashion circles.

Richard Burton. And John V. Lindsay, the young-in-heart Mayor of New York, endorsed the bare knee even while his own fussy high school principals were bewailing it. "It's a functional thing," the Mayor said. "It enables young ladies to run faster, and because of it, they may have to." His wife Mary also came out for the miniskirt—"on young girls, not on me." Tallulah Bankhead, registering the same qualified endorsement, suggested that twenty-one would be a suitable age limit for the bare-knee set. "You'll never catch me wearing one, Dahling," the actress told columnist Leonard Lyons. "I have beautiful feet and ankles, but knees like Daddy's." Miss Bankhead may have had in mind something once said by that peer among drama critics, Percy Hammond: "The human knee is a joint and not an entertainment." Without dwelling on the merits of that particular joint, Gina Lollobrigida set forth her own case against the miniskirt by saying that "it is better for men to discover than for women to reveal." How this squared with the solidly endowed Italian siren's lowcut upstairs fashion preferences was not explained in the overseas dispatches.

While all this was going on, a rather imposing dissent on the fashions of the Sixties in general wafted across the Atlantic from Paris. It came from Coco Chanel, the couturier, as follows:

It is a lousy time for women. If one isn't a Yé-Yé then you are washed up. *La mode* is now just a question of the length of the skirt. It is idiocy. Fashion cannot come up from the street; it can only go down into the street.

Phyllis Lee Levin, author of *The Wheels of Fashion*, quoted diverse authorities in a long look at the miniskirt in the New York *Times* magazine. "It's spitting in the eye, protesting against bourgeois values and generations past, against the Establishment," said fashion photographer Irving Penn. "It's real protest. Much of the news isn't fit to print. Things are happening, and that's what the young are lifting their skirts about." Bernard Barber, professor of sociology at Barnard College, saw larger implications. "We are living in a freer society and whether you call it a hedonistic revolution or a striking shift, there is an increasing appreciation of the sensual," he said. "Not just the pure hedonist philosophy of eat, drink and be merry, but of anything that delights the eye and senses. People are less puritanical." The professor made another interesting, if perhaps debatable observation. "It can't go too far," he told Miss Levin, "or it becomes self-defeating. If everyone were nude, it wouldn't be interesting."

H. L. Mencken must have had something like that in mind when he remarked that "if women, continuing their present tendency to its logical goal, end by going naked, there will be no more poets and painters, but only dermatologists." That was in 1916. An even half-century later, the girls went about as far as they could go, or so it seemed, and the issue of decency quickly came to the fore, with the predictable results: Across the country, assorted principals and college deans banned as "distracting" influences any teeny boppers whose knees were showing. This fresh war between students and constituted authority, with parental forces alternately appearing on both sides of the battle lines, represented a switch on an earlier engagement touched off, curiously, when some of the girls started showing up in the floor-scraping Granny dress. The Granny Look—a most conservative Empire model with lots of bows and frills—made its debut in Los Angeles, and wherever it dipped its ankles into areas of the nation that didn't quite swing like the West Coast, such as the Bible Belt, there was trouble. Thus John Nelson, principal of Soldan High School in St. Louis, barred sophomore Billie Morrison because her Granny dress seemed to him—you guessed it—to be a "distracting" influence. Billie's mother had to fetch her a shorter dress before she could go to class.

The miniskirt debate, understandably much more intense, ranged around the world. In Rome, the Communist Party's fashion vehicle, *Noi Donne* (We Women), hailed the thigh-scraper as a political weapon. "This skirt is the right outfit to wear not only for dances and the beach," said the magazine, "but for taking part in a strike or peace march or demonstrating against American bombings in Vietnam." In Dakar, Senegal, the gendarmes invoked the statutes governing indecent exposure against any girls—or women, for that matter—caught in the nonskirts on public beaches. In war-torn Saigon, where the traditional *ao dai* covers the feminine form from the neckline to the shoetops, the miniskirts drew angry frowns on the streets. In Greece, one of the first acts of the junta that took the government away from young King Constantine in 1967 was to rule the miniskirt illegal. The Russians, having neglected to invent the short skirt, saw to it that their designers—if you could call them that—never went more than two inches above the knobby knees over there. In the American South, Governor Lester Maddox of Georgia, a hard-rock segregationist suddenly turned so liberal that he posed for an arm-in-arm picture with Hubert Humphrey, hurt his developing new image with an edict banning the miniskirt among his employees in the capital in Atlanta. In Manila, the Superintendent of the Philippines National Penitentiary barred women visitors who wore the nonskirt; he said it disturbed the prisoners to see too much. On the Gaza Strip, the miniskirt stirred up some incidental trouble after Israel's six-day triumph over the Arab States in 1967: A few of the more daring Arabs made passes at Israeli girls dressed in the new style. And back here, General Eisenhower came out foursquare against the style. "I have been looking at girls since I was six, and I know what they are like," the General said. "Ankles are nearly always neat and good-looking, but knees are nearly always not."

In England, simply awash in debate over the way the Mod movement was making it so much harder to tell the girls from the boys, and vice versa, Dr. Geoffrey Taylor offered some advice to both sexes. He said the girls would be healthier and more efficient in their work if they wore ski pants instead of miniskirts, and that the boys in the tight pants might well consider long johns even if it made them bulge a bit. The doctor's point about the girls, working or otherwise, was well taken. Thus when 1966's first big freeze set in on the very Tight Little Isle a hundred girls had to flee the Reading College of Technology just because the furnace wasn't working right (you see, their knees turned blue).

When that sort of thing drew critical notice in the public prints here in the Colonies, Sir Patrick Henry Dean, British Ambassador to the Court of Lyndon Baines Johnson, took umbrage. "I sometimes think the people who write articles of this kind must have mini-minds," said Sir Patrick, "because they do not write about other aspects of modern Britain. Miniskirts are there, anyway, for all to see, and some are quite attractive." Back home, as it happened, the thing had stirred up quite a rumpus. Indeed, the stuffy old tax authorities dealt themselves in at the very outset. Widely published photographs of top fashion model Jean (The Shrimp) Shrimpton in the Nude Knee style led to a second look at the fine print in the laws lest the local merchants try to pass off the miniskirt as a tax-free children's garment instead of a grown-up's dress. A debate on the question of whether the skirt had gone too high or not high enough drew 1,200 students into Oxford Union Hall. The only distaff speaker, Daphne Triggs of St. Hilda's College, denounced the mini model as a "vestment of harlots." Appearing in a Roman toga and laurel wreath to speak for the style revolution, Leofranc Holford-Stevens of Christ Church College took a frank and forthright position. "A miniature skirt gives you the

opportunity of being able to inspect your wares before you buy," he said. The motion to raise them still higher lost just the same, but by a scant thirty-three votes.

Over here at that time, the Mod style, or Carnaby Street Look—high boots, tapered low-rise slacks set on the hips, floral print shirts, wide belts, double-breasted sports coats with nipped-in waists and deep side vents—was drawing its share of garlands and raps. The school authorities frowned on the Mod boys, invariably on the long-haired side, and girls alike. The industry had mixed views. The National Association of Men's Sportswear Buyers, meeting in New York, split on the new fashion while Michael Daroff, chairman of Botany Industries, Inc., made no secret of his stand. "Mod styling stinks," Daroff told the annual convention of the Men's Wear Retailers of America at Dallas. "When you talk about Mod you're talking about a complete look. This must include the long hair and bangs in the front. If this is the way some shmoes want to dress, let them. It's a free country." John D. Gray, president of Hart, Schaffner & Marx, wrote Mod off as sheer bad taste from top to bottom but Gus Van Sant, vice-president of McGregor-Doniger, Inc., said his company was very high on it. "I think it's a great thing, a real stimulus," said another manufacturer. Would he let his own son go to the style? "I'd break his head first," the man said.

To go back to the girls for a moment (oh, how this one hurts), a word is needed here about an item that came out of the fall showings in Paris in 1957. There were various names for it: the sack, the chemise, the silhouette, the relaxed look, the loose look, the unfitted look, the Moslem look, the limp look, the little-girl look and, not the least, the bag.

The men who designed that dress did not want us ordinary fellows to know, or even suspect, what might be under it. They didn't want anything to show, although that in itself wasn't a new concept at all. The flapper of F. Scott Fitzgerald's Jazz Age, wild as she was reputed to be, wore something quite like it; so did some of the Dogpatch girls in Al Capp's *L'il Abner* strip, although they leaned to the bargain-basement burlap models and never made *Vogue* or *Harper's Bazaar*.

The 1957 sack, in any case, stirred considerable controversy in and out of the home. The heart of the matter was best expressed by an authorized spokesman for Bergdorf-Goodman, the swank Fifth Avenue specialty shop, in response to an inquiry from *Business Week*. "The wearer," said this source, "should be a girl with plenty of chic. If she isn't, it really is a bag."

The long and the short: Wendy Hiller, accepting Paul Scofield's Oscar for *A Man for All Seasons*, wore a high-neck multicolored model. Julie Christie, a 1966 winner for *Darling*, presenting the Scofield award, wore a polka-dot minimodel, and Edith Head, style consultant for the Academy, spoke as follows: "I did not sanction that dress." *Wide World Photos*

That is our point of reference.

The sack was indeed worn by a great many American women who did not have "plenty of chic"—and by a great many who had no chic at all—and so, more often than not, it really was a bag. Within a year, happily, it was hanging, in its loose and formless way, on the mark-down rack.

And on that rack, come to think of it, the sack looked good. But then it's all so academic now as the Seventies draw to a close. The revolution in fashion goes on apace. Woody Allen, funny man, writer, actor, director, producer, even turned up in that minefield. In his widely hailed four-Oscar *Annie Hall*, voted 1977's best film, Allen dressed his favorite ex-roommate, Diane Keaton, in baggy pants, vest, a

This is a University of Houston coed competing in a fashion contest on the Texas campus in 1967.

Brigitte Bardot draws a most happy fan, an Italian soldier, on a shopping expedition in Rome. *WWP*

After a while, something more than the knees began to show. Here's Baby Jane Holzer, one of the early Andy Warhol "superstars," with designer Halston and his see-through gown.

But there was no way of getting away from the gal with the T-shirt and the jeans. Here Lisa Steele, since given to other pursuits but in her time one of the few models who could claim a degree or two from Yale, sports a T-shirt that says it all (in French): "The more I see of men the more I like my dog." *Paul Sann*

"I think miniskirts are super," said Marjorie Janney. "They express the freedom of our age." What made it news? She was the wife of the Reverend Dennis Janney, a Methodist minister in London. "By being modern," said the red-haired Mrs. Janney, "I feel I can encourage young people to realize that religion does not mean disapproval." The Reverend did not disapprove. *WWP*

229

mannish shirt with a net tie and tweedy jacket topped by a floppy felt hat. And so the Annie Hall Look was upon us, good for a strong run in at least its first two years. And once again, as in the time of the long hair fad, one might have had a spot of trouble telling who was who until the female breed began to switch back to the dressier jackets they belonged in, discarded the ties (not to mention the suspenders some had taken to wearing) and began to look like women again instead of Woody Allen.

Now, passing over the see-through or let-it-all-hang-out types, we're into the stocking suit pretty heavily. Disco Glitter, if it needs a name, but it goes well beyond the disco crowd. It starts with the leotard or Danskin, all in one piece and stopping at the panty line or going all the way to the ankles. Milady throws a sweater, shirt or jacket over that short one—day, or evening if there's some high living in prospect—and she's off and running without a bank loan. A current favorite in this department is the stretch fabric Lycra mixture which holds you up and in and moves with your hopefully beautiful and slender body. Nancy White, former executive editor of *Harper's Bazaar*, no less, went to the altar a while back in a short body suit with a shirt to match in deep fuchsia rose and looked almost as good as Grace Kelly marrying that fellow Grimaldi in his little kingdom of Monaco amidst all that pomp and ceremony or Jackie Kennedy tying the knot with Greek shipping billionaire Aristotle Onassis on his island of Skorpios in the blue chiffon gown slapped together for her by Italy's Valentino, one of her favorite couturiers. If there's a moral here for the men who are still the sole breadwinners in this time of Women's Lib, it is that the woman of your dreams needn't constitute quite that heavy a drain on your wallet anymore.

Diane Keaton in the new Annie Hall look which Woody Allen, the all-purpose movie man with her, had fashioned for the star's role opposite him in the smash 1977 film of the same name.

For the women who weren't into hotpants or knickers in the Seventies, Paris's Valentino came up with the midi or maxi skirt to make us forget the mini. This model's wearing a Mollie Parnis version of the more conservative design. *New York Post*

And Rudi Gernreich with his wide-open models.

Part XI

THE AMERICAN CAMPUS

How it all began: Lothrop Withington, Jr., swallows a three-inch goldfish at the Harvard Union to win a $10 bet. *WWP*

NIGHT OF THE GOLDFISH

"Each age has its own follies, as its majority is made up of foolish young people."
—RALPH WALDO EMERSON

WE COME NOW to a landmark date—March 3, 1939. On that day, in the venerable precincts of Harvard, Lothrop Withington Jr., sprung from the loins of the university's 1910 football captain and something of a football player himself, swallowed a four-inch goldfish. Months later, college students across the land were still vying with great intensity—and some scattered intestinal disturbances—for the goldfish-swallowing championship of the United States.

How did it fall to Lothrop Withington Jr. to start all that? You have to go back to 1928, when the boy was just ten and his parents took him to Honolulu to visit his grandmother. There, on the beach, the impressionable youngster saw a native eat a goldfish with no apparent ill effect. Four years later, during a party in the Withington summer home in Plymouth, the talk among the adults turned to strange stunts and—

"There was a goldfish bowl on the table and I scooped up a fish and ate it."

Skip seven years to 1935. Lothrop Withington Jr. was dining out with friends when someone offered to bet him the price of the meal that he wouldn't eat a fantail. He ate the fantail, of course.

And so to that fateful March day in 1939.

Withington, majoring in biology and sociology because he wasn't sure what he wanted to do, was dining with two classmates, Harry Newman of Hollywood and John Lacey of Brookline, when a fresh challenge was hurled at him, backed up by two five-dollar bills. "It looked like easy money," he recalls, "and I was all set to eat the fish then and there but the boys wanted their money's worth and stipulated that I perform the feat in public at the Harvard Union." The thing might have gone unnoticed outside that freshman dining hall at Cambridge, except that Newman and Lacey felt impelled to advise the *Crimson* of the impending event. The resulting headline in the undergraduate journal—YARDLING TO SWALLOW GOLDFISH—brought the Boston reporters hurrying to the scene on the appointed afternoon. As it must to all newspapers, the accounts of the feat varied, of course. The *Globe* reported that the boy took a few swallows of the evening meal selected by the Harvard culinary authorities, reached for the fantail reposing in a bowl in front of him, picked it up by the tail, dropped it into his mouth, and then—

Waves of perplexity passed over Withington's face once the fish had disappeared. There seemed to be some difficulty at first—some internal struggle—but after a brief moment of confusion the fisheater swallowed and all was well.

The *Globe* reported that Withington, limiting himself to the observation that it was easy, then produced a toothbrush, shampooed his molars, and that was it. The *Daily Record* said that after gulping down the fantail and gagging momentarily he smiled wryly, said "That's good," and then downed several swallows of water from the fishbowl with the remark, "Just like chowder." The man from the *Transcript,* supported by the *Post*'s eyewitness, confirmed the item about Withington using the fish's water for a chaser. Beyond this, the *Transcript* was able to reveal exclusively that the resourceful freshman had trained for the event on live minnows, smaller goldfish and guppies for several days, cashing another ten-dollar bet in that process.

Withington, now the father of four non-goldfish-swallowers and president and principal stockholder of the Pilgrim Petroleum Service, Inc., in Plymouth, has a pat explanation for the episode today. "Mind over matter," he says, "I didn't mind and the fish didn't matter." He confesses that he was a bit taken aback over the way the press displayed his small epicurean feat. This is something he attributes to the fact that it was a slow news time. He remembers, for example, that the reformed Austrian house painter who was then running Germany—and making menacing gestures in every possible direction—happened to be uncommonly quiet that first week in March of 1939. What he doesn't remember is that another momentous item of news—Eugenio Cardinal Pacelli's elevation to Pius XII—came from the Vatican on the very day that he swallowed the goldfish. So much for that. Let us examine, in any case, the consequences of Withington's deed, reconstructed from the faded clippings.

One of the first to accept the gauntlet when the Boston accounts hit the wires was Frank Pope, a student at little Franklin and Marshall College in Lancaster, Pennsylvania. He swallowed three fantails on a five-dollar bet and phoned a friend at Cambridge, Irving M. Clark, a sophomore, to tell him about it. "I did it just to show you Harvard bums," said Pope. "As a matter of fact, I don't like fish any other way." Oh, yeah? Clark knew how to deal with that kind of sarcasm. Using orange juice for a chaser, he promptly downed twenty-four goldfish in five minutes to win a fifty-dollar bet (there was money on the campus in those days, even though that left-wing Democratic crowd held the White House). "I could have eaten fifty just as easily," Clark said—and that was *his* mistake. On the University of Pennsylvania campus the very next day, Gilbert Hollandersky, a junior, sloshed down twenty-five goldfish, with a mix-ture of ketchup and orange juice for a chaser, and then, still uncommonly hungry, knocked off a steak dinner.

Hollandersky's record was short-lived. A youth named Jules Aisner, rising to the challenge, ate twenty-eight goldfish on the University of Michigan campus, only to see that record topple when Donald V. Mulcahy, a junior at Boston College, using milk for a chaser, put away twenty-nine before an audience of 300 cheering witnesses. Now, suddenly, there were consequences. Not in the least amused, Robert F. Sellar, president of the Boston Animal Rescue League, prevailed on the State Senate to order the Commonwealth's Department of Conservation to look into the manner in which the state's goldfish population was being ravaged. Why did Mr. Sellar react with such angry force? "Nobody knows how a fish feels," he said, "We can't sidestep this issue." The college itself quite plainly shared the Rescue League's view, for the Reverend Thomas A. Fay, Dean of Discipline, caused this notice to be posted on the student bulletin board:

NO MORE CONTESTS OF THE GOLDFISH-SWALLOWING TYPE WILL BE TOLERATED. OFFENDERS MAY EXPECT DRASTIC PUNISHMENT.

There is no evidence in the printed record to show that a single student on the campus defied this edict, but then, how far could the good Father's influence extend? On the Massachusetts Institute of Technology's campus, just down the hallowed road from the ivy-covered hall where the unwitting Lothrop Withington Jr. had set the fierce competition in motion, Albert E. Hayes undertook to eat forty-two goldfish because he happened to be in the Class of '42. Hayes accomplished his mission in fifty-two minutes and openly laid claim to the title, showing a mutual disdain both for the Animal Rescue League and the State Department of Conservation's assigned sleuths.

Now the month-old madness, reaching its height, was producing more widespread reaction.

"No college gold will come from goldfish," Dr. Dixon Ryan Fox, president of Union College at Schenectady, New York, told a meeting at Rensselaer Polytechnic Institute at Troy. Dr. Fox took a side-swipe at the Fourth Estate, too. He said that the press should be reporting the real story of higher education instead of wasting its substance on "frivolous campus pranks and insignificant activities." The New York *Herald Tribune* demurred on April 3.

"If students aren't swallowing goldfish," said Horace Greeley's old paper, now so sadly gone from

John Patrick, a University of Chicago student, didn't care for goldfish. He preferred phonograph records. Coed Ruth Whelan served as a volunteer waitress. The boy reported no aftereffects. *WWP*

The goldfish fad made a brief comeback on the campus in the spring of 1967 when Robert Auve, Thomas Bullock and Robert Cameron (left to right) got together for a Junior Week competition at St. Joseph's College in Philadelphia. Auve won handily, swallowing 199 live ones. Cameron dropped out early in the proceedings. Bullock quit after the first 147, went to see his doctor later and reported, "He said there was no need to do anything except see a head shrinker." *Philadelphia Evening Bulletin*

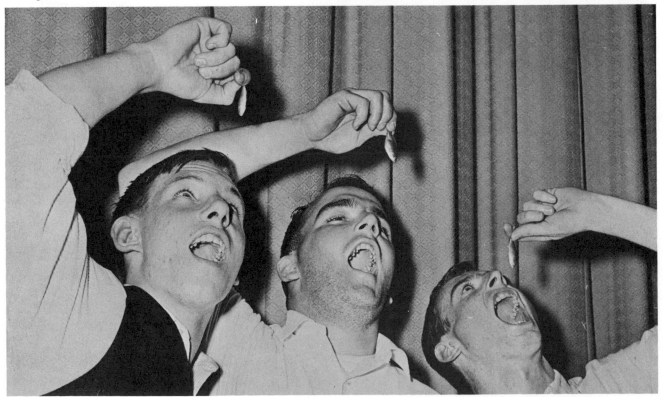

our midst, "they are up to something else just as foolish—and just as much fun at the moment. That's what keeps students from being dull—and campus life from being a bore. In any event, the goldfish mood will pass. Already news comes from the Middle West that students are eating phonograph records. There is no cause for alarm."

Perhaps spurred by word of this editorial, since the age of speedy communication was already upon us then, for better or worse, Howard Francis, a freshman at Kutztown State Teachers College in Reading, Pennsylvania, put away forty-three goldfish in fifty-four minutes and drew an immediate suspension from the institution's president, Q. A. W. Rohrbach. The charge: "conduct unbecoming a student in a professional course." On the side, Dr. Rohrbach made the point that several hundred students had cut classes to watch the boy perform his record-breaking feat. For young Francis, indeed, the whole thing was a total loss. Amidst great popular acclaim, Gordon Southworth of Middlesex University immediately restored the title to the Commonwealth by eating sixty-seven goldfish beneath the Soldier's Monument on Waltham Common, overlooking Mayor Arthur A. Hansen's office. C. Ruggles Smith, president of Middlesex, asked whether he contemplated any disciplinary action, issued an uncommonly succinct reply for an educator: "Nope." But the matter did not end there. Southworth, a pre-vet student, of all things, was ordered posthaste to the university's laboratory for an intensive investigation on his digestive tract, since Dr. Edwin E. Ziegler, the Federal Public Health Service's chief pathologist in the Boston area, had just warned that the nation's growing army of goldfish eaters was submitting itself to the risk of such dire afflictions as tapeworm and anemia. Happily, a fractional gastric analysis performed by the university's biochemists showed that Southworth enjoyed a digestion twice as fast as the average mortal of those times, so there was no reason to believe that the unfriendly elements in the goldfish had been permitted to settle in his intestinal tract long enough to wreak their damage. The scientific task force further explained that the youth's speedy digestive process accounted for the fact that he was able to put that ghastly repast away within fourteen minutes and then wash it down with milk and a peanut butter sandwich. Down at Franklin and Marshall, incidentally, George Rabb Jr., a member of the wrestling team, wound up in the hospital after eating a meager six goldfish and then going to the mat in a tournament. It was evident that for all his bulk that boy did not have the high-velocity, cast-iron insides of Gordon Southworth.

At this point, Professor Sarah Atsatt, zoologist at the University of California at Los Angeles, produced information that the human stomach had a physiological limit of 125 to 150 goldfish at a sitting and warned that any student foolish enough to try to pass that brave pinnacle might truly be courting danger. For the weight-conscious in those days before the no-cal dodge became a multimillion-dollar American industry, the Professor let it be known that 125 to 150 goldfish, taken in one sitting, constituted 1,000 calories, or the equivalent of a loaf of bread, twelve eggs or two hamburgers garnished with mayonnaise. Whether this intelligence had anything to do with it or not, the craze began to fade from the campuses around this moment in early April but not before the girls—in limited numbers, happily—had gotten into the act.

Marie Hansen of the University of Missouri held her nose one day in late March, ate one goldfish, followed by a pop soda and a piece of rye bread, and then remarked disdainfully, "My, my, doesn't that Eastern culture spread." Scottie Hunnicutt, a coed at Texas Western in El Paso, where girls were girls even in those days, thereupon downed three goldfish and claimed the national women's title.

The *Herald Tribune* editorial cited above mentioned reports of students in the Midwest eating phonograph records. For the record, so to speak, this was a reference to a University of Chicago junior named John Patrick, who had indeed munched on a couple of 78's (this was before the long-playing disc) before an admiring group of coeds. "Fellow students," Patrick said, "I did this for Alma Mater." There was another switch on the goldfish bit at Lafayette College in Easton, Pennsylvania. A sophomore from Brooklyn, Justin Stolitsky, ate a magazine from cover to cover because, he said, there were no goldfish on the campus. Neither the name of the magazine nor its dimensions were listed in the inadequate dispatches of the time.

University of California students mill outside Alpha Phi house as surrendered trophies float from windows. This 1956 raid turned into a near-riot. *WWP*

PANTIES
AND THINGS

"What is the panty raid except another expression of the older ones of receiving a lady's glove or handkerchief as a token of favor? You know, tournaments, jousting and that sort of thing . . . it's pretty primitive stuff."
—DR. MARYNIA FARNHAM, psychiatrist

No, MOTHER, they don't make panty raids like they used to.

The serious student of this aspect of life on the American campus will find that the Fifties was the decade of the panty raids; after that, with isolated exceptions, the midnight foray on the girls' dorms diminished in fervor. It would be wrong to assume that the boys lost their interest in the coeds' underthings, or that the need to go *get* them expired altogether. It is apparent that, come the Sixties, the boys had something better, perhaps more than one something better, to turn on with but that's another chapter.

Springtime, in any case, is when the undergraduate's fancy used to drift more forcibly to the mass assault on milady's underthings. Take the spring of 1952: 2,000 University of Missouri students went on a rampage through the coed dorms of the Columbia campus and then moved on to nearby Stephens and Christian colleges, desisting only when a call went out for the local militia. The next day the boys, contrite, assembled on the Missouri basketball court bearing bags full of panties, bras and slips earmarked for return to the coeds, along with a modest collection

of silver currency by way of further restitution. A similar outbreak at the University of Tennessee had to be put down by the Knoxville police. A raid on the girls domiciled at the University of Georgia at Athens went askew when the football squad blocked the dormitory portals. The girls, for their part, tossed undergarments out of the windows to the thwarted invaders, just as coeds at the University of Pennsylvania shouted encouragement to an eager force descending on them while the Philadelphia police were hauling the boys away on disorderly conduct charges.

A switch on the panty raid marked the next semester. Thirty-five girls raided a dormitory at Toledo University in a quest for men's shorts. "We were lucky," said one of the student victims. "They didn't try to get the shorts we were wearing." There was another switch at Indiana University. Mrs. Alice Nelson, director of the women's residence halls, looked on with a scowl as a band of panty collectors was driven off one night; then she announced that no further raids would be necessary. She said she would collect a barrel full of discarded female undergarments and make them available to the boys. That took care of *that*. Around the same time, Indiana's resident authority on sex and its assorted problems, Dr. Alfred C. Kinsey, begged off when he was asked whether his researches had given him any insight into the motivation behind panty raids. "It is somewhat out of my field," he said.

In June, 1954, Northwestern University in Evanston, Illinois, came up with a novel antidote for panty raids. Dean James McLeod greeted an onrushing force of 300 students with one crisp sentence: "I want your names and draft numbers." Given a choice between some secondhand pink underthings and a bleak two years in the Army, the boys retreated.

There were serious consequences on a few campuses in 1955. The University of Nebraska expelled seven students after a raid in which some coeds endured a little rough handling for refusing to surrender their most intimate apparel, while the University of Connecticut threw out eight freshmen caught in a foray in which the girls offered more encouragement than resistance. In contrast, just because the girls cheered them on, the University of Michigan elected not to punish the ringleaders of a band of 1,000 which had descended on three different dormitories on the Ann Arbor campus in a wild rampage. The University of Massachusetts recorded the worst raid in its history; before it ended at 6:00 A.M. some of the more eager students in that 600-man force were collecting undergarments from live bodies rather than bureau drawers or powder-room clotheslines. In the same semester, the Denver police had to be called out when coeds from the all-girl Loretto Heights College descended on the men of Regis College in the dark of night.

The University of California, fated within another decade to become the site of the most violent campus riots in the nation's history (on more serious issues, such as free speech), drew the blackest headlines as the panty raid contagion continued into 1956.

On a moonstruck night in May, the sprawling Berkeley complex bordered on terror as 3,000 students swept through twenty-two sororities and boardinghouses, leaving $10,000 worth of property damage and some damage to persons besides. The students' own daily, *The Californian,* reported that coeds were "knocked around, assaulted, carried outside in pajamas or nude," presumably protesting all the way. In an editorial entitled "The Masses Are Asses," *The Californian* denounced the whole performance as a "night of debauchery." The Berkeley police had to augment the university's own campus force to cool off the marauders. There would be nothing to compare with the uncontrolled violence of that night until two more years passed and thousands of students at the University of Ohio went on a panty-hunting expedition so wild that the Athens police had to use tear gas to drive them from the coeds' dorms. Once again, the girls waved their underthings out of the windows in support of the dispersing raiders.

The same thing happened in New York in 1957, by the way, when a delegation of Columbia undergraduates set out from the ivy halls to collect some lingerie from two girls' dorms at adjoining Barnard College. While forty-five city policemen held off the students, the girls tossed panties out of the windows to show which side they were on. Come the dawn, Dean Lawrence H. Chamberlain put forth a benignly tolerant view. "The campus is better for it this morning," he said. "No one got hurt and all the students had a good time." Mrs. Millicent C. McIntosh, president of Barnard, wasn't that sanguine at all. She withdrew behind a frosty "no comment."

Somebody solicited the views of Dr. Marynia Farnham on the campus phenomenon, and she was reminded of the ancient Roman Feast of Saturn when, courtesy of the god of harvest, all work ceased

1952: Northwestern University coeds wave undergarments at raiders. *WWP*

and everybody had fun. Was the panty raid a senseless thing?

"Sure it's senseless," said the lady psychiatrist, "but here it is, the Saturnalia. It is as old as mankind, and all societies have recognized that this will happen when there comes a release from tension, when the sun comes back. Now here we are again, with the sun over the Equator and everybody loosed from the bondage of ice and snow and—at the back of our minds—freed from the fear that when everything turned brown the sun might never come back to us. Older females buy new hats. Older men get out their golf clubs. The young are beside themselves. People even dye eggs—certainly a symbol of fertility. Everything, at this time, is a symbol of sex and birth. Naturally, man—and of course woman—is a cyclic animal. Usually, the girls get into this nonsense just as much as the boys do. It's quite clear that everybody involved recognizes the sexual symbols mixed up in all this."

Professor William J. Pinard, head of the psychology department at Boston University, also dipped back into history. He saw the college man's yearning for the lingerie of the opposite sex as a civilized version of the ancient tribal systems. He was talking, of course, about a time when the man went and collected the whole woman, not just her undergarments.

There was a brief resurgence of panty raiding, centered in the Ivy League, in 1963. New Haven police hauled in seventeen Yale boys after a mob descended on the graduate women's dormitory, screaming, "We want sex." In Providence, it took

This Southern Methodist University coed chose the water cure for one of the 300 rampaging males under a full moon over Dallas. *WWP*

It wasn't always just plain fun. An undergrad is lifted onto a stretcher after 2,500 University of Florida students, hailed by panty-waving coeds, rioted in 1964.

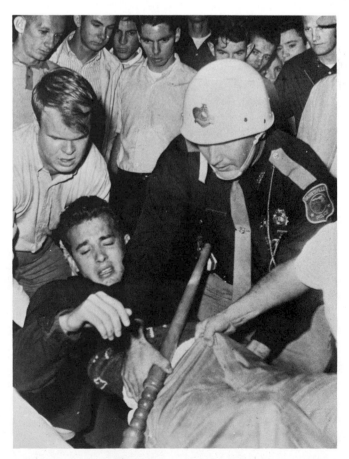

five hours to put down the rioting touched off when Brown University students set out to collect the spare lingerie of the girls at neighboring Pembroke. The more serious observers had quite a few things to say at the time.

Dr. Phillip Polatin, professor of clinical psychiatry at the College of Physicians and Surgeons at Columbia, put forth the view that students were under tremendous sexual pressures which could not be gratified, so—

They turn to violent forms of aggression. To some degree, they are rebelling against authority which restricts them from their fun-loving pleasures. You have to realize, too, that it's springtime. The boys had their noses to the grindstone all year. Examinations are coming up and suddenly they give vent to their creative impulses. They have a need for recreation and they resort to riot. The world today is more threatening. More aggressive weapons, such as H-bombs and A-bombs, can be released for destruction. It is a natural result that with some students their conduct will be more aggressive.

Dr. Renatus Hartogs, chief psychiatrist at New York's Youth House and medical officer of the Community Guidance Service, put it this way: "In this period of the school year before examinations, a student's aggressive condition can take flight into destructive action. Many students at this time live in anxiety, with a fear of failure in the upcoming exams, and they may be letting out their anger at college authorities. They're fed up, they've had enough and they let go." Dr. Hartogs also observed that (a) fathers were too weak, and (b) the colleges themselves were too lenient with their fun-loving charges.

Dr. Sydney E. Langer, of New York University, saw the panty raid as a display of misplaced anger. He noted that it was a time of accelerated living, extraordinary feats in outer space and the threat of The Bomb, all compounded by an attitude at once both hopeless and lonely. "It's like losing your taste for simple food," he said. "You suddenly want spicy food. You want new thrills."

So much for the innocent reveler who collects spices made for wearing. Between this character and the dead-serious types who have more fun carrying a picket sign in one cause or another, the American campus traditionally boasts an abundant supply of students prepared at all times to join in whatever happens to be at hand in the way of a passing fad.

While this chronicle of nonsense has recorded nothing quite as inane as the goldfish-swallowing binge of 1939, it is plain that the boys have not been idle in the intervening years. Indeed, they have kept a vigilant eye on their contemporaries in distant lands, just so nothing got away.

Thus the telephone-booth-jamming syndrome of 1959.

That one was touched off by a dispatch out of South Africa describing how twenty-five Durban students, none less than six feet tall, had succeeded in squashing themselves into a single telephone booth. For some obscure reason, this challenge, instantly picked up in London, hit our California campuses most forcibly. At Modesto Junior College, thirty-two students, presumably in junior sizes, squeezed into one booth. At St. Mary's College in Moraga, the total came to a modest twenty, still good enough to top by three bodies the showing made at UCLA. The highest figure that came out of Texas was twelve, presumably because they don't grow any small boys in that country. And the Queen's merry men? Campus leaders at Cambridge University and Hatfield Technical College, scornful of the tidings from South Africa, invoked a round of dieting and then made a run at the record. Cambridge managed fifteen and Hatfield nineteen, defending their dismal showings by observing that the Durbans' achievement was invalid because they had jammed their booth to the extent that the phone could not be used whereas, they said, the real trick was to stuff in as many undergraduates as you could and still make an outgoing call. As it happened, the fad did not last long enough for any definitive resolution of the issue.

Our British cousins, by the way, were responsible for a much more muscular seizure which had a limited run here in the Colonies four years later—piano wrecking. This one was touched off when a brawny team at the Derby College of Technology, armed with crowbars, sledgehammers, iron wedges and axes, battered an old piano into splinters in a matter of fourteen minutes and three seconds. The rules of the game: no more than six to eight in the demolition squad and no stopping until the last remaining piece of the instrument could be passed through a hole just under eight inches in diameter. At the California Institute of Technology a hastily organized Piano Reduction Study Group went right to work and showed the boys from Derby that the task could be accomplished in much quicker time, like ten minutes and 44.4 seconds. The Cal Tech group professed to be very serious indeed. "Piano reduction has psychological implications which are

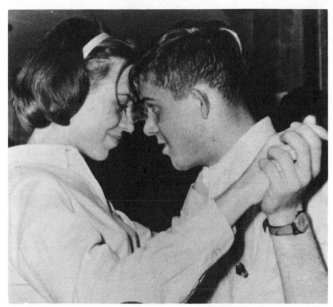

Speaking of fads, the trick here was to see how long you could dance with an ice cube on the bridge of your nose. Indiana students Jennie Englebright and Kent Wilson claimed a 1964 record of fifteen minutes and forty-five seconds. *WWP*

pretty dear to us," said Robert W. Diller, the team captain. "It is a satire on the obsolescence of today's society."

The Cal Tech record itself became obsolete in no time at all. Without delving into the psychological aspects of the thing, a brawny band at Wayne State University in Detroit lugged an old fraternity house piano into an empty lot and beat it to death in four minutes and fifty-one seconds.

To go back to Cambridge for a moment, a most imposing record, however pointless, came out of that hallowed educational foundry in 1960. Four undergraduates got together for a spot of bridge and managed to stay with it for seventy-three hours and forty-five minutes. In the Chi Phi fraternity house at Stevens Tech in Hoboken, New Jersey, a determined quartet consisting of Andrew Bradick, Douglas Wilkinson, Wayne Konopka and Joseph Zorskie set out to top that marathon performance but had to quit after a trifling forty-three and a half hours. "It turned out to be more of a test than we figured," Konopka said. "It stopped being fun." Bradick's experience was more harrowing. "After a while I started to have hallucinations," he said. "I thought I saw cards standing on tripods." So the long-distance bridge-playing crown reposes to this day in the Mother Country.

For something less sedentary, consider what was going on in the American Far West in the languid June of 1951. On the campus of Washington State College, some of the more athletic types put their bodies and minds into long-distance teeter-tottering. You can guess what happened: Two University of California students shamed the Washington State crowd by keeping a seesaw in action for seventy-two hours, whereupon Jim Lane and Duane Weaver of the College of the Pacific repaired to the nearest unoccupied teeter-totter and kept going past ninety hours. The secret? In the marathon teeter-totter set, the partners alternately rest their weary bones in sleeping sacks lashed to the boards, while the waking member keeps the seesaw going. This was just one of the things you had to go to college to learn back in what some observers called the Fabulous Fifties.

But, then, there has never been a lack of diversions to offset the increasingly more rigorous college grind. In 1961, the telephone talkathon briefly occupied some scattered campuses. Western Michigan University at Kalamazoo claimed the record when sixty boys and sixty girls, in relays, kept one phone going for 124 hours. In 1965, there was a small outbreak of marathon scooter riding. Six Sigma Alpha Mu boys at Long Island University, led by psychology major George Popper, kept a scooter in action on a nine-tenths-of-a-mile course in Brooklyn for sixty-one hours. Was it any sillier than the USC and UCLA teams pitted against each other in a "wine-walking" contest to see which barefoot squad could stomp the most grapes? Or the Delta Chi and Tau Epsilon fraternities out there mounting beds on wheels and pushing them over a forty-two-mile course (1961, Delta Chi won the race). Or the contest to select the girl with the most kissable lips at little Presbyterian College in Clinton, South Carolina? Or the recurring competitions to see who could toss an ice cube back and forth the most times? Or the girls of Alpha Phi Sorority at the University of Arizona lining up in a parking lot and throwing whipped cream pies at one another to relieve the tension of examination time in 1967? Or the short-lived hunkerin' fad in the Ozarks in 1959 in which the idle student did nothing more than squat on his haunches and kill time? Or the brief flurry of campus "murders" inspired in 1965 by *The Tenth Victim*, the movie in which Ursula Andress dispatches that bad Chinese fellow with the help of a two-gun brassiere? This unseemly diversion—no, not the Maidenform bit, just plain killing—left some assorted "corpses" on Midwestern campuses before the undergraduates lost their interest, happily, in simulated mayhem.

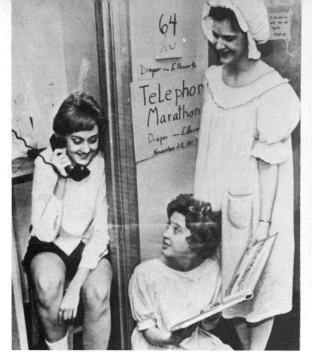

In 1961, it was the talkathon. How long could you tie up the phone? Western Michigan University's Kathy Vaughn and Jim Bruggema take their turns in the sixth day of a relay at the Kalamazoo school. *WWP*

1959: Something new in campus crazes. How many could you cram into one phone booth? The Men's Club at Southeast Missouri State claimed a record with this stunt—thirty-five, but some of them seemed more out than in. *WWP*

At Colorado State University in 1955 somebody wondered how many students this second-hand hearse could hold. The count: fifty, including four rather venturesome coeds. *WWP*

Toward the mid-Sixties, one campus fad turned on how many students could pile onto a single bed or just a mattress. The University of Oklahoma at Norman emerged with the record—fifty-six. *WWP*

Mario Savio, leader of Berkeley's Free Speech Movement—"Filthy Speech" to the school's administrators—addresses mass rally at height of the disorders. *WWP*

THE NEW REVOLT

"A university should be a place of light,
of liberty and of learning."
—DISRAELI

WHAT TURNED the college student on? Free speech? Vietnam? Civil rights? LSD?

Whatever it was—and it was all those things and more—the strong winds of revolt fanned the American campus in the Sixties. The new generation, damned unhappy about the world it was inheriting from its elders, plunged headlong into combat behind a truly formidable arsenal: massive picket lines, boycotts, sit-ins, teach-ins, marches, rallies and little bonfires fed by draft cards. This college crop, clamoring to be heard, also came armed with a thin skin and a ruggedly fierce determination not seen in our gigantic education foundry (five and a half million on the rolls) in thirty years. It was a generation that did not play by the rules because it did not respect them.

How do you change the rules in this kind of game? Direct action. You man the barricades.

In 1964, 679 students and 135 free-riding sympathizers were arrested during a "free-speech" sit-in at the University of California at Berkeley. In 1965, nearly 20,000 students swarmed to the White House to protest the ever-expanding bloodbath in Vietnam. Across the nation in this decade, few colleges and universities have escaped some kind of student wrath.

While the first outbreaks were touched off by the civil rights issue, the targets of the rebellion ultimately ranged all the way from bad cooking in campus kitchens to United States policy in Southeast Asia. In between, there were protests over dress and dormitory regulations, academic freedom, student drinking (they wanted the same rights as their parents in this department), and so on and on. Even little Slippery Rock State College in Pennsylvania faced a protest march from 300 students who, in the school's own words, were against "just about everything"—especially the rules covering their dress and their conduct in the dormitories.

The rule-breaking did not always spring from the loftiest or most deeply suffered motivation. Not by any means. While some students appeared moved by a social conscience, others showed no conscience at all. Senseless riots, particularly during Easter holidays, were staged in resort communities across the nation.

"We want whiskey! We want beer!" vacationing students chanted as they stormed through towns, destroying property and battling police. It happened in such places as Fort Lauderdale, Florida; Lake George, New York; Ocean City, Maryland; Wildwood, New Jersey; Hampton Beach, New Hampshire, and Cape Cod. At Princeton, 1,500 students launched the 1963 Intercollegiate Spring Riot Season by burning benches, smashing railroad cars, pushing autos over and storming Westminster Choir College, where the coeds tossed panties and potted plants from the windows. The Tigers, sacrificing fourteen men to the town jail, even threw cherry bombs on Governor Richard J. Hughes's lawn. He took it philosophically—"It's spring and the sap begins to run." At Yale, rioting to the cry of "We want sex." seventeen were jailed and one wound up in the hospital after some rough handling by the police.

Commenting on student riots in Oregon and New Hampshire in 1964, Harvard's Dr. Jerome S. Bruner, president of the American Psychological Association, said the "outbursts probably reflect a feeling of disengagement from society because of the complexity of modern life—a desire on the part of the demonstrators to express a feeling of control over their own destinies." Dr. Robert F. Goheen, Princeton's president, shunned any deep analysis, simply putting it all down as "a shocking display of individual and collective hooliganism on the part of young men who have no possible justification for sinking into it." But to Tom Kahn, executive director of the League for Industrial Democracy, it was a rebellion against the sorry record of the preceding decade. "The McCarthyite witch-hunt, the Eisenhower mediocrity, and the cold war prosperity had combined to repress dissent on the campus, giving rise to the so-called 'silent generation,' " Kahn wrote.

But if Ike was to be blamed for contributing to the lethargy of the Fifties, then perhaps another President—young, vibrant, vigorous—had to be taxed for inspiring the free-wheeling revolt that came later. John F. Kennedy could have been sounding a collegiate battle cry when he said:

> Let the word go forth . . . that the torch has been passed to a new generation of Americans—born in this country, tempered by war, disciplined by a hard and bitter peace, proud of our ancient heritage—and unwilling to witness or permit the slow undoing of those human rights to which this nation has always been committed. . . .

The word did go forth. There were sit-ins at Southern lunch counters, picket lines on Capitol Hill and along the iron fence of the Colonial mansion on Pennsylvania Avenue, riots against the House Un-American Activities Committee in San Francisco, demonstrations everywhere.

What was happening? When the products of the post-World War II "Baby Boom" came of age and swarmed onto the nation's campuses, the schools shoved back their walls to contain the human tide. The University of California's enrollment, for example, went from 43,000 to 87,000 in ten years. So much for the body. Capturing the *spirit* of the vibrant new generation was something else. The massive influx separated the student from the teacher—with an army in his class, how many could the man reach?—and turned university life into an assembly-line existence where the undergraduate could best be identified by a set of holes punched in an IBM card. Thus one Berkeley demonstrator once wore a sign reading:

I AM A U.C. STUDENT
PLEASE DO NOT FOLD, SPINDLE
OR MUTILATE ME

Faced with this atmosphere of bigness and depersonalization, the student became all the more concerned with his identity, his reason for being. But first, it appears, somebody else's reason for being came into play—the Southern black risking life and limb against night riders, sheriffs' billies, cattle prods, water hoses and dogs in a suddenly erupted struggle for "Freedom Now." Mario Savio, the bushy-haired New Yorker who emerged as the sparkplug of the Berkeley revolt, saw the 1964 Free Speech Movement "as an extension of either vicarious or actual involvement in the struggle for civil rights."

"It was easy," said Savio, "to draw upon this reservoir of outrage at the wrongs done to other people . . . the focus of our attention shifted from our deep concern with the victimization of others to outrage at the injustices done to ourselves."

It was easy for many reasons. At Berkeley it was easy because California in 1964 was leading the nation in a swing toward conservatism that posed a challenge to civil liberties and academic freedom. It was easy because a blundering university administration, in its anxiety to please conservative critics and win support for a forthcoming bond issue, whipped the student body into a frenzy. Most of all, it was easy because the Republicans that election year had Barry Goldwater as their front-running candidate and ex-Senator William F. Knowland turned up as his California campaign chairman.

The "free speech" rallying cry had not yet been heard in the summer of 1964 when the Grand Old Party assembled in San Francisco's Cow Palace to nominate the man from Arizona, but if a single event could trigger the uproar at Berkeley and its echoes across the nation, this was it. Such Berkeley groups as

1964: The big action was at the University of California in Berkeley. *WWP*

Campus CORE, sensing a threat in the Goldwater brand of conservatism, recruited students to go across the bay and picket the GOP conclave. The recruiting took place on a 26-by-60-foot brick walk at Bancroft Way and Telegraph Avenue—the only campus location where such political activity was permitted. Most people thought that strip was in Berkeley city territory. Actually, the university had acquired the land outside its historic gate but UC President Clark Kerr, aware that political fund-raising and recruiting violated campus rules, had been trying ever so quietly to transfer the strip back to the city.

During the Republican convention, the Oakland *Tribune,* published by Bill Knowland, sent a reporter to the nearby Berkeley campus to look into the anti-Goldwater activities. Knowland in turn felt the sting of student protest when chanting, placard-waving demonstrators marched on his plant to protest the *Tribune*'s allegedly discriminatory hiring practices. Knowland looked on in stony silence as pickets sat down in the plant's driveway, blocking circulation trucks. Soon police began hauling off the protesters.

Ten days later, the ax fell.

The Berkeley administration, headed by Chancellor Edward Strong, announced that the Bancroft Strip was campus property and that any political activity for "off-campus" organizations was illegal. Student reaction was swift. Leaders of nineteen student branches of "off-campus" groups formed a "United Front" to battle the new restrictions. Among those banding together were such diverse groups as the Students for Goldwater, the W. E. B. DuBois Club, Young Republicans, Students for Democratic Action, CORE, the Student Non-Violent Coordinating Committee (SNCC) and three Socialist clubs.

On September 21, first day of the fall term, the United Front confronted Dean Katherine A. Towle and rejected her offer to permit tables on the strip only on condition that no partisan activity, fund-raising or recruitment could take place there. By noon, the first protest demonstration—a 200-man picket line—was in full swing before Sproul Hall, the administration building. Clark Kerr wasn't at all happy about it.

"I don't think you have to have action to have intellectual opportunity," said the UC president. "Their actions—collecting money and picketing—aren't highly intellectual activity. It is not right to use the university as a basis from which people organize and undertake direct action in the surrounding community."

But by then the direct action was turning inward, toward the university itself. The United Front set up tables and resumed the prohibited activities. Two nights later the students staged a "Free Speech Vigil" on Sproul Hall steps, and a week after the term began 1,000 pickets marched on a university meeting, where Chancellor Strong surprised them by announcing a further compromise: Advocacy of election issues and

243

candidates would be permitted, but the ban stood against fund-raising, recruitment and promoting of off-campus social and political causes. The United Front's reply: "We will settle for nothing less than total victory." Two days later, five students were cited for manning tables on campus without permits and ordered to the office of Dean of Men Arleigh Williams. They showed up with 300 others and a petition signed by 600, all asking to share the blame. The instigators of the share-the-blame movement—Mario Savio, Arthur Goldberg and Sandor Fuchs—then were cited along with the other five. The 300 waiting outside sat down in the corridors and did not leave until early the next morning, October 1. By then, Strong and Kerr had suspended the eight cited students—a penalty traditionally not imposed without a hearing by the Faculty Student Conduct Committee.

Now the chasm between the students and the administration, with the faculty somewhere in between, began to widen by the hour, threatening to tear the university apart. Leaflets calling for a free speech rally at noon began to circulate, and forbidden tables suddenly went up. At 11:45 A.M., eight or ten people behind a Campus CORE table were doing a brisk business when Dean Van Hooten arrived with campus police. The Dean addressed himself to a single member of the CORE group, Jack Weinberg, a graduate student in mathematics who had dropped out, and advised him that he was trespassing and faced arrest unless he left. Instead, Weinberg made a speech for the constantly growing horde around him. He said the UC "knowledge factory" was unhappy because "certain of the products are not coming out to standard specifications" and urged everyone to stand up and be counted on such issues as segregation, poverty and unemployment. That was as far as he got. With reinforcements arriving, a police car was driven into the plaza and the youth was carried into it, whereupon some 100 students flopped down in front of the car and eighty sat down behind it. "Release him!" they chanted. "Let him go!" But the cops were not about to release Weinberg. The standoff would last for thirty-two hours.

It was in this absurd but tragically meaningful situation that Mario Savio, a twenty-one-year-old philosophy major, took over for the student activists. With permission from the police, Savio removed his shoes and scrambled to the patrol car roof to address the still-swelling crowd. He urged the students to spread the demonstration into Sproul Hall, and 150 responded while 500 remained around the car. All through the afternoon speakers held forth from the caved-in roof of the vehicle while efforts to medi-

Karen Lieberman of New York drew a year's suspension for her role in the student rebellion. *WWP*

ate faltered on the administration's insistence that campus discipline was not negotiable. By nightfall, 2,500 students surrounded the car, and the demonstrators who had filled Sproul Hall—400 strong at one point—came out to join the action. Weinberg still sat in the car, under arrest. About 200 students stayed all night, some in blankets or sleeping bags, and with daylight their numbers swelled again.

Now something had to give. While efforts to bring about a negotiated settlement were still under way, Kerr, Strong and Governor Edmund G. Brown decided that force might be necessary and began mobilizing 500 to 1,000 policemen from Berkeley, Oakland and nearby communities as well as the Alameda County Sheriff's Office and the California Highway Patrol. The armed, club-carrying force gathered behind Sproul Hall to await orders which would never come.

Instead, late in the afternoon, Kerr agreed to meet with the students, and shortly after 7:30 P.M. Savio clambered onto the prowl car again to announce a six-point agreement signaling an armistice: a halt in the demonstrations, formation of a joint committee to study campus political behavior, withdrawal of the charges against Weinberg (although he would have to be booked for his indiscretion), submission of the eight suspensions to an independent faculty group, restoration of the student organization's privileges, and intensified efforts to deed the Bancroft strip back to the city, its actual owner.

During the next two days, the United Front, minus some of its Goldwaterites, emerged as the Free Speech Movement. The truce between the Movement and the administration, however, crumbled quickly, with each side charging bad faith. As the debate wore on, the FSM began to lose its glamour for the students, and interest waned rapidly—until Strong wrote to Savio and three other student leaders, Arthur Goldberg, Jackie Goldberg and Brian Turner, as well as nineteen FSM-linked clubs, to announce that discipline would have to be invoked for the sit-in around the police car. To many, this appeared an outrageous violation of the six-point settlement, and the FSM was reborn, inspiring support on UC campuses throughout the state. The Movement issued an ultimatum: Drop the charges or face "massive direct action." A noon rally was scheduled for December 2 on the Sproul Hall plaza. "Bring books, food and sleeping bags," an FSM leaflet advised. The administration ignored the ultimatum, setting the stage for what history may record as the ultimate act in massive civil disobedience by the restless and rebellious university students of the Sixties. An army of 6,000 gathered for the noon rally and heard Savio say:

There is a time when the operation of the machine becomes so odious, makes you so sick at heart, that you can't take part, you can't even tacitly take part. And you've got to put your bodies upon the gears and upon the wheels, upon the levers, upon all the apparatus, and you've got to make it stop. And you've got to indicate to the people who run it, to the people who own it, that unless you're free, the machine will be prevented from working at all.

It was clear that the activist students were indeed going to throw their bodies upon the gears and wheels and levers that operated the university from inside Sproul Hall.

"When you go in," folk singer Joan Baez told them, "go with love in your hearts."

With Miss Baez leading to the strains of "We Shall Overcome," nearly 1,000 students—40 percent of them girls—filed slowly into Sproul Hall, not knowing when, or how, they would leave, and took it over. Graduate students organized classes in subjects ranging from aesthetics and biology to "The Nature of God and the Logarithmic Spiral." The fourth floor became a study hall. The second floor featured films with Charlie Chaplin and Laurel and Hardy. Some read, some sang, some talked, some laughed. Sandwiches were handed out. Sit-in leaders kept in walkie-talkie contact with the outside.

At 7:00 P.M. the doors were locked from the outside by university guards. By midnight, some of the invaders were sound asleep but FSM leaders awakened them at 2:30 A.M. The liberal Pat Brown, under increasing fire from California's flourishing right wing and fated to lose his office to the glamorously conservative Ronald Reagan, had called out the law. It wasn't Clark Kerr's idea, by the way. He wanted to let the mutineers hang on to Sproul Hall until they got weary enough to give it back to him. The University of Chicago had waited out a nine-day sit-in

The embattled UC president, Clark Kerr, talks to some of the rebels. Youth in center is Arthur Goldberg, one of Savio's lieutenants.

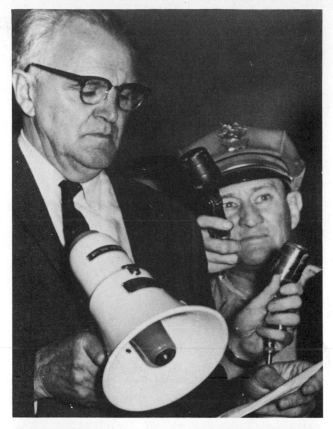

that way with no appreciable damage on either side. In any case, Dr. Strong showed up with a bullhorn at 3:15 A.M. and urged the students to abandon their "act of disobedience." He said the sit-in could no longer be tolerated because it had impaired "the purpose and work of the university." About 200 students left. More than 800 elected to stay.

It took 635 cops to shove, prod, drag and carry the rebels from Sproul Hall to be hauled off in vans and buses and distributed among the nearby jails, a National Guard Armory and a prison farm. And so the sit-in was smashed, but the great university had settled nothing.

The student body, with some faculty support, responded with a strike. The belabored administration made its next move on December 7. Kerr set up a mass meeting in the Greek Theater on the campus, and there 15,000 heard his peace proposals: new and liberalized political action rules and an offer to drop UC's charges against the students arrested in the sit-in and let the courts dispose of their cases. The meeting adjourned in some harmony but then Savio tried to approach the microphone and was jumped by two policemen. For a moment, it looked as though a riot might break out—until Savio was permitted to speak. "Please leave here," he said. "Clear this disastrous scene and get down to discussing the issues." As the students obeyed, Kerr sighed, "That was a hell of an ending."

Although the issues that separated the students and the school would not be resolved for years, if ever, the FSM was on the verge of its finest hour. It came the next day, when the Academic Senate gathered in Wheeler Hall and thousands of students clustered around loudspeakers outside to hear the issues debated. It wasn't much of a debate. When it was over, the faculty had voted 824–115 in favor of the FSM position, all the way.

The Berkeley story didn't end there, of course.

The trials growing out of the sit-in produced more than 700 convictions for trespassing, resisting arrest or both, with fines ranging from $50 to $300. Savio drew 120 days, including an extra month for rejecting

Above, Chancellor Edward W. Strong appeals to Sproul Hall sit-ins to return the administration building to the university, but it took the massed forces of the law to get that done. *WWP*

Below, A youth being hauled away after Governor Brown gave the order. *WWP*

Cordon of officers holds off students as sit-ins are dragged into police bus. *WWP*

During a winter protest over Navy recruiting at Berkeley that year, a beefy plainclothesman and the uniformed officer have a student sandwiched between them. There were ten arrests that day. *WWP*

probation. The university brass paid, too. First Strong went. Then Kerr was fired in 1967 by the Reagan-dominated Regents.

There were lots of other things happening on the nation's campuses in the lively mid-Sixties:

At the University of Kansas, 113 students were arrested for a campus sit-in protesting fraternity and sorority segregation. At the University of Chicago, 200 sang freedom songs in the snow while protesting curfew hours. At St. John's University in New York, students broke a long tradition of obedience by joining a faculty strike for academic freedom. At Antioch College in Yellow Springs, Ohio, the police used tear gas when students sat down outside a segregated barbershop. And the civil rights movement, where it all started, was continuing to attract large numbers in 1965. The Reverend Martin Luther King's Southern Christian Leadership Conference drew 5,000 students to a voter registration drive in the South that summer. When demonstrators marched at Selma, Alabama, undergraduates from Harvard, Yale and Princeton were in their ranks, as well as the omnipresent Savio.

Now the unrest on the campus swung more and more to Vietnam and the draft. Here University of Chicago students stage a peaceful sit-in—but there was more to come, lots more. *WWP*

"This generation of students has what other generations have lacked—a holy discontent, courage and the willingness to sacrifice," St. John's sociology professor William Osborne told *Time* magazine, which likes to call it the "Now Generation." To Yale president Kingman Brewster Jr., the unrest on the campus represented "a great and potentially constructive awakening on the part of the students to their own stake in education." Buell C. Gallagher, president of the City College of New York, had quite a different view. "Just as we have defended academic freedom from the onslaughts of McCarthy, the Ku Klux Klan and the John Birch Society," said Dr. Gallagher, "we must be on guard against the 'take-over mentality' when it shows up among students."

To the Senate Internal Subcommittee, the campus uprisings of 1964–65 fell, perhaps inevitably, into the well-worn mold of the Red plot. "These demonstrations seemed spontaneous at first," the subcommittee reported, "but a pattern emerged . . . which made it unmistakably clear that the Communist Party of the United States and its front organizations were playing a key role in organizing them." The Senators no doubt were exercised because the students had started to hit at a new target: the war in Vietnam. There is no question that such New Left groups as the Students for a Democratic Society furnished considerable impetus for the antiwar drive but the notion that its mass support was radically-oriented was patently silly. The movement drew the usual apolitical pacifist forces and a healthy sprinkling of students of varied persuasions sharing a wholly understandable attitude: They weren't too thrilled about the prospect of going from the campus to the mud and grime—and bloodletting—of Vietnam. And they had abundant faculty support, too. Thus the teach-in, born at the University of Michigan, rapidly gained popularity. This device, generally orderly but often lasting through the night, lacked the impact of the sit-in or the boycott but it did keep the issue of American political morality out where it could be weighed in the scales. Beyond the teach-ins, of course, the antiwar drive began to dominate the campus scene and inevitably spread beyond it. In the spring of 1965, 20,000 demonstrators, mostly students, marched on the White House. At the same time, the draft-card ritual came into vogue, succeeding primarily in getting the match-wielders arrested. There were also some futile attempts to block troop trains, and in the fall there were "International Days of Protest" and all manner of rallies and marches across the nation.

Berkeley remained the protest capital of the academic world, of course, and out there some 10,000 demonstrators tried to march on the Oakland Army Terminal only to be turned back by hundreds of police with what one reporter described as "preparations that would have been appropriate to repel a Viet Cong invasion." Around the same time, fifty students from the University of Wisconsin at Madison marched on the nearby Truax Air Force Base to make a citizen's arrest of Lieutenant Colonel Lester Arasmith, the commandant, as an accessory to "mass murder and genocide," and the police hauled in eleven of them on the more mundane charge of loitering and obstructing traffic. In Ann Arbor, thirty-eight persons, including students and professors from the University of Michigan, were arrested for staging a "lie-in" at Selective Service Headquarters. But one of the first of the pamphlets bearing advice on how to beat the draft came from ever-embattled Berkeley—

Be a C.O. Write your local draft board requesting the special conscientious objector form SS 150. . . . It's fairly certain that your local board will turn you down. Then you can appeal their decision, be investigated, appeal again and so on. . . .

Refuse to sign the loyalty oath. . . .

Be "gay." Play the homosexual bit. Besides flicking your wrist, move your body like chicks do—hold cigarette delicately, talk melodically, act embarrassed in front of the other guys when you undress. Ask your girl friend to give you lessons.

That sort of nonsense, coupled with the headline-making demonstrations across the country, may have suggested a great ferment on the campuses but closer inspection belied it. The Associated Press polled eighty-five colleges in the winter of '65 and reported that the antiwar forces—"Vietniks" to the other side —represented nothing more than a small but vocal minority, and in mid-1966 *Newsweek* spotted still another trend away from political activism on the campus:

Many students, and the large community of non-students surrounding the university, have reached out for a new Hippy culture of joy and introspection: the drug culture. Berkeley is a turned-on town . . .

Larry Gertner, city editor of the *Daily Californian* at Berkeley, put it this way: "The psychedelic culture is overwhelming everything else. More and more students would rather smoke pot than march in a Vietnam parade. We're going back to the Fifties when students were unconcerned."

While Gertner's eulogy for student activism was patently premature, there is no question that such mind-blowing agents as marijuana, mescaline, peyote and the much more perilous LSD made quite a few friends on the campus in the mid-Sixties. With these risky playthings came the pop culture of Folk Rock, Beatle hairdos, Mod styles, miniskirts, op art and the mystical introspection peddled by Timothy Leary.

"Marijuana has become this generation's alcohol," wrote Richard Goldstein, a Columbia journalism graduate who toured the nation for his book, *1 in 7: Drugs on Campus*. "In the Fifties, when the Kinsey report stunned a 'puritan' America, college students were experimenting with sex and bragging about it. Now, it is drugs." Goldstein equated narcotics—involving one out of every seven students, in his estimate— with bootleg liquor during Prohibition. "When you knew that liquor was harmless and fashionable, the fact that it was illegal was laughable. The same is true among students. . . . Pot smokers, to a man, find their vice 'enjoyable' and 'harmless.' "

By 1967, some surveys listed 15 to 20 percent of the students as users of drugs ranging from the so-called "up" pills to marijuana to the psychedelics (LSD, mescaline and psilocybin). The big one, of course, was grass. The Turned-On Generation appeared to be convinced that pot was no worse than the booze and barbiturates the grown-ups were using. Thus Eve Babitz, a twenty-three-year-old on the staff of New York's far-out *East Village Other*, told the Senate Judiciary Committee that "everybody I know, except for my grandmother and grandfather, just about, smokes marijuana."

LSD, of course, posed the more exotic and infinitely more serious problem. While there was nothing to indicate that anything more than a handful of students were toying with that kind of dynamite, Timothy Leary talked confidently of, oh, perhaps a third of them enjoying trips on LSD's magic carpet. It sounded more like the wish than the fact, happily. Dr. Ralph R. Greenson, then a UCLA psychiatrist and later head doctor for many movie stars, including Marilyn Monroe at the time of her OD death in 1962, suggested that drugs, in some cases, were replacing sex on the campus.

Maybe so, but to the average student today, like his predecessors in the panty-raiding Fifties and in all the decades before that, the opposite gender remains a most absorbing extracurricular activity. Even in the era of the free speech battles, there was also some unfettered talk about sex—and The Pill, of course. It is a fair assumption that there were at least as many coeds exercised over the brand of freedom implied in The Pill as there were over the issue of free speech.

Indeed, the boys themselves hardly overlooked the problem. At Columbia, for instance, they formed a Sexual Freedom Forum to encourage heterosexual activities by mature persons who feel affection for each other. At UCLA and elsewhere, there were drives to legalize abortion. Nearly a thousand Michigan State University students held a "kiss-in" to protest the "puritanical" chastisement of a couple caught in an innocent embrace in a dormitory lounge. The demonstrators gathered in the women's lounge and smooched away as sign-carriers waved placards proclaiming MAKE LOVE NOT WAR, LOVE THY NEIGHBOR and LIPS OF MSU UNITE. At Wheaton College in Norton, Massachusetts, coeds Doris G. Granoff and Catherine Allsup suggested mass sexual abstinence to protest the Vietnam War. It was a switch, of course, on Aristophanes' *Lysistrata*, in which the women withhold their charms to make their husbands desist from killing each other, but the Wheaton girls failed to win any appreciable support. That tells you something. But to go on, a sit-in started at the University of Florida when Pamela Brewer, eighteen, was placed on probation for displaying her nude form in the centerfold of an off-campus magazine. Uniting under the banner of "Nude Power," the busty Pamela's fellow students argued that no school regulation specifically barred a coed from posing in her birthday suit. The girl herself settled the argument. She left the university, fully dressed, in a huff.

Despite all the increased talk about sex, the New York *Times* in 1966 found little evidence that students were behaving any differently from the generation of the Thirties. "For instance," wrote reporter John Corry, "Dr. Kinsey and his associates, who began collecting their information in 1938, said in 1948 that perhaps 20 percent of college girls were not virgins. Subsequent studies indicate that this is still a true figure." And Harvard's Dr. Farnsworth, a Harvard psychiatrist, told an audience of 100 coeds: "Your behavior and your mothers' behavior are very similar. They were nice girls, too."

The college students, in fact, did appear to be a pretty damn nice bunch. Sure, some blew pot, ate acid, or carried their social protests to drastic, if not ridiculous, extremes. But listen to Dr. Grayson Kirk, president of Columbia:

The minority is noisy and some of its members are conspicuous by a studied eccentricity in dress and, perhaps, in personal hygiene. But, taken as a whole, students today are brighter, more hardworking, more intellectually mature and clearer in their career goals than at any time in the history of American higher education.

And Dr. Robert M. Hutchins, president of the Center for the Study of Democratic Institutions, seemed optimistic even about the noisy minority.

". . . Whether the students of the United States can constitute a permanent source of social criticism remains to be answered," said Hutchins. "I will say only one thing about this, and that is that this is a very encouraging development indeed, and one hopes that it will last."

It didn't just last. It exploded.

Sex came up too. Jan Lienke wrote the Minnesota *Daily*, the campus newspaper, a letter espousing premarital relations for those who were so disposed. The resulting furor was so great that the coed asked everybody to forget it, including her own legion of supporters. *WWP*

ALL THE WAY

...Kent State and Jackson State Close a New Chapter

"When dissent turns to
violence it invites tragedy."
—PRESIDENT RICHARD M. NIXON

WE COME NOW to a heart-wrenching moment when blood ran in buckets on the campus and a confrontation over black studies turned at least one university into an armed camp.

Throw out the Hippie time and such once-urgent matters as the "open door" warfare over the boys' and girls' dorms. Throw out a President too, for the college generation contributed its share to Lyndon Johnson's abdication—and that's the word—before the 1968 reelection campaign.

Let's start with the latter item, surely the one with the most momentous implications.

In the Storming of the Pentagon on October 21, 1967, there were students in the tens of thousands who joined the coalition of 150 antiwar and civil rights groups put together by David Dellinger's National Mobilization Committee to End the War in Vietnam. That demonstration, with 6,000 soldiers on hand and more than 2,000 National Guardsmen and U. S. marshals to augment the Washington police force, not to mention another 20,000 GIs on alert across the nation "in the event of a full-scale insurrection," did not achieve its stated aim of bringing our military establishment to a dead halt.

No way.

But it did something larger.

It took 'Nam, and the count through 1967 would be 14,592 dead bodies and another 92,820 broken with 31,898 more marked for flag-draped coffins before Richard Nixon ended it in his good time in 1973, within blocks of the White House itself. It took "Johnson's War" to Johnson's doorstep at the worst possible moment for the Tall Texan. He had the Viet Cong's TET offensive still hanging over his head. He had the polls showing his constituents' support for the war rapidly dwindling away. He had the specter of another Kennedy—Robert F.—as a possible contender for that Oval Office. And now he had a veritable army from across the broad and sorely beset land to remove from his troubled head any notions about maybe changing his mind and accepting a "draft" to go for those four more years and get the job done. There was no longer any way he could take the crucial vote of the young away from the likes of a Bob Kennedy or a Eugene McCarthy.

If the March on the Pentagon wasn't enough, the shame of Chicago was still to come. And again, amidst the Yippies and the Crazies and the New Left types who were fully prepared to see the streets of Mayor Richard Daley's Windy City turned into a river of crimson while the 1968 National Democratic Convention unfolded in his Amphitheater, were the students. And it didn't end there, not even with LBJ self-exiled to his rich acres outside of Austin. On Vietnam Moratorium Day on October 15 of the following year universities everywhere either ground to a virtual stop or, in a fair number of cases, shut down altogether as millions of Americans, young and old, joined in a day to do nothing but tell their government the no-win war had to be ended. At Whittier College in California, the alma mater of Mr. Nixon, who was going to get us out of Southeast Asia five minutes after he moved into the White House, the authorities let the students light a flame of life as a memorial to the dead.

Now go back a step.

In the Spring of 1968, a takeover sparked by Mark Rudd's left-wing Students for a Democratic Society at Columbia University put seventy-seven undergrad-

uates, two outside demonstrators, eight faculty members and sixteen New York cops into hospital emergency wards before it was over. The arrests in the course of the bloodletting which put down that weeklong revolt: 525 students and 167 outsiders. And what was it all about? Primarily, the SDS wanted the University to break its ties to the Institute for Defense Analysis, a think-tank operation funded by the Defense Department, although there was also an issue over a new gym Columbia was putting up without setting aside enough time and space for the use of the neighboring Harlem ghetto. Rudd, a local youth wanted for his role in the uprising, vanished into the Weather Underground for nine years after that, coming away with a $2,000 fine and two years probation.

The following Spring it was Berkeley again—the Battle of People's Park, launched by the street people from San Francisco but quickly joined by thousands of UC students. This time the issue was a 1.3 million-

The 1968 takeover at Columbia. Mark Rudd, the student leader, tells newsmen outside occupied Low Memorial Library that the university's policy of "racism and support for imperialism" has to go. *WWP*

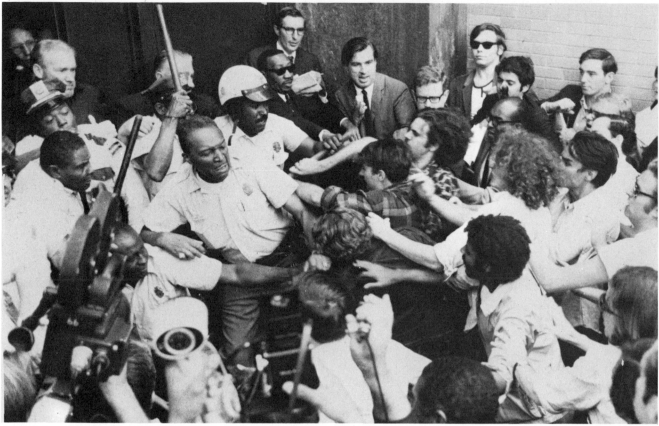

One of the many bloody student clashes with Columbia's outmanned guards before the police were brought in. Rudd (plaid shirt) is in the middle of this one. *WWP*

dollar piece of vacant land three blocks away from the campus that the university wanted to use either for additional dorms or a soccer field. Spurred by the underground *Berkeley Barb*, the Hippies, half-baked "revolutionaries," acidheads, potheads and what-have-you from the city across the bay decided instead that that piece of ground should be set aside for a "cultural, political freak out and rap center." Before that month-long frolic ended, the American campus witnessed some innovations: pepper gas, tear gas sprayed on demonstrators from a police helicopter and students passing into their classrooms through cordons of Guardsmen. On the bloodiest single afternoon, May 15, forty-three persons were treated for bullet wounds and scores of others for assorted injuries, while the police claimed ninety-eight casualties on their side. Count one death. James Rector, twenty-five, convicted burglar, junkie and parole violator from San Jose, was shot as he was either witnessing the warfare from a rooftop or throwing things at the lawmen. The total arrests among the students and the outsiders who started it: 900.

In that same year the war on "racism" in the universities came into full flower with a mounting chorus of demands for more black studies and even, here and there, autonomous Afro-American colleges within the universities. It was on that issue, at Cornell in upstate New York's Ithaca, where a truly menacing aresenal turned up in the hands of students rather than police or Guardsmen. The scene was Willard Straight Hall, the Student Union building, seized by 250 blacks to press their demands. When the university authorities talked the invaders out after thirty-six tense hours, seventeen rifles and shotguns were confiscated. Why the armor? The Afro-American force said they had the arsenal smuggled in only after hearing whispers that white students were going for *their* artillery to de-liberate that building. Without any prosecutions on either side, a rather ominous question would never be answered. How many guns were there on that Ivy League campus?

There was nothing unique about the Cornell experience except for all those rifles. There were outbreaks on sixty other campuses in twenty-three states

It's Berkeley again, this time in the 1969 Battle of People's Park, and something new: tear gas sprayed on demonstrators from a helicopter. *WWP*

Youth wounded by birdshot gets first aid on rooftop while shotgun-packing officer keeps alert for snipers. *WWP*

Facing masked National Guardsmen, demonstrators stage peaceful vigil for the one fatality in that Berkeley showdown.*WWP*

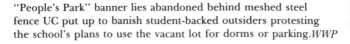

"People's Park" banner lies abandoned behind meshed steel fence UC put up to banish student-backed outsiders protesting the school's plans to use the vacant lot for dorms or parking.*WWP*

The scene shifts to Cornell with another, even more menacing innovation. Black students barricaded themselves in a campus building to protest university policies. Talked out thirty-six hours later, they were carrying a virtual arsenal. *WWP*

The ultimate tragedy and the ultimate shame: Kent State, 1970. A girl (not a student but a runaway teen-ager, it turned out) screaming and gesturing over the body of one of four students slain by National Guardsmen during a protest over the Nixon "Secret War" in Cambodia. This photo won a Pulitzer Prize for John Filo, a lab technician in the Ohio University's School of Journalism. *WWP*

during that same semester—some over Vietnam, some over demands for administration reforms, some spurred by the New Left and a very heavy proportion on the black issue. At the University of Wisconsin Governor Warren F. Knowles had to send in 1,900 Guardsmen to enable white students to get into their classrooms in the face of a strike by the Black Peoples Alliance. And the sting of tear gas was felt out there in Madison too. Berkeley—there's always Berkeley— suffered a seven-week strike spurred by the Third World Liberation Front and the Afro-American Student Union over ethnic issues. Governor Reagan kept 1,000 Guardsmen on alert until peace was restored— with no winners. New York's tuition-free City College had to be closed briefly in April when 200 black and Puerto Rican students seized the South Campus to demand a racial balance more closely reflecting the city's population breakdown, and there again it took the police to restore order. And at Harvard 197 were arrested and 41 injured in clashes with cops busting up a three-day takeover of University Hall by students who wanted the ROTC thrown off the campus, not an extraordinary demand by any means in that time.

The capstone on the endless strife came within a nine-day period in the spring of 1970 in two educational foundries as widely separated as Kent State University in Kent, Ohio, and the all-black Jackson State College in Jackson, Mississippi.

Kent State came first.

Embittered over the disclosure of the Nixon Administration's "secret war" in Cambodia, marked by more than 3,500 heavy bombing sorties covered up in faked Pentagon reports over a fourteen-month period that went back to March of 1969, Kent State students demonstrated for three nights and finally put the torch to the ROTC building, whereupon Governor James A. Rhodes declared a state of martial law.

And then came *the* day in infamy, a matter of no more than two or three seconds, actually, to wash all the turmoil of the Sixties out of our memories. It was May 5 and a crowd of some 1,000 assembled on the Commons, a grassy campus gathering spot, to press their protest. Guardsmen lobbing tear gas canisters pretty much took the edge off that noon rally without quite clearing the area. No harm done—except that twenty minutes later a volley of gunfire was aimed at the remaining students. Four of them—two men and two women—died in the senseless massacre and nine were wounded, some seriously.

Why? We still don't really know nine years later even though no less an author than James A. Michener put in a long stretch doing a book on Kent State.

From Columbus, Adjutant General Sylvester Del

Corso said his men had used their M-1 rifles only after a sniper opened fire against them from a nearby rooftop. On the scene, his assistant, Frederick P. Wenger, echoed him, stressing that his platoon was "under standing orders to take cover and return any fire" only if the students shot at them.

John Kifner, a fine young reporter for the *New York Times* who was with the rallying students from the outset, disputed those statements. He said that while some rocks had been thrown he heard no gunfire until the Guards let go.

The commander-in-chief of the "secret war" devastating our Vietnam ally's bordering neighbor to root out Communist strongholds lost no time in deploring the deaths—without failing to note, to be sure, that "when dissent turns to violence it invites tragedy." Presumably satisfied that the students—or a student— had touched off the gunfire, Mr. Nixon expressed the fervent hope that "this tragic and unfortunate incident will strengthen the determination of all the nation's campuses, administrators, faculty and students alike to stand firmly for the right which exists in this country of peaceful dissent and just as strongly against the resort to violence as a means of such expression."

Well, that settled that, didn't it?

There was nothing left to do but bury the dead.

Allison Krause, nineteen, of Pittsburgh.

Sandra Lee Scheuer, twenty, of Youngstown, Ohio.

Jeffrey Glenn Miller, twenty, of Plainview, Long Island.

William K. Schroeder, nineteen, of Lorain, Ohio.

But there was a lingering question.

Brigadier General Robert Canterbury, the actual commander of the troops on the campus, said they had been given *no official order* to start shooting.

The situation did not allow it. A crowd of 600 students had surrounded a unit of about 100 Guardsmen on three sides and were throwing rocks. Some of the rocks were the size of baseballs. The troops had run out of tear gas.

If that clears it up for you, we can go on to the postmortems.

Eight of those Guardsmen who had used up all their tear gas went to trial in Cleveland in 1974 but District Court Judge Frank J. Battisti threw the case out. He said the government had failed to establish "beyond a reasonable doubt" that the defendants had willfully intended to deprive those clay pigeons at Kent State of their civil rights (that is, the right not to get killed for protesting against something you're against).

Arthur Krause of Pittsburgh holds photo of his daughter Allison, one of the victims. That family's share of the 1979 settlement of the civil suits growing out of the massacre: $15,000

William Schroeder and Sandy Scheuer—also slain. They were both Ohioans. The fourth student cut down by the Guardsmen was Jeffrey Miller of New York. Why? The question hasn't been answered yet. The families of these three victims also were awarded $15,000 each.

There was another trial the following year after the parents of the dead and the wounded survivors filed a civil suit for $46 million in damages, naming as defendants Governor Rhodes, Messrs. Canterbury and Del Corso and former Kent State President Robert L. White along with twenty-seven Guardsmen. All thirty-one were found not liable by a six-man, six-woman jury that deliberated thirty-two hours and brought in a 10–2 verdict for them after hearing fifteen weeks of testimony. The ACLU appealed in 1977 and the United States Court of Appeals in Cincinnati reversed that finding and ordered a new trial for all but White, ruling that he had no control over the actions of the guard. That trial didn't find its way onto the calendar until December of the following year and was cut short by an out-of-court settlement awarding $675,000 to the plaintiffs minus $50,000 in lawyer's fees and $25,000 in out-of-pocket expenses.

Here is how the $600,000, paid by the state, was split:

The families of the dead and four wounded students—Alan Canfora, James D. Russell, Robert F. Stamps and Douglas Wrentmore—were awarded $15,000 apiece.

The healthier disbursements went to the more seriously wounded—$350,000 to Dean Kahler, $42,500 to Joseph Lewis, $37,500 to Tom Grace, $27,500 to Donald S. MacKenzie, and $22,500 to John Cleary.

So the slate was wiped clean at long last. Or was it? There wasn't enough money in this affluent land of the free to buy back that sun- and blood-spattered afternoon of May 5, 1970. But, then, you could throw in another item. The settlement required the governor and his co-defendants to sign a statement expressing their regret over the bloodletting.

The Jackson State incident—two dead blacks and twelve wounded—started on the night of May 13 on the thoroughfare that bisects the little college and bears the incredibly appropriate name of Lynch Street. It started small. There was just some rock throwing and some fires set. That was enough for Mayor Russell Davis to call for the National Guard, but a student delegation prevailed upon him to keep the campus clear of both police and troops. John A. Peoples, Jr., Jackson State's president, met with twenty-five of his charges at 1 A.M. and came out of that session satisfied that the incident was just a spontaneous, passing thing.

It wasn't.

The next night some 75 to 200 students assembled outside of the Alexander Hall coed dormitory and a smattering of rocks and bottles flew, along with some bad language, and this time the police wasted no time opening up on the demonstrators, separated from them by a four foot-high chain-link fence.

Count off twenty-eight seconds.

In that time, even as the students fled toward their dorms, more than 150 rounds of armor-piercing bullets and Double-O shotgun pellets raked the small area. No tear gas. No warning shots. No openly heard order to start firing.

Here is a portion of the report radioed back to headquarters by Inspector Lloyd Jones, commanding the contingent on the scene from the Mississippi Highway Safety Patrol:

I think there are about three more nigger males over there, one of 'em shot in the arm, one of 'em shot in the leg and one of 'em somewhere else. They ain't hurt all that bad. Them gals, it was two nigger gals . . . shot in the arm, I believe. . . . There are two nigger females and three males we just discovered, that's a total of 10. . . . Here's another one; let me see what this is. We got two students 10-7.

What 10-7 means over the lawman's radio in that Dixie city of 170,000, nearly half black, is "out of service," and what "out of service" means is dead. The Inspector was talking about Phillip Gibbs, a twenty-one-year-old junior with an eighteen-month-old son, and James Earl Green, seventeen, not a Jackson State student but a high school track star said to have been passing through the area on the way home from a side job.

What was the aftermath?

Outrage. Not clear across the landscape and in no way comparable with the uproar over the Kent State tragedy. Also, the usual postmortems. The FBI had a passel of agents scour that concrete campus. Two grand juries, one local and one federal, took testimony. Mayor Davis set up a biracial committee—three whites and two blacks—to look into the incident.

And what came of that frenzied flurry of activity?

Zero.

But President Nixon's Commission on Campus Unrest, headed by William W. Scranton, former governor of Pennsylvania and briefly a GOP presidential aspirant himself in 1964, also stepped into that bleak drama. And what emerged, on October 1, was a scathing eighty-six-page denunciation.

The commission found the lawmen not only guilty of "unreasonable, completely unwarranted and unjustified reaction" when they fired on the students but also guilty of all kinds of perjury in their reports on what happened. That second point is particularly in-

Two Jackson State coeds peer through window shot out by Mississippi police the night before, supposedly aiming at a "sniper" they could never prove even existed. *WWP*

teresting because Governor John Bell Williams had relied solely on his highway patrol's oral report on that one-sided battle when he went on TV June 4 with a complete whitewash of every last man involved in the bloodletting.

The key finds of the Scranton panel:

• The police testimony that they opened up only after "a colored male" broke a third-floor window in the dorm and shot twice at them was demonstrably false because FBI ballistics tests established that the window in question had been shattered by *incoming* bullets or shot-gun pellets fired from the ground. Moreover, the special sniper team had found no occasion to use their weapons at all.

• Police witnesses—and there were only two blacks out of a contingent of fifty-five, neither of whom used their weapons—lied not only to their superiors and the FBI but were responsible for "a number of inaccurate findings" by the county grand jury that cleared them.

• The police statements that they had confined their fire to the air to avert any casualties or at best confine them to a minimum were patently untrue because both fatalities died on the ground—one of

them *across the street* from the phantom sniper's position.

• Even if there had been sniper fire no case could be made for the assault force's use of bullets and buckshot instead of birdshot, which would have just as effectively broken up the demonstration, surely with fewer wounded and possibly with no dead. Item: Each load of Double-O buckshot carries the equivalent of nine .33 caliber bullets, "each of which travels along a different trajectory and can be lethal for a distance in excess of 40 yards."

• Apart from the missile hurling, termed minimal by the commission since no police injuries were reported, the spontaneous and undirected action of the lawmen appeared to have been spurred mainly by epithets like "pig" and "honky" and such reported rhetoric as "All the pigs will not walk away from the campus."

• The rifle and shotgun barrage stemmed at least in part from a combination of racial animosity "and the confidence of white officers that if they fire weapons during a black campus disturbance they will face neither stern departmental discipline nor criminal prosecution."

On that last point, the Jackson city fathers moved with due speed to prove the Scranton panel wrong with a firm pronouncement to the effect that any policemen found to have lied to the FBI or their own superiors on the "disturbance" in question would indeed face disciplinary action.

And how did it all end?

Another zero.

If a single officer was disciplined, then the form of it was too insignificant to generate any fat headlines.

And, unlike Kent State, nobody went to court to collect any cash damages. That would have been a loser's bet in any event, because both before and after the commission's report—bluntly dismissed as the work of "a kangaroo court" by Mississippi Attorney General A. F. Summer—the judgment of the white power structure in Jackson was firmly engraved on the record.

The police and highway patrolmen had conducted themselves in those early hours of May 18 strictly according to the procedures laid down in that Dixie stronghold in "riot" situations.

The wonder is that nobody picked up any decorations when all the noise died down.

THE STREAKERS

"Foreigners caught streaking will be deported in the nude," the vice president of Kenya, Daniel Moi, said today.

—AP dispatch from Nairobi in March 1974.

In Orwigsburg, Pennsylvania, the Reverend John Ness, Jr., posted a message for the streaking fraternity. That piece of madness was running its course by then in any case—and not a moment too soon. *WWP*

WE'RE STILL ON the campus here—on it and off it. The year is 1974. There is something going on in Washington, that little Watergate mess, but that's about all. The draft cards have all been burned. Vietnam and the "secret war" are both receding into bitter memory, that hard-won free speech is here to stay, and the Chinese wall separating the sexes in the dorms is about as impenetrable as the swinging door in the old-time saloons.

What, then, would an undergrad's fancy turn to for the rites of another Spring?

Streaking.

Take it all off and run.

Run past the coeds.

Run past the stuffy old prexy's house.

Run through the school cafeteria.

Run out and play in the traffic, or maybe even stop it.

That March, in a contagion akin only to the panty raids of the Fifties, streaking swept across the nation like a plague, sparing nothing in its barebacked assault on the silly convention that required the rest of us to keep our clothes on in public. Nothing. Not even the sacrosanct U. S. Military Academy. Not even

a Bible Belt college here or there. Certainly not the Ivy League.

How did that frolic start?

Here the historian runs into trouble.

There was a rumor that one hardy student made a nude dash across the University of Maryland campus in the preceeding November, but no eyewitness testimony emerged to support it. Perhaps the night was very dark. Small matter. The modern-day streaker—Adam had to be the first, no?—came in with the chill winds of March. The first week of that month had barely expired before all kinds of records were being claimed, led by the University of Colorado, where no fewer that 1,200 youths went for a fast sprint around the quad in their birthday suits. At Columbia University, backed up by an Ad-Hoc Streaking Band, a bare twenty freshmen went those Colorado kids one better. They assembled before the Sun Dial at 11:15 A.M. (some of the more modest types wore hats to go with their sneakers), raced around the steps of the Low Library, clambered aboard the Alma Mater statue for a photographic session and then scooted across Broadway to display their wares to the girls at Barnard. That romp caused something of a traffic problem, naturally, but the police simply waved the cars along until the freshmen—briefly joined by one Barnard coed—went back to their own turf and got dressed. Dr. William J. McGill, the school's president, took no disciplinary action, simply looking down his nose and remarking, "If these tactics are getting Columbia exposure, it's indecent exposure." At Princeton three streakers flashed through a classroom where a lecture on Roman history was in progress. At Harvard a lone streaker passed out leaflets in support of a new campus organization called FUDA, which stood for Fully Clothed Dashing Activists. "We have nothing to hide," the leaflet said. At Ole Miss, the new campus sport drew a strong denunciation from Governor Bill Waller, who proclaimed that "lewd exposure" could not be tolerated in the Magnolia State. At Eden College, a Presbyterian school in North Carolina, scores of streakers descended on the coed dorms crying "Take if off! Take it off!"—and a handful of the girls obliged. At the University of the South, an Episcopal bastion in Tennessee, three students made a naked run through the library. At West Point, dozens of cadets, some wearing neckties so they wouldn't be completely naked, romped across the post in the buff with some of the more stodgy officers in full pursuit. The plebes escaped punishment, whereas at New York's Fordham University a threat of instant suspension was posted after a trio of jaybirds displayed their wares in a tree outside one of the women's dorms.

Inevitably, the troubled political scene reared its ugly head. At Fairleigh Dickinson in Rutherford, New Jersey, a dozen students staged a "Streak for Impeachment"—an idle exercise with Mr. Nixon's voluntary if reluctant departure from the White House not far off.

Before it departed the campus scene, doomed to linger down to this day only as a permanent one-night spring ritual at Okahoma State University in Stillwater, the bareback craze swiftly spread to the world without, with the most spectacular incident adding a touch of spice to the Academy Awards ceremony in the Los Angeles Music Center. Offering his wares in full color not just before that always elegantly posh audience but seventy-six million NBC-TV viewers as well, Robert Opel, a thirty-five-year-old press agent without any clients, took it all off and

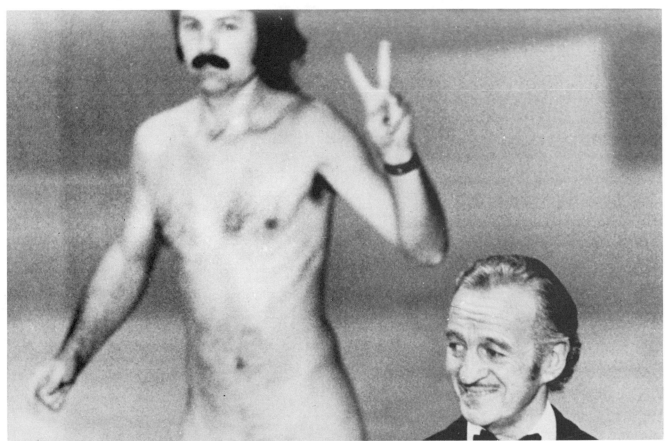

The high moment of the streakers' year: Robert Opel crosses the stage as David Niven is about to bring on Elizabeth Taylor at the 1974 Academy Awards dinner. Live and in color for 76 million television viewers. *WWP*

Part of a group of forty University of California at Los Angeles students who went to the undress bit to stir up some interest in an upcoming basketball game against USC. *WWP*

scampered across the stage of the Chandler Pavilion while David Niven was about to bring on Elizabeth Taylor to present the Oscar for *The Sting* as 1973's best film. The gentleman from the Mother Country, his suave manner intact, took it in stride, observing that it was "bound to happen" and adding rather acerbicly that "the only laugh that man will ever get in his life is stripping off his pants and showing his shortcomings." And from Miss Taylor: "That is a pretty hard act to follow. I'm nervous. That really upset me. I think I'm jealous." The star had no trouble, however, delivering the gold for the Paul Newman–Robert Redford movie.

As for Mr. Opel, that nude fling went unpunished—but not the next one. Arguing for nude beaches at a hearing in the L. A. City Hall, he doffed his blue track suit to make his point more forcibly, and that cost him four months in jailhouse denim.

The green playing fields weren't spared either. In Cincinnati's Riverfront Stadium, on the very day in March when the Atlanta Braves' Henry Aaron hit his 714th home run to tie Babe Ruth's record, a youth in

the upper left-field bleachers doffed all his garments and proceeded to jump up and down in the aisle. Needless to say, that character picked the wrong day for his brief moment in the sun. The Aaron feat drew all the ink while the stationary streaker attracted nothing but some police attention.

The Yankees ran into a more flagrant problem on their opening day in Shea Stadium, their temporary home in 1974, when Joseph Fleming, twenty-four, a beer truck driver, left his clothes in the stands and flashed across the infield. Nailed by a security guard, the youth was charged with disorderly conduct and criminal trespass and drew a sentence of fifteen days in jail or a $150 fine from a Queens Supreme Court Justice, M. Marvin Berger. Even worse, Fleming had to wade his way through an eleven-page decision in which the judge dug all the way back to ancient Greek times to satisfy himself that while the athletes of yore often performed with no more than a girdle around their loins there was nothing in our modern-day law that endowed nudity on a baseball diamond with any legal authority.

The green playing fields weren't spared, either. This is a non-college type braving a 38-degree April day to swing from the scoreboard during a Yankees-Tigers game in Detroit. *WWP*

Streaking also went classical that year on a rather special night when Rudolf Nureyev and the Royal Ballet were performing at New York's Metropolitan Opera House. While our gift from the Soviets was resting his feet and two young dancers were making their debuts a naked girl traipsed across the stage for a debut of her own. The Met would never be the same again after that.

And oh, yes, the fad took to the air, too. A man in his early thirties repaired to one of the numerous rest rooms on a Pan American 747 jet headed to London from New York, emerged in nothing more than his beard, and sprinted the length of the giant aircraft and back. There was no punishment to fit that infraction, of course, since it would be poor form for an airline to drop a paying fare into the Atlantic.

To get back to the educational foundries, there was no shortage of long-haired views on the whys and wherefors of the undress bit. First, no less an authority than Marshall McLuhan, the communications theo-

rist and director of the Center for Culture and Technology at the University of Toronto:

"Streaking is a put-on, a form of assault. It's an art form, of course. All entertainment has elements of malice and power in it. Streaking has a political point, too. It's a form of activism."

The professor threw in a touch of linguistics as well, observing that streakers may be nude but they're never naked. "It's only when you don't want to be seen that you're naked," said the author of *The Medium Is the Massage*. "A stripper backstage is naked, but when she is in front of an audience she is wearing her public." Your author leaves it to you to work on that one.

Dr. Robert J. Lifton, a Yale psychiatry professor, found a place for streaking in college tradition—"a challenge to authority and a mockery of authority" with touches of "the sexual revolution and sexual mores" at its roots. The doctor went further: "There are three things I'm sure it's not. It's not a return to the Fifties, it's not a sign of the corruption of American morality and it's not a threat to national security."

While that must have warmed a good many of the more timorous adult hearts in the time of Watergate, Dr. David Abrahamsen, a Manhattan psychoanalyst, put forth a more elementary view of the streaking fraternity. He said the young'uns were simply "trying to liberate themselves" after a "long winter without sexual outlets." What had made the preceding winter such a difficult time for the boys and girls to get together in the hay was not clear, but one had to listen to Dr. Abrahamsen. He was the author of ten books by then and his big one, *Nixon Vs. Nixon: An Emotional Tragedy*, in which he would manage to probe the depths of the busted President's mind without ever having the man on his couch or even listening to his extensive tape collection, was still to come.

Part XII

THE POP SCENE

THE NEW DANCE:

No Hands

"In my day, not only did boys and girls dance
together but you could tell at a glance
which was which."
— BENNY GOODMAN, 1966

ON HIS NATIVE soil in Abilene on May 2, 1962, Dwight D. Eisenhower made the dedication address for the Eisenhower Library, and he spoke these words:

> We venerate the pioneers who fought droughts and floods, isolation and Indians, to come to Kansas and westward to settle into their homes, to till the soil and raise their families. We think of their sturdiness, their self-reliance, their faith in God. We think of their glorious pride in America. Now, I wonder if some of these people could come back today and see us doing the Twist instead of the Minuet—whether they would be particularly struck by the beauty of that dance?

The former President said he had "no objection to the Twist as such" but went on to equate the new dance craze with the "vulgarity, sensuality, indeed downright filth" then rampant, as he saw it, in the movies, on the stage and in books and magazines. Along the way, he took a sideswipe at Pop Art, finally asking:

"What has happened to our concept of beauty and decency and morality?"

There was instant reaction, some of it angry, on the dance front.

From Janet Huffsmith, twenty-one, of New York's Peppermint Lounge, the Twist's shrine: "Eisenhower? Man, he's a square." From Marlene Klair, eighteen, a co-worker of Miss Huffsmith's: "Does Ike twist? Like if he doesn't twist I don't think he knows how to dance the Minuet either." From Meyer Davis, titan of the society bands: "The Minuet is completely divorced from what people want to do, from the tempo of the times. It's too conservative, too slow. The Twist has action." From Mrs. Horace E. Dodge of the automobile millions: "Moral decline? Some days are emotionally sunny when all's right with the world. Other days are gloomier. I think Ike just had a bad day. The Twist has brought fun and gaiety into people's lives."

And sex? Dr. Albert Ellis, author of such works as *An Encyclopedia of Sexual Behavior* and *The Folklore of Sex,* ventured into the Peppermint Lounge and came away with this pronouncement on the Twist:

> There is sex implied in it but it is not a social sex urge. The sex image is confined to the indi-

vidual. The partner might as well be a post. There is some stimulation from the dance but I don't believe it often leads to consummation. They must be too tired.

The psychologist concluded that the new dance craze represented nothing more than a return to the African ceremonial dances of yore and would disappear in no time at all.

Disappear? There were learned examinations of the thing still going on in 1967. Thus Edward M. Levine, Associate Professor of Political Science at the Illinois Institute of Technology, writing for the *Israel Annals of Psychiatry,* found that people do the Twist because they are "anxiously in search of, or uncertain about, their identity as individuals." And that's not all. "The music, rhythm, volume and tempo," the professor went on, "all converge to obliterate pulsating and deeply felt sensuality. An extremely eroticized sense of self-awareness is quickly aroused, as all else recedes into oblivion. Small wonder, then, that the dance is often characterized by orgastic movements and by flights into auto-erotic sensations. Almost wholly unfettered in its stimulation of the emotions, the Twist induces emotional introversion."

Marshall Fishwick, professor of American studies at Washington and Lee University in Lexington, Virginia, offered an explanation for the "Brave New Whirl" in the *Saturday Review.* "The Twist," said the professor, "is a valid manifestation of the Age of Anxiety; an outward manifestation of the anguish, frustration and uncertainty of the 1960's; an effort to release one of the tensions which, if suppressed and buried, could warp and destroy." Gerald Sykes, critic and novelist on the faculty of Columbia University's School of General Studies, singled out the Frug, one of the Twist's early offshoots, and attributed it to man's loss of separateness in what he termed our increasingly homogenized world. He noted that in the Frug, which could be danced alone (just swing your hips from side to side and throw your arms backward and forward or from side to side around your waist, or something), the emphasis is not on sex, which implies participation with someone else, but on the ego, and concluded that we were all doing that dance as a sheer gesture of independence. And where do you suppose Professor Sykes offered this observation? At a learned symposium at the Center for the Study of Democratic Institutions in Santa Barbara, California, in 1965.

As far as the Twist's origins went, Dr. Ellis had some support from the very youth taxed with in-

Mr. Checker: from the chicken market to the heights.

flicting it on the nation. "Take a look at some of those old TV shows like *Ramar of the Jungle,*" said Chubby Checker. "The natives have been doing something like the Twist for years."

Chubby Checker, for the record, was born Ernest Evans Jr. in Philadelphia, son of a stevedore and a seamstress. An industrious little fat boy, he worked in a chicken market from sunup until the school bell rang at 8:00 o'clock and then returned to his labors from 3:30 P.M. to 7:30, contributing his twenty-five-dollar paycheck to the family. Happily, the 220-pound Ernest could also dance and sing like anything, and

Hank Ballard (left), doing his thing at New York's Roundtable, was first with the Twist, but Chubby Checker's version two years later touched off the revolution in dance. *New York Post*

his employers, Henry Colt and part-time music man Kal Mann, had the good sense to get him a recording date. What came out was the Twist. Actually, Hank Ballard had recorded a Twist number down in Atlanta two years earlier, in 1959, but it was Checker's version—and his live performances on TV—that got the dance off the ground. It got Chubby—and, indeed, Colt and Mann—out of the chicken market, too. The boy's earnings reached close to a million dollars before he was twenty-one. And for what? *Anybody* could twist. Chubby himself, now below the 200-pound mark as a result of his strenuous exertions, explained how simple it was. "The first position of the stance is like a boxer's. Then you move your hips like you're wiping yourself with a towel. Your body goes back and forth in one direction and your hands go in the other direction. From that point on you ad-lib energetically." Never touching your partner, of course.

While Chubby credited *Ramar of the Jungle, Life* magazine, simply disgusted, traced the Twist to the Middle Ages, observing that in those times the plague-ridden people tried to shake off their worries in a "dancing madness" which only served to leave them prostrate. The same analogy, you will recall, was made when the marathon dances had their brief moment of fame in this country. But never mind *Life*'s short view. The weekly bulletin of the University of Ottawa went a little farther back and found the Twist in the writings of St. John Chrysostom, circa 390: "Dancing women roll their eyes, wave their hands and describe circles with their feet; they twist their whole body." The weekly recorded this bit of information under the heading *Nihil Novi Sub Sole*— there is nothing new under the sun. Another scholarly source traced the dance even further back, noting that 300 years before Christ the Greeks were doing something called the Cordax. In that one, the partners went through all kinds of wild gyrations while passing a rope back and forth. The story was that the dance made its way to pagan Rome, where it shook up Cicero no end when he found the younger set cordaxing—there's a word—at his wedding feast.

New or old, but relentlessly pushed on television and radio by such darlings of the younger generation as Dick Clark, Clay Cole and Murray the K, the dance swept the nation like a prairie fire, spawning the inevitable commercial binge. After a while you could buy Twist chairs, Twist hats, Twist shoes, Twist pajamas, Twist cuff links, Twist candy (nothing new there), Twist dresses ($5.99 at Gimbels), Twist belts and, of course, Twist garters. The beauty salons got on the bandwagon too, with a Twist hairdo. And the wild new American invention soon went around the world. Egypt's Nasser banned it as some kind of dangerous invention. President Sukarno of Indonesia, resting a bit more securely on his throne in those days, threatened to arrest anybody caught doing the Twist "at a time when our revolution is heightening and we are mobilizing our potentials." Saigon outlawed not only the dance but what passed for the music. In Formosa, the dancing schools were told to stick to ballet and folk dancing and never mind that wicked American thing. The Twist was also declared illegal in Beirut, Lebanon, but the police didn't do anything about it because they were never quite certain what it was when they saw people doing it.

The Soviets, of course, carried on the most heated debates. Igor Moiseyev, Russia's leading choreographer, said the Twist "expressed dirty feelings and dirty instincts." Yevgeny Yevtushenko, the rebellious poet, demurred and said he saw no real differences in the dances of the socialist and capitalist worlds. That was in 1962. Four years later, the argument was still going on over there. Tikhon Khrennikov, head of the Composers Union, charged in *Izvestia* that the Twist represented "bourgeois decadence" at its very worst and could never inspire heroic deeds in the Socialist state. *Komsomolskaya Pravda,* the Communist youth paper, quoted Pia and Aare Erb, the Estonian ballroom dancers, in reply: "Bourgeois dances like the Twist and the Shake should be performed by the young, not banned. Bans lead to vulgarization and parody."

On this side, inevitably, the Twist was banished in a scattered few places. In 1962 it was ruled out of all Catholic schools and parishes in Buffalo, New York, on the grounds of decorum and taste, and Tampa, Florida, declared it off limits in its community centers. The dance also drew some official attention on at least one other level. In Syracuse, New York, the widow of an auto salesman who died of a heart attack after twisting at a company party sued for workmen's compensation under the state law and won it. The ruling, in essence, was that the man had laid down his life in the line of duty.

The Twist in time gave birth to a whole variety of kindred dances—the Mashed Potato, the Pony, the Mess Around, the Majestic Slop, the Jerk, the Swim, the Mule, the Fly, the Monkey (make like you're climbing a tree), the Boston Monkey (just keep both feet still and shake the hips and hands), the Philly Dog, the Watusi, the Hully Gully and the Chicken Back. And it gave birth, for better or worse, to something new on the nightclub scene—the discothèque (record library), borrowed from the French.

In the early discothèques in New York, such as Oleg Cassini's Le Club, L'Interdit in the cellar of the Gotham Hotel and Shepheard's at the Drake, the dancers could contort themselves until unconscious to the overamplified sound of recorded music, but after a while most of the owners found it advisable to bring in live music and alternate it with the much more economic wax platters. In this process, by way of an incidental item in history, Sybil Burton, the silver-haired Welsh woman Richard abandoned for Elizabeth Taylor, acquired a new husband—Jordan Christopher, né Zankoff, son of a Macedonian tavern operator back in Akron, Ohio. The romance flowered while the twenty-five-year old youth was playing the electric guitar and shaking a tambourine in front of a Rock 'n' Roll combination called The Wild Ones in Arthur, the discothèque Mrs. Burton opened on the East Side of Manhattan in 1965 after wiggling her hips through the long hours in everybody else's joint.

Arthur established itself overnight as the new shrine of the Twist. It was so *in* that you needed a connection to get in; once Rock Hudson himself couldn't get by the muscular doorkeepers. Those who did make the sacred portals on any given night might be privileged, on the jam-packed dance floor, to bump against such diverse personalities as ex-King Peter of Yugoslavia, Sammy Davis Jr., Hope Hampton, Princess Lee Radziwill (and on at least one occasion her sister Jacqueline Kennedy), Leonard Bernstein, Anne Ford, Lynda Bird Johnson (complete with her non-Twisting escorts from Father's Secret Service), Lauren Bacall, Rudolf Nureyev of the Royal Ballet, Truman Capote, Carol Channing, Tennessee Williams, and the Republican Senator from New York, Jacob Javits, whose wife, Marion, will frug on a split second's notice. For that matter, you might even see the Democratic Senator, Robert Kennedy, some night when Ethel wasn't having a baby. Now if there are perchance any names in this galaxy that come as a shock to people who regard the dances of the Sixties with disdain, bear in mind that when the Right Rev. James A. Pike was the Episcopal Bishop of California he had a fling at the Twist himself during a church social out there. And the Bishop wasn't flouting Dwight Eisenhower alone. No less a social arbiter than Elsa Maxwell, since removed from this vale of bad manners, had cited Princess Olga of Yugoslavia as her authority for the view that the Twist by its very orgiastic nature should be reserved for private parties and never, but never, danced in public places.

Sybil Burton, who didn't need the money, wasn't the only person enriched overnight by the new dance craze. Frank (Killer Joe) Piro emerged as one of the most sought-after dance-masters in the land, putting the likes of Arthur Murray and Fred Astaire in the shadows. As a teen-ager, Piro won the National Jitterbugging Contest in the New York *Daily News's* Harvest Moon Ball—the only non-Negro who ever could claim that distinction. Back from wartime duty in the Pacific with the Coast Guard, Killer Joe, a five-foot-six-inch whirling dynamo with the face of your friendly neighborhood pizza chef, served as Master of Ceremonies at New York's Palladium dance hall and taught such dances as the Rumba, Cha-Cha, Meringue and Pachanga until he had enough of a stake to open his own studio and walk away from his other career as a plastics designer. When the Peppermint Lounge opened, he turned up as the Twister without peer, and in no time at all the Jet Set was banging on his

Killer Joe Piro, who found a big-money career in the Twist and its assorted variations, showing Luci Baines Johnson how to do the Watusi. *Washington Post*

Carol Channing, star of Broadway's *Hello, Dolly!*, doing the Twist at a Washington party with Henry H. Fowler, Secretary of the Treasury in the Johnson cabinet.

door. His fame, indeed, spread to such a degree that a ballad about him turned up in Julius Monk's satirical review at the Plaza—

> *Killer taught the Duke of Windsor*
> *How to Slop and how to Bug,*
> *At the Waldorf, in the foyer,*
> *Where there wasn't any rug.*
> *He showed Lady Milford-Haven*
> *How to Undulate her spleen,*
> *And Baroda's Maharani*
> *Is a Hully-Gully queen!* *

There was more hard truth than satire in that one, for Killer Joe's clientele did indeed include those cited in the lyrics, as well as Windsor's Duchess ("I think I'm too old for it, but it's very good exercise"), Dame Margot Fonteyn, ballerina Alicia Markova, Sybil Burton herself, that swingin' Adlai Stevenson when he was Ambassador to the United Nations, Luci Baines Johnson (with *her* Secret Service men), Mrs.

---

* From "The Saga of Killer Joe," from Julius Monk's "Plaza 9" review, *Pick a Number.* Lyrics by Nelson Garringer, music by Fred Silver.

Vincent Astor, Joseph E. Levine, the portly movie baron, Marlon Brando, Eva Gabor (Zsa Zsa didn't need any help, presumably), Shirley Booth, Hedda Hopper, Googie Withers (look, that's her name), the Duke and Duchess of Bedford and Ray Bolger, who must be listed here as another dancer of note. Jackie Kennedy not only took some lessons from Mr. Piro but had him preside over the dance floor when she threw a party for the Beautiful People, as her set is known, at New York's Sign of the Dove in 1966. Impressed? Hell, Arthur Schlesinger Jr. summoned the Killer to one of *his* parties. So did Elizabeth Arden—and the man's fees for gracing the more private bashes run all the way from $1,000 to $5,000 a night.

What with this assortment of customers, compounded by juicy commercial contracts for endorsements and such simple chores as inventing dances like the Smirnoff Mule for the vodka people and The Shake for one of the blue jean cartels, Killer Joe, son of an East Harlem tailor, was able to pick up the *Wall Street Journal* one day and read this: "The dancer seems assured of becoming a millionaire before long."

He could never have made it on the slow Minuet.

Since this chapter opened with the assault aimed at the Twist by General Eisenhower, it must be noted that few of the dances of modern times—let's say anything arriving after Ike's Minuet—escaped censure in one form or another. The Reverend Billy Sunday denounced the Tango in 1915 as "the most hellish institution that ever wriggled from the depths of perdition." Around the same time, the Mayor of Boston, John "Honey Fitz" Fitzgerald, grandfather of John F. Kennedy, banned the Turkey Trot, the Bunny Hug, the Grizzly Bear and everything else he could find that was danced to ragtime. In the Twenties, the United Dancing Masters of America, in convention assembled, debated whether that wicked new Charleston was too vulgar to deserve official recognition, and the *Catholic Telegraph* of Cincinnati carried this description of the Fox Trot: "The music is sensuous—the female only half-dressed. [It] is absolutely indecent; and the motions—they are such as may not be described. . . . Suffice it to say that there are certain houses appropriate for such dances; but those houses have been closed by law." In the Thirties, the Big Apple came out of an obscure Negro nightclub in Columbia, South Carolina, and suddenly was the rage, from the campus to the ballroom. One critic insisted that it combined all the worst elements of the Charleston, Black Bottom, Truckin', Suzy Q, Shag, Virginia Reel, Paul Jones and Schottische, and eventually it inspired so much discussion that it came up in a White House press conference. Did Franklin Delano Roosevelt have a position on the Big Apple or didn't he? The President took no sides. He said the thing was interesting but lacked rhythm. In the Forties, the nation began to jitterbug in zoot suits and the ensuing fuss reached all the way to the academic halls. This statement came from Fritz Redl of the School of Public Affairs and Social Work at Detroit's Wayne University:

This photo by Ollie Atkins won the White House Photographers Association's annual award for 1943, but Henry A. Wallace, FDR's Vice President, making the presentation, said the prize should have gone to something more consequential than a picture of a zoot suiter and his partner. *WWP*

The phenomenon is not entirely new. It has developed out of groups whose main objective was enjoyment of expressional orgies. Recently, in some places, the phenomenon has changed somewhat and assumed more epidemic forms. This means an increase not only in participation but also in vehemence and intensity. In some places and at certain times, the original basis of dance enjoyment seems to be brushed aside by an interest in tough-guy behavior, in alcoholic excesses and in rebelliously manifested freedom of inhibition in social relations with the other sex. It is, as yet, very hard to define just how much of this gang formational change is characteristic of the total movement, to what degree and where.

Professor Max Schoen of Carnegie Tech put forth a more philosophical view:

People have been jitterbugging, in some form or another, ever since they wore leopard skins and carried clubs. There is a deep-seated urge to revert to the primitive and the infantile behind every jitterbug. . . . For a few minutes they revert to live with their primitive ancestors and become a bundle of primary emotions and intense activity. After the spasm is over, they are right back in modern times and thirsty for an ice cream soda.

There was a war on then, of course, and the government was more concerned about the jitterbugs' manner of dress than the dance itself. The War Production Board's textile division protested that the zoot suit was "wasting a large amount of fabric that ought to be saved for our soldiers and for necessary civilian clothing."

The WPB offered this definition so that the masses would understand the problem: "A zoot suit in the parlance of the needle nuts and gandy dancers is a creation also known as a 'solid set of threads.' In order to be right with the rags, a hep cat has to have a jacket reaching approximately three inches above the knees." That wasn't all. The "solid set of threads" also had to have a three-inch overhang in the shoulders and cuffs twelve inches wide, so there truly was an awful lot of good cloth being worn away on dance-hall floors in a period of short supply.

Jitterbugging, like the Twist later with its broken ankles and slipped discs, produced its share of physical damage. In 1951, a widow in Detroit won a $7,145 judgment from an Arthur Murray dance studio there because she broke an arm doing the frenzied step. The plaintiff, fifty-four years old, was able to prove that one of the studio's instructors had talked her into trying it in the first place. The assumption

Today it's the Hustle. That's Margaret Trudeau, the young wife who walked out on Canadian Prime Minister Pierre Trudeau, teaming up with tennis star Vitas Gerulaitis at New York's Studio 54 in 1977.

here has to be that this woman later turned to the more conservative dances. Like the Minuet, perhaps.

For the rest of us, it went the other way.

Today, in the burgeoning new discotheques everywhere, it's the Hustle, where you touch your partner and all that, like in the good old days before the Twist. There are so many wrinkles to the Hustle—fancy dips, swings, spins—that you need an M.I.T. degree to master the new form. Maybe it's worth it all, since it's the first dance since the cha-cha of the Fifties were you can really get to know the other party. But then there are those who say it's just a variation on the Lindy Hop and those others who say it's something the gays invented. The fact is, it's danced to a mambo beat and the more earnest historians say it originated with the high-stepping Latins in New York. The Hustle and its offspring, the Rope, some kind of nonsense in which you swing your arms until they fall off, is so hot now that you have to stand on line at the dance studios for a lesson that may cost $7 to $9 a shot.

But for the late General of the Armies all hope is not lost. There's also a thing called the Walk now, and in that one, said to have enjoyed its birth on the West Coast, you don't touch the material. Whole armies can do the Walk. It's just a matter of traipsing back and forth in a series of complicated steps. Against the Hustle, of course, the Walk must count on a short life at best. Taking into account the high tabs in the current discos, a man has a right to get acquainted with the woman of his choice—even if it's his own wife.

Lillian (Miz) Carter, the President's mother, drops into Studio 54 for a spot of dancing (no, not the Hustle) at a benefit for the United Nations Children's Fund (UNICEF). *WWP*

The new disco scene brought some wacky no-limit fashions with it. *WWP*

THE BIG BEAT:

Rock 'n' Roll Came to Stay

Disc jockey Alan Freed was the bellringer for the Rock 'n' Roll revolution, only to be brought down by a payola scandal. *New York Post*

"It is easier to understand a nation by listening to its music than learning its language."

—ANON

IT WAS A mixed broth of the songs men chanted on railroad gangs or chain gangs or on the plantations which held them in bondage, with a touch of the spirituals that rocked the store-front churches of the black ghettos and a little "pleasure" music thrown in. It swelled up from the fields and the levees of the Delta after the Civil War, and they called it the Blues because they had the blues in abundance—"the low-down blues, the dirty mistreated blues, the broke and hungry blues, the loveless blues, the evil-hearted blues," as Alan Lomax said it so well. In time it all came together in Storyville, the New Orleans red-light district, and the name was Dixieland Jazz. But the police padlocked the temples of flesh and the wilder watering places in 1917 and the men who made the music there, men like Jelly Roll Morton, Sidney Bechet, Bunk Johnson and the young Louis Armstrong, had to pick up and follow the Mississippi to that "toddlin' town" to earn their bread. Then it was Chicago Jazz, black and white playing together, and after a while it moved to the Big Apple, New York, and it was just Jazz. In the Thirties, a man with a hot clarinet, Benny Goodman, began to play some sweet variations on it, and the word—put to music by Duke Ellington—was that "It don't mean a thing if you ain't got that Swing." Within another decade, the inventive Dizzy Gillespie was blowing strange new sounds on his trumpet and Be-Bop enjoyed a brief vogue. Gillespie wasn't alone, of course; the ill-starred Charlie Parker, called Yardbird, and Lester Young, called Prez, also were blowing pretty good in those trail-blazing days.

And then—

Rock 'n' Roll, the new beat and the ultimate mixture—back to the Blues, back to Country Western and Rhythm-and-Blues, back to the gospel shouters (listen to the great Mahalia Jackson's "He Said He Would" and the Soul music of Ray Charles's "Bye Bye Love" and see how far apart they are). When R & R came clattering on the scene, accompanied by a riot or two as the kids lost their heads, the purists put it down as another ridiculous musical fad which would consume the know-nothing young briefly and then disappear into limbo. How wrong they were. A quarter of a century later the Big Beat is still the thing. Hell, it has even outlived the very man who christened it and got if off the ground.

Alan Freed, born in Ohio, son of a clothing store

clerk, attended Ohio State University for two years, played the trombone out there and led a band called the Sultans of Swing. He broke into radio in New Castle, Pennsylvania, as the announcer on a longhair program that leaned heavily on Wagner (he said he was hung up on the *Ring*) with touches of Bach, Brahms, Beethoven and Tchaikovsky. Then he went to Cleveland, and in 1952, behind a hard sell that might as well have been fired out of a machine gun, started playing the race records of such little-known singers as Chuck Berry, Bo Diddley, Muddy Waters and John Lee Hooker. He borrowed a recurring, sex-orientated phrase from the Rhythm-and-Blues people and called it Rock 'n' Roll. For those who might have been a little slow in getting around to it, Bill Haley and His Comets arrived with a thunderbolt-style recording of "Rock Around the Clock" which reached for the libido in the plainest terms and proved to be inescapable either in the most remote American hamlet or the farthest reaches of the outside world. A quickie movie built around the song inspired wild disorders wherever it was shown.

Radio Station WINS brought the gravel-voiced Freed to New York four years later and he became the darling of the burgeoning teen-age musical underground, the Pied Piper of Rock. The revolution was going into high gear, and it burst wide open in the spring of 1956 when Elvis Presley turned up first on the Dorsey Brothers CBS-TV show and then on Milton Berle's NBC program and was permitted to wiggle his narrow hips with what some segments of the viewing population considered far too much abandon for the home screen. The ensuing storm of protest plastered R & R all over the front pages. In Atlanta, the police ruled that teen-agers could not dance to it in public without written parental consent. Asbury Park, New Jersey, barred all R & R after a Convention Hall riot sent twenty-five teen-agers to hospitals. In New York, a vocational high school suspended sixty students for daring to infuse that dull "Star-Spangled Banner" with the new beat. In Boston, Catholic leaders called for a boycott, and there was a movement afoot to appoint a music censor (they had every other kind up there). In the nation's capital, an R & R show in the National Guard Armory ended up in a free-for-all, so the police asked the Commanding General not to rent his military playpen to the new-breed musical entrepreneurs anymore.

The ensuing debate touched all the levels of our culture, from the lawmakers to the music makers to the head doctors and the courts to the racists. A Senate subcommittee talked about looking into the dark links between R & R and juvenile delinquency. Frank

Sinatra, not exactly high on the loud and lusty new singers, assailed R & R as "the martial music of every sideburned delinquent on the face of the earth" (how could the man know then that his own daughter Nancy was going to dig the Big Beat when she grew up and started to sing?).

Mitch Miller, the bearded master of pop, was bland but icy. "You can't call any music immoral," he said. "If anything is wrong with Rock 'n' Roll, it is that it makes a virtue out of monotony." Alfred D. Buchmueller, executive director of the Child Study Association of America, conceded that "kids, just like adults, get caught up in a mass kind of hysteria which is contagious" and that "some get hurt by it, physically and emotionally," but he cautioned parents that they could do more harm than good by taking too strong a stand against R & R. Judge Hilda Schwartz of New York's Adolescent Court denied that the new sound was in itself producing delinquency, but added, "for the disturbed, hostile and insecure youth, the stimulation of this frenzied, abandoned music certainly can't be therapy."

Dr. Philip Solomon of Harvard demurred. As a psychiatrist, he saw R & R as a healthy outlet "for restlessness, for unexpressed and sublimated sex desires." Dr. Jane Vorhaus Gang, a New York psychiatrist, had an even more benign view. "The teen-ager," she said, "is entitled to be young." *Look* magazine also was prompted to rise to the defense: "Rock 'n' Roll is a fad and eventually will be absorbed in the mainstream of American popular music. Is it music or

Few white performers hit the rock scene with the wallop of Bill Haley and His Comets. His "Rock Around the Clock," featured in the worldwide hit movie by that name, was practically the anthem of the Big Beat for quite a while.

madness? Perhaps it is a little of both. But it is no closer to insanity than those who attack it—or any form of musical expression—as morally bad."

From the South, predictably, there were anguished wails. Asa E. (Ace) Carter, head of the White Citizens Council in Northern Alabama, saw great peril for Dixie in the "Negro music" which, he said, "brings out animalism and vulgarity." Carter blamed the National Association for the Advancement of Colored People for Rock 'n' Roll and, for that matter, for all jazz, sensing somewhere, somehow a "plot to mongrelize America." That man wasn't too hip; he didn't understand that R & R, kicked off by the early race records, had become "white" music, leaving the exclusively Negro field to such items as the Soul sound of Mr. Charles. From Britain, witnessing its first R & R riots, along with Norway, Melbourne, Malaya and other distant way stations, symphony conductor Malcolm Sargent wrote off the Big Beat with total disdain. "It is nothing more than an exhibition of primitive tom-tom thumping," said Sir Malcolm, while the Lord Chamberlain, Britain's stage censor, banned a religious play which used R & R for background and portrayed Christ as a teen-ager in blue jeans.

Alan Freed, riding higher and higher even as an army of 3,500 disc jockeys around the nation began to walk in his footsteps and Dick Clark's *American Bandstand* cornered the TV market in Rock, coined big money in personal appearances with R & R stars until his screaming followers got out of hand and began to tear things—including the police—apart. In Boston, this sort of thing not only got Freed banned but indicted as well. It happened after 7,200 of his fans, roughly handled when they started dancing in the aisles of the Boston Arena, burst into the streets on a wild rampage. For the defense, no advocates arose in adequate haste to point out that the men and women who brought forth those children had themselves flipped once not only for some crooners—Rudy Vallee, Bing Crosby, Mr. Sinatra—but even for the sweet, soothing Swing of Benny Goodman, or that Orpheus had to flee from the wigged-out females when he turned on that hot lyre of his in ancient Greece. No, the watchdogs in Boston dug up an old anarchy statute and charged Freed with "unlawfully, wickedly and maliciously" inciting a riot. The case was dropped after a while but the incident caused other cities to cancel scheduled Freed "concerts." This dented the disc jockey's purse, but larger troubles lay ahead. The television quiz show scandal touched off an investigation of "payola" among the record spinners, and

Freed as well as Clark, not just the very image of the boy next door but so antiseptic you would hock the family jewels for the nuptials if he asked for your best daughter's hand, were caught up in it.

Clark, affirming that he never took a tainted dollar but simply had acquired some fairly lucrative business interests along the way, did his penance by fading from the scene until the odor of the scandal wafted away. Today he's back among the little screen's tall men. His "American Bandstand" is on the air again and he's also your host on one of TV's endlessly proliferating game shows—"The $20,000 Pyramid." In 1978 NBC starred him in a special called "Dick Clark's Good Old Days" (and weren't they good indeed?) filled with nostalgia from the Fifties and early Sixties. This was followed with "Dick Clark's Live Wednesday," a variety show that had the NBC flacks talking about their new boy—older, wiser and just as pretty as ever—as the new Ed Sullivan even before it hit the airwaves. That one, alas, failed to collect the kind of ratings it needed to get renewed into the 1979 season, but do not brood for Dick Clark. Apart from his TV labors, he has now been called upon to rescue the Westchester Premier Theater, a 3,500-seat showcase fallen not only upon hard times but bankruptcy as well amidst government charges that Mafia types had dipped too deeply into the till. Even as seven of the theatre's ex-operators were winning a mistrial on fraud charges, the bank stuck with the mortgage on the Tarrytown, New York, entertainment palace engaged Dick Clark Presentations to take it over with an option to buy the whole thing for between $3 million and $4 million.

With Alan Freed, it was quite another story. WABC fired that record spinner in 1959 for refusing to swear in writing that he had never taken money or gifts to plug records; later WNEW-TV dropped him in the same kind of argument.

The worst was yet to come. In 1960, Freed was indicted on a charge of having accepted $30,650 from six record companies for pushing their releases on the air. He denied it, insisting that it wasn't payola but fees for "services rendered" as a consultant. "This is the backbone of American business," he said; but he changed his mind about that line when the case came to court, pleading guilty in return for a six-month suspended sentence and a $300 fine. Later he was indicted on charges of evading payment of taxes on $37,920 worth of payola, but fate spared the dishonored prophet of the Big Beat.

In sunny exile in Palm Springs, Freed died early in 1965, a victim of uremia at forty-three. He left his

ers, The Shirelles, The Supremes (the gospel-tinted Detroit sound), The Impressions (the Chicago Sound), The Four Seasons, The Four Tops, The Lovin' Spoonful, The Mamas and the Papas, The Monkees, The Miracles, Sam the Sham and the Pharaohs. On top of all those, there came a plethora of combinations, generally hidden under a frightening abundance of hair and sometimes spoofing the whole bit, with such quaint designations as Judas and the Traitors, The Undertakers, Oedipus and the Mothers, Johny Hoar and the Hoar Masters, The Thirteen Screaming Niggers, Francis X and the Bushmen, Six and the Single Girl, Barry and the Remains, Cannibal and the Headhunters, Wolfgang and the Mozarts, Stark Naked and the Car Thieves, The Fugs (necessarily avoided by most disc jockeys), The Mothers of Invention (album title: *Freak Out!*), The Grateful Dead and, no kidding, Mogen David and the Grapes of Wrath.

Dick Clark, also on the ground floor, found himself stung by the payola thing too but bounced back nicely. Here he is in 1978 with recording star Barry Manilow. *Adam Scull/Black Star*

musical baby—and his racket too, for that matter, since payola indictments were still flowing out of grand jury rooms as late as 1977—in ravishing good health. The jazz lover had to scratch around to find his favorite performer playing in some cellar or in the few nightclubs still catering to that narrowed audience, and the radio listener who wanted to hear the tuneful melodies of Richard Rodgers or Harold Arlen had to twist the dials pretty feverishly. R & R, buttressed by Folk Rock, filled the airwaves.

Over the years, you needed a musical scorecard to keep up with the cast of characters. A whole assortment of names comes to mind, surely not complete: Dion, Frankie Avalon, Fabian (plucked off a Philadelphia stoop by a record scout), Bobby Rydell, Pat Boone (before he switched to Hollywood and the nicer songs), Fats Domino, Little Frankie Lymon, James Brown ("Mr. Dynamite"), Roger Miller (the Nashville Sound, with a touch of hillbilly), The Platters, The Pretenders, Little Anthony and the Imperials, The Chiffons, The Crystals, Ruby and the Romantics, the Righteous Brothers, the Everly Broth-

In truth, rock wasn't just "Negro music" at all. It was *everybody's* music, while the pure black Soul sound rested in the hands of such performers as Ray Charles. Sightless since he was six and orphaned in his teens, Charles learned to read Braille and play piano and clarinet in the St. Augustine School for the Blind in Florida. "I realized I had a choice of getting a cane and picking out a street corner," he said once, "or striding out as a musician." Whether it was Soul, Country Western or Rhythm-and-Blues, you had to reckon with Mr. Charles—and still do. Not many have matched those strides.

In 1965, nearly ten years after it was supposed to vanish into limbo as another fad, R & R was so healthy that some large brain in Sargent Shriver's Office of Economic Opportunity decided to employ it in a TV spectacular which was supposed to get the nation's dropouts to straighten up and fly right. For this purpose, the OEO enlisted the services of Murray Kaufman, who had identified himself as "The Fifth Beatle" somewhere along the frenetic way. The name of the show was "It's What's Happening, Baby!" and what happened was that the halls of Congress rang with angry protests. The OEO reported that thousands of dropouts, stirred by the message of Murray the K and his R & R stars, had written in to inquire about summer jobs and vocational training and all those good things, but the old men on the Hill insisted that there had to be a more tasteful way to reach our troubled youth. There was no encore, which is not to knock the Rock but only to say that the time was not at hand for it to serve as an adjunct of The Establishment.

Indeed, in the case of the high-flying Folk Rock, quite the opposite was true. The kids with the electric guitars, led by the fluffy-haired Bob Dylan, a

They came out of a Liverpool cellar joint called the Cavern in 1961, and within two years the driving sound of the Beatles was assailing the human ear all around a world drenched in hysteria. In the photo above, made by the author in Montreal's Forum when he covered their earth-rattling invasion of the United States and Canada in 1964, John Lennon and Paul McCartney, who collaborated on their biggest hits, are seated with George Harrison standing behind Lennon and drummer Ringo Starr in the center. The Beatle sound, inspired by Elvis Presley, made multimillionaires out of four kids who had to scratch around to buy their first musical instruments. The quartet came asunder in 1970 after selling something like 250 million records and coining another fortune on three movies—*Hard Day's Night, Help* and *Let It Be* (a fourth, *Yellow Submarine,* just used their names and voices). Lennon settled into the marital bed with a little Japanese artist, Yoko Ono—publicly, during the Vietnam War, in what he termed a "bed-in" for peace—and spent three years in a winning battle against a U.S. deportation order based on a 1968 marijuana conviction in England. McCartney eventually married Linda Eastman of New York and is touring with her today with a new combination of his own, Wings. Harrison, always on the mystic side, spent much time with the Indian TM man, Maharishi Mahesh Yogi, although he showed up at Madison Square Garden with Starr and Bob Dylan in 1971 to do two SRO appearances for the benefit of East Pakistani refugees (the famous Bangladesh concerts). Starr has been struggling with a movie career. The collapse of the Beatle empire, then said to be bringing in some $17 million a year, enriched a whole battery of lawyers on both sides of the Atlantic. *Paul Sann*

walking slum but the Poet Laureate of the Hipsters, were using the Big Beat to put protest to music—protest over Vietnam, protest over The Bomb, protest over segregation, protest over the PTA types who wanted them to get the hair out of their eyes, protest over the squares who said marijuana was bad, protest over . . . well, start with that strange Dylan, who literally came out of nowhere back in 1961 and can safely be identified today as a millionaire rebel (before taxes, of course). All he seemed to have, starting out at Gerde's Folk City in Greenwich Village on a coffee-and-cake date, was his guitar, the conventional round-the-clock wardrobe (high boots, beat-up jeans, work shirt, corduroy cap), the gaunt and unfed look and the dark glasses, called "shades" in that set. It turned out, very quickly, that the kid with the scratchy no-voice voice was simply bubbling over with the rage required by his generation; he had it to burn. Sprinkled amidst his ballads of lost love, he had something to say.

Bob Dylan came out of the West by way of Minnesota. He was born in Duluth on May 24, 1941, and brought up—when they could keep him home—in Hibbing, where his father, Abe Zimmerman, sold appliances and his mother sold dresses. The story originally was that he took the name of Dylan from Dylan Thomas because he loved the Irish poet but he said that wasn't so, adding, "I've read some of Dylan's stuff, and it's just not the same as mine. We're different."

It wasn't just the name in any case. The boy didn't dig Hibbing and he didn't dig his family ("I just don't have any family," he told the Chicago *Daily News* in 1965, "I'm all alone"). He once said that he ran away from that icy mining town on the Canadian border when he was ten, twelve, thirteen, fifteen, fifteen and a half, seventeen and eighteen ("I been caught and brought back all but once") and it would appear that he's still running. In any case, he bought his first guitar in Chicago when he was ten, taught himself to play it, and then tackled the piano, autoharp and harmonica. He said he was playing Rock in his early teens but had to quit "because I just couldn't make it that way—the image of the day was Frankie Avalon or Fabian, or this whole athletic supercleanliness bit, which if you didn't have that you couldn't make any friends." He attended the University of Minnesota for six months, spent most of his time in the coffeehouses of Dinkytown, on the edge of the campus, and then picked up his guitar and struck out for the West as an itinerant folk singer. The musical influences in his background, as he tells it, range all the way from

A commonplace scene wherever the Beatles showed up. Here they were leaving Kennedy Airport to go back to England and it was just too much for this teen-ager. *New York Post*

Odetta to Harry Belafonte, Leadbelly, Josh White, Hank Williams, Muddy Waters, Jelly Roll Morton, Big Joe Williams, Mance Lipscomb and, possibly above all, Woody Guthrie. Dylan met Guthrie once in California in his hitchhiking time, came East to visit him early in 1961 when the great dustbowl singer lay desperately ill in a New Jersey hospital, and included his "Song to Woody" in his first album that year.

Dylan has said that he wrote his first song when he was fifteen and that it was an ode to Brigitte Bardot—a far cry from the burning, come-of-age Dylan whose "Blowin' in the Wind" became the rallying anthem of the civil rights movement in 1962 ("Yes/'n' how many times can some people exist/Before they're allowed to be free?") when it issued forth in the put-on hillbilly tones of the oldest twenty-one-year-old in the world. And it's a far cry from a love ballad for the French sex kitten to the raging fury of "Masters of War" ("You hide in your mansion/As young people's blood/Flows out of their bodies/And is buried in the mud/") or the bruising lines of "A Hard Rain's A Gonna Fall" ("I saw ten thousand talkers whose tongues were all broken/I saw guns and sharp swords in the hands of young children").*

With fire-breathing messages like those, it didn't

_____

* All quoted Bob Dylan lyrics © M. Witmark & Sons.

The early Bob Dylan in a park-bench news conference in London with Joan Baez prior to a 1965 tour.

take long for the whole community of folk singers to embrace the disheveled, rail-thin runaway from the cornball milieu of the Twin Cities. The Dylan songs turned up, selling like pure gold, on the records of Peter, Paul and Mary, Joan Baez, Pete Seeger, Odetta, Judy Collins, Sonny and Cher, The Byrds, The Turtles, The Chad Mitchell Trio, The Kingston Trio and even Bobby Darin (a heart victim at thirty-seven in 1973) and, no less, Marlene Dietrich. And the new-breed writers were right behind the brooding Dylan, led by nineteen-year-old P. F. Sloan with his doomsong, "Eve of Destruction":

The Eastern world it is explodin',
Violence flarin', and bullets loadin',
You're old enough to kill, but not for votin' . . .
If the button is pushed, there's no runnin' away.
There'll be no one to save, with the world
*in a grave . . .**

In the tormented, alienated world of Bob Dylan and P. F. Sloan ("I'm bugged most of the time"), practically everybody must have believed it, because those black sentiments, sung by the mop-haired Barry McGuire, soared to the top of the 1965 best-seller lists. But something had happened to Dylan before "Eve of Destruction," the purest distillation of the bitter protest with which he had exploded on the

Dylan a decade later—in a 1976 appearance with The Band in San Francisco.

A sample of the latter-day stages of the R & R revolution. It's the Mothers of Invention with Frank Zappa, the head man, or No. 1 Mother, draped in the flag. Their lyrics, not always suitable for the airwaves, tended to put down the rock scene.

The young man with the horn, Herb Alpert, shook 'em all up in the mid-Sixties with the sound of the Tiajuana Brass, inspired by the music of the Mexican mariachi bands he heard on a trip to the bullfights. His records grossed $30 million in 1966, but he would never come that close again. But, then, he wouldn't need food stamps either.

musical scene, made it so big. In 1965, he turned up at the Newport Folk Festival with the Paul Butterfield Rock 'n' Roll band and got booed off the stage. Then he caught some more hell at a Forest Hills concert, and it wasn't just the big sound behind him. Unaccountably, Dylan was moving away from Folk Rock back to the love song, and he wasn't up there all alone with his guitar in that wrinkled work shirt and the threadbare jeans either. He had some strangers behind him, wired to the rafters with all those electronic gimmicks, and he was wearing a fancy Carnaby Street polka-dot shirt and singing songs like the Beatles sing. Nothing was the same except that wild upswept hairdo. So the kids in his old let's-make-love-not-war league were bound to ask why the war was gone from the Dylan lyrics and the artist himself was bound to shake 'em off; he has never been given to public pronouncements. His new albums, like *Highway 61 Revisited* and *Bringing It All Back Home*, left no doubt about where he was going. And in such items as "Like a Rolling Stone," "Positively 4th Street" and "Ballad of a Thin Man" and "I Want You," the kid who was so cool with the anti-everything Joan Baez in the early days appeared to be reminding the customers that, for better or worse, he was the same guy who once wrote a song under the distant inspiration of that Bardot babe over in France.

There was a tidbit here and there, however, to remind the far-out types that Bob Dylan still had some of the older notions. "Mr. Tambourine Man," a huge hit on records for The Byrds, brought suggestions that the hipster poet was borrowing a leaf (no pun) from the book of that other apostle of all the freedoms, Allen Ginsberg, and working in a plug for marijuana—"Take me disappearing through the smoke rings of my mind . . . far from the twisted reach of crazy sorrow." Some listeners detected a piece of drug promotion in "Rainy Day Women #12 and 35" as well. While Dylan would never discuss that sort of thing ("Don't interpret me"), his manager, Albert Grossman, took pains to deny any connection between his boy's new lyrics and the stuff of dreams. In a way, it was a secondary issue anyway. The larger thing was that Bob Dylan of "The Times They Are A-Changin'" and "A Hard Rain's A Gonna Fall" had taken the folk out of the rock and was now an R & R star. That's what was happening, baby.

Part XIII

SONGS FOR SALE

VALLEE TO CROSBY TO SINATRA TO PRESLEY

> "Let me make the songs of a nation,
> and I care not who makes its laws."
> —ANDREW FLETCHER

Rudy Vallee: The megaphone was an afterthought.
Besides, there was no microphone on the bandstand
when he started that wave of heartthrobs.

LET'S SKIP THE NAMES, because we're dealing here with a family skeleton that doesn't need rattling, but it happened on a Thursday night in Kansas City in 1931. This plumber came home, weary from the day's labors, and found his bride, as usual, cuddled up to the radio and so deep in reverie that she didn't even look up to greet him. She was listening to the soft nasal tones of Rudy Vallee, and the plumber went into a rage. He said he was sick and tired of playing second fiddle to the faraway voice of that damned singer. He wanted the radio turned off. His wife refused, turning up the volume instead. The plumber produced a revolver. In the ensuing struggle for it, as the widow told it, he was shot dead.

This is not to say that the Yale man in the white ducks, breathing tender ballads into a microphone, caused the American hearthside to be rent with small arms fire. He was responsible, however, for a solid decade of harsh words: husband against wife, father against daughter, brother against sister (in the author's instance, brother against the terrifying odds of *three* sisters). There were no neutrals in this warfare. You either surrendered the one and only Stromberg-Carlson to the girls and retreated, out of hearing, or you stood your ground and made some noise of your own. Rudy Vallee was more than just a singer; he was an issue. He came right into the home after the womenfolk—a "phantom Lothario," in the words of one of his more vivid detractors. His timing, an accident of history, could not have been better. The memory of Valentino, dead less than two years, evidently was still fresh in female hearts. Valentino, you will recall, had to work his magic from the remote fastness of the silent screen. He had to do it all with those flashing eyes. Vallee, swiftly anointed the Vagabond Lover, enjoyed the help of Mr. Marconi's little invention and a pleasantly warm tenor voice, and he had something to say: "I'm Confessing That I Love You," "What Good Am I Without You?" "If I Had a Girl Like You," "And Then Your Lips Met Mine." Things like that. "I feel myself only as a lover," said the troubadour. "My audience is a girl—or many girls. Sometimes I am thinking of a real girl, sometimes a dream girl, but when I sing I am always a lover." The girls had no trouble getting the message. Actually, nobody could have been more surprised than Vallee. He never saw himself, in the beginning, as the man come to douse the Valentino torch. He just wanted to play the saxophone.

Hubert Prior Vallee, son of an Irish mother and

French father, was born in 1901 in the papermill town of Island Pond, Vermont, and grew up in Westbrook, Maine, where his father had a drugstore. Hubert worked in the store after school but had no taste for the pharmacist's trade. He was more interested in music. He learned the clarinet and then, with the help of a correspondence course from Rudy Wiedoeft, a very large name in the field then, switched to the saxophone. He was so good on the instrument in his late teens that he left the University of Maine for Yale after his freshman year because New Haven offered a wider range for his musical sideline. London's famed Savoy Hotel lured him away one semester to sit in with the Savoy Havana Band, and he could have stayed over there to play and teach—the Prince of Wales, among others, wanted to take lessons from him—but elected to come back to Yale and work for his degree. On the side, he led the Yale Football Band and played dances and coming-out parties around New England with an orchestra of his own.

Armed with a degree in philosophy and a pretty good reputation on the sax, Vallee joined the Vincent Lopez orchestra but quickly left it to organize his own Connecticut Yankees. The band opened at Don Dickerman's Heigh Ho Club in Manhattan in January, 1928, and one night the handsome, wavy-haired leader put the sax aside, picked up a megaphone, closed his gray eyes, and started to sing. That was it. *Variety*'s Abel Greene swiftly rendered the judgment that Vallee, who by now had appropriated the first name of his mentor Wiedoeft, was very "pash," and whatever that meant it was good. Within a month, Station WABC was carrying the crooner's soft-sell arrangements, and by 1929 the man from Yale was digging in for his ten-year run astride the network radio charts. And there, by the way, lies the secret of Rudy Vallee's swiftly blooming fame. In the days before radio, Al Jolson, the great Mammy Singer, had to scrape his knees on the boards for twenty years, coast to coast, before he could say that he had been heard by two million people. When Vallee came along, lofted on the airwaves, there were 11,250,000 radio sets in the nation's homes. Is it any wonder that his name, naughty or otherwise, became a household word overnight? You have to shudder to think what might have happened if a singer with Vallee's built-in appeal had turned up, say, at a moment like this when there are more TV sets than bathtubs in the American home. Instant Madness, no doubt, as in the case of Elvis Presley and the Beatles after him. But let us not weep for the men born too far ahead of the ultimate revolution in communications.

Between his radio show and mob-scene personal

The old Eli, back from obscurity, with Robert Morse in the 1964 Broadway smash, *How to Succeed in Business Without Really Trying.*

appearances in such showplaces as the Palace and the cavernous Paramount theatres in New York and Brooklyn, Vallee's income soared as high as $20,000 a week. That may not sound like a staggering sum in this day of six-figure one-shot "concerts" by outfits like the Rolling Stones or the lush purses the networks and the Las Vegas and newly arrived Atlantic City gambling dens dish out for talent, but it wasn't bad for a guy who drew down seven dollars a week as a movie usher in his high school days and counted himself rich when his sax earned him thirty dollars a week to help pay his way through Yale. And it was just a start at that. Always quick to cash in on a new face, Hollywood speedily summoned Vallee to star in *The Vagabond Lover* (from his hit song of the same name) and he appeared in George White's *Scandals* on Broadway in 1934 and 1936. More than three decades and four wives later (how could the man fight them off?), he was to score heavily in both places as the stuffed-shirt tycoon of *How to Succeed in Business Without Really Trying.*

In his prime, Vallee encountered considerable hostility from the male animal, and it disturbed him. "From the attitude of some people you would think I was neither fish nor fowl—not a regular fellow," he told an interviewer in 1934. "Well, that's a cockeyed impression of men. Just because a fellow sings in a voice that isn't the usual robust baritone need not mean he is effeminate. I'm suffering from the same unfair prejudice that men felt against Rudolph Valentino." And so he was. The last quarrel of Valentino's young life—and surely one of the most painful—occurred when the Chicago *Tribune,* just kidding, equated him with the growing lifted pinky set. Angry and upset, the star vainly offered the *Tribune* editorial writer his choice of a duel or a fistfight. Rudy Vallee never had to resort to anything so extreme; nobody said anything that nasty about him in print. He had to take more kidding over his vaunted New England frugality. Thus there was a story about some hard bargaining between the Connecticut Yankee and the two city-slicker-type hoodlums who put the collar on him one night as he was leaving the Brooklyn Paramount for the Club Vallee in Manhattan. Removed to the gunmen's lair and told that he had to produce $50,000 in cold cash or suffer the application of a very hot flatiron to the soles of his feet, just for openers, Vallee was said to have talked the badmen into settling for $10,000.

So much for that. We're dealing here with the often inexplicable waves of popular adulation which lift one entertainer or another to incredible heights in the American playpen.

While Charles Alphonse Vallee's boy was killing 'em in his early days, there was a trio called The Rhythm Boys traveling with Paul Whiteman's band. Al Rinker, brother of Mildred Bailey, who was Whiteman's first vocalist, was one of them. Harry Barris, who wrote the big 1927 hit, "Mississippi Mud," was another. The third was Harry Lillis (Bing) Crosby, a dropout law student from Gonzaga University in Spokane, drummer in a schoolboy outfit of Rinker's called the Musicaladers, later with an aggregation called the Juicy Seven, still later the other half of Crosby & Rinker. The Rhythm Boys disbanded in 1929 and Bing Crosby, then twenty-five years old, struck out on his own with what he described as his "journeyman sea-level baritone."

Journeyman or otherwise, his voice carried him so far and so fast that the record salesmen were having trouble pushing Vallee's albums, for all his celebrity, by 1931. The new crooner, swiftly dubbed the King of the Groaners, had a much broader appeal. He could make the girls go limp with his rendition of "I Surrender, Dear" or "Sunday, Monday and Always," get to the menfolks with a cowboy song like "Don't Fence Me In" and tug at aging, sentimental heartstrings with "Home on the Range": In time, he would make the all-time best-selling recordings of "Silent Night" and "White Christmas."

In a word, this was the voice for everybody, and Crosby wasn't just an overnight sensation; he was for keeps. He went on to the movies and by 1944 he was Hollywood's Number 1 box office draw. When he won an Oscar for his role of the good Father O'Malley in *Going My Way* that year, *Time* looked back on his career in considerable wonderment, observing that he had been heard by more people than any other singer in history, that he had sold 75,000,000 recordings, that he was still among the top twelve names in radio, and that the end was nowhere in sight. Bob Hope, Crosby's co-star in that wearying flock of *Road To——*epics, knew why. "Don't worry about Bing," the comedian said when Frank Sinatra clamored onto the scene like an exploding rocket in the early Forties. "He is the man who made Sinatra's mother swoon, and in 1960 he'll be the man who will make Sinatra's daughter swoon." And Crosby did just that. Indeed, often in joint TV appearances with Sinatra. He just went on and on, working when he felt like it, going to the track or playing golf (an absolute addiction) and building a new life in 1957 with Kathryn Grant, twenty-three, an actress thirty-years his junior. This was five years after the death of his first wife, Dixie Lee. Der Bingle, as he was known to his huge circle of friends, was an avid sportsman, and among his varied interests he was owner of the Del Mar racetrack he built in California, part owner of the Pittsburgh Pirates for three decades, an early adviser to the struggling American Football League and sponsor of the Crosby National Pro-Am Tournament, one of golf's major events. He went on to the age of seventy-three and then died, very likely just the way he would have wanted, after finishing a round on a course in Madrid on October 14, 1977. He was survived by Kathy and their three children, Harry Lillis III, Nathaniel Patrick and Mary Frances, and the four sons of his twenty-two year union with Dixie Lee. A man who played benefits at the drop of a hat or an airline ticket, he was mourned all over the world.

This brings our narrative, without fear or favor, to the saga of the Kid from Hoboken, who was spawned

1944: Crosby and director Leo McCarey pick up their Oscars for *Going My Way*. The lady is Ingrid Bergman, winning for *Gaslight*.

by a generation of swooning bobby soxers who went onward and upward to a pinnacle of awesome power in the entertainment world. Chairman of the Board, The Man, The Leader, The Dago, The General, The Pope, *Il Padrone* or what-have-you. He remains a most interesting—if not always a most happy—fella and owes it all, strangely enough, to Bing Crosby. He became a singer in the first place because Crosby made it seem so easy.

Francis Albert Sinatra weighed in at 13 ½ pounds when he came into the world in that four-room cold-water flat with the toilet in the hall. The delivery was so difficult that the doctor thought he was stillborn and turned his attention to Natalie Sinatra, but the baby's grandmother held him under the kitchen faucet and he let out a lusty cry—not his last by any means. Except for bad neck scars and an ear-lobe nicked by the forceps, Frank Sinatra was alive and well in New Jersey. The date was December 12, 1915, and the next one that counted came in 1933. It was then that the boy took his teenage sweetheart, Nancy Barbato, a plasterer's daughter, to a Jersey City vaudeville house to hear Mr. Crosby. Sinatra, who had done some singing in high school before he departed the educational scene in his senior year,

"Der Bingle" with his first wife, Dixie Lee, an early cancer victim (above), and in 1977 with the second Mrs. Crosby, Kathryn Grant. *WWP* watched the effortless Crosby performance and knew that he could make some music too, only better.

The next day Sinatra quit the eleven-dollar-a-week job his father had gotten him as a helper on the Jersey *Journal*'s trucks. To Martin Sinatra, a saloon-keeper-turned-fire captain on the strength of his wife's long and dedicated performance as a Democratic district leader, it was a disappointment. Sinatra, once a bantamweight boxer under the name of Marty O'Brien, had the gloves on his son at a tender age. He would have preferred another fistfighter to a crooner but the boy never acquired the necessary physique, so there was no real argument. The rest is familiar history: Frank ran off with a singing contest in Jersey City, went on the Major Bowes amateur hour and won a thirty-nine-week contract to tour with a quartet called "The Hoboken Four," did sustaining radio programs for his carfare, took a fifteen-dollar-a-week job as a singing waiter in the Rustic Cabin outside of Hoboken, married Nancy Barbato when the roadhouse boosted his pay to twenty-five dollars, went to trumpeter Harry James's Band for seventy-five dollars a week in 1939 and scored his first big hit with "All Or Nothing at All," switched to the Tommy Dorsey orchestra to sing with the Pied Pipers for $125 a week, came up with a smash recording of "I'll Never Smile Again," and, late in 1942, bought his freedom from Dorsey so that he could be free to go out on his own.

From then on, it was Sinatra all the way.

Booked into the New York Paramount at the end of that December, the wafer-thin baritone, who could turn an everyday lyric into a melodic poem, brought out such an army of wailing, screaming teen-agers that police reserves had to be called. Day after day the bobby-sox brigades staged scenes of near-riot which made the earlier demonstrations for Rudy Vallee and Bing Crosby look like church socials by comparison. Sinatra needed a small army to help him negotiate his way into the theatre past hordes of panting, souvenir-hunting admirers bent on tearing the clothes from his bony frame. Wherever he went thereafter—to fill nightclub engagements, to the CBS studios to do the Lucky Strike *Hit Parade,* to Hollywood to make his first movies—Sinatra had to fight off the wild legions. In an appearance at the RKO in Boston in 1943, he drew 17,000 fans in a single day, shattering records previously set by Eddie Cantor and Deanna Durbin. In New York on Columbus Day in 1944, a crowd of 25,000 descended on the Paramount to hear him, and the box office itself, its windows smashed, was in danger of falling before the police restored order.

In those days, there was no end to the speculation, longhaired and otherwise, over the sources of the Sinatra magic. The Broadway columnists, taking the elementary view, labeled him the first of the great "bedroom singers," conveniently forgetting how female hearts had fluttered over Rudy Vallee. Psychiatrist Louis I. Berg put the raging new craze down to "mass frustrated love without direction." Professor Henry E. Garrett, head of Columbia's psychology department, viewed it as a case of mass hysteria in girls bereft because their true loves were away at war. (Sinatra was 4F because of a punctured eardrum.) "This little fellow represents some kind of idealized hero, much like Prince Charming," said Garrett. Another psychologist traced Sinatra's eminence to the fact that he was performing "a sort of melodic strip tease which lays bare his soul." An Indiana University professor insisted that the singer was riding the crest only because the nation's youngsters were in rebellion against the stuffy classical music foisted upon them in the schools. And amidst all the talk of mass love, mass hysteria and mass hypnotism, psychologist Donald A. Laird came forth with a somewhat more complex theory.

"The secret of Mr. Sinatra's appeal," Laird wrote, "is no problem to the psychologist. It proceeds from a well-recognized and familiar response to one of the elemental instincts of femalekind: the urge to feed the hungry." There was nothing startling about that, because we had already been told that Sinatra's lean and hungry small-boy look was stirring the most beautiful female emotions, but Laird went deeper. Observing that adolescent girls with suddenly developing busts were in the vanguard of the singer's fans, he observed that the physiological "preparation for motherhood naturally gives rise to unfamiliar sensations, among them increased emotional sensitivity due to mammary hyperesthesia. From time to time this hyperesthesia is more marked than at others; when it is most acute some girls are likely to swoon at any stimulating emotions." From all this, Laird deducted that Sinatra's appeal was "not to crude sex, but to the tenderest mothering instinct—the highest type of unselfish emotion."

After that—at least for those of us who understood mammary hyperesthesia—there was no further occasion to brood over the underlying sources of the great orgy of love which the scarred, hollow-cheeked crooner had set in motion. There was no trouble understanding why more than five hundred Sinatra fan clubs abounded in the land—including the Sighing Society of Sinatra Swooners, the Slaves of Sinatra and, if you have the time for a slow one, the

Frank Sinatra (right), then a member of the Hoboken Four, with Major Bowes of NBC's *Amateur Hour* in 1935.

Girls Who Would Lay Down Their Lives for Sinatra Fan Club.

The fall—and what a fall—came just about ten years after the glorious ascent began. Sinatra had trouble with his voice, his movie and TV career, his money and his private life, all at once. Hopelessly drawn to Ava Gardner, he divorced Nancy in 1951, giving her custody of Nancy, Frank Jr. and Christina and a healthy percentage of his future earnings. His songs lost some of their spell around that time and during his brief alliance with the beautiful Miss Gardner his career went into a precipitate decline. He rescued it himself. Killing some idle moments in Africa while his bride was there making *Mogambo* with Clark Gable, Sinatra read James Jones's *From Here to Eternity,* then being cast for the movies, and hungered after the role of the ill-fated Maggio, so he cabled Harry Cohn of Columbia Pictures and asked for it. Even though he was in a financial straitjacket and tangled up with the government over an item of $110,000 in back taxes, he agreed to do it for the rock-bottom price of $1,000 a week for eight weeks of shooting. He didn't have much of a choice at that, because his name carried little weight at the box office then. So all the brooding singer got for bringing Maggio to life on the screen was an Academy Award and a new lease on his own life which he would never relinquish. That was in 1954; the angry man from Hoboken ("I have a Sicilian temper") wasn't quite thirty-nine when his second career beckoned.

Now he could write his own ticket for his movies because either the Sinatra-owned Park Lake Enterprises or Artanis Productions made them (and Artanis spells Sinatra when you turn it around). He used the Warner lot for Artanis, and the word around there was that Jack Warner had designated him as his heir apparent. The top album seller of all time then (say a 100 million dollars' worth) he didn't have to dicker with record companies anymore; he owned his Reprise Records. In television, when the spirit moved him toward the little screen, he could name his price. In Las Vegas, long before the fees for the name entertainers soared into the six-figure class, the Sands paid him $50,000 a week or more to lure the high rollers into its casino. And that was just like singing for his own supper, because he held a 9 percent share in that gambling den—just a mere trifle against his 50 percent piece of the Cal Neva Lodge in Lake Tahoe. He had to divest himself of both those baubles, said to be worth $3.5 million, when Nevada's Gaming Control Board cracked down on him in 1953 for permitting Sam (Momo) Giancana, the Chicago Mafia Don, to dwell on the premises during one of singer Phyllis McGuire's engagements there. The racket boss's sojourn on those sun-kissed acres was perfectly innocent, since Miss McGuire happened to be his best girl at the time; the only problem was that his name graced the regula-

The man and his quartet of wives. Clockwise, with Nancy, the first and mother of his three children; then Ava Gardner, always identified as the love he never quite recovered from; at fifty with twenty-one-year-old Mia Farrow (very briefly); and in 1976 (*WWP*) with Barbara Marx, the ex- wife of Zeppo. That looked like the one to stick for Ol' Blue Eyes.

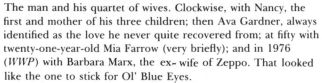

In John F. Kennedy's corner then (but destined to turn up on the GOP side with Richard Nixon later), Sinatra escorts the new First Lady into the capital's National Guard Armory for the 1961 Inaugural Gala.

tory board's "black book," which listed eleven underworld figures of varying degrees of fame barred from the state's casinos. Giancana, just one of the assorted mob luminaries linked with Sinatra by law enforcement authorities down through the years, also figured in a somewhat more momentous embarrassment for the singer in 1975 when the dalliance between John F. Kennedy and the sultry Judith Campbell Exner surfaced. The striking brunette let it be known that in 1960 another playmate of hers, the same Sinatra, had introduced her in turn first to JFK and then to Mr. Giancana, whereupon she proceeded to divide her favors between the Chief Executive and the gangland chieftain. Swift denials from ex-associates of the assassinated President failed to stand up against the White House's own telephone logs, which showed no less than seventy communications between the President and the party girl all the way into March of 1962, when J. Edgar Hoover dropped in on JFK to tell him that Mrs. Exner was killing

some of her spare time not only with Giancana but also an equally unsavory helpmate, John Roselli. Neither of those gentlemen—the pair recruited by the CIA in its abortive attempt to have Fidel Castro wasted—were around to comment, both since having been eliminated by Mafia executioners themselves. Sinatra did have something to say when the woman put it all into a book: "Hell hath no fury like a hustler with a literary agent."

The Sinatra–Kennedy connection itself, nurtured by Peter Lawford, husband of JFK's sister Pat and a member in good standing of the singer's inner social circle, alternately known as The Rat Pack and The Clan, came abruptly asunder when Attorney General Robert F. Kennedy began poking around the entertainer's seamier associations. Thus Sinatra, the honcho at the Inaugural Gala in 1961, turned up in the Nixon camp in 1968. Thereafter, he listed Spiro Agnew among his intimates, sticking with him even after the Vice-President had to step down when his own dirty linen from his days as governor of Maryland—like dollar bills changing hands and not showing on his tax returns—got hung out.

In the years between the short-tempered singer come to be known as Ol' Blue Eyes had his share of wins and losses.

In 1966, at fifty, he married Mia Farrow, Maureen O'Sullivan's wispy daughter, then twenty-one and starring in TV's "Peyton Place" serial. That May–December affair lasted just a little more than two years even though Miss Farrow took a long time out for a spot of Transcendental Meditation with India's Maharishi Mahesh Yogi, presumably to see whether there was any way a girl like her could make a life with an American Sultan like Sinatra. Another ten years passed before the man tried the marriage marts again, this time with the beautiful blonde Barbara Marx, forty-six, ex-model, ex-showgirl and ex-wife of Zeppo Marx. Those nuptials took place on the thousand-acre Palm Springs estate of former Ambassador to Britain Walter Annenberg, just down the road from Sinatra's own palatial desert enclave, with a guest list topped by such dignitaries as Mr. Agnew and Ronald Reagan.

Now about that temper. Except during the period of his brief "retirement" in 1972, it has kept Hoboken's most renowned alumnus in the headlines with a regularity skirting the edges of monotony. He came close to blowing an Australian tour in 1974 when he characterized Melbourne's newspaperwomen as "two-dollar hookers" and put down the male journalists not only as "bums and parasites" but "a bunch of fags" besides. Nothing short of a four-hour peace parley between Sinatra aides and Robert J. Hawke, president of the Australian Council of Trade Unions, patched that one up so the tour could proceed. That incident paled the following year at a pre-Inauguration party for Richard Nixon when Ol' Blue Eyes sailed into Maxine Cheshire, the Washington *Post*'s snydicated gossip columnist, with this rather strong tirade: "Two dollars. Two dollars. You've been laying down for that all your life. You're nothing but a cunt. That's spelled c-u-n-t. You know what that means, don't you?" The stunned writer, mother of four, said Sinatra topped that peroration by stuffing two $1 bills into her evening purse. In 1976 he called Chicago *Daily News* columnist Mike Royko a pimp for saying that he had used the local police as bodyguards during an appearance in the Windy City. That one was committed to writing, happily, so Royko auctioned off the letter for $400 and turned the money over to the Salvation Army.

That sale tells you something.

The Sinatra signature is still worth something. So's the talent. The only trouble down through the years, in the words of one of his own best standards, is that the man's always done it "my way." Endlessly generous both with the buck and the helping hand to a degree that may never be known, he has seemed content for the past two decades to come out on the short end in the public prints. It's those vocal chords of his—the chords that have left us a veritable treasury of songs for lovers.

This brings us to another singer of songs. His name was Elvis Aron Presley and he was just a couple of years past kindergarten, down in Tupelo, Mississippi, when Frank Sinatra touched off those riot calls in the East. Sinatra's earliest interest in music asserted itself when an uncle bought him a ukelele, Presley's when his father bought him a $2.98 guitar.

Elvis, in truth, owed his real surrender to the muse to a much more deeply rooted ideal: a boy's love for his mother. When he was in high school in Memphis and earning fourteen dollars a week as a part-time theatre usher he put out four dollars to record a scratchy little serenade, Rock 'n' Roll style, for his mother's thirty-sixth birthday. The song was something called "That's All Right, Mama." Sam Phillips, owner of the Sun Recording Company, where Elvis made the disc, heard a playback of it, and a year later, when Elvis was out of school and driving a truck for thirty-five dollars a week, called the kid back in and had him do it over with some professional backing. A local disc jockey played the thing and it sold 7,000 copies the next day. This was the beginning.

A robust nineteen-year-old six-footer who looked more like Marlboro Country than metropolitan Tennessee, Elvis came off the truck and set out to climb the gold-plated Everest of Rock 'n' Roll. He arrived with a hip wriggle calculated to stir all kinds of instincts, motherly and beyond. That was in 1954, and within two years, on the strength of such record hits as "Blue Suede Shoes" and "Hound Dog," delivered in a driving rockabilly style reminiscent of the unsung Chuck Berry, the New York television impresarios came looking for him. Marshall McLuhan, something of a one-man fad himself in the Deepthink Sixties, has told us that the medium is the message and also that the medium is the massage. Elvis serves as an exhibit here, if one may risk a play on the Professor's sometimes cloudy words, for there was both message and massage in it when the hazel-eyed kid with the sideburns set the nation's television screens aflame.

Elvis made two tame appearances on the Dorsey Brothers variety show on CBS in the spring of 1956, just for warm-ups, apparently, and then turned on the body English in a sizzling guest shot for Milton Berle which brought a flood of protests to NBC and some strong language from the critics. The New York *Times*'s influential Jack Gould, leading off for the forces of good, had this to say: "These gyrations have to concern parents—unless we're the kind of parents who approve of kids going around stealing hubcaps, indulging in promiscuity, and generally behaving like delinquents. . . . It isn't enough to say that Elvis is kind to his parents, sends money home, and is the same unspoiled kid he was before all the commotion began. That still isn't a free ticket to behave like a sex maniac in public before millions of impressionable kids." Gould put Presley down as nothing more than a "virtuoso of hootchy kootchy," while Hearst's Jack O'Brian reminded his readers that Fiorello LaGuardia had run burlesque out of New York in happier days and the *Daily News*'s Ben Gross dismissed the new star as a "grunt and groin" specialist. On the other end of the landscape, the San Francisco *Chronicle* said the whole thing was in "appalling taste." For the defense, the star himself, on the edge of great affluence, entered the most demure not-guilty plea. "Ma'am, ah'm not tryin' to be sexy," he told a lady reporter. "Ah didn't have any idear of trying to sell sex. It's just my way of expressin' how I feel when I move around. It's all leg movements. Ah don't do nothin' with my body." John Lardner took a lighthearted view of the debate in his *Newsweek* column. He said the boy's contortions reminded him of an outboard motor, and a Yale sociologist quickly amended that analysis to make it "a lovesick outboard motor."

The TV people, as it happened, knew all this well in advance of that wild display on the Berle show. Almost a year before that, a Presley performance in Jacksonville, Florida, had inspired an audience reaction so frantic that a bluenosed juvenile court judge threatened to lock him up on charges of impairing the morals of the town's minors. Elvis modified his torso-swinging for the second show and got the hell out of there. When he appeared later in the Municipal Auditorium of LaCrosse, Wisconsin, the local gazette skipped the larger cultural impact of his song styling and denounced him for performing "a strip tease with clothes on." Came the gray dawn, the parents of some of Elvis' ecstatic teen-age fans were forming a committee to bar him forever from those Victorian precincts.

Did NBC quail before the storm when its turn came? Of course not. The network, bless its corporate soul, observed that the reformed truck jockey had pushed Uncle Miltie's ratings past Phil Silvers' *Sergeant Bilko* for the first time and let Steve Allen book him in the all-important Sunday night spot against Ed Sullivan. There were some necessary refinements, of course: The brass sent a man around to take away Elvis's thigh-scraping jeans and sport shirt and drape him in white tie and tails and, on the side, cool the gymnastics lest his more severe critics mount an assault on the steel and concrete barricades of Radio City. Elvis complained to the New York *Post*'s Bob Williams that the NBC spoilsport had taken away 85 percent of the necessary exertions which accompanied his ballads, but even under that restraint he performed a small miracle for General Sarnoff's bouncing baby. He earned Allen 55.3 percent of the viewing audience against a staggeringly low 14.8 for its CBS rival. Sullivan, passed in the ratings for the first time since Dean Martin and Jerry Lewis had turned that trick two years before, read the Trendex on the wall and reached for his checkbook. Against the $5,500 Allen had paid to Presley, he went to Colonel Tom Parker, the old Tennessee carnival man who constituted the Presley brain trust, and signed the singer for three appearances in the fall for a round $50,000. In the process, the outspoken columnist-maestro knew he would have to swallow some disdainful remarks he had made earlier about the hillbilly from Memphis. In character, Sullivan took back the bad words, said he would let the boy do his act without handcuffs, and steeled himself for the voices of protest. But while the anti-Presley legions were still in full cry, the people in the great wasteland obviously were waiting with bated breath for him to show up before the unblinking CBS cameras. His first appearance with Sullivan, who did take the precaution of moving the cameras in above the waist when the boy lost his head and shook too much, skyrocketed the show to an eight-year high as an estimated 54,000,000 persons tuned in—a record due to stand until that Sunday in February, 1964, when the Beatles' American debut with Sullivan drew something like 67,500,000 viewers. Looking back, and bearing in mind that the advent of the Twist would bring all kinds of scantily clad Go-Go girls to the little screen (did you happen to catch Mitzi Gaynor slipping those grinds and bumps into the otherwise antiseptic 1967 Academy Award show on ABC?), you have to wonder what all the fuss over Presley was about. In any event, there was no evidence anywhere, not even in the J. Edgar Hoover archives, that the merger of Elvis and Ed Sullivan had in itself prompted any noticeable outbreak of hubcap stealing, promiscuity or delinquency. Like nothing happened, man.

Dr. Wilson Shaffer, professor of psychology at Johns Hopkins University, was among those who weren't a bit surprised when our more sacred institutions managed to survive the Presley invasion. "He is simply one more in a series of performers who incite a kind of hysterical reaction," Dr. Shaffer said, "but I don't think he is a serious menace to young people. Before him there was that Johnnie Ray, who cried and sang at the same time. And, as I recall, when Frank Sinatra was in the swooning teen-agers stage, he was considered offensive because he often seemed to be caressing the microphone while he sang." Dissenting, Dr. David H. Webster, of Temple University, said that Presley's music "emphasizes exhaustion, self-torture, frustration, and always a rhythm of sullen, ugly complaint." In Manhattan, The Rev. Charles Howard Graef, rector of St. John's in the Village, sadly observed that "Mr. Presley, using innuendo and suggestion, by curl of lip and shake of hip, represents the revolt from the tried and true." In *Harper's*, James and Annette Baxter put it this way:

Presley's stunning rapport with his own generation must hinge on something more than the ageless call of the wild. Appealing to the youthful imagination in some way inscrutable to the parents of the teen-agers who worship him, Elvis fills some kind of need that the older generation can't fathom, and more significantly, doesn't feel. Why? Perhaps because they have run out of dreams. Elvis is for real, and in his voice the

Backstage before his record-shattering stint on the Ed Sullivan show, Presley with his wily manager, Colonel Tom Parker, and the most durable of the television maestros (right).

teen-ager hears intimations of a world heavily weighted with real emotion.

But there is in Presley's delivery something much more subtle and hard to get at. From some fathomless and unstudied depth he has managed, in a whole series of songs, to call forth irony. Elvis is laughing at us and at himself, without knowing it, and while remaining altogether serious.

Laughing or not, let's see where Elvis Presley went once the magic tube took him, loose of limb and larger than life, into all those living rooms. In 1957, with a million dollars or so coming in from personal appearances and record royalties and some pocket money out of commercial endorsements (Elvis Presley lipstick in such shades as Hound Dog Orange and Tutti Frutti Red sold like the proverbial hotcakes that year), Colonel Parker set a TV price of $100,000 per on his dandy meal ticket's services and in one stroke eliminated the peril of overexposure; nobody could afford the boy. Then Elvis went into the service for two years, while the Colonel on the outside dispensed stored-up recordings to the mournful legions and Paramount Pictures tried to buttress our spirits with a Presley movie which happened to be called

G. I. Blues. A civilian again but minus the sideburns (you know those butchers in the Army), Elvis settled down in Hollywood to make a never-ending succession of·films which invariably would be damned by the critics and hailed by the men who count the returns. Good for a six- or seven-figure fee every time, he went before the cameras, and stepped up into the 5-to-6-million-dollar-a-year bracket, Elvis worked so much that he never took the time to let his antiseptic new image get tarnished by anything even remotely resembling a Sinatra-like image. Except for his ceaseless toil on the set, he lived the simple life of an Arabian oil potentate on an estate in Bel-Air, surrounded by his one and only wife, Priscilla Ann Beaulieu, an Air Force officer's daughter who was fourteen when he met her while doing his Army time in Germany, the ever-present Colonel in the counting room, and a small army of long-time buddies performing the numerous services a man of his station required.

But something happened along the line, and we would not know about it for seventeen years.

In 1960 Presley did a $125,000 guest shot on a Frank Sinatra TV special followed by a pronouncement from the Colonel that thereafter his price for gracing the little screen would be $150,000. A single released that year, "Are You Lonesome Tonight?," sold 20 million copies and made the Guinness record book, followed by another whopper in a spiritual vein, "His Hand in Mine." In 1961 RCA laid a plaque on Elvis to denote that since the four-dollar session which produced "That's All Right, Mama" the man had sold 76 million records. Beautiful, except that by then the quickie movies were dying at the box office and Elvis vanished from the boob tube as well. With something like $12 million a year in royalties and assorted pieces of change pouring in, he all but vanished from the scene. Eight years went by. Then, in the winter of 1968, Priscilla presented him with a bouncing baby girl, Lisa Marie, and the King of Rock surfaced again with an NBC-TV appearance and a four-week stint at Las Vegas' International Hotel worth a million dollars. The man was back in business, just as big as ever even against competition like the Beatles and Mick Jagger's Rolling Stones.

Skip a few years here.

Elvis and Priscilla break up. She goes off with Lisa and a settlement of $1.7 million plus $8,000 a month until 1983, and the troubled star settles down for the next five years in his palatial hometown retreat, Graceland Mansion, with the honey blonde Linda Thompson, a one-time Miss Tennessee beauty queen. Now, between occasional performances, the swivel-

One of the world's most eligible bachelors, the Pelvis surprised everybody in 1967 and married Priscilla Ann Beaulieu. They met in Germany when Presley was a GI and Priscilla, the Colonel's daughter, was attending school there. *UPI*

hipped body is a shapeless mass of fat. Now, paranoid or worse, and sustained by a plague of uppers, downers and what-have-you, the King of Rock is on the downhill slide. Come the Seventies, his playthings are an M-1 carbine and a .38 caliber Smith & Wesson revolver. If he sees anything on the TV screen that he doesn't like he blows it apart. As related by long-time bodyguards Robert (Red) West, Delbert (Sonny) West and Dave Hebler in Steve Dunleavy's *Elvis: What Happened?*, he wants a karate instructor named Mike Stone executed for pirating Priscilla's affections. The armored trio rejects that; they know their meal ticket has flipped out.

The end came on August 16, 1977.

Elvis Presley, forty-two, who made a revolution in music, was found dead in his mansion by his newest live-in companion, twenty-one-year-old Ginger Allen, Memphis's Miss Traffic Safety of 1976. The doctors put it down to arrhythmia, an irregular heartbeat that can be as deadly as an M-1 carbine. There was no evidence of drugs, although the man was a walking pharmaceutical house by then.

And what happened? As with Bing Crosby's passing, but much more so, the record manufacturers found that putting out 4 million long-playing discs a day wouldn't quite meet the demand. The Dunleavy book, with a first printing of 400,000 and another 250,000 rolling off the Ballantine presses, threatened to smash all the marks for the quickie paperback.

On the eve of his induction in 1958, Elvis comforts his parents in their Memphis home. *WWP*

Presley memorabilia—anything with the magic name on it, like T-shirts and toys—sold like gold bars before the price of gold went into the stratosphere. And Mama was dead and the fresh windfall would accrue to Presley's ailing sixty-two-year-old father, Vernon, and the pieceman Parker. Windfall? Record sales hit an estimated $400 million in the first year after the King of Rock's demise and the tie-in items about $100 million. In time, of course, what's left of a fortune that has to be staggering will go to Lisa, eleven now and living with her mother, thirty-three, in Beverly Hills.

On the first anniversary of Elvis's death Memphis geared itself for an invasion of tens of thousands of his fans—with a $3 price tag for a tour of the Cook County Convention Center just to steal a glance at Elvis paintings, Elvis buttons, Elvis clocks, Elvis belt buckles, a few locks of the star's hair or, God help us, a closeup view of the Presley trash can. For $5 you could have your picture taken in the man's old purple Cadillac. For $5.75 you could buy an 8x10 photo of him made with his daughter just four days before the end, and for $3.50 you could buy a dollar bill with Elvis's face on it.

It's hard to remember anything uglier or more commercial, but let's remember the kid from Memphis for songs like "Love Me Tender," "Heartbreak Hotel," "I Need Your Love Tonight," "You'll Never Walk Alone," "Jailhouse Rock," "I Want You, I Need You, I Love You," and all the others. He left his mark on this scene.

The now-overblown singer, on every kind of upper and downer and his wife discarded for a Tennessee beauty queen, in an infrequent appearance in Des Moines in June of 1977 two months before his heart gave out at forty-two. *WWP*

Something to remind you of the Rudolph Valentino obsequies a half-century back. The hordes gather outside Presley's Graceland Mansion in Memphis for a view of the body and a chance to buy some overpriced souvenirs. The money kept rolling in with the old hit recordings.

The funeral procession moves down Elvis Presley Boulevard in the city that spawned a flaming star who had it all but couldn't beat the death wish. *WWP*

Part XIV

〰〰〰〰〰〰〰〰〰〰〰〰〰〰〰〰〰〰〰〰〰〰〰〰〰〰〰

IN THE MATTER OF S-E-X

FROM KINSEY TO MASTERS AND JOHNSON

"There may be some things better than
sex, and some things may be worse. But
there is nothing exactly like it."
— W. C. FIELDS

Dr. William H. Masters with his assistant,
psychologist Virginia Johnson (later his wife),
when their *Human Sexual Response* headed for
the best-seller lists in 1966. *WWP*

IT ALL BEGAN, really, in the Garden of Kinsey. Dr. Alfred Charles Kinsey, the University of Indiana biologist who grew weary of probing into the life of the gall wasp and throwing nets over butterflies, took dead aim at people instead, and lit up our world with *Sexual Behavior of the Human Male* (1948) and *Sexual Behavior of the Human Female* (1953). Performing his wondrous labors eventually at the Intitute for Sex Relations in Bloomington, the reformed zoological wizard told us everything about our sex lives that we either didn't want to ask about or admit. It turned out, as everyone knows now, that ever so many of us had cast aside the Judeo-Christian ethics of our forefathers, not to mention the laws of the land, and were doing it all. Some of the time, perish the thought, with members of our own sex.

So much for Dr. Kinsey, now passed from this vale of rampant lovemaking.

Today, all hanging out, the problems associated with this area of our lives virtually borders on big business. The trick is to get the most for your money or your love, and it is a very crowded field, SRO to the degree that it has drawn the inevitable quacks alongside the qualified professionals. Our examina-

tion starts on the upbeat side with Dr. William H. Masters, out of Cleveland, and his longtime associate, psychologist Virginia E. Johnson.

Masters, a gynecologist and authority in hormone therapy, began to probe the sexual wilderness at the Washington University Medical School in Saint Louis in 1954 on the heels of the trailblazing Kinsey. It was the doctor's notion that it takes two to tango in the boudoir—two to do it wrong or two to do it right— and that the solution for whatever might be awry rested in the treatment of *both* partners. Thus his patient would be the marriage itself—under glass. And on tape. And with color cameras, electrodes and all manner of equipment.

Therapy at the Masters-Johnson Institute, which has had funding help from such as Hugh Hefner's Playboy Foundation, is not for your everyday couple with trouble in bed. The two-week course carries a grunt of $2,500, plus your travel and a room at the inn of your choice over that period unless you're one of the 25 percent who qualify on economic grounds for free treatment or a reduced fee. And you can't just drop in on the Missouri sexologists. You have to be recommended by a doctor, clergyman, social

Alfred Kinsey with one of his principal associates, Dr. Wardell Pomeroy, in 1953. *Institute for Sex Research/Dellenback*

any festering secrets, such as possible homosexual histories, traumatic sexual encounters, abortion or whatever. Except by mutual consent, the latter items are kept in confidence. On the third day, following physical tests to ascertain that nothing organic stands in the way of fulfillment for a particular couple, four-way rap sessions begin, informal to the degree that the therapists do not limit themselves to the stuffy jargon of their profession but talk the patients' language, whatever it may be.

And then, with exercises known as "sensate focus," the treatment gets under way. Stripped down, the couple is instructed to make an effort to give each other pleasure in turn by fondling, holding or stroking any parts of their bodies *except* the breasts and genital areas. This brief exercise, free of the anxiety very likely associated with the necessity for orgasm in the troubled pair, is described as an initial "deliberate expression of an undemanding sexual exchange." What's involved is touch, sight, sound, smell, empathy. The next day is devoted to the body and what it's about with some heavy discussion of such damaging myths as the widespread notion that it's always the man, only the man, who knows just what his sex partner needs—and when.

In the next step, the "sensate focus" exercise extends to the sex organs but without proceeding to climax. That—in the privacy of your own rented bedroom—occurs somewhere short of halfway through the treatment. When you head for your own marital bed, finally, you have been through between twenty-five and fifty hours of concentrated psychotherapy and have spent a solid two weeks, ideally, with nothing on your mind but the sex act and all of your other day-to-day concerns, the good and the bad, in cold storage.

In their runaway bestsellers, *Human Sexual Response* (1966) and *Human Sexual Inadequacy* (1970), based on years of case files all involving five-year follow-up checks, Masters and Johnson claim a record of success in the 80 to 85 percent area.

Now how about the *un*married party with the problem?

The Saint Louis team, courting fire, made an exception early on for the single male who could satisfy them that he had a serious purpose, like the love of his life was waiting at the airport for him to step off the jet in better shape than when he got on it. The procedure for the men was instituted in 1958 with the help of thirteen female surrogates—there were double that many volunteers—between the ages of twenty-three and forty-three. The women patients were admitted later, and there were also unmarried

worker, psychologist, marriage counselor or in some instances by a lawyer trying to keep you out of the divorce courts. And then you have to pass a screening to ascertain that neither partner is seriously disturbed mentally or afflicted with some ailment that would bar a satisfactory sexual relationship no matter what the treatment. Age is not a factor. The Masters-Johnson alumni—some from as far off as Pakistan, South Africa, Australia, South America and other outposts across the oceans—have ranged from their mid-twenties into their seventies.

There is nothing at all complicated about the procedure and no coaching from the sidelines, but there is one firm rule: the sex act itself must be shunned until the couple has undergone all of the initial ministrations as out-patients at the hospital.

The first step consists of two separate sessions. Dr. Masters and an associate tape the male partner's psychosocial history while Mrs. Johnson and a woman associate do the same with the wife, reversing the process the next day. In those seven hours, ideally, the patients are expected to tell it all—what they like and don't like in their lovemaking, prior experiences and

couples—serious types, of course—accepted for treatment. Missouri, along with some of our other provinces, still has one of those ancient Puritanical laws banning sex without that piece of paper, but it was never invoked against the Masters and Johnson operation and became academic in 1970 anyway. The sexology team dropped the Single-O's then, one reason stemming from a lawsuit filed against them by the somewhat angry husband of a supposedly single or divorced surrogate on their team, but continued to find room for unmarried couples (one out of eight of the patient load).

The surrogate, needless to say, never performed his or her wonders gratis, neither in the Masters-Johnson clinic nor the others which blossomed like wild flowers in its wake, such as the Berkeley Sex Therapy Group near the UC campus. It is a procedure which has drawn assaults from quite a few authorities in the field who equate the pinch-hitter with nothing more than a prostitute, male or female. Dr. Helen Kaplan, author of *The New Sex Therapy* and then running the therapy program at New York's Payne Whitney Clinic, has put it this way:

> Lonely people can be helped by surrogates, but I would try to work in psychotherapy to figure out why the person is lonely. We have to get humanity and eroticism back into sex. You can't do that if you pay someone $100 to go to bed with you.

And from Dr. John O'Connor, head of the sex therapy program at New York's Columbia Presbyterian Medical Center—

> A guy may be able to have sex with a surrogate, but what happens when he wants to have sex with his partner?

Good question.

Dr. Masters has an answer for it. He says that over an eleven-year span in his clinic the imported female partners overcame impotency problems in 75 percent of the fifty men treated.

A personal note on the doctor and his helpmate is in order here. In 1970 Masters, then fifty-four, was divorced by his wife, Elizabeth, on the grounds of desertion, with custody of their teen-age son and daughter split between them and the sexologist burdened with a $2,038-a-month alimony bite. The forty-six-year-old Virginia Johnson, mother of two and divorced back in 1956, became Mrs. Masters in a quiet Unitarian ceremony in Fayetteville, Arkansas, early in 1971.

How much of a growth industry is sex therapy?

Just a few years back Masters himself estimated that there were somewhere between 3,500 and 5,000 sex clinics in operation—not more than a hundred, in his view, in the hands of qualified professionals. There are some therapists, operating with price tags running as high as $4,000, who will never be candidates for food stamps. And the Masters-Johnson "sensate focus" device, which Dr. Kaplan has lauded as "an ingenious and invaluable tool in treating general female dysfunction," has been discarded in many clinics in favor of such more rapid stimulation as films showing assorted couples in the real act. Elsewhere, straight pornography is available for whatever therapeutic purpose that may have. You can also buy yourself treatments built around sado-masochistic exercises, the homosexual bit or, inevitably, the "cure" in which the therapist himself happily serves as your surrogate partner (you keep reading about one or another of those paid swordsmen hauled before the bar by patients who had not attained the promised ecstatic high). Or would you rather go the bisexual route? That's available too—at a price.

Why is this so?

You don't need a license to be a sex therapist. You just need an office or a bedroom, a movie projector or what-have-you. This is not to put down the respectable organizations and doctors in the field but it does raise a serious question: what's taking the state legislatures and the medical profession itself so long to do something about those that are not?

Former Attorney General Ramsey Clark and his wife, Georgia, with Harry Reems at a Manhattan benefit to raise money for the *Deep Throat* co-star's appeal against a five-year obscenity conviction in Memphis. *WWP*

THE OTHER THERAPY: PORN

"We are very much in a stage of transition sexually, and there is bound to be some exploitation."
—*Playboy*'s HUGH HEFNER

HEY, WHAT'S GOING ON in this Sodom and Gomorrah—or, more aptly, what's coming off?

Porn is rampant in the land. President Nixon's Commission on Obscenity and Pornography in 1970, not only taking that flourishing industry rather lightly but averring that there was no evidence that it was fostering more sex crimes or even soiling our moral character, put the dirt peddlers' haul at a mere $600 million a year. The estimates since then have run closer to the $2 and $3 billion range. But the coin of the realm is not the issue here. The issue is much larger: Where does that horde of paying clients come from? What were they doing before the peep shows, the massage parlors, the plotless X-rated sex movies and the bookstores specializing in rape, bestiality, sadism and child molestation came out of the woodwork not just in the big swinging cities on both coasts but even in the Bible Belt? We know about the second oldest profession. We know you could always buy yourself a stack of lewd photos or a 16-mm home movie with all the ways or, for that matter, answer a classified ad and do business with the real thing. The question is what brought the crowd out of the closet. What accounts for the man in the three-piece double-

knit suit with the attaché case in his hand walking into all the nudie service stations just as casually as if he were on the way to a board meeting? What accounts for the woman who has demanded—and won—the same right to patronize those sleazy joints? How did all the barricades fall in such a relatively short period of time? How did live sex shows come to the movie houses? And how silly can you get? The debate over legalizing prostitution goes on and on when as a matter of plain fact the entrepreneurs in the flesh-for-sale trade have effectively legalized it themselves, and the guardians of our morals, huffing and puffing, can't do a thing about it.

Hold on here. You're not reading a sermon. The author is neither clamoring for a special session of the Congress to deal with the problem nor calling down the wrath of the gods upon the women (and don't forget the teenagers) who are selling their bodies, either in the massage parlors or the streets, although he does have an antipathy toward the enormously prosperous gentlemen driving Pimpmobiles. No. This is just an inquiry into a phenomenon worthy of some diligent probing at this time because it has come such a long way since that Presidential commission put together its rather cavalier ten-volume report after two years of labor.

We're dealing now with something that in essence only began to happen the day before yesterday. That may sound a little casual, but the fact is that the lid began to come off only in the last decade when the bottomless bar blossomed in San Francisco, followed by the restaurant with the topless waitress, followed by the rapidly proliferating Mafia-connected whorehouses that went by the name of massage parlors, followed by the barebacked encounter "retreats" or "palaces" or "relaxation spas" where if you had the price you could buy everything but the proprietor's own best girl or, as the case may be, best fella. Remember when the first wife-swapping scandals hit the public prints around the Fifties or so? In Manhattan's once-venerated Ansonia Hotel today there's an establishment called Plato's Retreat where you can take your spouse (or someone you may like even better, for that matter), dance to some ear-bending disco tunes, frolic in a common bath, drop into the "mat room" to join in a jam-packed Bacchanalian orgy or slip into one of the twenty "miniswing" rooms limited to one to three couples. Admission: $25 per couple, $10 for unaccompanied women looking for some action (sorry, no unattached males allowed). Plato's, just one of a half-dozen similar "swinger" operations in New York, functions as a private club with a nominal six-week membership fee of $5. The food and drink, like the stranger who may catch your eye, is on the house. Sounds like a hard way to turn a profit, doesn't it? Hardly. The owners will tell you that with somewhere between 700 to 850 couples dropping in for their jollies every week Plato's is good for a million dollars in after-tax profits per year. It is by no means unique. There are other fun places like it in San Francisco, Chicago and Montreal, and there should be a plethora of others scattered around by the time you read this. The price is right and the law's no bother. Would the police bust down the door of the Women's National Republican Club in Manhattan if the GOP ladies turned it into a possibly more genteel version of Plato's? Or the Yale or Harvard clubs?

Back to the pleasure palaces. There's another Manhattan club, called Caesar's Retreat, that forgoes anything as pedestrian as orgies for private ministrations running all the way up to one rather special treatment, just $100 worth, furnished by three women all toiling at once. From that plush type of resort, one descends to the tawdrier massage parlors that for years turned Times Square into something approximating the world's largest brothel. In those traps, you could buy yourself a "local"—nothing more than a quick piece of masturbation by your hand-picked "masseuse"—or take the express for $25 to $50 and have all kinds of fun. The city fathers all but exhausted themselves padlocking those playpens with such devices as vice raids and building code violations only to have fresh arrivals hang out their neon shingles five minutes later. Then a citywide moratorium succeeded to some degree in banishing any parlors peddling flesh rather than those so-called massages and finally, in late 1978, an ingenious twist in the zoning laws may have sounded their eventual doom. The new legal assault cut the number down from sixty-four to twenty with the last of them set to close down by November of 1979. Assuming, of course, that the entrepreneurs running them, more often than not in the firm embrace of the underworld, haven't found a loophole somewhere in that legislation before then.

When the Hollywood authorities cracked down on a massage parlor called Chick's Delight in 1975 the enterprising owners switched to an "out-call service" advertising "finger-lickin' good" females who made house calls bearing "snack boxes, breasts, thighs, white meat and drink." That same year in the Iowa corn country, the Des Moines police busted twenty similar "out-call" operations, whereupon the owners converted them to out-call "modeling" services and stayed in business. At least one Mormon temple in Utah suddenly found some hardcore porn establishments among its neighbors. Atlanta's Peachtree Street sprouted all kinds of prostitution and grubby porn operations until the mayor himself, Maynard Jackson, was solicited by a streetwalker at the wheel of his car one afternoon when he was stalled in traffic on that once-proud thoroughfare. A swift crackdown followed, but the Georgia capital's venerable Baptist Book Store vanished in favor of a porn shop along the way. Omaha's Main Street found itself sullied and Wichita, Kansas, also known as "the buckle on the Bible Belt," fell host to its share of porn merchants. Five nude bars suddenly flourished in little Mason City, Iowa (pop. 32,000). Detroit went after its burgeoning smut trade in 1977 with the most effective zoning law in the nation, and Chicago, New Orleans, Pittsburgh, Los Angeles and Portland followed suit, but you can buy what you want in all those cities anyway; the laws weren't retroactive. Joel Gora, the ACLU's acting legal director then, opposed any such legislation on the grounds that "you can't zone free speech" (oh, yes, the sex peddlers have their absolutist First Amendment supporters in all kinds of quarters) but drew this dissent from Harvard Law's highly

Boston's Combat Zone—two square blocks of anything you want to buy if you have the guts to go into it. The authorities started a crackdown there in 1977, revoking the liquor licenses of the nudie playpens when the Harvard football team's cornerback, Andrew Puopolo, twenty-two, was fatally stabbed in a row after a prostitute made off with his wallet. A teammate survived his wounds. *UPI*

respected Alan Dershowitz: "I don't think there is a First Amendment right to have pornography available every place. Zoning is a reasonable idea." Boston went to a variation on that device in 1974 by setting up an "adult entertainment district" confined to just two blocks. This seven-acre anything-goes enclave of all the known pleasures (credit cards accepted) came to be known as the city's Combat Zone, and it has proved to be an apt term. It's not too safe, having chalked up at least one homicide—a college student—and any number of ambulance calls.

So much for this depressing scene. Nobody's come up with a way to do anything about it, although Congress in 1978 did enact a tough "kiddie porn" law in an effort to shut off the fairly new traffic in home movies featuring children as young as five in sex acts of every variety.

This brings us to the way-out sex cinema—Linda Lovelace in *Deep Throat*, Georgina Spelvin in *The Devil in Miss Jones*, Marilyn Chambers (the ex-model whose face once adorned the Ivory soap box) in *Behind the Green Door*, just to mention the triple-X blockbusters that in 1976 had found 780 movie houses dropping Hollywood's conventional fare to accommodate them,

often at $5 a head in the larger metropolitan centers. *Deep Throat*—and that was the only possible name for it—was made for $25,000 in 1972 and, still running, has coined millions. So has the Spelvin movie, another oldie by now. Ms. Chambers' starring vehicle cost $45,000 and had made it back twenty times over by 1976. All of those big-screen home movies have had their troubles getting shown here and there but the Supreme Court's 1973 decision leaving it to the individual communities to make their own determinations as to what constitutes obscenity has worked more for than against the promoters of the straight sex epics.

The most notable exception, still not over, has come in Memphis, where Assistant U.S. Attorney Larry Parrish, thirty-two, father of three and an elder in the First Evangelical Church, put on twelve obscenity trials in 1976 with his most publicized score coming in the conviction of superstud Harry Reems for his not-too-arduous labors opposite Linda Lovelace, who beat indictment by "cooperating" with the government. Reems, so marvelously endowed that he has appeared in more than 400 porn movies, was paid a big $100 for his role in *Deep Throat*, and is

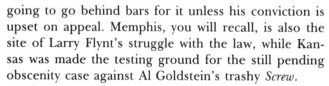

The Moonies invaded Boston's "adult entertainment district" in 1977, and Darlene Starr, a dancer in one of the joints, took some time out to hear what they had to say. *WWP*

Los Angeles: This was a just-plain movie house before the gold strike in triple-X rated entertainment.

San Francisco's gaudy Broadway in 1973 while the sex-peddlers were fighting off a clampdown by local officials. *WWP*

going to go behind bars for it unless his conviction is upset on appeal. Memphis, you will recall, is also the site of Larry Flynt's struggle with the law, while Kansas was made the testing ground for the still pending obscenity case against Al Goldstein's trashy *Screw*.

What accounts for all this, and where does it leave us?

Time made it a cover essay a couple of years ago and couldn't come up with the answer. From UCLA psychiatrist Robert J. Stoller, author of *Perversion: The Erotic Form of Hatred*: "Societies fear pornography as they fear sexuality, but perhaps there is a less sick reason—they (porn's paying clients) respond intuitively to the hostile fantasies disguised but still active in pornography." From psychologist Douglas Wallace of the University of California: "Are you to deny these victims of our socialization process [the sexual

300

B'nai Yeshua, an organization of Jewish students, pickets one of the many porn theaters in New York's Times Square. That 25-cent bit on the marquee was just a sales pitch. For a quarter all you could do was crank up one of those ancient home-movie machines. The live shows ran to $2.99.

Linda Lovelace when her starring vehicle, *Deep Throat,* hit the silver screen in 1972. It's still running.

losers] the satisfaction they might enjoy from looking at these kinds of stimuli?" But perhaps Marvin E. Wolfgang, a University of Pennsylvania sociologist, said it best: "There ought to be a way to limit pornography to those who want it."

Only one problem there.

The law, all but impotent, is fighting a rear-guard action at best. Pornography, a closet operation for so many years, has burst into ravishing good health as another growth industry and appears to be here to stay, as long as there are paying customers to keep it financially healthy. Approximately forever, let's say, since its strongest ally—the First Amendment—is also here to stay.

Ms. Spelvin, not a bit ruffled, eavesdrops outside a Memphis courtroom while awaiting a hearing on an obscenity indictment over *The Devil in Miss Jones.* She wouldn't have to do any time. *WWP*

Marilyn Chambers when she was making a living as a model—
before the porn movies beckoned.

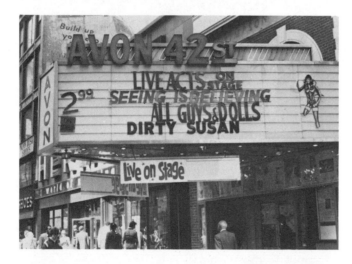

New York's Forty-Second Street. Take your pick. *Paul Sann*

〰〰〰

Part XV

THE SPORTING FRONT

NOTHING
BUT MONEY

Curt Flood with lawyer Arthur Goldberg in a park bench
strategy session during a recess in one of his endless court
sessions in his battle against baseball's reserve clause.

*"It's a little difficult
to find a job for a used center fielder.
You can't look in the want ads and
find a job like that."*
—CURT FLOOD, out of baseball

THIS ONE'S ABOUT another revolutionary movement—
not with guns but sheer determination. It happened
on the playing fields where that other underprivileged
class, the baseball players, toiled in broiling sun, or
rain, or toward season's end in cold and high autumn
winds. It's about guys with names like Flood and
Messersmith and McNally, who took on the Establishment with legal briefs and a tough labor negotiator,
ultimately buttressed by agents and accountants instead of artillery. It's about the new instant millionaires of the Seventies, not just in baseball but in the
other professional games. How did it happen in a
business—and sports *is* a business no different from
U. S. Steel or General Motors—where as recently as
the early Sixties you could buy yourself an athlete for
minimum scales as low as $7,500 a year?

While the revolt of the sweat-stained slaves was in
progress before then, since they had turned into just
plain union men in 1966, you have to start with the
handsome, gentle Curt Flood, full-time outfielder,
part-time portrait painter and an angry product of
Oakland's black ghetto. It was this man who in 1969
challenged the century-old reserve clause that made
the diamond's wage earners indentured servants, took

it all the way to the High Court, lost—and kicked
open the sacred door anyway. It was Flood, with the
Major League Players' Association behind him, who
paved the way for the national pastime's free agent.
Free, that is, to say something after a while about
where he wants to play, for whom and for how much.
You could compare it to Mr. Lincoln's Emancipation
Proclamation, although that hasn't worked quite as
well.

Here is how it happened:

Flood, who played two years for the Cincinnati
Reds and twelve for the Anheuser-Busch beer cartel's
Saint Louis Cardinals, compiling an eminently respectable .293 batting average and winning the
Golden Glove Award for center fielders seven times
in a row, found himself traded to Philadelphia at the
end of the 1969 season. Well, Mr. Flood, having
played for so many years alongside such neon-lit colleagues as slugging Stan (The Man) Musial, pitcher
Bob Gibson and base-stealing Lou Brock, did not
wish to end his career in a club invariably identified
by the sportswriters as the "lowly Phillies." So he
didn't pack his gear for Quaker Town. He went to
New York instead and engaged the services—gratis—

With his agent, Herb Osmond, the Dodgers' Andy Messersmith awaits a session with Baseball Commissioner Bowie Kuhn on the validity of his claimed new status as a free agent. The pitcher won the argument. *WWP*

of Arthur J. Goldberg, a former Associate Justice of the Supreme Court and at the time a candidate for governor of the Empire State. Philadelphia, as it happened, was prepared to pay Flood a big $8,000 in spring training money as well as his healthy $90,000 Saint Louis salary, but the man wasn't interested in money. He preferred to go against the reserve clause, which dated back to the 1870s and owed its charmed life to a 1922 Supreme Court ruling that held that the sport of baseball (and baseball *alone*, by the way) was not a business engaged in interstate commerce and therefore not subject to the provisions of the Sherman Anti-Trust Act. Three separate challenges to that dictum had fallen short in the Fifties, but Curt Flood felt that the time had come to take away the license that made the ball players slaves. It was his view that the Cardinals could not simply discard him like a spiked shoe that had gone bad but that he had a right to a say in any trade. Mr. Goldberg and his associate, Jay Topkis, argued that the reserve clause amounted to nothing more than a "contract for perpetual service" and therefore constituted "an unreasonable restraint of trade." The suit asked for $3 million in damages and named Commissioner Bowie Kuhn, the presidents of both the National and American Leagues and all twenty-four clubs. The defendants, fretting more over the high principle involved than the trifling cash at stake with all the TV gold flowing into their coffers, contended that the slightest bend in the reserve clause would not only produce instant chaos but shatter the "fine rapport" between the players and their owners. The trial before Federal Judge Irving Ben Cooper in the spring of 1970 occupied fifteen court sessions and built up a 2,000-page record, but even in the face of testimony that none of the other professional sports were operating with contracts quite as binding as baseball's Flood lost and headed for Washington. And there, two years later, he lost again. The High Court, 5–3, ruled that the sport was indeed free of all anti-trust restraints and had a right to stay that way unless Congress elected to do something about it—a rather idle notion in view of the fact that the game's devoted fans on Capitol Hill had turned away prior efforts in that direction.

But that wasn't the end of it.

Marvin Miller, the highly skilled one-time negotiator for the steelworkers, got the reserve clause loosened up a bit in his negotiations for the Players Association the following year and come 1976 the barricades collapsed altogether, thanks to a couple of pretty fair country pitchers with minds as strong as their arms—Andy Messersmith of the Los Angeles Dodgers and southpaw Dave McNally of the expansion Montreal Expos. Messersmith, with his contract running out, sold himself to the New York Yankees on a four-year deal worth $2 million, found that owner George Steinbrenner had scribbled in some provisions he didn't care for, and wound up with Atlanta on quite the same arrangement—$330,000 per season in pay and a $500,000 bonus for signing. He threw out his shoulder fielding a hard-hit ball and the Braves happily gave him back to Mr. Steinbrenner the next summer, another bad time because then an elbow problem put him out of action. In the interim, amidst agonized wails over what those radical athletes were doing, the whole argument wound up in the hands of arbitrator Peter Seitz, who ruled that the owners' time-honored hold on their chattels—the contract phrase was "in perpetuity"—had no validity whatever. McNally, leaving the sport anyway because his time, patience and some of his arm had wilted, stayed with the case as a matter of principle. What came out of it all, writing the closing chapter in the long-running drama that had seen baseball hit by an unprecedented players' strike during spring training in 1969, Curt Flood's two-year court battle and another strike that knocked out the first five games of the 1972 season, was a whole new ball game. The owners couldn't trade away a player with ten years in the sport, the last five years on a single club, without giving him a veto power over where he was being shipped. Still juicier, your sixth season became an option year—nothing on paper—after which you were free to negotiate for yourself with any other club hungering after your services. This marked the birth of baseball's free agents—a breed of men of such remarkable upward ability that they might be just as apt to read the *Wall Street Journal* as *The Sporting News*. Thus when Charles O. Finley started to dismantle his world champion Oakland Athletics a few years back to cut his burgeoning payroll, the Yanks picked up the powerful right arm of James Augustus (Catfish) Hunter on a five-year contract with a $3.5 million price tag (for the record, Mr. Finley wasn't all that anxious to see that particular fireballer go but Hunter became a free agent when the club violated his contract by neglecting to make a $50,000 insurance deposit called for in the small print). Rich Gossage, a refugee from the Pittsburgh Pirates who is now one of the throwers behind the Catfish, burdened with all kinds of arm miseries from '76 way into '79, occupies the New York bullpen on a contract worth $2.748 million over six years. In right field, where his labors at times fall short of the spectacular, the Yanks employ another Finley discard, the power-hitting Reggie Jackson, lured into the family in 1976, after one semester in Baltimore, for $2.9 million for five seasons in the Bronx ball yard. Then there's the $3.155 million the Milwaukee Brewers are paying outfielder Larry Hisle for the next six summers and the $2.955 million the Texas Rangers are spending on the big bat of Richie Zisk, the right fielder who drifted over

from the Chicago White Sox. Gene Autry, Hollywood's reformed singing cowboy, put down $2 million and change to steal free agent Lyman Bostock from Minnesota only to lose him before he had that big bat—ninth best in the American League at .296— through his first season. The twenty-seven-year-old superstar outfielder was shotgunned to death in September 1978 by the estranged husband of a woman he was driving with in Gary, Indiana. The man had nothing against the ballplayer. He was trying to kill the wife who had fled his bed and board.

Some of the numbers cited above, by the way, turned rather paltry even as this essay was being written. The Cincinnati Reds' Pete Rose squeaked past the Mount Everest peak of 3,000 career hits, throwing in a forty-four game streak to edge the senior league record set in the Forties by the Boston Braves' Tommy Holmes, and decided that $365,000 per annum didn't quite cover that kind of ditch-digging labor. So the third baseman known as Charlie Hustle left the banks of the Ohio after sixteen years and, at age thirty-seven, went to the Philadelphia Phillies to play first base for $3.2 million and a guarantee that he would still be roaming the infield, or somewhere, at the ripe old age of forty-one. The Red Sox's slugging young outfielder, Jim Rice, the AL's Most Valuable Player for that same '78 season, had his agent wrangle a new contract worth $5.7 million over the next seven years even if he doesn't live that long. That was just a farthing or so behind Mr. Rose's arrangement in Quaker Town.

Shall we go on? Rose's old team came up with a new three-year contract worth between $700,000 and $800,000 per for its fence-busting outfield patrolman, George Foster. Pittsburgh surrendered to the free-agent process with a four-year contract extension for Dave Parker—not just the NL's MVP but the game's heaviest hitter—larded with a $625,000 bonus for signing, $625,000 a season and deferred payments at 8.5 percent interest, which could add up to between $7.5 and $9 million before the Pirates are finished paying the man in the year 2007. Finally, there's first baseman Rod Carew, just an odd point or so behind Parker and the big bat of the Minnesota Twins, plucked away by Mr. Autry with a five-year, $4.5 million piece of paper that starts at $800,000 and could go to a million in 1982 and $1.1 million in 1983 with cost-of-living boosts (well, the old high cost of living does keep going up, doesn't it, fellow workers?)

The owners and the suddenly rich players, it follows, do not share the same view of these recent developments. Twins President Calvin Griffith, brushing away tears, has complained that the ball clubs

Haywood Sullivan, the Red Sox General Manager, can still manage a smile after signing his slugging outfielder, Jim Rice, to a seven-year contract worth $5.4 million. And Rice, the AL's MVP in the 1978 season, collects it even if he breaks both legs and never plays another game. *WWP*

But Pete Rose, the Cincinnati Reds' Charlie Hustle, topped that bonanza by jumping to the Philadelphia Phillies for a four-year $3.2 million contract. That's $800,000 per season against Rice's paltry $770,000. *New York Post*

staggered into 1979 owing their chattels $240 million, including deferments. The man noted along the way that average salaries which ranged between $22,000 and $23,000 a decade earlier had climbed to $97,000. For the athletes, in turn, Marvin Miller responded with some numbers of his own: the owners' combined revenue in the preceeding season exceeded $278 million, thanks to the paying customers, soaring concession prices and more and more TV and radio money, whereas their combined payrolls of $68.5 million ate up a mere 24.6 percent of total income.

So much for the telephone numbers in the sport where a home-run hitter named Babe Ruth got all the way up to $80,000 a year in the Twenties and a pretty good center fielder, Joe DiMaggio, extracted $100,000 a year from the same Yankees before he hung up his golden glove in 1951.

Now we come to some athletes who came upon the big bucks via another route altogether. In professional basketball, football and hockey the more explosive talents got lucky when something new—competing leagues—suddenly sprang into existence. It started in 1960 when some upstarts calling themselves the American Football League set themselves up in business against the National Football League. Then in 1967 some entrepreneurs with tax money to burn (and did it burn) launched the American Basketball Association to challenge the National Basketball Association's long and happy monopoly, and in 1972 the National Hockey League found itself bargaining for talent against the newly formed World Hockey Association. Now the oldest established mints in the big-money games had to dig down in their vaults to hang on to their stars—and dig they did. In due

Slugger Rod Carew, having jumped Minnesota to spend five years in the sun with the California Angels for $4.5 million, doesn't look a bit unhappy. *WWP*

course, before they got emptied out altogether, the dual football and basketball leagues merged. Hockey's still in there slugging it out. Let's see what happened when the marketplace for the beautiful bodies opened up.

In roundball, the Philadelphia 76ers are paying Julius Erving, an ABA import better known as Dr. J because of the way he operates on the court in his short pants, $3.1 million on a six-year deal. Washington's Bullets signed their star forward, Elvin Hayes, to a three-year $1.3 million extension of his contract in 1977 when he was in his eleventh season and getting a little older, like thirty-three. Kareem Abdul-Jabbar—listed at a modest seven feet two inches but closer to seven-four—is drawing $3.1 million from the Los Angeles Lakers on a five-year deal. That's $625,000 per, the same pittance the high-scoring Pete Maravich of the New Orleans Jazz is managing to subsist on. In 1978, crying all the way from the bank because his team was simply awful, the New York Knickerbockers' Sonny Werblin invested $3 million in Marvin Webster, the Seattle Supersonics' seven-one "human eraser," for five seasons. The Chicago Bulls dipped into their till for a five-year extension on their seven-two man in the middle, Artis Gilmore, carrying a price tag of $4.5 million, or $900,000 per season. And that topped the $800,000 paycheck of Denver's dead-eyed David Thompson, which had created a problem for Portland with their man Bill Walton. That club signed the six-eleven redhead out of UCLA on a five-year $2 million deal and ran into trouble when his contract ran out in 1977. The league's MVP that semester even with assorted leg ailments keeping him on the bench much of the time, Walton announced that he wasn't going to play for anybody for one dime less than Mr. Thompson. As it turned out, amidst charges that the Trail Blazers' doctors had compounded his injuries with painkillers, Walton skipped the next season altogether, making the tiff over the dollar bill academic. Then Walton settled it all by signing with the San Diego Clippers for seven years for something more than Thompson's $800,000 per, plus two new Mercedes-Benz each season and some assorted odds and ends in fringe benefits.

Pirates' manager Chuck Tanner telling the press that the big man with the beard, Dave Parker, heaviest hitter in the NL, has just picked up a four-year contract extension worth so much only the accountants could figure it out. *WWP*

Philadelphia's Julius Erving, a "small" forward in modern basketball because he's a mere 6-6, dropping one into the hoop as the Knicks' Butch Beard, a midget of 6-3, looks on in anger. *New York Post*

Bill Walton, Portland's prize possession before they ran out of the kind of record-setting money he needed to live on, stuffing one in against the New Jersey Nets in the 1977–78 season. *WWP*

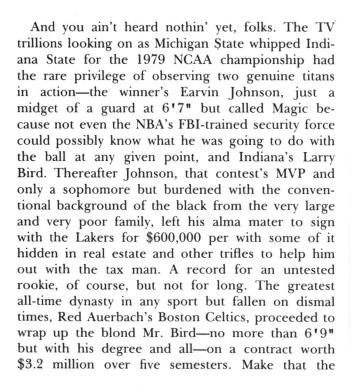

And you ain't heard nothin' yet, folks. The TV trillions looking on as Michigan State whipped Indiana State for the 1979 NCAA championship had the rare privilege of observing two genuine titans in action—the winner's Earvin Johnson, just a midget of a guard at 6'7" but called Magic because not even the NBA's FBI-trained security force could possibly know what he was going to do with the ball at any given point, and Indiana's Larry Bird. Thereafter Johnson, that contest's MVP and only a sophomore but burdened with the conventional background of the black from the very large and very poor family, left his alma mater to sign with the Lakers for $600,000 per with some of it hidden in real estate and other trifles to help him out with the tax man. A record for an untested rookie, of course, but not for long. The greatest all-time dynasty in any sport but fallen on dismal times, Red Auerbach's Boston Celtics, proceeded to wrap up the blond Mr. Bird—no more than 6'9" but with his degree and all—on a contract worth $3.2 million over five semesters. Make that the

O. J. Simpson carrying the ball for the Buffalo Bills before he sold himself to the San Francisco team for the same modest salary—a record $733,358 per season even with his best years behind him and the end not far at hand.

highest salary ever paid to a newcomer in basketball or any other game. This is where it's at now, a fact worth noting if you have fully grown boys around the house who want to go to college and work hard in the gym.

In football, the fleet O. J. Simpson, while also running for Avis Rent-A-Car in those TV spots, drew $733,358 per from the Buffalo Bills in 1976 and 1977 and then moved on to the San Francisco 49ers at the same stipend even with his diesel-powered legs slowing down a bit in his ninth year. Pretty good money when you consider that Derek Sanderson, too soon a victim of alcohol and drugs, became the world's highest paid athlete when the World Hockey Association's Philadelphia Blazers got him to jump from the Boston Bruins for $500,000 per in 1972 only to buy back his contract for a million dollars, or $333,330 for each goal he had put into the net, eight games into the season. Also on the ice, superstar defense man Bobby Orr jumped Boston for the Chicago Black Hawks in 1976 with $3 million in his sights over five seasons (well, none of those millionaires actually draw it all because they're surrounded by big brains like Boston lawyer Bob Woolf, an agent on the side, New York's Irwin Weiner and Larry Fleisher and hockey-specialist Alan Eagleson out of Canada) only to call it quits last year at thirty after his sixth knee operation.

For comparative purposes, a couple of postscripts: Chicago's Bobby Hull, the all-time great scoring machine who jumped to the Winnipeg Jets in 1972 for a

Superstar Bobby Hull pushing the puck for the Chicago Black Hawks before he jumped the NHL for greener ice in Canada. *WWP*

$1 million cash bonus and $250,000 a year, was risking his limbs on the ice just ten years earlier for $25,000; one of the game's all-time great scorers through twenty-two seasons, Hull retired in 1978 at thirty-nine. Carl Yastrzemski (called Yaz) labored in the Boston Red Sox outfield for $25,000 in 1962 and got up to $270,000 fifteen years later. And now that baseball has slipped back into this essay in high finance, a word about the man who dared to take the moguls into court.

For Curt Flood, who was thirty-two when he carried the standard, there was no personal gain. He sat out the 1970 season, which cost him $98,000. Then the Washington Senators' Bob Short hired him for $110,000 on a no-trade contract for the next semester but Flood unaccountably quit in less than a month and went to live—and paint—abroad. He came back into the game in 1978 as color man for the Oakland A's radio broadcasts. Never made the Hall of Fame but his name looms larger to day than some of the forgotten baseball slaves whose busts grace the museum at Cooperstown.

Finally, a word about that all-but-sacred "fine rapport" between the athletes and the owners. It wasn't there before and it isn't there today, no more than it is in the coal mines. The pro in all the games is just a guy working for a salary, as often as not on a career doomed to a fairly short run. He brings the customers into the house—and at constantly escalating prices. The owner just comes in on the cuff with his circle of intimates. And no owner's career ever was shortened either by an injury suffered on the field of battle or by some whiz kid coming up from the minors, the colleges or the sandlots. And there's something else worth noting about the breed. More and more, with one muncipality after another subsidizing new stadia for them, they've got us taxpayers as silent partners and the networks as enormously free-handed patrons. Football's collecting $656 million from TV in 1979, baseball $92.8 million and basketball $74 million. Hockey, something of a stepchild when it comes to selling soaps, deodorants, automobiles, beer and those little cigars and things, had to settle for a piddling $180,000. Are the big television brains getting their money's worth? Well, the commericals snapped up for the 1978 Super Bowl cost $325,000 for each 60 seconds.

Indiana State's Larry Bird, at $640,000 per season the highest-paid rookie in the history of sports, is flanked by Boston Celtics general manager Red Auerbach and the basketball team's new coach, Bill Fitch (right). *UPI*

The 1978 New York City Marathon kicks off in 72-degree heat from the Verrazano Bridge linking Brooklyn and Staten Island, with 9,875 runners, 1,134 of them women, off on their five-borough 26-mile run. *New York Post*

ANYONE FOR JOGGING?

"I used to be a weekly Mass goer. Now I'm not. I'm like Emily Dickinson. I keep my Sabbath in Central Park on Sunday."
—Dr. George A. Sheehan, jogger

We know who started it and when. It was Pheidippides, the Athenian courier, circa 490 B.C., who was dispatched to Sparta to get the reserves out when the Persians landed at Marathon. Pheidippides made the 25-mile run four times but dropped dead on the last lap to Athens to break the news that their side had won. There's a reference to the gallant Greek earlier in this book in the chapter on C. C. Pyle's Bunion Derby.

The point here is that our piece of Planet Earth is now inhabited, or so Mr. Gallup tells us, by no less than 23 million men and women who would rather run than eat. There are places where the streets aren't even safe because you may get knocked down by a jogger coming full speed—or even slow speed—around the corner. Oh, the party in the short pants may puff out a small "so sorry" but he—or she, and there are more and more from the Ms. side of the fence—won't lose a stride.

Now is all this good or bad? As ever, you can get an argument on it.

The preponderant view of the medical profession is that the serious joggers—and who isn't?—are running to live and living pretty good because they're doing all kinds of good for their hearts, lungs, blood pressure and even their heads, assuming the absence of any demons one can't outrun. It is by no means an easy task today to find a cardiologist who will not list running or swimming or the bicycle among the Rxs for patients who have bounced back from coronaries. Why? The heart can pump more blood with less effort for the man or woman on a regular regime in those exercise areas, and that cuts down on the danger of clots leading to fresh cardiac seizures. Let alone jogging, there hasn't been a marathon in recent years without its share—small, to be sure—of heart cases.

The catch, so elementary, is that there are joggers, especially among those thirty-five or older, who have jumped aboard that bandwagon without benefit of medical advice even though they may have shunned any kind of exercise since they were kids. This is where the doctors haul out the warning flags, because there's nothing all that unusual about coronary artery deficiencies exploding into heart attacks with sudden bursts of strenuous, unregulated athletic activity.

Thus nobody in the over-thirty-five group coming off a prolonged sedentary regime should join the running legions without a stress test and without finding out what that rugged sport entails. You don't just haul on shorts and sneakers and go dashing out into the nearest park or the carbon monoxide-filled streets. You need a five-to-ten minute warmup. You need to condition and loosen the leg and thigh muscles. You need to run regularly, not just when the spirit moves you. You need to know how to cool down after a workout to let your heart come down to its normal levels. If you know all that and will do it, your doctor's going to tell you to go buy those running shoes.

It is not all that easy to nail down the jogging boom.

Not too many years ago you could walk into any YMCA or YMHA that had a track and buy yourself a membership in five minutes. Now there are waiting lists as often as not. Not too long ago it took the hardiest of souls to run around the reservoir in New York's Central Park either too early in the morning or too long after dusk because there might be a mugger or two lurking in the bushes. The mugging fraternity and the rapists as well are still there, but business has dropped off badly. Too many joggers. And this must be true in urban centers throughout the country, not just in that otherwise perilous sylvan retreat in the heart of Manhattan.

Running, happily, has no age limits. Your correspondent, a couple of years back, was jogging alongside a gentleman who had competed in the 1920 Olympics. In this vein, consider the experiment undertaken in 1969 by Herbert A. de Vries, a University of Southern California physical education instructor. He found himself forty-one dead-game men ranging in age from fifty to eighty-seven and put them through a three-times-a-week regime of jogging and calisthenics for six weeks and then checked them against twenty-six sedentary types in the same age brackets. What he found: a 4.9 percent drop in body fat, a 6 percent cut in diastolic blood pressure, a 9.2 percent jump in maximum oxygen consumption and a 15 percent reduction in nervous tension as measured by pulse rates. There have been later tests just as impressive.

And, inevitably, we are now witnessing an undreamed-of boom in the book marts. The 1978 nonfiction best-seller lists heralded James F. Fixx's *The Complete Book of Running* and Dr. George A. Sheehan's *Running and Being* for what seemed like forever, right into 1979. Fixx, forty-five, a one-time editor at *Life* and top man at *McCall's*, traded in his cigarettes and lunchtime martinis for a pair of running shoes in 1967 and has since done 30,000 miles. He has com-

peted in twenty marathons, seldom runs less than ten miles a day, and at 160 looks nothing like the 220-pounder who sat behind magazine desks for seventeen years. His bank account looks better too. The book that hit, his third on the subject, passed 155,000 hardcover copies and earned him $200,000 in no time at all. Dr. Sheehan, a fifty-nine-year-old cardiologist from Red Bank, New Jersey, started jogging at forty-five and has rarely missed a marathon since.

Speaking of marathons, the will, total dedication and sheer brute strength of the people who enter those romps, challenging their bodies almost beyond the point of no return, is too well known to belabor. Let a single story tell it all. It happened last November in the 26-mile Grand Valley Marathon in Allendale, Michigan.

Passing the 10-mile point and moving along nicely, Dennis Rainear, twenty-six, felt a thud against the back of his head that almost knocked him off his feet. Assuming that some fun-loving idiot along the route had aimed a stone at him, he quickly regained his stride and kept running. He made the finish line in just nine minutes over the three hours needed to qualify for the next Boston Marathon and then asked the doctors to check the swelling goose-egg-sized bump on his head. No, it wasn't a stone. It was a .22 caliber bullet that had flattened against his skull without causing any bleeding. In the hospital, the bullet was removed and the wound stitched together. Rainear wasted no time brooding about it, except to note remorsefully that the hand behind the gun very likely had cost him his shot at the Boston race.

To get back to Jim Fixx and Dr. Sheehan, two other committed souls who probably couldn't be stopped by bullets either, they are a pair who got healthy in more ways than one when they left their swivel chairs and started to run. The people who sell the shoes aren't doing badly either, and don't put jogging down as just another fad. It's here to stay. On the indoor tracks, in the parks, on the byways, in hardback and softback and what-have-you. The Fixx and Sheehan books had quite a tussle with two paperbacks—*The Complete Runner*, by the editors of *Runner's World* magazine, and *The Runner's Handbook*, by Bob Glover and Jack Sheppherd—before the whole fraternity ran into a totally unexpected piece of competition. Vic Ziegel and Lewis Grossberger, two escapees from the New York *Post* writing staff, knocked out something called *The Nonrunner's Book* and found themselves aboard the trade paperback best-selling list early in 1979. The title tells it all. Those two funny men, who wouldn't run if their Greenwich Village apartments caught fire, count King Tut among

Opposite: Grete Waitz, a junior high school teacher from Oslo, took the women's share of that October race in New York in 2:32:30—two minutes faster than the world record pace. Was this twenty-five-year-old possessor of the 1978 record for the women's mile at 4:26:9 a bit tired? "I don't know if I'll ever do one of these again," she said.

Bill Rodgers, thirty, out of Boston, winning for the third time in a row, crosses the Central Park finish line in 2:12.12, his slowest time but with no other male runner on his heels. *New York Post*

Joan Benoit, twenty-one, a Bowdoin College senior from Brunswick, Maine, set a new women's record of 2:35:15 in 1979 in the eighty-third edition of the Boston Marathon. It was just her second marathon. Who's that next to her? Bill Rodgers, of course. He took the men's title for the third time in five years, breaking the record he set in 1975 by covering the grueling 26.2-mile course in 2 hours, 9 minutes and 27 seconds. The classic drew a mere 7,877 contestants. *WWP*

James Fixx: the track shoes changed his life and his big book on running did some things for his bank account.

Age doesn't count for the joggers. Look at this trio going around the Central Park reservoir in Manhattan. *Paul Sann*

their heroes just for "lying around a thousand years" and not having a single pair of running shoes encumbering his tomb.

Jim Fixx has offered one explanation for the raging phenomenon.

"I think the U.S. is in a terribly inward-looking, narcissistic frame of mind; we've lost faith in a lot of the important institutions in our society, like government and marriage."

Is *that* what it's all about? Joggers, examine thyselves—unless, of course, you're on the public payroll or running with your own wife.

Dennis Rainear of Midland, Michigan, finished the 1978 marathon out there with a .22-caliber rifle slug embedded in his head at the 10-mile mark. He didn't know it was a bullet and would have kept going even with a "silly thing" like that befalling him during the long grind. *WWP*

314

A NATION ON (SMALL) WHEELS

So MUCH FOR the footsore but happy joggers. There's another breed—men, Ms.'s and a veritable legion of the young—that brought back the roller skate in the late Seventies. But big. If the numbers are right, there are more people on skates today than in sneakers, with 3,000 rinks claiming a whirling clientele of 28,000,000 against the mere 23,000,000 runners. As far as the teens go, a 1978 Gallup poll listed that revived exercise as the sixth most popular participation sport behind basketball, baseball, softball, swimming and bowling. Mr. Gallup had the tennis players, skiers, fishermen and hunters dragging behind the skating crowd.

It does get tiresome after a while, but once again if you look hard enough you find that this revival is still another product of the sunny, fun-loving West Coast. The locale this time: Venice, California, a couple of years back the boardwalk out there suddenly bloomed with a whole flock of roller skaters, and pretty soon you were hearing that the entire state was into the sport that boomed in the Thirties with a big assist from Fred Astaire and Ginger Rogers on roller skates in 1937's *Shall We Dance* and then died a none-too-slow death. As in all the turn-ons, some glittering names quickly appeared in the shoes-on-wheels set. Television's Cher, or Cher Bono Allman if you want to go all the way, started throwing roller-rink soirees,

and one report had Linda Ronstadt roller-skating to a luncheon with Governor Edmund G. Brown, Jr.

Today's wheels, as you must know if you've been out of your knee pants long enough, bear no resemblance at all to the tinny things you strapped onto your shoes with clamps in the olden days, hoping against hope that they would hold. No. Now the nice round wheels come attached to boots just like ice skates, and the better ones are made out of durable substances like polyurethane or a fancy plastic. Cost: anywhere from $30 up to $145 or so.

But you don't need to dig into your pocket for any kind of money unless your thing is skating in the streets. The great bulk of the new army is in the rinks zinging along carefully manicured high-density chipboard floors on rented skates at rates running as low as $2 an hour. This, of course, is for the lower classes.

The more recent disco skating rage is quite another ball game. Soft lights, hard disco tunes and knee-deep carpeted areas around the floor where the liquid refreshments don't come cheap. And that's not the half of it, especially for the females. There's also the matter of the proper dress, not that the generally acceptable leotard or Danskin is all that expensive. But that really won't do in the more chic roller discos, will it? Milady can run into some money when

Between the roller skates and that German Shepherd this pretty girl had a right to feel moderately safe in New York's Central Park. *New York Post*

Finally, a postscript for the masses under scorn and indictment for lugging around too much weight: every twenty miles an hour you put in on roller skates means 400 calories down the drain. Think about that, but don't get careless. Even without that rickety old clamp, there are people falling off skates and getting hurt. Nothing at all comparable with the perils of skateboarding, to be sure. Let us give thanks for that.

Another Manhattan scene to illustrate the skating boom. *New York Post*

she drapes those bodysuits in fluffy satin or silk skirts.

Put the just-plain commercial neighborhood rinks together with the plush joints and the sizable army plucking the shelves of the sporting goods and department stores empty for their own skating in the parks, playgrounds or streets and what have you got? If you listen to Irwin Rosee, executive secretary of the flourishing Roller Skating Foundation of America, public relations arm of the revived fad, you have a $600 million-a-year industry.

~~~~~~

Part XVI

A MISCELLANY

The Communes:

One Big Happy Family

> "Communes are a device to
> make up for some of the things
> now lost in family life."
> —MITCHELL I. GINSBERG
> Dean, Columbia University
> School of Social Work

Their names were Reggie and Barb and that teepee was home to them in the Morning Star Ranch Commune at Occidental, California, in 1971. *WWP*

THERE'S NOTHING NEW about the commune. Hundreds and hundreds of them dotted this landscape once, led by such as John Humphrey Noyes' famous Oneida Community in upstate New York. That one, radically oriented, started out in 1848 built around total celibacy but had to switch to a form of "complex marriage"—*everybody* was husband and wife—when too many of the 300 Noyes followers talked about switching to the nearby Shakers, also known as the Shaking Quakers, because their belief in the imminent Second Coming of Christ led to all kinds of wild, trembling emotion. The Oneida group expired in 1881, while the Shakers, organized seventy-two years earlier and flourishing in eight states as far west as Indiana by 1826, counted 6,000 members before the movement began to lose its hold in 1860. The Shakers, by the way, also were celibate, but evidently not *that* celibate; there were still a few of them around in the early Seventies. Then there were—still are—the Hutterites, or Hutterian Brethren, who exploded from a small band in Tabor, South Dakota, in 1874 into a sect with more than 200 communities scattered through the Dakotas, Montana and even into Canada. The Hutterites, built along much the same religious principles as the Protestant Christian Mennonites,

who had their birth in Germantown, Pennsylvania, in 1683, encouraged family living but strictly enforced the rule of monogamy.

Today's commune—no, no, not the Amish or the Hutterites—is in quite another genre, more like the "complex marriage" of the Oneida Community. Born out of the turbulence and strife of the Angry Decade of the Sixties, part of it an outgrowth of the Hippie-Flower Children underculture, part of it religious or semi-religious in its origins, part of it just a withdrawal from the nine-to-five square society with its mortgages, two-car garages, private schools for one's heirs and all that, it has enjoyed a revival not all that large but with a respectable staying power. Live off the land and your own handicrafts—and in some instances handouts from your occasionally friendly rural neighbors without the blue noses—and the hell with the rest of it. Back to Thoreau and the good earth. It was all there in *Walden Two*, the 1948 novel by Harvard psychology professor B. F. Skinner and such later fictional outpourings as Robert A. Heinlein's *Stranger in a Strange Land* and Aldous Huxley's *Island*. One word, hardly new, summed up the good, carefree road: Utopia. *Easy Rider*, the 1969 Dennis Hopper–Peter Fonda film, a classic of sorts, didn't hurt either with its celebration of the communal life framed around a drug deal intermixed with the violence of that decade. In yet another sense, it may be said that the new collective way evolved from the "crash pads" of Haight–Ashbury and New York's East Village in the time of turn on/tune in/drop out (Dr. Leary again).

The modern commune came on like Heinz's 57 varieties or, to put it another way, with enough variations to suit every conceivable taste. What'll *you* have? Sex around the clock? Drugs? Zen Buddhism? The Hindu bit? Yoga? Name it. There was—and still is to a dwindling degree—a place for you somewhere.

A notable, early exception to what's been listed above was the much-celebrated Drop City outside the town of Trinidad in southern Colorado. One story is that a Boulder artist, Gene Bernofsky, bought up a sheep pasture out there in 1965 and settled down with nine other artists to form a self-sustaining retreat in which you could paint, sculpt or just sit around and soak in the good mountain air between essential chores. The other is that four college dropouts acquired that six-acre tract for $450 to furnish a haven for other refugees from the sick society. Either way, what evolved was a self-built community of nine kerosene-lit geodesic domes made of wood and tar-impregnated fiber with the tops of wrecked cars for roofs, two tents, a chicken coop and an outhouse. R. Buckminster Fuller, father of the dome concept, was sufficiently impressed at the outset to contribute $1,000 to that commune, which enjoyed a varying population that never exceeded twenty-eight or so and quickly drew sour notices as a haven not for serious artists but for beatniks, Flower Children, Hippies and deadbeats. Not happy with its reception in such journals as the *Rocky Mountain News* and *Denver Post*, the Droppers eventually barred the local press while welcoming such media intruders as a TV film crew from Britain's BBC.

The fact is that Drop City started out with some pretty good notices. An early *Post* story headed WORK, THRIFT, ARTISTIC CREATIVITY described in glowing terms how that commune shunned drugs and alcohol and was toiling strenuously to be self-sustaining although not averse to outside donations to make ends meet. Another noted that the Droppers, a strong tourist attraction from the start, were quite generous about giving away what little they had to give in the way of souvenirs, such as small art objects of their own craftsmanship. All well and good, but after a while the twelve adults and thirteen children then abiding in the commune were living off government handouts in the form of food stamps and in trouble with Welfare Director Charline J. Birkins, who took the view that the grown-ups—young, healthy, educated—ought to go out and get jobs. Come September 1967 the Droppers lost their certification, even with the ACLU stepping in to argue their case, and the end of that dream was at hand. Neither the sovereign state of Colorado nor the federal government was going to pay the bills for the new subculture, period. Three years later one of the Drop City founders who went by the name of Peter Rabbit set up a new commune called Libre on the south slope of Greenhorn Mountain near Gardner, this time bearing a message of love, brotherhood and a touch of drugs on the side. That one also was destined for a short life.

In those same early days there was a group living on a falling-down farm, called Oz, borrowed rent-free from a kindly owner in Meadville, Pennsylvania. There twenty men and fourteen women settled, among them seven couples either married or just sharing the same mattress or sleeping bag between love-ins in a nearby creek which served as their powder room. Many of them left not only their prior existences but their names as well behind, preferring to be known by such handles as Dancing Bear or Patty-Pooh. They worked the fields, harvesting corn, squash, turnips, tomatoes and berries to supplement a diet heavily spiced with brown rice, soy beans and soup. Some made beads or other souvenirs for sale to gawking tourists. Some of the men worked nearby farms to supplement their insufficient crop. Some—college dropouts with an allowance from home, or teachers with the remnants of a bank book—chipped in with cash when the going was too rough. One of the women took a sabbatical to go to New York and pose for some porno art to make enough money to buy a goat so there would be some milk in the larder. There was no wardrobe problem, of course. The men wore jeans, the women leaned to the granny dress— and both sides also found it quite comfortable with no gear at all when the weather permitted. But that candlelit oasis of a communal peace was doomed to an early death. Four members of the Oz family were arrested as vagrants in a nearby town and then the farm was raided by state police as "a disorderly house" under an 1860 law barring idleness, gaming, drinking, misbehaving and that sort of thing. The gendarmes posted a notice on the farmhouse barring "fornication, assignation and lewdness" and the stores where they were buying essential supplies started turning them away. The local prosecutor came up with a ready solution: get out of town and we'll forget the whole thing, so the Family Oz, only four

"Michele" and her two-year-old daughter at Drop City in Colorado after moving in from Texas with her husband Rick (no last names there). "We've never been happier," the woman told reporters. "Some people don't think we've got a chance, but I think we do." She was wrong. The Droppers couldn't make it. *WWP*

months old, packed up its scant belongings and left.

In the more hospitable Southwest in the same year—1969—twenty or more communes began to dot the New Mexican landscape, mostly around the writers' colony of Taos north of Santa Fe. The biggest name to come out of that flight from the ugly urban life was Hog Farm, so named because its Flower Children in the town of Llano happily went to work slopping the necessary vittles to a farmer's forty pigs in return for free quarters bereft of any elaborate conveniences. The Hog Farm gurus were middle-aged Hugh Romney, who had worked in the California school system and as an acting instructor at Columbia Pictures, and his wife, Bonnie Jean, a refugee from the TV acting scene. While it may have been carefree, Hog Farm fell somewhat short of Utopia, unless your idea of Utopia is all the sex you can get plus a reasonable supply of the Dream Street accoutrements, including LSD and mescaline. Norman Pearlstine, a *Wall Street Journal* reporter who found his way to that paradise (it wasn't easy), filed a story which suggested that Hog Farm wasn't an inappropriate name for that

communal resort at all. He found its denizens barely subsisting on brown rice, salad and homemade bread and dreaming of greasy hamburgers from fast food joints, for even with all those pigs around there seldom was any meat on the communal table.

Health was another problem in many of the communes. Such afflications as hepatitis and dysentery were not uncommon, and New Mexico frowned on the strange invaders as having a venereal disease rate double that of the rest of the state, which certainly gave one pause about the heralded virtues of free love in the new free society dedicated to washing out the bad memory of urban life. There is still something to be said for hot and cold running water and the flushing toilet versus the primitive outhouse and all those flies. Hog Farm, and so many others like it, carried the seeds of its own doom. The hogs had it better than the people.

None of the above, of course, is meant to damn the communal life in its entirety. As noted, there are all kinds of ways to live together and beat the system. Clear across the country, the idea continues to pay off on a limited scale, depending on the minds and purpose behind it. There's something to be said for banding together, sharing the good and the bad. What is the Israeli *kibbutz*, born in blood and strife in 1948, except a commune that works, everybody pulling his share of the burden? Sociology professor Benjamin Zablocki of Columbia University surveyed the communes in the early Seventies and found the rampant sex-sharing that had captured all the media coverage present in only about one out of ten of the group-living situations. On the same campus, Dr. Amitai Etzioni, another psychologist, viewed the better communes as "inexpensive mental hospitals." It was his view that those collectives had saved the lives of any number of neurotic, hard-drug cases who would have been candidates for suicide via the OD route if they hadn't found a family in which they could find a purposeful life. Drugs or whatever, there is ample support for these views. The fact is, we have been misled by the headline hunters running down the skinny-dippers and the turned-on types. There are all kinds of communes today. Some very select, some large, some religious-based, some benignly tolerant toward the marijuana set—and some, alas, that come and go. Why? Because the concept behind them is basically deficient in the fundamentals, and as often as not it's just a romp in the hay with some faceless figure. And you don't have to go into self-exile for that joyful purpose at all, because it's just as available in the Establishment. Indeed, the Establishment has the edge: privacy. You can do your thing, with your woman or your man, without a built-in family on the adjoining mattress. Of course, if your thing is religion that's something else. There's room for everybody in the commune that's celebrating God or waiting for the Second Coming.

A Marine veteran of Korea and a former acidhead from Haight-Ashbury, Stephen Gaskin presided over the commune An Om outside of San Francisco in 1970, moving on to the edge of Summerton, Tennessee, a year later to set up what would prove to be the nation's most successful experiment in communal living—The Farm. In the kitchen you're looking at, meat is banned. *WWP*

Part of Gaskin's flock of hundreds, many of them ex-Hippies and Flower Children, load sorghum for processing into molasses at a nearby mill to help pay off their $70,000 1,014-acre homestead. Early on, the commune also was growing its own marijuana until the local authorities confiscated 1,000 plants and ordered Gaskin and three of his helpmates into prison, shunting aside their claim that the grass was being grown strictly for use in religious rites. *WWP*

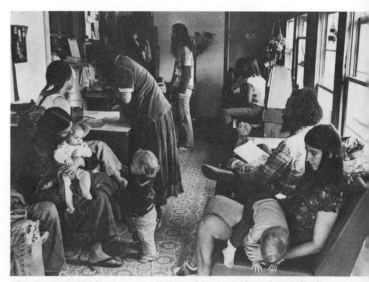

The Farm maintains its own clinic and has members in medical schools, all expenses paid, pledged to come back and minister to the communal family. The tall and gaunt Gaskin, forty-three, once taught creative writing at San Francisco State College, but as The Farm's guru he's into Oriental mysticism and the Biblical mandates of peace and love. And they've worked for him. *UPI*

SECURITY AREA PASSENGERS ONLY BEYOND THIS POINT

ONE PASSENGER AT A TIME PLEASE

PASSENGERS MAY SUBMIT TO PHYSICAL SEARCH IF DESIRED

NO JOKING MATTER!

This is why the skyjackers are pretty much out of business today.

THE SKYJACKERS:

Fly Now, Pay Later

"I've been in this place [Cuba] six years
and I'm out of my mind. Believe me, I'm all for
the United States now. I'd even wear
a Nixon button."
—GARLAND GRANT, twenty-seven, an ex-
Black Panther from Milwaukee who
hijacked a Northwest Airlines jet in 1971.

MARK THE YEAR: 1961. That's when skyjacking, a dread mixture of peril and terror all but universally without profit for its practitioners, came into vogue on these shores. For a time, it reached the proportions of a popular sport, soaring toward the 200 mark before the slow-moving federal aviation watchdogs and the airlines bestirred themselves and made it all but impossible to carry an arsenal of weapons or homemade bombs in your flight bag along with your paperbacks, pill boxes, snacks and other personal necessities. What took so long? Presumably, the carriers needed time to weigh the cost of electronic detection devices and extra personnel against the burgeoning waste of their highly expensive fuel and the emotional trauma of the paying customers who, as often as not, found themselves paying an unplanned call on Fidel Castro in Havana.

It started May 1 in that first year of Camelot when a man armed with a pistol and knife directed the pilot of a National Airlines twin-engine Convair bound from Miami to Key West to drop him off in Cuba. Mr. Castro let the other seven passengers and the three crewmen go back to Key West at once but didn't chase out the skyjacker. On July 24 an Eastern Airlines turbo-prop Electra on a Miami–Tampa flight

was diverted to the misnamed Isle of Freedom by a lone gunman, and on that occasion Castro made the thirty-three passengers and five crewmen stay overnight before returning them on another plane while he kept the $2.5 million Electra, offering to surrender it only to the United Nations Security Council. In both those situations, the identity of the skyjackers—Hispanics—remained obscure.

The more interesting—and much more frightening—adventure in the blue occurred on August 3 when ex-con Leon Bearden drew a .38 on a Continental Airlines flight headed for Houston from Los Angeles and announced that he and his son Cody, sixteen, who was toting a .45, wished to be dropped off in Cuba. The heads-up pilot, Captain B. D. Rickards, said he was sorry but he couldn't manage that unscheduled stop without touching down at El Paso to refuel. What ensued there was a nine-hour drama marked by the first sounds of gunfire in the skyjacking trade. Met by a swarm of FBI agents, Texas border patrolmen, police and deputy sheriffs, Bearden let it be known that the crew of six and four volunteers among the sixty-seven terrified passengers would be held hostage until all those lawmen went away and the captain took the jet up. This one ap-

321

peared to have such a high potential for tragedy that the FBI checked the White House itself before determining how far its men should go. The answer from John Kennedy was pretty forthright: in essence, do what you have to do. Pilot Rickards eventually was given the go-ahead and the thirty-eight-year-old Bearden looked like a winner—except that as the 707 taxied down the runway the heavy artillery came into action, riddling all ten tires and one engine with machine-gun fire. FBI man Francis E. Crosby put aside his revolver and went aboard to have a chat with Bearden while a colleague, Robert Nagel, crept into the jet with a border patrolman and took away young Cody's .45. Dad, a wiry felon who had started out as a horse thief in 1941 and moved on to auto theft, forgery and robbery, messing up every time, elected to stand and fight but got off just one shot before one of the hostages, Leonard Gilman of the Immigration Service, felled him with a blow to the jaw. The bullet came to rest in the floor of the jet and Bearden headed for twenty years behind bars while the boy was ordered imprisoned until he reached twenty-one. Back in Chandler, Arizona, Mrs. Bearden, like any proper wife, rose to her husband's defense, saying he had always been a model husband and father to their brood (whenever he was home, presumably). Why he wanted to go to Cuba in the first place never was made clear.

In the next seven years forty-six more planes were skyjacked to Cuba, with a peak of twenty-eight in 1968. Then, in 1969 fifty-seven jets, counting a few strays from Colombia, Mexico and Venezuela, made that stop at José Martí Airport. By that time their bearded host was granting most of the self-appointed flyboys asylum in his prisons, although many of them had initially been welcomed as heroes fleeing imperialist America to enjoy the good life on the left. There was a small sprinkling of Black Power types in that select group.

The first skyjacker to face an American court was Robert McRae Helmley, a special forces reservist from Savannah who in January 1969, armed with a gun and the nom de plume "El Rojo," commandeered a United Pittsburgh–Miami flight and forced it to set down in Castroland. How he got out of Cuba is rather vague but he was picked up in Canada and returned to Miami, where he won an acquittal on the grounds of temporary insanity.

While all this was going on Juanita Castro, the dictator's self-exiled sister, was laying all the blame at the feet of the United States and its hemispheric neighbors for not taking any effective action against Big Brother's regime. The International Federation of

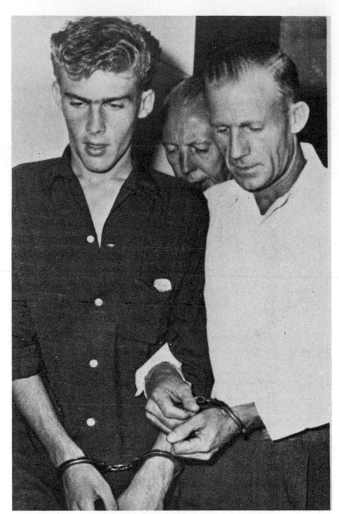

Leon Bearden and his teen-age son Cody after their bungled adventure into skyjacking. *WWP*

Airline Pilots Association (IFALPA), representing 44,000 pilots in fifty-four countries, wasn't exactly silent either. The pilots threatened reprisals against all nations that refused to institute "appropriate punishment" for skyjackers and even talked about a worldwide strike.

That September, Cuba at long last announced that it would permit extradition of skyjackers deemed to be common criminals while granting asylum "to those persons who, for political reasons, arrive in our country having found themselves in the necessity of using this extreme means to elude a real danger of death or grave repression." Our State Department welcomed the Castro pronouncement as a constructive contribution to air safety. It was in that autumn—rather late, it would seem—that our airlines, led by Eastern and TWA, began to install weapons-screening

The former Countess Christina Paolozzi, wife of Dr. Howard T. Bellin of New York, carries son from Eastern Airlines jet hijacked to Cuba by a black gunman and a woman helper in 1968. Mrs. Bellin was allowed to return to Miami immediately with fourteen of the other 136 passengers because the child was ill. The Cuban authorities sent the rest back later that day. *WWP*

Captains R. H. Hastings and Billy N. Williams, and pointed toward Rome before anybody got killed. Just for insurance, the one-man army took a customs official along as a hostage. When the 707 touched down it marked the end of an odyssey that had used up seventeen hours and 6,900 miles. Minichiello managed to get out of the Rome airport with no difficulty, even acquiring a car and taking the customs man along for a brief look at the countryside before turning him loose. The police picked up the flying Corporal five hours later in a village church and announced that he would be held on charges of hijacking, kidnapping, armed threats and illegal possession of firearms adding up to a possible thirty years in prison. Our side submitted that we would rather have the youth flown home, all expenses paid, where he would face life imprisonment for kidnapping or even a possible if unlikely death sentence for air piracy. The Italians turned that down on the grounds that hijacking was not among the misdeeds on *their* criminal statutes and thus our extradition agreement with

devices at an undisclosed number of airports. Los Angeles, alas, was not among them, and that's where the high moment of the air-pirate fraternity—the first international skyjacking—had its origin.

The star of that saga, appropriately unveiled on Halloween, was twenty-year-old Marine Lance Corporal Raffaele Minichiello, who had broken away from two MPs just the day before while being led before the brass to face a charge of breaking into the PX at Camp Pendleton, California. The boy boarded a cross-country TWA flight at Los Angeles with enough arms to overthrow a banana republic: an M-1 carbine, 250 rounds of ammo, ten dynamite caps and a hunting knife for good measure, and he knew how to use that arsenal because he had served in Vietnam. A citizen of Seattle who had a terrible yearning for his native Italian soil, Minichiello took command of the Boeing 707 over Fresno, freed all thirty-nine passengers and three of the four stewardesses during a refueling stop at Denver, and then took on the waiting FBI at Kennedy Airport in New York with considerable ease. The moment a party in mechanic's gear (a familiar FBI device) approached the plane a warning shot went zinging over his head. The jet's skipper, Captain Donald Cook, later would term the G-Men "idiots" who had come close to setting off a massacre, putting himself on J. Edgar Hoover's permanent Bad Boy list. In any case, the better part of wisdom thereupon dictated that the youth should be furnished with two veterans of the trans-Atlantic run,

Raffaele Minichiello pulled off the big one the following year—taking a TWA jet all the way from California to his native Italy with some stops for fuel and other things along the way. Here he's in a Rome courtroom demonstrating how he pointed one item in his arsenal—an unloaded rifle—at an Italian police officer he abducted when the 707 got him home. He beat extradition and got off with an 18-month sentence over there. *WWP*

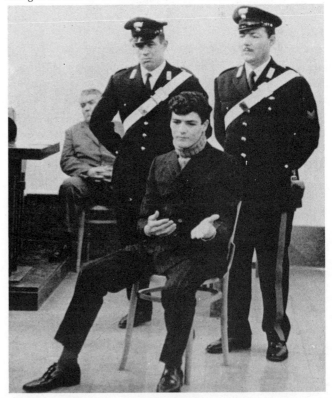

them did not apply. Minichiello drew a seven-and-a-half-year term over there but was a free man after a mere eighteen months. Free, back where he wanted to be, something of a folk hero, and ever so happy with a job as a bus boy in some pasta palace.

The forty-six-year-old Captain Williams, by the way, was drawn into a rather bizarre skyjacking the following June *between* flights. It happened when Arthur G. Barkley, forty-nine, a former bakery truck driver, boarded a Phoenix-to-Washington 707 at Phoenix, dropped into the cockpit waving a gun and ordered the pilot to bypass a St. Louis stop and go straight on to Dulles Airport. En route, Barkley ordered a communiqué sent to the Supreme Court, of all places, announcing that he would need an even $100 million in small bills when he got to the capital. There, the plane sat on the apron for an hour and then Williams was delegated to go aboard with a satchel containing a compromise bundle of $100,700 hastily gathered from a number of District banks. The new commander of the TWA plane barely had time to start counting when FAA agents shot out the 707's tires and rushed the plane as the fifty-one passengers scampered to safety and Barkley put a bullet into the stomach of co-pilot Dale C. Hupe before he was subdued. Hupe survived. The Phoenix man beat prosecution on the grounds of insanity and was consigned to a mental hospital.

Skyjacking on this side of the water—fad, folly, delusion, madness?—slowed down considerably after 1969 as the electronic detection devices became an ornament of virtually all the airports of any size and the government put armed sky marshals on all flights. By comparison with the overseas record—most often the work of Arab terrorists and highlighted by the incredible drama played out at Entebbe Airport in Idi Amin's Uganda in 1976 when so much blood flowed as the Israelis staged that better-than-fiction Commando rescue—the American experience with air piracy has been relatively free of casualties. The toll, with the skyjacker himself almost always the victim, either by his own hand or the FBI's, is too small to count off, especially when you consider that the total number of skyjackings passed 160 in late 1977. Today that particular form of lunacy is all but out of style here.

Who are the people who rode that rickety roller coaster when the fever was at its highest pitch? There has been only one serious study, *The Skyjacker: His Flight of Fantasy*, written by Dallas psychiatrist David Graham Hubbard in 1971. After interviewing twenty of the breed that doctor profiled the skyjacker as a twenty-nine-year-old white from the lower economic

Arthur G. Barkeley, shackled to another prisoner, is led into Federal Court in Alexandria, Virginia, in 1970 after hijacking a TWA Phoenix-Washington flight and demanding $100 million in small bills. He wound up in a mental hospital. *WWP*

scale generally free of any criminal record except possibly for something like petty theft. Psychotic, very likely, but not dumb. Why does he venture into that deep water? In the Hubbard analysis it is because his whole life had been marked by one failure after anther. What better way to repair that dismal picture than to commandeer a multimillion-dollar jet in midair and, for once, take charge? There's something sickeningly familiar in that profile, for it brings to mind some of the assassins and mass killers of the Sixties, the ones who never amounted to a damn and wanted to see their names in the papers.

A notable exception to that Hubbard profile surfaced August 1978 on a TWA 707 carrying seventy-eight passengers from New York to Geneva. Over the Irish Sea one of those fares handed a stewardess a rambling nineteen-page statement saying that the jet would be blown up by remote control unless the pilot received a rather wild set of assurances including immediate freedom for Sirhan B. Sirhan, the assassin of Robert F. Kennedy; ex-Hitler deputy Rudolf Hess, the last Nuremberg defendant languishing in West

Berlin's Spandau Prison; and five Croatian hijackers in U.S. jails. The note bore the signature of the "United Revolutionary Soldiers of the Reciprocal Relief Alliance for Peace Justice and Freedom Everywhere." Captain Robert Hamilton did nothing more than radio European control towers that his craft was "under control by elements" and when he set it down at Geneva's Cointrin Airport a small army of antiterrorist police gave the plane an eight-hour scouring before letting *all* the passengers alight. And the pseudo-skyjacker? The stewardess couldn't identify him, but a wig, false mustache, eyeglasses and coat were found in the 707's men's room. So that one might well have been put down as a hoax. Or a prank. Or somebody's notion of a real belly laugh. The culprit simply strolled out of that airport with his seventy-seven thoroughly terrified fellow passengers. It seemed such a pity, because the man sounded like he would have made a splendid companion for Rudolf Hess, all alone in Spandau these many years.

But it wasn't over, because the Swiss police are anything but Keystone Cops. One by one, they investigated every adult who was on that flight and in due course they came up with a Mr. X who filled the bill. In a check with the FBI two different names fit the gentleman—Rudi Siegfried Kuno Kreitlow and Charles Frank Metel, and it turned out he had an arrest record in the States dating back to the Sixties when he beat a charge involving some funny business with a passport. In November, the German-born Kreitlow-Metel, sixty-three, was picked up in Manhattan while killing some time in a chess club. He was charged not with hijacking but the not-often encountered crime of "intimidation"—in that particular case interfering with a flight in midair and furnishing false information to the crew. The punishment to fit those crimes, respectively, is twenty years and five years. The accused pleaded innocent and was sent off for psychiatric tests pending trial. Was he just a guy having some fun? No. He was a card-carrying, Gestapo-trained Nazi in Hitler's Germany. He did want Mr. Hess turned loose, and it appeared that Mr. Sirhan was one of his favorite people because he hated Jews. Nailed by fiber tests linking the false wig and other objects of his clothing to that caper over the Atlantic, he drew seven years in prison.

The last illicit flyboy worthy of mention here is Garrett Brock Trapnell, and if you stick around you'll find out why.

A blond and bearded six-footer with an IQ of 130, this man emerged from the union of a Radcliffe graduate from a highly placed Massachusetts family and a Navy commander relieved of his stripes for operating

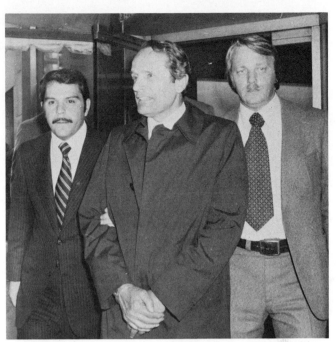

Rudi Siegfried Kuno Kreitlow, a/k/a Charles Frank Metel, in custody in Manhattan two months after staging a phony hijack scare on a TWA flight from Kennedy to Geneva. *UPI*

a bordello while stationed in the Panama Canal Zone. Small stuff. The scion's own career produced a 1976 book by Eliot Asinof concisely titled *The Fox Is Crazy Too: True Story of Garrett Trapnell, Adventurer, Skyjacker, Con Man, Lover.* He ran guns for Mr. Castro when he was twenty, robbed a minimum of seven banks, wrote rubber checks in carload lots and pulled off a $100,000 jewel robbery in the Bahamas, just to mention some highlights. He fell into police hands some twenty times but spent less than two years behind bars because the men in the black robes almost invariably bought his insanity defense. That device, however, failed him in 1972 after he skyjacked a Los Angeles-to-New York jet over the Midwest and then was shot by an FBI agent posing as a crew member when he came down at Kennedy Airport with his 101 captives. Recovered nicely, he drew one life sentence compounded by still another and spiced with an additional 110 years recently for trying to break out of the Federal Penitentiary at Marion, Illinois.

Forty now and with two children and a minimum of two wives in his past, Garrett Trapnell recently filed the necessary papers with the Federal Election Commission to stand among the aspirants for the Presidency in 1980 as a candidate of his own Nationalist Christian Democratic Party. That tells you something about the long-time felon's sense of humor, doesn't it though?

PATTY HEARST AND THE SLA:

A New Turn in Social Protest

BEING KIDNAPPED MEANS ALWAYS
HAVING TO SAY YOU'RE SORRY.
——Legend on a T-shirt
worn in prison by Patty Hearst

Patty Hearst manages a clenched fist salute despite the handcuffs
shortly after her arrest in 1975. In her trial later, she ascribed
the gesture to "profound confusion" over whether her bizarre
experience in the underground was at long last over. *WWP*

LET'S GO NOW to the drama that unfolded on the night of February 4, 1974, with a terrified scream and a blaze of senseless gunfire on a quiet street off the University of California campus. The principals: Patricia Campbell Hearst, nineteen, daughter of publisher Randolph Apperson Hearst, and a band of ten predominantly black Maoist revolutionaries calling themselves the Symbionese Liberation Army, working shorthanded because two of their soldiers were in San Quentin in the preceding November's slaying of Oakland's black schools superintendent, Marcus Foster. The blond newspaper heiress, an art history sophomore, was in the apartment she shared with twenty-six-year-old teacher and philosophy major Steven A. Weed when three SLA delegates burst in. A woman with a .38 and two men with heavy weapons slugged Weed and dragged their tiny, half-naked prey out to be deposited in the trunk of a car and whisked away while they sprayed the street with bullets.

It had the sound of any conventional kidnapping.

No one doubted that the second act would open with a demand on the fifty-eight year-old chairman of the Hearst Corporation and proprietor of the San Francisco *Examiner* for a sky-high chunk of ransom

money in small, unmarked bills, and then Patty would be back in her family's arms.

But the little-known SLA, all guerilla trained, hadn't kidnapped the girl to fill its own coffers. The SLA didn't want one thin dime for itself. The first word that came to the Hillsborough estate of the Hearsts was that the third eldest of their five daughters would be killed unless they dipped into their bank account and came up with enough cash to feed the state's needy families—each and every one of them. In receipt of tape-recorded pleas from Patty, the anguished Hearst lost no time in moving to set up a $2 million People in Need (PIN) program designed to operate out of seventeen distribution centers in the Bay Area's slum districts. While fresh SLA tapes rejected that windfall as nothing more than "a few crumbs" Hearst launched the food giveaway on February 21 just the same, accompanied by a pledge that another $4 million would be placed in escrow by the parent Hearst Corporation to triple the PIN operation upon Patty's release.

What the SLA had brought about was a mint-new twist in social reform—a political kidnapping. Now the poor would be fed not with meager government handouts, nor on soup lines reminiscent of the Great Depression, but with the boundless fortune amassed by their captive's grandfather, William Randolph Hearst, Sr., and passed on to his five sons. The word "revolution" hardly seemed adequate to describe that accomplishment of the SLA, but it wasn't good enough at that. The initial distribution to the hordes—mostly black or Chicano—that descended on the centers consisted of frozen turkey hindquarters, two 12-ounce cans of tomato juice, two cans of luncheon meat pretty close to the Army's Spam and a large box of Saltine crackers. The SLA swiftly rejected that fare as nothing more than supplemental groceries that fell short of the real needs of the poor. Given no choice with his daughter's life believed to be at stake, Hearst had PIN switch to individual handouts roughly equivalent to about $25 worth of food at supermarket prices—steaks, frozen fish and chicken and turkey along with eggs, milk, rice, macaroni and cheese, potatoes and fresh fruits.

Now that was more like it—except that the more lavish fare also fell short for the band pulling the strings via their tape-recorded communiqués. The SLA view was that Hearst should provide no less than $70 worth of vittles per recipient as a "good faith gesture" before it would entertain active negotiations for Patty's return, and the publisher had ample warning on that score. A taped message from Patty on March 9 complained that he wasn't doing enough to satisfy her captors' demands.

It would all prove academic in any case.

The first $2 million ran out on March 26, an indeterminate chunk of it evidently ripped off either by internal thefts at the distribution points or simply gone astray in sloppy administration by the poverty-area community leaders named to oversee the giveaway.

The next $4 million—the escrow money—would not have to be spent, for on April 3 a stunning new tape from Patty reached her parents:

I have been given the choice of one, being released in a safe area, or, two, joining the forces of the Symbionese Liberation Army and fighting for my freedom and the freedom of all oppressed people. I have chosen to stay and fight.

A photo, delivered by the underground, came with it, and Randolph and Catherine Hearst looked at their daughter in a military jacket with a machine gun in her arms. She wasn't even Patty Hearst anymore. She said her name was Tania, borrowed from a woman who had been a member of Che Guevera's guerilla band before Bolivian government troops trapped the ex-Castro lieutenant and shot him to death in 1967.

A scant few weeks later the Hearsts had another picture to look at—Patty, or Tania, holding a sawed-off M-1 carbine on some of the customers while an SLA troupe swept up $10,690 from the Hibernia Bank in San Francisco. The bank's own cameras made that shot but it wasn't really needed, for a fresh tape in her voice, branding her parents as "pigs," advised the family that Patty had participated in that stickup and reaffirmed her commitment to the SLA. Now the girl no longer was a kidnap victim with some 8,000 FBI agents on the prowl to rescue her. No. She was a fugitive from justice, and on May 16 the heiress-turned-revolutionary was identified as the machine-gun wielder who had sprayed a Los Angeles sporting goods store with bullets while two white SLA associates, William and Emily Harris, caught shoplifting, made a successful getaway. The day after that SLA "Field Marshal" Donald DeFreeze, known as Cinque, died with five of his key helpers in their flaming L.A. hideout in a shootout with the police.

What followed, inexplicably, was a sixteen-month hegira in which Patty Hearst roamed the country from one end to the other without ever being caught, without ever seeking to break loose from the remnants of the SLA, without ever calling her parents to come and get her if, say, she was really an involuntary captive who had had no choice from the start. The end didn't come until September 18, 1975, when the FBI, acting on information, caught up with Patty in a San Francisco apartment and miniarsenal (two sawed-off shotguns, six pistols) she was sharing with Wendy Masako Yoshimura, thirty-two, a Bay Area artist on the run since 1972 after vanishing from Berkeley while under a charge of possessing weapons and explosives. The capture of the young Harris couple swiftly followed.

Embraced by her parents and her sisters Anne and Vicki, little Patty would now enjoy the best legal defense money could buy—nobody less than the Great Defender, F. Lee Bailey. In her thirty-nine-day trial on the robbery charge the following spring, Bailey argued that his client, nothing more than a brainwashed prisoner, had gone to the Hibernia Bank under duress and thus should be declared innocent. Patty's story was that she had been drugged, raped, tortured, imprisoned in a closet for fifty-seven days and threatened with death until she was prepared to do the bidding of the ex-con called Cinque. But whether or not Bailey should have put her on the stand is another question. The girl didn't help her case at all when

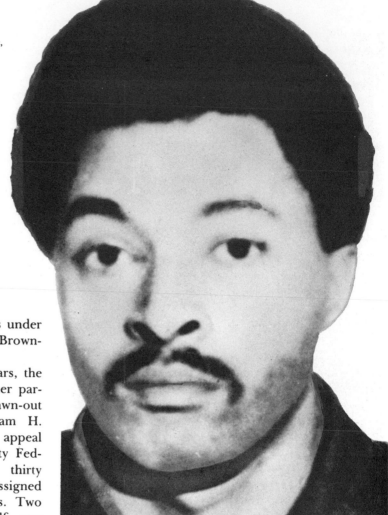

The Symbionese Liberation Army leader behind the kidnapping—"Field Marshal" Donald (Cinque) DeFreeze, later slain in a shootout with Los Angeles police. *WWP*

she took the Fifth Amendment forty-two times under cross-examination by U. S. Attorney James L. Browning.

Found guilty and facing up to thirty-five years, the fragile defendant eventually was released to her parents on $1.2 million bail pending the long-drawn-out appeals process. U. S. District Judge William H. Orrick sentenced her to seven years when the appeal failed and she went into the minimum-security Federal Correctional Institution at Pleasanton, thirty miles from San Francisco, in May of 1978, assigned to the mess hall as dishwasher and waitress. Two fresh arguments later were offered in her behalf—one that she should be freed because the very busy Bailey had not adequately presented her case ("a crock of horseshit," the counselor said in rebuttal) and the other claiming that a 1977 guilty plea made by the Harrises in the kidnapping established that she had told the truth from the start. William Harris was in the kidnap trio, while his wife was at the wheel of one of the two getaway cars. That couple already had been hit with sentences of eleven years to life on charges stemming from that shoplifting and shootout in 1974, with an incidental kidnapping thrown in because the trio borrowed some youth and his van to make their escape (the heiress got off with probation in that case). Harris, thirty-three, denied that Patty had been either brainwashed, beaten, tortured, raped, locked in a closet or even "coerced into rejecting her family and remaining with the people in the SLA." In what must rank as one of the classic plea-bargaining arrangements of all time in a nation where all the courts have become cut-rate sentencing outlets because there is more crime than they can handle, Harris and his thirty-one-year-old wife came out of it all

in 1978 with fresh concurrent terms of ten years to life. With credit for time served and a touch of good behavior, that deal left them in a position to be freed in 1983 to pursue their lingering commitment to the SLA road to the America of their revolutionary dreams.

The news of the pair's plea, by the way, came to inmate No. 00077-81 at Pleasanton along with a revoltingly gruesome memento: someone deposited a decomposing rat on her bunk.

But the end of that girl's nightmare was approaching by then, thanks to a Free Patty campaign of towering proportions. A clemency petition bearing 40,000 names, among them more than 100 members of Congress, including California Democratic Senators Alan Cranston and John V. Tunney as well as GOP Presidential hopeful Ronald Reagan and John Wayne, went to the Justice Department. Charles Bates, the since-retired West Coast FBI bureau chief

Patty Hearst's parents in a press-conference appeal for their daughter's return. They repeated this scene over and over outside their Hillsborough mansion, but the SLA wasn't listening. The couple later separated, the breakup of their forty-year marriage attributed in part to disagreements stemming from their daughter's ordeal and its aftermath. *WWP*

tressed by no fewer than twenty-five gunbearers from the Pleasanton staff and police helicopters hovering above as well, the country's most celebrated female prisoner stepped briskly through the twin glass doors of the home she had known for twenty-two months. Up twenty pounds from the ninety-five she was carrying when she went in and looking just as healthy as she was happy, Patty opened her blue ski parka to bare a T-shirt that said PARDON ME and chatted amiably with the eighty-man media army on hand as her new flaming red hairdo waved in a gentle breeze. She thanked her family, all those petition signers and her most recent lawyer, George Martinez, and joyfully

Part of the throng massed outside one of the San Francisco distribution centers as the Hearst family launched the $2-million food-giveaway program demanded by the SLA in return for Patty's life. *WWP*

who headed the $5 million, nineteen-month case from the start, pitched in with a statement to the effect that Patty "got a little tougher sentence than most bank robbers who have long rap sheets"—a debatable point to say the least. (Without questioning Bates' sincerity, it bears mention here that he had a TV special coming up on the Hearst saga.) The pro-Patty forces, encountering only the barest opposition, wanted not only an early parole but a Presidential pardon. What they got, in January of 1979, was the parole—five months ahead of Patty's first eligible date and only the fifth commutation of Jimmy Carter's two years in office. During the four-month Free Patty drive, by the way, the White House counted some 1,500 letters with more than 90 percent in the girl's favor. Strangely, the mail that came in later was more heavily weighted against the President's action.

In any case, at 7:30 on the morning of February 1, with a quartet of four family-hired bodyguards but-

The SLA symbol graces one of the centers. *WWP*

Emily and William Harris, members of the kidnap band, head for separate prisons after their first trial in 1976. The couple drew additional ten-years-to-life terms on additional charges two years later in a plea-bargaining arrangement that should see them freed around 1983. *WWP*

held aloft that White House commutation. She said nothing about the fact that a pardon would have been so much better because it would not only have relieved her of the usual requirements of parole but also restored her civil rights.

There was one more thank-you—the big one.

That was reserved for the brawny, mustachioed hunk of man who had slipped an engagement ring on her finger—not that she could wear it in there—in the Pleasanton visitor's lounge the year before. No

socialite and no Joe College but a thirty-three-year-old cop, eight years her senior, with whom she fell in love while he was moonlighting as part of the twenty-man guard detail her parents had around her when she was out on bail. This was Bernard Shaw, ex-GI, ex-shipping clerk, ex-longshoreman and a black belt in karate. His wife, Valerie, mother of two youngsters, divorced him while he was on the Hearst assignment. Put it down to a tragic stroke of fate that brought the 5'10" Shaw and little Patty together. Working on the docks, the native Californian was set to join the San Francisco Fire Department when a brother of his was murdered and he decided he would rather become a cop.

There were no members of Patty's family outside the prison doors. Instead, the Hearsts—their long union broken in 1978 by a separation which some attributed to differences arising from the handling of the girl's case—waited at the Hillsborough mansion with their four other daughters until Bernard Shaw and George Martinez pulled into the driveway with the guest of honor for a regal homecoming breakfast. And pretty soon Patty and Shaw, granted two weeks off by the PD, vanished to an undisclosed vacation hideaway.

The couple did not surface again until April 1, and that was for their wedding, under heavy security, on the Treasure Island Naval Base in the middle of San Francisco Bay not far from another prison—the government's abandoned Alcatraz. It was an Episcopal ceremony performed by the Reverend Edward Dumke of San Mateo, who had converted the white-gowned Patty from Catholicism, and it was marked by a touch of Old Testament wrath. This was a verse, chosen by the bride, which said "O, bring back on evildoers their iniquity and wipe them out for their wickedness." Patty Hearst's final words for the SLA, presumably.

There was a nice touch of irony in the selection of the maid of honor—the new Mrs. Shaw's friend Trish Tobin, whose father owns the Hibernia Bank. The 300 guests were shielded from the press under an arrangement through which the exclusive coverage was sold for $50,000 to a troika consisting of *Look* magazine, Rupert Murdoch's weekly *Star* and the Sygma photo agency. Robert Gutwilling, *Look's* editor, quoted George Martinez as saying the heiress wanted it that way because she needed the money and was tired of being exploited.

And the future?

Patty has said that she wanted a family, wanted to raise dogs, preferably German shepherds, and planned to work as a volunteer with the new Women's Equal Rights Legal Defense and Education Fund based in Los Angeles. What would she do there? She would counsel victims of wife-beating—*and rape*.

So much for all that.

The fact is that even to this day, even with the muddled self-serving confessionals of the Harris duo, we don't really know the whole Patty Hearst story. Perhaps we never will.

We do know, from the pitiful results of that $2 million giveaway engineered by the departed Cinque and his troops, that the Symbionese formula for social reform wasn't the answer at all. We know that it will take more than political kidnappings, terror, machine guns and taped commands to feed this nation's poor according to the way-out precepts of the SLA types in our midst.

A free woman again, Patty Hearst waves President Carter's clemency order. Behind her, Bernard Shaw, the cop she lost her heart to when he was part of her bodyguard detail while she was out on bail. *WWP*

INDEX

Page numbers in italics refer to illustrations.